❧ Feminist Philosophies ❧

Problems, Theories, and Applications

Edited by

Janet A. Kourany
University of Notre Dame

James P. Sterba
University of Notre Dame

Rosemarie Tong
Davidson College

PRENTICE HALL, Englewood Cliffs, New Jersey 07632

Library of Congress Cataloging-in-Publication Data

Feminist philosophies : problems, theories, and applications / edited
   by James P. Sterba, Janet A. Kourany, Rosemarie Tong.
         p.   cm.
      Includes bibliographical references.
      ISBN 0-13-313560-8
      1. Feminist theory.   I. Sterba, James P.   II. Kourany, Janet A.
   III. Tong, Rosemarie.
   HQ1190.F463 1992
   305.42′01—dc20   91-27009
                                                        CIP

Editorial/production supervision and interior design: **Michael R. Steinberg**
Cover Design: **Barbara Singer**
Cover Photo: **Diana Ong** (Superstock), *Portrait in Orange*
Prepress Buyer: **Herb Klein**
Manufacturing Buyer: **Patrice Fraccio**
Acquisitions Editor: **Ted Bolen**

© 1992 by Prentice-Hall, Inc.
A Simon & Schuster Company
Englewood Cliffs, New Jersey 07632

Printed in the United States of America

10   9   8   7   6   5   4   3   2   1

ISBN 0-13-313560-8

PRENTICE-HALL INTERNATIONAL (UK) LIMITED, *London*
PRENTICE-HALL OF AUSTRALIA PTY. LIMITED, *Sydney*
PRENTICE-HALL CANADA INC., *Toronto*
PRENTICE-HALL HISPANOAMERICANA, S.A., *Mexico*
PRENTICE-HALL OF INDIA PRIVATE LIMITED, *New Delhi*
PRENTICE-HALL OF JAPAN, INC., *Tokyo*
SIMON & SCHUSTER ASIA PTE. LTD., *Singapore*
EDITORA PRENTICE-HALL DO BRASIL, LTDA., *Rio de Janeiro*

Toward a feminist future for our children:

Paul Shih-mien Tong,

John Joseph Tong,

Sonya Kourany Sterba.

❧ Contents ❧

The World of Work

The Domestic Scene

Cultural Invisibility

FEMINIST THEORIES AND APPLICATIONS: EXPLAINING THE PRESENT AND CHANGING THE FUTURE

Liberal Feminism

Radical Feminism

Psychoanalytic Feminism

Marxist/Socialist Feminism

Postmodern Feminism

Methodological Postscripts

Suggested Reading   *405*

❧ Preface ❧

This anthology is designed to be a basic text for a first course in feminist philosophy or a first course in women's studies. Part I deals with a broad range of the most significant problems confronting women today. It deals with them from perspectives as diverse as those of the psychologist, sociologist and economist on the one hand and those of the philosopher, poet and children's story writer on the other. Part II presents some of the most promising theoretical frameworks thus far proposed to explain and resolve these problems. No other anthology combines so extensive and detailed a treatment of the problems confronting women today with the most current theoretical and practical means for resolving them.

Without the help of many people, this anthology would never have come to be. First of all, we want to thank the 120 friends and colleagues who provided us with the syllabi from which the basic structure of the anthology emerged. Second, we want to give particular thanks to Sandra Bartky of the University of Illinois at Chicago, Iris Young of the University of Pittsburgh, Barbara Corrado Pope of the University of Oregon, Ann Garry of California State College at Los Angeles, Cynthia Freeland of the University of Houston, Thomas Moody of California State University at San Bernardino, and Suzanne Marilley of the University of Notre Dame. Their suggestions proved invaluable as we worked to select the most appropriate articles for our readers. Finally, we want to thank Ted Bolen, the Philosophy Editor at Prentice Hall, and Michael Steinberg, Production Editor at Prentice-Hall, for their understanding, patience and technical assistance in bringing this anthology to press.

Janet A. Kourany

James P. Sterba

Rosemarie Tong

❧ Introduction ❧

Feminism. For many women as well as men this term evokes an image of strident, unattractive women angrily demanding the abandonment of the family, the desertion of husbands, the killing of fetuses, or perhaps just the burning of bras. But this picture of feminism grossly misrepresents its real nature and significance. To be sure, feminists sometimes have controversial ideas about the family, sexual relations, the mother-child relationship, and the female body. But these controversial ideas are far less "radical" than the public has been led to believe. Therefore, one of the central aims of this anthology is to provide a vision of feminism that communicates its positions accurately.

In contrast to media misrepresentations of feminists as look-alike women cut from the same ideological cloth, feminists differ, one from the other, in a variety of ways. Feminists come from all types of religious, educational, ethnic, racial, and class backgrounds; they are of different ages, body sizes, and sexual orientations; and they include men as well as women. Yet despite the fact that no single profile of the "typical feminist" exists, feminists do have some things in common: a firm commitment to gender equality, a painful awareness that such equality is far from achieved, and a continuing desire to work toward such equality. In the past, feminists pressed for such social transformations as the abolition of slavery, the inauguration of universal suffrage, free public education, affordable health care, accessible birth-control clinics, and improved working conditions for women and children. More recently, feminists have sought the passage of the Equal Rights Amendment, quality child care facilities, equal pay for equal work (or work of comparable worth), reproductive rights, and an end to sexual violence against women (rape, pornography, sexual harassment, wife beating, etc.).

The fact that feminists have generally pursued such goals does not mean that each individual feminist has pursued them with equal conviction. Feminists disagree about many matters including the original causes of gender inequality, the factors that continue to perpetuate it, and the actions that should be taken to end it. That feminists should disagree even about these fundamental matters should not surprise us, however. After all, any feminist who seeks to understand the present condition of women requires knowledge from such diverse fields as biology, psychology, anthropology, sociology, political science, economics, history, religion, and philosophy—knowledge that is oftentimes confusing and complex, and sometimes unavailable and unreliable. Small wonder, then, that feminists are greatly challenged by the problems that routinely confront women.

In this anthology we provide several descriptive accounts of problems confronting women together with a variety of feminist theories that address them. Because both these descriptive accounts and these theories are partial and provisional in nature, it is vital that we neither accept nor reject them at face value.

With respect to any one of the descriptive accounts in Part I, we must ask ourselves whether it portrays a pressing and present problem for women, or whether it portrays instead a pseudo or past problem that no longer holds. What evidence does the author offer to support her or his account? How are the problems that the author analyzes related to each other? Which seem the most important and why? Does the author gloss over or omit problems of equal or greater significance? Do our experiences bolster the author's account, or is there an enormous gap between our lived reality and what the author tells us to think about it?

With respect to the theories in Part II, we should also raise serious questions about each of them:

1. How well does the theory explain women's problems? How convincing is it?
2. How sound and complete is the evidence that the theory provides for its claims? (This evidence can be abstract or concrete; general or specific; biological, psychological, anthropological, sociological, political, economic, historical, religious, and/or philosophical).
3. How useful is the theory? Does it provide concrete strategies for dealing with women's concerns? If these strategies have been tried, have they worked? Why or why not? If they have not been tried, do they seem promising? Why or why not?

Although these questions are very basic ones, they are not the only ones we need to ask about the theories of Part II. Feminists have advanced these theories in order to explain gender inequality and to suggest ways to eliminate it. But gender inequality is an enormously complex phenomenon. It is not the case either that all men are equal and on one level, or that all women are equal and on another, lower level. On the contrary. There are inequalities among men related to class, race, ethnicity, sexual orientation, and the like, and corresponding inequalities among women. Therefore, any adequate feminist theory must relate gender issues to those of race, class, ethnicity, and sexual orientation.

PROBLEMS OF INEQUALITY

Gender Socialization

In every society, men are thought to be independent, aggressive, competitive, rational, and physically strong, while women are thought to be passive, nurturant, cooperative, emotional, and physically weak. These masculine and feminine gender characteristics are distinct from male and female sex characteristics. The fact that masculine and feminine gender characteristics vary not only in different cultures but also in our own culture provides some evidence that biological sex has little, if anything, to do with social gender. Studies of hermaphrodite babies, whose sex is difficult to determine at birth, also provide some evidence that sex and gender are separable phenomena. When hermaphrodite babies are assigned to the "wrong" sex—that is, when they are reared as girls when they are really boys, or vice versa—they cultivate the gender identities, traits, and behaviors associated with this "wrong" sex.

Whether gender is able to keep biological sex at bay permanently remains controversial, however. Nevertheless, very few people deny that the process by which female and male babies are turned into "feminine" and "masculine" adults is heavily social. Numerous studies show that adults teach children their gender identities in subtle as well as blatant ways. For example, parents send specific gender messages to their children—messages that girls are passive and nurturant and that boys are independent and aggressive. Mothers and fathers convey these messages to their sons and daughters through words and gestures; through the toys and clothes they buy them; and by the rights and responsibilities they give or do not give them.

Consider, for example, the astronaut or superman pajamas that boys wear versus the dainty, ruffled nighties that girls wear; or the floral arrangements and pastel bedspreads in girls' rooms versus the animal wallpaper and baseball pennants in boys' rooms. These parental messages are reinforced by teachers and peers who have their own strong ideas about how girls and boys should think, talk, and act. Clearly, society deliberately channels girls and boys in different directions, oftentimes irrespective of their individual needs, abilities, and interests. This channeling process promotes a sex-segregation that denies children of both sexes valuable opportunities to sample one another's interests and activities. As a result, children and adolescents tend to be far more comfortable in same-sex groups than in mixed-sex groups—a feeling that many children and adolescents carry with them, as adults, into the public realm.

That gender socialization psychologically and socially underdevelops boys and girls in certain areas is undeniable, but according to Claire Renzetti and Daniel Curran (authors of the first reading in the text) these developmental distortions limit girls even more than they do boys. After all, "feminine" characteristics such as passivity and physical weakness do seem objectively inferior to "masculine" characteristics such as activity and physical strength. Moreover, society still tends to regard other, arguably *good* "feminine" characteristics (for example, cooperativeness) as somehow inferior to their arguably *bad* "masculine" counterparts (for example, competitiveness), and as somehow inappropriate ones for persons in positions of power to cultivate. As a result, girls tend to have lower career aspirations and expectations for themselves than boys have for themselves.

Would gender-free socialization be better? In " 'X': A Fabulous Child's Story," novelist Lois Gould relates a tale about a child who is brought up in a gender-free way—as an X. The story describes the ways in which society pressures boys and girls to conform to its gender roles. It also suggests what it would take and what it would mean for individuals to depart from these gender roles. As Gould sees it, such departures would make for happier, more well-adjusted individuals. But what happens to "gender-free" children when they grow up and their biological sex becomes apparent? How does a person confront fundamental difference after he or she has been instructed that everyone is exactly the same? Gender socialization is debilitating and destructive when it is imposed rigorously and without opportunity for variation; but we may ask whether all acknowledgments of and appreciation for difference are necessarily wrong.

Sexuality

The process of gender socialization obviously includes learning, using, and attending to language. In " 'Pricks' and 'Chicks': A Plea for Persons," Robert Baker argues that our language does not serve women well. First, it regards man as "essentially human, while woman is only accidentally so." Thus, " 'Humanity' is synonymous with 'mankind' but not with 'womankind' " (p. 52). Second, women are linguistically related, at least in men's speech, to certain types of animals (chick, fox), playthings (babe, doll), items of clothing (skirt), and anatomical parts associated with sexual intercourse (snatch, cunt). Third, our language embeds a conception of sexual intercourse in which men play the role of active victimizers and women play the role of passive victims (men "screw" women and not vice versa). In sum, says Baker, our language teaches us that what makes men fully human is, paradoxically, the fact that they use sex to make women less than fully human. But, continues Baker, if this is the way we speak, then this must be the way we think. Speech not only shapes but reflects the way we think; and thought, as we know, guides action. Therefore, concludes Baker, if we want to change our deleterious sexual practices, we must revise our conception of heterosexuality and the words we use to articulate it. This revision and others like it, however, will require us to eliminate gender from our conceptual-linguistic schema.

To be sure, concedes Baker, this is no easy task since gender is probably the central feature of our language. When a baby is born, the first thing everyone wants to know is whether it is a "he" or a "she." Baker's call for gender-free language seems, then, far more radical than Lois Gould's plea for gender-free child rearing. But is it possible to change our thoughts and words before we change our practices, or must we change our thoughts, words, and practices simultaneously?

These last questions are urgent ones with implications for the world in which we live. If Baker is correct, for example, about the disturbing conception of heterosexuality that is revealed in our speech, then we can understand the pervasiveness of sexual violence against women in our society. This sexual violence takes many forms—rape, woman-battering, sexual harassment, and the sexual abuse of children—and is so prevalent that Carole Sheffield terms it and the fear it evokes "sexual terrorism":

The word terrorism invokes images of furtive organizations of the far right or left, whose members blow up buildings and cars, hijack airplanes, and murder innocent people in some country other than ours. But there is a different kind of terrorism, one that so pervades our culture that we have learned to live with it as though it were the natural order of things. Its targets are females—of all ages, races, and classes. It is the common characteristic of rape, wife battery, incest, pornography, harassment, and all forms of sexual violence. I call it sexual terrorism because it is a system by which males frighten and, by frightening, control and dominate females. (p. 61)

Sexual terrorism knows no bounds. It is committed by men of all ages, races, and religions, from all socioeconomic classes and educational levels, and whether these men are married, single, separated, or divorced. Most of this violence goes unreported; and when it is reported, unpunished (rape, for example, has the lowest conviction rate of all violent crimes). When society does take sexual violence against girls and women at all seriously, it still tends to blame the victims and to excuse the offenders. What is even worse than its "blame the victim" attitude, however, is the fact that society usually jokes about, outrightly denies, or misunderstands the nature and function of sexual violence. The motivation for rape is rooted not "in sexual frustration or sexual prowess," argues Sheffield, but in "the need to assert a masculine image or a masculine privilege as defined by the culture" (p. 71).

If any man who wants to be "masculine" is a potential perpetrator of sexual violence against women, and if society does little to protect women from this violence, or even to acknowledge it, we can understand why some women eschew heterosexual relations, preferring instead to form lesbian relationships with women. But, as Julia Penelope points out in "The Lesbian Perspective," women who choose to love women are usually penalized for this choice. Our society clearly tries to instruct women that heterosexuality is the only love possible: "Being a Lesbian or a heterosexual isn't a matter of 'choosing' a lifestyle or a 'sexual preference' from the table spread before us by parents, teachers, and other authority figures. There's only one dish on the social menu—heterosexuality—and we are given to understand that we swallow it or go without" (p. 73). As a result of society's injunctions, lesbians are forced to live on the margins of society as deviants with little political or personal support. What we need, says Julia Penelope, is a new social order in which lesbians live and love as happily as heterosexuals do. Never again should lesbians be "rejected, ridiculed, committed to psychiatric hospitals, jailed, or tortured" (p. 74); and never again should a woman be driven to suicide for daring to love women more than men.

Reproduction

Although American women have greater reproductive options than they have had in the past, their freedom to procreate or not to procreate remains subject to certain limits. One problem is cost: Contraception, sterilization, abortion, artificial insemination by donor, and in vitro fertilization are all expensive and beyond the economic means of many women. But there are other problems as well, insist Rachel Gold and Cory Richards in "Women and Reproduction." Frequently, much-needed reproductive services are unavailable and/or inaccessible; and even when these services are available and accessible, many of the women who need them are unaware of their existence. Women will never be able to control their fertility/infertility unless they are educated and encouraged to do so.

In "Abortion: Is a Woman a Person?," Ellen Willis raises the additional concern, that if Right-to-Life advocates have their way, the hard-won reproductive options of American women may be significantly eroded. Since there is no foolproof method of contraception, save for complete abstinence from heterosexual sex, any heterosexually active woman risks getting pregnant at any time. Such a woman may well wish to exercise her abortion option. Depending on what else is or is not going on in her life, she may regard pregnancy as an invasion—akin to an act of rape—and abortion as an act of self-defense.

We live in a society that defines child rearing as the mother's job; a society in which most women are denied access to work that pays enough to support a family, childcare facilities they can afford, or any relief from the constant, daily burdens of motherhood; a society that forces mothers into dependence on marriage or welfare and often into permanent poverty; a society that is actively hostile to women's ambitions for a better life. Under these conditions the unwillingly pregnant woman faces a terrifying loss of control over her fate. Even if she chooses to give up the baby, unwanted pregnancy is in itself a serious trauma. There is no way a pregnant woman can passively let the fetus live; she must create and nurture it with her own body, in a symbiosis that is often difficult, sometimes dangerous, always uniquely intimate. (p. 84)

As Ellen Willis sees it, those who would ban abortions are not simply interested in asserting that the fetus's right to life trumps a woman's right to bodily integrity. On the contrary. They are also interested in curbing a woman's sexual freedom. Abortion control, suggests Willis, is a form of sex control, a way to reassert the very traditional view that, at least insofar as women are concerned, sex is not about pleasure but about procreation. If Willis's analysis is correct, we need to ask ourselves whether women can ever be sexually free as long as they are required to pay the procreative piper in ways that men are not.

As bad as the present situation is for abled women, in "Claiming All of Our Bodies: Reproductive Rights and Disability," Anne Finger points out that it is far worse for disabled women. Here the problem is not that disabled women feel constrained by their limits, but that the larger society tends to define such women by their disabilities. Disabled women are abnormal women rather than women who happen to have atypical limits. Because abled people regard disabled people as other than "normal," they doubt that disabled people engage in "normal" sexual practices. As a result, the larger society assumes either that disabled people never engage in sex or that they engage in "kinky" and/or "irresponsible" sex. If the larger society makes the former assumption, then, for example, its researchers fail to devise birth control methods with the disabled in mind. In contrast, if the larger society makes the latter assumption, then, for example, its policymakers recommend restrictive measures, including coercive sterilization, to limit the sexual activities of at least developmentally disabled individuals.

Moreover, abled women carrying "defective fetuses" are routinely counseled to have abortions; and the killing or "letting die" of disabled infants—through the withholding or withdrawing of medical treatment—is urged. Rarely are these abled women given the opportunity to talk to the parents of disabled children who are not only surviving but thriving. Nor are they told that, if they choose to bear a disabled child but not to rear it, the child has a good chance of being adopted—sometimes within twenty-four hours. Although Finger is certainly correct to point out that disabled women's sexual and reproductive options are fewer than those of abled women, and that the larger society discriminates against disabled adults and children in both overt and subtle ways, we may nonetheless want to assess more carefully the situation of disabled infants. Is it always discriminatory to choose death over life for a severely disabled infant? Are there always enough adults who are willing to adopt disabled infants?

The newer reproductive technologies would seem to increase women's reproductive choices. Artificial insemination by donor permits fertile women who are married to infertile men, who are unmarried, or who are lesbian to have children who are genetically related to them. In vitro fertilization (that is, the ex utero fertilization of an ovum with sperm) allows women with fertility-related problems to beget, bear, and give birth to children. Finally, the social arrangement of surrogate, or contracted motherhood, enables certain men—fertile males married to infertile females, unmarried males, or gays—to beget a child. Critics of these collaborative modes of reproduction have argued, however, that contrary to appearances, these technologies and arrangements actually decrease rather than increase women's reproductive freedom. Commercial surrogacy is held out for special scrutiny. In "Selling Babies and

Selling Bodies," Sara Ann Ketchum suggests that commercial surrogacy cannot be distinguished either from selling babies or from selling (or renting out) women's bodies. Because it is wrong to treat babies and women as objects rather than as persons, Ketchum concludes that commercial surrogacy is a morally objectionable practice:

> Producing a child to order for money is a paradigm case of commodifying children. The fact that the child is not being put up for sale to the highest bidder, but is only for sale to the genetic father, may reduce some of the harmful effects of an open market in babies but does not quiet concerns about personhood. . . . (p. 98)

> A market in women's bodies—whether sexual prostitution or reproductive prostitution—reveals a social ontology in which women are among the things in the world that can be appropriately commodified—bought and sold and, by extension, stolen. (p. 100)

Commercial surrogacy has other negative features as well, not the least of which is the specter of rich infertile couples "harvesting" the babies of poor contracted mothers. Also of concern is the tendency in these contractual arrangements to focus on the interests of the genetic fathers and, correspondingly, to lose sight of the interests of the gestational mothers, their families, and the offspring produced in the process. For these reasons and others like them, Ketchum recommends the prohibition and/or the nonenforcement of *commercial* surrogacy. We may want to ask, however, whether the only thing that makes such arrangements suspect is their commercial nature. Could it be that there is something morally wrong about deliberately conceiving a child with no intention of participating in that child's life whether or not one is paid to do so?

Self-Images

When we discussed gender socialization above, we noted that females are thought to be passive, nurturant, cooperative, emotional, and physically weak. By no means do these gender characteristics totally exhaust society's notion of "femininity." In "Foucault, Femininity, and the Modernization of Patriarchal Power," Sandra Bartky sketches out in more detail our current understanding of femininity, touching on body size and configuration, gestures, facial expressions, postures, styles of movement, and styles of ornamentation. She also describes the "disciplinary practices," or forms of subjection (dieting, exercise, skin care, hair care, makeup, etc.) that females undergo to produce the ideal woman—all for the sake of being attractive to men. Because the "ideal woman" standard is impossible to ever achieve fully, or to achieve for very long, a real woman may regard her body as grossly inadequate: "The disciplinary project of femininity is a 'setup': it requires such radical and extensive measures of bodily transformation that virtually every woman who gives herself to it is destined in some degree to fail. Thus, a measure of shame is added to a woman's sense that the body she inhabits is deficient . . ." (p. 110). Sadly, even when a woman manages to achieve near physical perfection, all she will gain is some attention and admiration. What she will not gain is real respect and social power. Nevertheless, because she fears the loneliness that comes with rejection, such a woman may swallow her pride and continue to do whatever she has to do to earn the male gaze. Comments Bartky:

Insofar as the disciplinary practices of femininity produce a "subjected and practiced," an inferiorized, body, they must be understood as aspects of a far larger discipline, an oppressive and inegalitarian system of sexual subordination. This system aims at turning women into the docile and compliant companions of men just as surely as the army aims to turn its raw recruits into soldiers. (p. 110)

If Bartky is correct, we must ask ourselves what it will take to motivate women to rebel, or at least conscientiously to object to "beauty" service.

In "Mammies, Matriarchs, and Other Controlling Images," Patricia Hill Collins describes four images of African-American women prevalent in society: (1) the *Mammy*, who typifies the faithful, obedient, self-sacrificial black mother-figure in a white home; (2) the *Matriarch*, who typifies the unfeminine, castrating, working black mother-figure in a black home; (3) the *Welfare Mother*, an updated version of the breeder woman who is lazy, prolific, and a totally irresponsible mother; and (4) the *Jezebel*, the whore, or hypersexed black temptress. Collins maintains that these images function to oppress African-American people. For example, the Mammy image causes black children to behave deferentially toward whites even when such deference is not warranted; the Matriarch and Welfare Mother images cause black women to be blamed for the problems black children experience in society; and the Jezebel images causes black women to be blamed for the rapes and beatings men inflict upon them. Furthermore

these controlling images remain powerful influences on our relationships with whites, black men, and each other. Dealing with issues of beauty, particularly skin color, facial features and hair texture, is one concrete example of how controlling images denigrate African-American women. . . . Blue eyed, blond, thin white women could not be considered beautiful without the Other—black women with classical African features of dark skin, broad noses, full lips and kinky hair. (p. 125)

If what Collins says is correct, we need to spell out in detail the relationship between the "femininity" of African-American women and that of white women. As hard as it is for a white woman to be a perfect woman in this society, it seems virtually impossible for an African-American woman to achieve this imposed goal.

In "The Women in the Tower," Cynthia

Rich analyzes a 1982 *Boston Globe* article about a group of black women, aged 66 to 81, who demanded a meeting with the Boston Housing Authority to complain about the intolerably unsafe conditions in the "housing tower for the elderly" where they lived. Throughout the newspaper article, old women are portrayed as ugly (crow's feet, liver spots), unnatural, powerless, touchy, excitable, quarrelsome, quirky, quaint, annoying, endearing but not to be taken seriously, unkempt, senile, meek, pitiful, and definitely having nothing in common with either young or middle-aged people. But are *all* old women really like this? Is being an old woman that "bad"? Is life no longer worth living after menopause? Are young, abled, white women the only women worth knowing and loving?

The World of Work

Ever since World War II, American women have increasingly moved into the paid labor force owing to factors such as relaxed attitudes about proper gender roles, expanded job opportunities, decreased family size, the need for a second income, and higher divorce rates. In spite of legislative initiatives, court rulings, and affirmative-action programs, however, women's salaries still lag behind those of men. Indeed, full-time women workers earn approximately 69 percent of what full-time male workers earn; they enjoy fewer benefits, such as the chance to train for better jobs; and they are more subject to layoffs and firings.

Analysts have offered various explanations for the differences in wages and benefits between women and men. According to one explanation, these differences are due to inequalities in "human capital." Because men have accumulated more than women in the way of education, on-the-job training, and work experience, they can produce more for their employers than can women. Therefore, it is only fair that employers pay their male employees more than their female employees. According to another explanation, these differences are due to occupational segregation by sex. Women are clustered in a narrow range of low-paying jobs, whereas men are spread across a broader range of more highly paid occupations. Still another explanation for these differences points to the difficulties women have in combining work and family responsibilities. Family women usually cannot work long hours, choose jobs involving travel, or accept promotions with added responsibilities since these factors conflict with their role as child rearers and homemakers. A final explanation for these differences is conscious or unconscious discrimination against women. Employers' attitudes toward women are unduly influenced by the stereotypes that women are less committed to and less serious about their work than men are; that women's wages are second incomes and not really needed; and that women cannot handle job-related stresses and strains. So powerful are these stereotypes that one-third of the total wage difference between women and men has been attributed to discrimination.

In "Women Wage Earners," Marie Richmond-Abbott discusses the ways in which African-American women and women in blue-collar jobs are particularly hard hit by gender discrimination in the workplace. Many of these women are forced to work because they are the primary or sole support of one or more children. Not only are these women in need of parental leaves, adequate health care, affordable child care, and decent wages, but they are also in need of protection from sexual harassment on the job. Regrettably, an employer or manager may force himself upon a female worker precisely because he knows he can threaten to fire her if she does not comply with his wishes. Whereas a woman with some degree of economic security may be able to bluntly rebuff such advances, a woman who is poor, relatively unskilled, and in fear of winding up on welfare may feel that she has to acquiesce to his demands.

In contrast to Richmond-Abbot, Debra Renee Kaufman focuses on the situation of white-collar women in "Professional Women: How Real Are the Recent Gains?" She observes that nearly ten million women, one out of every five employed, hold white-collar jobs and that their number has increased significantly over the last decade. Even so, "what women are allowed to do remains limited, and barriers still restrict their mobility in the professional world" (p. 150). The professions, says Kaufman, are divided into the lower-paying, less prestigious female-dominated professions—for example, elementary school teaching, nursing, social work, and library science—and the higher-paying, more prestigious male-dominated professions— medicine, law, science, college teaching, and business administration. Female-dominated professions depend on skilled but abundant labor; they are structured for the lives that women lead (for example, career continuity is not essential); they tend to reserve their most respected positions for men; and they typically lack the kind of authoritarian and monopolistic controls that characterize the male-dominated professions.

In contrast, male-dominated professions reserve their lowest-paying, lowest-prestige subspecialities for women; they are structured for the lives that men lead (they demand great investments of time, energy, and commitment away from family life); and they require the exhibition of the more aggressive masculine gender traits. Comments Kaufman:

The high status professions and the prestige specialties in our society are identified with the instrumental, rigorous, "hard-nosed" qualities identified as masculine, not with the "softer," more expressive, nurturing modes of behavior identified as feminine. Since the characteristics associated with the most valued professions are also those associated with men, women fail to meet one of the most important professional criteria: They are not men." (p. 154)

Interestingly, even if a woman exhibits masculine gender traits, she will not be readily ac-

cepted in a male-dominated profession. She will tend to be excluded altogether, or at least left out of the power networks that make the difference when decisions for promotion partnership, tenure, research grants, and co-editorships are under consideration. The woman who manages to break through these barriers will probably do so only because she has paid some extremely high dues. Professional women often give up personal relationships, delay having children, and/or add on major domestic responsibilities to their already demanding workday. Small wonder that Kaufman wonders whether women's professional gains are worth the personal price.

But what of fields such as literature and the arts, disciplines that seem to transcend some of the rigors of gender's rules? In "Women and Creativity," Simone de Beauvoir points out that even in these fields women do less well than do men. Statistics have something to do with this situation. Because fewer women than men have become artists or writers, fewer women than men have produced great works of art or literature. But statistics are not the entire story, suggests de Beauvoir. If a woman chooses to be a painter or a sculptor, for example, public opinion and her own upbringing will work against her—especially if she lives a bohemian existence in squalid surroundings with neither husband nor children. Forced to use much of her energy to combat negative social pressures and her own ambivalence about being an artist, a woman will find herself much less able than a man to concentrate single-mindedly on her creative projects. To make matters worse, careers in painting or sculpture require a considerable amount of financial support. Studios are expensive as are the materials necessary for producing art. Unfortunately, family and friends are less likely to subsidize a woman than a man. And even when family and friends do provide their daughters, wives, and girlfriends with the material means for pursuing careers in art, art dealers and art collectors may show little interest in women artist's work. Comments de Beauvoir:

They always assume that the time will come when a woman will give up [abandon art for marriage or motherhood] and, therefore, that she is a bad investment. . . . Thus they deny her the means to develop her talent and to prove that she has some; which amounts to reinforcing the same old prejudice: she is a woman, therefore she cannot be talented. (p. 164)

A career in writing would seem to be a more viable choice for women, suggests de Beauvoir, since all that is needed for it is pen, paper, and "a room of one's own" (to quote Virginia Woolf). Furthermore, women are in a privileged position with regard to producing great literature—that is, the kind of literature that sees what all too many people fail to see. Not being a part of man's world, women have a certain distance from it, and thus can see it for what it is. Unfortunately, says de Beauvoir, women do not often push themselves to use their remarkable insights:

Women do not have enough faith in themselves, because others have not had faith in them; neither do they make the most extreme demands of themselves, which alone allow the individual to attain the greatest heights of achievement. . . . These qualities are denied them not by virtue of any flaw in their nature, but by virtue of the conditioning they have undergone. (p. 170)

De Beauvoir concludes that, since creativity is not "some sort of natural secretion" but "an extremely complex process, conditioned by all aspects of society" (p. 170), women will not be able to realize their full creative potential until they have the same opportunities for success as men have.

Of course, there is one occupation that women are welcome in and that they excel in, and that is the occupation of housewife. Even though the proportion of adult women engaging exclusively in housework has been dwindling in recent years, it is still the largest single occupation for American women. That this should be the case should not surprise us. After all, the family that includes a housewife devoted full time to child care, food preparation, housecleaning, laundry, grocery shopping, and the like generally benefits from high-quality and timely services. Nevertheless, as Barbara Bergmann points out in "The Job of Housewife," "housewifing" is a very peculiar occupation: "The nature of the duties to be performed, the method of payment, the form of supervision, the tenure system, the 'market' in which the 'workers' find 'jobs,' and the physical hazards are all very different from the way things are in other occupations" (p. 171). So great are these differences that people frequently say that housewives "don't work." Bergmann assures us, however, that housewives *do* work, performing servantlike tasks seven days a week and potentially twenty-four hours a day.

Unlike servants, however, housewives are usually expected to add sexual and other emotional services to their list of chores. In return for her labor, the housewife receives food, clothing, shelter, and even a share in whatever luxuries her husband's salary provides. What she does not receive, however, is any monetary reward designated as her own to be used as she sees fit. With his monopoly on the household's money, the husband of a housewife is in a position of power over her. He gives her as much or as little money as he chooses to; and if she protests in any way, he may react harshly toward her, reminding her that without him she will be poor indeed. For these and other reasons, Bergmann suggests that "the housewife occupation is one of the most problem-ridden in the economy" (p. 172).

Despite all these problems, however, present laws favor families with full-time housewives in several ways. For example, a man married to a woman with no income pays considerably less in taxes than he would as a single person, and also less, on a percentage basis, than if his wife worked for a wage. Moreover, many women who have worked outside the home and made substantial contributions to

Social Security receive the same Social Security benefits they would have received had they stayed at home. Bergmann discusses some of the proposals that have been made to rectify such shortcomings in our laws, as well as such related issues as paid maternity and child-rearing leaves. She also discusses the possibility of paying housewives wages for their work, an idea that we must consider carefully. Who would pay these wages? Would it not be preferable to require men to work as hard around the house as women do, thereby permitting both husbands and wives to work outside the home without either of them having to hold down a second, full-time job within the home? Is all the time that a woman spends with her spouse and children "work"?

Traditionally, marriage has been a lifelong partnership between a man and a woman in which their individual resources, interests, and even identities fully merge. For two-earner as well as one-earner families, marriage has also been an economic partnership in which a woman gives priority to homemaking and child care, while a man gives priority to his career. Over the centuries, a distinctive ideology has come to surround not only marriage but also motherhood. This ideology of motherhood finds expression everywhere: in novels and works of art, in the booklets found in obstetricians' waiting rooms, and even in the lectures handed down by mothers and mothers-in-law. According to this ubiquitous ideology, once a woman becomes a mother, she no longer has an identity and interests of her own. Henceforth, she is simply the instrument of her children's needs and wants. No matter what, the "maternal" show must go on, a drama in which each and every mother is supposed to repeat endlessly the small, routine chores of socializing young human beings. Though father may "help out" whenever he feels like it, raising children is mother's responsibility. "Normal" women love to mother, and there is something "abnormal" about any woman who does not

want to sacrifice herself totally in acts of unconditional love for her children.

The Domestic Scene

The ideology of motherhood not withstanding, some women are not always willing or even able to fulfill its terms. They have other identities besides that of mother, and other interests besides those of the children. To the degree that the mothering role conflicts with these other interests and identities, such women may experience their maternal tasks as suffocating. Moreover, they may get physically and psychologically exhausted—tired of the demands made upon them, and resentful of husbands who lift relatively few of their fingers around the house. Nevertheless, these women may also feel guilty precisely because their feelings about mothering are ambivalent. In "Anger and Tenderness," Adrienne Rich articulates these and other maternal feelings. She shares with us her own mothering experiences—her love-hate relationship with her sons. We need, she says, to ask ourselves if there are ways for women to mother that do not demand unconditional surrender to the needs and wants of their children. Under what set of circumstances can mothering be a relatively joyful—or at least healthy—experience for all considered?

If traditional marriage has brought with it problems such as those sketched above, then perhaps the solution is to replace traditional marriage with a new type of marriage in which the roles of husband and wife are fully equal. Perhaps a married couple should both work outside the home and within the home, thereby overcoming traditional gender roles and responsibilities. In "The Divorce Law Revolution and the Transformation of Legal Marriage," Lenore Weitzman observes that this new ideology of marriage is the one that is implicit in the new no-fault divorce laws. The old divorce laws assumed that a husband's role was to support a wife and children during marriage, and to continue to support them after divorce; and that a wife's role was to take care of home and children during marriage and to continue to care for them after divorce.

In contrast, the new divorce laws treat wives and husbands as fully equal partners in marriage *and* divorce. Thus, at divorce both partners are responsible for self-support and child support, and both are eligible for child custody. Alimony is awarded only according to need, and property is divided equally. Moreover, in most states no ground or fault is necessary to obtain a divorce. All that is required, according to the new divorce laws, is the desire of at least one partner in the marriage to end it. This is in sharp contrast to the old divorce laws, according to which a marriage could be dissolved only if at least one of the parties was judged guilty of some serious indiscretion, such as adultery, physical abuse, or mental cruelty. In such cases, the law punished the guilty party and rewarded the innocent one through suitable alimony and property awards.

However enlightened the new divorce laws seem, Weitzman argues that they worsen rather than improve women's condition. Even when both members of a married couple work outside the home, the woman's job is still the second job: the part-time job, the dead-end job, the luxury job. Women still tend to choose family responsibilities over career opportunities when push comes to shove, a tendency that is far less prevalent among men. As a result, at the time of a divorce a woman's earning capacity may have been impaired by the marriage relationship, while a man's earning capacity may have been enhanced. But the new divorce laws do not take this phenomenon into account. No matter what, divorce courts currently treat men and women equally at divorce, and decide property settlements, alimony awards, and child support accordingly. What makes this "new deal" a particularly difficult one for ex-wives, who get child custody 90 percent of the time, is that their ex-husbands rarely pay even half of the

expenses associated with rearing a child to adulthood. As a result, women and children now experience a sharp decline in their standard of living subsequent to a divorce, while men experience a steady rise in theirs. (Weitzman originally reported an average 73 percent decline in women and children's standard of living in the first year after divorce versus an average 42 percent rise in men's standard of living. However, Saul Hoffman and Greg Duncan suggest that 30 percent may be a more accurate figure for the decline in women and children's standard of living.)

According to Weitzman, another significant consequence of the new divorce laws is that they have "shifted the legal criteria for divorce—and thus for viable marriage—from fidelity to the marriage contract to individual standards of personal satisfaction" (p. 200). As a result, marriage is increasingly understood as a "time-limited, contingent arrangement rather than a lifelong commitment" (p. 201). In addition, the new divorce laws "alter the traditional legal view of marriage as a partnership by rewarding individual achievement rather than investment in the family partnership" (p. 204). Instead of "the traditional vision of a common financial future within marriage," the new laws "convey a new vision of independence for husbands and wives in marriage," and they "confer economic advantages on spouses who invest in themselves at the expense of the marital partnership" (p. 204). Given this new understanding of marriage, Weitzman predicts that fewer people are going to "tie the marriage knot." Therefore, we need to ask ourselves whether the demise of the traditional marriage is an event that we should celebrate with unalloyed glee, or one that we should worry about—if only a bit.

If both the old inegalitarian marriage and the new egalitarian marriage pose problems for women, no marriage at all often poses even greater problems for them. In "The Feminization of Poverty," Diana Pearce points out that the average income of the female-headed family has recently fallen to 46 percent of that of the average male-headed family, and that there are now three and one-half million female-headed families that fall below the poverty level. These trends are even worse within some minority communities. For example, about three out of four poor black families are now maintained by females alone. No wonder that Pearce concludes her article with a chilling observation: "If one simply extrapolated the present trends and did not take into account any other factors, all of the poor by the year 2000 would be women and children" (p. 207).

Given the increased unavailability of both low-cost housing and modestly priced rental units, one consequence of the "feminization of poverty" is that more and many female-headed families are becoming homeless. What makes the plight of these women particularly sad is that if no social-service agency or charitable organization houses them, then government officials may place their children in foster care. Since it is "extremely difficult" to get one's children back after they have been placed with foster parents, many homeless mothers avoid the welfare system, choosing to live with their children in condemned houses, abandoned cars, or cardboard boxes. Pearce proposes to eliminate this intolerable state of affairs by providing homeless women with decent temporary housing, quality childcare, and good jobs so that they can earn enough money to feed, clothe, and house themselves and their children.

Cultural Invisibility

Although women's physical presences are difficult to deny—after all, they do constitute over one-half of the population—lamentably, their mental abilities and achievements are all too often discounted, discredited, or denigrated. Whereas men's contributions to literature, history, religion, and science are routinely pronounced "great," women's contributions are regularly presented as minor, trivial, or periph-

eral. The writings in this section of the text each outline strategies to overcome this state of affairs. For example, in "Dancing Through the Minefield: Some Observations on the Theory, Practice, and Politics of a Feminist: Literary Criticism," Annette Kolodny describes what feminist literary scholars are doing to remedy women's exclusion from literature. In the first place, feminist scholars are rediscovering, republishing, and returning to circulation previously lost or otherwise ignored works by women writers—stories, novels, poems, essays, plays, and other genres popular with readers and critics in their own times and still interesting to us today. Second, they are developing new methodologies to interpret these works—methods that enable readers to appreciate recurrent symbols in women's writings, such as the "madwoman" who represents resistance to male domination. Third, feminist critics are questioning the norms and standards that underlie the discipline of literature. Far from being "objective," these norms and standards are often informed by male biases and sexist assumptions that serve to discount women's writing as "poor," "unimportant," "overly melodramatic" and the like.

Fourth, critics are seeking to make the evaluatory criteria for "great" literature truly objective; that is, open to women's as well as men's insights. Only when this fundamental change is made will women's writings take their rightful place: in widely read textbooks, in highly regarded anthologies, in the proceedings of national and international language and literature symposia, and in course syllabi. Finally, feminist critics are investigating the female traditions and themes that constitute women's writings, comparing as well as contrasting them with the male traditions and themes that constitute men's writings. Needless to say, observes Kolodny, each of these feminist initiatives has met with the resistance of the "authorities," the "Fathers," the patriarchs who wish to maintain the status quo.

In "Women in History: The Modern Period," Joan Scott describes what feminist historians are doing to include women in history. First, some feminist historians are rewriting *"his/story"* as *"her/story."* Usually they write "her/story" by moving the new subject, women, entirely outside of the framework of "his/story," offering a narrative that focuses exclusively on women's world-making experiences. Since women's story "remains separate" from men's (p. 239), Scott suggests that "her/story" remains subsidiary to "his/story." For this reason, other feminist historians are working in those fields of traditional history that are open to the thought that women's experiences are just as important and interesting as men's experiences.

One of these fields is social history, which "is ultimately about processes or systems" but which "is told through the lives of various groups of people who are the ostensible, though not always the actual subjects of the narrative" (p. 240). A social-historical approach, therefore, is one that tells us about the ways in which women, as a group, were affected by phenomena such as industrialization, urbanization, technological development, modernization, capitalism, and so on. Like the "her/story" approach to women's history, the social history approach is not unproblematic. Comments Scott: "If 'her-story' tends to be too separatist a position, much of the social history of women has been too integrationist, subsuming women within received categories of analysis" (p. 241). Women are understood not as individual agents but as group representatives who play predictable roles in that abstraction termed "social change."

To overcome the drawbacks of the "her/story" and "social history" approaches to women's history, other feminists are redoing "his/story." They seek to make gender as fundamental to historical analysis as race and class are. Because she favors this last approach, Scott argues on its behalf as follows:

Feminist desires to make woman a historical subject cannot be realized simply by making her the agent or principal character of a historical narrative. To discover where women have been throughout history it is necessary to examine what gender and sexual difference have had to do with the workings of power. By doing so historians will both find women and transform political history. (p. 242)

In "The Feminist Critique in Religious Studies," Rosemary Radford Ruether outlines the ways in which feminist theologians are struggling to overcome women's invisibility and negative treatment in Western religions, but especially in Judaism and Christianity. First, they are documenting instances of male bias in the Judeo-Christian tradition. Here the aim is to show how the male point of view dominates the Western religious tradition and how it shapes in conscious and unconscious ways official doctrine and practice.

Second, feminist theologians are discovering that deep within Christianity and Judaism there are unofficial doctrines and practices that welcome women's ideas and initiatives. Recent studies have revealed, for example, that women in first-century Judaism were not uniformly excluded from study in the synagogues; and that women in first-generation Christianity participated in leadership, teaching, and ministering roles. The feminist theologians who are making these discoveries are not simply interested in supplementing male religious tradition, however. Rather, they are interested in replacing its hierarchical values with a set of egalitarian values that celebrate *both* genders as well as all races and classes. This attempt, says Ruether, "will create a radical reappraisal of Jewish or Christian traditions, since much that has been regarded as marginal, and even heretical, must now be seen as efforts to hold onto an authentic tradition of women's equality" (p. 248); and much that has been regarded as "mainstream" will be seen as a failure to appreciate the depth and breadth of God's love for one and all.

This work, concludes Ruether, is not for

the faint of heart, for it "might lead to a new religion as momentous in its break with old religions as Christianity was with the religions of the Semites and the Greeks" (p. 250).

Finally, in "Re-visioning Clinical Research: Gender and the Ethics of Experimental Design," Sue Rosser details some of the necessary conditions for making clinical research and medical practice more responsive to women's needs.

First, research on conditions specific to females must receive higher priority, funding, and prestige. Second, since "many diseases have different frequencies (heart disease, lupus), symptoms (gonorrhea), or complications (most sexually transmitted diseases) in the two sexes, scientists should construct their studies with these differences in mind. For example, when exploring the metabolism of a particular drug, one should routinely run tests in both males and females" (p. 254).

Third, although guidelines now require federally funded research projects to ensure humane treatment of human subjects and to obtain their fully informed consent, more needs to be done with regard to subject involvement in research design and implementation so that subjects become actively involved in the production, evaluation, and uses of the knowledge relating to their own experience.

Finally, "the community of scientists undertaking clinical research needs to include individuals from backgrounds of as much variety and diversity as possible with regard to race, class, gender, and sexual preference. . . . Only then is it less likely that the perspective of one group will bias research design, approaches, subjects, and interpretations" (p. 258). Rosser concludes with a quote from Lynda Birke, a feminist biologist:

Perhaps this discussion of creating a feminist science seems hopelessly utopian. Perhaps. But feminism is, above all else, about wanting and working for change, change towards a better society in which women of all kinds are not devalued, or oppressed in any way.

Working for change has to include changing science, which not only perpetuates our oppression at present, but threatens also to destroy humanity and all the other species with whom we share this earth. (pp. 259–260)

THEORETICAL EXPLANATIONS: MOVING TOWARD A SOLUTION

Every once in a while feminists wonder whether twentieth-century feminists are making real progress toward gender equality, or whether they are simply treading water. Unfortunately, feminists have reason to be somewhat pessimistic. In the first place, gender and sex roles have not changed that much over the last century. Despite the fact that many men and women acknowledge that "masculinity" and "femininity" are cultural contructs, that "female sexuality" is no more or less passive (active) than "male sexuality" is, and that heterosexuality is not the only or even the best way for a woman (man) to express her (his) sexual needs and desires, these same men and women often behave in largely stereotypical ways.

Second, the reproductive roles of today's population are not appreciably different from those of past generations. Major developments in reproductive technology (for example, contraception, sterilization, abortion, artificial insemination by donor, and in vitro fertilization) have not substantially changed what it means to be a mother or a father for the vast majority of people.

Third, the rights and responsibilities that men and women currently have in both the public and private spheres bear strong resemblances to those of their nineteenth-century counterparts. Although women are entering the professions and occupations at an increasing rate, and although men are showing greater interest in the home, women still occupy less prestigious and less lucrative positions in the work force than do men, and men still spend less time working around the house and tending the children than do women.

Still another fact that has not altogether changed over the last century is women's relatively low self-image. No matter her race or class, her religion or ethnicity, a woman is still likely to worry too much about what men think about her physical appearance and sexual attractiveness.

Finally, despite the fact that many women have entered the academies of the arts and sciences, they remain largely unseen and unheard there.

Given the persistence of gender inequality, it is no wonder that feminists are eager to overcome it once and for all. Over the years, feminists have urged society to look at its sexist systems and structures through a variety of theoretical lenses. Although these theories are difficult to define (because they are still developing), many feminists have nonetheless named them "liberal," "radical," "psychoanalytic," "socialist," and "postmodern." To be sure, these labels are imperfect. Often they distort the precise meaning behind a feminist thinker's ideas and words. Nevertheless, they are helpful, each of them suggesting a partial and provisional answer to women's oppressed, repressed, and/or suppressed "condition," and what, if anything, can and ought to be done about it.

Although many feminists are in the process of conceiving the kind of feminist theories that are not limited by labels, we believe that it is important to study feminists' *past* attempts to explain the hows and whys behind women's oppression, repression, and/or suppression. Only then will we fully appreciate how much progress feminists have made in the struggle to liberate women from all the forces that limit their potential.

Liberal Feminism

Liberal feminism is probably the most widely recognized mode of traditional feminist thought. In his nineteenth-century classic *The Subjection of Women*, philosopher John Stuart Mill argues that no reflective student of human history can assert that *all* men are stronger and smarter than *all* women. That an average woman cannot do something an average man can is no reason to bar an exceptional woman from attempting that activity. Indeed, says Mill, even *if* it turns out that all women are worse than all men at some activity, say lifting weights, this is still no reason to bar women from trying to lift weights anyway, for "what women by nature cannot do, it is quite superfluous to forbid them from doing. What they can do, but not so well as the men who are their competitors, competition suffices to exclude them from" (p. 267). Although Mill believes that women are in fact men's equals, he concedes that there may be some biological sex differences between males and females. However, he does not concede that there are any *intellectual* and/or *moral* differences between men and women:

For, however great and apparently ineradicable the moral and intellectual differences between men and women might be, the evidence of their being natural differences could only be negative. Those only could be inferred to be natural which could not possibly be artificial—the residuum, after deducting every characteristic of either sex which can admit of being explained from education or external circumstances. The profoundest knowledge of the laws of the formation of character is indispensable to entitle any one to affirm even that there is any difference, much more what the difference is, between the two sexes considered as moral and rational beings; and since no one, as yet, has that knowledge, . . . no one is thus far entitled to any positive opinion on the subject. (p. 267)

Later in the *Subjection*, Mill suggests that men and women should become androgynous persons, a perfect blend of the best character and personality traits that "masculinity" and "femininity" have to offer. Interestingly, Mill fails to trace out the implications of his urging men and women to be androgynous. One would think, for example, that androgynous female persons would assume approximately the same roles in society that androgynous male persons would. However, Mill maintains that in the best of all possible worlds—with marriage a voluntary contract between real equals, with legal separation and divorce easily available to wives, and with high-paying jobs open to women—most women would continue to choose the "career" of family over other competing careers (business, law, and medicine), and most men would continue to choose public life over private life.

That Mill fails to appreciate the full implications of his androgynous ideal should not surprise us. It is difficult enough to be a reformer, let alone a revolutionary. Nevertheless, in "Feminist Justice and the Family," James Sterba, a twentieth-century philosopher, husband, and father, demonstrates what Zillah Eisenstein has elsewhere argued—namely, that liberal feminism may have a radical future.[1] Sterba shows that, carefully interpreted, an androgynous ideal has salutary implications for the kind of justice feminists believe should characterize male-female relationships in all human institutions. To avoid interminable discussions about whether existing "feminine" and "masculine" traits are "good" or "bad," Sterba defines the androgynous ideal abstractly. As he sees it, all that this ideal requires is that men and women be given equal opportunities for self-development; specifically, that "the traits that are truly desirable in society be equally available to both women and men, or in the care of virtues, equally inculcated in both women and men" (pp. 269–70).

Although many feminists have rightly objected to other versions of androgyny on the grounds that they tend to "Scotch-tape" together distorted extremes of "femininity" (Farrah Fawcett-Majors) and "masculinity" (John Travolta),[2] Sterba thinks that his version of androgyny avoids such ridiculous consequences. Indeed, as Sterba sees it, his androgynous ideal is the one that other feminists have sought to derive from either a Welfare Liberal Conception of Justice or a Socialist Conception of Justice.

According to the Welfare Liberal Conception of Justice, the androgynous ideal will remain just that—an ideal—unless all men and women "who have the same natural assets and the same willingness to use them" are given the "necessary resources to achieve similar life prospects" (p. 271); and according to the Socialist Conception of Justice, men's and women's basic and non-basic needs will never be satisfied unless capitalism is replaced by socialism. Whether feminists use a "liberal" or a "socialist" framework, however, they must challenge and change the structures that limit women (pp. 271–73).

First and foremost among these structures is the traditional family. Given that private as well as public day-care facilities are largely "inadequate" (p. 274), argues Sterba, ways must be found to permit young children to stay at home without reinstating the non-androgynous ideal of Public Man/Private Woman[3]; that is, without recreating the world in which daddy goes off to work each morning and mommy stays behind to take care of the children. Sterba suggests "that to truly share child-rearing within the family what is needed is flexible (typically part-time) work schedules that also allow both parents to be together with their children for a significant period every day" (p. 275); and it is this suggestion that distinguishes Sterba from Mill who, though Mill imagined women in the workplace, never imagined men in the nursery.

To the same degree that it is useful to juxtapose Mill's and Sterba's arguments, it is helpful to couple the speeches of the nineteenth-century suffragist Elizabeth Cady Stanton with those of twentieth-century political activist Gloria Steinem. When Susan B. Anthony, Lucy Stone, Isabella Beecher Hooker, and Elizabeth Cady Stanton addressed the U.S. Senate Committee on Women Suffrage, Stanton argued that women require all the rights that men have, especially the right to vote, so that they can assume "personal responsibility" for their lives (p. 276). A woman who lacks a "complete education," the "right of property," and "political equality" is a woman who lacks the means to make her way in the world (p. 277).

Interestingly, like their nineteenth-century counterparts, twentieth-century women are still fighting for their rights. When the suffragists finally won the right to vote, little did they suspect that their great-granddaughters would fail (at least for now) to secure passage of an Equal Rights Amendment. No wonder that Gloria Steinem exhorts contemporary feminists to learn the lessons that will help them survive the next stages of women's liberation. The lessons are somber ones: (1) Feminists must realize that to the extent that they are resisted, to that same extent they are being successful; (2) feminists must resist the type of thinking that focuses on a woman's "political correctness" rather than on her sincere desire to improve women's everyday lot; (3) feminists must be historians who derive plans of action as well as inspiration from their foremothers; and (4) feminists must realize that not moving ahead is the same as falling behind.

That women have come a long way since the time of Mill and Stanton is clear. Had liberal feminists not secured crucial educational, legal, and economic rights for women, there would be no female professors and college presidents, no women governors and senators, and no women physicians and lawyers today. Nevertheless, it is also true that the coin of liberal feminism has a "down" side as well as an "up" side. All too often liberal feminists have either implicitly or explicitly counselled women that, in order to be successful, women must (1) cultivate men's *negative* as well as positive character and personality traits, and (2) eschew women's *positive* as well as negative character and personality traits.

Radical Feminism

No wonder, then, that radical feminists believe that their liberal sisters have not gone far enough. They argue that it is patriarchy that oppresses women: a system characterized by power, dominance, hierarchy, and competition—a system that cannot be reformed but only extirpated root and branch. It is not just patriarchy's legal, political, and economic structures that must be overturned; it is also its social and cultural institutions (especially the family, the Church, and the academy).

Although radical feminist writings are as distinct as they are myriad, many of them trace the effects of female biology on women's self-perception, status, and function in the private and public domains. When an antifeminist says that biology is destiny, that individual means that (1) people are born with the hormones, anatomy, and chromosomes of either a male or a female; (2) females are destined to have a much more burdensome reproductive role than males are; (3) males will, other things being equal, exhibit "masculine" psychological traits, whereas females will, other things being equal, exhibit "feminine" psychological traits; and (4) society should preserve this natural order, making sure that its men remain "manly" and its women "womanly." Radical feminists, however, have no interest in preserving a biological status quo that subordinates women to men. Rather, their aim is to overcome whatever *negative* effects biology has had on women and perhaps also on men.

Although most radical feminists now view women's biology and psychology as potential sources of women's liberation, they initially saw them as the actual causes of women's enslavement. In *The Dialectic of Sex,* Shulamith Firestone argues that no matter how much educational, legal, political, and economic equality women achieve, nothing fundamental will change for women as long as biological reproduction remains the rule rather than the exception. As Firestone sees it, biological reproduction is neither in women's best interests nor in those of the children so reproduced. The joy of giving birth—invoked so frequently in this society—is a patriarchal myth. In fact, pregnancy is "barbaric," and natural childbirth is "at best necessary and tolerable," at worst, "like shitting a pumpkin" Moreover, biological motherhood is the root of further evils, especially the vice of possessiveness that generates feelings of hostility and jealousy among human beings. As Firestone sees it, the vice of possessiveness—the favoring of one child over another on account of its being the product of one's ovum or sperm—is precisely what must be overcome in order to secure not only women's liberation from men but also all people's liberation from divisive hierarchies.

Whether women's monopoly over the power to give birth is *the* paradigm for power relations is controversial both inside and outside the radical feminist community. So too is the notion that bearing and rearing children are necessarily oppressive. As we noted above, most radical feminists no longer agree with Firestone that the "technological fix" of artificial reproduction will secure women's liberation. What is oppressive is not female biology per se, but rather the fact that men have controlled women as bearers and rearers of children. Thus, if women are to be liberated, each woman must determine for herself when to use or not to use reproduction-controlling technologies (for example, contraception, sterilization, abortion) and reproduction-aiding technologies (artificial insemination by donor and in vitro fertilization); and each woman must also determine for herself whether she is going to rear her children alone or in collaboration with a spouse, some relative(s), some friend(s), and/or some privately paid or publicly subsidized employees (babysitters, nannies, day-care professionals, nursery teachers).

Not all radical feminists focus on the biological origins of women's oppression, however.

Indeed, most of them stress the ways in which gender (rigid ideas about "femininity") and sexuality (rigid ideas about "heterosexuality") have been used to subordinate women to men. Although radical feminists seldom separate their discussions of gender and sexuality, preferring instead to discuss the sex/gender system *in toto*, moments of emphasis do punctuate their writings. Like many liberal feminists, many radical feminists have espoused a nurture theory of gender differences according to which "masculine" and "feminine" traits are the products of socialization. However, unlike liberal feminists, who tend to de-emphasize men's power over women, and who quite often suggest "that men are simply fellow victims of sex-role conditioning,"[4] radical feminists insist that men have guided the social construction of gender and sexuality for their own purposes. Through education, law, and economics; through pornography, prostitution, sexual harassment, rape, and woman battering; and through foot binding, suttee, purdah, clitoridectomy, witch-burning, and gynecology, men have controlled women's "femininity" and sexuality for male pleasure.[5]

Given the ways in which society has permitted men to abuse and misuse women, it is no wonder that some radical feminists have insisted that women must (1) reinterpret femininity as a way of being that is independent of masculinity; and (2) escape the confines of heterosexuality, creating an exclusively female sexuality through celibacy, autoeroticism, or lesbianism. Alone, or with other women, a woman can discover the true pleasures of sex. Women must learn how to stand separate from men so as to experience the fullness of their female persons.

To be certain, "separatism" is an idea that threatens not only men but many women. In her brilliant essay, "Some Reflections on Separatism and Power," Marilyn Frye approaches separatism as something practiced by a variety of individuals—especially those concerned with social change. We all participate in a multitude of relations, most often unreflectively. When we begin to question the "goodness" of some of these relations, we also begin to question the value of our participating in them. To reject some relations—to resist paying income tax for nuclear weapons, to divest from South African stock, or to engage in conscientious objection, for example—is to engage in noncooperation, in nonparticipation, in *separatism*. What distinguishes feminist from non-feminist separatism, says Frye, is that the former is a separation "from men and from institutions, relationships, roles and activities which are male-defined, male-dominated and operating for the benefit of males and the maintenance of male privilege—this separation being initiated or maintained at will, *by women*" (pp. 288–9). By refusing to approve the status quo for women, and by creating women's consciousness-raising groups, rape crisis centers, all-women social events, battered-women's shelters, and women's art galleries—feminists engage in acts of separatism.

Of course, feminist separation takes forms other than these. Some feminists refuse to change their career plans simply because the men in their lives ask them to; they refuse to have sexual intercourse with their boyfriends or husbands on demand; they refuse to say yes simply because the men in their lives wish they would. Indeed, as Frye sees it, "access is the crucial battle to be fought in the struggle for women's liberation from patriarchy, for the "Patriarchal Imperative" teaches that "males *must have access* to women" (p. 292). Women must remove (redirect, reallocate) goods and services from men in order to weaken, and even destroy, patriarchal power. Because the most vital goods and services that women have provided for men have tended to be sexual in nature, a call for *feminist* separatism sometimes leads to a call for *lesbian* separatism (nonparticipation in the institution of heterosexuality). Although radical feminists agree that female sexuality should not

be defined in terms of men's needs and wants, they do not want to impose lesbianism on all women. Indeed, as most radical feminists see it, no specific kind of sexual experience should be prescribed as *the* best kind for a liberated woman. Each and every woman should be encouraged to experiment sexually with herself, with other women, and even with men. As dangerous as heterosexuality is for a woman within a patriarchal society—that is, as difficult as it can be for a woman to know whether *she* wants to say yes or no to a *man*'s sexual advances—she must feel free to follow the lead of her own desires.

One of the most debated issues in the radical feminist community is related to what sorts of sexual desires men and women *should* feel free to follow. Should men and, for that matter, women have access to pornographic material—that is, to a continuum of material that ranges from pulpy romance novels, which tell stories of thinly disguised male domination and female submission, to soft-core magazines such as *Playboy*, which feature depictions of quivering young bunnies disrobing in front of elderly Great White Hunters, to hard-core magazines such as *Bondage*, which highlight scenes of men torturing women (for example, photos of businessmen systematically applying hot irons, scissors, torches, and knives to the breasts and vaginas of their secretaries)?[6] As some feminists, including some radical feminists, see it, both men and women should have access to this material provided that it benefits them in some way; for example, by helping them to overcome sexual hang-ups. As other feminists, including the majority of radical feminists, see it, however, pornography never benefits women; rather, it always harms them. How could it be otherwise, asks Catharine MacKinnon, since pornography is

the graphic sexually explicit subordination of women through pictures or words that also includes women dehumanized as sexual objects, things or commodities; enjoying pain or humiliation or rape; being tied up, cut up, mutilated, bruised, or physically hurt; in postures of sexual submission or servility or display; reduced to body parts, penetrated by objects or animals, or presented in scenarios of degradation, injury, torture; shown as filthy or inferior; bleeding, bruised, or hurt in a context that makes these conditions sexual. (p. 300)

Pornography is not about free speech and the First Amendment, says MacKinnon. Rather, it is about civil rights and the Fourteenth Amendment. Premised as it is on inequality, pornography leads men (and to some degree women) not only to think less of women, but to treat women as second-class citizens, or less than fully human persons. For this reason, MacKinnon argues that pornography can and ought to be controlled as a civil rights violation. Any woman—or man, child, or transsexual used in the place of a woman—should be granted a legal cause of action if that individual is coerced into a pornographic performance, has pornography forced on her, or has been assaulted or attacked because of a particular piece of pornography. Further, any woman should be able to bring suit against traffickers in pornography on behalf of all women.

Clearly, MacKinnon's ideas and those of Andrea Dworkin, her collaborator, are controversial. To their credit, MacKinnon and Dworkin have noticed what we all should have noticed years ago: that the pornographic imagination distorts, degrades, and demeans the bodies of women far more than those of men. With rare exception, pornography is something men do to women. Nevertheless, many feminists, especially liberal feminists, resist the argument that pornography is *central* to women's subordination. To suggest that pornography contributes to women's oppression more than does lack of access to good jobs, affordable child care, and quality education is, they insist, to suggest something about

which the typical woman on welfare can only shake her head in disbelief.[7]

Psychoanalytic Feminism

The fact that radical feminists focus more on pornography than do liberal feminists underscores the additional fact that, unlike liberal feminists, radical feminists believe that women's reproductive and sexual roles are the primary cause of women's oppression. Interestingly, psychoanalytic feminists agree with radical feminists that reproduction and sex are the primary source of women's oppression, but they offer a different account of why this is so.

For radical feminists, the centrality of sexuality emerges "from feminist practice on diverse issues, including abortion, birth control, sterilization abuse, domestic battery, rape, incest, lesbianism, sexual harassment, prostitution, female sexual slavery, and pornography."[8] For psychoanalytic feminists, however, the centrality of sexuality arises out of Freudian theory and such theoretical concepts as the pre-Oedipal stage (the stage in which all infants are symbiotically attached to their mother, whom they perceive as omnipotent) and the Oedipus complex (the process by which boys and girl submit their sexual desires to society's conscience—that is, to society's rules and regulations). To resolve the Oedipus complex successfully, and to escape castration at the hand of his father, the boy must give up his first love object—his mother. As a result of submitting his id (or desires) to the superego (collective social conscience), the boy is fully integrated into culture. In contrast to the boy, the girl, who has no penis to lose, separates slowly from her first love object—her mother. As a result, the girl's integration into society is supposedly less complete, and she never becomes as obedient to society's rules and regulations as does her male counterpart.

Among the psychoanalytic feminists who

have focused on the pre-Oedipal stage and the Oedipus complex is sociologist Nancy Chodorow. For years, the fact that women *want* to mother even when they do not *have* to mother puzzled Chodorow. Unsatisfied either by the "nature" theory of motherhood (female anatomy destines women to mother) or by the "nurture" theory of motherhood (society socializes women to mother), Chodorow found in psychoanalytic theory the answer to her questions about women's penchant for mothering. As we noted above, boys separate from their mothers to a degree that girls do not. This difference in the psychosexual development of boys and girls has significant social repercussions.

According to Chodorow, the boy's separateness from his mother is the source of his inability to relate deeply to others, including his own wife and children: an inability that prepares him, however, for work in the public sphere, which values single-minded efficiency, a down-to-business attitude, and competitiveness.

Similarly, the girl's oneness with her mother is the source of her capacity for relatedness: a capacity that enables her to meet the needs and desires of those to whom she is related but that often prevents her from meeting her own needs and desires—indeed, from being a person in her own right. What this means is that men are underdeveloped relationally and overdeveloped occupationally, whereas women are underdeveloped occupationally and overdeveloped relationally. Not until fathers and mothers "dual-parent" their children, argues Chodorow, will this lopsided state of affairs be repaired. Were both men and women to spend approximately the same time in the private domain, they would also be able to spend approximately the same time in the public domain. The consequence of this more balanced approach to life would be *well-developed* men and women, equally capable of intimacy and separation.

Despite their general admiration for Chodorow's ideas, critics have leveled three specific objections against her work. The first is simply that Chodorow focuses too much on the inner dynamics of the psyche and not enough on the external structures of society as the *primary* source of women's oppression. Despite some disclaimers to the contrary, Chodorow ultimately suggests that feminine personality causes family structure, when it seems more likely that family structure causes feminine personality. The second objection is that far from ending women's oppression, dual parenting may actually exacerbate it. Once men take over the nursery, they will have more power than ever—emotional power within the family as well as political and economic power outside the family. The third objection voiced by critics is that Chodorow wrongly uses one kind of family and one kind of mother—the capitalist, middle-class, white, heterosexual one—as the paradigm for all types of families and all types of mothers.

The last of these criticisms is the one that Elizabeth Spelman elaborates in "Gender in the Context of Race and Class." As Spelman sees it, Chodorow does not pay nearly enough attention to the ways in which race and class as well as gender "reproduce" mothers. In particular, Chodorow does not specifically address questions such as the following:

(1) Does race or class identity affect gender identity? For example, are there elements of race and class in notions of masculinity and femininity?

(2) Does a child's sense of self include a conscious or unconscious sense of race or class?

(3) What are the hierarchies in the world into which children are born and socialized? Is sexual privilege or domination affected by the race and class of the men and women in question?

(4) What are the ways in which sexism might be related to other forms of oppression? For example, is

sexism a support or cause of racism or classism? Or is it in some sense more closely intertwined with them? (pp. 328–9)

As a result of paying scant attention to race and class, says Spelman, Chodorow "tends to write as if the kind of care mothers provide is everywhere the same—despite her acknowledgement of the likelihood of cultural differences on this score". A relatively disadvantaged black woman in a racist society will mother her children very differently than will a relatively advantaged white woman in that same society. Unlike the white mother who has the luxury of telling her sons and daughters stories with happy endings, the black mother may have to tell her sons and daughters stories with sad endings in order to prepare them for the injustices and cruelties that await them in the larger world. There is no such creature, says Spelman, as a "woman in general" or, we may add, a mother in general. The only kind of women and mothers we know are particular women and mothers: women with concrete histories and specific identities. We must ask not only why women in general mother, but why this woman in particular mothers. However related the answers to these two separate questions may be, they are not identical, says Spelman.

Marxist/Socialist Feminism

Rather than choosing among the liberal, radical, and psychoanalytic explanations, some feminists seek to weave these strands of feminist theory together. This task seems to have been taken up most effectively by socialist feminists. Although the socialist feminist approach to women's oppression differs from the Marxist feminist approach, it shares enough ideas with its historic antecedent to warrant a discussion of Friedrich Engel's "The Origin of the Family, Private Property, and the State." Like all Marxist feminists, Engels claims that women's oppression originated in the introduction of private property, an institution that ended whatever equality the human community had previously enjoyed. Private ownership of the means of production by relatively few persons, originally all male, inaugurated a class system whose contemporary manifestations are corporate capitalism and imperialism. Reflection on this state of affairs suggests that not so much patriarchy as capitalism is the root cause of women's oppression. If all women—not just the relatively privileged or exceptional ones—are ever to be liberated, the capitalist system must be replaced by a socialist system in which the means of production belong to one and all. Because no one would be economically dependent on anyone else under socialism, women would be economically liberated from men. Thus freed, women would enter into sexual relations with men for one reason only: their own desire to do so. Comments Engels:

Full freedom of marriage can therefore only be generally established when the abolition of capitalist production and of the property relations created by it has removed all the accompanying economic considerations which still exert such a powerful influence on the choice of a marriage partner. For them there is no other motive left except mutual inclination.

Unconvinced that the entrance of women into the workplace will automatically make women men's equals, socialist feminists argue that women's condition is overdetermined by the structures of production (from Marxist feminists), reproduction and sexuality (from radical feminists), and the socialization of children (from liberal feminists). In other words, a woman's status and function in *all* of these structures, and not just the production-related ones, must change if she is to achieve anything approximating full liberation. Furthermore, woman's interior world (her psyche) must also be transformed (as emphasized by psychoanalytic feminists); for without such a change, improvements in woman's exterior world will not liberate her from the kind of patriarchal thoughts that undermine her self-concept and self-confidence.

In "The Unhappy Marriage of Marxism and Feminism," Heidi Hartmann, a leading socialist feminist, maintains that although the categories of Marxist analysis—for example, "class," "reserve army of labor," "wage laborer"—help explain the constitution of a particular occupational structure, they leave unexplained why it is that *women* play the subordinate and submissive roles both in the workplace and in the home. To understand women's relation to men as well as workers' relation to capital, says Hartmann, a feminist analysis of patriarchy must accompany a Marxist analysis of capitalism. The partnership between capitalism and patriarchy—"a set of social relations between men which have a material base, and which, though hierarchical, establish or create interdependence and solidarity among men that enable them to dominate women" (p. 345)—is most complex, says Hartmann, because capitalism's interests in women are not always the same as patriarchy's interest. In the nineteenth century, for example, male workers wanted "their women at home to personally service them" (p. 350), whereas male capitalists wanted women (excluding their own, of course) to work in the wage-labor market. Only if male workers and male capitalists could find some mutually agreeable way to handle this particular "women question" could the interests of capitalism and patriarchy be harmonized.

Initially, the way was for male capitalists to pay male workers a "family wage" large enough to permit their wives and children to stay at home. Male capitalists struck this bargain with male workers because they believed that (1) stay-at-home housewives would produce and maintain healthier and happier male workers than would working wives; and (2) women and children could always be persuaded at a later date to reenter the work force for low wages should men demand overly high wages. As it so happens, many women and children are currently entering the work force for low wages not so much because men are demanding too much in the way of remuneration, but simply because many families can no longer make it on *one* family income—even a good one.

However, the move of women into the workplace has not fundamentally diminished men's power over women. Through the sexual division of labor, patriarchy maintains the subordinate status of women in the workplace as well as in the home. In a workplace that is divided into high-paying, male-dominated jobs and low-paying, female-dominated jobs, men earn $1.00 for every $.69 women earn. In the home, working women, but not working men, experience the stresses and strains of the "double day." Numerous studies show that the husbands of working women do not do much more work around the house than do the husbands of stay-at-home housewives.[9] Most working women have two full-time jobs: one in the home and one outside the home.

Reflecting on the present sexual division of labor, which results in *women* getting the "short end of the stick" in the home and/or the workplace, Hartmann concludes that men's desire to control women is at least as strong as capitalism's desire to control workers. Capitalism and patriarchy must be fought simultaneously. However, since war on two fronts is enormously taxing, women must pick their battles carefully. And given that it is easier for working women to form coalitions than it is for housewives to do so, women might as well begin their "war" in the workplace by demanding that they be paid as well as men are paid. Not only must women demand "equal wages for equal work," but they must also demand "comparable wages for comparable work," for only then will the workplace by truly socialized rather than merely liberalized.

As many socialist feminists see it, the ultimate aim of the so-called comparable worth movement is not simply to make women the economic equals of men but to break down what is an increasingly scandalous hierarchy of wages, providing some people with seven-figure salaries and others with a pittance. The justification generally given for this skewed state of affairs is that the market pays the highest price to those who do the most valuable work. But as socialist feminists see it, it is doubtful that the market always rewards the "right" people; and it is even more doubtful that anyone's work is worth astronomically more than anyone else's. Is a college professor's work really worth eight or nine times that of a secretary's? The comparable worth debate is an opportunity, therefore, to flatten the hierarchy of wages by demonstrating the ways in which most female-dominated occupations require as much knowledge, skills, mental acuity, and accountability as do most male-dominated occupations. It is also an opportunity to argue the point that all jobs are of approximately equal worth. Comment Teresa Amott and Julie Matthaei in "Comparable Worth and Incomparable Pay":

if [the] discussion of what makes work worthy extended to the grass roots, we may decide that workers in unskilled, routinized jobs may be doing the hardest work of all, for such work saps and denies their very humanity. Why should those whose work give them the most opportunity to develop and use their abilities also be paid the most? The traditional argument—that higher pay must be offered as an incentive for workers to gain skills and training—is contradicted by the fact that our highly paid jobs attract many more workers than employers demand. (p. 363–4)

To be sure, it will be difficult for mainstream Americans to accept not only that women deserve as much pay as men do for comparable work, but also that no one really deserves that much more money than anyone else. But even if Americans accept only the first of these arguments, capitalism and patriarchy will be weakened. For example, because nearly half of all poor families are female-headed, and because women are the primary recipients of food stamps, legal services, and Medicare, if wage-earning women were paid what their jobs are worth, these women would be able to support themselves and their families adequately without being forced, in one way or another, to attach themselves to men as an additional source of income.

Postmodern Feminism

Interestingly, the socialist feminist effort to find integration and agreement, to establish *one* specifically feminist standpoint that could represent how *women* see the world, has not gone unchallenged. Postmodern feminists regard this effort as yet another example of "phallologocentric" thought. It is typical "male thinking" to seek the "one, true, feminist story of reality."[10] For postmodernists, such a synthesis is neither feasible nor desirable. It is not *feasible* because women's experiences differ across class, racial, and cultural lines. It is not *desirable* because the "One" and the "True" are philosophical myths that culture has used to club into submission the differences that, in point of empirical fact, best describe the human condition. That feminism is many and not one is to be expected because women are many and not one. The more feminist thoughts, the better. By refusing to center, congeal, and cement separate thoughts into a unified and inflexible truth, feminists resist patriarchal dogma.

In their attempt to articulate feminist diversities, postmodern feminists make fascinating connections between the ways in which women's "sexuality" and women's "textuality" merge. As Annie Leclerc sees it in her article "Woman's Word," the fact that men's sexuality is linear and unitary, doggedly focused as it is on the penis's penetration of the vagina, is not unrelated to the fact that men's writing is overly regimented (ideas are marshalled rather than diffused). Likewise, the fact that women's sexuality is cyclical and multifaceted is not unrelated to that fact that women's writing is without definite boundaries. These ideas are developed in full by Helene Cixous who objects to masculine writing and thinking because they are cast in binary oppositions. Man has unnecessarily segmented reality by coupling concepts and terms in pairs of polar opposites, one of which is always privileged over the other. In her essay "Sorties," Cixous lists some of these dichotomous pairs:

> Activity/Passivity
> Sun/Moon
> Culture/Nature
> Day/Night
> Thought has always worked through opposition.
> Speaking/Writing
> Parole/Écriture
> High/Low
> Through dual, hierarchical oppositions (p. 369).

In Cixous's view, all of these dichotomies find their inspiration in the fundamental dichotomous couple—man/woman—in which man is associated with all that is active, cultural, light, high, or generally positive, and woman with all that is passive, natural, dark, low, or generally negative. Moreover, the first term of the man/woman dichotomy is the term from which the second departs or deviates. Man is the self; woman is his Other. Thus, woman exists in man's world on his terms. She is either the Other for man, or she is "unthinkable," "unthought" (p. 370).

Cixous challenges women to write themselves out of the world that men have constructed for them by putting into words the unthinkable/unthought. The type of writing that Cixous identifies as woman's own—marking, scratching, scribbling, jotting down—connotes movements that bring to mind Heraclitus's ever-changing river. In contrast, the type of writing that Cixous associates with man connotes Parmenides's static world: what *is* has always been and will always be. Once it is stamped with the official seal of patriarchal approval, a thought is no longer permitted to move or change. Thus, for Cixous, feminine writing is not merely a new style of writing; it is "the very possibility of change, the space that can serve as a springboard for subversive thought, the precursory movement of a transformation of social and cultural standards".

In the process of further distinguishing between men's and women's writing, Cixous draws many connections between male sexuality and masculine writing on the one hand and female sexuality and feminine writing on the other. Male sexuality, which centers on what Cixous calls the "big dick," is ultimately boring in its pointedness and singularity. Like male sexuality, masculine writing, usually termed "phallocentric" writing by Cixous, is also ultimately boring. Men write the same old things with their "little pocket signifier"—the trio of penis/phallus/pen. Fearing the multiplicity and chaos that exist outside their Symbolic Order, men always write in black ink, carefully containing their thoughts in a sharply defined and rigidly imposed structure. In contrast, female sexuality is, for Cixous, anything but boring; and just as exciting as female sexuality is feminine writing that is open and multiple, varied and rhythmic, full of pleasures and, perhaps more importantly, of possibilities. When a woman writes, said Cixous, she writes in "white ink," letting her words flow freely where she wishes them to go.

Luce Irigaray ("Questions") agrees with Cixous that female sexuality is the source of feminine writing, but she resists what she regards as the temptation to define the "feminine feminine." As Irigaray sees it, any statement that definitively asserts what the real, or true "feminine" is will re-create the "phallic," or "masculine" feminine: "To claim that the feminine can be expressed in the form of a concept is to allow oneself to be caught up again in a system of 'masculine' representations, in which women are trapped in a system or meaning which serves the auto-affection of the (masculine) subject". What obstructs the progression of women's thoughts out of this trap is the concept of Sameness, the ideational result of masculine narcissism and singularity.

Although Irigaray finds Sameness everywhere in Western philosophy and psychoanalysis, she finds it omnipresent in the work of Sigmund Freud, especially in Freud's writings on female sexuality. According to Irigaray, Freud sees the little girl not as feminine in any positive sense but only in her negativity, as a "little man" without a penis. Freud suppresses the notion of difference, characterizing the feminine instead as a lack of something. Woman is a reflection of man, the Same as a man, except in her sexuality. Female sexuality, because it does not mirror the male's, is an absence, or lack of the male's sexuality. Where woman does not reflect man, she does not exist and, suggests Irigaray, will never exist until the Oedipus complex is exploded and the *"feminine* feminine" released from its repression.

In realizing that Western culture is loathe to abandon accounts of how the self—that is, the male self—is constituted, Irigaray suggests several strategies aimed at enabling woman to experience herself as something other than "waste" or "excess" in the structured margins of a dominant ideology. One of these strategies is to mime the mimes men have imposed on women. If women exist only in men's eyes, as images, women should take those images and reflect them back to men in magnified proportions. As Toril Moi notes:

Through her acceptance of what is in any case an ineluctable mimicry, Irigaray doubles it back on itself, thus raising the parasitism to the second power. . . . Miming the miming imposed on woman, Irigaray's subtle specular move (her mimicry mirrors that of all women) intends to undo the effects of phallocentric discourse simply by overdoing them. [11]

To be sure, concedes Irigaray, mimicking is not without its perils. The distinction between mimicking the patriarchal definition of woman in order to subvert it and merely fulfilling this definition is not clear. In their attempts to overdo this definition, women may be drawn back into it. Nevertheless, despite this risk, no female should lose the opportunity to break out of the male straitjacket that has been misshaping her female form.

Methodological Postscripts

As attractive as the postmodern approach to feminism may be, some feminist theorists worry that an overemphasis on difference and a rejection of unity may lead to intellectual and political disintegration. If feminism is to be without any standpoint whatsoever, it becomes difficult to ground feminist claims about what is good for women. Contemporary feminism's major challenge is, therefore, to reconcile the pressures for diversity and difference with those for integration and commonality. Feminists need a home in which each woman has a room of her own, but one in which the walls are thin enough to permit a conversation, a community of friends in virtue and partners in action. Only in such a community are feminist ethics and politics possible.

Contemporary feminists are not shirking from this challenge. Indeed, in "Have We Got a Theory for You! Feminist Theory, Cultural Imperialism and the Demand for 'The Woman's Voice,' " Maria Lugones and Elizabeth Spelman challenge feminists to do what has never been done before—to conceive a theory that celebrates women's different ways of thinking, doing, and being without separating women from each other on account of these

differences. They also challenge feminist theo-
reticians not to write about "Woman" in general, for no such abstraction exists. Finally, they
challenge feminist theorists to ferret out the racism, classism, ethnocentrism, imperialism, and
heterosexism in feminist writings—"isms" that
prevent women from becoming *friends.*

Naturally, it is very difficult to meet all of
Spelman and Lugones's challenges, especially
the one regarding "isms." In "Sisterhood: Political Solidarity between Women," Bell Hooks
reminds feminists that confronting one's own
ugly "isms" and those of others is a painful process. Hurtful words will be shouted and angry
glances will be exchanged. Yet as Hooks sees it,
"sustained woman bonding" between black and
white women, or between Anglo-American and
Hispanic women, or between any two women
who really differ from each other, will never
occur unless all women learn to do what
Lugones and Spelman have obviously learned
to do—namely, to confront each other's limits
lovingly.

The type of feminist theory that Spelman,
Lugones, and Hooks envision has not been written yet, but feminists have taken out their
scratch pads. The "scribbling" that is going on
is about expanding narrowness of mind and removing constrictions of heart, and that, says
Lugones and Spelman, takes "openness, sensitivity, concentration, self-questioning" (p.
393). To say "we women think" is both a privilege and an achievement. Only friends can say
"we"—proudly, defiantly, joyfully, angrily,
hopefully. And it is not always easy to make
friends. But friendship is precisely what feminists are committed to creating.

We hope this anthology has shown how incredibly diverse feminists are. As we look back over
the readings in this book, we take vicarious pleasure and pride in the different ideas that feminists have conceived about justice and caring,
about difference and unity, about individuality

and community. To be sure, some of these
ideas have caused women (and men) to stumble
down cul-de-sacs; but most of them have
brought women (and men) at least a few steps
closer to liberation. Because feminist thought is
kaleidoscopic, our first impression of it may be
one of chaos and confusion, of dissension and
disagreement, of fragmentation and splintering.
But first impressions are often unreliable, and if
we reflect more closely on the kaleidoscope of
feminist thought, new visions, new structures,
and new relationships for personal and political
life will emerge. What is to be treasured about
feminist thought, then, is its creativity, its fe-
cundity. Feminist ideas have many beginnings;
they have no one end. They allow each of us
permission to think new feminist thoughts and
to shape the type of communities in which these
thoughts and ideas can be lived in friendship.

NOTES

1. Zillah Eisenstein, *The Radical Future of
Liberal Feminism* (Boston: Northeastern University
Press, 1986).

2. Mary Daly, *Gyn/Ecology: The Metaethics of
Radical Feminism* (Boston: Beacon Press, 1978),
p. xi.

3. Jean Elshtain uses this phrase as the title of
her book *Public Man, Private Woman* (Princeton,
NJ: Princeton University Press, 1981).

4. Ellen Willis, "The Conservatism of *Ms.*," in
Feminist Revolution (New York: Random House,
1975), p. 170.

5. Daly, *Gyn/Ecology: The Metaethics of Radical Feminism*, pp. 107-312.

6. Laura Lederer, ed., *Take Back the Night:
Women on Pornography* (New York: William Morrow, 1980).

7. There is another way to interpret MacKinnon's and Dworkin's claim about the centrality of
pornography—an interpretation that strengthens their
claim. If, for example, pornography does not refer
simply to the women-hating depictions that litter
books, magazines, and films, but rather to the way in
which male-female relationships have been con-

structed under the institution of compulsory hetero-sexuality—an institution that, according to radical feminists, forces women to live not for themselves but exclusively for the emotional gratification and sexual satisfaction of men—then pornography may indeed be the *sine qua non* of women's oppression.

8. Catharine A. MacKinnon, "Feminism, Marxism, Method, and the State: An Agenda for Theory," *Sign: Journal of Women in Culture and Society* 7, no. 3 (Spring 1982):528.

9. Barbara Bergmann, *The Economic Emergence of Women* (New York: Basic Books, 1986), pp. 266–269.

10. Sandra Harding, *The Science Question in Feminism* (Ithaca, NY: Cornell University Press, 1986), p. 28.

11. Toril Moi, *Sexual/Textural Politics: Feminist Literary Theory* (New York: Methuen 1985), p. 140.

❧ Sex-Role Socialization ❧

Gender Socialization

Claire Renzetti
Daniel Curran

Imagine that it is ten years from now. You are married and would like to start a family, but you and your spouse have just been told that you can have only one child. Which would you prefer that child to be: a boy or a girl?

If you are like most American college students, you would prefer your only child to be a boy. Indeed, since the 1930s, researchers have documented that Americans in general have a clear "boy preference." Not only do we prefer boys as only children, but in larger families, we also prefer sons to outnumber daughters, and we have a strong preference for sons as first-borns. There is some evidence to suggest that this may be weakening a bit in the United States; for instance, several recent studies have reported an increasing tendency for people to express no preference rather than an explicit son or daughter preference. Outside the United States, however, boy preference remains so strong that in some countries, such as India and Egypt, it is estimated that if parents could choose the sex of

their offspring, the resulting ratio of boys to girls would range from 162:100 to as high as 495:100.

It appears, then, that children are born into a world that largely prefers boys over girls. Some of the common reasons that adults give for this preference are that boys carry on the family name (assuming that a daughter will take her husband's name at marriage) and that boys are both easier and cheaper to raise. The small minority that prefers girls seems to value them for their traditionally feminine traits: they are supposedly neater, cuddlier, cuter, and more obedient than boys. Although it is uncertain whether children perceive their parents' sex preferences, it is clear that these preferences are closely associated with parental expectations of children's behavior and tend to reflect gender stereotypes.

*   *   *

GROWING UP FEMININE OR MASCULINE

If you ask parents whether they treat their children differently simply on the basis of sex, most

From *Women, Men and Society* (1989), Chapter 4. Reprinted by permission.

would probably say no, and there is some research to back up their claims. In Maccoby and Jacklin's review of the literature, for instance, no consistent sex differences in parent–infant interaction were found. Nevertheless, there is considerable evidence that what parents *say* they do and what they *actually* do are often not the same.

It appears, in fact, that gender socialization gets underway shortly after a child is born. Although there are few physiological or behavioral differences between males and females at birth, parents do tend to respond differently to their newborns on the basis of sex. For example, when asked to describe their babies within twenty-four hours of birth, new parents frequently use gender stereotypes. Infant girls are described as tiny, soft, and delicate, but parents of infant boys use adjectives such as strong, alert, and coordinated to describe their babies. Interestingly, fathers provide more stereotyped descriptions than mothers do.

It is not unreasonable for us to suspect that parents' initial stereotyped perceptions of their children may lay the foundation for the differential treatment of sons and daughters. Maccoby and Jacklin did find that parents tend to elicit more gross motor activity from their sons than from their daughters, but there appears to be little if any difference in the amount of affectionate contact between mothers and their sons and daughters. Additional research indicates that parents tend to engage in rougher, more physical play with infant sons than with infant daughters. In this way, parents may be providing early training for their infant sons to be more independent and aggressive than their daughters.

This pattern continues through the preschool years. For example, Fagot [and colleagues] discovered that adults respond differently to boys' and girls' communicative styles. Although thirteen- and fourteen-month-old children showed no sex differences in their attempts to communicate, adults

tended to respond to boys when they "forced attention" by being aggressive, or by crying, whining, and screaming. Similar attempts by girls were usually ignored, but adults were responsive to girls when they used gestures or gentle touching, or when they simply talked. Significantly, when Fagot and her colleagues observed these same children just eleven months later, they saw clear sex differences in their styles of communication: boys were more assertive, whereas girls were more talkative. In a study with a related theme, Weitzman et al. found that mothers communicate differently with toddler sons and daughters. They speak to their sons more explicitly, teach and question them more, and use more numbers and action verbs in speaking to them. In short, mothers provide their sons more than their daughters with the kind of verbal stimulation thought to foster cognitive development. What is perhaps as important, however, is the fact that Weitzman and her colleagues included in this study mothers who profess not to adhere to traditional gender stereotypes. Although the differential treatment of sons and daughters was by no means absent, it was less pronounced among these mothers.

The studies discussed so far have been based on samples of white, middle-class, two-parent families, making generalizations with regard to other types of families' socialization practices unreliable at best. Despite the limitations of such studies, they do help to explain why sex differences that are absent in infancy . . . begin to emerge during early childhood. But, as we have already mentioned, gender socialization is accomplished not only through parent–child interaction, but also through the ways parents structure their children's environment. Let's turn, then, to a discussion of this latter aspect of the socialization process, keeping in mind that this research, too, tends to be race- and class-specific. We will return to examine more carefully the variables of race and social class later in the chapter.

The Gender-Specific Nature of Children's Environments

What is the easiest and most accurate way for a stranger to determine the sex of an infant? According to Madeline Shakin and her associates, a baby's clothing provides the best clues. Ninety percent of the infants they observed in suburban shopping malls were dressed in sex-typed clothes. The color of the clothing alone supplied a reliable clue for sex labeling: the vast majority of the girls wore pink or yellow, whereas most boys were dressed in blue or red. The style of children's garments also varies by sex. On special occasions, girls wear dresses trimmed with ruffles and lace and at bedtime, nighties with more of the same; for leisure activities, their slacks sets may be more practical, but chances are they are pastel in color and decorated with motifs such as hearts or flowers. In contrast, boys wear three-piece suits on special occasions and at bedtime, astronaut, athlete, or super-hero pajamas; and for leisure activities, their overalls or slacks sets are in primary colors with sports or military decorations.

All this may seem insignificant, even picky, to you. However, what we must emphasize here is that clothing plays a significant part in gender socialization in two ways. First, by informing others about the sex of the child, clothing sends implicit messages about how the child should be treated. "We know . . . that when someone interacts with a child and a sex label is available, the label functions to direct behavior along the lines of traditional [gender] roles." Second, certain types of clothing encourage or discourage particular behaviors or activities. Girls in frilly dresses, for example, are discouraged from rough-and-tumble play, whereas boys' physical movement is rarely impeded by their clothing. Boys are expected to be more active than girls are and the styles of the clothing designed for them reflect this gender stereotype. Clothing,

then, serves as one of the most basic means by which parents organize their children's world along gender-specific lines.

Parents also more directly construct specific environments for their children with the nurseries, bedrooms, and playrooms that they furnish and decorate. The classic study in this area was conducted by Rheingold and Cook, who actually went into middle-class homes and examined the contents of children's rooms. Their comparison of boys' and girls' rooms is a study of contrasts. Girls' rooms reflected traditional conceptions of femininity, especially in terms of domesticity and motherhood. Their rooms were usually decorated with floral designs and ruffled bedspreads, pillows, curtains, and rugs. They contained an abundance of baby dolls and related items (e.g., doll houses) as well as miniature appliances (e.g., toy stoves). Few of these items were found in boys' rooms where, instead, the decor and contents reflected traditional notions about masculinity. Boys' rooms had more animal motifs and were filled with military toys and athletic equipment. They also had building and vehicular toys (e.g., blocks, trucks, wagons). Importantly, boys had more toys overall as well as more types of toys, including those considered educational. The only items girls were as likely to have as boys were musical instruments and books (although, as we will see shortly, the content of children's books is rarely gender-neutral). Given that similar findings were obtained more than ten years later, it appears that Rheingold and Cook's conclusion remains applicable, at least with regard to the socialization of white, middle-class children:

The rooms of children constitute a not inconsiderable part of their environment. Here they go to bed and wake up; here they spend some part of every day. Their rooms determine the things they see and find for amusement and instruction. That their rooms have an effect on their present and subsequent behavior can be assumed; a standard is set that may in part account for some differences in the behavior of girls and boys. [1]

The Rheingold and Cook study also highlights the importance of toys in a young child's environment. Toys, too, play a major part in gender socialization. Toys not only entertain children, they also teach them particular skills and encourage them to explore through play a variety of roles they may one day occupy as adults. Thus, if we provide boys and girls with different types of toys, we are essentially training them for separate (and unequal) roles as adults. What's more, we are subtly telling them that what they *may* do, as well as what they *can* do, is largely determined (and limited) by their sex.

Are there clear differences in the toys girls and boys are expected to play with and, if so, just what are these differences? Rheingold and Cook's research already answered these questions to some extent, but a quick perusal of most contemporary toy catalogs further addresses the issue. The toys for sale are frequently pictured with models; pay careful attention to which toys are pictured with female models and which are shown with males. In the catalog we picked up, most of the toys were obviously gender-linked. We found, for instance, that little girls were most frequently shown with dolls or household appliances. The only "dolls" boys were pictured with were "action figures," such as Rambo and Masters of the Universe. On one page, a boy was shown pushing a toy lawn mower that blows bubbles but, almost as if to intentionally delineate for youngsters the "appropriate" sexual division of household labor, a little girl was pictured on the opposite page pushing a toy vacuum cleaner with "dust bunnies" inside the canister. On other pages, little boys were shown writing the ABCs on a chalkboard or examining a leaf under a plastic microscope, while little girls were pictured cooking in a "storybook kitchen" or sleeping peacefully under a bed canopy designed to look like a tent. Even the stuffed

animals were gender-linked: a smiling female model cuddled a cheery Popples bear, while a snarling male model held his "pet monster" with "break-apart plastic chains and removable wrist bands."

Even though toy catalogs are directed primarily to parents—in the United States parents make over 70 percent of all toy purchases—many children spend considerable time looking at the catalogs and often ask their parents to buy specific toys they see advertised. If the catalog we examined is typical of toy catalogs in general—and we have no reason to doubt that it is—then children are receiving very clear gender messages about the kinds of toys they are supposed to want. These messages are reinforced by the pictures on toy packaging, by the way toy stores often arrange their stock in separate sections for boys and girls, and by sales personnel who frequently recommend gender-stereotyped toys to potential customers. It is no wonder that by two and a half years of age, children request mostly gender-stereotyped toys. Are they ever really given a choice?

The toys themselves foster different traits and abilities in children, depending on their sex. Toys for boys tend to encourage exploration, manipulation, invention, construction, competition, and aggression. In contrast, girls' toys typically rate high on manipulability, but also creativity, nurturance, and attractiveness. As one researcher concluded, "These data support the hypothesis that playing with girls' versus boys' toys may be related to the development of differential cognitive and/or social skills in girls and boys."

Apart from toys, what other items stand out as a central feature of a child's environment? You may recall from the Rheingold and Cook study that books are one of only two items that boys and girls are equally likely to have. Unfortunately, children's literature has traditionally ignored females or has portrayed males and females in a blatantly stereotyped fashion. For example, Lenore Weitzman and her colleagues found in their now-classic analysis of award-winning picture books for preschoolers that males were usually depicted as active adventurers and leaders, whereas females were shown as passive followers and helpers. Boys were typically rewarded for their accomplishments and for being smart; girls were rewarded for their good looks. Books that included adult characters showed men doing a wide range of jobs, but women were restricted largely to domestic roles. In about one-third of the books they studied, however, there were no female characters at all.

In a recent replication of the Weitzman research, Williams et al. noted significant improvements in the visibility of females. Only 12.5 percent of the 1980s books they examined had no females, while a third had females as central characters. Nevertheless, although males and females are now about equal in their appearance in children's literature, the ways they are depicted remain largely unchanged. According to Williams et al., "With respect to role portrayal and characterization, females do not appear to be so much stereotyped as simply colorless. No behavior was shared by a majority of females, while nearly all males were portrayed as independent, persistent, and active. Furthermore, differences in the way males and females are presented is entirely consistent with traditional culture." In short, the gender stereotypes fostered by much toy play continue to be promoted in children's books.

Importantly, considerable attention has been given to the problem of sexism in children's literature, resulting in an effort to change it. Publishers, for instance, have developed guidelines to help authors avoid sexism in their works, and a number of authors and writers' collectives have set to work producing egalitarian books for youngsters. Research on the success of these endeavors is limited, however, and the findings are mixed. On the one hand, it has been argued that the so-called nonsexist picture books frequently advantage female characters at the expense of male characters, thus simply re-

versing traditional depictions of gender rather than portraying gender equality. On the other hand, Davis praises the nonsexist books for their depictions of females as highly independent and males as nurturant and nonaggressive. However, he also points out that the nonsexist books continue to reinforce some traditional gender stereotypes in that they still tend to portray females as more emotional and less physically active than males. It remains to be seen, therefore, whether this new genre can overcome the gender biases that have traditionally pervaded children's literature.

One way that writers and publishers have tried to overcome sexism in children's literature is to depict characters as genderless or gender neutral. But recent research casts doubt on the potential success of this approach, since it has been found that parents who read these books to their children almost always label the characters in gender-specific ways. In 95 percent of these cases the labeling is masculine. In this study, the only pictures that prompted feminine labels were those showing an adult helping a child, an interpretation consistent with the gender stereotypes that females need more help than males and that females are more attentive to children. Based on this research, then, it appears that "picturing characters in a gender-neutral way is actually counterproductive, since the adult 'reading' the picture book with the child is likely to produce an even more gender-biased presentation than the average children's book does."

To summarize our discussion so far, we have seen that virtually every significant dimension of a child's environment—his or her clothing, bedroom, toys, and books—is structured according to cultural expectations of appropriate gendered behavior. If, as cognitive-developmental theorists maintain, young children actively try to organize all the information they receive daily, their parents and other adults are clearly providing them with the means. Despite their claims, even most parents who see themselves as egalitarian tend to provide their children with different experiences and opportunities and to respond to them differently on the basis of sex. Consequently, the children cannot help but conclude that sex is an important social category. By the time they are ready for school, they have already learned to view the world in terms of a dichotomy: his and hers.

THE INTERVENING VARIABLES OF RACE AND SOCIAL CLASS

Again, we must emphasize that much of the research on early-childhood gender socialization has recruited subjects from white, middle- and upper-class, two-parent families. There are indications, however, that the findings of such studies may not be representative of the socialization practices of families of other races and social classes. The work of Janice Hale-Benson is instructive on this point.

Hale-Benson has studied the socialization goals and practices of black families. She emphasizes the dual nature of the socialization that takes place in black households. "One of the challenges Black families must face in socializing their children is to understand and assist their children to function within their peer group. In addition, Black parents must also provide them with the skills and abilities they will need to succeed in the outside society." For both male and female children, black parents stress heavily the importance of hard work, ambition, and achievement. Thus, black children of both sexes tend to be more independent and self-reliant than their white peers. They are also imbued at an early age with a sense of financial responsibility to earn income for themselves and to contribute to the support of their families.

Still, the socialization experiences of young black males and females is not identical. Hale-Benson points out, for example, that among the traits and skills taught to black boys (largely in the context of their peer group) are the ways to move their bodies distinctively, athletic prowess, sexual competence, and street savvy, including how to fight. In contrast, black girls are socialized into "a very strong motherhood orientation," although this does not preclude the general expectation that they will also work outside the home. The development of personal uniqueness or distinctiveness is also emphasized, with special attention given to sexuality, clothing, and body movement.

It is important to note that black children are frequently socialized in social contexts different from traditional white, middle-class family structure; . . . black children are often exposed to women and men sharing tasks and assuming collective responsibility. In two-parent black families, women are typically employed outside the home, and men participate in child care. But over half of black children live with just one parent, usually the mother, compared with 18 percent of white children. . . . In black single-parent households, the parent may be aided in the care and socialization of the children by an extended kin and friendship network. In addition, Hale-Benson notes that the black church offers "a kind of extended family fellowship that provides other significant adults to relate to the children, and it also provides material and human resources to the family."

In light of these data, it is not surprising that Hale-Benson and others have found that black children are not taught to perceive gender in completely bipolar terms. Instead, both males and females are expected to be nurturant and expressive emotionally as well as independent, confident, and assertive. Bardewell et al. have also found that black children are less gender-stereotyped than white children are. Importantly, Isaaks obtained similar results in a comparison of Hispanic and white children. However, there is some research that reports contradictory findings. For instance, Gonzalez and Price-Bonham and Skeen found at least as much, if not more, gender stereotyping among blacks and Hispanics as among whites.

The picture becomes blurred or more complex when social class is taken into account. For example, there is modest support for the hypothesis that gender stereotyping decreases as one moves up the social class hierarchy. However, if parental educational level may be used as an indicator of a family's social class, it appears that gender stereotyping may be greater the higher a family's social class position, at least among whites. Research that examines the interaction of social class with race and ethnicity indicates that the latter is the more important variable; that is, it has a stronger influence on child-rearing practices, although this research did not examine gender socialization specifically. We can only conclude that much more research is needed to elucidate the rich diversity of gender socialization practices and their outcomes among various races and social classes.

* * *

EDUCATING GIRLS AND BOYS: THE ELEMENTARY SCHOOLS

Just like parents, elementary school teachers when asked will state that they treat all their students fairly regardless of their sex. Research findings indicate, however, that in practice, teachers typically interact differently with their male and female students. For one thing, most teachers continue to use various subtle forms of sex segregation in their classrooms. For example, they seat girls on one side of the room, boys on the other; or they ask girls and boys to form separate lines; or they may organize teams for a spelling competition according to students' sex. It is also not uncommon for teachers to assign girls and boys different classroom chores; for instance, girls may be asked to dust or water the plants, whereas boys carry books, rearrange desks, or run equipment.

Subtle though they may be, these kinds of sex segregation have at least three interrelated consequences. First, sex segregation in and of itself prevents boys and girls from working together cooperatively, thus denying children of both sexes valuable opportunities to learn about and sample one another's interests and activities. Second, it makes working in same-sex groups more comfortable than working in mixed-sex groups—a feeling that children may carry with them into adulthood and that may become problematic when they enter the labor force. And finally, sex segregation reinforces gender stereotypes, especially if it involves differential work assignments.

But separating students by sex is neither the only nor the most significant way that teachers treat their male and female pupils differently. It also appears that teachers respond more to boys than girls, in both positive and negative ways. For example, one recent study of fourth-, sixth-, and eighth-grade classes in the Washington, D.C., and New England areas found that "teachers were more likely to provide remediation and challenge for male students. They gave boys more help in finding errors and correcting problems. They were also more likely to challenge a male student to achieve the best possible academic response." Other studies confirm these findings. Boys get more praise for the intellectual quality of their work, whereas girls are praised more often for the neatness of their work. In addition, teachers typically provide boys with detailed instructions for completing a complex task, but they are more likely to simply do the task for girls, thereby depriving girls of the valuable experience of independent learning through doing.

Although boys engage in more positive interactions with teachers, they are also more likely than girls to incur their teachers' wrath. Boys are subject to more disciplinary action in elementary school classrooms, and their punishments are harsher and more public than those handed out to girls. Of course, this may be because boys misbehave more than girls. . . . We pointed out that preschool boys are encouraged to be active and aggressive, while preschool girls are rewarded for quiet play and passivity. It may be that the early childhood socialization of girls better prepares them for the behavioral requirements of elementary school. Yet, this fails to explain why, when boys and girls are being equally disruptive, it is the boys that teachers most frequently single out for punishment. The one exception appears to be when answers are called out in class: "When boys call out comments without raising their hands, teachers accept their answers. However, when girls call out, teachers reprimand this 'inappropriate' behavior with messages such as, 'In this class we don't shout out answers, we raise our hands'." Clearly, gender stereotypes have a strong influence on teacher–student interactions.

It is hardly surprising that teachers respond to their students in these ways given that few teacher-preparation programs do anything to prevent it. In one study of teacher-education textbooks, for instance, researchers found that the problem of sexism in the schools is rarely addressed. In fact, the authors of these texts are sometimes guilty of sexism themselves.

The gender messages that teachers send to students are further reinforced by the traditional curricular materials available in elementary schools; . . . students learn not only the academic subjects of their school's formal curriculum, but also a set of values and expectations of a hidden curriculum. We can see the hidden curriculum at work in the selective content of textbooks and other educational materials. Even though the United States is a country with citizens of both sexes who share a rich and varied racial and ethnic heritage, there is a conspicuous absence of racial minorities and women in elementary school textbooks. In history texts, for example, Native Americans and Chicanos are rarely mentioned apart from such events as Custer's last stand or the Alamo, and in both cases, it is made abundantly clear who the "bad guys" were. Blacks are typically discussed in the context of slavery, the Civil War, and perhaps the civil rights movement, but Harriet Tubman

and the Rev. Martin Luther King, Jr. are often the only blacks singled out as history makers. When women are mentioned, it is usually in terms of traditional feminine roles: for example, for nursing, Florence Nightingale; for sewing, Betsy Ross; for being married to famous men, Dolly Madison and Jackie Kennedy Onassis. The heterosexist bias of the texts goes without saying. . . .

The use of history texts as an example is not meant to imply that a hidden curriculum is prevalent only in the material taught to older children. Researchers have found the hidden curriculum at work even in the early grades. Consider the books used to teach children to read. As the following example illustrates, these books may also teach children particular lessons about gender:

A book in the easy-to-read section of the library taught the children that: "Boys eat, girls cook; boys invent things, girls use what boys invent; boys build houses, girls keep house."[2]

Just as their later history texts will implicitly teach them that racial minorities and women rarely make significant contributions to our society, young children also learn from their readers that there are things only boys can do and things only girls can do. Some publishers of children's readers have made a serious effort in recent years to eliminate gender as well as racial stereotyping from these texts. Systematic research to gauge their success remains to be done, but the importance of this task is underlined by evidence that indicates that children do learn their lessons quite well. Consider, for instance, the findings of one researcher who asked a group of second- and third-graders what they wanted to be when they grow up. Typical responses from boys included "A pro football player because I would make a lot of money"; "A spy chief, I like to spy"; and "A motorcycle racer, it is fun." In contrast, the girls replied, "I want to be a plain old woman wife, it is fun"; "A mother, I want to have a baby, it is fun"; "I want to be a nurse so I can help people when they are sick"; and "I want to be a teacher, I just like it."

Finally, children receive messages about gender simply by the way adult jobs are distributed in their schools. Although approximately 84 percent of elementary school teachers and 94 percent of teachers' aides are women, less than 18 percent of principals and assistant principals are women. Importantly, research indicates that the sex of a school principal does have a measurable effect on children's gender-role perceptions. According to one study of first-graders, for instance, children who attended a school headed by a female principal held fewer gender stereotypes than those who went to a school with a male principal.

In light of our discussion so far, it is hardly surprising to find that, although girls outperform boys academically in the early grades, their achievement test scores decline significantly as they progress through school. As we will see next, this pattern continues in high school.

EDUCATING TEENAGE GIRLS AND BOYS: THE SECONDARY SCHOOLS

Both parents and teenagers will attest that adolescence is one of the more stressful periods of the life cycle. As one's body changes and matures, so do one's interests, and the opinions of friends take on greater significance in the formation of one's self-concept. Young men and women both feel the need to be popular with their peers, but the means and measures of their success at this are somewhat different.

For teenage boys, the single most important source of prestige and popularity is athletic achievement. The teenage boy tends to measure "himself by what he can do physically compared with others his age, and how he stacks up determines to a great extent his social acceptance by others and his own self-esteem." The "nonjock" is at an obvious disadvantage, so-

cially and psychologically. It is the athlete who is looked to as a leader, not only by his peers, but also by teachers and parents. Moreover, on the court or on the playing field, boys are taught a variety of stereotypically masculine skills and values: aggression, endurance, competitiveness, self-confidence, and teamwork.

It is also in high school that young men are expected to formulate their career goals. For those not planning to attend college, there are vocational training programs that provide the educational background needed for jobs in the skilled trades or in preparation for technical school. Most boys, though, study an academic or college prep curriculum, which may seem a bit surprising given their greater likelihood for academic difficulties in the lower grades. Importantly, however, boys' academic performance usually improves during high school—to such an extent, in fact, that their SAT scores are higher on average than those of girls.

And what about girls? How does their high school experience differ from that of boys? For one thing, physical prowess and athletic ability are not their chief sources of prestige and popularity. Indeed, most teenage girls learn that to be athletic is to be unfeminine and . . . schools reinforce this message with inadequate funding for girls' sports programs. Instead, what contributes most to a teenage girl's prestige and popularity is having a boyfriend. "A girl may be bright, friendly, competent, and attractive, but without a boyfriend she lacks social validation of these positive attributes. It is as though being selected by a boy tells others that a girl is worthwhile."

Of course, it is during high school that young women also begin to plan for their futures. However, the career aspirations of teenage girls appear to be significantly lower than those of teenage boys with similar backgrounds and abilities. Even though teenage girls now see the majority of adult women around them working full-time outside the home, they continue to expect a rather traditional future for themselves. A number of studies have found that although many high school girls today express a preference for an egalitarian division of labor in the household, most still favor an arrangement in which the husband is the primary breadwinner and the wife is responsible for housework and child care, especially when there are young children at home.

These traditional expectations are reflected in the coursework teenage girls most often undertake in preparation for their future careers. Those not planning to attend college are typically enrolled in sex-typed vocational training courses, such as home economics, cosmetology, and secretarial programs that prepare them to be homemakers or for jobs with salaries far lower than the skilled trades that employ mostly men. But even college-bound girls shy away from courses such as those in advanced mathematics and science that will prepare them to pursue further study for the most highly paid and prestigious professions (See box on page 41).

Interestingly, the low career aspirations of teenage girls are usually unrelated to their academic achievement. For example, Bernice Lott reports that in one study of midwestern high school students, "the girls who anticipated working in the lowest status occupations had higher grade point averages than the boys who anticipated working in medium status occupations." Thus, girls tend to underestimate their academic ability, which in turn may lead them to lower their educational and career plans for the future.

An obvious question at this point is why do young women develop such perceptions of themselves? One explanation, offered by psychologist Matina Horner, is that women fear success. In her research, Horner asked female and male subjects to write stories based on information with which she provided them, in some cases dealing with success. She found that 62 percent of the women but only 9 percent of the men wrote stories containing negative imagery in response to success-related cues. She

subsequently discovered that these women tended to perform better on word-game tasks when they worked alone rather than in mixed-sex groups. This led her to conclude that women's fear of success was related to a discomfort they experienced when competing with men. Horner argued that women may deliberately, though perhaps unconsciously, underachieve because they fear the consequences that success in high-achievement situations might bring—specifically, that they might appear to be unfeminine and, therefore, might be rejected socially.

Empirical research on the "fear of success" theory, however, has yielded inconsistent findings. There is evidence that girls tend to feel uneasy and embarrassed about academic success, and that they often avoid subjects defined as masculine because they think boys will not like them. Yet, fear of success seems to decrease as girls progress through adolescence, and it is certainly the case, too, that girls do excel in many areas—that our male-centered culture devalues what it defines as feminine accomplishments should not detract from their successes. In addition, replications of Horner's research have produced no significant differences between females and males in their use of negative imagery in response to success-related cues. In other words, male subjects in subsequent experiments were just as likely as female subjects to exhibit fear of success.

By focusing on the psychology of the adolescent girl, the fear of success argument also ignores the "invisible ceiling" that others frequently impose on young women's ambitions. This invisible ceiling takes a variety of forms. First, there is the widespread belief that girls are not as intellectually gifted as boys and, therefore, cannot be expected to do as well in school. Research reveals, for example, that both parents and teachers tend to attribute boys' academic achievements to intellectual prowess and to explain their failures in terms of factors such as "bad luck." They do just the opposite for girls;

Are Boys Naturally Gifted with Greater Math Ability Than Girls?

Fact: On average, males score significantly higher than females on math tests. Is this difference the result of some inborn talent in males, or are there social factors at work that foster math achievement for males but hamper it for females? This question has long been the focus of a heated and still-unresolved debate. Although we certainly cannot hope to settle the argument here, we can review some of the evidence that has been gathered.

Boys tend to outperform girls on tasks involving spatial skills. Since many math problems require a strong spatial orientation, some observers argue that boys do better at math because of their greater visualspatial ability. Is this ability natural, or is it nurtured? Sex differences in spatial skills are actually small and appear to be developmental; that is, they emerge over time as children get older. Consequently, some researchers maintain that these differences may be due to the fact that "boys more than girls may be allowed to explore and manipulate their environment and/or encouraged to play with materials, such as mechanical toys that develop spatial skills." Would sex differences in spatial abilities, and hence math achievement, disappear if girls were given the same opportunities? Unfortunately, we know of no research to date that provides a definitive answer.

Other factors associated with sex differences in math achievement are as follows: (1) the extent to which math is oriented to males; (2) teacher–student interaction; and (3) parental encouragement. With regard to the first, several observers have noted that math word problems are often oriented toward traditionally masculine-typed areas and interests. Frieze and her colleagues cite as a typical example a problem that involves mixing cement—an activity girls rarely (are permitted to) engage in. Research, however, indicates that girls perform significantly better on problems with feminine-typed content, so they suggest varying the gender-orientation of word problems by changing the focal activity, for instance, from cement mixing to cake mixing.

More recent research has pointed to the masculine orientation of much computer software, particularly computer games, as well as the male-dominated environment of most public game rooms. Hess and Muira also found that the educational software programs most likely found in math and science classes center around male themes of violence and adventure. Consequently, girls may come to see math, science, and computer-related activities as masculine—a perception that may affect not only their performance, but also their career aspirations.

Significantly, Fennema and Sherman discovered that the major difference between males and females with regard to mathematics is not math ability, per se, but rather extent of exposure to mathematics. Girls and boys with identical math backgrounds show little difference in performance on math tests. Yet girls are less likely than boys to pursue math training beyond their schools' requirements for graduation, and two critical factors influencing their decisions appear to be their interactions with teachers and the encouragement of their parents. Sherman for example, reports that girls (33 percent) are much more likely than boys (10 percent) to cite a teacher as the factor that most discouraged them from studying math. In addition, girls who pursue math training tend to be closer to their parents and more influenced by them. Although few parents openly discourage their daughters from studying math or math-related fields, the message may be communicated indirectly. For instance, recent research indicates that parents are much less likely to enroll daughters than sons in computer camps, especially when the cost of the camps is high. Importantly, although girls and boys both recognize that computers will have a significant impact on their personal futures, boys are more likely to report having access to computers at home.

In summary, the weight of the evidence points to a variety of social factors as responsible for observed differences in math achievement between males and females. In one sense, this is encouraging since, as we have argued previously, socially induced conditions are more easily changed than those biologically caused. Indeed, the solution seems obvious: educators and parents must consciously commit themselves to providing a more supportive and less sex-segregated learning environment for both girls and boys. Until such steps are taken, math will probably remain a "critical filter" that blocks females' advancement into the lucrative and prestigious scientific professions.

if they are successful, they were lucky or the task itself was easy; if they do poorly, it is because they are not smart. Consequently, teachers appear to offer male students more encouragement, to publicly praise their scholastic abilities, and to be friendlier toward them than they are toward female students. Importantly, as Bush notes, "These findings are analogous to those for teacher expectations linked to class and/or race" in which teachers respond more positively to middle- and upper-class students than to working-class and poor students or to white students relative to minority students. We can only speculate on the impact that the intersection of teachers' sexism, racism, and classism may have on students, but there is evidence that students internalize these beliefs, which, if one is female, could reasonably lead to a scaling down of aspirations—not for fear of success, but for fear of failure.

Curriculum materials and school personnel may also place a ceiling on girls' ambitions. We have already seen that women are underrepresented in elementary school textbooks. Reskin and Hartmann cite research that shows gender stereotyping in math and foreign language texts as well as in other higher educational materials. At the same time, high school guidance counselors may channel male and female students into different (i.e.,

gender-stereotyped) fields and activities. There is evidence that gender stereotyping is common among counselors, and that they often steer female students away from certain college prep courses, particularly in mathematics and the sciences. Finally, although elementary school girls can at least identify with their teachers, whom we have noted are almost all women, this becomes increasing difficult in high school where men are almost 57 percent of teachers. High school students are especially likely to have a male teacher for their math courses (57.7 percent) and science courses (65.4 percent).

Given the rather discouraging nature of their high school experience, it is somewhat surprising that so many young women choose to go on to college. Nevertheless, they now constitute a slight majority of college students. Unfortunately, the education they receive continues to differ in many important respects from that of their male peers.

NOTES

1. H. L. Rheingold and K. V. Cook, "The Content of Boys' and Girls' Rooms as an Index of Parents' Behaviors," *Child Development* (1975) 463.

2. R. Best, *We've Got Scars: What Boys and Girls Learn in Elementary School*, Bloomington: Indiana University Press (1983) p. 62

"X": A Fabulous Child's Story

Lois Gould

Once upon a time, a Baby named X was born. It was named X so that nobody could tell whether it was a boy or a girl.

Its parents could tell, of course, but they couldn't tell anybody else. They couldn't even tell Baby X—at least not until much, much later.

You see, it was all part of a very important Secret Scientific Xperiment, known officially as Project Baby X.

This Xperiment was going to cost Xactly 23 billion dollars and 72 cents. Which might seem like a lot for one Baby, even if it was an important Secret Scientific Xperimental Baby.

But when you remember the cost of strained carrots, stuffed bunnies, booster shots, 28 shiny quarters from the tooth fairy . . . you begin to see how it adds up.

Long before Baby X was born, the smartest scientists had to work out the secret details of the Xperiment, and to write the *Official Instruction Manual*, in secret code, for Baby X's parents, whoever they were.

These parents had to be selected very carefully. Thousands of people volunteered to take thousands of tests, with thousands of tricky questions.

Almost everybody failed because, it turned out, almost everybody wanted a boy or a girl, and not a Baby X at all.

Also, almost everybody thought a Baby X would be more trouble than a boy or a girl. (They were right, too.)

There were families with grandparents named Milton and Agatha, who wanted the baby named Milton or Agatha instead of X, even if it *was* an X.

There were aunts who wanted to knit tiny dresses and uncles who wanted to send tiny baseball mitts.

Worst of all, there were families with other children who couldn't be trusted to keep a Secret. Not if they knew the Secret was worth 23 billion dollars and 72 cents—and all you had to do was take one little peek at Baby X in the bathtub to know what it was.

Finally, the scientists found the Joneses, who really wanted to raise an X more than any other kind of baby—no matter how much trouble it was.

The Joneses promised to take turns holding X, feeding X, and singing X to sleep.

And they promised never to hire any babysitters. The scientists knew that a babysitter would probably peek at X in the bathtub, too.

The day the Joneses brought their baby home, lots of friends and relatives came to see it. And the first thing they asked was what kind of a baby X was.

When the Joneses said "It's an X!" nobody knew what to say.

From A *Fabulous Child's Story*. Reprinted by permission of the Charlotte Sheedy Literary Agency Inc.

They couldn't say, "Look at her cute little dimples!"

On the other hand, they couldn't say "Look at his husky little biceps!"

And they didn't feel right about saying just plain "kitchy-coo."

The relatives all felt embarrassed about having an X in the family.

"People will think there's something wrong with it!" they whispered.

"Nonsense!" the Joneses said cheerfully. "What could possibly be wrong with this perfectly adorable X?"

Clearly, nothing at all was wrong. Nevertheless, the cousins who had sent a tiny football helmet would not come and visit anymore. And the neighbors who sent a pink-flowered romper suit pulled their shades down when the Joneses passed their house.

The *Official Instruction Manual* had warned the new parents that this would happen, so they didn't fret about it. Besides, they were too busy learning how to bring up Baby X.

Ms. and Mr. Jones had to be Xtra careful. If they kept bouncing it up in the air and saying how *strong* and *active* it was, they'd be treating it more like a boy than an X. But if all they did was cuddle it and kiss it and tell it how *sweet* and *dainty* it was, they'd be treating it more like a girl than an X.

On page 1654 of the *Official Instruction Manual*, the scientists prescribed: "plenty of bouncing and plenty of cuddling, *both*. X ought to be strong and sweet and active. Forget about *dainty* altogether."

There were other problems, too. Toys, for instance. And clothes. On his first shopping trip, Mr. Jones told the store clerk, "I need some things for a new baby." The clerk smiled and said, "Well, now, is it a boy or a girl?" "It's an X," Mr. Jones said, smiling back. But the clerk got all red in the face and said huffily, "In *that* case, I'm afraid I can't help you sir."

Mr. Jones wandered the aisles trying to find what X needed. But everything was in sections marked BOYS or GIRLS: "Boys' Pajamas" and "Girls' Underwear" and "Boys' Fire Engines" and "Girls' Housekeeping Sets." Mr. Jones went home without buying anything for X.

That night he and Ms. Jones consulted page 2326 of the *Official Instruction Manual*. It said firmly: "Buy plenty of everything!"

So they bought all kinds of toys. A boy doll that made pee-pee and cried "Pa-Pa." And a girl doll that talked in three languages and said, "I am the Pres-i-dent of Gen-er-al Mo-tors."

They bought a storybook about a brave princess who rescued a handsome prince from his tower, and another one about a sister and brother who grew up to be a baseball star and a ballet star, and you had to guess which.

The head scientists of Project Baby X checked all their purchases and told them to keep up the good work. They also reminded the Joneses to see page 4629 of the *Manual*, where it said, "Never make Baby X feel *embarrassed* or *ashamed* about what it wants to play with. And if X gets dirty climbing rocks, never say, 'Nice little Xes don't get dirty climbing rocks.'"

Likewise, it said, "If X falls down and cries, never say, 'Brave little Xes don't cry.' Because, of course, nice little Xes *do* get dirty, and brave little Xes *do* cry. No matter how dirty X gets, or how hard it cries, don't worry. It's all part of the Xperiment."

Whenever the Joneses pushed Baby X's stroller in the park, smiling strangers would come over and coo: "Is that a boy or a girl?" The Joneses would smile back and say, "It's an X." The strangers would stop smiling then and often snarl something nasty—as if the Joneses had said something nasty to *them*.

Once a little girl grabbed X's shovel in the sandbox, and zonked X on the head with it. "Now, now, Tracy," the mother began to scold, "little girls mustn't hit little—" and she turned to ask X, "Are you a little boy or a little girl, dear?"

Mr. Jones, who was sitting near the sandbox, held his breath and crossed his fingers.

X smiled politely, even though X's head

had never been zonked so hard in its life. "I'm a little X," said X.

"You're a *what?*" the lady exclaimed angrily. "You're a little b-r-a-t, you mean!"

"But little girls mustn't hit little Xes, either!" said X, retrieving the shovel with another polite smile. "What good's hitting, anyway?"

X's father finally X-haled, uncrossed his fingers, and grinned.

And at their next secret Project Baby X meeting, the scientists grinned, too. Baby X was doing fine.

But then it was time for X to start school. The Joneses were really worried about this, because school was even more full of rules for boys and girls, and there were no rules for Xes.

Teachers would tell boys to form a line, and girls to form another line.

There would be boys' games and girls' games, and boys' secrets and girls' secrets.

The school library would have a list of recommended books for girls, and a different list for boys.

There would even be a bathroom marked BOYS and another one marked GIRLS.

Pretty soon boys and girls would hardly talk to each other. What would happen to poor little X?

The Joneses spent weeks consulting their *Instruction Manual.*

There were 249 and one-half pages of advice under "First Day of School." Then they were all summoned to an Urgent Xtra Special Conference with the smart scientists of Project Baby X.

The scientists had to make sure that X's mother had taught X how to throw and catch a ball properly, and that X's father had been sure to teach X what to serve at a doll's tea party.

X had to know how to shoot marbles and jump rope and, most of all, what to say when the Other Children asked whether X was a Boy or a Girl.

Finally, X was ready.

X's teacher had promised that the class could line up alphabetically, instead of forming separate lines for boys and girls. And X had permission to use the principal's bathroom, because it wasn't marked anything except BATHROOM. But nobody could help X with the biggest problem of all—Other Children.

Nobody in X's class had ever known an X. Nobody had even heard grown-ups say, "Some of my best friends are Xes."

What would other children think? Would they make Xist jokes? Or would they make friends?

You couldn't tell what X was by its clothes. Overalls don't even button right to left, like girls' clothes, or left to right, like boys' clothes.

And did X have a girl's short haircut or a boy's long haircut?

As for the games X liked, either X played ball very well for a girl, or else played house very well for a boy.

The children tried to find out by asking X tricky questions, like, "Who's your favorite sports star?" X had two favorite sports stars: a girl jockey named Robyn Smith and a boy archery champion named Robin Hood.

Then they asked, "What's your favorite TV show?" And X said: "Lassie," which stars a girl dog played by a boy dog.

When X said its favorite toy was a doll, everyone decided that X must be a girl. But then X said the doll was really a robot, and that X had computerized it, and that it was programmed to bake fudge and then clean up the kitchen.

After X told them that, they gave up guessing what X was. All they knew was they'd sure like to see X's doll.

After school, X wanted to play with the other children. "How about shooting baskets in the gym?" X asked the girls. But all they did was make faces and giggle behind X's back.

"Boy, is *he* weird," whispered Jim to Joe.

"How about weaving some baskets in the arts and crafts room?" X asked the boys. But they all made faces and giggled behind X's back, too.

"Boy, is *she* weird," whispered Susie to Peggy.

That night, Ms. and Mr. Jones asked X how things had gone at school. X tried to smile, but there were two big tears in its eyes. "The lessons are okay," X began, "but . . ."

"But?" said Ms. Jones.

"The Other Children hate me," X whispered.

"Hate you?" said Mr. Jones.

X nodded, which made the two big tears roll down and splash on its overalls.

Once more, the Joneses reached for their *Instruction Manual.* Under "Other Children," it said:

"What did you Xpect? Other Children have to obey silly boy-girl rules, because their parents taught them to. Lucky X—you don't have rules at all! All you have to do is be yourself.

"P.S. We're not saying it'll be easy."

X liked being itself. But X cried a lot that night. So X's father held X tight, and cried a little, too. X's mother cheered them up with an Xciting story about an enchanted prince called Sleeping Handsome, who woke up when Princess Charming kissed him.

The next morning, they all felt much better, and little X went back to school with a brave smile and a clean pair of red and white checked overalls.

There was a seven-letter-word spelling bee in class that day. And a seven-lap boys' relay race in the gym. And a seven-layer-cake baking contest in the girls' kitchen corner.

X won the spelling bee. X also won the relay race.

And X almost won the baking contest, Xcept it forgot to light the oven. (Remember, nobody's perfect.)

One of the Other Children noticed something else, too. He said: "X doesn't care about winning. X just thinks it's fun playing boys' stuff *and* girls' stuff."

"Come to think of it," said another one of the Other Children, "X is having twice as much fun as we are!"

After school that day, the girl who beat X in the baking contest gave X a big slice of her winning cake.

And the boy X beat in the relay race asked X to race him home.

From then on, some really funny things began to happen.

Susie, who sat next to X, refused to wear pink dresses to school any more. She wanted red and white checked overalls—just like X's.

Overalls, she told her parents, were better for climbing monkey bars.

Then Jim, the class football nut, started wheeling his little sister's doll carriage around the football field.

He'd put on his entire football uniform, except for the helmet.

Then he'd put the helmet *in* the carriage, lovingly tucked under an old set of shoulder pads.

Then he'd jog around the field, pushing the carriage and singing "Rockabye Baby" to his helmet.

He said X did the same thing, so it must be okay. After all, X was now the team's star quarterback.

Susie's parents were horrified by her behavior, and Jim's parents were worried sick about his.

But the worst came when the twins, Joe and Peggy, decided to share everything with each other.

Peggy used Joe's hockey skates, and his microscope, and took half his newspaper route.

Joe used Peggy's needlepoint kit, and her cookbooks, and took two of her three babysitting jobs.

Peggy ran the lawn mower, and Joe ran the vacuum cleaner.

Their parents weren't one bit pleased with Peggy's science experiments, or with Joe's terrific needlepoint pillows.

They didn't care that Peggy mowed the

lawn better, and that Joe vacuumed the carpet better.

In fact, they were furious. It's all that little X's fault, they agreed. X doesn't know what it is, or what it's supposed to be! So X wants to mix everybody *else* up, too!

Peggy and Joe were forbidden to play with X any more. So was Susie, and then Jim, and then *all* the Other Children.

But it was too late: the Other Children stayed mixed-up and happy and free, and refused to go back to the way they'd been before X.

Finally, the parents held an emergency meeting to discuss "The X Problem."

They sent a report to the principal stating that X was a "bad influence," and demanding immediate action.

The Joneses, they said, should be *forced* to tell whether X was a boy or a girl. And X should be *forced* to behave like whichever it was.

If the Joneses refused to tell, the parents said, then X must take an Xamination. An Impartial Team of Xperts would Xtract the secret. Then X would start obeying all the old rules. Or else.

And if X turned out to be some kind of mixed-up misfit, then X must be Xpelled from school. Immediately! So that no little Xes would ever come to school again.

The principal was very upset. X, a bad influence? A mixed-up misfit? But X was a Xcellent student! X set a fine Xample! X was Xtraordinary!

X was president of the student council. X had won first prize in the art show, honorable mention in the science fair, and six events on field day, including the potato race.

Nevertheless, insisted the parents, X is a Problem Child. X is the Biggest Problem Child we have ever seen!

So the principal reluctantly notified X's parents and the Joneses reported this to the Project X scientists, who referred them to page 85769 of the *Instruction Manual*. "Sooner or later," it said "X will have to be Xamined by an Impartial Team of Xperts.

"This may be the only way any of us will know for sure whether X is mixed up—or everyone else is."

At Xactly 9 o'clock the next day, X reported to the school health office. The principal, along with a committee from the Parents' Association, X's teacher, X's classmates, and Ms. and Mr. Jones, waited in the hall outside.

Inside, the Xperts had set up their famous testing machine: the Superpsychiamedicosocioculturometer.

Nobody knew Xactly how the machine worked, but everybody knew that this examination would reveal Xactly what everyone wanted to know about X, but were afraid to ask.

It was terribly quiet in the hall. Almost spooky. They could hear very strange noises from the room.

There were buzzes.

And a beep or two.

And several bells.

An occasional light flashed under the door. Was it an X ray?

Through it all, you could hear the Xperts' voices, asking questions, and X's voice, answering answers.

I wouldn't like to be in X's overalls right now, the children thought.

At last, the door opened. Everyone crowded around to hear the results. X didn't look any different, in fact, X was smiling. But the Impartial Team of Xperts looked terrible. They looked as if they were crying!

"What happened?" everyone began shouting.

"*Sssh*," ssshed the principal. "The Xperts are trying to speak."

Wiping his eyes and clearing his throat, one Xpert began: "In our opinion," he whispered—you could tell he must be very upset—"in our opinion, young X here—"

"Yes? Yes?" shouted a parent.

"Young X," said the other Xpert, frowning, "is just about the *least* mixed-up child we've ever Xamined!" Xclaimed the two Xperts, together. Behind the closed door, the Superpsychiamedicosocioculturometer made a noise like a contented hum.

"Yay for X!" yelled one of the children. And then the others began yelling, too. Clapping and cheering and jumping up and down.

"*SSSH!*" SSShed the principal, but nobody did.

The Parents' Committee was angry and bewildered. How *could* X have passed the whole Xamination?

Didn't X have an *identity* problem? Wasn't X mixed up at *all*? Wasn't X *any* kind of a misfit?

How could it *not* be, when it didn't even *know* what it was?

"Don't you see?" asked the Xperts. "X isn't one bit mixed up! As for being a misfit— ridiculous! X knows perfectly well what it is! Don't you, X?" The Xperts winked. X winked back.

"But what *is* X?" shrieked Peggy and Joe's parents. "*We* still want to know what it is!"

"Ah, yes," said the Xperts, winking again. "Well, don't worry. You'll all know one of these days. And you won't need us to tell you."

"What? What do they mean?" Jim's parents grumbled suspiciously.

Susie and Peggy and Joe all answered at once. "They mean that by the time it matters which sex X is, it won't be a secret any more!"

With that, the Xperts reached out to hug Ms. and Mr. Jones. "If we ever have an X of our own," they whispered, "we sure hope you'll lend us your instruction manual."

Needless to say, the Joneses were very happy. The Project Baby X scientists were rather pleased, too. So were Susie, Jim, Peggy, Joe, and all the Other Children. Even the parents promised not to make any trouble.

Later that day, all X's friends put on their red and white checked overalls and went over to see X.

They found X in the backyard, playing with a very tiny baby that none of them had ever seen before.

The baby was wearing very tiny red and white checked overalls.

"How do you like our new baby?" X asked the Other Children proudly.

"It's got cute dimples," said Jim. "It's got husky biceps, too," said Susie.

"What kind of baby is it?" asked Joe and Peggy.

X frowned at them. "Can't you tell?" Then X broke into a big, mischievous grin. "*It's a* Y!"

❧ Sexuality ❧

"Pricks" and "Chicks": A Plea for "Persons"

Robert Baker

There is a school of philosophers who believe that one starts philosophizing not by examining whatever it is one is philosophizing about but by examining the words we use to designate the subject to be examined. I must confess my allegiance to this school. The import of my confession is that this is an essay on women's liberation.

There seems to be a curious malady that affects those philosophers who in order to analyze anything must examine the way we talk about it; they seem incapable of talking about anything without talking about their talk about it—and, once again, I must confess to being typical. Thus I shall argue, first, that the way in which we identify something reflects our conception of it; second, that the conception of women embedded in our language is male chauvinistic; third, that the conceptual revisions proposed by the feminist movement are con-

From *Philosophy and Sex*, new revised eidtion, edited by Robert Baker and Frederick Elliston (Buffalo, N.Y.: Prometheus Books). Copyright © 1984 by Robert Baker and Frederick Elliston. Reprinted by permission of the publisher.

fused; and finally, that at the root of the problem are both our conception of sex and the very structure of sexual identification.

IDENTIFICATION AND CONCEPTION

I am not going to defend the position that the terms we utilize to identify something reflect our conception of it; I shall simply explain and illustrate a simplified version of this thesis. Let us assume that any term that can be (meaningfully) substituted for x in the following statements is a term used to identify something: "Where is the x?" "Who is the x?" Some of the terms that can be substituted for x in the above expressions are metaphors; I shall refer to such metaphors as metaphorical identifications. For example, southerners frequently say such things as "Where did that girl get to?" and "Who is the new boy that Lou hired to help out at the filling station?" If the persons the terms apply to are adult Afro-Americans, then "girl" and "boy" are metaphorical identifications. The fact that the metaphorical identifications in question are standard in the language reflects the fact that ccrtain characteristics of the objects properly classified as boys and girls (for example, immaturity, inability to take care of themselves, need for guidance) are generally held by those who use identifications to be properly attributable to Afro-Americans. One might say that the whole theory of southern white paternalism is implicit in the metaphorical identification "boy" (just as the rejection of paternalism is implicit in the standardized Afro-American forms of address, "man" and "woman," as in, for example, "Hey, man, how are you?").

Most of what I am going to say in this essay is significant only if the way we metaphorically identify something is not a superficial bit of conceptually irrelevant happenstance but rather a reflection of our conceptual structure. Thus if one is to accept my analysis he must understand the significance of metaphorical identifications. He must see that, even though the southerner who identifies adult Afro-American males as "boys" feels that this identification is "just the way people talk"; but for a group to talk that way it must think that way. In the next few paragraphs I shall adduce what I hope is a persuasive example of how, in one clear case, the change in the way we identified something reflected a change in the way we thought about it.

Until the 1960s, Afro-Americans were identified by such terms as "Negro" and "colored" (the respectable terms) and by the more disreputable "nigger," "spook," "kink," and so on. Recently there has been an unsuccessful attempt to replace the respectable identifications with such terms as "African," and "Afro-American," and a more successful attempt to replace them with "black." The most outspoken champions of this linguistic reform were those who argued that nonviolence must be abandoned for Black Power (Stokely Carmichael, H. Rap Brown), that integration must be abandoned in favor of separation (the Black Muslims: Malcolm X, Muhammad Ali), and that Afro-Americans were an internal colony in the alien world of Babylon who must arm them-

selves against the possibility of extermination (the Black Panthers: Eldridge Cleaver, Huey Newton). All of these movements and their partisans wished to stress that Afro-Americans were different from other Americans and could not be merged with them because the differences between the two was as great as that between black and white. Linguistically, of course, "black" and "white" are antonyms; and it is precisely this sense of oppositeness that those who see the Afro-American as alienated, separated, and nonintegratable wish to capture with the term "black." Moreover, as any good dictionary makes clear, in some contexts "black" is synonymous with "deadly," "sinister," "wicked," "evil," and so forth. The new militants were trying to create just this picture of the black man—civil rights and Uncle Tomism are dead, the ghost of Nat Turner is to be resurrected, Freedom Now or pay the price, the ballot or the bullet, "Violence is as American as cherry pie." The new strategy was that the white man would either give the black man his due or pay the price in violence. Since conceptually a "black man" was an object to be feared ("black" can be synonymous with "deadly," and so on), while a "colored man" or a "Negro" was not, the new strategy required that the "Negro" be supplanted by the "black man." White America resisted the proposed linguistic reform quite vehemently, until hundreds of riots forced the admission that the Afro-American was indeed black.

Now to the point: I have suggested that the word "black" replaced the word "Negro" because there was a change in our conceptual structure. One is likely to reply that while all that I have said above is well and good, one had, after all, no choice about the matter. White people are identified in terms of their skin color as whites; clearly, if we are to recognize what is in reality nothing but the truth, that in this society people are conscious of skin color, to treat blacks as equals is merely to identify them by their skin color, which is black. That is, one might argue that while there was a change in words, we have no reason to think that there was a parallel conceptual change. If the term "black" has all the associations mentioned above, that is unfortunate; but in the context the use of the term "black" to identify the people formerly identified as "Negroes" is natural, inevitable, and, in and of itself, neutral; black is, after all, the skin color of the people in question. (Notice that this defense of the natural-inevitable-and-neutral conception of identification quite nicely circumvents the possible use of such seemingly innocuous terms as "Afro-American" and "African" by suggesting that in this society it is *skin color* that is the relevant variable.)

The great flaw in this analysis is that the actual skin color of virtually all of the people whom we call "black" is not black at all. The color tones range from light yellow to a deep umber that occasionally is literally black. The skin color of most Afro-Americans is best designated by the word "brown." Yet "brown" is not a term that is standard for identifying Afro-Americans. For example, if someone asked, "Who was the brown who was the architect for Washington, D.C.?" we would not know how to construe the question. We might attempt to read "brown" as a proper name ("Do you mean Arthur Brown, the designer?"). We would have no trouble understanding the sentence "Who was the black (Negro, colored guy, and so forth) who designed Washington, D.C.?" ("Oh, you mean Benjamin Banneker"). Clearly, "brown" is not a standard form of identification for Afro-Americans. I hope that it is equally clear that "black" has become the standard way of identifying Afro-Americans not because the term was natural, inevitable, and, in the context, neutral, but because of its occasional synonymy with "sinister" and because as an antonym to "white" it best fitted the conceptual needs of those who saw race relations in terms of intensifying and insurmountable antonymies. If one accepts this point, then one must admit that there is a close connection between the way in which we identify things and the way in which we conceive them—and thus it should be also clear why I wish to talk about the way in which women are identified in English. (Thus, for example, one would expect Black Muslims, who continually use the term "black *man*"—as in "the black *man's* rights"—to be more male chauvinistic than Afro-Americans who use the term "black *people*" or "black *folk*.")

WAYS OF IDENTIFYING WOMEN

It may at first seem trivial to note that women (and men) are identified sexually; but conceptually this is extremely significant. To appreciate the significance of this fact it is helpful to imagine a language in which proper names and personal pronouns do not reflect the sex of the person designated by them (as they do in our language). I have been told that in some oriental languages pronouns and proper names reflect social status rather than sex, but whether or not there actually exists such a language is irrelevant, for it is easy enough to imagine what one would be like. Let us then imagine a language where the proper names are sexually neutral (for example, "Xanthe"), so that one cannot tell from hearing a name whether the person so named is male or female, and where the personal pronouns in the language are "under" and "over." "Under" is the personal pronoun appropriate for all those who are younger than thirty, while "over" is appropriate to persons older than thirty. In such a language, instead of saying such things as "Where do you think *he* is living now?" one would say such things as "Where do you think *under* is living now?"

What would one say about a cultural community that employed such a language? Clearly, one would say that they thought that for purposes of intelligible communication it was more important to know a person's age grouping than the person's height, sex, race, hair color, or parentage. (There are many actual cultures, of course, in which people are identified by names that reflect their parentage; for example, Abu ben Adam means Abu son of Adam.) I think that one would also claim that this people would not have reflected these differences in the pronominal structure of their language if they did not believe that the differences between unders and overs was such that a statement would frequently have one meaning if it were about an under and a different meaning if it were about an over. For example, in feudal times if a serf said, "My lord said to do this," that assertion was radically different from "Freeman John said to do this," since (presumably) the former had the status of a command while the latter did not. Hence the conventions of Middle English required that one refer to people in such a way as to indicate their social status. Analogously, one would not distinguish between pronominal references according to the age differences in the persons referred to were there no shift in meaning involved.

If we apply the lesson illustrated by this imaginary language to our own, I think that it should be clear that since in our language proper nouns and pronouns reflect sex rather than age, race, parentage, social status, or religion, we believe one of the most important things one can know about a person is that person's sex. (And, indeed, this is the first thing one seeks to determine about a newborn babe— our first question is almost invariably "Is it a boy or a girl?") Moreover, we would not reflect this important difference pronominally did we not also believe that statements frequently mean one thing when applied to males and something else when applied to females. Perhaps the most striking aspect of the conceptual discrimination reflected in our language is that man is, as it were, essentially human, while woman is only accidentally so.

This charge may seem rather extreme, but consider the following synonyms (which are readily confirmed by any dictionary). "Humanity" is synonymous with "mankind" but not with "womankind." "Man" can be substituted for "humanity" or "mankind" in any sentence in which the terms "mankind" or "humanity" occur without changing the meaning of the sentence, but significantly, "woman" cannot. Thus, the following expressions are all synonymous with each other: "humanity's great achievements," "mankind's great achievements," and "man's great achievements." "Woman's great achievements" is not synonymous with any of these. To highlight the degree to which women are excluded from humanity, let me point out that it is something of a truism to say that "man is a rational animal," while "woman is a rational animal" is quite debatable. Clearly, if "man" in the first assertion embraced both men and women, the second assertion would be just as much a truism as the first. Humanity, it would seem, is a male prerogative. (And hence, one of the goals of women's liberation is to alter our conceptual structure so that someday "mankind" will be regarded as an improper and vestigial ellipsis for "humankind," and "man" will have no special privileges in relation to "human being" that "woman" does not have.)

The major question before us is, How are women conceived of in our culture? I have been trying to answer this question by talking about how they are identified. I first considered pronominal identification; now I wish to turn to identification through other types of noun phrases. Methods of nonpronominal identification can be discovered by determining which terms can be substituted for "woman" in such sentences as "Who is that woman over there?" without changing the meaning of the sentence. Virtually no term is interchangeable with "woman" in that sentence for all speakers on all occasions. Even "lady," which most speakers would accept as synonymous with "woman" in that sentence, will not do for a speaker who applies the term "lady" only to those women who display manners, poise, and sensitivity. In most contexts, a large number of students in one or more of my classes will accept the following types of terms as more or less interchangeable with "woman." (An asterisk indicates interchanges acceptable to both males and females; a plus sign indicates terms restricted to black students only. Terms with neither an asterisk nor a plus sign are accepted by all males but are not normally used by females.)

A. NEUTRAL TERMS: *lady, *gal, *girl (especially with regard to a coworker in an office or factory), * + sister, *broad (originally in the animal category, but most people do not think of the term as now meaning pregnant cow)

B. ANIMAL: *chick, bird, fox, vixen, filly, bitch (Many do not know the literal meaning of the term. Some men and most women construe this use as pejorative; they think of "bitch" in the context of "bitchy," that is, snappy, nasty, and so forth. But a large group of men claim that it is a standard nonpejorative term of identification—which may perhaps indicate that women have come to be thought of as shrews by a large subclass of men.)

C. PLAYTHING: babe, doll, cuddly

D. GENDER (association with articles of clothing typically worn by those in the female gender role): skirt, hem

E. SEXUAL: snatch, cunt, ass, twat, piece (of ass, and so forth), lay, pussy (could be put in the animal category, but most users associated it with slang expression indicating the female pubic region), + hammer (related to anatomical analogy between a hammer and breasts). There are many other usages, for example, "bunny," "sweat hog," but these were not recognized as standard by as many as 10 percent of any given class.

The students in my classes reported that the most frequently used terms of identification are in the neutral and animal classifications (although men in their forties claim to use the gender classifications quite a bit) and that the least frequently used terms of identification are sexual. Fortunately, however, I am not interested in the frequency of usage but only in whether the use is standard enough to be rec-

ognized as an identification among some group or other. (Recall that "brown" was not a standardized term of identification and hence we could not make sense out of "Who was the brown who planned Washington, D.C.?" Similarly, one has trouble with "Who was the breasts who planned Washington, D.C.?" but not with "Who was the babe (doll, chick, skirt, and so forth) who planned Washington, D.C.?")

Except for two of the animal terms, "chick" and "broad"—but note that "broad" is probably neutral today—women do not typically identify themselves in sexual terms, in gender terms, as playthings, or as animals; *only males use nonneutral terms to identify women*. Hence, it would seem that there is a male conception of women and a female conception. Only males identify women as "foxes," "babes," "skirts," or "cunts" (and since all the other nonneutral identifications are male, it is reasonable to assume that the identification of a woman as a "chick" is primarily a male conception that some women have adopted).

What kind of conception do men have of women? Clearly they think that women share certain properties with certain types of animals, toys, and playthings; they conceive of them in terms of the clothes associated with the female gender role; and, last (and, if my classes are any indication, least frequently), they conceive of women in terms of those parts of their anatomy associated with sexual intercourse, that is, as the identification "lay" indicates quite clearly, as sexual partners.

The first two nonneutral male classifications, animal and plaything, are prima facie denigrating (and I mean this in the literal sense of making one like a "nigger"). Consider the animal classification. All of the terms listed, with the possible exception of "bird," refer to animals that are either domesticated for servitude (to *man*) or hunted for sport. First, let us consider the term "bird." When I asked my students what sort of birds might be indicated, they suggested chick, canary (one member, in his forties, had suggested "canary" as a term of identification), chicken, pigeon, dove, parakeet, and hummingbird (one member). With the exception of the hummingbird, which like all the birds suggested is generally thought to be diminutive and pretty, all of the birds are domesticated, usually as pets (which reminds one that "my pet" is an expression of endearment). None of the birds were predators or symbols of intelligence or nobility (as are the owl, eagle, hawk, and falcon); nor did large but beautiful birds seem appropriate (for example, pheasants, peacocks, and swans). If one construes the bird terms (and for that matter, "filly") as applicable to women because they are thought of as beautiful, or at least pretty, *then there is nothing denigrating about them*. If, on the other hand, the common properties that underlie the metaphorical identification are domesticity and servitude, then they are indeed denigrating (as for myself, I think that both domesticity and prettiness underlie the identification). "Broad," of course, is, or at least was, clearly denigrating, since nothing renders more service to a farmer than does a pregnant cow, and cows are not commonly thought of as paradigms of beauty.

With one exception all of the animal terms reflect a male conception of women either as domesticated servants or as pets, or as both. Indeed, some of the terms reflect a conception of women first as pets and then as servants. Thus, when a pretty, cuddly little chick grows older, she becomes a very useful servant—the egg-laying hen.

"Vixen" and "fox," variants of the same term, are the one clear exception. None of the other animals with whom women are metaphorically identified are generally thought to be intelligent, aggressive, or independent—but the fox is. A chick is a soft, cuddly, entertaining, pretty, diminutive, domesticated, and dumb animal. A fox too is soft, cuddly, entertaining, pretty, and diminutive, but it is neither dependent nor dumb. It is aggressive, intelligent, and

a minor predator—indeed, it preys on chicks—and frequently outsmarts ("outfoxes") men.

Thus the term "fox" or "vixen" is generally taken to be a compliment by both men and women, and compared to any of the animal or plaything terms it is indeed a compliment. Yet, considered in and of itself, the conception of a woman as a fox is not really complimentary at all, for the major connection between *man* and fox is that of predator and prey. The fox is an animal that men chase, and hunt, and kill for sport. If women are conceived of as foxes, then they are conceived of as prey that it is fun to hunt.

In considering plaything identifications, only one sentence is necessary. *All the plaything identifications are clearly denigrating since they assimilate women to the status of mindless or dependent objects.* "Doll" is to male paternalism what "boy" is to white paternalism.

Up to this point in our survey of male conceptions of women, every male identification, without exception, has been clearly antithetical to the conception of women as human beings (recall that "man" was synonymous with "human," while "woman" was not). Since the way we talk of things, and especially the way we identify them, is the way in which we conceive of them, any movement dedicated to breaking the bonds of female servitude must destroy these ways of identifying and hence of conceiving of women. Only when both sexes find the terms "babe," "doll," "chick," "broad," and so forth, as objectionable as "boy" and "nigger" will women come to be conceived of as independent *human beings*.

The two remaining unexamined male identifications are gender and sex. There seems to be nothing objectionable about gender identifications per se. That is, women are metaphorically identified as skirts because in this culture, skirts, like women, are peculiarly female. Indeed, if one accepts the view that the slogan "female and proud" should play the same role for the women's liberation movement that the slogan "Black is beautiful" plays for the black-liberation movement, then female clothes should be worn with the same pride as Afro clothes. (Of course, one can argue that the skirt, like the cropped-down Afro, is a sign of bondage, and hence both the item of clothing and the identification with it are to be rejected—that is, cropped-down Afros are to Uncle Tom what skirts are to Uncle Mom.)

The terms in the last category are obviously sexual, and frequently vulgar. For a variety of reasons I shall consider the import and nature of these identifications in the next section.

MEN OUGHT NOT TO THINK OF WOMEN AS SEX OBJECTS

Feminists have proposed many reforms, and most of them are clearly desirable, for example, equal opportunity for self-development, equal pay for equal work, and free day-care centers. One feminist proposal, however, is peculiarly conceptual and deeply perplexing. I call this proposal peculiarly conceptual because unlike the other reforms it is directed at getting people to think differently. The proposal is that *men should not think of women (and women should not think of themselves) as sex objects*. In the rest of this essay I shall explore this nostrum. I do so for two reasons: first, because the process of exploration should reveal the depth of the problem confronting the feminists; and second, because the feminists themselves seem to be entangled in the very concepts that obstruct their liberation.

To see why I find this proposal puzzling, one has to ask what it is to think of something as a sex object.

If a known object is an object that we know, an unidentified object is an object that we have not identified, and a desired object is an object that we desire, what then is a sex object? Clearly, a sex object is an object we have sex with. Hence, to think of a woman as a sex object is to think of her as someone to have sexual

relations with, and when the feminist proposes that men refrain from thinking of women in this way, *she is proposing that men not think of women as persons with whom one has sexual relations.*

What are we to make of this proposal? Is the feminist suggesting that women should not be conceived of in this way because such a conception is "dirty"? To conceive of sex and sex organs as dirty is simply to be a prude. "Shit" is the paradigm case of a dirty word. It is a dirty word because the item it designates is taboo; it is literally unclean and untouchable (as opposed to something designated by what I call a curse word, which is not untouchable but rather something to be feared—"damn" and "hell" are curse words; "piss" is a dirty word). If one claims that "cunt" (or "fuck") is a dirty word, then one holds that what this term designates is unclean and taboo; thus one holds that the terms for sexual intercourse or sexual organs are dirty, one has accepted puritanism. If one is a puritan and a feminist, then indeed one ought to subscribe to the slogan *men should not conceive of women as sexual objects*. What is hard to understand is why anyone but a puritan (or, perhaps, a homosexual) would promulgate this slogan; yet most feminists, who are neither lesbians nor puritans, accept this slogan. Why?

A word about slogans: Philosophical slogans have been the subject of considerable analysis. They have the peculiar property (given a certain seemingly sound background story) of being obviously true, yet obviously false. "Men should not conceive of women as sex objects" is, I suggest, like a philosophical slogan in this respect. The immediate reaction of any humanistically oriented person upon first hearing the slogan is to agree with it—yet the more one probes the meaning of the slogan, the less likely one is to give one's assent. Philosophical analysts attempt to separate out the various elements involved in such slogans—to render the true-false slogan into a series of statements, some of which are true, some of which are false,

and others of which are, perhaps, only probable. This is what I am trying to do with the
slogan in question. I have argued so far that one
of the elements that seems to be implicit in the
slogan is a rejection of women as sexual partners
for men and that although this position might
be proper for a homosexual or puritanical movement, it seems inappropriate to feminism. I
shall proceed to show that at least two other
interpretations of the slogan lead to inappropriate results; but I shall argue that there are at
least two respects in which the slogan is profoundly correct—even if misleadingly stated.

One plausible, but inappropriate, interpretation of "men ought not to conceive of women
as sex objects" is that men ought not to conceive
of women *exclusively* as sexual partners. The
problem with this interpretation is that everyone can agree with it. Women are conceived of
as companions, toys, servants, and even sisters,
wives, and mothers—and hence not exclusively
as sexual partners. Thus this slogan loses its
revisionary impact, since even a male chauvin-
ist could accept the slogan without changing his
conceptual structure in any way—which is only
to say that men do not usually identify or conceive of woman as sexual partners (recall that
the sexual method of identification is the least
frequently used).

Yet another interpretation is suggested by
the term "object" in "sex object," and this interpretation too has a certain amount of plau-
sibility. Men should not treat women as
animate machines designed to masturbate men
or as conquests that allow men to "score" for
purposes of building their egos. Both of these
variations rest on the view that to be treated as
an object is to be treated as less than human
(that is, to be treated as a machine or a score).
Such relations between men and women are
indeed immoral, and there are, no doubt, men
who believe in "scoring." Unfortunately, however, this interpretation—although it would
render the slogan quite apt—also fails because
of its restricted scope. When feminists argue

that men should not treat women as sex objects
they are not *only* talking about fraternity boys
and members of the Playboy Club; they are talking about all males in our society. The charge is
that in our society men treat women as sex objects rather than as persons; it is this universality
of scope that is lacking from the present interpretation. *Nonetheless, one of the reasons that
we are prone to assent to the unrestricted charge
that men treat women as sex objects is that the
restricted charge is entirely correct.*

One might be tempted to argue that the
charge that men treat women as sex objects is
correct since such a conception underlies the
most frequently used identifications, as animal
and plaything; that is, these identifications indicate a sexual context in which the female is
used as an object. Thus, it might be argued that
the female fox is chased and slayed if she is
four-legged, but chased and layed if she is two.
Even if one admits the sexual context *implicit*
in *some* animal and plaything identifications,
one will not have the generality required; because, for the most part, the plaything and animal identifications themselves are nonsexual—
most of them do not involve a sexual context. A
pregnant cow, a toy doll, or a filly are hardly
what one would call erotic objects. Babies do
not normally excite sexual passion; and anyone
whose erotic interests are directed toward
chicks, canaries, parakeets, or other birds is
clearly perverse. The animals and playthings to
whom women are assimilated in the standard
metaphorical identifications are not symbols of
desire, eroticism, or passion (as, for example, a
bull might be).

What is objectionable in the animal and
plaything identifications is not the fact that
some of these identifications reflect a sexual
context but rather that—regardless of the
context—these identifications reflect a conception of women as mindless servants (whether
animate or inanimate is irrelevant). The point
is not that men ought not to think of women in
sexual terms but that they ought to think of

them as human beings; and the slogan *men should not think of women as sex objects* is only appropriate when a man thinking of a woman as a sexual partner automatically conceives of her as something less than human. It is precisely this antihumanism implicit in the male concept of sex that we have as yet failed to uncover—but then, of course, we have not yet examined the language we use to identify sexual acts.

OUR CONCEPTION
OF SEXUAL INTERCOURSE

There are two profound insights that underlie the slogan "men ought not conceive of women as sexual objects"; both have the generality of scope that justifies the universality with which the feminists apply the slogan; neither can be put as simply as the slogan. The first is that the conception of sexual intercourse that we have in this culture is antithetical to the conception of women as human beings—as persons rather than objects. (Recall that this is congruent with the fact we noted earlier that "man" can be substituted for "humanity," while "woman" cannot.)

Many feminists have attempted to argue just this point. Perhaps the most famous defender of this view is Kate Millett, who unfortunately faces the problem of trying to make a point about our conceptual structure without having adequate tools for analyzing conceptual structures.

The question Millett was dealing with was conceptual—Millett, in effect, asking about the nature of our conception of sexual roles. She tried to answer this question by analyzing novels; I shall attempt to answer this question by analyzing the terms we use to identify coitus, or more technically, in terms that function synonymously with "had sexual intercourse with" in a sentence of the form "A had sexual intercourse with B." The following is a list of some commonly used synonyms (numerous others that are not as widely used have been omitted, for example, "diddled," "laid pipe with"):

screwed
laid
fucked
had
did it with (to)
banged
balled
humped
slept with
made love to

Now, for a select group of these verbs, names for males are the subjects of sentences with active constructions (that is, where the subjects are said to be doing the activity); and names for females require passive constructions (that is, they are the recipients of the activity—whatever is done is done to them). Thus, we would not say "Jane did it to Dick," although we would say "Dick did it to Jane." Again, Dick bangs Jane, Jane does not bang Dick; Dick humps Jane, Janes does not hump Dick. In contrast, verbs like "did it with" do not require an active role for the male; thus, "Dick did it with Jane, and Jane with Dick." Again, Jane may make love to Dick, just as Dick makes love to Jane; and Jane sleeps with Dick as easily as Dick sleeps with Jane. (My students were undecided about "laid." Most thought that it would be unusual indeed for Jane to lay Dick, unless she played the masculine role of seducer-aggressor.)

* * *

It should be clear, therefore, that our language reflects a difference between the male and female sexual roles, and hence that we conceive of the male and female roles in different ways. The question that now arises is, What difference in our conception of the male and female sexual roles requires active constructions for males and passive for females?

One explanation for the use of the active construction for males and the passive construction for females is that this grammatical asymmetry merely reflects the natural physiological asymmetry between men and women: the asymmetry of "to screw" and "to be screwed," "to insert into" and "to be inserted into." That is, it might be argued that the difference between masculine and feminine grammatical roles merely reflects a difference naturally required by the anatomy of males and females. This explanation is inadequate. Anatomical differences do not determine how we are to conceptualize the relation between penis and vagina during intercourse. Thus one can easily imagine a society in which the female normally played the active role during intercourse, where female subjects required active constructions with verbs indicating copulation, and where the standard metaphors were terms like "engulfing"—that is, instead of saying "he screwed her," one would say "she engulfed him." It follows that the use of passive constructions for female subjects of verbs indicating copulation does not reflect differences determined by human anatomy but rather reflects those generated by human customs.

What I am going to argue next is that the passive construction of verbs indicating coitus (that is, indicating the female position) can *also* be used to indicate that a person is being harmed. I am then going to argue that the metaphor involved would only make sense if we conceive of the female role in intercourse as that of a person being harmed (or being taken advantage of).

Passive constructions of "fucked," "screwed," and "had" indicate the female role. They also can be used to indicate being harmed. Thus, in all of the following sentences, Marion plays the female role: "Bobbie fucked Marion"; "Bobbie screwed Marion"; "Bobbie had Marion"; "Marion was fucked"; "Marion was screwed"; and "Marion was had." All of the statements are equivocal. They might literally mean that someone had sexual intercourse with Marion (who played the female role); or they might mean, metaphorically, that Marion was deceived, hurt, or taken advantage of. Thus, we say such things as "I've been screwed"

("fucked," "had," "taken," and so on) when we have been treated unfairly, been sold shoddy merchandise, or conned out of valuables. Throughout this essay I have been arguing that metaphors are applied to things only if what the term *actually* applies to shares one or more properties with what the term *metaphorically* applies to. Thus, the female sexual role must have something in common with being conned or being sold shoddy merchandise. The only common property is that of being harmed, deceived, or taken advantage of. *Hence we conceive of a person who plays the female sexual role as someone who is being harmed* (that is, "screwed," "fucked," and so on).

It might be objected that this is clearly wrong, since the unsignated terms do not indicate someone's being harmed, and hence we do not conceive of having intercourse as being harmed. The point about the unsignated terms, however, is that they can take both females and males as subjects (in active constructions) and thus *do not pick out the female role*. This demonstrates that we conceive of sexual roles in such a way that only females are thought to be taken advantage of in intercourse.

The best part of solving a puzzle is when all the pieces fall into place. If the subjects of the passive construction are being harmed, presumably the subjects of the active constructions are doing harm, and indeed, we do conceive of these subjects in precisely this way. Suppose one is angry at someone and wishes to express malevolence as forcefully as possible without actually committing an act of physical violence. If one is inclined to be vulgar one can make the sign of the erect male cock by clenching one's fist while raising one's middle finger, or by clenching one's fist and raising one's arm and shouting such things as "screw you," and "up yours" or "fuck you." In other words, one of the strongest possible ways of telling someone that you wish to harm him is to tell him to assume the female sexual role relative to you. Again, to say to someone "go fuck yourself" is to order him to harm himself, while to call someone a "mother fucker" is not so much a play on his Oedipal fears as to accuse him of being so low that he would inflict the greatest imaginable harm (fucking) upon that person who is most dear to him (his mother).

Clearly, we conceive of the male sexual role as that of hurting the person in the female role—but lest the reader have any doubts, let me provide two further bits of confirming evidence: one linguistic, one nonlinguistic. One of the English terms for a person who hurts (and takes advantage of) others is the term "prick." This metaphorical identification would not make sense unless the bastard in question (that is, the person outside the bonds of legitimacy) was thought to share some characteristics attributed to things that are literally pricks. As a verb, "prick" literally means "to hurt," as in "I pricked myself with a needle"; but the usage in question is as a noun. As a noun, "prick" is a colloquial term for "penis." Thus, the question before us is what characteristic is shared by a penis and a person who harms others (or, alternatively, by a penis and by being stuck by a needle). Clearly, no physical characteristic is relevant (physical characteristics might underlie the Yiddish metaphorical attribution "schmuck," but one would have to analyze Yiddish usage to determine this); hence the shared characteristic is nonphysical; the only relevant shared nonphysical characteristic is that both a literal prick and a figurative prick are agents that harm people.

Now for the nonlinguistic evidence. Imagine two doors: in front of each door is a line of people; behind each door is a room; in each room is a bed; on each bed is a person. The line in front of one room consists of beautiful women, and on the bed in that room is a man having intercourse with each of these women in turn. One may think any number of things about this scene. One may say that the man is in heaven, or enjoying himself at a bordello; or perhaps one might only wonder at the oddness of it all. One does not think that the man is

being hurt or violated or degraded—or at least the possibility does not immediately suggest itself, although one could conceive of situations where this was what was happening (especially, for example, if the man was impotent). Now, consider the other line. Imagine that the figure on the bed is a woman and that the line consists of handsome, smiling men. The woman is having intercourse with each of these men in turn. It immediately strikes one that the woman is being degraded, violated, and so forth—"that poor woman."

When one man fucks many women he is a playboy and gains status; when a woman is fucked by many men she degrades herself and loses stature.

Our conceptual inventory is now complete enough for us to return to the task of analyzing the slogan that men ought not to think of women as sex objects.

I think that it is now plausible to argue that the appeal of the slogan "men ought not to think of women as sex objects," and the thrust of much of the literature produced by contemporary feminists, turns on something much deeper than a rejection of "scoring" (that is, the utilization of sexual "conquests" to gain esteem) and yet is a call neither for homosexuality nor for puritanism.

The slogan is best understood as a call for a new conception of the male and female sexual roles. If the analysis developed above is correct, our present conception of sexuality is such that to be a man is to be a person capable of brutalizing women (witness the slogans "The marines will make a man out of you!" and "The army builds *men!*" which are widely accepted and which simply state that learning how to kill people will make a person more manly). Such a conception of manhood not only bodes ill for a society led by such men, but also is clearly inimical to the best interests of women. It is only natural for women to reject such a sexual role, and it would seem to be the duty of any moral person to support their efforts—to redefine our conceptions not only of fucking, but of the fucker (man) and the fucked (woman).

This brings me to my final point. We are a society preoccupied with sex. As I noted previously, the nature of proper nouns and pronouns in our language makes it difficult to talk about someone without indicating that person's sex. This convention would not be part of the grammar of our language if we did not believe that knowledge of a person's sex was crucial to understanding what is said about that person. Another way of putting this point is that sexual discrimination permeates our conceptual structure. Such discrimination is clearly inimical to any movement toward sexual egalitarianism and virtually defeats its purpose at the outset. (Imagine, for example, that black people were always referred to as "them" and whites as "us" and that proper names for blacks always had an "x"

suffix at the end. Clearly any movement for integration as equals would require the removal of these discriminatory indicators. Thus at the height of the melting-pot era, immigrants Americanized their names: "Bellinsky" became "Bell," "Burnstein" became "Burns," and "Lubitch" became "Baker.")

I should therefore like to close this essay by proposing that contemporary feminists should advocate the utilization of neutral proper names and the elimination of gender from our language (as I have done in this essay); and they should vigorously protest any utilization of the third-person pronouns "he" and "she" as examples of sexist discrimination (perhaps "person" would be a good third-person pronoun)—for, as a parent of linguistic analysis once said, "The limits of our language are the limits of our world."

Sexual Terrorism

Carole Sheffield

No two of us think alike about it, and yet it is clear to me, that question underlies the whole movement, and our little skirmishing for better laws, and the right to vote, will yet be swallowed up in the real question, viz: Has a woman a right to herself? It is very little to me to have the right to vote, to own property, etc., if I may not keep my body, and its uses, in my absolute right. Not one wife in a thousand can do that now.
        LUCY STONE, in a letter to Antoinette Brown, July 11, 1855

The right of men to control the female body is a cornerstone of patriarchy. It is expressed by their efforts to control pregnancy and childbirth

and to define female health care in general. Male opposition to abortion is rooted in opposition to female autonomy. Violence and the threat of violence against females represent the need of patriarchy to deny that a woman's body is her own property and that no one should have

From *Women: A Feminist Perspective*, 3rd ed., edited by Jo Freeman. Reprinted by permission.

access to it without her consent. Violence and its corollary, fear, serve to terrorize females and to maintain the patriarchal definition of woman's place.

The word *terrorism* invokes images of furtive organizations of the far right or left, whose members blow up buildings and cars, hijack airplanes, and murder innocent people in some country other than ours. But there is a different kind of terrorism, one that so pervades our culture that we have learned to live with it as though it were the natural order of things. Its targets are females—of all ages, races, and classes. It is the common characteristic of rape, wife battery, incest, pornography, harassment, and all forms of sexual violence. I call it *sexual terrorism* because it is a system by which males frighten and, by frightening, control and dominate females.

The concept of terrorism captured my attention in an "ordinary" event. One afternoon I collected my laundry and went to a nearby laundromat. The place is located in a small shopping center on a very busy highway. After I had loaded and started the machines, I became acutely aware of my environment. It was just after 6:00 P.M. and dark; the other stores were closed; the laundromat was brightly lit; and my car was the only one in the lot. Anyone passing by could readily see that I was alone and isolated. Knowing that rape is a crime of opportunity, I became terrified. I wanted to leave and find a laundromat that was busier, but my clothes were well into the wash cycle, and, besides, I felt I was being "silly," "paranoid." The feeling of terror persisted, so I sat in my car, windows up, and doors locked. When the wash was completed, I dashed in, threw the clothes into the drier, and ran back out to my car. When the clothes were dry, I tossed them recklessly into the basket and hurriedly drove away to fold them in the security of my home.

Although I was not victimized in a direct, physical way or by objective or measurable standards, I felt victimized. It was, for me, a terrifying experience. I felt controlled by an invisible force. I was angry that something as commonplace as doing laundry after a day's work jeopardized my well-being. Mostly I was angry at being unfree: a hostage of a culture that, for the most part, encourages violence against females, instructs men in the methodology of sexual violence, and provides them with ready justification for their violence. I was angry that I could be victimized by being "in the wrong place at the wrong time." The essence of terrorism is that one never knows when is the wrong time and where is the wrong place.

Following my experience at the laundromat, I talked with my students about terrorization. Women students began to open up and reveal terrors that they had kept secret because of embarrassment: fears of jogging alone, dining alone, going to the movies alone. One woman recalled feelings of terror in her adolescence when she did child care for extra money. Nothing had ever happened and she had not been afraid of anyone in particular, but she had felt a vague terror when being driven home late at night by the man of the house.

The men listened incredulously and then demanded equal time. The harder they tried the more they realized how very different— qualitatively, quantitatively, and contextually— their fears were. All agreed that, while they experienced fear in a violent society, they did not experience terror; nor did they experience fear of rape or sexual mutilation. They felt more in control, either from a psychophysical sense of security that they could defend themselves or from a confidence in being able to determine wrong places and times. All the women admitted fear and anxiety when walking to their cars on the campus, especially after an evening class or activity. None of the men experienced fear on campus at any time. The men could be rather specific in describing when they were afraid: in Harlem, for example, or in certain parts of downtown Paterson, New Jersey— places that have a reputation for violence. But they could either avoid these places or, if not, the men felt capable of self-protective action.

Above all, male students said that they *never* feared being attacked simply because they were male. They *never* feared going to a movie or to dinner alone. Their daily activities were not characterized by a concern for their physical integrity.

As I read the literature on terrorism it became clear that both sexual violence and nonviolent sexual intimidation could be better understood as terrorism. For example, although an act of rape, an unnecessary hysterectomy, and the publishing of *Playboy* magazine appear to be quite different, they are in fact more similar than dissimilar. Each is based on fear, hostility, and a need to dominate women. Rape is an act of aggression and possession, not of sexuality. Unnecessary hysterectomies are extraordinary abuses of power rooted in man's concept of woman as primarily a reproductive being and in his need to assert power over reproduction. *Playboy*, like all forms of pornography, attempts to control women through the power of definition. Male pornographers define women's sexuality for their male customers. The basis of pornography is men's fantasies about women's sexuality.

COMPONENTS OF SEXUAL TERRORISM

The literature on terrorism does not provide a precise definition. Mine is taken from Hacker, who says that "terrorism aims to frighten, and by frightening, to dominate and control." Writers agree more readily on the characteristics and functions of terrorism than on a definition. This analysis will focus on five components to illuminate the similarities of and distinctions between sexual terrorism and political terrorism. The five components are ideology, propaganda, indiscriminate and amoral violence, voluntary compliance, and society's perception of the terrorist and the terrorized.

An *ideology* is an integrated set of beliefs about the world that explains the way things are

and provides a vision of how they ought to be. Patriarchy, meaning the "rule of the fathers," is the ideological foundation of sexism in our society. It asserts the superiority of males and the inferiority of females. It also provides the rationale for sexual terrorism. The taproot of patriarchy is the masculine/warrior ideal. Masculinity must include not only a proclivity for violence but also all those characteristics necessary for survival: aggression, control, emotional reserve, rationality, sexual potency, etc. Marc Feigen Fasteau, in *The Male Machine*, argues that "men are brought up with the idea that there ought to be some part of them, under control until released by necessity, that thrives on violence. This capacity, even affinity, for violence, lurking beneath the surface of every real man, is supposed to represent the primal untamed base of masculinity."

Propaganda is the methodical dissemination of information for the purpose of promoting a particular ideology. Propaganda, by definition, is biased or even false information. Its purpose is to present one point of view on a subject and to discredit opposing points of view. Propaganda is essential to the conduct of terrorism. According to Francis Watson, in *Political Terrorism: The Threat and the Response*, "Terrorism must not be defined only in terms of violence, but also in terms of propaganda. The two are in operation together. Violence of terrorism is a coercive means for attempting to influence the thinking and actions of people. Propaganda is a persuasive means for doing the same thing." The propaganda of sexual terrorism is found in all expressions of the popular culture: films, television, music, literature, advertising, pornography. The propaganda of sexual terrorism is also found in the ideas of patriarchy expressed in science, medicine, and psychology.

The third component, which is common to all forms of political terrorism, consists of "indiscriminateness, unpredictability, arbitrariness, ruthless destructiveness and amorality."

Indiscriminate violence and amorality are also at the heart of sexual terrorism. Every female is a potential target of violence—at any age, at any time, in any place. In her study of rape, Susan Brownmiller argues that rape is "nothing more or less than a conscious process of intimidation by which all men keep all women in a state of fear." Further, as we shall see, amorality pervades sexual violence. Child molesters, incestuous fathers, wife beaters, and rapists often do not understand that they have done anything wrong. Their views are routinely shared by police officers, lawyers, and judges, and crimes of sexual violence are rarely punished in American society.

The fourth component of the theory of terrorism is "voluntary compliance." The institutionalization of a system of terror requires the development of mechanisms other than sustained violence to achieve its goals. Violence must be employed to maintain terrorism, but sustained violence can be costly and debilitating. Therefore, strategies for ensuring a significant degree of voluntary compliance must be developed. Sexual terrorism is maintained to a great extent by an elaborate system of sex-role socialization that in effect instructs men to be terrorists in the name of masculinity and women to be victims in the name of femininity.

Sexual and political terrorism differ in the final component, perception of the terrorist and the victim. In political terrorism we know who is the terrorist and who is the victim. We may condemn or condone the terrorist depending on our political views, but we sympathize with the victim. In sexual terrorism, however, we blame the victim and excuse the offender. We believe that the offender either is "sick" and therefore in need of our compassion or is acting out normal male impulses.

TYPES OF SEXUAL TERRORISM

Many types of sexual terrorism are crimes. Yet when we look at the history of these acts we see that they came to be considered criminal not so much to protect women as to adjust power relationships among men. Rape was originally a violation of a father's or husband's property right; consequently, a husband by definition could not rape his wife. Wife beating was condoned by the law and still is condemned in name only. The pornographic presentation of sexual violence serves to direct male violence against women and girls and to contain male violence toward other men. Although proscriptions against incest exist, society assumes a more serious posture toward men who sexually abuse other men's daughters. Sexual harassment is not a crime, and only recently has it been declared an actionable civil offense. Crimes of sexual violence are characterized by ambiguity and diversity in definition and interpretation. Because each state and territory has a separate system of law in addition to the federal system, crimes and punishments are assessed differently throughout the country.

Rape

The most generally accepted definition of rape is "sexual intercourse with a female, not the wife of the perpetrator, without the consent of the female." Seventeen states punish rape within marriage.

Because rape is considered a sexual act, evidence of force and resistance (that is, nonconsent) plays a major role in the conviction or acquittal of rapists. Proof of nonconsent and resistance is not demanded of a victim of any other crime. If one is stopped on the street and robbed one never has to justify nonresistance or prove resistance and nonconsent. Females are expected to resist rape as much as possible, otherwise "consent" is assumed.

John M. MacDonald, in *Rape Offenders and Their Victims*, offers the following advice to law enforcement officials: "To constitute resistance in good faith it must have been commenced at the inception of the advances and continued until the offense was consummated. Resistance by mere words is not sufficient, but such resistance must be by acts, and must be reasonably proportionate to the strength and opportunities of the woman." Passive resistance or compliance, even in a situation that is perceived to be life-threatening, is not, to many prosecutors, clear evidence that the rape was against one's will.

Wife Assault

For centuries it has been assumed that a husband had the right to punish or discipline his wife with physical force. The popular expression, "rule of thumb," originated from English common law, which allowed a husband to beat his wife with a whip or stick no bigger in diameter than his thumb. The husband's prerogative was incorporated into American law. Several states had statutes that essentially allowed a man to beat his wife without interference from the courts.

In 1871, in the landmark case of *Fulgham v. State*, an Alabama court ruled that "the privilege, ancient though it be, to beat her with a stick, to pull her hair, choke her, spit in her face or kick her about the floor or to inflict upon her other like indignities, is not now acknowledged by our law." The law, however, has been ambiguous and often contradictory on the issue of wife assault. While the courts established that a man had no right to beat his wife, it also held that a woman could not press charges against her abusive husband. In 1910, the U.S. Supreme Court ruled that a wife could not charge her husband with assault and battery because it "would open the doors of the courts to accusations of all sorts of one spouse against the other and bring into public notice complaints for assaults, slander and libel." The courts virtually condoned violence for the purpose of maintaining peace.

Laws and public attitudes about the illegality of wife assault and the rights of the victim have been evolving slowly, and attempts are being made to resolve the contradictions. Only three states (California, Hawaii, and Texas) define wife abuse as a felony. In other states, laws applicable to wife battery include assault, assault and battery, aggravated assault, intent to assault or to commit murder, and possession of a deadly weapon with intent to assault.

Sexual Abuse of Children

Defining sexual abuse of children is very difficult. The laws are complex and often contradictory. Generally, sexual abuse of children includes statutory rape, molestation, carnal knowledge, indecent liberties, impairing the morals of a minor, child abuse, child neglect, and incest. Each of these is defined and interpreted differently in each state. Convictions run the gamut from misdemeanors to various degrees of assault and felony. Punishments vary widely from state to state as well.

The philosophy underlying statutory-rape laws is that a child below a certain age—arbitrarily fixed by law—is not able to give meaningful consent. Therefore, sexual intercourse with a female below a certain age, with or without the use of force, is a criminal act of rape. Punishment for statutory rape, although rarely imposed, can be as high as life imprisonment. Coexistent with laws on statutory rape are laws on criminal incest. Incest is generally interpreted as sexual activity, most often intercourse, with a blood relative. The difference, then, between statutory rape and incest is the relation of the offender to the child. Statutory rape is committed by someone outside the family; incest, by a member of the family. The penalty for incest, also rarely imposed, is usually no more than ten years in prison. This contrast suggests that sexual abuse of children is tolerated when it occurs within the family and that unqualified protection of children from sexual assault is not the intent of the law.

Sexual Harassment

Sexual harassment is a new term for an old phenomenon. The research on sexual harassment, as well as the legal interpretation, centers on acts of sexual coercion or intimidation on the job and at school. Lin Farley, in *Sexual Shakedown: The Sexual Harassment of Women on the Job*, describes sexual harassment as "unsolicited nonreciprocal male behavior that asserts a woman's sex role over her function as a worker. It can be any or all of the following: staring at, commenting upon, or touching a woman's body; requests for acquiescence in sexual behavior; repeated nonreciprocated propositions for dates; demands for sexual intercourse; and rape."

Sexual harassment is now considered a form of sex discrimination under some conditions and is therefore a violation of Title VII of the 1964 Civil Rights Act, which prohibits sex discrimination in employment, and of Title IX of the 1972 Education Amendments, which prohibits sex-based discrimination in education.

CHARACTERISTICS OF SEXUAL TERRORISM

Those forms of sexual terrorism that are crimes share several common characteristics. Each will be addressed separately, but in the real world these characteristics are linked together and form a vicious circle, which functions to mask the reality of sexual terrorism and thus to perpetuate the system of oppression of females. Crimes of violence against females (1) cut across socioeconomic lines; (2) are the crimes least likely to be reported; (3) when reported, are the crimes least likely to be brought to trial or to result in conviction; (4) are often blamed on the victim; (5) are generally not taken seriously; and (6) are not really about sex.

Violence Against Females Cuts Across Socioeconomic Lines

The question "Who is the typical rapist, wife beater, incest offender, etc?" is raised constantly. The answer is simple: men. Even among those who commit incest, women are exceedingly rare. The men who commit acts of

sexual terrorism are of all ages, races, and religions; they come from all communities, income levels, and educational levels; they are married, single, separated, and divorced. The typical sexually abusive male does not exist.

One of the most common assumptions about sexual violence is that it occurs primarily among the poor, uneducated, and predominately nonwhite populations. Instead, violence committed by the poor and nonwhite is simply more visible because these people lack the resources to ensure the privacy that the middle and upper classes can purchase. Most rapes, indeed most incidents of sexual assault, are not reported, and therefore the picture drawn from police records must be viewed as very sketchy.

The data on sexual harassment in work situations indicate that it occurs among all job categories and pay ranges. Sexual harassment is committed by academic men, who are among the most highly educated members of society.

All the studies on wife battery testify to the fact that wife beating crosses socioeconomic lines. Wife beaters include high government officials, members of the armed forces, businessmen, policemen, physicians, lawyers, clergy, blue-collar workers, and the unemployed. According to Maria Roy, founder and director of New York's Abused Women's Aid in Crisis: "We see abuse of women on all levels of income, age, occupation, and social standing. I've had four women come in recently whose husbands are Ph.D.s—two of them professors at top universities. Another abused woman is married to a very prominent attorney. We counseled battered wives whose husbands are doctors, psychiatrists, even clergymen."

Similarly, in Vincent De Francis's classic study of 250 cases of sexual crimes committed against children, a major finding was that incidents of sexual assault against children cut across class lines.

Since sexual violence is not "nice," we prefer to believe that nice men do not commit these acts and that nice girls and women are not victims. Our refusal to accept the fact that violence against females is widespread on all levels of society strongly inhibits our ability to develop any meaningful strategies directed toward the elimination of sexual violence. Moreover, because of underreporting, it is difficult to ascertain exactly how widespread it is.

Crimes of Sexual Violence Are the Least Likely to Be Reported

The underreporting issue, often called the "tip-of-the-iceberg theory," is common to all crimes against females. The FBI recognizes that rape is the most frequently committed violent crime that is seriously underreported. According to FBI data for 1987, 91,111 rapes were reported. The FBI and other criminologists suggest that this figure be multiplied by at least a factor of ten to compensate for underreporting. The FBI *Uniform Crime Report* for 1987 estimates that a forcible rape occurs every six minutes. This estimate is based on reported cases; to account for the high rate of underreporting the FBI estimates that a rape occurs every two minutes. The number of forcible rapes reported to the police has been increasing every year. Between 1978 and 1987, there was a 21 percent increase in reported forcible rapes. It is estimated that one-half of all rape victims are under eighteen years of age and 25 percent of rape victims are under twelve years of age.

The FBI's *Uniform Crime Report* indexes 10 million reported crimes a year but does not collect statistics on wife abuse. Since statutes in most states do not identify wife beating as a crime, incidents of wife beating are usually classified under "assault and battery" and "disputes." However, the FBI estimates that wife abuse is three times as common as rape. Estimates that 50 percent of American wives are battered are not uncommon in the literature.

"The problem of sexual abuse of children is of unknown national dimensions," according to Vincent De Francis, "but findings strongly point to the probability of an enormous national incidence many times larger than the reported incidence of physical abuse of children." He discussed the existence of a wide gap between the reported incidence and the actual occurrence of sexual assault against children and suggested that "the reported incidence represents the top edge of the moon as it rises over the mountain."

Incest, according to author and researcher Florence Rush, is the *Best Kept Secret*. The estimates, however speculative, are frightening. Alfred Kinsey, in a study involving 4,441 female subjects, found that 24 percent had been approached sexually by an adult male prior to their adolescence; in 23 percent of the cases that adult male was a relative. Significantly, all the respondents in the Kinsey study were white and predominately middle class. The Child Sexual Abuse Project in San Jose, California, estimates that there are approximately 26,000 cases of father–daughter incest each year. This estimate excludes incestuous behavior by grandfathers, uncles, brothers, cousins. Cases reported to the Santa Clara Child Sexual Abuse Treatment Program increased from 31 in 1974 to 269 in 1976, suggesting that the incidence of incest may be grossly underestimated. Child-protection organizations estimate that the number of reported incidents of child sexual abuse ranges from one hundred thousand to 1 million and that the majority of sexual assaults against children are not reported.

Accurate data on the incidence of sexual harassment are impossible to obtain. Women have traditionally accepted sexual innuendo as a fact of life and only recently have begun to report and analyze the dimensions of sexual coercion in the workplace. Research indicates that sexual harassment is pervasive. Lin Farley found that accounts of sexual harassment within the federal government, the country's largest single employer, are extensive and that surveys of working women in the private sector indicate "a dangerously high rate of incidence of this abuse."

In 1976, over nine thousand women responded to a survey on sexual harassment conducted by *Redbook* magazine. More than 92 percent reported sexual harassment as a problem; a majority of the respondents described it as serious; and nine out of ten reported that they had personally experienced one or more forms of unwanted sexual attentions on the job. The Ad Hoc Group on Equal Rights for Women attempted to gather data on sexual harassment at the United Nations. The questionnaire was confiscated by UN officials, but 875 staff members had already responded; 73 percent were women, and more than half of them said that they had personally experienced or were aware of incidents of sexual harassment at the UN. In May 1975, the Women's Section of the Human Affairs Program at Cornell University, Ithaca, New York, distributed the first questionnaire on sexual harassment. Of the 155 respondents, 92 percent identified sexual harassment as a serious problem; 70 percent had personally experienced some form of sexual harassment; and 56 percent reported incidents of physical harassment.

A pilot study conducted by the National Advisory Council on Women's Educational Programs on Sexual Harassment in Academia concluded:

The sexual harassment of postsecondary students is an increasingly visible problem of great, but as yet unascertained, dimensions. Once regarded as an isolated, purely personal problem, it has gained civil rights credibility as its scale and consequences have become known, and is correctly viewed as a form of illegal sex-based discrimination.

Crimes of Violence Against Females Have the Lowest Conviction Rates

The common denominator in the underreporting of all sexual assaults is fear. Females have been well trained in silence and passivity. Early and sustained sex-role socialization teaches that women are responsible for the sexual behavior of men and that women cannot be trusted. These beliefs operate together. They function to keep women silent about their victimization and to keep other people from believing women when they do come forward. The victim's fear that she will not be believed and, as a consequence, that the offender will not be punished is not unrealistic. Sex offenders are rarely punished in our society.

Rape has the lowest conviction rate of all violent crimes. On a national average, one rapist in twenty is arrested, one out of thirty prosecuted, and one in sixty is convicted. In *Forcible Rape: The Crime, the Victim, and the Offender*, the authors report that the conviction rate for Los Angeles County is less than 10 percent and that "in no recent year have more than eight percent of rape arrests resulted in rape convictions" in New York City. The authors conclude that rapists in New York City have enjoyed "almost complete immunity" from prosecution.

Data on prosecution and conviction of wife beaters are practically nonexistent. According to Roger Langley and Richard Levy, authors of *Wife-Beating: The Silent Crisis*, "the vast majority of wife-beaters are never prosecuted. In fact, they are seldom even charged. The battered wife has to overcome an incredible array of roadblocks and detours built into the legal system before she can prosecute her husband."

The roadblocks are both technical and attitudinal. The laws on wife beating are confusing and vary from state to state. Their application varies with the attitudes and beliefs of law-enforcement personnel. Police indifference to wife beating has been extensively documented by victims.

Dee Zurbrium of Laurel, Maryland, says she called police for help and was told, "We can't get involved in a domestic quarrel, Lady. The best thing you can do is get out of there because next time you may be dead."

The *Detroit Free Press*, in an article headlined "Emergency Number Still Has Kinks," reports: "A near-breathless woman, beaten by her husband, dialed 911 to ask for police assistance. 'Does he have a weapon?' the operator asked.

"She answered he did not.

" 'Then I am sorry. We won't be able to help you,' the operator said to the dismayed woman."

One woman called the police after her husband broke her nose. They took her to the hospital, bleeding and with both eyes swelling shut, but they refused to arrest her husband. "You don't want to do that, honey," said the cop, reassuringly. "It's something that happens in every man's life."

It is routine policy for police officers and lawyers to discourage women from filing charges against an abusive husband. The instructors at the Police Training Academy in Michigan use the following guidelines in teaching police officers how to convince a woman not to press charges:

a. Avoid arrest if possible. Appeal to their vanity.
b. Explain the procedure of obtaining a warrant.
    1. Complainant must sign complaint.
    2. Must appear in court.
    3. Consider loss of time.
    4. Cost of court.
c. State that your only interest is to prevent a breach of the peace.
d. Explain that attitudes usually change by court time.
e. Recommend a postponement.
    1. Court not in session.
    2. No judge available.
f. Don't be too harsh or critical.

It is also common practice for police officers and lawyers to use outright intimidation to convince battered women not to pursue the matter legally. Battered wives are confronted with statements or questions such as these: "You know he could lose his job." "Who will support you if he is locked up?" "Why don't you just kiss and make up?" "What did you do to make him hit you?" "Lady, why do you want to make trouble?"

It is ironic that police officers do not view what they call a "domestic disturbance," "lover's quarrel," or "family spat" as serious. The category of "answering family disturbance calls" accounts for about 20 percent of the incidents of police killed on duty.

According to Detroit Police Commander James Bannon:

The attrition rate in domestic violence cases is unbelievable. In 1972, for instance, there were 4,900 assaults of this kind which had survived the screening process long enough to at least have a warrant prepared and the complainant referred to the assault and battery squad. Through the process of conciliation, complainant harassment and prosecutor discretion, fewer than 300 of these cases were ultimately tried by a court of law. And in most of these the court used the judicial process to attempt to conciliate rather than adjudicate.

Mr. Bannon argues: "You can readily understand why the women ultimately take the law into their own hands or despair of finding relief at all. *Or why the male feels protected by the system in his use of violence.*" (emphasis mine).

In his study of child sexual abuse, Vincent De Francis found that plea-bargaining and dismissal of cases were the norm. The study sample consisted of 173 cases brought to prosecution. Of these, 44 percent (seventy-six cases) were dismissed; 22 percent (thirty-eight cases) voluntarily accepted a lesser plea; 11 percent (six cases) were found guilty of a lesser charge; and 2 percent (four cases) were found guilty as charged. The remaining thirty-five cases were either pending (fifteen); terminated because the offender was committed to a mental institution (five) or because the offender absconded (seven); or no information was available (eight).

Of the fifty-three offenders who were convicted or pleaded guilty, thirty offenders escaped a jail sentence. Twenty-one received suspended sentences and were placed on probation; seven received suspended sentences without probation; and two were fined a sum of money. The other 45 percent (twenty-three offenders) received prison terms from under six months to three years; five were given indeterminate sentences—that is, a minimum term of one year and a maximum term subject to the discretion of the state board of parole.

Most of the victims of sexual harassment in the Cornell University study were unwilling to use available procedures, such as grievances, to remedy their complaints, because they believed that nothing would be done. Their perception is based on reality; of the 12 percent who did complain, over half found that nothing was done in their cases. The low adjudication and punishment rates of sexual-harassment cases are particularly revealing in light of the fact that the offender is known and identifiable and that there is no fear of "mistaken identity," as there is in rape cases. While offenders accused of familial violence—incest and wife abuse—are also known, the courts' posture is heavily in favor of keeping the family intact, or so they say. There is no such motivation in cases of sexual harassment.

Blaming the Victim of Sexual Violence Is Pervasive

The data on conviction rates of men who have committed acts of violence against females must be understood in the context of sociopolitical attitudes about women. The male-dominated society has evoked powerful myths to justify male violence against females and to ensure that these acts will rarely be punished. Victims of sexual violence are almost always suspect. We have developed an intricate network of beliefs and attitudes that perpetuate the idea that "victims of sex crimes have a hidden psychological need to be victimized." We tend to believe either that the female willingly participated in her victimization or that she outright lied about it. Either way, we blame the victim and excuse or condone the offender.

Consider, for example, the operative myths about rape, wife battery, incest, and sexual harassment.

Rape

> All women want to be raped.
> No woman can be raped if she doesn't want it (you-can't-thread-a-moving-needle argument).
> She asked for it.
> She changed her mind afterwards.
> When she says no she means yes.
> If you are going to be raped you might as well enjoy it.

Wife Battery

> Some women need to be beaten.
> A good kick in the ass will straighten her out.
> She needs a punch in the mouth every so often to keep her in line.
> She must have done something to provoke him.

Incest

> The child was the seducer.
> The child imagined it.

Sexual Harassment

> She was seductive.
> She misunderstood, I was just being friendly.

Underlying all the myths about victims of sexual violence is the belief that the victim causes and is responsible for her victimization. Underlying the attitudes about the male offender is the belief that he could not help himself; that is, he was ruled by his biology and/or he was seduced. The victim becomes the offender and the offender becomes the victim. Clearly, two very important processes are at work here: blaming the victim and absolving the offender. These serve a vital political purpose: to protect our view of the world as orderly and just and to help us make sense of sexual violence. The rationale is that sexual violence against an innocent female is unjustifiable; therefore, she must have done something wrong or it would not have happened. Making a victim believe she is at fault erases not only the individual offender's culpability but also the responsibility of the society as a whole. Sexual violence becomes an individual problem, not a sociopolitical one.

One need only read the testimony of victims of sexual violence to see the powerful effects of blaming the victim. From the National Advisory Council on Women's Educational Programs Report on Sexual Harassment of Students:

I was ashamed, thought it was my fault, and was worried that the school would take action against me (for "unearned" grades) if they found out about it.

This happened seventeen years ago, and you are the first person I've been able to discuss it with in all that time. He's still at _____, and probably still doing it.

I'm afraid to tell anyone here about it, and I'm just hoping to get through the year so I can leave.

From *Wife-Beating: The Silent Crisis*, Judge Stewart Oneglia comments:

Many women find it shameful to admit they don't have a good marriage. The battered wife wraps her bloody head in a towel, goes to the hospital, and explains to the doctor she fell down the stairs. After a few years of the husband telling her he beats her because she is ugly, stupid, or incompetent, she is so psychologically destroyed that she believes it.

A battered woman from Boston relates:

I actually thought if I only learned to cook better or keep a cleaner house, everything would be okay. I put up with the beatings for five years before I got desperate enough to get help.

Another battered woman said,

When I came to, I wanted to die, the guilt and depression were so bad. Your whole sense of worth is tied up with being a successful wife and having a happy marriage. If your husband beats you, then your marriage is a failure, and you're a failure. It's so horribly the opposite of how it is supposed to be.

Katherine Brady shared her experience as an incest survivor in *Father's Days: A True Story of Incest*. She concluded her story with the following:

I've learned a great deal by telling my story. I hope other incest victims may experience a similar journey of discovery by reading it. If nothing else, I would wish them to hear in this tale the two things I needed most, but had to wait years to hear: "You are not alone and you are not to blame."

Sexual Violence Is Not Taken Seriously

Another characteristic of sexual violence is that these crimes are not taken seriously. Society manifests this attitude by simply denying the existence of sexual violence, denying the gravity of these acts, joking about them, and attempting to legitimate them.

Many offenders echo the societal norm by expressing genuine surprise when they are confronted by authorities. This seems to be particularly true in cases of sexual abuse of children, wife beating, and sexual harassment. In her study of incest, Florence Rush found that child molesters very often do not understand that they have done anything wrong. This is true as well for men who beat their wives. Many men still believe that they have an inalienable right to rule "their women." Batterers, for example, often cite their right to discipline their wives; incestuous fathers cite their right to instruct their daughters in sexuality. Clearly, these men are acting on the belief that women are the property of men.

The concept of females as property of men extends beyond the family unit, as the evidence on sexual harassment indicates. "Are you telling me that this kind of horsing around may constitute an actionable offense?" queried a character on a recent television special on sexual harassment. This represents the typical response of a man accused of sexual harassment. Men have been taught that they are the hunters, and women—all women—are fair game. The mythology about the workaday world abounds with sexual innuendo. Concepts of "sleazy" (read "sexually accessible") nurses and dumb, big-breasted, blond secretaries are standard fare for comedy routines. When the existence of sexual violence can no longer be denied, a common response is to joke about it in order to belittle it. "If you are going to be raped, you might as well enjoy it" clearly belittles the violence of rape. The public still laughs when Ralph threatens Alice with "One of these days, POW—right in the kisser." Recently, a television talk-show host remarked that "incest is a game the whole family can play." The audience laughed uproariously.

Sexual Violence Is Not Motivated by Sex

The final characteristic common to all forms of violence against females is perhaps the most difficult to comprehend. Sexual assault, contrary to popular belief, is not about sex. The research that has been done in every area of sexual assault suggests that while the motivation is complex, it is not rooted in sexual frustration or sexual prowess. Rather, the motivation for the violent abuse of women has to do with the need to assert a masculine image or a masculine privilege as defined by the culture. In an article in *Ms.* magazine, "I Never Set Out to Rape Anybody," a rapist talked about his motivation to rape. He said that the image of men (masculinity) as hypersexual, violent, and dominant and the image of women (femininity) as liking tough men made him feel compelled to live up to this standard.

A rapist is usually regarded as a healthy male who was the victim of a seductive and vengeful woman, a sexually frustrated man who was no longer able to control his desires, or a "pervert" or "sex fiend." These views all suggest that the rapist's behavior is motivated by sexual desire. The assumption that rape, forceful and often violent, is about the satisfaction of sexual need or desire is entirely false. In his study *Men Who Rape: The Psychology of the Offender*, A. Nicholas Groth reports that "careful clinical study of offenders reveals that rape is in fact serving primarily nonsexual needs. It is the sexual expression of power and anger."

Men do not rape for sexual pleasure. They rape to assert power and dominance. Jack Fremont's interviews with several rapists revealed the notion of masculine privilege as a dominant motive. For example:

INTERVIEWER: Do you think many men commit rape?

JIMMY: Oh, yes, I know damn well they do! With no more feeling involved and no more neurosis than just, I want you, and I can't have you, so I'll take you.

David Finkelhor, in his study *Sexually Victimized Children*, argues that the sexual exploitation of women and children is made easier in a society that is dominated by men. "Sex in any society is a valuable commodity, and a dominant group—such as men—will try to rig things to maximize their access to it." He maintains that "the cultural beliefs that underpin the male-dominated system contribute to making women and children sexually vulnerable. For example, to the extent that family members are regarded as possessions, men can take unusual and usually undetected liberties with them." Research by Robert Geiser supports the conclusion that sexual gratification is not the dominant motive in the abuse of children. A daughter asked her father, "Why did you do it to me?" He replied, "You were available and you were vulnerable." Research on offenders suggests that men turn to children because their adult relationships are complicated, unsatisfying, stressful, or anxiety-laden. According to Geiser, child molesters need to exercise authority and to avoid rejection: "The child's vulnerability and helplessness make her easier to overpower and dominate."

Husbands who batter their wives are often trying to prove their superiority. Del Martin found that wife beating is unquestionably an example of power abuse. Martin characterized the battering husband this way:

He is probably angry with himself and frustrated by his life. He may put up a good front in public, but in the privacy and intimacy of his home he may not be able to hide, either from himself or his wife, his feelings of inadequacy and low self-esteem. The man who is losing his grip on his job or his prospects may feel compelled to prove that he is at least the master of his home. Beating his wife is one way for him to appear a winner.

Sexual harassment is also not about sex but about power. Farley argues that the sexual harassment of women at work arose from men's need to maintain control of women's labor. Sexual harassment serves to keep women (individually and collectively) economically inferior and ensures the system of male dominance.

Conclusion

Sexual terrorism is a system that functions to maintain male supremacy through actual and implied violence. Violence against the female body (rape, battery, incest, and harassment) and the perpetuation of fear of violence form the basis of patriarchal power. Both violence and fear are functional. If men did not have power to intimidate and to punish, their domination of women in all spheres of society—political, social, and economic—could not exist.

The Lesbian Perspective

Julia Penelope

WHAT'S WRONG WITH THIS PICTURE?

Where do we begin to define our Selves? How are Lesbians unique? In spite of our occasional craving to be "like everybody else," we know

From *Lesbian Philosophies*, edited by Jeffner Allen. Reprinted by permission.

that we **aren't**. If we were, we wouldn't be Lesbians. Some deep-seated consciousness knows that the world presented to us as "real" is false. There's something wrong with the picture. The Lesbian Perspective originates in our sense of "difference," however vague the feeling may be, however much we resist that knowledge, and in our certainty that what others seem happy to accept as "real" is seriously flawed. In order to conceive and define ourselves as Lesbians, we have to defy the "wisdom of the ages." Nobody held up a picture of a wonderful dyke for us and said, "You could grow up to be strong and defiant like her." From the day a girl child is born, everyone who exercises control and authority in her life assumes that she will grow up to "fall in love" with a male, as though that were an "accidental" misstep, and that she will inevitably marry one. All the messages she hears about WHO she is and WHO she's expected to become assume that there's only one kind of love and one kind of sexuality, and that's HETEROSEXUAL. One of those messages informs us that we possess a biologically-determined "maternal instinct"; another croons at us, "Every woman needs a man." Imagine how many Lesbians there would be in the world if we got the kind of air-time and publicity that heterosexuality gets. In spite of liberal feminist proclamations to the contrary, we're a long, long way from Marlo Thomas's world of "Free to Be You and Me." What we're "free to be" is heterosexual. That, and that only.

If we must speak of choice, it is the Lesbian who **chooses** to accept the terms of the heterosexual imperative, not the heterosexual. Heterosexuals don't choose their sexuality, because they believe it's "natural," the only way there is to be. Only Lesbians can choose to define ourselves. Being a Lesbian or a heterosexual isn't a matter of "choosing" a lifestyle or a "sexual preference" from the table spread before us by parents, teachers, and other authority figures. There's only one dish on the social menu—heterosexuality—and we are given to understand that we swallow it or go without. The only options we have are those we create for ourselves because we must do so. Who we decide we are isn't a matter of "taste," although some Lesbians do try to acquire a "taste" for heterosexuality.

There's a large difference between "being heterosexual" and "being" a Lesbian. "Being" heterosexual means conforming, living safely, if uncomfortably, within the limits established by men. "Being" a Lesbian means living marginally, often in secrecy, often shamefully, but always as different, as the "deviant." Some Lesbians have sex with men, often marry one, two, three, or four men, have numerous children, and may even live as heterosexuals for some portion of their lives. Lesbians are coming out at every age, and, regardless of how old we are when we decide to act on our self-knowledge, we say, "I've always been a Lesbian." Some Lesbians die without once acting on their deep feelings for other wimmin. Some Lesbians live someone else's life. Deciding to act on our emotional and sexual attractions to other wimmin is usually a long-drawn-out process of introspection and self-examination that can take years, because the social and emotional pressure surrounding us is so powerful and inescapable. There's no visible, easily accessible support in our society for being Lesbians, which explains why we have so much trouble imagining what "being Lesbian" means. In many ways, we remain opaque even to our Selves because we haven't yet developed a language that describes our experiences.

The differences among us have to do with our level of tolerance for discomfort, how thoroughly we have learned to mistrust and deny our Lesbian selves. Lesbians can deny ourselves endlessly because we are told that we "should." Being heterosexual is the only identity offered, coerced, supported and validated by male society. Male society makes it easy to deny our inner selves, to disbelieve the integrity of our feelings, to discount the necessity of our love for each other, at the same time making it difficult for us to act on our own behalf. Ask a Lesbian who has lived as a heterosexual if she knew she was a Lesbian early in her life, and most will say "yes." Maybe some didn't know the world *Lesbian*, but they'll talk about their childhood love for teachers and girlfriends. Most will say, after they've named themselves Lesbians, "I've always been a Lesbian." Most will say, "I didn't believe there were others like me. I thought I was the only one." This is reinterpretation of experience from a new perspective, *not* revision. Once a Lesbian identifies herself as *lesbian*, she brings all of her earlier experiences with and feelings for other women into focus; she crosses the conceptual line that separates the known (the "safe") of the social validation awarded to heterosexuals and the tabooed unknown of deviance. Crossing into this territory, she begins to remember experiences she had "forgotten," recalling women and her feelings for them that she had analyzed or named differently; she examines memories of her past from a new perspective. Events and experiences that once "made no sense" to her are now full of meanings she had ignored, denied, or discarded. Reconceiving herself as Lesbian, she doesn't change or revise women, events, and experiences in her past, she reinterprets them, understanding them anew from her Lesbian Perspective in the present.

When we fail to be visible to each other, we invalidate the Lesbian Perspective and the meanings it attaches to our experiences. Each of us pays a price for Lesbian invisibility, in our self-esteem, in years of our lives, in energy spent trying to deny our Selves. But it is a fact that millions of us name ourselves "Lesbian" even when we have no sense of a community, when we know no one else who is like us, when we believe we will live as outcasts and alone for the remainder of our lives. How do we become that which is nameless, or, named shameful, sinful, despised? The Lesbian stands against the world created by the male imagination. What **willfulness** we possess when we claim our lives!

The Lesbian Perspective develops directly out of our experiences in the world: How other people treat us as Lesbians, the negative and positive reactions we get in specific situations, what we're told (and believe) we "ought" to feel about ourselves as Lesbians, and the degree of honesty we come to feel we can exercise in our various relationships. What appear to be impor-

tant differences among Lesbians are survival skills that enable us to survive in hostile territory. Some of us, for example, have had mostly positive or less damaging reactions to our Lesbianism from others who "count" in our estimation. Some Lesbians have experienced varying degrees of acceptance, tolerance, and open-heartedness from their heterosexual families and friends. Some Lesbians say they've had "no problems" in their lives connected with their Lesbianism. Not every Lesbian has had portions of her mind destroyed by drugs and repeated shock treatments, or been disowned by her genetic family, or had to survive on her own in the streets, but lots of Lesbians have suffered greatly, have been abused, rejected, ridiculed, committed to psychiatric hospitals, jailed, and tortured. For some, the pain of loving as a Lesbian made death a reasonable choice, and many Lesbians have killed themselves rather than endure an existence that seemed to have no hope. Suicide is a valid choice. Whatever our personal experience is, we are always at risk in this society.

CHOOSING OUR SELVES

Being a Lesbian isn't a "choice." We **choose** whether or not we'll live as **who we are.** Naming ourselves *Lesbian* is a decision to ACT on our truest feelings. The Lesbian who decides to live as a heterosexual does so at great cost to her self-esteem. Heterosexuals don't have to question the assumptions on which they construct their lives and then defend them to a hostile society. I can't estimate the damage done to our emotional lives by the dishonesty forced on us by male dogma, but I know how much of my own life has been lies, lies, and more lies.

We live in a society where dishonesty is prized far above honesty, and Lesbians learn the necessity of lying early on. Parents may tell us to "be ourselves," but we find out quickly, after only one or two "experiments," that honesty is punished, that "being ourselves" really means "Be who we want you to be." I know how much of myself I've tried to cover up, deny, and lie about in order to escape the most violent, lethal methods of suppression. The people who represent "society" for us when we're growing up teach us all we need to know about what being an "adult" means. "Growing up" for females in male societies means *choosing men*, and then lying about how "happy" they are. Naming ourselves Lesbian is one of the most significant steps we take to affirm our integrity, to choose honesty over deception, and to become real to ourselves.

This is why the consensus reality of heteropatriarchy describes Lesbianism as "a phase," as something we're supposed to "grow out of." Adopting the protective coloration of heterosexuality is thus equated with "maturity." "Growing up" is a code phrase signalling one's willingness to perform in specific ways: compromise principles, deny feelings, provide **and** accept descriptions one knows to be false, and read along from the heteropatriarchal script. Some are more adept and credible at acting "mature," but adults lie, and they lie all the time—to their children, loved ones, friends, bosses—but mostly to themselves.

Even after we've begun to explore and expand the meanings of our Lesbian Perspective, we bring that learned dishonesty, and our painful experiences about the cost of being honest, into our Lesbian lives. Unlearning years of heterosexual training isn't something we can expect to accomplish quickly or easily. Staying honest about ourselves takes lots of practice. We bring our lessons about the necessity of disguising ourselves, of lying about our innermost feelings, and a sincere reluctance to self-disclose with us when we become members of Lesbian society. The results can be far more damaging to our attempts to communicate and create a community than they are in male society.

On the one hand, lying, not being honest about who we are or how we feel, is a **survival skill** we have developed. We have to lie to get

by in most heterosexual contexts. I realize there are some exceptions to this—there are always exceptions to any generalization. But a majority of Lesbians—today, in 1990—are **afraid** to be honest about their Lesbian identity, and with good reason. As an outfront Lesbian, one of the exceptions, I want to validate their fear. It's real, it's based on real or likely experiences, and no Lesbian should feel she's expected to apologize for protecting herself in the only way she knows.

On the other hand, we've internalized the ethic of fear and secrecy so thoroughly that we discover we can't simply shed it when we're in Lesbian contexts. Again, though, previous experiences suggest that self-disclosure and honesty aren't entirely wise even among Lesbians. Too many Lesbians simply don't feel "safe" among other Lesbians on an emotional level, because of previous experiences, and so we're constantly on guard, prepared to protect ourselves. If we're committed to creating Lesbian communities in which we can work together, we have to deal up front with the fact that Lesbians hurt other Lesbians, not just sometimes, but frequently. We can only stop it when we recognize it, name it for what it is, resolve not to do it, and eliminate it as a behavior.

* * *

THE BIG PICTURE

It's been a scary ten or eleven years for Lesbians, and many of us have slipped into an uneasy silence or slammed shut the doors of the closets behind us for a second or third time. We need to keep reminding each other that, *as far as we know*, **nothing like us has ever happened before**. *As far as we know*, there has never been a Lesbian Move-ment, and we are *global* in our connectedness. Too many Lesbians have learned, again, to think of themselves as "small," "tiny," insignificant. We've heard so much about "broader issues" and "the big picture" that some may think that the Lesbian Perspective is a "narrow" one, restricted to an "insignificant" minority.

"Narrow," when applied to concrete, physical dimensions, is used positively, because it means 'slender' in width, and being 'slender' in our society has become a moral imperative for those born female. But "narrow," used abstractly to describe ideas, implies a primarily negative evaluation of whatever concepts it's used of. We speak, for example, of "narrow opinions," "narrow perspectives," "narrow concerns," and we're much taken by points of view that advertise themselves as part of "the broader picture," as affording us "a broader perspective," a "wider scope," or an opportunity to join the "larger revolution." The word "narrow" is used to trivialize, diminish, and discredit a point of view that some people, usually those with socially-validated power, find threatening, repugnant, and downright outrageous. It is my intention to be outrageous. The "Lesbian Perspective" is certainly no less "real" or compelling than the dominant perspective of the white, heterosexual majority, and it is by no means as "narrow" in the negative sense of that word. We rightly avoid the "straight and narrow path."

Our unacknowledged allegiance to male thought patterns can hypnotize us into passivity, and men frequently succeed in paralyzing us with that word (and others). There is nothing "narrow" about being and thinking **Lesbian**. What I'm warming up to here is a discussion of "category width" in English and where we think we might "fit" into the categories of the man-made framework. The language most Lesbians in the U.S. speak, by choice or coercion, is English (Native American, Black, and Hispanic Lesbians know first-hand about the cultural imperialism of imposed language), and it's the semantic structure of English that binds our minds, squishing our ideas into tidy, binary codes: this/not-this, female/male, big/small, Black/White, poor/rich, fat/thin, seeing/unseeing, powerless/powerful, wide/narrow, guilty/innocent. These are narrow concepts in the most negative sense of the word, but they are the semantic basis of the pale male perspective,

and we need to understand the conceptual territory those semantic categories map before we can set about the task of creating a new map that charts the territory of the Lesbian Perspective.

Learning a first language socializes us, and we're dependent creatures when our minds are guided into the conceptual grooves created by the map of the territory men want us to follow. The language forces us to perceive the world as men present it to us. If we describe some behaviors as "feminine" and others as "masculine," we're perceiving ourselves in male terms. Or, we fail to perceive what is not described for us and fall back on male constructs, such as "butch" and "femme," as inherently explanatory labels for our self-conceptions.

Those of us raised speaking English weren't offered any choice in the matter. While we were passive in the indoctrination process for the first few years, however, there comes a time when we have to put aside the fact that we began as innocent victims and undertake the active process of self-reclamation that starts with understanding what happened to us and questioning the conceptual premises on which male societies are based. Learning to think around categorial givens is hard, but it's something we have to do in order to think well of ourselves. If we refuse to do this, we abandon our Selves.

What is called "consensus reality" is the male-defined, male-described version of "what is," and we are obliged to live around, under, and sometimes within what men say is "reality," even as we strive to conceive and define a Lesbian "consensus reality." The duality of our position as Lesbians, simultaneously oppressed by a society in which we are unwanted and marginal and envisioning for ourselves a culture defined by our values, with Lesbian identity at its core, is, I maintain, a position of strength if we take advantage of it.

First, we must undertake the tedious process of examining and re-examining **every** aspect of how we've been taught to "think," including the process of thinking itself. Every one of us raised in an English-speaking household was programmed to perceive the world, and ourselves in the world, according to the special map of the pale male perspective. Any map is always, and only, a **partial description** of the territory it claims to chart. Each map draws attention only to those topographical features that the map creator thinks are "relevant" or "significant"; each map creator perceives only some of the aspects of the territory while other, perhaps equally important features, remain invisible, unperceived. Some things are left out on purpose, others are distorted. Black and dark, for example, are given negative values in the pale male conceptual structure, while white and light are assigned positive values; being able to see is a "good thing"; not being able to see is a "bad thing." These descriptions, and the values attached to them, are not "the nature of the world," and that is not a coincidence. Whatever conceptual changes are eventually condoned by male culture can occur only by enlarging existing category widths, in particular the referential scope of words like *people* and *gay*. The semantic categories themselves don't change; they aren't allowed to change. They expand and contract, but the essential thought structures remain the same.

One of our difficulties with describing a Lesbian consensus reality is a language problem, the contradictory labels we use to name ourselves, a terminology that's sometimes useful, and often divisive. The way we name ourselves reflects how we understand what we mean in the world. We call ourselves, for example, "people," "human beings," "women," "gays," "Lesbians," "Dykes." Because we're biologically categorized as female, it seems meaningful to say that, by inclusion with heterosexual women, we're oppressed as "women," and our experience of socialization confirms this category overlap. Likewise, because we aren't hetero, we're also oppressed as "homosexuals," so some Lesbians identify with gay men, in which case they call themselves "gay women," as I did

for many years. Our invisibility, even to ourselves, is at least partially due to the fact that our identity is subsumed by two groups: women and gays. As a result, Lesbian issues seem to find their way, by neglect or elimination, to the bottom of both liberation agendas. The liberation of Lesbians is supposed to wait for the liberation of all women, or be absorbed and evaporate into the agenda compiled by gay men. Instead of creating free space for ourselves, we allow men to oppress us invisibly in both categories, as "women" or as "gays," without even the token dignity of being named "Lesbians." How we name ourselves determines how visible we are, even to each other.

If we allow ourselves to imagine ourselves as something other than "woman" or "gay," if we try to conceive of our Selves beyond those labels, what comes into our minds? Is it nothing, or is it some-thing? Even if it is hazy, vague, without clear definition, isn't it something we know but haven't yet been able to articulate? The issue here is making explicit the basis of our prioritizing, which is the idea that we are "sub-" somebody else. I think we are much, much more if we choose our Selves. The problem, as I identify it, is calling ourselves *women*. Monique Wittig and others have argued that the category *woman* is a man-made category that serves men's purposes. In this case, the label *woman* diffuses Lesbian movement toward our Selves, to divert our attention from Lesbian issues and Lesbian needs. The label shifts our focus, directing our attention away from Lesbian community. As soon as we name ourselves Lesbians, we step outside of the category 'woman'. What we experience as Lesbians and identify as "women's oppression" is the socialization process that tried to coerce us into 'womanhood'. As a result of this tailoring of our identities, when we change categories from 'woman' to 'lesbian', we're still oppressed as 'female' and oppressed for daring to be 'non-woman'. While both Lesbians and hetero women experience misogyny as biological females, our experience of that oppression is very different.

The L-word continually disappears into the labels "gay" and "woman," along with our energy, our money, and our hope. So much Lesbian creativity and activity is called "women's this" or "gay that," making Lesbians invisible and giving heterosexual women or gay men credit for what they can't imagine and haven't accomplished. We need to think LESBIAN. We need to think DYKE. We need to stop being complacent about our self-erasure.

The male map cannot be trusted because the territory it describes isn't a healthy place for us to live in. Accepting male descriptions of the world endangers Lesbians. We can fight for inclusion within already sanctioned categories, such as *people*, *human being*, or *woman*, thereby forcing other speakers to enlarge them, or we can remain outside of patriarchally-given categories and endeavor to construct a different, more accurate map of the Lesbian conceptual territory. We have internalized a description of the world that erodes our self-esteem, damages our self-image, and poisons our capacity for self-love. If the children we were lacked options for the process of self-creation, the Lesbians we've become have the potential, as well as the responsibility, for redefining ourselves, learning to perceive the world in new and different ways from what we were taught, and setting about making maps that accurately describe the territory of our envisioning.

We can choose whether or not we will conform to heterosexual values, and even the degree to which we'll conform to the map men have imposed on reality. How we choose to deal with the defining categories of male culture places us within its boundaries or at its periphery. (See my essay, "Heteropatriarchal Semantics: 'Just Two Kinds of People in the World'," for an analysis of these defining categories.) We are never "outside" the reach of society, because even the negative evaluation of who we are can limit and control our lives. How we

describe for ourselves that first wary step into an uncharted world determines how we think of ourselves as Lesbians. The Lesbian situation is essentially **ambiguous,** and that ambiguity provides the foundation of the Lesbian perspective. We must start from where we are.

TERRA INCOGNITA

Deciding to act on our Lesbian perceptions requires each of us to conceive ourselves as someone other than what male society has said we are. The Lesbian process of self-definition, however long it takes, begins with the recognition and certainty that our perceptions are fundamentally accurate, regardless of what male societies say. This is a STRONG place in us. In order to trust ourselves, we have to be able to push through the lies and contradictions presented to us as "truths," cast them aside, and stand, for that moment, in our own clarity. Every Lesbian takes that step into *terra incognita*, the undescribed or falsely described, the "unknown," beyond the limits posted by the pale male map of reality. Picture for yourself the map of the "known" world presented to us every moment, every day of our lives. Label that map HETEROPATRIARCHY out to the very neatly trimmed edges. Now read the warning signs along the edge: "Dangerous," "monstrous," "sick," "sinful," "illegal," "unsafe," "Keep Out! Trespassers will be violated!" Remember how long you deliberated with yourself before stepping across that boundary, before you decided you had to ignore the warning signs and take your chances in an ill-defined geography.

It's the clarity of that moment, the confidence of self-creation, that creates the "euphoria" so many Lesbians experience when we first come out. We do not forget that moment of clarity, ever. Lesbians think and behave differently because we've had to fight constantly to establish and maintain our identity in spite of covert and overt attempts, some of them violent, all of them degrading, to coerce us into heterosexuality. The Lesbian Self must stand alone, sometimes for years, against the force of the heterosexual imperative, until she can find other Lesbians who will support and affirm her. The out Lesbian has denied the validity of what men call "reality" in order to be Her Self. We do think differently. We perceive the world as aliens, as outcasts. No matter how hard some Lesbians try to "fit in," pale male societies define us as outside the boundary of the categories that maintain its coherence. We are made outcasts, but we can empower our Selves on that ground.

Although we may look back at times with yearning toward the heterosexual land of make-believe, we know that delusion for what it is: a man-made smog that pollutes and poisons all life. We must choose our own clarity, our willfulness, and reject the orthodoxy, "right-thinking," of men. Being Lesbian is nonconforming. The Lesbian perspective demands heterodoxy, deviant and unpopular thinking, requires us to love ourselves for being outcasts, not in spite of it, to create for ourselves the grounds of our being. The Lesbian Perspective isn't something we acquire as soon as we step out of our closets. It's as much a process of unlearning as it is learning. It's something we have to work at, nurture, encourage, and develop. The Lesbian Perspective is furious self-creation.

If we can imagine ourselves into being, if we can refuse to accept the labels and descriptions of men, the "possibilities **are** endless." We **are** outcasts from male society. We have no choice in that. What we can choose is how we define ourselves with respect to our outcast status. The Lesbian Perspective always asks "unpopular" questions. They're not popular because they threatened the interior structure of societies erected by men. What, exactly, does the Lesbian Perspective look like? Because we're already living in a way that men say is impossible, we gradually shed the dichotomies and distinctions we learned as children. The labels, names, and compartmentalizations that accompany those ways come to have less and less relevance in our thought processes, and we find new ways of interpreting our experience in the world because we perceive it differently. What we once memorized and accepted as "facts" no longer accurately describes our perceptions of reality. We realize that what we were taught to think was "real" or "natural" are only man-made constructs imposed on acts and events, ready-made representations of thoughts and feelings that we can, and must, reject. This is a difficult, gradual, uncertain process only because male societies don't want us to enjoy being outcasts. It's definitely **not** in the interests of men for us to like ourselves. Although it's men who established the boundaries that made us outcasts, what counts is how we organize that information in our minds and act on it in our lives.

The Lesbian Perspective challenges what heterosexuals choose to believe is "fact." As our joy in being outcasts expands, so does our ability to ask dangerous questions and dis-cover magical answers. We have no "givens" beyond that which is "other than": "deviant," "abnormal," "unnatural," "queer," false descriptions we begin with and cannot afford to forget. Indeed, we should wear them proudly. But our major endeavor must be self-definition. We have much to learn yet about ourselves, *our* culture, and we have new maps to draw that show the significant features of our worlds. The Lesbian Perspective makes it possible to challenge the accuracy of male consensus reality, and to create a reality that is Lesbian-defined and Lesbian-sustaining. Once we learn to perceive the world from our own perspective, outside the edges of the pale male map, we'll find it not only recognizable, but familiar.

❧ Reproduction ❧

Women and Reproduction

Rachel Gold
Cory Richards

Bearing children and raising a family are central to the aspirations of most American women. Equally important is the ability to do so under the best possible circumstances. Over the course of a woman's "childbearing years" (roughly, between the ages of fifteen and forty-four), she faces a series of reproductive options and opportunities, but also a series of challenges and obstacles.

Since most American women want to have only a few children, the challenge they face for most of their childbearing years is avoiding an unintended pregnancy. Of the 55 million women of reproductive age in the United States in 1982, the most recent year for which data are available, one-third were pregnant, seeking to become pregnant, infertile or not in a sexual relationship, but the remaining two-thirds, 36 million women, were at risk of an unintended pregnancy. (Unless otherwise indicated, all data are from the Alan Guttmacher Institute.)

More than 90 percent of these women used some method of contraception. Nearly one-third of them reported that either they or their partners had been sterilized, making surgical sterilization the most common form of contraception. Nearly 29 percent of users relied on oral contraceptives, and 23 percent used a barrier method such as the diaphragm, condom, or foam. Seven percent reported using an intrauterine device (IUD), although the number of women using IUDs will likely drop dramatically, since virtually all IUDs have been removed from the U.S. market as a result of the crisis in liability insurance. The remaining contraceptive users relied on periodic abstinence, withdrawal, or other methods.

The kind of contraceptive a woman uses typically varies with her age, marital status, race, and socioeconomic status. Oral contraceptive use is the most common method among teenagers, and use of the pill peaks at ages twenty to twenty-four. Sterilization is the most common method for women over thirty. Poor

The American Woman 1987–88: A Report in Depth, Ed. Sara Rix. W.W. Norton, New York, 1987. © The Women's Research and Education Institute of the Congressional Caucus for Women's Issues.

women and white women are most likely to rely on contraceptive sterilization, and nonwhite women are more likely than white women to use oral contraceptives.

Not all women, however, are protected from risk of unintended pregnancy by contraceptive use. Teenagers are less likely than women in any other age group to use contraception: one-fifth of all sexually active teenagers use no method of contraception at all. Unmarried women and black women are also less likely to be contraceptive users than their married or white counterparts. The reasons why women do not use contraception are complex and varied. Cost is clearly one important factor. The average first-year cost for oral contraceptives is nearly $200, and the cost of using a diaphragm with spermicide is over $150. Obtaining an IUD usually costs well over $100. While historic differentials in contraceptive-use patterns between rich and poor women and black and white women in the United States have narrowed significantly, the gap is far from closed. Although nearly five million women are able to receive family planning services through federally subsidized clinics, more than four in ten of the low-income and teenage women in need of subsidized contraceptive care do not receive medically supervised family planning services. In addition, some women are deterred from using the most effective methods of contraception because they misunderstand the risks (and underestimate or are unaware of the benefits) or because they feel that the currently available methods of contraception are too intrusive or otherwise "inappropriate" for their lifestyles.

Partially because contraceptive use is not universal and partially because even the most effective methods of contraception are not foolproof, some three million-plus American women still become pregnant unintentionally each year. Among American teenagers, unintended pregnancy is twice as likely as it is in France, Canada, and Great Britain, three times as likely as it is in Sweden, and seven times as

likely as it is in the Netherlands. Black women in the United States are 2 1/2 times more likely than white women to become pregnant unintentionally. Similarly, unmarried women are more likely than married women to do so.

While 13 percent of all unintended pregnancies end in miscarriage, 46 percent, or about 1.5 million, are terminated by abortion each year. Eight in ten abortions are obtained by unmarried women, who are seven times more likely than married women to obtain one. Black women confronted with unintended pregnancies choose abortion in roughly the same proportion as white women; however, since more black women than white women are faced with unintended pregnancies, black women are more than twice as likely as white women to have abortions.

Not all women who need abortions are able to obtain them: poor women, teenagers, and women in non-urban areas have the greatest difficulty in obtaining abortions. Public funding for abortions is available in only fourteen states and the District of Columbia, and even there only to the very poor, i.e., those eligible for Medicaid. And, even though nearly half of all metropolitan areas have no abortion provider, abortion services are highly concentrated in urban areas. Nearly 90 percent of all nonmetropolitan areas, where more than a quarter of all women of reproductive age live, have no abortion provider at all. Furthermore, the later in pregnancy an abortion is needed, the more difficult it is for any woman, but particularly for young and rural women, to find abortion providers. Fewer than one-third of all abortion providers will perform procedures past the end of the first trimester of pregnancy.

About 3.6 million women gave birth in 1982. Even when joyously anticipated, pregnancy and childbirth can be a financial strain. The cost of even an uncomplicated delivery averages $5,000 nationwide, and the cost in some areas may be considerably higher. Although most families can defray at least some of the cost of childbirth through either public or private insurance, nearly one in five women of reproductive age has no insurance coverage.

Although no data are available at this time to link lack of insurance coverage directly to an inability to obtain adequate prenatal care, it is known that the same groups of women who are likely not to have insurance coverage are the same groups of women who are most likely to receive either late prenatal care or no care at all during pregnancy. Failure to obtain adequate prenatal care is closely tied to poor birth outcomes, and especially with low birthweight, a major factor associated with infant mortality. Although some women may forgo prenatal care because of financial constraints, most pregnant women are able to gain hospital admission for deliveries. However, they may not be able to pay for the care if they have no insurance coverage. One study found that patients admitted for delivery accounted for 37 percent of all surgical patients who received care for which the hospital was not compensated.

For yet another group of women the problem is neither avoiding pregnancy nor affording pregnancy-related care but rather becoming pregnant. Approximately 15 percent of all married couples in the United States are estimated to be infertile for various reasons. Treatment for infertility is expensive, frequently not covered by health insurance, and uncertain to produce favorable results. For those couples whose infertility problems cannot be solved through either corrective surgery or drug therapy, artificial insemination and *in vitro* fertilization are sometimes viable options, depending on the cause of the infertility problem. However, neither of these options is widely available in the United States, and both have significant price tags.

In short, American women may have greater reproductive options, both legally and technologically, now than ever before, but exercising those options in the context of real life is another matter. For a variety of reasons, some of which are understandable, American women—and particularly American teenagers—seem to have less success in controlling their fertility than their counterparts in most other developed countries. At least insofar as the prevention of unintended pregnancy is concerned, this appears to be true for American women as a whole, not just for minorities and the disadvantaged. Still, minority status and poverty, as well as residence in a rural area, are important factors. In the United States today, a woman who is likely to be disadvantaged in making and effecting one reproductive choice at one point in her life runs a high risk of being disadvantaged in making and effecting other reproductive choices at other points along the thirty year continuum of her reproductive life.

Abortion: Is a Woman a Person?

Ellen Willis

If propaganda is as central to politics as I think, the opponents of legal abortion have been winning a psychological victory as important as their tangible gains. Two years ago, abortion was almost always discussed in feminist terms—as a political issue affecting the condition of women. Since then, the grounds of the debate have shifted drastically; more and more, the Right-to-Life movement has succeeded in getting the public and the media to see abortion as an abstract moral issue having solely to do with the rights of fetuses. Though every poll shows that most Americans favor legal abortion, it is evident that many are confused and disarmed, if not convinced, by the anti-abortionists' absolutist fervor. No one likes to be accused of advocating murder. Yet the "pro-life" position is based on a crucial fallacy—that the question of fetal rights can be isolated from the question of women's rights.

Recently, Garry Wills wrote a piece suggesting that liberals who defended the snail-darter's right to life and opposed the killing in Vietnam should condemn abortion as murder. I found this notion breathtaking in its illogic. Environmentalists were protesting not the "murder" of individual snail-darters but the

practice of wiping out entire species of organisms to gain a short-term economic benefit; most people who opposed our involvement in Vietnam did so because they believed the United States was waging an aggressive, unjust, and/or futile war. There was no inconsistency in holding such positions and defending abortion on the grounds that women's welfare should take precedence over fetal life. To claim that three very different issues, each with its own complicated social and political context, all came down to a simple matter of preserving life was to say that all killing was alike and equally indefensible regardless of circumstances. (Why, I wondered, had Wills left out the destruction of hapless bacteria by penicillin?) But aside from the general mushiness of the argument, I was struck by one peculiar fact: Wills had written an entire article about abortion without mentioning women, feminism, sex, or pregnancy.

Since the feminist argument for abortion rights still carries a good deal of moral and political weight, part of the anti-abortionists' strategy has been to make an end run around it. Although the mainstream of the Right-to-Life movement is openly opposed to women's liberation, it has chosen to make its stand on the abstract "pro-life" argument. That emphasis has been reinforced by the movement's tiny left wing, which opposes abortion on pacifist

grounds and includes women who call themselves "feminists for life." A minority among
pacifists as well as Right-to-Lifers, this group
nevertheless serves the crucial function of making opposition to abortion respectable among
liberals, leftists, and moderates disinclined to
sympathize with a right-wing crusade. Unlike
most Right-to-Lifers, who are vulnerable to
charges that their reverence for life does not
apply to convicted criminals or Vietnamese
peasants, anti-abortion leftists are in a position
to appeal to social conscience—to make analogies, however facile, between abortion and na-
palm. They disclaim any opposition to women's
rights, insisting rather that the end cannot justify the means—murder is murder.

Well, isn't there a genuine moral issue
here? If abortion *is* murder, how can a woman
have the right to it? Feminists are often accused
of evading this question, but in fact an evasion
is built into the question itself. Most people
understand "Is abortion murder?" to mean "Is
the fetus a person?" But fetal personhood is ultimately as inarguable as the existence of God;
either you believe in it or you don't. Putting the
debate on this plane inevitably leads to the non-
conclusion that it is a matter of one person's
conscience against another's. From there, the
discussion generally moves on to broader issues:
whether laws defining the fetus as a person violate the separation of church and state; or conversely, whether people who believe an act is
murder have not only the right but the obligation to prevent it. Unfortunately, amid all this
lofty philosophizing, the concrete, human reality of the pregnant woman's dilemma gets lost,
and with it an essential ingredient of the moral
question.

Murder, as commonly defined, is killing
that is unjustified, willful, and malicious. Most
people would agree, for example, that killing in
defense of one's life or safety is not murder. And
most would accept a concept of self-defense that
includes the right to fight a defensive war or revolution in behalf of one's independence or free-

dom from oppression. Even pacifists make
moral distinctions between defensive violence,
however deplorable, and murder; no thoughtful
pacifist would equate Hitler's murder of the Jews
with the Warsaw Ghetto rebels' killing of Nazi
troops. The point is that it's impossible to judge
whether an act is murder simply by looking at the
act, without considering its context. Which is to
say that it makes no sense to discuss whether
abortion is murder without considering why
women have abortions and what it means to
force women to bear children they don't want.

We live in a society that defines childrearing as the mother's job; a society in which most
women are denied access to work that pays
enough to support a family, childcare facilities
they can afford, or any relief from the constant,
daily burdens of motherhood; a society that
forces mothers into dependence on marriage or
welfare and often into permanent poverty; a society that is actively hostile to women's ambitions for a better life. Under these conditions
the unwillingly pregnant woman faces a terrifying loss of control over her fate. Even if she
chooses to give up the baby, unwanted pregnancy is in itself a serious trauma. There is no
way a pregnant woman can passively let the
fetus live; she must create and nurture it with
her own body, in a symbiosis that is often difficult, sometimes dangerous, always uniquely
intimate. However gratifying pregnancy may be
to a woman who desires it, for the unwilling it
is literally an invasion—the closest analogy is to
the difference between lovemaking and rape.
Nor is there such a thing as foolproof contraception. Clearly, abortion is by normal standards an act of self-defense.

Whenever I make this case to a Right-to-
Lifer, the exchange that follows is always substantially the same:

RTL: If a woman chooses to have sex, she
        should be willing to take the conse-
        quences. We must all be responsible for
        our actions.

EW: Men have sex, without having to "take the consequences."

RTL: You can't help that—it's biology.

EW: You don't think a woman has as much right as a man to enjoy sex? Without living in fear that one slip will transform her life?

RTL: She has no right to selfish pleasure at the expense of the unborn.

It would seem, then, that the nitty-gritty issue in the abortion debate is not life but sex. If the fetus is sacrosanct, it follows that women must be continually vulnerable to the invasion of their bodies and loss of their freedom and independence—unless they are willing to resort to the only perfectly reliable contraceptive, abstinence. This is precisely the "solution" Right-to-Lifers suggest, usually with a touch of glee; as Representative Elwood Rudd once put it, "If a woman has a right to control her own body, let her exercise control before she gets pregnant." A common ploy is to compare fucking to over-eating or overdrinking, the idea being that pregnancy is a just punishment, like obesity or cirrhosis.

One hundred and fifty years after Freud it is depressing to have to insist that sex is not an unnecessary, morally dubious self-indulgence but a basic human need, no less for women than for men. Of course, for heterosexual women giving up sex also means doing without the love and companionship of a mate. (Presumably, married women who have had all the children they want are supposed to divorce their husbands or convince them that celibacy is the only moral alternative.) "Freedom" bought at such a cost is hardly freedom at all and certainly not equality—no one tells men that if they aspire to some measure of control over their lives, they are welcome to neuter themselves and become social isolates. The don't-have-sex argument is really another version of the familiar anti-feminist dictum that autonomy and femaleness—that is, female sexuality—are in-

compatible; if you choose the first, you lose the second. But to pose this choice is not only inhumane; it is as deeply disingenuous as "Let them eat cake." No one, least of all the anti-abortion movement, expects or wants significant numbers of women to give up sex and marriage. Nor are most Right-to-Lifers willing to allow abortion for rape victims. When all the cant about "responsibility" is stripped away, what the Right-to-Life position comes down to is, if the effect of prohibiting abortion is to keep women slaves to their biology, so be it.

In their zeal to preserve fetal life at all costs, anti-abortionists are ready to grant fetuses more legal protection than people. If a man attacks me and I kill him, I can plead self-defense without having to prove that I was in danger of being killed rather than injured, raped, or kidnapped. But in the annual congressional battle over what if any exceptions to make to the Medicaid abortion ban, the House of Representatives has bitterly opposed the funding of abortions for any reason but to save the pregnant woman's life. Some Right-to-Lifers argue that even the danger of death does not justify abortion; others have suggested "safeguards" like requiring two or more doctors to certify that the woman's life is at least 50 percent threatened. Anti-abortionists are forever worrying that any exception to a total ban on abortion will be used as a "loophole": better that any number of women should ruin their health or even die than that one woman should get away with not having a child "merely" because she doesn't want one. Clearly this mentality does not reflect equal concern for all life. Rather, anti-abortionists value the lives of fetuses above the lives and welfare of women, because at bottom they do not concede women the right to an active human existence that transcends their reproductive function. Years ago, in an interview with Paul Krassner in *The Realist*, Ken Kesey declared himself against abortion. When Krassner asked if his objection applied to victims of rape, Kesey replied—I may not be remembering the exact words, but I will never forget the substance—"Just because another man planted the seed, that's no reason to destroy the crop."[1] To this day I have not heard a more eloquent or chilling metaphor for the essential premise of the Right-to-Life movement: that a woman's excuse for being is her womb. It is an outrageous irony that anti-abortionists are managing to pass off this profoundly immoral idea as a noble moral cause.

The conservatives who dominate the Right-to-Life movement have no real problem with the anti-feminism inherent in their stand; their evasion of the issue is a matter of public relations. But the politics of anti-abortion leftists are a study in self-contradiction: in attacking what they see as the violence of abortion, they condone and encourage violence against women. Forced childbearing does violence to a woman's body and spirit, and it contributes to other kinds of violence: deaths from illegal abortion; the systematic oppression of mothers and women in general; the poverty, neglect, and battering of unwanted children; sterilization abuse.

Radicals supposedly believe in attacking a problem at its roots. Yet surely it is obvious that restrictive laws do not keep women from seeking abortions; they just create an illicit, dangerous industry. The only way to drastically reduce the number of abortions is to invent safer, more reliable contraceptives, ensure universal access to all birth control methods, eliminate sexual ignorance and guilt, and change the social and economic conditions that make motherhood a trap. Anyone who is truly committed to fostering life should be fighting for women's liberation instead of harassing and disrupting abortion clinics (hardly a nonviolent tactic, since it threatens the safety of patients). The "feminists for life" do talk a lot about ending the oppression that drives so many women to abortion; in practice, however, they are devoting all their energy to increasing it.

Despite its numerical insignificance, the anti-abortion left epitomizes the hypocrisy of the Right-to-Life crusade. Its need to wrap misogyny in the rhetoric of social conscience and even feminism is actually a perverse tribute to the women's movement; it is no longer acceptable to declare openly that women deserve to suffer for the sin of Eve. I suppose that's progress—not that it's much comfort to women who need abortions and can't afford them.

NOTE

1. A reader later sent me a copy of the Kesey interview. The correct quotation is "You don't plow under the corn because the seed was planted with a neighbor's shovel."

Reproductive Rights and Disability

Anne Finger

Just as I can't remember a time of my life when I wasn't a feminist, I can't remember not believing in disability rights. From the time I was a very young child, I understood that I was "more handicapped" by people's perceptions and attitudes towards me than I was by my disability (I had polio shortly before my third birthday). Although as a child I didn't have the word "disability," never mind "oppression" or "attitudinal barriers" to describe my experience, what I *did* have was the example of the black civil rights movement, then beginning in the South. From about the age of five or six, I used to think, "People are prejudiced against me the same way that they are against Negroes."

While increased understanding has led me to see the differences as well as the similarities between Black experiences and my own, my belief that disability in and of itself was much less of a problem than social structures and attitudes towards disability has never changed. In part because I was exempted from traditional feminine roles—*no one* ever so much as mentioned the possibility of my having babies when I grew up—I was also a feminist, at least in some incipient form, as far back as I can remember.

But it has not always been easy building a

From *Test-Tube Women*. Reprinted by permission.

politics that connects these two parts of my experience. The feminist movement—the movement which has been my home for most of my adult life—has by and large acted as if disabled women did not exist. For instance, the 1976 edition of *Our Bodies, Our Selves* mentioned disability only twice—both times speaking of fetuses with potentially disabling conditions, not disabled women. In the early years of the feminist movement I heard constantly about how women were sex objects—I could see that that was true for a lot of my abled sisters, but there were no voices saying that being stereotyped as asexual was also oppressive—and also was part of our female experience. More recently, the disability rights movement and the women's movement have seemed to be at loggerheads with each other over issues of reproductive technologies, genetics, and fetal and neonatal disabilities. I hope this article will be a step towards helping us to claim *all* of our selves.

Most discussions of disability begin with a laundry list of disabling conditions. Disability, we are told, does not just mean being in a wheelchair. It also includes a variety of conditions, both invisible and visible. These include being deaf or blind, having a heart condition, being developmentally disabled or being "mentally ill." While this is necessary to an understanding of disability, thinking about disability only in medical or quasi-medical terms limits our understanding: disability is largely a social construct.

Women, like disabled people, can be defined in terms of physical characteristics that make us different from males (only women menstruate; only women get pregnant; women tend to be shorter than men). We can also be defined socially. A social description would include all of the above physical characteristics, but would emphasize that, in our society, we are paid far less than men; we are less likely to vote Republican; and more likely to be emotional and empathetic.

In the same manner, when we start looking at disability socially, we see not only the medically defined conditions that I have described, but the social and economic circumstances that limit the lives of disabled people. We look, for instance at the fact that White disabled women earn 24 cents for every dollar that *comparably qualified* nondisabled men earn; for Black disabled women, the figure is 12 cents. (Figures for other racial groups were not reported.) Media images almost always portray us as being either lonely and pitiful or one-dimensional heroes (or, occasionally, heroines) who struggle valiantly to "overcome our handicaps." Many of us are still being denied the free public education that all American children supposedly receive; and we have a (largely unknown) history of fighting for our rights that stretches back at least to the mid-nineteenth century (and probably further). To understand that disability is socially constructed means understanding that the economic, political, and social forces which now restrict our lives can (and will) change.

THE EUGENICS MOVEMENT AND STERILIZATION ABUSE

The reproductive rights movement has, by and large, failed to address the ways that sterilization abuse has affected disabled people. Compulsory and coerced sterilization of the disabled began in the late nineteenth century. The eugenics movement provided the ideological basis for these actions (as well as providing a similar rationale for racist actions). The term "eugenics" was coined by Sir. Francis Galton; the *Oxford English Dictionary* defines the word as "pertaining or adapted to the production of fine offspring, esp. in the human race." The aim of this movement was to apply the same principles of improving "stock" that were used for horses and vegetables to human beings. This movement has strong roots in Social Darwinism—the idea that life is a struggle between the fit and the unfit. The unfit—which includes the "feeble minded, insane, epileptic, diseased, blind, deaf, [and] deformed" were to be bred out of existence.

Based on the mistaken notion that all disabilities were inherited, there were several factors that contributed to the growth of the eugenics movement at this period. One factor was the prevalent assumption of nineteenth-century science that human perfection could be achieved through a combination of technological and social manipulation, an increased understanding of heredity, and the fact that surgical techniques for sterilization had become available. But any discussion of the eugenics movement which leaves out the changing social role of disabled people at this period fails to grasp the true nature of this movement.

As America industrialized, there was less room for those who had physical or mental limitations to adapt their work environment to their needs. Our history as disabled people has yet to be written. But from what I have been able to glean, I believe that in rural societies disabled people had far more of a social role than they have had in the more urban and industrialized world. The fact that folk tales and rhymes refer to "the simple;" that "the village idiot" was a stock figure; that blind and other disabled people appear in the myths and legends of many places, all indicate that in the past, disabled people had more of a daily presence in the world.

As work became more structured and formalized, people who "fit" into the standardized factories were needed. Industrializing America not only forbade the immigration of disabled people from abroad, it shut the ones already here away in institutions. The growth of social welfare organizations and charities which "helped" those with disabilities did provide jobs for a certain segment of the middle class; and volunteer charity fit in with the Victorian notion of women's duties and sphere.

This change in attitudes towards disabled people can be traced in language. The word *defective*, for instance, was originally an adjective meaning faulty or imperfect: it described one aspect of a person, rather than defining that person totally. By the 1880s, it had become a noun: people were considered not merely to have a defective sense of vision or a defective gait—they had become totally defined by their limitations, and had become *defectives*. A similar transformation took place a few decades later with the word *unfit*, which also moved from being an adjective to being a noun. The word *normal*, which comes from the Latin word *norma*, square, until the 1830s meant standing at a right angle to the ground. During the 1840s it came to designate conformity to a common type. By the 1880s, in America, it had come to apply to people as well as things.

Close on the heels of the rise of institutions for disabled people was an increase in forced and coerced sterilization. Adele Clarke has pointed out that "the intentional breeding of plants and animals is almost exclusively undertaken to improve the products . . . [to increase] profitability from the products, whether they be Arabian horses or more easily transportable tomatoes or peaches. Eugenics applies, I believe, the same profit motive to the breeding of people." Since disabled people were of little or no use to the profit-makers, and since they were thought likely to become burdens on the state coffers, they were to be stopped from producing others like themselves.

Compulsory sterilization laws were passed in the early 1900s. By the 1930s, in addition to sterilization laws, forty-one states had laws which prohibited the marriage of the "insane and feeble-minded," seventeen prohibited the marriage of people with epilepsy; four outlawed marriage for "confirmed drunkards." More than twenty states still have eugenics laws on their books.

Coerced sterilization is still very much a reality, especially among the developmentally disabled. "Voluntary" sterilizations are sometimes a condition for being released from an institution; there has been at least one recent case of a "voluntary" sterilization being performed on a six-year-old boy.

It is important to understand the connections between sterilization abuse of disabled people and of Third World people. The U.S. Senate Committee on Nutrition and Human Needs reported in 1974 that between 75 percent and 85 percent of the "mentally defective and retarded children" who are born each year are born into families with incomes below the poverty line. This means that a large number of those who are labeled as "retards" are people of color. The vast majority of people who get diagnosed as being mentally retarded have no definite, identifiable cause for their retardation: they are called the "mildly retarded," the "educable," and those with "cultural-familial" retardation. The same IQ tests which "prove" that Black people as a whole are less intelligent than Whites label a far greater percentage of individual Black children as "retarded."

The Eugenics Movement in Nazi Germany. The Model Sterilization Law of Harry Laughlin, which I cited earlier, was never passed in its totality by any state in this country; however, a version of it was adopted in Nazi Germany. American eugenicists were often enthusiastic supporters of Hitler's attempt to rid Germany of "defectives."

Nazi ideology stressed purity, fear of disease, and the importance of heredity, intertwining these concepts with racism. In *Mein Kampf*, Hitler calls syphilis "the Jewish disease"; Jewish people (and other "sub-humans") are portrayed as being weak, sickly, and degenerate, in contrast with healthy blonde Aryans. Before the start of World War II, Nazi eugenics courts had forced hundreds of thousands of disabled people to be sterilized. This forced sterilization helped to pave the way for the wartime genocide of Germany's disabled population.

THE REPRODUCTIVE RIGHTS MOVEMENT

Many disabled women find involvement in the reproductive rights movement problematic. Not only have many activists in this movement talked about the issues raised by disabled fetuses in ways that are highly exploitative and prey upon fears about disability, the movement also has, by and large, failed to address the denial of reproductive rights to disabled women and men. It has also failed to make itself physically accessible to disabled women.

I often hear an argument in favor of abortion rights that says, "The right-wing would even force us to give birth to a child who was deformed." ("Deformed" is mild in this context. I've heard "defective," "grossly malformed," and "hideously deformed.") This attitude has become so widespread that at a recent conference on reproductive rights I heard disabled infants referred to as "bad babies." *Off Our Backs* parodied a conversation between Nathanson and Hatch on "the joys of having a mongoloid [*sic*] child."*

No woman should be forced to bear a child, abled or disabled; and no progressive social

movement should exploit an oppressed group to further its end. We do not need, as Michelle Fine and Adrienne Asch point out in their article "The Question of Disability: No Easy Answers for the Women's Movement" to list conditions—such as the presence of a fetus with a disability—under which abortion is acceptable. The right to abortion is not dependent on certain circumstances: it is our absolute and essential right to have control over our bodies. We do not need to use ableist arguments to bolster our demands. There are racist and classist arguments that can be made for abortion: to argue against them does not compromise our insistence on abortion rights.

Issues Raised by Fetal Diagnosis.   When we first fought for and won abortion rights, we focused on the situation of the *woman* herself. Most women who choose abortion do so early on in pregnancy, having made the decision that they do not want a child, any child, at the time. Now, however, the availability of techniques for diagnosis of fetal disabilities (such as amniocentesis, ultrasonography, and fetoscopy) means that women can now choose not to give birth to a *particular* fetus. This is a radical shift, one which raises profound and difficult questions. Perhaps some of the kneejerk reaction to the issues of disabled fetuses reflect our unwillingness to fully explore these hard issues.

It is a little too pat to say that decisions about whether to have amniocentesis or to abort a disabled fetus are personal ones. Ultimately, of course, they are and must remain so. But we need to have a feminist, political language and ways of thinking about this issue to aid us in making those personal decisions and discussing these issues.

As Adrienne Asch has pointed out, discussions about whether or not to carry to term a pregnancy where the fetus will be born with a disability are clouded when we think in terms of the "severity" of the "defect." Rather, potential parents need to consider who *they* are and what

---

* The term "mongoloid" to describe children with the chromosonal disorder now termed "Down syndrome" originated in the mid-nineteenth century. It was thought that the birth of these children to White parents was a "hereditary throwback" to the "lower race" of Mongols (Asians) from which the White race had ascended.

they see as *their* strengths and weaknesses as parents making these decisions.

In choosing to be a parent, none of us knows what we are getting into: prenatal diagnosis may shed a little light, but everyone who becomes a parent takes a giant leap into the unknown. We need to remember that there is no such thing as a "perfect" child; that all children, abled and disabled, are going to experience suffering and joys in this world.

One thing that feminists should push for is good amniocentesis counseling. Unfortunately, despite my attempts, I haven't been able to witness any such counseling first hand. I was able to interview one disabled woman who had amniocentesis. She was having amnio not because she intended to abort if her fetus had a potential disability, but because she felt that, given her special needs, she needed to be able to make plans if her child was going to have a disability. She was shocked at the assumptions made by the counselors that any woman who was carrying a fetus with Down's syndrome or spina bifida would of course abort. After the group counseling session, she called the clinic to voice her objections about their presentation of disability. She was told by counselors at the clinic that they felt they should provide as *negative* a picture as possible.

Much of this stems from medical attitudes towards physical impairment. One woman did an informal survey in which she asked doctors, "What things would be worse than death?" They answered, being paraplegic, or being deaf, or partially sighted or not having both arms. I think having attitudes like that is a fate worse than death. Too often, people who see physical and mental limitations as tragedies are counseling women following amniocentesis. Are women who are told they are carrying a Down's fetus told that, due to deinstitutionalization and better educational methods, some people with Down's now go to school in regular classrooms, live in their own apartments and hold jobs? Are they told that 95 percent of Down's people have

moderate to mild retardation? Are they told that if they choose to bear their child, but not raise her or him, the child can be adopted immediately—usually within twenty-four hours? Do they have anything more to go on than fear, shame, and their own prejudices combined with those of the medical profession? Women who are considering aborting a disabled fetus must have the opportunity to talk to disabled people and the parents of disabled children. Anything less is not real reproductive freedom.

Women considering whether or not to give birth to a disabled child have few, if any, positive role models. Mothers who remain the primary caregivers of disabled children are seen as being either self-sacrificing saints or bitter, ruined women. These popular images get carried into the "objective" scientific literature. Wendy Carlton reviewed the studies done of mothers of disabled children: they were seen as either being "rejecting" or "overprotecting"; they denied the child's condition or had unrealistic expectations; they are "unconcerned or overinvolved." No matter what they did, they couldn't seem to get it right. One in every twenty children is born with some sort of disability—a quarter of a million children a year. In addition, many become disabled during childhood. There are millions of mothers of disabled children in the U.S., most of whom, I am sure, manage to do a halfway decent job of childrearing, despite stereotypes, social service cutbacks, and the limitations of the nuclear family.

Dealing with Fears. This article grew out of a talk that I gave to a reproductive rights group on this issue. In the discussion that followed, I was very disappointed that women in the audience never once addressed the reproductive rights of disabled women and men, despite extensive presentation of such issues. Instead, the discussion focused on disabled infants and, more specifically, on their personal fears of having a disabled child. The women I talked to are hardly alone.

For instance, Sheila Kitzinger, well-regarded in the alternative birth movement, has a chapter on "The Psychology of Pregnancy" in her book *The Experience of Childbirth*. In the subsection entitled "Fear that the baby will be malformed," she states:

Any time after about the fifth month of pregnancy, when the child begins to move and becomes a reality to the mother, she may start to think about her baby as possibly deformed. . . . What if this thing I am nourishing and cherishing within my own body, around which my whole life is built now, whose pulse beats fast deep within me—what if this child should prove to be *a hideous deformed creature, subhuman, a thing I should be able to love, but which I should shudder to see?* (emphasis added)[1]

Kitzinger deals with this issue solely on the level of a neurotic fear, never once discussing what happens when a child is actually born with a disability.

The deeply rooted fears that many women have of giving birth to a disabled child extend to our politics. They need to be worked through. But please don't expect disabled women to sit there and listen to you while you do so.

Killing Babies, Left and Right.   Infanticide of the disabled has gone on at least as long as history has been recorded. (Although the Reagan administration would like us to believe that it has gotten worse in the past ten years—*i.e.*, since the legalization of abortion.) Killing of disabled infants continues today—sometimes through denial of nutrition, more often through withholding of medical treatment.

"Baby Doe" is probably the best-known case. A Down's syndrome infant, born with a blocked esophagus, his parents and the doctors involved decided to deny him standard live-saving surgery, resulting in his death by starvation. This happened despite the fact that child welfare workers went to court to try to get an injunction to force the surgery to be performed, and despite the fact that there were twelve families ready to adopt the child, and a surgeon willing to perform the surgery for free. Nearly all Down syndrome children, up to about the age of five, are now adoptable—thanks in large part to the baby shortage caused by legal abortion and the increased number of single women who keep their children.

I believe that it is inconsistent with feminism for us to say that human beings should be killed (or allowed to die, if you prefer) because they do not fit into oppressive social structures. "Anatomy is destiny" is a right-wing idea. It is right-wing whether it is applied to women or whether it is applied to disabled children by the people I usually think of as my sisters and brothers.

So-called "right-to-lifers" are among the loudest voices heard in defense of these children's lives, and I have heard the argument made that it is dangerous for us to sound like we are on "their" side. But if we fail to call for full rights for *all* disabled people, we will have allowed right-wing, anti-feminist forces to totally define the terrain on which we struggle. And we can distinguish ourselves from the Right on this issue, by standing for full rights for disabled people—not just the right to live so that we can, in the words of anti-abortionist Nathanson, "evoke pity and compassion" from the abled.

SEXUALITY, BIRTH CONTROL, AND PARENTAL RIGHTS

Occasionally, reproductive rights groups make a token mention of disabled women. When we are included, it is usually at the end of a long list. But our particular needs and concerns are rarely addressed, much less fought for. One reproductive rights activist said to me, "We always used to talk about the rights of disabled women, but I was never sure exactly what that meant." Lack of access to our offices, newsletters, demonstrations and meetings remains a barrier, preventing many disabled women from being physically present within the movement to voice their concerns.

Part of this problem lies in the pervasive stereotype of disabled women as being asexual. Disabled women have been asked, "What do you need birth control for?" or "How did *you* get pregnant?" In 1976, SIECUS, the Sex Information and Education Council on the United States, which is a quite respectable organization, prepared a booklet on "Sexuality and the Handicapped" which was sent to the 1976 White House Conference on the Handicapped—and promptly rejected as "inappropriate."

At least some of this prevalent stereotype of asexuality stems from seeing disabled people as eternal children. Telethons and other charitable activities have played a large role in creating this image. They portray us as being wan, pathetic, pitiful. The Jerry Lewis telethon even showed a series of film clips of adult disabled people saying, "I'm forty-seven years old and I'm one of Jerry's kids," "I'm fifty-five years old and I'm one of Jerry's kids." I won't go into the way that children's sexuality is treated in this society.

This asexual image is often prevalent among doctors and counselors as well. Women who have had spinal cord injury report that when they asked questions about their sexual functioning they were given the information that they could still have children—and nothing more. Or else, they received sexist and heterosexist information, typified by the following:

. . . a female paraplegic can have intercourse more easily than a male paraplegic, since she does not have to participate actively. Although some such women have no subjective feeling of orgasm [as opposed to an objective feeling of orgasm?] they are perfectly capable of satisfying their husbands.[2]

All human bodies are sexual. People without genital sensation (which is a fairly common occurrence following spinal cord injury) can have orgasms through the stimulation of other parts of their bodies, such as their breasts, earlobes, or necks. One measure of the rigid structure which the medical profession imposes on our bodies is that these non-genital orgasms are sometimes referred to by clinicians as "phantom orgasms." These are not genuine, medically-approved orgasms—they only *feel* like the real thing.

There is an opposite stereotype, in some ways similar to the madonna-whore dichotomy which women face. Disabled people (particularly men, although also women) are sometimes seen as being filled with diseased lusts. Lewis Terman, one of the early authorities on what was then called "feeble-mindedness," said that all developmentally disabled women were "potential prostitutes" since moral values could not "flower" without full intelligence. Media images portray disabled men—whether they are physically disabled or "escaped mental patients"—as rapists and potential rapists. The chilling realities about rape of disabled people, particularly within institutions, has been largely ignored both by the public at large and within the women's movement.

Disabled lesbians are rarely seen as having made a choice about their sexuality. Many people see them as having had to take "second best" because of their disability, or as having relationships which must be asexual. For mentally retarded lesbians the "normalization" which is a part of moving developmentally disabled people into the community holds pitfalls. "Normal" women are supposed to curl their hair, wear makeup and dresses, giggle, and sleep with men. Many who argue for the sexual rights of developmentally disabled people point out that if they aren't allowed to form heterosexual relationships that they will form—horror of horrors—homosexual ones.

Birth Control. The stereotype of asexuality persists in information that comes from the women's health movement. I have never seen a discussion of birth control methods—no matter how extensive—that talks about how a particular method works for a woman who is blind, or has cerebral palsy, or is developmentally disabled. *Our Bodies, Our Selves*, for instance, warns that the pill should not be taken by women who have a "disease or condition associated with poor blood circulation," without mentioning what those diseases or conditions are. Unfortunately, many of us with disabilities are far from fully informed about our medical conditions. I had no idea (and neither, apparently, did any of the gynecologists I saw) that, due to my disability, taking birth control pills put me at great risk of thromboembolism.

When we work for improved birth control, we need to remember that there are many disabled women for whom there is *no* method that comes close to being safe and effective. The pill is contraindicated for most women in wheelchairs because of circulation problems. Many women who have paralysis cannot insert a diaphragm, and these same women may have problems with an IUD, especially if they do not have uterine sensation and cannot be warned by pain and cramping of infection or uterine perforation.

The 1983 hearings in Washington about the possible licensing of Depo-Provera highlight another area of contraceptive abuse of which feminists must be aware. Depo-Provera is an injectable contraceptive. Because it is not user-controlled, it is often recommended for women who have developmental disabilities. (It also has the "beneficial" effect of doing away with menstruation; for developmentally disabled women, this is supposed to be a special plus, since it is more "hygenic." (Is it disability or menstruation that is unclean?)

Part of the problem with this use of Depo is that many of those who are considered severely or profoundly retarded also have physical disabilities. One study found that users of Depo "are several times as likely to undergo thromboembolic (blood clotting) disease without evident cause as nonusers." It seems likely that their physical disabilities would put them at increased risk.

Depo-Provera, because of the many side effects that have occurred with its use, is only licensed for use as a treatment for cancer. However, individual doctors can prescribe Depo for any reason they choose; and developmentally disabled women are probably receiving it now, with no method of reporting the side effects and problems they experience. (*Toward Intimacy*, an otherwise excellent booklet about contraception for disabled women, lists only a few of the known side-effects associated with Depo, and candidly notes: "Available only through private physicians until FDA approval is obtained for Depo-Provera's use as a contraceptive. Family planning clinics can often refer you to private physicians if you are interested in this method.")

Parenting, Custody Issues, and Adoption.   In preparing this article, I looked for, but was unable to find, any statistics about the number or percentage of disabled people who have children. I did find lots of anecdotal information about disabled people being told they *shouldn't* have children, and heard some chilling stories from disabled women about being pressured into having abortions. There is almost no public image of disabled people as parents, and I do not know of a single book about being a disabled parent—although there are probably hundreds about having a disabled child.

There have been two fairly well-known cases in which a disabled parent fought to win or keep custody of a child. One of these concerned a single mother who had been born without arms or legs: welfare workers attempted to take her child away from her. After demonstrating to the judge that she was able to care for her child's needs herself, she won the right to custody. In the second case, a divorced quadraplegic father won custody of his sons.

It is particularly important that we in the women's movement take up these issues, since too often they are ignored when demands for disability rights are raised. The American Civil Liberties Union puts out a handbook called *The Rights of Physically Handicapped People* which contains no mention of parental rights, sexual rights, rights to adoption, or rights to safe and effective birth control.

The many political issues around adoption are too complex for me to delve into here. We do need to be sure that people are not denied the right to adopt on the basis of their disability. This has a special importance for two reasons: a small percentage of people with disabilities are unable to become biological parents. In addition, there is a growing tendency for disabled people to adopt children with disabilities, so that they can be raised within our community.

Because both the reproductive rights movement and the disability rights movement are rooted in our rights to control our bodies and our lives, there are strong links between the two. Just as there needs to be a realization within the disabled rights movement that the rights of disabled women must be fought for, so there needs to be an awareness within the reproductive rights movement that those of us who are disabled can no longer be exploited and ignored.

NOTES

1. Kitzinger, Shiela, *The Experience of Childbirth*, Penguin Books (1988).

2. Becker, Elle, *Female Sexuality Following Spinal Cord Injury*, Accent Special Publications: Bloomington, Indiana (1978).

Selling Babies and Selling Bodies

Sara Ann Ketchum

The "Baby M" case has turned into something approaching a national soap opera, played out in newspapers and magazines. The drama surrounding the case tends to obscure the fact that the case raises some very abstract philosophical and moral issues. It forces us to examine questions about the nature and meaning of parenthood, of the limits of reproductive autonomy,

From *Hypatia* (1989). Reprinted by permission.

of how the facts of pregnancy should affect our analysis of sexual equality, and of what counts as selling people and of what forms (if any) of selling people we should honor in law and what forms we should restrict. It is this last set of questions whose relevance I will be discussing here. One objection to what is usually called "surrogate motherhood" and which I will call "contracted motherhood" (CM) or "baby contracts"[1] is that it commercializes reproduction and turns human beings (the mother and/or the baby) into objects of sale. If this is a compelling objection, there is a good argument for prohibiting (and/or not enforcing contracts for) commercial CM. Such a prohibition would be similar to laws on black market adoptions and would have two parts, at least: (1) a prohibition of commercial companies who make the arrangements and/or (2) a prohibition on the transfer of money to the birth mother for the transfer of custody (beyond expenses incurred). I will also argue that CM law should follow adoption law in making clear that pre-birth agreements to relinquish parental rights are not binding and will not be enforced by the courts (the birth mother should not be forced to give up her child for adoption).

CM AND AID: THE REAL DIFFERENCE PROBLEM

CM is usually presented as a new reproductive technology and, moreover, as the female equivalent of AID (artificial insemination by donor) and, therefore, as an extension of the right to privacy or the right to make medical decisions about one's own life. There are two problems with this description: (1) CM uses the same technology as AID—the biological arrangements are exactly the same—but intends an opposite assignment of custody. (2) No technology is necessary for CM as is evidenced by the biblical story of Abraham and Sarah who used a "handmaid" as a birth mother. Since artificial insemination is virtually uncontroversial it seems clear that what makes CM controversial is not the technology, but the social arrangements—that is, the custody assignment. CM has been defended on the ground that such arrangements enable fertile men who are married to infertile women to reproduce and, thus, are parallel to AID which enables fertile women whose husbands are infertile to have children. It is difficult not to regard these arguments as somewhat disingenuous. The role of the sperm

donor and the role of the egg donor/mother are distinguished by pregnancy, and pregnancy is, if anything is, a "real difference" which would justify us in treating women and men differently. To treat donating sperm as equivalent to biological motherhood would be as unfair as treating the unwed father who has not contributed to his children's welfare the same as the father who has devoted his time to taking care of them. At most, donating sperm is comparable to donating ova; however, even that comparison fails because donating ova is a medically risky procedure, donating sperm is not.

Therefore, the essential morally controversial features of CM have to do with its nature as a social and economic institution and its assignment of family relationships rather than with any technological features. Moreover, the institution of CM requires of contracting birth mothers much more time commitment, medical risk, and social disruption than AID does of sperm donors. It also requires substantial male control over women's bodies and time, while AID neither requires nor provides any female control over men's bodies. Christine Overall notes that when a woman seeks AID, she not only does not usually have a choice of donor, but she also may be required to get her husband's consent if she is married. The position of the man seeking CM is the opposite; he chooses a birth mother and his wife does not have to consent to the procedure (although the mother's husband does). The contract entered into by Mary Beth Whitehead and William Stern contains a number of provisions regulating her behavior, including: extensive medical examinations, an agreement about when she may or may not abort, an agreement to follow doctors' orders, and agreements not to take even prescription drugs without the doctor's permission. Some of these social and contractual provisions are eliminable. But the fact that CM requires a contract and AID does not reflects the differences between pregnancy and ejaculation. If the sperm donor wants a healthy child (a good product), he needs to control the woman's behavior. In contrast, any damage the sperm-donor's behavior will have on the child will be present in the sperm and could, in principle, be tested for before the woman enters the AID procedure. There is no serious moral problem with discarding defective sperm; discarding defective children is a quite different matter.

COMMODIFICATION

There are three general categories of moral concern with commercializing either adoption (baby selling) or reproductive activities. The three kinds of argument are not always separated and they are not entirely separable:

(1) There is the Kantian argument, based on a version of the Second Formulation of the Categorical Imperative. On this argument, selling people is objectionable because it is treating them as means rather than as ends, as objects rather than as persons. People who can be bought and sold are being treated as being of less moral significance than are those who buy and sell. Allowing babies to be bought and sold adds an extra legal wedge between the status of children and that of adults, and allowing women's bodies to be bought and sold (or "rented" if you prefer) adds to the inequality between men and women. Moreover, making babies and women's bodies available for sale raises specters of the rich "harvesting" the babies of the poor. (2) Consequentialist objections are fueled by concern for what may happen to the children and women who are bought and sold, to their families, and to the society as a whole if we allow an area of this magnitude and traditional intimacy to become commercialized. (3) Connected to both 1 and 2, are concerns about protecting the birth mother and the mother-child relationship from the potential coerciveness of commercial transactions. These arguments apply slightly differently depending on whether we analyze the contracts as baby contracts (selling babies) or as mother contracts (as a sale of women's

bodies), although many of the arguments will be very similar for both.

Selling Babies. The most straightforward argument for prohibiting baby-selling is that it is selling a human being and that any selling of a human being should be prohibited because it devalues human life and human individuals. This argument gains moral force from its analogy with slavery. Defenders of baby contracts argue that baby selling is unlike selling slaves in that it is a transfer of parental rights rather than of ownership of the child—the adoptive parents cannot turn around and sell the baby to another couple for a profit. What the defenders of CM fail to do is provide an account of the wrongness of slavery such that baby-selling (or baby contracts) do not fall under the argument. [Some defenders of CM] in particular, would, I think, have difficulty establishing an argument against slavery because they are relying on utilitarian arguments. Since one of the classic difficulties with utilitarianism is that it cannot yield an argument that slavery is wrong in principle, it is hardly surprising that utilitarians will find it difficult to discover within that theory an argument against selling babies. Moreover, their economic argument is not even utilitarian because it only counts people's interest to the extent that they can pay for them.

Those who defend CM while supporting laws against baby-selling distinguish CM from paid adoptions in that in CM the person to whom custody is being transferred is the biological (genetic) father. This suggests a parallel to custody disputes, which are not obviously any more appropriately ruled by money than is adoption. We could argue against the commercialization of either on the grounds that child-regarding concerns should decide child custody and that using market criteria or contract considerations would violate that principle by substituting another, unrelated, and possibly conflicting, one. In particular, both market and contract are about relations between the adults involved rather than about the children or about the relationship between the child and the adult.

Another disanalogy cited between preadoption contracts and CM is that, in preadoption contracts the baby is already there (that is, the preadoption contract is offered to a woman who is already pregnant, and, presumably, planning to have the child), while the mother contract is a contract to create a child who does not yet exist, even as an embryo. If our concern is the commodification of children, this strikes me as an odd point for the *defenders* of CM to emphasize. Producing a child to order for money is a paradigm case of commodifying children. The fact that the child is not being put up for sale to the highest bidder, but is only for sale to the genetic father, may reduce some of the harmful effects of an open market in babies but does not quiet concerns about personhood.

Arguments for allowing CM are remarkably similar to the arguments for legalizing black-market adoptions in the way they both define the problem. CM, like a market for babies, is seen as increasing the satisfaction and freedom of infertile individuals or couples by increasing the quantity of the desired product (there will be more babies available for adoption) and the quality of the product (not only more white healthy babies, but white healthy babies who are genetically related to one of the purchasers). These arguments tend to be based on the interests of infertile couples and obscure the relevance of the interests of the birth mothers (who will be giving the children up for adoption) and their families, the children who are produced by the demands of the market, and (the most invisible and most troubling group) needy children who are without homes because they are not "high-quality" products and because we are not, as a society, investing the time and money needed to place the hard to adopt children. If we bring these hidden interests to the fore, they raise a host of issues about consequences—both utilitarian issues and issues about the distribution of harms and benefits.

Perhaps the strongest deontological argument against baby-selling is an objection to the characterization of the mother-child relationship (and, more generally, of the adult-child relationship) that it presupposes. Not only does the baby become an object of commerce, but the custody relationship of the parent becomes a property relationship. If we see parental custody rights as correlates of parental responsibility or as a right to maintain a relationship, it will be less tempting to think of them as something one can sell. We have good reasons for allowing birth-mothers to relinquish their children because otherwise we would be forcing children into the care of people who either do not want them or feel themselves unable to care for them. However, the fact that custody may be waived in this way does not entail that it may be sold or transferred. If children are not property, they cannot be gifts either. If a mother's right is a right to maintain a relationship, it is implausible to treat it as transferrable; having the option of terminating a relationship with A does not entail having the option of deciding who A will relate to next—the right to a divorce does not entail the right to transfer one's connection to one's spouse to someone else. Indeed, normally, the termination of a relationship with A ends any right I have to make moral claims on A's relationships. Although in giving up responsibilities I may have a responsibility to see to it that someone will shoulder them when I go, I do not have a right to choose that person.

Selling Women's Bodies.   Suppose we do regard mother contracts as contracts for the sale or rental of reproductive capacities. Is there good reason for including reproductive capacities among those things or activities that ought not to be bought and sold? We might distinguish between selling reproductive capacities and selling work on a number of grounds. A conservative might argue against commercializing reproduction on the grounds that it disturbs family relationships, or on the grounds that there are some categories of human activities that should not be for sale. A Kantian might argue that there are some activities that are close to our personhood and that a commercial traffic in these activities constitutes treating the person as less than an end (or less than a person).

One interpretation of the laws prohibiting baby selling is that they are an attempt to reduce or eliminate coercion in the adoption process, and are thus, based on a concern for the birth mother rather than (or as well as) the child. All commercial transactions are at least potentially coercive in that the parties to them are likely to come from unequal bargaining positions and in that, whatever we have a market in, there will be some people who will be in a position such that they have to sell it in order to survive. Such concerns are important to arguments against an open market in human organs or in the sexual use of people's bodies as well as arguments against baby contracts of either kind.

As Margaret Radin suggests, the weakness of arguments of this sort—that relationships or contracts are exploitative on the grounds that people are forced into them by poverty—is that the real problem is not in the possibility of commercial transactions, but in the situation that makes these arrangements attractive by comparison. We do not end the feminization of poverty by forbidding prostitution or CM. Indeed, if we are successful in eliminating these practices, we may be reducing the income of some women (by removing ways of making money) and, if we are unsuccessful, we are removing these people from state protection by making their activities illegal. Labor legislation which is comparably motivated by concern for unequal bargaining position (such as, for example, minimum wage and maximum hours laws, and health and safety regulations) regulates rather than prevents that activity and is thus less vulnerable to this charge. Radin's criticism shows that the argument from the coerciveness of poverty is insufficient as a support for laws rejecting

commercial transactions in personal services. This does not show that the concern is irrelevant. The argument from coercion is still an appropriate response to simple voluntarist arguments—those that assume that these activities are purely and freely chosen by all those who participate in them. Given the coerciveness of the situation, we cannot assume that the presumed or formal voluntariness of the contract makes it nonexploitative.

If the relationship of CM is, by its nature, disrespectful of personhood, it can be exploitative despite short-term financial benefits to some women. The disrespect for women as persons that is fundamental to the relationship lies in the concept of the woman's body (and of the child and mother-child relationship) implicit in the contract. I have argued elsewhere that claiming a welfare right to another person's body is to treat that person as an object:

An identity or intimate relation between persons and their bodies may or may not be essential to our metaphysical understanding of a person, but it is essential to a minimal moral conceptual scheme. Without a concession to persons' legitimate interests and concerns for their physical selves, most of our standard and paradigm moral rules would not make sense; murder might become the mere destruction of the body; assault, a mere interference with the body . . . and so on. We cannot make sense out of the concept of assault unless an assault on S's body is ipso facto an assault on S. By the same token, treating another person's body as part of my domain—as among the things that I have a rightful claim to—is, if anything is, a denial that there is a person there.[2]

This argument is, in turn, built on the analysis of the wrongness of rape developed by Marilyn Frye and Carolyn Shafer in "Rape and Respect":

The use of a person in the advancement of interests contrary to its own is a limiting case of disrespect. It reveals the perception of the person simply as an object which can serve some purpose, a tool or a bit of material, and one which furthermore is dispensable or replaceable and thus of little value even as an object with a function.[3]

We can extend this argument to the sale of persons. To make a person or a person's body an object of commerce is to treat the person as part of another person's domain, particularly if the sale of A to B gives B rights to A or to A's body. What is objectionable is a claim—whether based on welfare or on contract—to a right to another person such that that person is part of my domain. The assertion of such a right is morally objectionable even without the use of force. For example, a man who claims to have a *right* to sexual intercourse with his wife, on the grounds of the marriage relationship, betrays a conception of her body, and thus her person, as being properly within his domain, and thus a conception of her as an object rather than a person.

Susan Brownmiller, in *Against Our Will*, suggests that prostitution is connected to rape in that prostitution makes women's bodies into consumer goods that might—if not justifiably, at least understandably—be forcibly taken by those men who see themselves as unjustly deprived.

When young men learn that females may be bought for a price, and that acts of sex command set prices, then how should they not also conclude that that which may be bought may also be taken without the civility of a monetary exchange? . . . legalized prostitution institutionalizes the concept that it is a man's monetary right, if not his divine right, to gain access to the female body, and that sex is a female service that should not be denied the civilized male.[4]

The same can be said for legalized sale of women's reproductive services. The more hegemonic this commodification of women's bodies is, the more the woman's lack of consent to sex or to having children can present itself as unfair to the man because it is arbitrary.

A market in women's bodies—whether sexual prostitution or reproductive prostitution—reveals a social ontology in which women are among the things in the world that can be appropriately commodified—bought and sold and, by extension, stolen. The purported freedom that such institutions would give women to enter into the market by selling their bodies is paradoxical. Sexual or reproductive prostitutes enter the market not so much as *agents* or subjects, but as commodities or objects. This is evidenced by the fact that the pimps and their counterparts, the arrangers of baby contracts, make the bulk of the profits. Moreover, once there is a market for women's bodies, all women's bodies will have a price, and the woman who does not sell her body becomes a hoarder of something that is useful to other people and is financially valuable. The market is a hegemonic institution; it determines the meanings of actions of people who choose not to participate as well as of those who choose to participate.

Contract.   The immediate objection to treating the Baby M case as a contract dispute is that the practical problem facing the court is a child custody problem and to treat it as a contract case is to deal with it on grounds other than the best interests of the child. That the best interests of the child count need not entail that contract does not count, although it helps explain one of the reasons we should be suspicious of this particular contract. There is still the question of whether the best interests of the child will trump contract considerations (making the contract nonbinding) or merely enter into a balancing argument in which contract is one of the issues to be balanced. However, allowing contract to count at all raises some of the same Kantian objections as the commodification problem. As a legal issue, the contract problem is more acute because the state action (enforcing the contract) is more explicit.

Any binding mother contract will put the

state in the position of enforcing the rights of a man to a woman's body or to his genetic offspring. But this is to treat the child or the mother's body as objects of the sperm donor's rights, which, I argued above, is inconsistent with treating them as persons. This will be clearest if the courts enforce specific performance and require the mother to go through with the pregnancy (or to abort) if she chooses not to or requires the transfer of custody to the contracting sperm-donor on grounds other than the best interests of the child. In those cases, I find it hard to avoid the description that what is being awarded is a person and what is being affirmed is a right to a person. I think the Kantian argument still applies if the court refuses specific performance but awards damages. Damages compensate for the loss of something to which one has a right. A judge who awards damages to the contracting sperm donor for having been deprived of use of the contracting woman's reproductive capacities or for being deprived of custody of the child gives legal weight to the idea that the contracting sperm donor had a legally enforceable *right* to them (or, to put it more bluntly, to those commodities or goods).

The free contract argument assumes that Mary Beth Whitehead's claims to her daughter are rights (rather than, for example, obligations or a more complex relationship), and, moreover, that they are alienable, as are property rights. If the baby is not something she has an alienable right to, then custody of the baby is not something she can transfer by contract. In cases where the state is taking children away from their biological parents and in custody disputes, we do not want to appeal to some rights of the parents. However, I think it would be unfortunate to regard these rights as rights to the child, because that would be to treat the child as the object of the parents' rights and violate the principles that persons and persons' bodies cannot be the objects of other people's rights. The parents' rights in these cases should be to consideration, to nonarbitrariness and to respect for the relationship between the parent and the child.

CONCLUDING REMARKS

The Kantian, person-respecting arguments I have been offering do not provide an account of all of the moral issues surrounding CM. However, I think that they can serve as a counterbalance to arguments (also Kantian) for CM as an expression of personal autonomy. They might also add some weight to the empirical arguments against CM that are accumulating. There is increasing concern that women cannot predict in advance whether or not they and their family[5] will form an attachment to the child they will bear nor can they promise not to develop such feelings (as some on the contracts ask them to do). There is also increasing concern for the birth-family and for the children produced by the arrangement (particularly where there is a custody dispute). A utilitarian might respond that the problems are outweighed by the joys of the adopting/sperm donor families, but, if so, we must ask: are we simply shifting the misery from wealthy (or wealthier) infertile couples to poorer fertile families and to the "imperfect" children waiting for adoption?

These considerations provide good reason for prohibiting commercialization of CM. In order to do that we could adopt new laws prohibiting the transfer of money in such arrangements or simply extend existing adoption laws, making the contracts non-binding as are prebirth adoption contracts and limiting the money that can be transferred. There are some conceptual problems remaining about what would count as prohibiting commodification. I find the English approach very attractive. This approach has the following elements (1) it strictly prohibits third parties from arranging mother contracts; (2) if people arrange them privately, they are allowed, (3) the contracts are not binding. If the birth-mother decides to keep the baby, her decision is final[6] (*and* the father may be required to pay child-support; that may be too much for Americans). (4) Although, in theory, CM is covered by limitations on money for adoption, courts have approved payments for contracted motherhood, and there is never criminal penalty on the parents for money payments.

NOTES

1. Terms such as "surrogate mother" and "renting a womb" are distortions—the surrogate mother *is* the mother, and she is giving up her child for adoption just as is the birth mother who gives up her child for adoption by an unrelated person. This language allows the defenders of paternal rights, to argue for the importance of biological (genetic) connection when it comes to the *father's* rights, but bury the greater physical connection between the mother and the child in talk that suggests that mothers are mere receptacles (shades of Aristotle's biology) or that the mother has a more artificial relationship to the child than does the father or the potential adoptive mother. But, at the time of birth, the natural relationship is between the mother and child. (I discuss this issue further in "New Reproductive Technologies and the Definition of Parenthood: A Feminist Perspective" [1987].) A relationship created by contract is the paradigm of artificiality, of socially created relationship, and the most plausible candidate for a natural social relationship is the mother-child bond. I will be using "contracted motherhood" and "baby contracts" (a term offered by Elizabeth Bartholet) rather than "surrogate motherhood" and "surrogacy." I will use "baby contracts" as the more general term, covering paid adoption contracts as well as so called "surrogate mother" arrangements. I have not yet found a term that is either neutral between or inclusive of the motherhood aspects and the baby-regarding aspects.

2. Ketchum, Sara Ann, "The Moral Status of the Bodies of Persons, *Social Theory and Practice* (1984), 25–38.

3. Frye, Marilyn and Carolyn Shafer "Rape and Respect" in *Feminism and Philosophy*. Mary Vetterling-Braggin et al. Totowa, NJ, Littlefield and Adams, 1977.

4. Brownmiller, Susan *Against Our Will*, New York: Simon and Schuster, 1975

5. One former surrogate reports that her daughter (11 at the time of the birth and now 17) is still having problems:

> Nobody told me that a child could bond with a baby while you're still pregnant. I didn't realize then that all the times she listened to his heartbeat and felt his legs kick that she was becoming attached to him.

Another quotes her son as having asked, "You're not going to give them me, are you?"

6. This presupposes a presumption in favor of the birth-mother as custodial or deciding parent. I have argued for that position on the grounds that, at the time of birth, the gestational mother has a concrete relationship to the child that the genetic father (and the genetic mother, if she is not the gestational mother) does not have. Without that presumption and without a presumption of sale or contract, each case would be subject to long custody disputes.

❧ Self-Images ❧

Foucault, Femininity and the Modernization of Patriarchal Power

Sandra Bartky

I

In a striking critique of modern society, Michel Foucault has argued that the rise of parliamentary institutions and of new conceptions of political liberty was accompanied by a darker countermovement, by the emergence of a new and unprecedented discipline directed against the body. More is required of the body now than mere political allegiance or the appropriation of the products of its labor: the new discipline invades the body and seeks to regulate its very forces and operations, the economy and efficiency of its movements.

The disciplinary practices Foucault describes are tied to peculiarly modern forms of the army, the school, the hospital, the prison, and the manufactory; the aim of these disci-

From *Feminism and Foucault: Reflections on Resistance*, edited by Irene Diamond and Lee Quinby. Copyright © 1988 by Irene Diamond and Lee Quinby. Reprinted with the permission of Northeastern University Press, Boston.

plines is to increase the utility of the body, to augment its forces:

What was then being formed was a policy of coercions that act upon the body, a calculated manipulation of its elements, its gestures, its behaviour. The human body was entering a machinery of power that explores it, breaks it down and rearranges it. A "political anatomy," which was also a "mechanics of power," was being born; it defined how one may have a hold over others' bodies, not only so that they may do what one wishes, but so that they may operate as one wishes, with the techniques, the speed and the efficiency that one determines. Thus, discipline produces subjected and practiced bodies, "docile" bodies.[1]

The production of "docile bodies" requires that an uninterrupted coercion be directed to the very processes of bodily activity, not just their result; this "micro-physics of power" fragments and partitions the body's time, its space, and its movements.

The student, then, is enclosed within a

classroom and assigned to a desk he cannot leave; his ranking in the class can be read off the position of his desk in the serially ordered and segmented space of the classroom itself. Foucault tells us that "Jean-Baptiste de la Salle dreamt of a classroom in which the spatial distribution might provide a whole series of distinctions at once, according to the pupil's progress, worth, character, application, cleanliness and parents' fortune." The student must sit upright, feet upon the floor, head erect; he may not slouch or fidget; his animate body is brought into a fixed correlation with the inanimate desk.

The minute breakdown of gestures and movements required of soldiers at drill is far more relentless:

Bring the weapon forward. In three stages. Raise the rifle with the right hand, bringing it close to the body so as to hold it perpendicular with the right knee, the end of the barrel at eye level, grasping it by striking it with the right hand, the arm held close to the body at waist height. At the second stage, bring the rifle in front of you with the left hand, the barrel in the middle between the two eyes, vertical, the right hand grasping it at the small of the butt, the arm outstretched, the triggerguard resting on the first finger, the left hand at the height of the notch, the thumb lying along the barrel against the moulding. At the third stage. . . .[2]

These "body-object articulations" of the soldier and his weapon, the student and his desk effect a "coercive link with the apparatus of production." We are far indeed from older forms of control that "demanded of the body only signs or products, forms of expression or the result of labour."

The body's time, in these regimes of power, is as rigidly controlled as its space: the factory whistle and the school bell mark a division of time into discrete and segmented units that regulate the various activities of the day. The following timetable, similar in spirit to the ordering of my grammar school classroom, is suggested for French "écoles mutuelles" of the early nineteenth century:

8:45 entrance of the monitor, 8:52 the monitor's summons, 8:56 entrance of the children and prayer, 9:00 the children go to their benches, 9:04 first slate, 9:08 end of dictation, 9:12 second slate, etc.

Control this rigid and precise cannot be maintained without a minute and relentless surveillance.

Jeremy Bentham's design for the Panopticon, a model prison, captures for Foucault the essence of the disciplinary society. At the periphery of the Panopticon, a circular structure; at the center, a tower with wide windows that opens onto the inner side of the ring. The structure on the periphery is divided into cells, each with two windows, one facing the windows of the tower, the other facing the outside, allowing an effect of backlighting to make any figure visible within the cell. "All that is needed, then, is to place a supervisor in a central tower and to shut up in each cell a madman, a patient, a condemned man, a worker or a schoolboy." Each inmate is alone, shut off from effective communication with his fellows, but constantly visible from the tower. The effect of this is "to induce in the inmate a state of conscious and permanent visibility that assures the automatic functioning of power"; each becomes to himself his own jailer. This "state of conscious and permanent visibility" is a sign that the tight, disciplinary control of the body has gotten a hold on the mind as well. In the perpetual self-surveillance of the inmate lies the genesis of the celebrated "individualism" and heightened self-consciousness that are hallmarks of modern times. For Foucault, the structure and effects of the Panopticon resonate throughout society: Is it surprising that "prisons resemble factories, schools, barracks, hospitals, which all resemble prisons"?

Foucault's account in *Discipline and Punish* of the disciplinary practices that produce the "docile bodies" of modernity is a genuine *tour de force*, incorporating a rich theoretical account of the ways in which instrumental reason takes hold of the body with a mass of historical detail. But Foucault treats the body throughout as if it were one, as if the bodily experiences of men and women did not differ and as if men and women bore the same relationship to the characteristic institutions of modern life. Where is the account of the disciplinary practices that engender the "docile bodies" of women, bodies more docile than the bodies of men? Women, like men, are subject to many of the same disciplinary practices Foucault describes. But he is blind to those disciplines that produce a modality of embodiment that is peculiarly feminine. To overlook the forms of subjection that engender the feminine body is to perpetuate the silence and powerlessness of those upon whom these disciplines have been imposed. Hence, even though a liberatory note is sounded in Foucault's critique of power, his analysis as a whole reproduces that sexism which is endemic throughout Western political theory.

We are born male or female, but not masculine or feminine. Femininity is an artifice, an achievement, "a mode of enacting and reenacting received gender norms which surface as so many styles of the flesh." In what follows, I shall examine those disciplinary practices that produce a body which in gesture and appearance is recognizably feminine. I consider three categories of such practices: those that aim to produce a body of a certain size and general configuration; those that bring forth from this body a specific repertoire of gestures, postures, and movements; and those that are directed toward the display of this body as an ornamented surface. I shall examine the nature of these disciplines, how they are imposed and by whom. I shall probe the effects of the imposition of such discipline on female identity and subjectivity. In the final section I shall argue that these disciplinary practices must be understood in the light of the modernization of patriarchal domination, a modernization that unfolds historically according to the general pattern described by Foucault.

II

Styles of the female figure vary over time and across cultures: they reflect cultural obsessions and preoccupations in ways that are still poorly understood. Today, massiveness, power, or abundance in a woman's body is met with distaste. The current body of fashion is taut, small-breasted, narrow-hipped, and of a slimness bordering on emaciation; it is a silhouette that seems more appropriate to an adolescent boy or a newly pubescent girl than to an adult woman. Since ordinary women have normally quite different dimensions, they must of course diet.

Mass-circulation women's magazines run articles on dieting in virtually every issue. The *Ladies' Home Journal* of February 1986 carries a "Fat Burning Exercise Guide," while *Mademoiselle* offers to "Help Stamp Out Cellulite" with "Six Sleek-Down Strategies." After the diet-busting Christmas holidays and, later, before summer bikini season, the titles of these features become shriller and more arresting. The reader is now addressed in the imperative mode: Jump into shape for summer! Shed ugly winter fat with the all-new Grapefruit Diet! More women than men visit diet doctors, while women greatly outnumber men in such self-help groups as Weight Watchers and Overeaters Anonymous—in the case of the latter, by well over 90 percent.

Dieting disciplines the body's hungers: appetite must be monitored at all times and governed by an iron will. Since the innocent need of the organism for food will not be denied, the body becomes one's enemy, an alien being bent on thwarting the disciplinary project. Anorexia nervosa, which has now assumed epidemic proportions, is to women of the late twentieth century what hysteria was to women of an earlier day: the crystallization in a pathological mode of a widespread cultural obsession. A survey taken recently at UCLA is astounding: of 260 students interviewed, 27.3 percent of women but only 5.8 percent of men said they were "terrified" of getting fat; 28.7 percent of women but only 7.5 percent of men said they were obsessed or "totally preoccupied" with food. The body images of women and men are strikingly different as well: 35 percent of women but only 12.5 percent of men said they felt fat though other people told them they were thin. Women in the survey wanted to weigh ten pounds less than their average weight; men felt they were within a pound of their ideal weight. A total of 5.9 percent of women and no men met the psychiatric criteria for anorexia or bulimia.

Dieting is one discipline imposed upon a body subject to the "tyranny of slenderness"; exercise is another. Since men as well as women exercise, it is not always easy in the case of women to distinguish what is done for the sake of physical fitness from what is done in obedience to the requirements of femininity. Men as well as women lift weights and do yoga, calisthenics, and aerobics, though "jazzercise" is a largely female pursuit. Men and women alike engage themselves with a variety of machines, each designed to call forth from the body a different exertion: there are Nautilus machines, rowing machines, ordinary and motorized exercycles, portable hip and leg cycles, belt massagers, trampolines, treadmills, and arm and leg pulleys. However, given the widespread female obsession with weight, one suspects that many women are working out with these apparatuses in the health club or at the gym with an aim in mind and in a spirit quite different from men's.

But there are classes of exercises meant for women alone, these designed not to firm or to reduce the body's size overall, but to resculpture its various parts on the current model. M. J. Saffon, "international beauty expert," assures us that his twelve basic facial exercises can erase frown lines, smooth the forehead, raise hollow cheeks, banish crow's feet, and tighten the muscles under the chin. There are exercises to build the breasts and exercises to banish "cellulite," said by "figure consultants" to be a special type of female fat. There is "spot-reducing," an umbrella term that covers dozens of punishing exercises designed to reduce "problem areas" like thick ankles or "saddlebag" thighs. The very idea of "spot-reducing" is both scientifically unsound and cruel, for it raises expectations in women that can never be realized—the pattern in which fat is deposited or removed is known to be genetically determined.

It is not only her natural appetite or unreconstructed contours that pose a danger to woman: the very expressions of her face can subvert the disciplinary project of bodily perfection. An expressive face lines and creases more readily than an inexpressive one. Hence, if women are unable to suppress strong emotions, they can at least learn to inhibit the tendency of the face to register them. Sophia Loren recommends a unique solution to this problem: a piece of tape applied to the forehead or between the brows will tug at the skin when one frowns and act as a reminder to relax the face. The tape is to be worn whenever a woman is home alone.

III

There are significant gender differences in gesture, posture, movement, and general bodily comportment: women are far more restricted than men in their manner of movement and in their spatiality. In her classic paper on the subject, Iris Young observes that a space seems to surround women in imagination that they are hesitant to move beyond: this manifests itself both in a reluctance to reach, stretch, and extend the body to meet resistances of matter in motion—as in sport or in the performance of physical tasks—and in a typically constricted posture and general style of movement. Woman's space is not a field in which her bodily intentionality can be freely realized but an enclosure in which she feels herself positioned and by which she is confined. The "loose woman" violates these norms: her looseness is manifest not only in her morals, but in her manner of speech and quite literally in the free and easy way she moves.

In an extraordinary series of over two thousand photographs, many candid shots taken in the street, the German photographer Marianne Wex has documented differences in typical masculine and feminine body posture. Women sit waiting for trains with arms close to the body, hands folded together in their laps, toes pointing straight ahead or turned inward, and legs pressed together. The women in these photographs make themselves small and narrow, harmless; they seem tense; they take up little space. Men, on the other hand, expand into the available space; they sit with legs far apart and arms flung out at some distance from the body. Most common in these sitting male figures is what Wex calls the "proffering position": the men sit with legs thrown wide apart, crotch visible, feet pointing outward, often with an arm and a casually dangling hand resting comfortably on an open, spread thigh.

In proportion to total body size, a man's stride is longer than a woman's. The man has more spring and rhythm to his step; he walks with toes pointed outward, holds his arms at a greater distance from his body and swings them farther; he tends to point the whole hand in the direction he is moving. The woman holds her arms closer to her body, palms against her sides; her walk is circumspect. If she has subjected herself to the additional constraint of high-heeled shoes, her body is thrown forward and off balance: the struggle to walk under these conditions shortens her stride still more.

But women's movement is subjected to a still finer discipline. Feminine faces, as well as bodies, are trained to the expression of deference. Under male scrutiny, women will avert

their eyes or cast them downward; the female gaze is trained to abandon its claim to the sovereign status of seer. The "nice" girl learns to avoid the bold and unfettered staring of the "loose" woman who looks at whatever and whomever she pleases. Women are trained to smile more than men, too. In the economy of smiles, as elsewhere, there is evidence that women are exploited, for they give more than they receive in return; in a smile elicitation study, one researcher found that the rate of smile return by women was 93 percent, by men only 67 percent. In many typical women's jobs, graciousness, deference, and the readiness to serve are part of the work; this requires the worker to fix a smile on her face for a good part of the working day, whatever her inner state. The economy of touching is out of balance, too: men touch women more often and on more parts of the body than women touch men: female secretaries, factory workers, and waitresses report that such liberties are taken routinely with their bodies.

Feminine movement, gesture, and posture must exhibit not only constriction, but grace and a certain eroticism restrained by modesty: all three. Here is field for the operation for a whole new training: a woman must stand with stomach pulled in, shoulders thrown slightly back and chest out, this to display her bosom to maximum advantage. While she must walk in the confined fashion appropriate to women, her movements must, at the same time, be combined with a subtle but provocative hiproll. But too much display is taboo: women in short, low-cut dresses are told to avoid bending over at all, but if they must, great care must be taken to avoid an unseemly display of breast or rump. From time to time, fashion magazines offer quite precise instructions on the proper way of getting in and out of cars. These instructions combine all three imperatives of women's movement: a woman must not allow her arms and legs to flail about in all directions; she must try to manage her movements with the appearance of grace—no small accomplishment when one is climbing out of the back seat of a Fiat—and she is well-advised to use the opportunity for a certain display of leg.

All the movements we have described so far are self-movements; they arise from within the woman's own body. But in a way that normally goes unnoticed, males in couples may literally steer a woman everywhere she goes: down the street, around corners, into elevators, through doorways, into her chair at the dinner table, around the dance floor. The man's movement "is not necessarily heavy and pushy or physical in an ugly way; it is light and gentle but firm in the way of the most confident equestrians with the best trained horses."

IV

We have examined some of the disciplinary practices a woman must master in pursuit of a body of the right size and shape that also displays the proper styles of feminine motility. But woman's body is an ornamented surface too, and there is much discipline involved in this production as well. Here, especially in the application of makeup and the selection of clothes, art and discipline converge, though, as I shall argue, there is less art involved than one might suppose.

A woman's skin must be soft, supple, hairless, and smooth; ideally, it should betray no sign of wear, experience, age, or deep thought. Hair must be removed not only from the face but from large surfaces of the body as well, from legs and thighs, an operation accomplished by shaving, buffing with fine sandpaper, or applying foul-smelling depilatories. With the new high-leg bathing suits and leotards, a substantial amount of pubic hair must be removed too. The removal of facial hair can be more specialized. Eyebrows are plucked out by the roots with a tweezer. Hot wax is sometimes poured onto the mustache and cheeks and then ripped

away when it cools. The woman who wants a more permanent result may try electrolysis: this involves the killing of a hair root by the passage of an electric current down a needle that has been inserted into its base. The procedure is painful and expensive.

The development of what one "beauty expert" calls "good skincare habits" requires not only attention to health, the avoidance of strong facial expressions, and the performance of facial exercises, but the regular use of skincare preparations, many to be applied more often than once a day: cleansing lotions (ordinary soap and water "upsets the skin's acid and alkaline balance"), wash-off cleansers (milder than cleansing lotions), astringents, toners, makeup removers, night creams, nourishing creams, eye creams, moisturizers, skin balancers, body lotions, hand creams, lip pomades, suntan lotions, sunscreens, and facial masks. Provision of the proper facial mask is complex: there are sulfur masks for pimples; oil or hot masks for dry areas; if these fail, then tightening masks; conditioning masks; peeling masks; cleansing masks made of herbs, cornmeal, or almonds; and mudpacks. Black women may wish to use "fade creams" to "even skin tone." Skincare preparations are never just sloshed onto the skin, but applied according to precise rules: eye cream is dabbed on gently in movements toward, never away from, the nose; cleansing cream is applied in outward directions only, straight across the forehead, the upper lip, and the chin, never up but straight down the nose and up and out on the cheeks.

The normalizing discourse of modern medicine is enlisted by the cosmetics industry to gain credibility for its claims. Dr. Christiaan Barnard lends his enormous prestige to the Glycel line of "cellular treatment activators"; these contain "glycosphingolipids" that can "make older skin behave and look like younger skin." The Clinique computer at any Clinique counter will select a combination of preparations just right for you. Ultima II contains "procollagen" in its anti-aging eye cream that "provides hydration" to "demoralizing lines." "Biotherm" eye cream dramatically improves the "biomechanical properties of the skin." The Park Avenue clinic of Dr. Zizmor, "chief of dermatology at one of New York's leading hospitals," offers not only such medical treatment as derma-brasion and chemical peeling, but "total deep skin cleansing" as well.

Really good skincare habits require the use of a variety of aids and devices: facial steamers, faucet filters to collect impurities in the water, borax to soften it, a humidifier for the bedroom, electric massagers, backbrushes, complexion brushes, loofahs, pumice stones, and blackhead removers. I will not detail the implements or techniques involved in the manicure or pedicure.

The ordinary circumstances of life as well as a wide variety of activities cause a crisis in skincare and require a stepping-up of the regimen as well as an additional laying-on of preparations. Skincare discipline requires a specialized knowledge: a woman must know what to do if she has been skiing, taking medication, doing vigorous exercise, boating, or swimming in chlorinated pools; or if she has been exposed to pollution, heated rooms, cold, sun, harsh weather, the pressurized cabins on airplanes, saunas or steam rooms, fatigue, or stress. Like the schoolchild or prisoner, the woman mastering good skincare habits is put on a timetable: Georgette Klinger requires that a shorter or longer period of attention be paid to the complexion at least four times a day. Haircare, like skincare, requires a similar investment of time, the use of a wide variety of preparations, the mastery of a set of techniques, and, again, the acquisition of a specialized knowledge.

The crown and pinnacle of good haircare and skincare is, of course, the arrangement of the hair and the application of cosmetics. Here the regimen of haircare, skincare, manicure, and pedicure is recapitulated in another mode.

A woman must learn the proper manipulation of a large number of devices—the blow dryer, styling brush, curling iron, hot curlers, wire curlers, eye-liner, lipliner, lipstick brush, eyelash curler, and mascara brush. And she must learn to apply a wide variety of products— foundation, toner, covering stick, mascara, eyeshadow, eyegloss, blusher, lipstick, rouge, lip gloss, hair dye, hair rinse, hair lightener, hair "relaxer," and so on.

In the language of fashion magazines and cosmetic ads, making-up is typically portrayed as an aesthetic activity in which a woman can express her individuality. In reality, while cosmetic styles change every decade or so, and while some variation in makeup is permitted depending on the occasion, making-up the face is, in fact, a highly stylized activity that gives little rein to self-expression. Painting the face is not like painting a picture; at best, it might be described as painting the same picture over and over again with minor variations. Little latitude is permitted in what is considered appropriate makeup for the office and for most social occasions; indeed, the woman who uses cosmetics in a genuinely novel and imaginative way is liable to be seen not as an artist but as an eccentric. Furthermore, since a properly made-up face is, if not a card of entree, at least a badge of acceptability in most social and professional contexts, the woman who chooses not to wear cosmetics at all faces sanctions of a sort that will never be applied to someone who chooses not to paint a watercolor.

V

Are we dealing in all this merely with sexual *difference*? Scarcely. The disciplinary practices I have described are part of the process by which the ideal body of femininity—and hence the feminine body-subject—is constructed; in doing this, they produce a "practiced and subjected" body, that is, a body on which an inferior status has been inscribed. A woman's face must be made-up, that is to say, made-over, and so must her body: she is ten pounds overweight; her lips must be made more kissable, her complexion dewier, her eyes more mysterious. The "art" of makeup is the art of disguise, but this presupposes that a woman's face, unpainted, is defective. Soap and water, a shave, and routine attention to hygiene may be enough for *him*; for *her* they are not. The strategy of much beauty-related advertising is to suggest to women that their bodies are deficient; but even without such more or less explicit teaching, the media images of perfect female beauty that bombard us daily leave no doubt in the minds of most women that they fail to measure up. The technologies of femininity are taken up and practiced by women against the background of a pervasive sense of bodily deficiency: this accounts for what is often their compulsive or even ritualistic character.

The disciplinary project of femininity is a "setup": it requires such radical and extensive measures of bodily transformation that virtually every woman who gives herself to it is destined in some degree to fail. Thus, a measure of shame is added to a woman's sense that the body she inhabits is deficient: she ought to take better care of herself; she might after all have jogged that last mile. Many women are without the time or resources to provide themselves with even the minimum of what such a regimen requires, for example, a decent diet. Here is an additional source of shame for poor women, who must bear what our society regards as the more general shame of poverty. The burdens poor women bear in this regard are not merely psychological, since conformity to the prevailing standards of bodily acceptability is a known factor in economic mobility.

The larger disciplines that construct a "feminine" body out of a female one are by no means race- or class-specific. There is little evidence that women of color or working-class women are in general less committed to the incarnation of an ideal femininity than their more privileged sisters: this is not to deny the many ways in which factors of race, class, locality, ethnicity, or personal taste can be expressed within the kinds of practices I have described. The rising young corporate executive may buy her cosmetics at Bergdorf-Goodman, while the counter-server at McDonald's gets hers at the K-Mart; the one may join an expensive "upscale" health club, while the other may have to make do with the $9.49 GFX Body-Flex II Home-Gym advertised in the *National Enquirer*: both are aiming at the same general result.

In the regime of institutionalized heterosexuality, woman must make herself "object and prey" for the man: it is for him that these eyes are limpid pools, this cheek baby-smooth. In contemporary patriarchal culture, a panoptical male connoisseur resides within the consciousness of most women: they stand perpetually before his gaze and under his judgment. Woman lives her body as seen by another, by an anonymous patriarchal Other. We are often told that "women dress for other women." There is some truth in this: who but someone engaged in a project similar to my own can appreciate the panache with which I bring it off? But women know for whom this game is played: they know that a pretty young woman is likelier to become a flight attendant than a plain one, and that a well-preserved older woman has a better chance of holding onto her husband than one who has "let herself go."

Here it might be objected that performance for another in no way signals the inferiority of the performer to the one for whom the performance is intended: the actor, for example, depends on his audience but is in no way inferior to it; he is not demeaned by his dependency. While femininity is surely something enacted, the analogy to theater breaks down in a number of ways. First, as I argued earlier, the self-determination we think of as requisite to an artistic career is lacking here: femininity as spectacle is something in which virtually every woman is required to participate. Second, the precise nature of the criteria by which women are judged, not only the inescapability of judgment itself, reflects gross imbalances in the social power of the sexes that do not mark the relationship of artists and their audiences. An aesthetic of femininity, for example, that mandates fragility and a lack of muscular strength produces female bodies that can offer little resistance to physical abuse, and the physical abuse of women by men, as we know, is widespread. It is true that the current fitness movement has permitted women to develop more muscular strength and endurance than was heretofore allowed; indeed, images of women have begun to appear in the mass media that seem to eroticize this new muscularity. But a woman may by no means develop more muscular strength than her partner; the bride who would tenderly carry her groom across the threshold is a figure of comedy, not romance.

Under the current "tyranny of slenderness" women are forbidden to become large or massive; they must take up as little space as possible. The very contours a woman's body takes on as she matures—the fuller breasts and rounded hips—have become distasteful. The body by which a woman feels herself judged and which by rigorous discipline she must try to assume is the body of early adolescence, slight and unformed, a body lacking flesh or substance, a body in whose very contours the image of immaturity has been inscribed. The requirement that a woman maintain a smooth and hairless skin carries further the theme of inexperience, for an infantilized face must accompany her infantilized body, a face that never ages or furrows its brow in thought. The face of the ideally feminine woman must never display the marks of character, wisdom, and experience that we so admire in men.

To succeed in the provision of a beautiful or sexy body gains a woman attention and some admiration but little real respect and rarely any social power. A woman's effort to master feminine body discipline will lack importance just because she does it: her activity partakes of the general depreciation of everything female. In spite of unrelenting pressure to "make the most of what she has," women are ridiculed and dismissed for their interest in such "trivial" things as clothes and makeup. Further, the narrow identification of woman with sexuality and the body in a society that has for centuries displayed profound suspicion toward both does little to raise her status. Even the most adored female bodies complain routinely of their situation in ways that reveal an implicit understanding that there is something demeaning in the kind of attention they receive. Marilyn Monroe, Elizabeth Taylor, and Farrah Fawcett have all wanted passionately to become actresses-artists—and not just "sex objects."

But it is perhaps in their more restricted motility and comportment that the inferiorization of women's bodies is most evident: women's typical body-language, a language of relative tension and constriction, is understood to be a language of subordination when it is enacted by men in male status hierarchies. In groups of men, those with higher status typically assume looser and more relaxed postures: the boss lounges comfortably behind the desk, while the applicant sits tense and rigid on the edge of his seat. Higher-status individuals may touch their subordinates more than they themselves get touched; they initiate more eye contact and are smiled at by their inferiors more than they are observed to smile in return. What is announced in the comportment of superiors is confidence and ease, especially ease of access to the Other. Female constraint in posture and movement is no doubt overdetermined: the fact that women tend to sit and stand with legs, feet, and knees close or touching may well be a coded declaration of sexual circumspection in a society that still maintains a double standard, or an effort, albeit unconscious, to guard the genital area. In the latter case, a woman's tight and constricted posture must be seen as the expression of her need to ward off real or symbolic sexual attack. Whatever proportions must be assigned in the final display to fear or deference, one thing is clear: woman's body language speaks eloquently, though silently, of her subordinate status in a hierarchy of gender.

VI

If what we have described is a genuine discipline—a system of "micropower" that is "essentially non-egalitarian and asymmetrical" —who then are the disciplinarians? Who is the top sergeant in the disciplinary regime of femininity? Historically, the law has had some responsibility for enforcement: in times gone by, for example, individuals who appeared in public in the clothes of the other sex could be arrested. While cross-dressers are still liable to some harassment, the kind of discipline we are considering is not the business of the police or the courts. Parents and teachers, of course, have extensive influence, admonishing girls to be demure and ladylike, to "smile pretty," to sit with their legs together. The influence of the media is pervasive, too, constructing as it does an image of the female body as spectacle, nor can we ignore the role played by "beauty experts" or by emblematic public personages such as Jane Fonda and Lynn Redgrave.

But none of these individuals—the skin-care consultant, the parent, the policeman— does in fact wield the kind of authority that is typically invested in those who manage more straightforward disciplinary institutions. The disciplinary power that inscribes femininity in the female body is everywhere and it is nowhere; the disciplinarian is everyone and yet no one in particular. Women regarded as overweight, for example, report that they are regularly admonished to diet, sometimes by people they scarcely know. These intrusions are often softened by reference to the natural prettiness just waiting to emerge: "People have always said that I had a beautiful face and 'if you'd only lose weight

you'd be really beautiful.' " Here, "people"— friends and casual acquaintances alike—act to enforce prevailing standards of body size.

Foucault tends to identify the imposition of discipline upon the body with the operation of specific institutions, for example, the school, the factory, the prison. To do this, however, is to overlook the extent to which discipline can be institutionally *unbound* as well as institutionally bound. The anonymity of disciplinary power and its wide dispersion have consequences that are crucial to a proper understanding of the subordination of women. The absence of a formal institutional structure and of authorities invested with the power to carry out institutional directives creates the impression that the production of femininity is either entirely voluntary or natural. The several senses of "discipline" are instructive here. On the one hand, discipline is something imposed on subjects of an "essentially non-egalitarian and asymmetrical" system of authority. Schoolchildren, convicts, and draftees are subject to discipline in this sense. But discipline can be sought voluntarily as well—for example, when an individual seeks initiation into the spiritual discipline of Zen Buddhism. Discipline can, of course, be both at once: the volunteer may seek the physical and occupational training offered by the army without the army's ceasing in any way to be the instrument by which he and other members of his class are kept in disciplined subjection. Feminine bodily discipline has this dual character: on the one hand, no one is marched off for electrolysis at gunpoint, nor can we fail to appreciate the initiative and ingenuity displayed by countless women in an attempt to master the rituals of beauty. Nevertheless, insofar as the disciplinary practices of femininity produce a "subjected and practiced," an inferiorized, body, they must be understood as aspects of a far larger discipline, an oppressive and inegalitarian system of sexual subordination. This system aims at turning women into the docile and compliant companions of men just as surely as the army aims to turn its raw recruits into soldiers.

Now the transformation of oneself into a properly feminine body may be any or all of the following: a rite of passage into adulthood, the adoption and celebration of a particular aesthetic, a way of announcing one's economic level and social status, a way to triumph over other women in the competition for men or jobs, or an opportunity for massive narcissistic indulgence. The social construction of the feminine body is all these things, but at its base it is discipline, too, and discipline of the inegalitarian sort. The absence of formally identifiable disciplinarians and of a public schedule of sanctions only disguises the extent to which the imperative to be "feminine" serves the interest of domination. This is a lie in which all concur: making-up is merely artful play; one's first pair of high-heeled shoes is an innocent part of growing up, not the modern equivalent of footbinding.

Why aren't all women feminists? In modern industrial societies, women are not kept in line by fear of retaliatory male violence; their victimization is not that of the South African black. Nor will it suffice to say that a false consciousness engendered in women by patriarchal ideology is at the basis of female subordination. This is not to deny that women are often subject to gross male violence or that women and men alike are ideologically mystified by the dominant gender arrangements. What I wish to suggest instead is that an adequate understanding of women's oppression will require an appreciation of the extent to which not only women's lives but their very subjectivities are structured within an ensemble of systematically duplicitous practices. The feminine discipline of the body is a case in point: the practices that construct this body have an overt aim and character far removed, indeed, radically distinct, from their covert function. In this regard, the system of gender subordination, like the wage-bargain under capitalism, illustrates in its own way the

ancient tension between what-is and what-appears: the phenomenal forms in which it is manifested are often quite different from the real relations that form its deeper structure.

VII

The lack of formal public sanctions does not mean that a woman who is unable or unwilling to submit herself to the appropriate body discipline will face no sanctions at all. On the contrary, she faces a very severe sanction indeed in a world dominated by men: the refusal of male patronage. For the heterosexual woman, this may mean the loss of a badly needed intimacy; for both heterosexual women and lesbians, it may well mean the refusal of a decent livelihood.

As noted earlier, women punish themselves too for the failure to conform. The growing literature on women's body size is filled with wrenching confessions of shame from the overweight:

I felt clumsy and huge. I felt that I would knock over furniture, bump into things, tip over chairs, not fit into VW's, especially when people were trying to crowd into the back seat. I felt like I was taking over the whole room. . . . I felt disgusting and like a slob. In the summer I felt hot and sweaty and I knew people saw my sweat as evidence that I was too fat.

I feel so terrible about the way I look that I cut off connection with my body. I operate from the neck up. I do not look in mirrors. I do not want to spend time buying clothes. I do not want to spend time with make-up because it's painful for me to look at myself.[3]

I can no longer bear to look at myself. . . . Whenever I have to stand in front of a mirror to comb my hair I tie a large towel around my neck. Even at night I slip my nightgown on before I take off my blouse and pants. But all this has only made it worse and worse. It's been so long since I've really looked at my body.[4]

The depth of these women's shame is a measure of the extent to which all women have internalized patriarchal standards of bodily acceptability. A fuller examination of what is meant here by "internalization" may shed light on a question posed earlier: Why isn't every woman a feminist?

Something is "internalized" when it gets incorporated into the structure of the self. By "structure of the self" I refer to those modes of perception and of self-perception that allow a self to distinguish itself both from other selves and from things that are not selves. I have described elsewhere how a generalized male witness comes to structure woman's consciousness of herself as a bodily being. This, then, is one meaning of "internalization." The sense of oneself as a distinct and valuable individual is tied not only to the sense of how one is perceived, but also to what one knows, especially to what one knows how to do; this is a second sense of "internalization." Whatever its ultimate effect, discipline can provide the individual upon whom it is imposed with a sense of mastery as well as a secure sense of identity. There is a certain contradiction here: while its imposition may promote a larger disempowerment, discipline may bring with it a certain development of a person's powers. Women, then, like other skilled individuals, have a stake in the perpetuation of their skills, whatever it may have cost to acquire them and quite apart from the question whether, as a gender, they would have been better off had they never had to acquire them in the first place. Hence, feminism, especially a genuinely radical feminism that questions the patriarchal construction of the female body, threatens women with a certain de-skilling, something people normally resist: beyond this, it calls into question that aspect of personal identity that is tied to the development of a sense of competence.

Resistance from this source may be joined by a reluctance to part with the rewards of compliance; further, many women will resist the abandonment of an aesthetic that defines what they take to be beautiful. But there is still another source of resistance, one more subtle, perhaps, but tied once again to questions of identity and internalization. To have a body felt to be "feminine"—a body socially constructed through the appropriate practices—is in most cases crucial to a woman's sense of herself as female and, since persons currently can *be* only as male or female, to her sense of herself as an existing individual. To possess such a body may also be essential to her sense of herself as a sexually desiring and desirable subject. Hence, any political project that aims to dismantle the machinery that turns a female body into a feminine one may well be apprehended by a woman as something that threatens her with desexualization, if not outright annihilation.

The categories of masculinity and femininity do more than assist in the construction of personal identities; they are critical elements in our informal social ontology. This may account to some degree for the otherwise puzzling phenomenon of homophobia and for the revulsion felt by many at the sight of female bodybuilders; neither the homosexual nor the muscular woman can be assimilated easily into the categories that structure everyday life. The radical feminist critique of femininity, then, may pose a threat not only to a woman's sense of her own identity and desirability but to the very structure of her social universe.

Of course, many women *are* feminists, favoring a program of political and economic reform in the struggle to gain equality with men. But many "reform," or liberal, feminists (indeed, many orthodox Marxists) are committed to the idea that the preservation of a woman's femininity is quite compatible with her struggle for liberation. These thinkers have rejected a normative femininity based upon the notion of "separate spheres" and the traditional sexual division of labor, while accepting at the same time conventional standards of feminine body display. If my analysis is correct, such a feminism is incoherent. Foucault has argued that modern bourgeois democracy is deeply flawed in that it seeks political rights for individuals constituted as unfree by a variety of disciplinary micropowers that lie beyond the realm of what is ordinarily defined as the "political." "The man described for us whom we are invited to free," he says, "is already in himself the effect of a subjection much more profound than himself." If, as I have argued, female subjectivity is constituted in any significant measure in and through the disciplinary practices that construct the feminine body, what Foucault says here of "man" is perhaps even truer of "woman." Marxists have maintained from the first the inadequacy of a purely liberal feminism: we have reached the same conclusion through a different route, casting doubt at the same time on the adequacy of traditional Marxist prescriptions for women's liberation as well. Liberals call for equal rights for women, traditional Marxists for the entry of women into production on an equal footing with men, the socialization of housework, and proletarian revolution; neither calls for the deconstruction of the categories of masculinity and femininity. Femininity as a certain "style of the flesh" will have to be surpassed in the direction of something quite different—not masculinity, which is in many ways only its mirror opposite, but a radical and as yet unimagined transformation of the female body.

VIII

Foucault has argued that the transition from traditional to modern societies has been characterized by a profound transformation in the exercise of power, by what he calls "a reversal of the political axis of individualization." In older authoritarian systems, power was embodied in the person of the monarch and exercised upon a largely anonymous body of subjects; violation of the law was seen as an insult to the royal individual. While the methods employed to enforce compliance in the past were often quite brutal, involving gross assaults against the body, power in such a system operated in a haphazard

and discontinuous fashion; much in the social totality lay beyond its reach.

By contrast, modern society has seen the emergence of increasingly invasive apparatuses of power: these exercise a far more restrictive social and psychological control than was heretofore possible. In modern societies, effects of power "circulate through progressively finer channels, gaining access to individuals themselves, to their bodies, their gestures and all their daily actions." Power now seeks to transform the minds of those individuals who might be tempted to resist it, not merely to punish or imprison their bodies. This requires two things: a finer control of the body's time and of its movements—a control that cannot be achieved without ceaseless surveillance and a better understanding of the specific person, of the genesis and nature of his "case." The power these new apparatuses seek to exercise requires a new knowledge of the individual: modern psychology and sociology are born. Whether the new modes of control have charge of correction, production, education, or the provision of welfare, they resemble one another; they exercise power in a bureaucratic mode—faceless, centralized, and pervasive. A reversal has occurred: power has now become anonymous, while the project of control has brought into being a new individuality. In fact, Foucault believes that the operation of power constitutes the very subjectivity of the subject. Here, the image of the Panopticon returns: knowing that he may be observed from the tower at any time, the inmate takes over the job of policing himself. The gaze that is inscribed in the very structure of the disciplinary institution is internalized by the inmate: modern technologies of behavior are thus oriented toward the production of isolated and self-policing subjects.

Women have their own experience of the modernization of power, one that begins later but follows in many respects the course outlined by Foucault. In important ways, a woman's behavior is less regulated now than it was in the past. She has more mobility and is less confined to domestic space. She enjoys what to previous generations would have been an unimaginable sexual liberty. Divorce, access to paid work outside the home, and the increasing secularization of modern life have loosened the hold over her of the traditional family and, in spite of the current fundamentalist revival, of the church. Power in these institutions was wielded by individuals known to her. Husbands and fathers enforced patriarchal authority in the family. As in the ancien régime, a woman's body was subject to sanctions if she disobeyed. Not Foucault's royal individual but the Divine Individual decreed that her desire be always "unto her husband," while the person of the priest made known to her God's more specific intentions concerning her place and duties. In the days when civil and ecclesiastical authority were still conjoined, individuals formally invested with power were charged with the correction of recalcitrant women whom the family had somehow failed to constrain.

By contrast, the disciplinary power that is increasingly charged with the production of a properly embodied femininity is dispersed and anonymous; there are no individuals formally empowered to wield it; it is, as we have seen, invested in everyone and in no one in particular. This disciplinary power is peculiarly modern: it does not rely upon violent or public sanctions, nor does it seek to restrain the freedom of the female body to move from place to place. For all that, its invasion of the body is well-nigh total: the female body enters "a machinery of power that explores it, breaks it down and rearranges it." The disciplinary techniques through which the "docile bodies" of women are constructed aim at a regulation that is perpetual and exhaustive—a regulation of the body's size and contours, its appetite, posture, gestures and general comportment in space, and the appearance of each of its visible parts.

As modern industrial societies change and as women themselves offer resistance to patriar-

chy, older forms of domination are eroded. But new forms arise, spread, and become consolidated. Women are no longer required to be chaste or modest, to restrict their sphere of activity to the home, or even to realize their properly feminine destiny in maternity: normative femininity is coming more and more to be centered on woman's body—not its duties and obligations or even its capacity to bear children, but its sexuality, more precisely, its presumed heterosexuality and its appearance. There is, of course, nothing new in women's preoccupation with youth and beauty. What is new is the growing power of the image in a society increasingly oriented toward the visual media. Images of normative femininity, it might be ventured, have replaced the religiously oriented tracts of the past. New too is the spread of this discipline to all classes of women and its deployment throughout the life cycle. What was formerly the speciality of the aristocrat or courtesan is now the routine obligation of every woman, be she a grandmother or a barely pubescent girl.

To subject oneself to the new disciplinary power is to be up-to-date, to be "with-it"; as I have argued, it is presented to us in ways that are regularly disguised. It is fully compatible with the current need for women's wage labor, the cult of youth and fitness, and the need of advanced capitalism to maintain high levels of consumption. Further, it represents a saving in the economy of enforcement: since it is women themselves who practice this discipline on and against their own bodies, men get off scot-free.

The woman who checks her makeup half a dozen times a day to see if her foundation has caked or her mascara has run, who worries that the wind or the rain may spoil her hairdo, who looks frequently to see if her stockings have bagged at the ankle or who, feeling fat, monitors everything she eats, has become, just as surely as the inmate of the Panopticon, a self-policing subject, a self committed to a relentless self-surveillance. This self-surveillance is a form of obedience to patriarchy. It is also the reflection in woman's consciousness of the fact that *she* is under surveillance in ways that *he* is not, that whatever else she may become, she is importantly a body designed to please or to excite. There has been induced in many women, then, in Foucault's words, "a state of conscious and permanent visibility that assures the automatic functioning of power." Since the standards of female bodily acceptability are impossible fully to realize, requiring as they do a virtual transcendence of nature, a woman may live much of her life with a pervasive feeling of bodily deficiency. Hence a tighter control of the body has gained a new kind of hold over the mind.

Foucault often writes as if power constitutes the very individuals upon whom it operates:

The individual is not to be conceived as a sort of elementary nucleus, a primitive atom, a multiple and inert material on which power comes to fasten or against which it happens to strike. . . . In fact, it is already one of the prime effects of power that certain bodies, certain gestures, certain discourses, certain desires, come to be identified and constituted as individuals.[5]

Nevertheless, if individuals were wholly constituted by the power-knowledge regime Foucault describes, it would make no sense to speak of resistance to discipline at all. Foucault seems sometimes on the verge of depriving us of a vocabulary in which to conceptualize the nature and meaning of those periodic refusals of control that, just as much as the imposition of control, mark the course of human history.

Peter Dews accuses Foucault of lacking a theory of the "libidinal body," that is, the body upon which discipline is imposed and whose bedrock impulse toward spontaneity and pleasure might perhaps become the locus of resistance. Do women's "libidinal" bodies, then, not rebel against the pain, constriction, tedium, semistarvation, and constant self-surveillance to which they are currently condemned? Certainly

they do, but the rebellion is put down every time a woman picks up her eyebrow tweezers or embarks upon a new diet. The harshness of a regimen alone does not guarantee its rejection, for hardships can be endured if they are thought to be necessary or inevitable.

While "nature," in the form of a "libidinal" body, may not be the origin of a revolt against "culture," domination (and the discipline it requires) are never imposed without some cost. Historically, the forms and occasions of resistance are manifold. Sometimes, instances of resistance appear to spring from the introduction of new and conflicting factors into the lives of the dominated: the juxtaposition of old and new and the resulting incoherence or "contradiction" may make submission to the old ways seem increasingly unnecessary. In the present instance, what may be a major factor in the relentless and escalating objectification of women's bodies—namely, women's growing independence—produces in many women a sense of incoherence that calls into question the meaning and necessity of the current discipline. As women (albeit a small minority of women) begin to realize an unprecedented political, economic, and sexual self-determination, they fall ever more completely under the dominating gaze of patriarchy. It is this paradox, not the "libidinal body," that produces, here and there, pockets of resistance.

In the current political climate, there is no reason to anticipate either widespread resistance to currently fashionable modes of feminine embodiment or joyous experimentation with new "styles of the flesh"; moreover, such novelties would face profound opposition from material and psychological sources identified earlier in this essay (see section VII). In spite of this, a number of oppositional discourses and practices have appeared in recent years. An increasing number of women are "pumping iron," a few with little concern for the limits of body development imposed by current canons of femininity. Women in radical lesbian communities have also rejected hegemonic images of femininity and are struggling to develop a new female aesthetic. A striking feature of such communities is the extent to which they have overcome the oppressive identification of female beauty and desirability with youth: here, the physical features of aging—"character" lines and graying hair—not only do not diminish a woman's attractiveness, they may even enhance it. A popular literature of resistance is growing, some of it analytical and reflective, like Kim Chernin's *The Obsession*, some oriented toward practical self-help, like Marcia Hutchinson's recent *Transforming Body Image, Learning to Love the Body You Have*. This literature reflects a mood akin in some ways to that other and earlier mood of quiet desperation to which Betty Friedan gave voice in *The Feminine Mystique*. Nor should we forget that a mass-based women's movement is in place in this country that has begun a critical questioning of the meaning of femininity, if not yet in the corporeal presentation of self, then in other domains of life. We women cannot begin the re-vision of our own bodies until we learn to read the cultural messages we inscribe upon them daily and until we come to see that even when the mastery of the disciplines of femininity produces a triumphant result, we are still only women.

NOTES

1. Michel Foucault, *Discipline and Punish: The Birth of the Prison*, trans. Alan Sheridan (New York: Vintage Books, 1979), p. 138.

2. Ibid., p. 28.

3. Millman, *Such a Pretty Face*, pp. 80, 195.

4. Chernin, *The Obsession*, p. 53.

5. Foucault, *Power/Knowledge*, p. 98. In fact, Foucault is not entirely consistent on this point. For an excellent discussion of contending Foucault interpretations and for the difficulty of deriving a consistent set of claims from Foucault's work generally, see Nancy Fraser, "Michel Foucault: A 'Young Conservative'?" *Ethics* 96 (October 1985): 165-84.

Mammies, Matriarchs and Other Controlling Images

Patricia Hill Collins

Called Matriarch, Emasculator and Hot Momma. Sometimes Sister, Pretty Baby, Auntie, Mammy and Girl. Called Unwed Mother, Welfare Recipient and Inner City Consumer. The Black American Woman has had to admit that while nobody knew the troubles she saw, everybody, his brother and his dog, felt qualified to explain her, even to herself.
TRUDIER HARRIS, from Mammies to Militants (1982)

Race, class, and gender oppression could not continue without powerful ideological justifications for their existence. As Cheryl Gilkes contends, "Black women's assertiveness and their use of every expression of racism to launch multiple assaults against the entire fabric of inequality have been a consistent, multifaceted threat to the status quo. As punishment, Black women have been assaulted with a variety of negative images." Portraying African-American women as stereotypical mammies, matriarchs, welfare recipients, and hot mammas has been essential to the political economy of domination fostering Black women's oppression. Challenging these controlling images has long been a core theme in Black feminist thought.

As part of a generalized ideology of domination, these controlling images of Black womanhood take on special meaning because the authority to define these symbols is a major in-

From *Black Feminist Thought* (1990). Reprinted by permission.

strument of power. In order to exercise power, elite white men and their representatives must be in a position to manipulate appropriate symbols concerning Black women. They may do so by exploiting already existing symbols, or they may create new ones relevant to their needs. Hazel Carby suggests that the objective of stereotypes is "not to reflect or represent a reality but (is) to function as a disguise, or mystification, of objective social relations." These controlling images are designed to make racism, sexism, and poverty appear to be natural, normal, and an inevitable part of everyday life.

* * *

The first controlling image applied to African-American women is that of the mammy—the faithful, obedient domestic servant. Created to justify the economic exploitation of house slaves and sustained to explain Black women's long-standing restriction to domestic service, the mammy image represents the normative yardstick used to evaluate all Black women's behavior. By loving, nurturing, and caring for her white children and "family" better than her own, the mammy image symbolizes the dominant group's perceptions of the ideal Black female relationship to elite white male power. Even though she may be well-loved and may wield considerable power in her white "family," the mammy still knows her "place" as obedient servant. She has accepted her subordination.

Black women intellectuals have aggressively deconstructed the image of Black women as contented mammies by challenging traditional views of Black women domestics. Literary critic Trudier Harris's volume, *From Mammies to Militants: Domestics in Black American Literature*, investigates key differences in how Black women have been portrayed by others in literature and how they portray themselves. In her work on the difficulties faced by Black women leaders, Rhetaugh Dumas describes how Black women executives are hampered by being treated as mammies and penalized if they do not appear warm and nurturing. But, in spite of these works, the mammy image lives on in scholarly and popular culture. Audre Lorde's account of a shopping trip offers a powerful example of its tenacity: "I wheel my two-year-old daughter in a shopping cart through a supermarket in . . . 1967, and a little white girl riding past in her mother's cart calls out excitedly, 'Oh look, Mommy, a baby maid!'"

The mammy image is central to interlocking systems of race, gender, and class oppression. Since efforts to control African-American family life require perpetuating the symbolic structures of racial oppression, the mammy image is important because it aims to shape Black women's behavior as mothers. As the members of African-American families who are most familiar with the skills needed for Black accommodation, Black women are encouraged to transmit to their own children the deference behavior many are forced to exhibit in mammy roles. By teaching Black children their assigned place in white power structures, Black women

who internalize the mammy image potentially become effective conduits for perpetuating racial oppression. In addition, employing mammies buttresses the racial superiority of white women employers and weds them more closely to elite white males as the source of power.

The mammy image also serves a symbolic function in maintaining gender oppression. Black feminist critic Barbara Christian argues that images of Black womanhood serve as a reservoir for the fears of Western culture, "a dumping ground for those female functions a basically Puritan society could not confront." Juxtaposed against the image of white women promulgated through the cult of true womanhood, the mammy image as the Other symbolizes the oppositional difference of mind/body and culture/nature thought to distinguish Black women from everyone else. Christian comments on the mammy's gender significance: "all the functions of mammy are magnificently physical. They involve the body as sensuous, as funky, the part of woman that white southern America was profoundly afraid of. Mammy, then, harmless in her position of slave, unable because of her all-giving nature to do harm is needed as an image, a surrogate to contain all those fears of the physical female." The mammy image buttresses the ideology of the cult of true womanood, one where sexuality and fertility are severed. "Good" white mothers are expected to deny their female sexuality and devote their attention to the moral development of their offspring. In contrast, the mammy image is one of an asexual woman, a surrogate mother in blackface devoted to the development of a white family.

No matter how loved they were by their white "families," Black women domestic workers remained poor because they were economically exploited. The restructured post–World War II economy where Black women moved from service in private homes to jobs in the low-paid service sector has produced comparable economic exploitation. Removing Black women's labor from African-American families and exploiting it denies Black extended family units the benefits of either decent wages or Black women's unpaid labor in their homes. Moreover, many white families in both the middle class and working class are able to maintain their class position because they have long used Black women as a source of cheap labor. The mammy image is designed to mask this economic exploitation of social class.

For reasons of economic survival, African-American women may play the mammy role in paid work settings. But within African-American communities, these same women often teach their own children something quite different. Bonnie Thornton Dill's work on childrearing patterns among Black domestics shows that while the participants in her study showed deference behavior at work, they discouraged their children from believing that they should be deferent to whites, and encouraged their children to avoid domestic work. Barbara Christian's analysis of the mammy in Black slave narratives reveals that, "unlike the white southern image of mammy, she is cunning, prone to poisoning her master, and not at all content with her lot."

The mammy image's inability to control Black women's behavior as mothers is tied to the creation of the second controlling image of Black womanhood. While a more recent phenomenon, the image of the Black matriarch fulfills similar functions in explaining Black women's placement in interlocking systems of race, gender and class oppression. Ironically, Black scholars like William E. B. DuBois and E. Franklin Frazier both describe the connections among higher rates of female-headed households in African-American communities, the importance that women assume in Black family networks, and the persistence of Black poverty. However, neither scholar interprets Black women's centrality in Black families as a *cause* of African-American social class status. Both see so-called matriarchal families as an *outcome* of racial oppression and poverty. Dur-

ing the eras when DuBois and Frazier wrote, the oppression of African-Americans was so total that control was maintained without the controlling image of matriarch. But what began as a muted theme in the works of these earlier Black scholars grew into a full-blown racialized image in the 1960s, a time of significant political and economic mobility for African-Americans. Racialization involves attaching racial meaning to a previously racially unclassified relationship, social practice or group. Prior to the 1960s, female-headed households were certainly higher in African-American communities, but an ideology racializing female-headedness as a causal feature of Black poverty had not emerged. Moreover, "the public depiction of Black women as unfeminine, castrating matriarchs came at precisely the same moment that the feminist movement was advancing its public critique of American patriarchy."

While the mammy typifies the Black mother-figure in white homes, the matriarch symbolizes the mother-figure in Black homes. Just as the mammy represents the "good" Black mother, the matriarch symbolizes the "bad" Black mother. The modern Black matriarchy thesis contends that African-American women fail to fulfill their traditional "womanly" duties. Spending too much time away from home, these working mothers ostensibly cannot properly supervise their children and are a major contributing factor to their children's school failure. As overly aggressive, unfeminine women, Black matriarchs allegedly emasculate their lovers and husbands. These men, understandably, either desert their partners or refuse to marry the mothers of their children. From an elite white male standpoint, the matriarch is essentially a failed mammy, a negative stigma applied to those African-American women who dared to violate the image of the submissive, hardworking servant.

Black women intellectuals examining the role of women in African-American families discover few matriarchs and even fewer mammies. Instead, they portray African-American mothers as complex characters who show tremendous strength under adverse conditions. In *A Raisin in the Sun*, the first play presented on Broadway written by a Black woman, Lorraine Hansberry (1959) examines the struggles of widow Lena Younger to actualize her dream of purchasing a home for her family. In *Brown Girl, Brownstones*, novelist Paule Marshall (1959) presents Mrs. Boyce, a Black mother negotiating a series of relationships with her husband, her daughters, the women in her community and the work she must perform outside her home. Ann Allen Shockley's *Loving Her* (1974) depicts the struggle of a lesbian mother trying to balance her needs for self-actualization with the pressures of childrearing in a homophobic community. Black women's scholarship on Black single mothers also challenges the matriarchy thesis.

Like the mammy, the image of the matriarch is also central to interlocking systems of race, gender and class oppression. Portraying African-American women as matriarchs allows the dominant group to blame Black women for the success or failure of Black children. Assuming that Black poverty is passed on intergenerationally via value transmission in families, an elite white male standpoint suggests that Black children lack the attention and care that white middle-class mothers allegedly lavish on their offspring and that this deficiency seriously retards Black children's achievement. Such a view diverts attention from the political and economic inequality affecting Black mothers and children and suggests that anyone can rise from poverty if he or she only received good values at home. Those African-Americans who remain poor are blamed for their own victimization. Using Black women's performance as mothers to explain Black economic subordination links gender ideology to explanations of class subordination.

The source of the matriarch's failure is her inability to model appropriate gender behavior. In the post–World War II era, increasing numbers of white women entered the labor market, limited their fertility, and generally challenged their proscribed roles in white patriarchal institutions. The image of the Black matriarch emerged at that time as a powerful symbol for both Black and white women of what can go wrong if white patriarchal power is challenged. Aggressive, assertive women are penalized—they are abandoned by their men, end up impoverished, and are stigmatized as being unfeminine.

The image of the matriarch also supports racial oppression. Much social science research implicitly uses gender relations in African-American communities as one putative measure of Black cultural disadvantage. For example, the Moynihan Report (1965) contends that slavery destroyed Black families by creating reversed roles for men and women. Black family structures are seen as being deviant because they challenge the patriarchal assumptions underpinning the construct of the ideal "family." Moreover, the absence of Black patriarchy is used as evidence for Black cultural inferiority. Black women's failure to conform to the cult of true womanhood can then be identified as one fundamental source of Black cultural deficiency. Cheryl Gilkes posits that the emergence of the matriarch image occurred as a counterideology to efforts by African-Americans and women who were confronting interlocking systems of race, gender and class oppression: "The image of dangerous Black women who were also deviant castrating mothers divided the Black community at a critical period in the Black liberation struggle and created a wider gap between the worlds of Black and white women at a critical period in women's history."

Taken together, images of the mammy and the matriarch place African-American women in an untenable position. For Black women workers in domestic work and other occupations requiring long hours and/or substantial emotional labor, becoming the ideal mammy means precious time and energy spent away from husbands and children. But being employed when Black men have difficulty finding steady work exposes African-American women to the charge that Black women emasculate Black men by failing to be submissive, dependent, "feminine" women. Moreover, Black women's financial contributions to Black family well-being have also been cited as evidence supporting the matriarchy thesis. Many Black women are the sole support of their families and labelling these women "matriarchs" erodes their self-confidence and ability to confront oppression. In essence, African-American women who must work are labelled mammies then are stigmatized again as matriarchs for being strong figures in their own homes.

A third, externally defined, controlling image of Black womanhood, that of the welfare mother, appears tied to Black women's increasing dependence on the post–World War II welfare state. Essentially an updated version of the breeder woman image created during slavery, this image provides an ideological justification for efforts to harness Black women's fertility to the needs of a changing political economy.

During slavery, the breeder woman image portrayed Black women as more suitable for having children than white women. By claiming that Black women were able to produce children as easily as animals, this objectification of Black women as the Other provided justification for interference in the reproductive rights of enslaved Africans. Slaveowners wanted enslaved Africans to "breed" because every slave child born represented a valuable unit of property, another unit of labor and, if female, the prospects for more slaves. The externally defined, controlling image of the breeder woman served to justify slaveowner intrusion into Black women's decisions about fertility.

The post–World War II political economy has offered African-Americans rights not available in former historical periods. African-

Americans have successfully acquired basic political and economic protections from a greatly expanded welfare state, particularly, Social Security, Aid to Families with Dependent Children, unemployment compensation, affirmative action, voting rights, antidiscrimination legislation, and the minimum wage. In spite of sustained opposition by Republican administrations in the 1980s, these programs allow many African-Americans to reject the subsistence level, exploitative jobs held by their parents and grandparents. Job export, de-skilling, and increased use of illegal immigrants have all been used to replace the loss of cheap, docile Black labor. The large numbers of undereducated, unemployed African-Americans, most of whom are women and children, who inhabit inner cities cannot be forced to work. From the standpoint of the dominant group, they no longer represent cheap labor but instead signify a threat to political and economic stability.

Controlling Black women's fertility in such a political economy becomes important. The image of the welfare mother fulfills this function by labelling as unnecessary and even dangerous to the values of the country the fertility of women who are not white and middle-class. A closer look at this controlling image reveals that it shares some important features with its mammy and matriarch counterparts. Like the matriarch, the welfare mother is labelled a bad mother. But unlike the matriarch, she is not too aggressive—rather, she is not aggressive enough. While the matriarch's unavailability contributed to her children's poor socialization, the welfare mother's accessibility is deemed the problem. She is portrayed as being content to sit around and collect welfare, shunning work and, passing on her bad values to her offspring. The image of the welfare mother represents another failed mammy, one who is unwilling to become "de mule uh de world."

The image of the welfare mother provides ideological justifications for interlocking systems of race, gender and class oppression.

African-Americans can be racially stereotyped as being lazy by blaming Black welfare mothers for failing to pass on the work ethic. Moreover, the welfare mother has no male authority figure to assist her. Typically portrayed as an unwed mother, she violates one cardinal tenet of Eurocentric masculinist thought—she is a woman alone. As a result, her treatment reinforces the dominant gender ideology positing that a woman's true worth and financial security should occur through heterosexual marriage. Finally, in the post–World War II political economy, one out of every three African-American families is officially classified as poor. With such high levels of Black poverty, welfare state policies supporting poor Black mothers and their children have become increasingly expensive. Creating the controlling image of the welfare mother and stigmatizing her as the cause of her own poverty and that of African-American communities shifts the angle of vision away from structural sources of poverty and blames the victims themselves. The image of the welfare mother thus provides ideological justification for the dominant group's interest in limiting the fertility of Black mothers who are seen as producing too many economically unproductive children.

The fourth controlling image—the Jezebel, whore or sexually aggressive woman—is central in this nexus of elite white male images of Black womanhood because efforts to control Black women's sexuality lie at the heart of Black women's oppression. The image of Jezebel originated under slavery where Black women were portrayed as being, to use Jewelle Gomez's words, "sexually aggressive wet nurses." Jezebel's function was to relegate all Black women to the category of sexually aggressive women, thus providing a powerful rationale for the widespread sexual assaults by white men typically reported by Black slave women. Yet Jezebel served another function. If Black slave women could be portrayed as having excessive sexual appetites, then increased fertility should be the expected outcome. By sup-

pressing the nurturing that African-American women might give their own children that would strengthen Black family networks, and forcing Black women to work in the field or "wet nurse" white children, slaveowners effectively tied the controlling images of Jezebel and Mammy to the economic exploitation inherent in the institution of slavery.

The fourth image of the sexually denigrated Black woman is the foundation underlying elite white male conceptualizations of the mammy, matriarch and welfare mother. Connecting all three is the common theme of Black women's sexuality. Each image transmits clear messages about the proper link between female sexuality, fertility and Black women's roles in the political economy. For example, the mammy, the only somewhat positive figure, is a desexed individual. The mammy is typically portrayed as overweight, dark, and with characteristically African features, in brief, as an unsuitable sexual partner for white men. She is asexual, and therefore is free to become a surrogate mother to the children she acquired not through her own sexuality. The mammy represents the clearest example of the split between sexuality and motherhood present in Eurocentric masculinist thought. In contrast, both the matriarch and the welfare mother are sexual beings. But their sexuality is linked to their fertility, and this link forms one fundamental reason why they are negative images. The matriarch represents the sexually aggressive woman, one who emasculates Black men because she will not permit them to assume roles as Black patriarchs. She refuses to be passive and thus is stigmatized. Similarly, the welfare mother represents a woman of low morals and uncontrolled sexuality, factors identified as the cause of her impoverished state. In both cases, Black female control over sexuality and fertility is conceptualized as being antithetical to elite white male interests.

Taken together, these four prevailing interpretations of Black womanhood form a nexus of elite white male interpretations of Black female sexuality and fertility. Moreover, by meshing smoothly with systems of race, class and gender oppression, they provide effective ideological justifications for racial oppression, the politics of gender subordination, and the economic exploitation inherent in capitalist economies.

CONTROLLING IMAGES IN EVERYDAY LIFE: COLOR, HAIR TEXTURE AND STANDARDS OF BEAUTY

Like everyone else, African-American women learn the meaning of race, gender and social class without obvious teaching or conscious learning. The controlling images of Black women are not simply grafted onto existing social institutions but are so pervasive that, even though the images themselves change in the popular imagination, Black women's portrayal as the Other persists. Particular meanings, stereotypes and myths can change but the overall ideology of domination itself seems to be an enduring feature of interlocking systems of race, gender, and class oppression.

African-American women encounter this ideology through a range of unquestioned, daily experiences. But when the contradictions between Black women's self-definitions and everyday treatment are heightened, controlling images become increasingly visible. Karen Russell, the daughter of basketball great Bill Russell, describes how racial stereotypes affect her:

How am I supposed to react to well-meaning, good, liberal white people who say things like: "You know, Karen, I don't understand what all the fuss is about. You're one of my good friends, and I never think of you as black." Implicit in such a remark is, "I think of you as white," or perhaps just, "I don't think of your race at all."[1]

Ms. Russell was perceptive enough to see that remarks intended to compliment her actually insulted African-Americans. As the Others, African-Americans are assigned all of the negative characteristics opposite to and inferior to those reserved for whites. By claiming that Ms. Russell is not really "black," her friends unintentionally validate this system of racial meanings and encourage her to internalize those images.

While Black women typically resist being objectified as the Other, these controlling images remain powerful influences on our relationships with whites, Black men, and each other. Dealing with issues of beauty, particularly skin color, facial features and hair texture, is one concrete example of how controlling images denigrate African-American women. A children's rhyme often sung in Black communities proclaims:

> Now, if you're white you're all right,
> If you're brown, stick around,
> But if you're black, Git back! Git back! Git back!

Externally defined standards of beauty long applied to African-American women claim that no matter how intelligent, educated, or "beautiful" a Black woman may be, those Black women whose features and skin color are most African must "git back." Blue eyed, blond, thin white women could not be considered beautiful without the Other—Black women with classical African features of dark skin, broad noses, full lips and kinky hair.

Race, gender and sexuality converge on this issue of evaluating beauty. Judging white women by their physical appearance and attractiveness to men objectifies them. But their white skin and straight hair privilege them in a system where part of the basic definition of whiteness is its superiority to blackness. Black men's blackness penalizes them. But because they are men, their self-definitions are not as heavily dependent on their physical attractiveness as those of all women. But African-American women experience the pain of never being able to live up to externally defined standards of beauty, standards applied to us by white men, white women, Black men and, most painfully, by each other.

Exploring how externally defined standards of beauty impact on Black women's self images, our relationships with each other, and our relationships with Black men, has been one recurring theme in Black feminist thought. The longstanding attention of musicians, writers and artists to this theme reveals African-American women's deep feelings concerning skin color, hair texture, and standards of beauty. In her autobiography, Maya Angelou records her painful realization that the only way that she could become truly beautiful was to become white:

Wouldn't they be surprised when one day I woke out of my black ugly dream, and my real hair, which was long and blond, would take the place of the kinky mass that Momma wouldn't let me straighten? . . . Then they would understand why I had never picked up a Southern accent, or spoke the common slang, and why I had to be forced to eat pigs' tails and snouts. Because I was really white and because a cruel fairy stepmother . . . had turned me into a too-big Negro girl, with nappy black hair.[2]

Gwendolyn Brooks also explores the meaning of skin color and hair texture for Black women. During Brooks' childhood, having African features was so universally denigrated that she writes, "when I was a child, it did not occur to me even once, that the black in which I was encased . . . would be considered, one day, beautiful." Early on, Brooks learned that a clear pecking order existed among African-Americans, one based on one's closeness to whiteness. As a member of the "Lesser Blacks," those farthest from white, Brooks saw firsthand the difference in treatment of her group and the "Brights":

One of the first "world"-truths revealed to me when I at last became a member of SCHOOL was that, to be socially successful, a little girl must be Bright (of skin). It was better if your hair was curly, too—or at least Good Grade (Good Grade implied, usually, no

involvement with the Hot Comb)—but Bright you marvelously *needed* to be.[3]

This division of African-Americans into two categories, the "Brights" and the "Lesser Blacks," affects dark-skinned and light-skinned women differently. Darker women face being judged inferior and receiving the treatment afforded "too-big Negro girls with nappy hair." Institutions controlled by whites clearly show a preference for lighter-skinned Blacks, discriminating against darker ones or against any African-Americans who appear to reject white images of beauty. Sonia Sanchez reports that, "sisters tell me today that when they go out for jobs they straighten their hair because if they go in with their hair natural or braided, they probably won't get the job."

Sometimes the pain most felt is the pain that Black women inflict on one another. Marita Golden's mother told her not to play in the sun, because "you gonna have to get a light husband anyway, for the sake of your children." In *Color*, a short film exploring the impact of skin color on Black women's lives, the dark-skinned character's mother tries to get her to sit still for the hot comb, asking "don't you want your hair flowing like your friend Rebecca's?" We see the sadness of a young Black girl sitting in a kitchen, holding her ears so that they won't get burned by the hot comb that will straighten her hair. Her mother cannot make her beautiful, only "presentable" for church. Marita Golden's description of a Black beauty salon depicts the internalized oppression that some African-American women feel about African features:

Between customers, twirling in her chair, white-stockinged legs crossed, my beautician lamented to the hairdresser in the next stall, "I sure hope that Gloria Johnson don't come in here asking for me today. I swear 'fore God her hair is this long." She snapped her fingers to indicate the length. Contempt riding her words, she lit a cigarette and finished, "Barely enough to wash, let alone press and curl."[4]

African-American women who are members of the "Brights" fare little better, for they too receive special treatment because of their skin color and hair texture. Harriet Jacobs, an enslaved light-skinned woman, was sexually harassed because she was "beautiful," for a Black woman. Her straight hair and fair skin, her appearance as a dusky white woman, made her physically attractive to white men. But the fact that she was Black, and thus part of a group of sexually denigrated women, made her available to white men as no group of white women had been. In describing her situation, Jacobs notes, "if God has bestowed beauty upon her, it will prove her greatest curse. That which commands admiration in the white woman only hastens the degradation of the female slave."

This difference in treatment of dark-skinned and light-skinned Black women creates issues in relationships among African-American women. Toni Morrison's novel *The Bluest Eye* (1970) explores this theme of the tension that can exist among Black women grappling with the meaning of externally defined standards of beauty. Freida, a dark-skinned "ordinary" Black girl, struggles with the meaning of these standards. She wonders why adults always got so upset when she rejected the white dolls they gave her and why light-skinned Maureen Peal, a child her own age whose two braids hung like "lynch-ropes down her back," got the love and attention of teachers, adults and Black boys alike. Morrison explores Freida's attempt not to blame Maureen for the benefits her light skin and long hair afforded her as part of Freida's growing realization that the "Thing" to fear was not Maureen herself, but the "Thing" that made Maureen beautiful.

Gwendolyn Brooks captures the anger and frustration experienced by dark-skinned women in dealing with the differential treatment that they and their lighter skinned sisters receive. In her novel *Maud Martha*, the dark-skinned heroine ponders actions she could take against a red-headed Black woman that her husband found so attractive. "I could," considered Maud Martha, "go over there and scratch her upsweep down. I could spit on her back. I could scream. 'Listen,' I could scream, 'I'm making a baby for this man and I mean to do it in peace.' " But Maud Martha rejects these actions, reasoning "if the root was sour what business did she have up there hacking at a leaf?"

This "sour root" also creates issues in relationships among African-American women and men. Maude Martha explains:

it's my color that makes him mad. I try to shut my eyes to that, but it's no good. What I am inside, what is really me, he likes okay. But he keeps looking at my color, which is like a wall. He has to jump over it in order to meet and touch what I've got for him. He has to jump away up high in order to see it. He gets awful tired of all that jumping.[5]

Her husband's attraction to light-skinned women hurt Maude Martha because his inability to "jump away up high" over the wall of color limited his ability to see her for who she truly was.

* * *

CONSTRUCTING AN AFROCENTRIC FEMINIST AESTHETIC FOR BEAUTY

Developing much-needed redefinitions of beauty must involve the critical first step of learning to see African-American women who have classical African features as being capable of beauty. Lorraine Hansberry describes this need for a changed consciousness about African-American women's beauty:

Sometimes in this country maybe just walking down a Southside street . . . Or maybe suddenly up in a Harlem window . . . Or maybe in a flash turning the page of one of those picture books from the South you will see it—*Beauty* . . . stark and full. . . . No *part* of this—but rather Africa, simply Africa. These thighs and arms and flying winged cheekbones, these hallowed eyes—without negation or apology. A *classical people demand a classical art.*[6]

But proclaiming Black women "beautiful" and white women "ugly" merely replaces one set of controlling images with another and fails to challenge how Eurocentric masculinist aesthetics foster an ideology of domination. Current standards require either/or dichotomous thinking—in order for one individual to be judged beautiful, another individual, the Other, must be deemed ugly. Accepting this underlying assumption avoids a more basic question concerning the connections among controlling images, either/or dichotomous thinking, and unequal power relationships among groups. Creating an alternative feminist aesthetic involves deconstructing and rejecting existing standards of ornamental beauty that objectify women and judge us by our physical appearance. Such an aesthetic would also reject standards of beauty that commodify women by measuring various quantities of beauty that women broker in the marital marketplace.

African-American women can draw upon traditional Afrocentric aesthetics that potentially free women from standards of ornamental beauty. While present in music, dance, and language, quiltmaking offers a suggestive model for an Afrocentric feminist aesthetic. African-American women quiltmakers do not seem interested in a uniform color scheme but instead use several methods of playing with colors to create unpredictability and movement. For example, a strong color may be juxtaposed with another strong color, or with a weak one. Contrast is used to structure or organize. Overall, the symmetry in African-American quilts does not come from uniformity as it does in Euro-American quilts. Rather, symmetry comes through diversity. Nikki Giovanni points out that quilts are traditionally formed from scraps. "Quilters teach there is no such thing as waste," she observes, "only that for which we currently see no purpose." In describing Alice Walker's reaction to a quilt done by an anonymous Black woman, Barbara Christian notes that Walker "brings together . . . the theme of the black woman's creativity, her transformation, despite opposition, of the bits and pieces allowed to her by society into a work of functional beauty."

This dual emphasis on beauty occurring via individual uniqueness juxtaposed in a community setting, and on the importance of creating functional beauty from the scraps of everyday life, offers a powerful alternative to Eurocentric aesthetics. The Afrocentric notions of diversity in community and functional beauty potentially heal many of the oppositional dichotomies inherent in Western social thought. From an Afrocentric perspective, women's beauty is not based solely on physical criteria because mind, spirit, and body are not conceptualized as separate oppositional spheres. Instead, all are central in aesthetic assessments of individuals and their creations. Beauty is functional in that it has no meaning independent of the group. Deviating from the group "norm" is not rewarded as "beauty." Instead, participating in the group and being a functioning individual who strives for harmony is key to assessing an individual's beauty. Moreover, participation is not based on conformity, but instead is seen as individual uniqueness that enhances the overall "beauty" of the group. Using such criteria, no individual is inherently beautiful because beauty is not a state of being. Instead, beauty is always defined in a context as a state of becoming. All African-American women as well as all humans become capable of beauty.

NOTES

1. Karen Russell, "Growing up with Privilege and Prejudice," *New York Times Magazine* June 14, 1987.

2. Maya Angelou, "I Know Why Caged Birds Sing" New York: Bantam (1969).

3. Gwendolyn Brooks, *Report from Part One*, Detroit: Broadside Press (1972).

4. Marita Golden, *Migrations of the Heart*, New York: Ballantine.

5. Mary Helen Washington, *Invented Genes*, Garden City: Anchor.

6. Lorraine Hansberry, *To Be Young Gifted and Black* New York: Signet.

The Women in the Tower

Cynthia Rich

In April, 1982 a group of Black women demand a meeting with the Boston Housing Authority. They are women between the ages of sixty-six and eighty-one. Their lives, in the "housing tower for the elderly" where they live, are in continual danger. "You're afraid to get on the elevator and you're afraid to get off," says Mamie Buggs, sixty-six. Odella Keenan, sixty-nine, is wakened in the nights by men pounding on her apartment door. Katherine Jefferson, eighty-one, put three locks on her door, but "I've come back to my apartment and found a group of men there eating my food."

The menace, the violence, is nothing new, they say. They have reported it before, but lately it has become intolerable. There are pictures in the *Boston Globe* of three of the women, and their eyes flash with anger. "We pay our rent, and we're entitled to some security," says Mamie Buggs. Two weeks ago, a man attacked and beat up Ida Burres, seventy-five, in the recreation room. Her head wound required forty stitches.

"I understand your desire for permanent security," says Lewis Spence, the BHA representative. "But I can't figure out any way that the BHA is going to be offering 24-hour security in an elderly development." He is a white man, probably in his thirties. His picture is much larger than the pictures of the women.

The headline in the *Boston Globe* reads, "Elderly in Roxbury building plead with BHA for 24-hour security." Ida Burres is described in the story as "a feisty, sparrow-like woman with well-cared for gray hair, cafe au lait skin and a lilting voice." The byline reads "Viola Osgood." The story appears on page 19.

I feel that in my lifetime I will not get to the bottom of this story, of these pictures, of these words.

Feisty, sparrow-like, well-cared for gray hair, cafe au lait skin, lilting voice.

Feisty. Touchy, excitable, quarrelsome, like a mongrel dog. "Feisty" is the standard word in newspaperspeak for an old person who says what she thinks. As you grow older, the younger person sees your strongly felt convictions or your protest against an intolerable life situation as an amusing over-reaction, a defect of personality common to mongrels and old people. To insist that you are a person deepens the stigma of your Otherness. Your protest is not a specific, legitimate response to an outside threat. It is a generic and arbitrary quirkiness, coming from the queer stuff within yourself—sometimes annoying, sometimes quaint or even endearing, never, never to be responded to seriously.

Sparrow-like. Imagine for a moment that you have confronted those who have power over you, demanding that they do something to end the

Cynthia Rich, "The Women in the Tower," from *Look Me in the Eye* by Barbara Macdonald with Cynthia Rich: Spinsters Book Company, 1983. (Available for $6.50 from Spinsters Book Company, P.O. Box 410687, San Francisco, CA 94141). Reprinted by permission.

terror of your days and nights. You and other women have organized a meeting of protest. You have called the press. Imagine then opening the newspaper and seeing yourself described as "sparrow-like." That is no simple indignity, no mere humiliation. The fact that you can be described as "sparrow-like" is in part why you live in the tower, why nobody attends. Because you do not look like a natural person—that is, a young or middle-aged person—you look like a sparrow. The real sparrow is, after all, a sparrow and is seen merely as homely, but a woman who is sparrow-like is unnatural and ugly.

A white widow tells of smiling at a group of small children on the street and one of them saying, "You're ugly, ugly, ugly." It is what society has imprinted on that child's mind: to be old, and to look old, is to be ugly, so ugly that you do not deserve to live. Crow's feet. Liver spots. The media: "I'm going to wash that gray right out of my hair and wash in my 'natural' color." "Get rid of those unsightly spots." And if you were raised to believe that old is ugly, you play strange tricks in your own head. An upper middle class white woman, a woman with courage and zest for life, writes in 1982: "When we love we do not see our mates as the young view us—wrinkled, misshapen, unattractive." But then she continues: "We still retain, somewhere, the *memory* of one another as beautiful and lustful, and we see each other at our *once-best*."

Old is ugly and unnatural in a society where power is male-defined, powerlessness disgraceful. A society where natural death is dreaded and concealed, while unnatural death is courted and glorified. But old is ugliest for women. A white woman newscaster in her forties remarks to a sportscaster who is celebrating his sixtieth birthday: "What women really resent about men is that *you* get more attractive as you get older." A man is as old as he feels, a woman as old as she looks. You're ugly, ugly, ugly.

Aging has a special stigma for women. When our wombs are no longer ready for pro-

creation, when our vaginas are no longer tight, when we no longer serve men, we are unnatural and ugly. In medical school terminology, we are a "crock"; in the language of the street, we are an "old bag." The Sanskrit word for widow is "empty." But there is more than that.

Sparrow-like. The association of the old woman with a bird runs deep in the male unconscious. Apparently, it flows back to a time when men acknowledged their awe of what they were outsiders to—the interconnected, inseparable mysteries of life and death, self and other, darkness and light. Life begins in genital darkness, comes into light, and returns to darkness as death. The child in the woman's body is both self and other. The power to offer the breast is the power to withhold it. The Yes and the No are inextricable. In the beginning was the Great Mother, mysteriously, powerfully connected to the wholeness of Nature and her indivisible Yeses and Nos. But for those outside the process, the oneness was baffling and intolerable, and the Great Mother was split. Men attempted to divide what they could not control—nature and women's relationship to it. The Great Mother was polarized into separate goddesses or into diametrically opposed aspects of a single goddess. The Good Mother and the Terrible Mother. The Good Mother created life, spread her bounty outward, fertilized the crops, nourished and protected, created healing potions. The Terrible Mother, the original old Witch, dealt in danger and destruction, devoured children as food for herself, concocted poisons. Womb ≠ tomb, light ≠ darkness, other ≠ self. A world of connectedness was split down the middle.

The Terrible Mother was identified with the winged creatures that feed on mammals: vultures, ravens, owls, crows, bats. Her images in the earliest known culture of India show her as old, birdlike, hideous: "Hooded with a coif or shawl, they have high, smooth foreheads above their staring circular eye holes, their owl-beak nose and grim slit mouth. The result is terrifying . . . the face is a grinning skull."

Unable to partake of the mystery of wholeness represented by the Great Mother, men first divided her, then wrested more and more control of her divided powers. The powerful Good Mother—bounteous life-giver, creator and nurturer of others—became the custodian of children who "belong" to the man or the male state. She can no longer even bear "his" child without the guiding forceps or scalpel of a man. She is the quotidian cook (men are the great chefs) who eats only after she has served others. She is the passive dispenser—as nurse, mother, wife—of the "miracles" of modern medicine created by the brilliance of man.

The Terrible Mother—the "old Woman of the West," guardian of the dead—represented men's fear of the powerful aspect of woman as intimate not only with the mysteries of birth but also of death. Today men are the specialists of death—despite a recent study that suggests that men face natural death with much more anxiety than women do. Today male doctors oversee dying, male priests and rabbis perform the rituals of death, and even the active role of laying out the dead no longer belongs to woman (now the work of male undertakers). Woman is only the passive mourner, the helpless griever. And it is men who vie with each other to invent technologies that can bring about total death and destruction.

The Terrible Mother—the vulture or owl feeding on others—represented the fear of death, but also the fear of woman as existing not only to create and nurture others but to create and nurture her Self. Indeed, the aging woman's body is a clear reminder that women have a self that exists not only for others; it descends into her pelvis as if to claim the womb-space for its own. Woman's Self—her meeting of her own needs, seen by men as destructive and threatening—has been punished and repressed, branded "unnatural" and "unwomanly."

In this century, in rural China, they had a practice called "sunning the jinx." If a child died, or there was some similar misfortune, it was seen as the work of a jinx. The jinx was always an old, poor woman, and she was exposed to the searing heat of the summer sun until she confessed. Like the witches burned throughout Europe in the fifteenth to seventeenth centuries, she was tortured by doublethink. If she died without confessing, they had eliminated the jinx. If she confessed her evil powers, she was left in the sun for three more days to "cure her." In Bali today, the Terrible Mother lingers on in magic plays, as Ranga, the witch who eats children, "a huge old woman with drooping breasts and a mat of white hair that comes down to her feet." It is a man who plays her part, and he must be old since only an old man can avoid the evil spirit of the Terrible Mother.

In present-day white culture, men's fear of the Terrible Mother is managed by denial: by insisting on the powerlessness of the old woman, her harmless absurdity and irrelevance. The dread of her power lingers, reduced to farce—as in the Hansel and Gretel story of the old witch about to devour the children until the boy destroys her, or in the comic juxtaposition of *Arsenic and Old Lace*. The image of her winged power persists, totally trivialized, in the silly witch flying on her broomstick, and in "old bat," "old biddy," "old hen," "old crow," "crow's feet," "old harpy." Until, in April of 1982, an old woman's self-affirmation, her rage at her disempowerment, her determination to die naturally and not at the hands of men, can be diminished to feistiness, and she can be perceived as sparrow-like.

Sparrow-like. Writing for white men, did Viola Osgood unconsciously wish to say, "Ida Burres is not a selfish vulture—even though she is doing what old women are not meant to do, speak for their own interests (not their children's or grandchildren's but their own). She is an innocent sparrow, frail and helpless"? Or had she herself so incorporated that demeaning image—sparrow-like—that she saw Ida Burres through those eyes? Or both?

Well-Cared for Gray Hair.   Is that about race? About class? An attempt to dispel the notion that a poor Black woman is unkempt? Would Viola Osgood describe a Black welfare mother in terms of her "well-groomed afro"? Or does she mean to dispel the notion that this *old* woman is unkempt? Only the young can afford to be careless about their hair, their dress. The care that the old woman takes with her appearance is not merely to reduce the stigma of ugly; often it is her most essential tactic for survival: it signals to the person who sees her, I am old, but I am not senile. My hair is gray but it is well-cared for. Because to be old is to be guilty of craziness and incapacity unless proven otherwise.

Cafe au Lait Skin.   Race? Class? Age? Not dark black like Katherine Jefferson, but blackness mitigated. White male reader, who has the power to save these women's lives, you can't dismiss her as Black, poor, old. She is almost all right, she is almost white. She is Black and old, but she has something in common with the young mulatto woman whose skin you have sometimes found exotic and sensual. And she is not the power of darkness that you fear in the Terrible Mother.

A Lilting Voice.   I try to read these words in a lilting voice: "I almost got my eyes knocked out. A crazy guy just came in here and knocked me down and hit me in the face. We need security." These words do not lilt to me. A woman is making a demand, speaking truth to power, affirming her right to live—Black, Old, Poor, Woman. Is the "lilting" to say, "Although her words are strong, although she is bonding with other women, she is not tough and dykey"? Is

the "lilting" to say, "Although she is sparrow-like, although she is gray-haired, something of the mannerisms you find pleasing in young women remain, so do not ignore her as you routinely do old women"?

I write this not knowing whether Viola Osgood is Black or white. I know that she is a woman. And I know that it matters whether she is Black or white, that this is not a case of one size fits all. But I know that Black or white, any woman who writes news articles for the *Globe*, or for any mainstream newspaper, is mandated to write to white men, in white men's language. That any messages to women, Black or white, which challenge white men's thinking can at best only be conveyed covertly, subversively. That any messages of appeal to those white men must be phrased in ways that do not seriously threaten their assumptions, and that such language itself perpetuates the power men have assumed for themselves. And I know that Black or white, ageism blows in the wind around us and certainly through the offices of the *Globe*. I write this guessing that Viola Osgood is Black, because she has known that the story is important, cared enough to make sure the photographer was there. I write this guessing that the story might never have found its way into the *Globe* unless through a Black reporter. Later, I find out that she is Black, thirty-five.

And I think that Viola Osgood has her own story to tell. I think that I, white Jewish woman of fifty, still sorting through to find the realities beneath the lies, denials and ignorance of my lifetime of segregations, cannot write this essay. I think that even when we try to cross the lines meant to separate us as women—old and young, Black and white, Jew and non-Jew—the seeds of division cling to our clothes. And I think this must be true of what I write now. But we cannot stop crossing, we cannot stop writing.

Elderly in Roxbury Building Plead with BHA for 24-hour Security.   Doubtless, Viola Osgood did not write the headline. Ten words and it contains two lies—lies that routinely obscure the struggles of old women. *Elderly.* This is not a story of elderly people, it is the story of old women, Black old women. Three-fifths of the "elderly" are women; almost all of the residents of this tower are women. An old woman has half the income of an old man. One out of three widows—women without the immediate presence of a man—lives below the official poverty line, and most women live one third of their lives as widows. In the United States, as throughout the world, old women are the poorest of the poor. Seven percent of old white men live in poverty, 47 percent of old Black women. "The Elderly," "Old People," "Senior Citizens," are inclusive words that blot out these differences. Old women are twice unseen—unseen because they are old, unseen because they are women. Black old women are thrice unseen. "Elderly" conveniently clouds the realities of power and economics. It clouds the convergence of racial hatred and fear, hatred and fear of the aged, hatred and fear of women. It also clouds the power of female bonding, of these women in the tower who are acting together as women for women.

Plead. Nothing that these women say, nothing in their photographs, suggests pleading. These women are angry, and if one can demand where there is no leverage—and one can—they are demanding. They are demanding their lives, to which they know full well they have a right. Their anger is clear, direct, unwavering. "Pleading" erases the force of their confrontation. It allows us to continue to think of old women, if we think of them at all, as meek, cowed, to be pitied, occasionally as amusingly "feisty," but not as outraged, outrageous women. Old women's anger is denied, tamed, drugged, infantilized, trivialized. And yet anger in an old woman is a remarkable act of bravery, so dangerous is her world, and her status in that world so marginal, precarious. Her anger is an act of insubordination—the refusal

to accept her subordinate status even when everyone, children, men, younger women, and often other older women, assumes it. "We pay our rent, and we're entitled to some security." When will a headline tell the truth: Old, Black, poor women confront the BHA demanding 24-hour security?

The Housing Tower for the Elderly. A tall building filled with women, courageous women who bond together, but who with every year are less able to defend themselves against male attack. A tower of women under seige. A ghetto within a ghetto. The white male solution to the "problem of the elderly" is to isolate the Terrible Mother.

That tower, however, is not simply architectural. Nor is the male violence an "inner city problem." Ten days later, in nearby Stoughton, a man will have beaten to death an eighty-seven-year-old white woman, leaving her body with "multiple blunt injuries around her face, head, and shoulders." This woman was not living in a housing tower for the elderly. She lived in the house where she was born. "She was very, very spry. She worked in her garden a lot and she drove her own car," reports a neighbor. She had the advantages of race, class, a small home of her own, a car of her own. Nor did she turn away from a world that rejects and demeans old women ("spry," like "feisty," is a segregating and demeaning word). At the time of her murder, she was involved in planning the anniversary celebration at her parish.

Yet she was dead for a week before anyone found her body. Why? The reporter finds it perfectly natural. "She outlived her contemporaries and her circle of immediate relatives." Of course. How natural. Unless we remember de Beauvoir: "One of the ruses of oppression is to camouflage itself behind a natural situation since, after all, one cannot revolt against nature." How natural that young people, or even the middle aged, should have nothing in common with an old woman. Unthinkable that she should have formed friendships with anyone who was not in her or his seventies or eighties or nineties. It is natural that without family, who must tolerate the stigma, or other old people who share the stigma, she would have no close ties. And it is natural that no woman, old or young, anywhere in the world, should be safe from male violence.

But it is not natural. It is not natural, and it is dangerous, for younger women to be divided as by a taboo from old women—to live in our own shaky towers of youth. It is intended, but it is not natural that we be ashamed of, dissociated from, our future selves, sharing men's loathing for the women we are daily becoming. It is intended, but it is not natural that we be kept ignorant of our deep bonds with old women. And it is not natural that today, as we re-connect with each other, old women are still an absence for younger women.

As a child—a golden-haired Jew in the segregated South while the barbed wire was going up around the Warsaw ghetto—I was given fairy tales to read. Among them, the story of Rapunzel, the golden-haired young woman confined to a tower by an old witch until she was rescued by a young prince. My hair darkened and now it is light again with gray. I know that I have been made to live unnaturally in a tower for most of my fifty years. My knowledge of my history—as a woman, as a lesbian, as a light-skinned woman in a world of dark-skinned women, as the Other in a Jew-hating world—shut out. My knowledge of my future—as an old woman—shut out.

Today I reject those mythic opposites: young/old, light/darkness, life/death, other/self, Rapunzel/Witch, Good Mother/Terrible Mother. As I listen to the voices of the old women of Warren Tower, and of my aging self, I know that I have always been aging, always been dying. Those voices speak of wholeness: To nurture Self = to defy those who endanger that Self. To declare the I of my unique existence = to assert the We of my connections with other women. To accept the absolute rightness of my natural death = to defend the absolute value of my life. To affirm the mystery of my daily dying and the mystery of my daily living = to challenge men's violent cheapening of both.

But I cannot hear these voices clearly if I am still afraid of the old witch, the Terrible Mother in myself, or if I am estranged from the real old women of this world. For it is not the wicked witch who keeps Rapunzel in her tower. It is the prince and our divided selves.

Note: There was no follow-up article on the women of the tower, but Ida Burres, Mamie Buggs, Mary Gordon, Katherine Jefferson, Odella Keenan, and the other women of Warren Tower, did win what they consider to be adequate security—"of course, it is never all that you could wish," said Vallie Burton, President of the Warren Tower Association. They won because of their own bonding, their demands, and also, no doubt, because of Viola Osgood.

❧ The World of Work ❧

Women Wage Earners

Marie Richmond-Abbott

In this century in the United States, women have moved in ever increasing numbers into the labor force. Between 1900 and 1980, female labor force participation grew from 18 percent to 50 percent. (The number of women who work for pay or who are trying to find a job almost doubled between 1950 and 1974 alone.) By 1988, 56 percent of all women were in the work force. These labor force participation rates are projected to continue to rise to the year 2000, but at a slower pace than in the last twenty years. This movement into paid market activity has had profound consequences for women's lives and for the economics of our society. The reasons for the movement are varied and are closely connected with world events as well as with the economic scene in our own country.

HISTORICAL PERSPECTIVES ON WOMEN'S WORK IN THIS COUNTRY

The historical pattern of women's market work in the United States shows that women were heavily involved in economic production in our

From *Masculine and Feminine*, 2nd edition. Reprinted with permission.

early history. In the agrarian society of early America, women had to plant and harvest crops, tend animals, and do other things that produced a money income, as well as work within the household to produce cloth, make clothes, make butter and cheese, preserve food, and the like. In addition, with the short life expectancy, many women became widows and ran businesses or farms; other women were midwives, nurses, teachers, printers, laundresses, and innkeepers. Many middle-class women also worked invisibly by taking in boarders or sewing at home. In the early 1830s and 1840s, women worked in textile mills and tobacco factories. By 1890, estimates are that at least 1 million women were employed in factories, with others working in agricultural and domestic service. Many of these were immigrants. An 1887 Bureau of Labor study found that of 17,000 factory workers surveyed, 75 percent were of immigrant stock. Black women were also more likely to work; the 1900 census showed that 41 percent of all nonwhite women worked outside the home, while only 17 percent of white women were employed. The great majority of white women did not work outside the home: their proper work was considered to be that of homemaker and mother.

Most of those who worked before the 1940s were young, single, or poor. They were segregated into occupations that were defined as "work for women." Thirty percent were clerical workers, and many of the rest were in textile or food-processing factories. Of the few women who were professionals, three out of four worked in elementary-school teaching or in nursing. As one of the well-known historians of this era points out, there was a "woman's place" in the paid work force as well as at home. Not only was certain work considered women's work, but it was presumed that women should not be paid as much as men and that women should never be placed in a position competitive with or superior to that of men. There was almost no support for the employment of middle-class homemakers.

It was World War II that marked the real turning point in women's employment in the United States. In 1940, 25.6 percent of all women worked; by 1945, that figure had risen to 36 percent, as 6 million women entered the job market to take the place of men who had been called into military service. These women did not fit the stereotype of young, single, or poor. Women who entered the labor market at this time were married and over thirty-five. By the end of the war, it was just as likely for a wife over forty to be employed as for a single woman under twenty-five. At the end of the war, quite a few of these working women returned home to make room for the returning soldiers, but the boom in the economy enabled some in service and clerical work to keep their jobs. In spite of the "feminine mystique," which insisted that women should gain their greatest fulfillment as homemakers and mothers, many women— single and married—continued to work for pay outside the home. During the 1950s, the employment of women increased four times faster than that of men. By 1960, 37 percent of the women in the country were in the labor force, and 30 percent of these were married. By 1987, 56 percent of all women worked outside the home, including almost 56 percent of all married women, 61 percent of separated women, and 75 percent of those who were divorced.

One of the striking trends of female employment during the 1960s and 1970s was the increasing number of mothers who were working. The fastest rise of all took place in the employment of mothers with preschool children. From 1959 to 1974, the employment rate for mothers with children under three more than doubled, from 15 to 31 percent. By 1987, 56 percent of the mothers of children under six were in the labor force. While some of this rise was due to the need for greater family income, these young women also had more education and thus had greater job opportunities and changing sex-role attitudes to support their employment.

Although they were in conflict with the actual economic behavior of women, traditional attitudes about "women's place" persisted. William Chafe has stated that this gap between traditional attitudes and actual behavior ironically facilitated expansion of the female labor force. As traditional values were given lip service, women could enter the labor force "to help out" and were not resisted as crusaders who would change the status quo.

REASONS WHY WOMEN ENTERED THE PAID LABOR FORCE

There were many reasons why women continued to enter the labor force after World War II. Real wages rose and job opportunities in the service sector expanded as the economy boomed. Women were also getting more education, which made the type of working opportunities available more attractive. There was a slow change in gender-role attitudes as well, and by the mid-1960s the revival of feminism made it difficult to maintain the traditional view of women's place as being in the home. These changing attitudes influenced and combined with several demographic changes. Women began to marry later and were thus more likely to be in the labor force longer in their early single years. They also had fewer children, so that their last child was born sooner in their lives and they were freed from child care earlier to reenter the paid economy. As divorce rates rose, many more women had to rely on themselves for support.

Other demographic and technical changes also helped women enter the labor market. The move from rural areas to the cities made it easier for many women to find jobs. The development of many labor-saving devices (like washing machines and frozen foods) also meant that they could, at least theoretically, spend less time in housework and food preparation. In addition, the 1970s were a period of economic inflation in the United States. Families had gotten used to a higher standard of living, frequently maintaining a large home and two cars, sending children to college, and enjoying expensive leisure-time activities. It was difficult to maintain this standard of living with inflation and, as a result, there was more pressure for married women to enter the work force to provide a second income.

THE PRESENT PICTURE: PROBLEMS OF WORKING WOMEN

Salary Problems

In spite of increased employment, Supreme Court rulings, and affirmative action programs, women's salaries today still lag far behind those of men. If one looks at full-time workers, women still earn approximately 69 percent of what men earn. (White females earn approximately 67 percent of what white males earn; black females earn approximately 82 percent of what black males earn.) In comparing weekly earnings, men earn an average of $419 per week and women earn $290. Women are also more likely to work part-time so their earnings are even lower than the figures above. In addition, they are more subject to layoffs during bad economic times and they get fewer benefits like health insurance.

The salary figures are also skewed by the fact that most of the improvement in women's salaries has come in the professional and managerial occupations. Women have greatly increased their numbers in law, medicine, and a few other professional fields and the pay that these few women receive makes the picture look far rosier than it is. Women who are college graduates but have no professional training get less pay than men who have the same credentials, and the great majority of women (55 percent) are still clustered in clerical and service occupations where they receive low wages.

While differences in pay between black and white men have declined and differences in wages between black and white women have been virtually eliminated, the difference in earnings between all women and white men has remained virtually the same over the last twenty years.

Other Inequities

In addition to low pay, women in the labor force suffer from other deficits. The National Commission on Working Women, a Washington-based arm of the National Manpower Institute, surveyed 150,000 women and discovered that although wages were a major difficulty for many, other problems were also severe. The women complained of differentials in fringe benefits, no chance to train for better jobs, increasing pay differentials as men got promoted, sexual harassment on the job, inadequate child care facilities, the stress of the multiple roles of wife-worker-mother, and extremely limited leisure time. (Fifty-five percent of the professional women surveyed and 50 percent of the clerical, sales, and blue-collar workers said they had *no* leisure time!) These women wanted additional education but lacked the time and money to get it; they wanted job counseling but could not find it. Their husbands did not object to their jobs but were of almost no help with household chores. The women described themselves as frustrated, working in a dead-end job with no chance in sight for advancement or training. They felt underpaid, underutilized, and afforded little or no respect for the work contributed. Let us look at these wage and non-wage problems one by one.

The National Research Council of the Academy of Sciences completed an assessment of job discrimination for the Equal Employment Opportunity Commission in 1983. In this assessment, they tried to pinpoint the reasons for the differential between men's and women's wages. The factors they found that affect wage rates and other benefits basically divide into measurable parts: human capital inequalities and institutional barriers, with a third residual category of discrimination.

Human Capital Inequities.   According to human capital theory, some differences in earnings are due to inequalities in human capital, or characteristics of workers that enable them to produce more for the firm. Such characteristics would include education, experience, training, and commitment to work. Believers in this theory say that men usually have more human capital than women do and thus command higher wages.

There are many basic difficulties with this theory, including the fact that productivity is almost impossible to measure in some jobs, that wages may not reflect the entire reward paid for a job, and that we do not have an open, competitive market for all jobs (remember the "old boy" network). Beyond the basic difficulties, however, the statistics show that women get less return on investments in their own human capital than men do. For example, women with college educations get lower annual mean earnings than men who are high-school dropouts.

The major difference in the amount of wages accounted for under human capital is attributed to differences in work experience: overall work experience, on-the-job training, and the like. Women are less likely to get on-the-job training than men are, as employers may believe that women are less committed workers and will not stay with the company. Women are also less likely to have continuous work experience. They may enter their careers after child bearing or interrupt them to raise children.

Women are the losers when they drop out of market. One study that documents the gains from continuous work experience is the National Longitudinal Survey of the Work Experience of Mature Women, which interviewed a national representative sample of 5,000 women aged thirty to forty-four eight times in the ten-year period between 1967 and 1977. Women who worked continuously had real wage gains of about 20 percent, while those who entered and left employment were no better off in 1977 than they were on average in 1967. Even the women with continuous experience, however, got less of a return on their experience than men did.

Taking all these factors—education, on-the-job training, and continuous work experience—together, the National Research Council's report shows that only a relatively small percentage of the gap in salaries between men and women is explained by human capital factors. Other studies have shown a slightly larger percentage of the wage differential accounted for by human capital, but all current research believes that it accounts for less than half the gap in earnings between men and women. We must look elsewhere to find out why women earn so much less than men.

Occupational Segregation and the Dual Labor Market.   Other factors such as institutional barriers and job segregation seem to be more important than work experience in explaining the wage gap. One of the major reasons that women's earnings tend to be so low is that women are clustered in a narrow range of jobs. One-third work in clerical occupations. Another quarter work in the fields of health care (not including physicians), education, domestic service, and food service. Many of these jobs require higher than average educational levels (teacher, social worker, nurse) but pay low salaries. Few women have until very recently entered male-dominated professions, which are more highly paid. As of 1986, women were only 17.6 percent of the physicians, 4.4 percent of the dentists, 18.1 percent of the lawyers and judges and 6 percent of the engineers.

Job segregation by sex seems to be an important factor in wage differentials. If we look at the twelve major occupational categories—such as professional and technical, managerial, sales, clerical, and so on—we do not see much difference in male and female salaries, as the categories are so broad and job classifications differ markedly. When 479 job categories are used, however, studies show job segregation accounts for a substantial amount of the gap in earnings. In one study that used both human capital and job segregation variables, every additional percentage of females in an occupation meant that workers in that job got an average of about $42 less in annual income.

Fifty percent of employed women work in only 20 occupations. Wage differentials occur with job segregation because, by concentrating in only certain fields, women increase the supply of workers for these jobs and decrease their own wages. Economic theorists call this the *crowding theory*. In contrast, the short supply of engineers and physicians elevates wages in these male-dominated professions. Some of the jobs that have been designated for women are also contracting as a result of population trends and changes in our technology. Low-level clerks and secretaries may be replaced as word processing becomes more automatic. Elementary-school teachers are less needed as people have fewer children. Yet women continue to enter the jobs traditionally designated as female. As these fields become crowded, wages go down.

Are women restricted to these jobs? Socialization, training, and custom have made it difficult for women to enter male-dominated fields, although more are doing so. While there are some indications of change (women entering law and medicine, for example), occupational segregation by sex is likely to continue. It has hardly decreased at all among whites for several decades, although it has decreased substantially among minorities. Women seldom have the full information or mobility needed to choose jobs. Employers seldom have access to all possible employees and are also constrained by other factors, such as union agreements and agreements to promote from within.

Women are willing to take low pay and to enter occupations that may, in addition, have low status because most of these jobs blend well with the stereotype of being "feminine." Many of the jobs with the highest percentage of female workers are nurturing in nature (teacher, social worker, nurse). In addition, some of these jobs have fairly flexible hours, which may aid a woman in combining them with domestic responsibilities. The professions traditionally designated for men, such as engineering, business management, and medicine, may also require proficiency in mathematics or science, and women have been discouraged from taking courses in those areas. Thus, many women do not have the necessary prerequisites to enter those professions.

The Dual Burden Theory of Job Inequities

The concept of the "dual burden" proposes that whatever job women pick, their family duties will make it difficult for them to do the same work and reap the same rewards as men. A woman may have to choose between career and family responsibilities in a way that a man does not have to do. Women may be reluctant to work long hours or to choose jobs that mean travel because these things conflict with what they perceive as their responsibility to be the primary child rearer. Women may refuse promotions because of the added burdens that conflict with home responsibilities or because of the fear of equaling or exceeding their husbands' salaries. Women who try to integrate their work lives with their family lives may find that employers are reluctant to grant maternity leaves, resent time taken off to be with sick children, and generally believe that a woman's commitment to work is lessened if she becomes a mother. This employer perception may mean fewer promotions and lower salaries.

The plight of this dual burden has been summed up in Sylvia Hewitt's *The Lesser Life* in which she compares the traditional American workplace to the more enlightened Swedish version. It has also been the subject of a recent Diane Keaton movie, *Baby Boom*, in which a rising young female lawyer has to choose between a partnership in the firm and spending time with a baby.

Still more recently, the whole idea of the dual burden has been formalized by Felicia Schwartz in an article in *The Harvard Business Review*. She discusses the problems that women executives have in combining work and family responsibilities and suggests that corporations officially recognize these difficulties with flexible, slower-paced jobs for women. Women without children could still be on the fast track career path with men. Feminists of course have been horrified at the idea of a formalized "mommy track" and singling out women with child-care responsibilities for less favorable treatment in the business world. Yet Schwartz has been willing to discuss a very real problem shared by many aspiring career women. . . .

It is instructive to give some examples here as support for the theory of the "dual burden" being part of the reason for the wage gap between men and women.

Sylvia Hewlett in *A Lesser Life* points out

that the family responsibilities borne by women exert strong pulls that lead to a woman receiving lower wages. Employment that is broken for child rearing, the inability to put in overtime hours, or the decision not to travel for the company may make it difficult for a woman to get promotions. Hewlett shows that never-married women have complete wage parity with never-married men while the wage gap between married men and women is extremely large. For women to move up in the managerial ranks, they must frequently cut their family responsibilities, perhaps by deciding not to have children or even not to get married. More than 50 percent of managerial jobs are held by women who are childless and have continuous work histories. Hewlett believes that this dual burden of carrying family responsibilities in addition to a paid job affects women's salaries more than any other kind of discrimination.

She asserts that many highly educated professional women put their careers on hold, cut back to part time, or have various kinds of discontinuities in their work lives because of the problems of combining raising children and paid labor outside the home. She says that even for the superwomen who try to do it all, there is just not enough time and energy to equal that of male colleagues who are unencumbered with such tasks. She points out that in spite of the greatly increased number of women who work outside the home, recent studies show that American men still do less than 25 percent of all household tasks and that in the last twenty years, the time spent by married men on housework has only increased 6 percent. One study finds that the workweek of American women is twenty-one hours longer than the workweek of American men.

Hewlett points out that there is a catch-22 in the "dual burden" hypothesis. One of the reasons that men are unwilling to help more with the housework is that their wives tend to make less money than they do. Remember, resources often determine the power you have to decide to do work or have other people do it. Obviously, if women continue to do the lion's share of housework and raising children, they will not be able to work in a way that will give them good salaries and related family power.

The Residual Category of Discrimination

When men and women work in the same fields, men still make more money than women do. It is not just the nature of the job, but nature (sex) of the person that accounts for the difference in amount of pay. Thus, men who work in "women's" fields still earn $1,200 more annually than women do on the average, and in male-dominated occupations, men's salaries exceed those of women by an average of $2,400.

Segregation *within* professions may also mean different pay scales. Male computer specialists get $3,714 more than their female counterparts. In retail sales, women and men are often in subcategories that pay differently. Men are more likely to sell the big-ticket items like appliances or furniture, which consequently carry higher commissions.

In addition, certain firms within the same occupational category are more likely to hire male workers, and others are more likely to hire a greater percentage of female workers. Without exception, the firms that are larger and more prestigious are more likely to hire men and to pay them more money. We see this in law firms, accounting firms, and even in restaurants, where the more prestigious restaurants (where bills and tips are larger) hire only male table servers. More segregation occurs in this fashion than by a random hiring process. This difference among firms is believed to account for more of the wage gap than the difference in any particular firm in the jobs that men and women will take.

Even within the same firm in an occupational category, men and women are still likely to have different jobs. Even if they do not start

in different categories, promotions may soon serve to separate the sexes. One prime example of this situation occurred in an insurance company that was sued for sex discrimination. In this company, men were given "claims adjuster" jobs, and recruited women got jobs entitled "claims representatives." Each job required a college degree, yet not only were "claim adjusters" paid $2,500 more in wages than the "claims representatives" who did the same work, but only the adjusters could obtain promotions.

Thus, a differential exists between men's and women's wages that cannot be accounted for by the human capital or job segregation explanation. Reasons for this gap probably comprise various factors that we can lump under the terms *stereotypes* and *discrimination*. The proportion of pay differential attributed to discrimination is estimated to be approximately one-third of the gap between female and male earnings. When we talk about discrimination in this sense, we are not necessarily talking about an overt attempt to discriminate against women. We are also talking about the complex of customs, traditions, and understandings that lead to stereotyping and beliefs about who should do what work.

MYTHS THAT JUSTIFY DISCRIMINATION

Why would women in the labor force face such discrimination? To answer this question, we need to look at some of the stereotypes about women workers. One of the first stereotypes is that she is a secondary worker, that her income is a second income for the household, and that she does not really need the money. This myth persists in spite of facts that contradict it. The truth is that most of the women who work need money badly. (While all people who work need money as a basis of independence, a large percentage of working women need the money they earn as basic self-support.) Twenty-three percent of working women are single, and an additional 19 percent are widowed, divorced, or separated and are their family's main support. An additional 26 percent have husbands earning less than $10,000. Of course, whether or not women really need the money is not supposed to be an issue: if they do equal work, they should get equal pay. We do not usually ask whether a man needs the money when it is time to adjust his salary or to assess his promotion qualifications.

Women are also seen as workers who are not serious about their work and are less committed and reliable than men. Employers expect them to be absent more than men and are reluctant to invest in them because they may quit. There seems to be no time when a woman worker is freed from this stigma. When she is single, employers are afraid she will quit to get married. When she is married, they are afraid she will quit to have children or will follow her husband to a better job. If she already has had her children, employers are afraid she will be absent a great deal because of child-care demands; and if she is older and her children have left home, she may be considered too old and unattractive for the job. The actual facts are that women are not absent from work any more than men (which is rather remarkable considering that many of them do have primary child-care responsibilities). Women and men are both absent an average of five and a half days a year. While the overall quit rates of women are higher than those of men, women do not quit more from the *same* jobs. The job attachment of anyone in a dead-end job is less than someone in a career that offers opportunity for advancement. Men who are bank tellers quit as often as women who are bank tellers; men who are physicians are no more or less committed to their work than women who are physicians.

Employers also say that they do not promote women because people don't want to work for a woman boss, that women don't want the top jobs, that they can't handle responsibility, and that they are too emotional to be in management. The first two statements are probably true in many cases. Traditional gender-role stereotypes have dictated that women be dominated by men and not vice versa. Many people are uncomfortable when these stereotypes are reversed. Even women workers may accept the stereotype and not wish to be supervised by another woman. Sometimes they are accurate in their perception that "Queen Bees" who have reached the top are not eager to help other women up the ladder. In addition, women may not admit to wanting higher-echelon jobs because they know that the probability of their getting such a job is low and that to accept such a job may be to accept job responsibility that may conflict with home and family commitments.

Rosabeth Kanter has pointed out in *Men and Women and the Corporation* that women managers may also be put in a position where it is difficult for them to supervise and to help their subordinates advance. Some women may not want supervisory positions or promotions that entail additional responsibility, but in most cases this is because such a promotion means that they do not have enough time to handle family responsibilities or they fear the difficulties that may come in exercising authority if co-workers resent them. . . . Kanter also points out that a great deal of the interchange in higher-echelon professional or business positions depends on common understanding and values. Men often prefer to work with a *homosocial* group (a group of people who are alike in race, sex, approximate age, and socioeconomic status) because they believe such a group will share their values. Men may fear that someone of a different status who does not share their background will make working situations more difficult. In addition, many men are used to dealing with women only as secretaries or wives and may have a difficult time adjusting to dealing with a woman on a parallel level. Thus, for many reasons, women may not want to be managers and others may not want them in managerial positions.

SEX AS A STATUS CHARACTERISTIC

As we examine the facts about women workers, we begin to see that sex is a status characteristic. It is used as a category to discriminate at work and elsewhere in much the same way that other statuses such as race, religion, and age are used. It is the status of being a woman that influences a woman's career aspirations, hiring possibilities, promotion chances, and salary as much as the personal qualifications she possesses or gains through her education.

When we think of sex as a status, we can see that some of the discrimination against women is a matter of the upper-status group (men) retaining power and privilege. As the work and abodes of men have always been more prestigious than those of women, men may consciously or unconsciously fear the dilution of their power and privilege if women join their ranks. The resistance of all-male clubs like The Harvard Club to opening their doors to women is a case in point. Men may feel their status, and thus their masculinity, threatened when women advance to parallel or supervisory positions in the work force.

To get around this difficulty of status, organizations use various techniques (consciously or unconsciously) to keep women out of the mainstream of advancement and decision making. Women's jobs may be reclassified to a lower category or women may not be trained on the job as men are to be eligible for promotion. Women may also be shifted into fields that do not lead to higher positions, such as personnel jobs. (Personnel is usually considered an area that is a service function to the organization and those in it are not on the upward track.)

In the blue-collar areas, unions have blatantly discriminated against women. Women were formally barred from craft unions for many years, and even today requirements for membership may be difficult for women to meet. Union meetings may be held in halls or clubs where women feel uncomfortable going or at hours after work or in the evening when women have primary responsibilities at home. Harassment on blue-collar jobs may be overt and sexual; on white-collar jobs it may take the form of isolation, but the intent is the same: to show the woman that she should stay in her place.

In a more radical perspective on the relationship between job segregation and discrimination, Heidi Hartmann suggests that as industrial society developed, men could not as easily maintain the control over women's work that they had in the more personal preindustrial economic system. As jobs were more impersonal, control had to be more institutionalized. She postulates that such control was continued by segregating industrial jobs by sex, with women making less money or possibly unable to get any work at all. Because of this segregation, women were and are partially or totally dependent on men for support, and as a result they perform domestic chores for their husbands. Thus men maintain control at home and are aided in their jobs by having domestic support. They also get higher wages because the labor supply is limited by women remaining home. Capitalism benefits because men are defined as the primary breadwinners and must work long hours to support their "idle" or partially employed wives.

Hartmann concludes that one cannot change women's position in the economic system without changing their household roles and cannot change household roles without changing job segregation in the economic system. As it is not to the benefit of those in power to change the system, it is unlikely that the system will be changed without conflict.

Hartmann's inference that segregation of

jobs by sex and discrimination against women are deliberate devices to enforce women's dependency may not be accepted by everyone. Yet at the same time it is quite clear that occupational segregation by sex as well as conscious and unconscious discrimination accounts for a great deal of the discrepancy in women's and men's wages and does perpetuate women's secondary status as workers.

WOMEN IN BLUE-COLLAR JOBS

We want to look separately at women in blue-collar jobs because while they share certain kinds of discrimination with female white-collar workers, they also have unique problems of their own. In the late 1980s, women manual laborers who are employed in blue-collar industrial and service occupations comprise 38 percent of all employed women, or some 12.5 million women in all. Most of these women are white, but three out of five black women work in blue-collar jobs.

While women have gone from 4 percent to 18 percent of the lawyers and even from 0.8 percent to 6.8 percent of the engineers between 1960 and 1985, the proportion of women carpenters rose only from 0.03 percent to 1.2 percent in the same period. There are several reasons for that difference. There are two and a half times as many carpenters as doctors and the relative size of the crafts means that more women are needed to produce a similar proportion of females. There has been an expansion in the number of professional jobs while the number of craft jobs has not grown substantially. Access to skilled craft jobs is via union apprenticeship, and entry is difficult because of union discrimination against women. Masculinity and work are particularly interwoven in these blue-collar jobs, and women in them often face a great deal of resistance. They are often subject to sexual and other forms of harassment; they may be resegregated into jobs that are automated or due to be eliminated altogether.

PROBLEMS FOR BLUE-COLLAR WORKERS

Occupational Segregation and the Dual-Labor Market in Blue-Collar Jobs

As in the white-collar organizations, blue-collar jobs are sex segregated. Certain industries have traditionally hired women: garment industries, laundry establishments, assemblers of small electric equipment, operators in communications industries, beauticians, waitresses, hospital aides, and household domestics. When both sexes are employed in the same industry, men hold the more prestigious and higher-paying jobs. In the apparel industry, for example, men are the skilled cutters, pressers, and tailors, while women are the mass-production sewing machine operators.

The usual consequence of this segregation is lower pay for women. The women in industrial and service jobs earn about 60 percent of the men's wages. In addition, many of the industries in which they work have poor fringe benefits, unstable employment, and exploitative part-time work. Many of the industries in which women work are not unionized at all. While unions have not treated men and women equally, the wages of women in unionized fields is still somewhat better than the salaries of those in non-union areas.

Women have not recently rushed to labor unions to relieve their problems. We have seen that blue-collar unions have not generally been supportive of their female members. In particular, they have not supported wage equality for their female employees, and during periods of high unemployment, seniority demands and the desire to keep men on the job have taken precedence over any union demands for affirmative action. There are few women in leadership position who could change this situation. Yet union membership among women workers is slowly increasing. Women have recognized that ultimately in most—but not all—cases, unionization improves their wages.

Even the women in unions who get good wages face many difficult situations. They often face male co-workers' hostility and undesired sexual advances. The men seldom help them learn their job, although they readily help another man. Yet it is estimated that as much as 80 percent of some kinds of work is learned informally from others on the job. Manual jobs may also mean changing shifts and forced overtime, which wreak havoc with a working mother's child-care arrangements and family obligations.

Union women have become more aware of the fact that they must push their unions to work for benefits for female members. In 1974, 3,500 women formed the Coalition of Labor Union Women (CLUW) to attempt to put more women into union leadership roles and to work for affirmative action and legislation for women. One of the major thrusts of their action is an attempt to reclassify women's jobs so that they can get into apprenticeship programs and also receive higher wages. Many women's jobs are now erroneously classified at such low skill levels that they not only pay poverty wages, but their classification keeps women from getting training to move into better-paid employment.

BLACK WOMEN IN THE LABOR FORCE

Fifty-eight percent of all black women work, and they have traditionally been in the labor force in large numbers. Only Asian-American women have more paid workers than blacks, although as white women have entered the labor force in greater and greater numbers, their percentage is close to that of black working women.

Striking changes have occurred in the jobs and earnings of black women in the last two decades. Traditionally, the median income among employed black women was very low, with a large proportion of them working in domestic service and the less-skilled manual trades. The early textile jobs were usually closed to black women, as were clerical and secretarial positions. During the 1980s, however, nearly one-fourth of black women changed jobs and shifted into clerical occupations and the female-dominated professions. The shift in occupation caused a marked improvement in occupational prestige and in earnings as they became nurses, teachers, and librarians among other things.

Black women thus increased their earnings, and by 1987, they earned an average of 98 percent of what white women were making. They work harder and longer for the same pay, however. They are often still in jobs with lower occupational prestige and wages. They compensate by working longer hours and remaining in the labor force rather than interrupting employment for long periods while children are small.

Of course, there are many variations among black women workers. This fact is particularly clear in differences between age groups, where older black females are more likely to be in domestic and other service and the younger ones are more likely to be in the professions. As 54 percent of black women workers are also likely to be single heads of families or to have husbands who earn lower incomes, it is particularly necessary for them to work.

Differences also exist between black women and black men workers. By 1986, black women still had slightly higher educational attainment than black men, yet black women were earning only 62 percent of a black man's annual salary. Sex segregation again tells the story. Black women, like their white counterparts, are in the "feminine" and low-paid occupations. Black women are 79 percent of the black librarians, 97 percent of the black nurses and 78 percent of the non-college teachers. They are also 46 percent of the black professionals, but only 7 percent of the engineers, 14 percent of the lawyers and 24 percent of the physicians and dentists of their race.

One disturbing trend is the possible loss of

jobs for many black women. For young black women, clerical work is the dominant occupation, and they have been concentrated in the routine jobs like typing and filing. But many of these jobs are being eliminated with automation. Black clerical workers are also more likely to work for the government than private employers and may lose jobs through recent governmental budget cuts.

Thus, it is sex discrimination rather than racial discrimination that now seems to be the basic problem for black women workers. They approximate white women in labor force participation, occupational prestige, education and earnings.

ISSUES OF EQUALITY FOR MEN AND WOMEN WORKERS

Legislation

The revival of the feminist movement and the increased numbers of working women have interacted to generate concern about the differential between women's and men's wages and about sex discrimination in the marketplace. A spate of laws and court interpretations have resulted from women agitating for legal protection.

There are four basic measures that prohibit discrimination on the basis of sex. The Equal Pay Act of 1963 (Section 6d of the Fair Labor Standards Act of 1939, as amended) requires that employees receive equal wages for "equal work on jobs the performance of which are performed under similar working conditions." This act does not prohibit discrimination in hiring or promotions, however. It was designed to aid women who were doing work equal to that done by men but were being paid less. In 1974, the Supreme Court interpreted this act to mean equal pay in all remuneration from the employer, including fringe benefits such as medical insurance and pension plans. However, *bona fide* (proved to be legitimate) seniority and merit systems were exempted.

Title VII of the Civil Rights Act of 1964 prohibits discrimination by race, color, religion, sex or national origin in hiring, firing, promotion, training, seniority, retirement and all other aspects of employment. The act also prohibits classification of employees in a way that will deprive an individual of employment opportunities. It applies to employment agencies and unions as well as to business. Feminists lobbied strongly for inclusion of sex as one of the categories against which one could not discriminate. While there was opposition to doing this, those opposed finally allowed sex included as a category because they really wanted to defeat the entire bill and thought that including sex would cause that defeat. However, Title VII passed, and for the first time, women were given a legal basis for insisting that they be allowed to compete with men for jobs and promotions. Even then, the Equal Employment Opportunity Commission (EEOC) refused for some time to enforce the sex provision and allowed employers to advertise "male jobs" and "female jobs."

By 1966, pressure from feminist groups resulted in stricter enforcement of sex discrimination rules, and a 1972 amendment to Title VII (Title IX) expanded the law to include educational institutions and state and local governments, as well as employers with fifteen or more employees. Since 1972, the EEOC can bring suits against all those (except government agencies) who violate the act. Two executive orders in 1965 and 1969 extended prohibitions against sex discrimination to federal contractors and to the federal government, itself.

One other important piece of legislation was the Age Discrimination Employment Act of 1967, which prohibited government, private employers, employment agencies and unions from discriminating against persons between forty and sixty-five years of age. As many women had not been hired or were fired for being "too old" or "old and unattractive," this was an important protection for older women.

There have been major tests of all these laws. Various groups and agencies have taken cases to the courts to see if the laws would be judged to be in line with the intent of the Constitution. The particular court which hears the case uses a variety of legal "tests" to see if the law is, indeed, constitutional. For example, there is a limitation in Title VII that sex can be used to discriminate in jobs when sex is a "bona fide occupational qualification reasonably necessary to the normal operation of that particular business or enterprise." The courts have narrowly interpreted this provision, however, and in most cases have held that being a certain sex was not a "bona fide occupational requirement" for hiring. One example of a result was the decision that men as well as women had to be hired as flight attendants.

Pregnancy insurance and pension benefits have been other areas legally tested under the law. For a time, the courts ruled that pregnancy and childbirth disabilities should be covered by health insurance, but recently, they have ruled that normal pregnancy is not covered. The issue of pension benefits has never been legally resolved. Since women live longer than men on the average, insurance companies have regularly given them smaller monthly retirement sums than men—contending that the total sum paid would equal out over the long run. Women have contested these smaller payments but have not yet won their suits.

A final area of concern has been the problem of seniority. The last-hired and first-fired policies that operate under seniority mean that those usually laid off would disproportionately be minorities and women. Despite disagreement in the court system, an appellate court ruled that under due process "if present hiring practices were nondiscriminatory, an employer's use of a long-established seniority system to establish the order of layoff and recall of employees was not a violation of Title VII."

The 1980s and Affirmative Action

During the 1980s, the Reagan administration deemphasized affirmative action. In fact, it fol-lowed the premise that affirmative action amounts to unlawful reverse discrimination against white males. Boris and Honey state that "The Office of Civil Rights within the Labor Department now deals with enforcement in the context of reducing Government spending and resulting paperwork." Federal funds were cut and the Women's Bureau programs for displaced homemakers and new immigrants had to rely upon the private sector. Federal job creation programs were decimated. 300,000 workers were cut from **CETA** in 1981 and cutbacks in the Labor Department reduced staff available for implementation of affirmative action and wage and hour regulations. The Office of Federal Contract Compliance adopted a 'nonconfrontational' approach, emphasizing technical services for employers. It urged voluntary compliance, rewrote guidelines to eliminate claims and eliminated the need for small contractors to adhere to affirmative action guidelines. "It appeared to civil rights and equal rights proponents that vigorous Federal affirmative action programs and public employment programs belonged to the past."

It is noteworthy that the Supreme Court has not upheld the Reagan administration's affirmative action philosophy. The Court has consistently upheld affirmative action decisions of the lower courts provided they did not unduly harm innocent white males. It has, however, prohibited preferential treatment for Blacks during layoffs, preserving seniority rules in such cases. It has also forbidden rigid, permanent quotas as a mechanism to achieve affirmative action.

In a recent Supreme Court decision which was hailed as a major victory for women and Blacks the court stated that affirmative action violated neither the Constitution nor Title VII of the Civil Rights Act of 1964. In a case in Santa Clara County, California where a woman was promoted to the post of road dispatcher over a man who scored two points higher on a qualifying interview, the Court held that the agency had appropriately taken into account as one factor the sex of the applicants. Three justices dissented from the majority opinion: Byron White, William Rehnquist and Anthony Scalia, who was appointed by President Reagan.

The dissent by Scalia included a provocative paragraph in which he blamed the victims, in this case women, for their own fate. He said it was "absurd to think" that road crew positions were "traditionally segregated" job categories because of a systematic exclusion of women "eager to shoulder pick and shovel." They were male-dominated he said because they have "not been regarded *by women themselves* as desirable work." This approach of blaming women for their own labor-force segregation is one that has been more and more frequently used. In the case of the EEOC vs. Sears, Roebuck and Company, the court ruled in favor of the Sears Company on the grounds that women have *chosen* their part-time and poorer paying jobs as a way of balancing their home and family lives. Ironically, the female lawyer defending Sears against the EEOC claim used feminist scholarly works dealing with the segregated position of women in the labor force to make her case. The path pursued by George Bush has not been very different from that of the Reagan administration. While he has not as actively attempted to dismantle more affirmative action machinery, he has not pushed for enforcement of non-discrimination.

OTHER IMPORTANT WORK ISSUES

Family Leaves and Maternity Health Coverage

One of the problems that working women who wish to have children have had to face is lack of parental leaves and maternity health coverage. The United States is the only industrialized country that has no statutory maternity leave as such. Over one thousand industrialized nations have family leave policies, most of which are paid leaves.

Some corporations do offer their own maternity policies and the best are to be found in the large corporations. A 1981 survey of 250 large corporations found 88 percent offering some type of maternity leave usually 6 weeks paid and 6 weeks unpaid leave. However, only about 25 percent of all working women work in these large corporations. For the great majority, maternity leave with some financial benefits is only a dream.

Hewlett points out in *The Lesser Life* that fewer than 40 percent of the working women in the United States have maternity coverage.

Much of this coverage is provided under an Amendment to Title VII of the Civil Rights Act which states that an employer can no longer fire a worker solely because she is pregnant. Pregnant women are also eligible for the same fringe benefits as workers with other disabilities. This would seem to indicate the right to use temporary disability insurance for pregnancy, but the catch is that the federal government does not require employers to provide disability insurance. Only five states (California, Hawaii, New Jersey, New York, Rhode Island) require such coverage. Even this coverage only amounts to usually 6-10 weeks at partial wage replacement.

Attempts have been made to pass Family and Medical Leave legislation but these attempts have been thwarted by big business which balks at the cost.

Child Care for Working Parents

Child Care is another important issue for working women. Providing adequate child care and subsidies for such care are another way to deal with the "dual burden." Hewlett points out that the United States is far behind other industrialized nations in providing such care. Public day care centers in the United States provide approximately ten percent of the child care used by working mothers. About half of these centers cater to poor families and are publicly subsidized. However, the Reagan budget cuts have cut the funding for these centers 21 percent since 1980.

The other half are private day care centers and can cost from 80 to 200 dollars a week per child. While they have to make a profit to exist, many of these centers seem more interested in making money than in giving quality care. Low salaries for their staffs may keep the centers open but often means lack of qualified, consistent workers. By contrast, many other nations spend considerable amounts to provide for childcare for working mothers because they consider it a good investment in raising children who will be future citizens. France, for example, spends more than 4 percent of its Gross National product on subsidies to preschool children. Yet in the United States, there is decreasing public support for children. "Since 1980, an additional 3 million children have fallen into poverty. 700,000 poor children have been struck from the Medicaid rolls and 200,000 have lost their day-care subsidies."

IN SUMMARY

In summary, we see that women in the job market suffer lower wages and lower job status than men for a number of reasons. As a matter of choice or discrimination, they may not make the investment in their human capital that gives them access to the more prestigious and well-paying jobs. They are likely to enter jobs that are segregated, which pay less and many of which may be glutted in the near future. They are also discriminated against for a variety of reasons, which include myths and the weight of cultural tradition. As unequal pay "per se" is illegal, the means for this discrimination is usually to place women in different jobs of secondary status. Government laws and policies add to the secondary status of women workers. Thus, institutional discrimination against women (conscious or unconscious) means that they retain their status as secondary workers with unequal wages and job status.

Professional Women: How Real Are the Recent Gains?

Debra Renee Kaufman

Today there are just under 50 million women in the civilian labor force. Nearly 10 million women, or one out of every five of those employed, hold professional or managerial posi-

From *Women: A Feminist Perspective* 3rd ed. edited by Jo Freeman. Reprinted with permission.

tions. In law, medicine, postsecondary education, and business, the number of women has increased significantly during the last ten years. But the gains that women have made in the professions have been hard won and may well prove even harder to maintain. As Epstein warned in 1970, "No matter what sphere of work women are hired for or select, like sediment in a wine bottle they seem to settle to the bottom." What women are allowed to do remains limited, and barriers still restrict their mobility in the professional world. In professions that are as male-dominated today as they were a decade ago, women are still likely to be overrepresented in low-paid and low-prestige subspecialities. However, when men enter female-dominated professions, they usually rise to the top.

Society has various expectations of and beliefs about its professionals. It assumes that they will abide by a code of ethics in dealing with their colleagues and clients and that they will belong to a professional association entrusted with enforcing this code. Since professionals are considered best qualified to judge each other's work, they are expected to submit to the judgment of their colleagues. Professionals are expected to make decisions without pressure from clients, the public, or an employing agency. It is believed that professional work benefits the public.

In many respects, professionals represent the elite cadre of society's work force. Since professions carry a high degree of honor and status in our society, their members can expect greater rewards for their services. Professional prestige is partly attributable to the fact that professionals are highly educated. Their specialized training allows them to draw on a body of knowledge unavailable to lay people. The exclusivity of the professions is also a result of their legal right to exercise a virtual monopoly over the delivery of their service. Professionals are thought to derive a great deal of fulfillment from their work and to enjoy a high degree of autonomy. It is not clear, however, that professional women enjoy these advantages to the same extent as do their male colleagues. Even when women are willing and able to make the commitment to a professional career, most find themselves located in subsidiary positions within prestige professions or in positions that do not accord them the autonomy, prestige, or

pay customarily associated with the professional image (See table on page 151)

The table shows that, from the beginning of this century to the present, the professions have been clearly sex-segregated. Although comparable data cannot be obtained until the next decennial census of the United States is taken, there are clear indicators that the prestige professions remain male-dominated. In 1987, only 6.9 percent of the clergy, 19.7 percent of lawyers and judges, 19.5 percent of physicians, and 37.1 percent of college and university teachers were women. Conversely, the percentages of women who are social workers (65.6 percent), teachers except college and university (73.6 percent), registered nurses (95.1 percent), and librarians (85.6 percent) indicate that those professions remain female-dominated. Perhaps even more revealing about women's status in the professions is that the female-dominated occupations, although classified by the Bureau of the Census as professions, are often referred to in the sociological literature as the "semiprofessions."

We see that this distinction is more than academic when we realize that the term *profession* seems to be reserved for only those careers structured for the lives that men lead. Such careers are predicated on the notion that the professional is relatively free from child-care and home responsibilities. This permits great investments of time, energy, devotion, and "overtime" work, which are not possible for someone whose primary obligation is to a family. Extensive, difficult, and often expensive schooling is also required for the pursuit of such careers. "Continuity is usually essential," writes Oppenheimer, "and the freedom to move or to stay put, depending on the exigencies of the career, may be an important factor in whether or not success is achieved."

THE FEMALE-DOMINATED PROFESSIONS

While the female-dominated occupations, like other professions, require advanced education

Percent Female in Eight Selected Professions, 1900–1980

PROFESSION	1980	1970	1960	1950	1940	1930	1920	1910	1900
Physicians	13.4	9.3	6.8	6.5	4.7	4.4	5.0	6.0	5.6
Lawyers and judges	12.8	4.9	3.5	3.5	2.5	2.1	1.4	0.5	0.8
Clergy	5.8	2.9	2.3	4.1	2.7	2.2	1.4	0.5	3.1
Professors	36.6	28.6	21.9	23.3	26.5	32.5	30.2	18.9	6.3
Social workers	64.9	62.8	62.7	69.1	64.3	78.7			
Nurses	95.9	96.1	97.5	97.6	97.8	98.1	96.3	92.9	93.6
Librarians	82.5	82.0	85.5	88.5	89.5	91.3	88.2	78.5	74.7
Teachers	70.8	69.5	72.5	78.8	75.3	81.8	84.5	80.1	74.5

Sources: For 1980: *Supplementary Report from the 1980 Census of Population*, Table 1, "Detailed Occupations and Years of School Completed by Age for Civilian Labor Force, by Sex, Race, and Spanish Origin: 1980." PC80-51-8. For 1970: *Nineteenth Decennial Census of the United States*, Vol. 1, *Characteristics of the Population*, Part 1, Section 2, Table 221. "Detailed Occupations of Experienced Civilian Labor Force and Employed Persons by Sex, 1970 and 1960," p. 1–718. For 1960 and 1950: *Eighteenth Decennial Census of the United States*, Vol. 1, *Characteristics of the Population*, Part 1, Table 201. "Detailed Occupations of Experienced Labor Force, by Sex, for the United States, 1960 and 1950," p. 1–522. For 1940: *Sixteenth Decennial Census of the United States: Population: Comparative Occupation Statistics for the United States, 1870 to 1940*. Table 2, "Persons 14 Years Old and over in the Labor Force (except New Workers), 1940." p. 49. For 1930, 1920, and 1910: *Fifteenth Decennial Census: Population: General Report on Occupations*, Table 1, "Gainful Workers 10 Years Old and over, by Occupation and Sex, with the Occupations Arranged according to the Classification of 1930, for the United States, 1930, 1920, and 1910," Vol. 5, p. 20. For 1900: *Twelfth Decennial Census: Population:* Part 2, Table 91, "Total Persons 10 Years of Age and over in the United States Engaged in Each Specified Occupation (in Detail), Classified by Sex, 1900," p. 505.

and specific credentials, they often lack the authority, autonomy, and monopoly over a knowledge base that characterize the prestige and male-dominated professions. Oppenheimer suggests that the major female-dominated professions stand in direct contrast to the male-dominated ones:

All of [the female-dominated professions] depend on skilled but cheap labor in fairly large quantities . . . most of the training for them is acquired *before* employment, and career continuity is not essential. They exist all over the country, and hence mobility—or the lack of it—is not usually a serious handicap. Diligence and a certain devotion to the job are required, but long-range commitments and extensive sacrifices of time and energy are not necessary. Employment in most of these occupations relatively infrequently puts the female worker in a supervisory position over male employees, though she may be in a position of relative power over those outside the organization. Nurses, for example, may initiate action for patients, but their authority to do so is derived from the attending physician; furthermore, the authority and the task have a distinctly feminine flavor—that of the nurturing female. Social workers are often in power positions vis-à-vis clients, but these clients are not in the work organization and are in a notoriously poor position to effect changes anyway.[1]

While all women are affected by this pattern, black professional women are especially vulnerable. They are heavily concentrated in the lower-paying specialties in the female-dominated professions, serving black clients and generally poor and working-class people in the public sector.

Men assume the more respected positions of authority and power in female-dominated professions, positions quite consonant with societal views about men's "natural" roles. Male nurses, for instance, tend to be promoted to administrative jobs more frequently than are female nurses. Likewise, a 1987 survey of 3,577 public- and private-school administrators showed that men are more likely than are women to be superintendents and principals. Among teachers, women are more likely to teach at less prestigious levels of education than are men. In 1987, 98.4 percent of prekindergarten and kindergarten and 85.3 percent of elementary-school teachers were women, compared to 54.3 percent of secondary-school teachers.

THE PRESTIGE PROFESSIONS

Despite the increasing number of women earning doctorates, completing professional degrees, and entering the professions, the prestige professions and the prestige specialities within them still remain male-dominated. Medicine, law, academia, and science have a similar gender hierarchy.

Medicine

Throughout the first seventy years of this century, the proportion of women among active American physicians remained essentially unchanged, at around 7 percent. Many factors have contributed to this low percentage—from early gender-role socialization to discrimination in admission practices and polices of medical schools. However, in the last two decades, changes in federal law and in custom have helped women more than quadruple their enrollment in medical schools. In 1964–1965, 7.7 percent of the first-year medical students in America were women; in 1987–1988, 36.5 percent of them were women. In 1976–1977, women accounted for 19.2 percent of all those who obtained medical degrees in America; by 1985–1986, they made up 30.8 percent of those receiving professional degrees in medicine. As of 1987, women constituted 19.5 percent of all practicing physicians, and 27.0 percent of all medical residents in America.

However, it is after medical school that the recent gains women have made come into question. Female physicians, for instance, tend to concentrate in such specialities as pediatrics, psychiatry, public health, physical medicine (rehabilitation), and preventive medicine, while men concentrate in high-status and high-pay surgical specialities. Despite steady increases, women are primarily located in the less prestigious areas of the medical profession and earn less in each speciality. In part, this may be because men are more likely to practice in independent or group practices and women are more likely to be found in salaried positions.

Law

Women have made great strides in the legal profession, increasing from 22.5 percent of those receiving law degrees in 1976–1977 to 38.5 percent in 1984–1985. In 1987, 19.6 percent of all lawyers were women. The figure increases only slightly (19.7 percent) when judges are included. However, as with medicine, the gains women have made are tempered by the different career patterns women lawyers face compared to those of their male colleagues. While women have been able to enter areas formerly denied to them—such as small private companies, large corporate firms, law school faculties, and the judiciary—they are still heavily clustered in the less prestigious areas of family law, trusts and estates, and tax. Even their Wall Street advances from associates to partners must be interpreted with caution. Although more women are making gains in the profession, such advancements may have a different meaning now than they would have had earlier.

For women and minority associates, there is a greater chance of becoming partner, but that position may be a junior partnership bringing a proportionately smaller share of profits at the end of the year. It may also have less power and influence attached to it. There is some suspicion on the part of older women attorneys that this is the kind of partnership young women are likely to get as the firms are feeling pressed to promote their women associates. Although this is definitely a step upward compared to the past, it does not mean that women have "made it" in relation to men who are rising in the hierarchy.[2]

Academe

Many disparities exist between male and female professors. Academic women are concentrated in lower-ranked and nontenured positions; they work mainly in less prestigious institutions and fields; they are often segregated in areas with predominantly female student bodies; and, even within the same academic rank or category of institutional affiliation, they do not earn as much as men do. Even in traditional women's fields, men are more likely to be at the top of the professions within them. Men direct the libraries, schools of social work, and teacher-training institutions for elementary and secondary education. Outside of education departments, employment of minority women is virtually nonexistent in all types of schools.

Women in science and math fare particularly poorly compared to men in the academic world. For instance, women are twice as likely as men are to be on a nontenure track. For men and women first appointed to medical school faculties in 1976, 16.6 percent of the men are currently tenured, compared to 11.5 percent of the women. In addition, women are more likely than are men to be located in the lower ranks of medical faculties. If women are disproportionately on nontenure track appointments, and if such appointments are in the lower ranks, as the data suggest, it is not certain that women, over time, will achieve either professional security or equality in ranks with men.

Science and Engineering

In 1986, women accounted for 15 percent of the science and engineering work force, up from 9 percent in 1976. Women account for a larger share of employment in science than they do in engineering. For instance, in 1986, while more than one in four scientists was a woman, only one in twenty-five engineers was a woman. Again, as with the other male-dominated professions, women are not randomly distributed in science or engineering. Among women sci-entists, only 5.5 percent are in the physical sciences, and only 4.9 percent are in mathematics, whereas 25.3 percent are computer specialists. In engineering, women represent 3 percent of both mechanical and electronics engineers. The most recent National Science Foundation report states that salaries for women are lower than are those for men in essentially all fields of science and engineering and at all levels of professional experience. In 1986, the overall annual salaries for women averaged 75 percent of those for men. In that same year, the unemployment rate for women was about double for that of men.

Sokoloff suggests that a split is developing in the organization of law, medicine, and university teaching. Two sets of jobs seem to be emerging: those with high prestige, good pay, autonomy, and opportunity for growth, and those that are more routinized, poorly paid, and less autonomous. She also notes that shifts in sex segregation have been often followed by declines in earnings or career possibilities. Therefore, numerical growth may not offset segregation patterns within the professions. This has led some authors to conclude that desegregation in the male-dominated professions has not substantially changed the sex-segregation patterns within those professions.

In conclusion, there are fewer women in the prestige professions than there are men, female professionals generally still occupy the least prestigious specialities within those professions, and females earn less for comparable work. These facts suggest that women still face stern barriers to their entry into and advance through the professional ranks.

SEX-TYPING AND THE PROFESSIONS

Not only have the professions been segregated by sex, but also they have been greatly affected by the even more invidious process of sex-typing. When a majority of those in a profession are of one sex, the "normative expectation" develops that this is how it *should* be. The model of the practitioner then takes on the personality and behavioral characteristics associated with that sex. For instance, in my study of accountants, the quality most frequently cited for success and mobility by both young and old, male and female respondents was "executive presence." This term almost perfectly matches what is called in the sociological literature the *male managerial behavioral model*—characterized by aggressiveness, decisiveness, competitiveness, and risk taking. In fact, so identified is *male* with *manager* that one writer has stated:"The good manager is aggressive, authoritative, firm and just. He is not feminine." The high-status professions and the prestige specialties in our society are identified with the instrumental, rigorous, "hard-nosed" qualities identified as masculine, not with the "softer," more expressive, nurturing modes of behavior identified as feminine. Since the characteristics associated with the most valued professions are also those associated with men, women fail to meet one of the most important professional criteria: They are not men.

Research on the subject has clearly shown that traits customarily associated with femininity, and consequently with women, are not as highly valued in our society as are traits stereotypically associated with men. The belief in strong sex differences persists, although leading scholars clearly state that the overlap between the sexes on most personality and behavioral measures is extensive. Jacklin and Maccoby, for instance, in a thorough review of the subject, argue that whether there are sex differences in fear, timidity, anxiety, competitiveness, and dependence among young children remains open to debate because of insufficient or ambiguous evidence. They also assert that there is little scientific support for sex differences in such areas as achievement motivation, risk taking, task persistence, or other related skills. Yet these traits are typically associated with men in our

society and with the pursuit of a successful professional career.

Other studies have revealed a deep conviction in our society that men and women manifest different characteristics, as well as showing that there is a more positive valuation of those characteristics ascribed to men. Perhaps their most surprising finding was that even mental-health clinicians ascribed specific traits to each sex and agreed that a normal, healthy adult more closely reflects those traits ascribed to a healthy male than it does those ascribed to a healthy female. The clinicians portrayed healthy female adults as more submissive, less independent, less adventurous, less objective, more easily influenced, less aggressive, less competitive, more excitable in minor crises, more emotional generally, more conceited about their appearance, and more apt to have their feelings hurt. This childlike portrait led the authors to remark that "This constellation seems a most unusual way of describing *any* mature healthy individual."

Such stereotypes follow women into the work place. Even when women do the same work as men, they are not perceived as being as competent as men, and their work is not perceived to be as prestigious. In a fine and thorough review of the social-psychological literature on sex-related stereotypes, O'Leary notes that Feldman-Summers and Kiesler were unable to find a single occupation in which women were expected to outperform males, even in elementary-school teaching and nursing. Toughey emphasizes that anticipating greater participation by women in high-status professions has resulted in a decline in the way both males and females perceive the prestige of these occupations. However, the converse was found when men entered female-dominated professions. In a study by Bass, Krussell, and Alexander, 174 male managers and staff personnel perceived women as unable to supervise men and as less dependable than men. In another study of managers' perceptions of sex differences, particularly perceptions relevant to the promotion of women, Rosen and Jerdee found that male managers and administrators held uniformly more negative perceptions of women compared to men on each of four scales: aptitudes, knowledge, and skills; interest and motivation; temperament; and work habits and attitudes. Generally, women were perceived as having aptitudes, knowledge skills, and interests and motivations compatible with routine clerical roles and not managerial roles. In this study, virtually every perceived difference between male and female employees was unfavorable to women aspiring to higher-level occupations. On the other hand, Reskin and Hartmann cite other studies that suggest that negative correlations about women supervisors are weaker among women, well-educated males, and workers with female bosses.

In their study, Rosen and Jerdee found that males and females often were treated differently in their managerial roles. In a simulated situation, "supervisor" subjects promoted men more often, gave men more career development opportunities, trusted men more in handling personnel problems, and granted men leaves of absence for child-care duties less often than they did with hypothetical female counterparts. However, we need not rely on hypothetical supervisors to know that sex biases exist. Women earn less than men do for comparable work in almost every occupation and within almost all specialties. Perhaps the best indicator that women are less valued in our society simply because they are female comes from a number of studies documenting that women possessing the *identical* qualifications and skills as men fare more poorly in obtaining professional-type jobs.

The Fidell study in 1970 was particularly eye-opening for people at that time just entering graduate school and planning for an academic career. Fidell sent one of two forms to all colleges and universities that were offering graduate degrees in psychology in 1970. Each form contained ten paragraphs describing professional characteristics of ten hypothetical psychologists. The person most closely associated with departmental hiring was asked to participate in the study by judging the "candidates" and their chances of obtaining full-time positions. Form A used masculine first names; form B, feminine first names. Except for the names and pronouns, the wording on both forms was identical. Fidell found that men received higher levels of appointments; the positions were more likely to be on tenure track; and only men were offered full professorships.

Since the prestige professions are sex-typed, the expectations for men and women differ from the moment people make a decision to train for a career. As graduate students, women are not expected to be as dedicated, ambitious, or serious about their studies as men are. It is assumed that marriage and childrearing will eventually interrupt their studies and certainly their careers. The data suggest that such interruptions are indeed more disruptive for women than they are for men. In a reanalysis of a nationwide sample of graduate students, Feldman found that divorced men were unhappier with the graduate-student role than were single or married men, whereas divorced women among all graduate students were the happiest. He concluded that "apparently divorced men are burdened with greater responsibilities than their single or married counterparts, while divorced women have reduced their responsibilities and are thus freer to pursue the student role."

Such disparities persist beyond graduate school. Of the twenty-four women partners on Wall Street interviewed by Epstein, nineteen were mothers, and some had serious problems arising from motherhood. While marriage for most of Epstein's sample was not regarded as an impediment to career commitment, children were often perceived as a source of problems.

The full-time employed wife–mother bears the largest burden for managing the home and children. Her share of domestic activities is three times as great as that of her full-time employed husband. These findings may not simply reflect a generation lag: in Komarovsky's study of Columbia University male students, even the "liberated" males in her sample expressed concern about the combination of motherhood and career for their future wives. The majority of the men believed that home and child-care responsibilities were still primarily the concern of the wife–mother. Professional careers are designed not for women with families, but rather for men who are free of family obligations. For the professional man, frequent absences from home, tardiness for dinner, and "overtime" work are not only expected but also accepted as evidence that he is a good provider and therefore a good parent and spouse. Such is not the case for the professional woman.

Multiple-role conflict is but one area in which differences exist between men and women who pursue professional careers. Another difference has to do with the timing of that endeavor. Hochschild argues that age is measured against one's achievements. Getting there first is an important element of success. "If jobs are scarce and promising reputations important, who wants a 50-year-old mother-of-three with a dissertation almost completed?" Referring specifically to the academic arena, Hochschild states that "time is objectified in the academic vita, which grows longer with each article and book, and not with each vegetable garden, camping trip, political meeting or child." A successful professional career requires early achievement and uninterrupted competition for continued success—timing based on a male pattern.

In almost every particular, professional life is oriented more toward males than toward females. Because women are expected to behave in a generally "softer" way than are men, they may be perceived as unsuited for the combative style expected from many professionals. Even smiling might be bad for women's business careers because it is interpreted by male co-workers as a sign of submission. This is substantiated by studies suggesting that the way women talk, gesture, smile, touch, sit, walk, and use space communicates their dependent and inferior status in our society. Some feminists have openly challenged the "success ethic" and the values of the professional life, arguing for a more humane (if not feminine) style in the workplace. However, such changes demand a total restructuring of the attitudes and behavior now common in the professions and a redefining and revaluing of what is feminine. The incentives for such change are few, particularly in a tight economy, and, as the following section shows, change generally comes quite slowly.

HISTORICAL REVIEW

The discouraging picture painted in the preceding discussion still represents an improvement over the past. The professions at the top of the American occupational hierarchy—medicine, law, and higher education—began as medieval guilds from which women were virtually excluded. In the thirteenth century, European medicine became firmly established as a secular science, and physicians were trained in the universities. Since females were excluded from the universities, they were denied the key resource to become professionals. However, there was little that we would recognize as science in the late medieval training. Physicians rarely saw any patients, and no experimentation of any kind was taught. Medicine was sharply differentiated from surgery; the dissection of bodies was considered sacrilegious. In contrast, women healers of the same time, who were often labeled witches, had an experimental and empirical base to their healing. "It was witches who developed an extensive understanding of bones, muscles, herbs, and drugs, while physicians were still deriving their prognoses from astrology"; in fact, "Paracelsus, considered the 'father of modern medicine,' burned his text on pharmaceuticals, confessing that he had learned from the Sorceress all he knew."

The key point is that neither knowledge nor

techniques, nor results, defined the professional. What defined the professional was access to the universities. Society barred women from practicing medicine as professionals by denying them access to university training. By the fourteenth century, the church had explicitly legitimized the professionalism of male practitioners by denouncing healing without university training as heresy. Medieval writings on the subject asserted that "if a woman dare to cure without having studied, she is a witch and must die."

The development of the American medical profession was quite different, but the results were the same—women were effectively barred from the profession. By the early nineteenth century, there were many formally trained doctors—"regular" doctors, as they called themselves. At the same time, the Popular Health Movement and numerous other groups with new medical philosophies were establishing their own schools, which were open to women and to blacks. Frightened by these new movements, the "regulars" established the American Medical Association, in 1847, thereby asserting themselves as the only legitimate spokespersons for the medical profession. Noting that by definition a profession has authority to select its own members and to regulate their practice, Ehrenreich and English emphasize that the "regular" doctors were a formidable obstacle to women. The rare woman who did make it into a "regular" medical school faced a series of "sexiest hurdles" that only the most motivated women could manage:

First there was the continuous harassment—often lewd—by the male students. There were professors who wouldn't discuss anatomy with a lady present. There were textbooks like a well-known 1848 obstetrical text which states, "She (Woman) has a head almost too small for intellect but just big enough for love." There were respectable gynecological theories of the injurious effects of intellectual activity on the female reproductive organs. . . . Having completed her academic work, the would-be woman doctor usually found the next steps blocked. Hospitals were usually closed to women doctors, and even if they weren't, the internships were not open to women. If she did finally make it into practice, she found her brother "regulars" unwilling to refer patients to her and absolutely opposed to her membership in their medical societies. [3]

By the early twentieth century, "irregular" schools and their students were routinely closed out of the medical profession. Tough licensing laws requiring extended college and clinical training sealed the doctors' monopoly on medical practice.

Law, like medicine, began as a medieval guild and has been, until very recently, a male bastion. Women in law, until the last decade, have been "sex segregated in an occupational hierarchy: the lawyers and judges are almost invariably men, while the clerks, paralegal workers and secretaries who work for them are usually women."

It was even more difficult for women to enter the legal profession than it was for them to become doctors. The first woman to be admitted to the practice of law in the United States was Belle Mansfield in 1869. Less than one year later, Myra Bradwell was refused admission to the bar in Illinois solely on the basis of her sex. In the nineteenth century, the legal profession was more highly organized and protected by government than was medicine. Law schools did not admit women until the 1890s, and then did so only reluctantly. And after completing their studies, "even if women did achieve professional acceptance, they usually supported themselves through salaried positions, generally with insurance companies or government agencies, rather than through independent practice." Patterson and Engleberg note that even now women lawyers are still more likely than are men to turn to government positions. But what is more important, the authors find that when a man enters a government position, he uses it as a stepping-stone into private practice, whereas a woman tends to stay put, making it a career.

Prior to 1920, women's admission to law schools was not critical because preparation to practice law could be done by apprenticeships. In 1920, the American Bar Association officially endorsed law school as the desired preparation for the practice of the profession. But it was not until 1972 that women were finally admitted to *all* law schools. In addition, there has been evidence of "low quotas and higher entrance standards for women at many law schools."

The recruitment of women into the now female-dominated professions has had a different historical pattern. Shortages of cheap skilled labor—particularly during wars, recessions, and depressions—have accounted for a good deal of the recruitment of women into teaching and nursing. There were several advantages to using females as teachers. Women were available in great numbers and they were willing to work for low wages. Moreover, this profession did not challenge the cultural ideal of women's "natural" place. Who could be more "naturally" equipped to teach children than women?

Nursing, too, began as an occupation dominated by men. But, when the Civil War created a shortage of male nurses, women entered the field in significant numbers. The Brownlees contend that the transformation of nursing into a woman's profession did not occur until there was a "sustained entry of educated women who reduced wages below what productivity justified." These were, for the most part, educated women who had been closed out of the prestige professions. Ehrenreich and English, for instance, note that Dorothea Dix and Florence Nightingale did not "begin to carve out their reform careers until they were in their thirties and faced with the prospect of a long useless spinsterhood."

In nursing, female attributes seemed more important than competence or skill; good nurses were essentially ones who looked good and possessed "character." Ehrenreich and English suggest that the "ideal lady" of the nineteenth century was simply transplanted from home to hospital.

To the doctor, she brought the wifely virtue of absolute obedience. To the patient, she brought the selfless devotion of a mother. To the lower level hospital employee she brought the firm but kindly discipline of a household manager accustomed to dealing with servants.[4]

Nursing itself was hard labor; therefore, while the educators remained upper class, the practitioners were mostly working-class and middle-class women. When a group of English nurses proposed that nursing model itself after the medical profession, with examinations and licensing, Nightingale claimed that "nurses cannot be examined any more than mothers." The occupations of nursing and teaching were extensions of women's "natural" domestic roles.

KEEPING WOMEN DOWN: THE SUBTLE ART OF PRACTICING THE PROFESSIONS

How can we explain women's continuing secondary status within the professions? As we have seen, the prestige professions are defined primarily in terms of men and the lives they lead. The processes that maintain this male model are usually well beyond a woman's control, however committed or dedicated she may be. No matter what her personal characteristics, a woman is often assigned the stereotypical characteristics of her sex, and despite her efforts to transcend these stereotypes, certain structural features of the professions work against her upward mobility.

"Interaction in professions, especially in their top echelons," Epstein points out, "is characterized by a high degree of informality, much of it within an exclusive, club-like context." Hughes notes that the "very word 'profession' implies a certain social and moral solidarity, a strong dependence of one colleague upon the opinions and judgments of others." Those who bear certain characteristics (black, Jewish, female, etc.) are at an immediate disadvantage in such a collegial context. As Hughes suggested years ago, such statuses condition what is considered an "appropriate" set of characteristics for acceptance by one's peers as a professional; he describes these as "auxiliary characteristics." Such auxiliary characteristics as race, religion, ethnicity, and sex are "the bases of the colleague group's definition of its common interests, of its informal code, and of selection of those who become the inner fraternity." Hughes's fraternal imagery is apt; like fraternal societies, the collegial group depends on "common background, continual association and affinity of interest." Almost by definition, women and other low-status groups are excluded from such brotherly associations.

Professional "standards of excellence" allegedly establish the criteria for recruitment and advancement in one's field. Excellence, however, like any other social reality, is not universally manifest, but must be defined and interpreted. As Epstein notes, fine distinctions between good and superior performances require subtle judgments, and such judgments are rendered by one's peers. In many ways, one's acceptance into and success within the professions are contingent on one's acceptance into the informal circles.

The professions depend on intense socialization of their members, much of it by immersion in the norms of professional culture even before entry; and later by the professional's sensitivity to his peers. . . . Not only do contacts with professional colleagues act as a control system, they also provide the wherewithal by which the professional may become equipped to meet the highest standards of professional behavior.[5]

Those who do not conform because they lack important "auxiliary characteristics" create dilemmas for themselves and for others. For example, the protégé system is one of the mechanisms whereby one's name and work become known in the upper echelons of one's profession. According to Epstein and White, the men who dominate the top echelons of most professions may be reluctant to adopt female protégés.

White claims that "a man . . . may believe that she is less likely to be a good gamble, a risk for him to exert himself for, or that she is financially less dependent upon a job." The man may also fear others' suspicion of a sexual liaison as a byproduct of such close and intense work. Although it is not unusual for a senior executive to be a mentor to a rising male star, this acceptable practice immediately becomes suspect if a young female receives it. A lack of sponsorship means a woman is more likely to be excluded from those crucial arenas where professional identity and recognition are established.

Collegial contacts are important for more than one's professional identity and acceptance into the profession. Social psychologist White interviewed women scholars at the Radcliffe Institute who had been awarded fellowships to continue their professional interests on a part-time basis while raising their families. The women thought that access to stimulating colleagues was as important as was the opportunity to be intellectually engaged in a project. White concluded that "appraisals of their work by others, coupled with acceptance and recognition by people whose professional opinions were relevant and appropriate, made a significant difference in determining whether a woman felt like a professional, and whether she in turn had a strong sense of commitment to future work." Furthermore, she suggests that "challenging interaction with other professionals is frequently as necessary to creative work as is the opportunity for solitude and thought."

Collegial contacts are also crucial for survival.

There are elaborate social systems in all parts of academic and business life, and purely technical training is rarely enough. The aspiring young scientist must be knowledgeable about many aspects of institutions, journals, professional meetings, methods of obtaining source materials, and funding grant applications. Knowing how to command these technical and institutional facilities requires numerous skills, many unanticipated by the young student. . . . This is the kind of learning we speak of as "caught," and not taught, and it is a valued by-product of acceptance and challenging association with other professionals.[6]

If women are excluded from male networks, they remain not only marginal but also invisible when such important professional decisions as selection for promotion, tenure, research grants, coeditorships, summer teaching, and departmental privileges are under consideration. My research suggests that women academicians are less likely than are men to include people of higher rank in their collegial networks, and are more likely to claim their colleague-friends as professionally unimportant to their careers.

It is within the collegial arena that judgments are made and standards are set. It is within the collegial arena that the ongoing dynamics of professional life are carried out. If women are denied access to this arena (even if they have formed their own networks), they are left out of the power centers of their professions. Moreover, their exclusion from male networks prevents the breakdown of myths about professional women. If women and men operate in different networks, gender-role stereotypes remain unchallenged.

CONCLUSION

How real are women's most recent gains in the professions? Despite their increasing numbers in male-dominated professions, women still constitute a disproportionately small percentage of those practicing the professions. Moreover, even in female-dominated professions, women are second to men in that their positions tend to carry less prestige.

Perhaps the most difficult task in assessing women's gains is measuring the "cost" of success. Even when women have been able to achieve high-pay, high-prestige positions within the professions, the costs for such success have been high. Many have had to give up or delay marriage, family, and significant relationships. Those who have not given up family have had to add to their demanding career commitments the major responsibilities of managing home and child-care tasks. In our society, both families and professional careers are "greedy" institutions. Until changes occur, women who want both can expect to face conflicting and overwhelming demands. Moreover, until we change the normative expectations about a woman's place both within the professions and within the home, so that both demands and rewards are equal to those of men, we must continue to question the gains women have made.

NOTES

1. Oppenheimer V.K., *The Female Labor Force in the US*, University of California at Berkeley Population Monographs, No. 5 Berkeley; University of California Press (1970).

2. Epstein, C. *Women in Law*, New York: Basic Books (1981).

3. Ehrenreich B. and English D. *Witches, Midwives and Nurses*, Old Westbury, NY: Feminist Press (1973).

4. *Ibid.*

5. White, M., "Psychological and Social Barriers to Women in Science," *Science* (1970) 413–416

6. *Ibid.*

Women and Creativity

Simone de Beauvoir

I am going to speak to you again today about the condition of women, because it seems to be just as burning an issue here in Japan as it is in France. I want to approach the subject from a particular angle. The question I would like to examine is the following: throughout history, it is clear that the achievements of women in every sphere—politics, the arts, philosophy, etc., —have been, in terms both of their quantity and of their quality, inferior to the achievements of men. Why? Could it be, as the anti-feminist lobby claims, that women are by nature inferior and therefore incapable of attaining the same level of achievement as men? Or is it the socially determined condition of women, confining them as it does to an inferior position, that influences their ability to act? Clearly, I am of the latter opinion and I would like to explain why. There is a famous woman novelist whom I greatly admire, and with whom some of you are particularly familiar; her name is Virginia Woolf. In one particular sphere she has furnished an answer to the same question I am asking today. She asked herself why it was that, in the literary sphere, works by English women were so rare, and generally of inferior quality. And in an admirable little work entitled *A Room of One's Own*, she provided the answer, very simply and in my view very correctly. The first thing necessary in order to be able to write is to

have a room of your own, a place to which you can retreat for a few hours; a place where, without risk of interruption, you can think, write, reread what you have written, criticize what you have done, be left to yourself. In other words, the room is at one and the same time a reality and a symbol. In order to be able to write, in order to be able to achieve anything at all, you must first of all belong to nobody but yourself. Now, traditionally, women are not independent, but rather the property of their husbands and their children. At any moment, their husbands or their children can come and demand explanations, support or assistance, and women are obliged to comply. Women belong to the family or the group; and not to themselves. And in such conditions, writing becomes, if not an impossibility, then at least a very difficult task indeed. Virginia Woolf takes Shakespeare as an example. She imagines what would have happened if instead of Shakespeare, exactly in his position, an extremely talented little girl had been born. She shows that it would have been virtually impossible for her to create anything at all. She would have stayed at home, learnt to cook and to sew, got married and had children; it is absolutely inconceivable that she would have had the education Shakespeare had, that she would have become an actor and a playwright; she would not have been Shakespeare; she would have been a nobody. In *The Second Sex* (1949), I myself attempted a similar analysis with reference to Van Gogh. I tried to show that

From *French Feminist Thought*, edited by Toril Moi. Reprinted with permission.

had a girl been born instead of Van Gogh, she would not have had the same opportunities; experiences such as his life in the Borinage mining district, the social contacts which allowed him to develop his ideas and his personality, all the ensuing events in his life. In short, I totally agree with Virginia Woolf; our conclusions are exactly the same: however gifted an individual is at the outset, if his or her talents cannot be exploited because of his or her social condition, because of the surrounding circumstances, these talents will be still-born. Stendhal has expressed the same thing—great feminist that he was—in a particularly striking phrase:"Every genius born a woman is lost to humanity."

Just so, you will say; that is how things were until relatively recently. But for the past twenty years or so, women have had the same opportunities as men; they can vote, they can enter the profession of their choice, and yet we have not seen much in the way of great achievements by women. True. But what I want to show is that it is absolutely fallacious to claim that the opportunities of men and women have been equal over the last twenty years. I intend to show you exactly why they are not.

Let us begin by looking at the question of women's careers—something which I touched upon in my previous lecture, but which I would like to return to now from a slightly different angle. It is certainly true that there are indeed women lawyers, women doctors, women engineers and women architects; and yet all the famous names in France, in the areas of law, engineering, medicine and architecture, are men's names. Why? Is there something about women that means they are doomed to mediocrity? Let us look at the issue in a little more detail. Firstly, as I said the other day, only a tiny number of women actually enter these professions. Now there is a statistical law which states that the larger the group, the more likely it is that one of its members will be exceptional. If I take at random, all things besides being equal, one hundred medical students on the one hand,

and a dozen on the other, and if I am asked in which group there is likely to be found a great doctor in the making, *a priori* I would place my bet on the group of a hundred. I would have a ten to one chance of winning. It is an elementary truth, but one too often ignored. In all these areas there are far fewer women than men, and so it is infinitely more likely that in these professions a man rather than a woman will achieve something exceptional. Secondly, there is a major obstacle in the way of women in every profession, one which prevents them from progressing beyond a certain point: they do not earn as much money as men, they are not given the same level of office or the same official positions; and more importantly, or so it would seem to me, they do not succeed in acquiring the same talents. Talent is not something you are born with, any more than is genius. It is something which is acquired by dint of effort; if you have to face up to difficulties, and if you struggle to overcome them, you are forced to excel. If you confine yourself to doing things which are easy, you manage only to acquire a certain facility. If, as a result of anti-feminist prejudices, people refuse to refer difficult disputes to woman lawyers, difficult cases to woman doctors, women will never have the opportunity to show their true ability. To show your true ability is always, in a sense, to surpass the limits of your ability, to go a little beyond them: to dare, to seek, to invent; it is at such a moment that new talents are revealed, discovered, realized. Now, such opportunities are denied women. They themselves are reluctant to venture into difficult areas. Firstly, they are tied down by the various forms of domestic drudgery I mentioned the other day. They have a variety of things to worry about; they are obliged to concern themselves with things other than their careers; they have to divide their time between their professional and their domestic lives. Consequently, they dare not contemplate launching themselves into anything too arduous. And it is here, I believe, that we come to the crucial issue. Women themselves, insofar as they attempt to achieve anything, never do so with the same audacity, with the same confidence as men. They see themselves as doomed from the start because they know that society will not give them a fair chance. What point is there in even trying to practice as a GP or become a famous psychiatrist or specialist, when you know that you will have neither the necessary backing nor the necessary number of patients? So, very wisely, you settle for gynaecology, or paediatrics, or social medicine; you accept the minor posts which your male colleagues would not touch, because you think that in any case you would only break your back over your work if you were more ambitious. This has in fact happened to many women, thus providing the others with a discouraging example.

Besides, given all the things I have just mentioned—the small number of women who actually work, the fact that working women are still viewed as something of an exception—women's ambitions automatically become more limited than men's. I was very struck by the reaction of a young female film director, in the days when this profession was still exclusively male. I asked her about her ambitions, her plans. And she replied: "Oh, it is already quite hard. Even to be a female film director in France is unusual enough. If on top of everything else I had to be a major director, it would be too much!" She was quite happy just to be a director, even a mediocre one. Her ambitions were limited both because she never imagined that she would have the means to make major films, and because for her it was enough, given the situation, to be able to make minor ones.

Finally, there is another reason which encourages women to settle for very little: given women's double role, given that the woman who works also wants to have a happy life, a lover, a successful home, she finds it advisable to take a back seat on the professional plane. A man has the advantage that the better a doctor, a surgeon or a lawyer he is, the more attractive he is considered to be; his wife admires him and is happy for him. A woman who is too successful however, risks upsetting, annoying, humiliating her husband. She does not dare. When, twenty years ago, I visited a number of women's colleges in the United States, I spoke to some students who seemed, judging by their conversation, to have the potential to go far; and yet their tutors told me that they only handed in mediocre work. So I asked them why? Many of them told me quite frankly:"Well, we have to avoid getting really bad marks, or people will think we are stupid; but if our marks are too good, people will think that we are pedantic or intellectual, and nobody will want to marry us. We want to do as well in our studies as possible without making marriage impossible." I have found similar examples amongst married people. I had a friend, younger than myself, who was preparing for the *agrègation* in philosophy. So was her husband. My friend only had one thing on her mind, that she might pass and her husband fail. And, in the end, although she was perfectly well prepared, she went all out to fail while her husband passed. The couple are happy enough, but the young woman still has some regrets, because she feels that she could have been more successful in her professional life. There are many such cases in the France of today. One could argue, then, that the professional mediocrity of women can be explained by a wide range of circumstances which are a product not of their nature but of their situation.

Let us now turn to the sphere with which this lecture is principally concerned, artistic and literary creativity. You will doubtless say to me that the individual here is much less dependent upon others than in the case of a more conventional career. Bosses and clients are not an issue. A woman who stays at home has plenty of free time. She has much more time to create, to realize her ambitions, than the man who spends his days at the office. Why does she not make better use of her freedom?

First of all, let us ask ourselves why, throughout history and right up to the present day, we find so few women painters or sculptors. Let us try to look at their situation in detail. We will see at once that the same factors come in to play as in the case of a career. A boy who wants to be a sculptor or painter rarely gets much family support; he more or less has to struggle throughout his long apprenticeship as painter or sculptor. But for a woman the situation is even worse; people think she is mad; she is told to do something more lady-like, typing or dress-making for instance. Only very rarely do women manage seriously to undertake an apprenticeship as a painter or a sculptor. Here again, statistics have a part to play: the fewer women there are who attempt to become either painters or sculptors, the fewer there will be who produce great works of art. And then the obstacle that I mentioned before is also a factor here, because these are occupations which in fact require considerable amounts of capital. Maintaining a studio, obtaining plaster or marble, tubes of paint and canvasses—these things cost money: such occupations therefore require a considerable amount of financial support. True, this support is sometimes provided by friends or family; but they will only provide it for a man, not for a woman. Remember the support Theo Van Gogh gave to his brother, providing his keep throughout his life and thus allowing him to become a great painter—it is hard to imagine a brother or father doing the same for a sister or daughter. They would not have enough confidence in her; they would find the idea abnormal; there is not a single recorded example of this actually happening.

Moreover, in order to make money, the backing of art dealers and art collectors is essential. Now I am reasonably well acquainted with the art world, and I know for a fact that art collectors and dealers will not back a young woman. They justify their stance by arguing that she will get married and give up painting; or, if she is already married, that she will start a family and give up painting; or, if she already has children, that she will have more children and give up painting. They always assume that the time will come when a woman will give up and, therefore, that she is a bad investment. In reality, such rationalizations disguise a much less rational train of thought; what they are really thinking is:"She is a woman, therefore she cannot be very talented." Thus they deny her the means to develop her talent and to prove that she has some; which amounts to reinforcing the same old prejudice: she is a woman, therefore she cannot be talented.

In addition, the difficulties a woman has to face if at the outset she is unable to earn a living from her art, are quite terrifying. A young man who has to struggle to make a living as a painter, who leads what is called a bohemian existence, who lives in squalid accommodation, who is badly dressed, who has no social position, who hangs out in a variety of cafes, is viewed as an artist. He is categorized, and accepted; his eccentricity is evidence of his vocation, proof of his talent. If a woman adopts the same life-style, the cost is much greater: not to have a nice home and decent clothes are things which blatantly contradict the traditional self-image inculcated in most women. It must be understood that every woman, however emancipated, is profoundly influenced by her education and her upbringing. So a woman will hesitate; many will not have the courage to lead such a life; and the one who does will find herself scornfully pointed at in the streets, viewed not as an artist, but as a madwoman or a monster. It takes much greater courage for a woman to accept such an existence than it does for a man. And then again, if she gets married and has a family, it is virtually impossible for her to continue to work. I know many young girls who had started to paint, and who then had to give up because such an occupation required eight or ten hours' work per day, and so much time simply could not be found at the same time as assuming the roles of housekeeper, wife and mother. At a stretch, if the husband is extremely well-disposed, his wife will still be able to sculpt or paint, provided she has no children. But this is a very serious decision for a woman to take; for many women the obligation to choose between motherhood and a creative career entails a bitter struggle. Men do not have to make such a choice; they can easily be fathers, have a home life, a wife and family, a full and successful emotional life, and still be artists.

There are some determined women who choose to give up everything else, in order to paint or to sculpt. But they use up so much energy in the process, it takes so much to resist the pressures of public opinion and to overcome their own internalized resistance, that they find themselves much less free in their work than the man who is spared all these difficulties. Now freedom [*disponibilité*] is one of the conditions most necessary for what we call genius to flourish. In order to achieve the highest levels of creativity one has to set one's sights exclusively on this goal, in complete freedom and without any disturbing external worries. There is a very important artist whom I knew very well and whom I greatly admire; you have no doubt heard of him: Giacometti. His life-style was quite extraordinary. Even when he was earning a lot of money, material concerns mattered so little to him that he lived in a sort of hovel which let in the rain; he caught the water in bowls which were themselves full of holes; water ran across the floor, but it was all the same to him. He had a tiny, extremely uncomfortable studio in which he worked throughout the night; he slept when it suited him, normally from about five or six o'clock in the morning; at mid-day he would get himself dressed any old how; a string served as a belt to hold his trousers up; his hands were covered in plaster. He didn't give a damn and everyone else found it quite normal that he should choose to live like that; he was an artist; anything was permissible; and in particular, his wife accepted this kind of existence. So he had absolutely no worries, other

than his sculpture. It does not take much imagination to realize what would happen to a woman who tried to follow the example of Giacometti: she would be locked up, or at least treated as if she were mad. It is impossible to imagine a husband adapting himself to this sort of life-style; he would become a social outcast. And in fact the woman herself would refuse to lead such a life; she would not find within herself the supreme sense of freedom which Giacometti felt. And for that reason, while there are women sculptors in France and women painters—and even some whom we rate as artists of considerable merit: Germaine Richier, Vieira da Silva—we have none who has attained the heights of a Giacometti or a Picasso. And here we come to the crucial point which should enable us to understand why in a sphere which seems so readily accessible to women, the literary sphere, women remain, save for a few exceptions, inferior to men. The internal conditioning of women is much more important in explaining the limitations of their achievements than the external circumstances which I have dealt with up to now.

With literature we come to the sphere where the anti-feminists appear to have the most trump cards. In effect, while a young girl of eighteen lacks the rudiments of sculpture and frequently even of painting, every young girl belonging to the privileged classes has been schooled, and often to quite an advanced level, in the art of writing. Literature is not something which is foreign to her. She has read books, she has written dissertations, essays and letters; she knows how to speak, how to express herself; she has in this sphere just as solid a background as her brother. Moreover, it is much easier to sit in a corner at a table, with pen and paper, than to obtain a studio, canvas and paints.

Yes, at first sight, things look promising for the woman who wants to write. There are of course some women who live in the sort of conditions Virginia Woolf described, without a room of their own. But there are others who, once their children have grown up—and even sooner in the case of the more well-to-do who generally have a certain amount of domestic help—have time to themselves; it is neither lack of training nor a shortage of time that prevents their achieving something. The best proof of this is that there are plenty of women who do write. Of the avalanche of manuscripts received by French editors each year, a third are written by women. I know from experience that women have the time to write because I myself receive a large number of manuscripts sent by women who, having nothing else to do, decide to embark upon a literary career. Why is it then that of this number there are so few that amount to much? And amongst those that are of some worth, why is it that so few are really first-rate?

The first reason is that—contrary to the beliefs of those women who write because they have not got anything else to do—it is not possible to become a writer just like that. Writing is a vocation; it is a response to a calling, and to a calling which normally makes itself heard early in one's life. There are exceptions, vocations discovered late in life, as for example in the case of Jean-Jacques Rousseau. But in the end, for the majority, it is something rooted in the individual from childhood. Mozart's vocation was clear from the age of five, Flaubert's from the age of nine, and I could cite numerous other examples. Now, in relation to this, everything conspires to encourage the young boy to be ambitious, while nothing encourages the young girl to be likewise. In order to want to write, that is to say to want to refashion the world in a particular way, to want to take responsibility for it in order to reveal it to others, you need to be incredibly ambitious. Ambition is something which is encouraged in a male child, by virtue of the fact that he belongs to the superior caste. He is told, right from the start: "you are a boy, you must not act like that: you are a boy, you must do well at school: you must not cry, etc."; an ideal of virility is held up before his eyes right from the start, its purpose being to encourage

him constantly to excel. The young boy is taught to excel himself. Moreover, psychoanalysis informs us that for the young boy the Oedipal complex takes the form of love for the mother, coupled with violent rivalry with the father. He wants to equal his father, to surpass him even. The seeds of ambition are thus sown in him by virtue both of his education and of his spontaneous emotional responses. Moreover, this social demand placed upon him leads to a somewhat tragic impression of abandonment and solitude. He is required to stand out from the crowd, to do better than his peers; he feels himself to be alone; he is afraid, crushed; he feels what in existentialist terms is called *abandonment* and he feels it with anguish. Now one of the things which has driven the vast majority of artists and writers to create, is precisely a refusal to accept this abandonment, this anguish. Simultaneously ambitious, and feeling himself to be contingent and abandoned, the young boy has every reason to want to "do something," and in particular to want to create, to write.

In the case of a little girl the situation is completely different. She starts classically by identifying with her mother who, in the majority of cases, is a traditional woman, a relative being, a secondary being. She thus learns to identify herself with a relative and secondary being; in her games, her fantasies and her myths, she dreams of herself in such terms, which amounts to denying or suppressing all ambition. Later, she identifies to some extent with her father. But at this stage, when the Oedipal complex develops in her, when she begins to view her mother as a rival and to come to be more or less in love with her father, she is already eleven or twelve years of age; she is already accustomed to being modest; she loves her father humbly, seeing herself as inferior to him, not even contemplating the idea of trying to be his equal. All she wants is to be his disciple, his shadow, something very modest by comparison with what he himself is. And since she loves her father, if the latter, like most men, has a traditional view of women, if he wishes his daughter to be a devoted wife, a devoted mother, a woman of the world, an accomplished home-maker, she will keep in check whatever little bit of ambition she might have, and will choose to be a successful mother. Moreover, because she lacks ambition, because she thinks of herself as a relative being, she feels protected by society; she is not required to stand out, to be self-supporting. She thinks that throughout her life, first her family and then her husband will look after her; she feels less abandoned than the little boy, and suffers much less the anguish of existence, and thus she has less need to transcend or to refashion the world into which she is thrown. She feels less need to produce a work of art; she is more conformist than the boy, and conformity is the very antithesis of creativity, which has its source in the contestation of the existent reality. So, for all these reasons, little girls have a creative vocation far less frequently than little boys.

Some do, however; and though this is something which I do not have time to dwell on here, I think it would be interesting to discover what the particular conditions are which cause certain women to discover within themselves, at an early stage, the vocation to be a writer. In looking at a number of cases, one thing has struck me: that in the case of most of the women who have had a vocation to write, they have been spared the identification with the mother; or at least they have had a father who was ambitious for them, and who pushed them to write. A striking example of this is the case of Virginia Woolf herself. In her early childhood, her father treated her as if she were a boy; he transferred on to her all the ambitions which he would have had for a son. She was always encouraged to write; she became the writer she was in accordance with the wishes of her father. I was very interested too, when reading about your great writer, Murasaki Shikibu, to discover references to the figure of her father in her

childhood memories. She tells how when her brother was studying Chinese he had difficulty learning the Chinese characters, while she was able to master them very quickly indeed; and her father said what amounted to: what shame that she is not a boy! This is no more than a pointer, and she does not go into much detail about her childhood, but it is a pointer which I found very interesting because it suggests that at the origins of this great work written by a woman—the greatest work in the world, I believe, written by a woman—there was, from early childhood, a paternal presence. It is not something that I have time to develop; that would require a detailed and nuanced study. I simply want you to recognize and understand that talent and genius are the result of a vocation; and that this is not something which is generally fostered in a woman, whereas, in contrast, everything in the education of the young boy conspires to cultivate it in him.

Let us now turn to the situation of the adult woman; what we find is that to a certain extent her situation is a favourable one as far as the production of a literary work is concerned, but only to a certain extent. In order to create, as I was saying earlier, it is necessary to want to reveal the world to others; consequently, one must be able to see the world, and in order to do so one must attain a certain distance from it. When totally immersed in a situation, you cannot describe it. A soldier in the midst of the fighting cannot describe the battle. But equally, if totally alien to a situation, you cannot write about it either. If somebody were to try to provide an account of a battle without having seen one, the result would be awful. The privileged position is that of a person who is slightly on the side-lines: for example a war correspondent who shares some of the risks of the fighting forces, but not all, who is involved in the action, but not totally; he is best placed to describe the battle. Well, the situation of women is akin to this. As this world is a man's world, the important decisions, the important responsibilities, the important actions fall to men. Women live on the side-lines of this world; they have contact with it only through their private lives, through men, in a mediated rather than an immediate way; they have a lot more free time than men do, and not just the time but also the internal disposition which permits them to watch, to observe, to criticize; they are used to being spectators, and this is a privileged position for anyone who wants to write. Here again, I will take the example of your great writer, Murasaki Shikibu. She was wonderfully well placed to write the great novel she wrote, a novel which provides the most extraordinary picture imaginable of court life at the beginning of the eleventh century. She lived at court, she was what we in France call a lady-in-waiting, and was very close to the empress; and yet she did not have the same kind of responsibilities as a man would have had, she was important neither as an official, nor as a soldier or minister; she was not required to act. She was party to the action, without participating in it. This was a privileged position, and it is thus not so surprising, when you stop to think about it, that it was a woman rather than a man who wrote the tale of Genji. I would compare her to a woman whose work is considerably less important, but who means a great deal to us in France, and whom we greatly admire: Mme de La Fayette. She too, a few centuries later, described the manners of the French court in a novel. She described them with considerable skill as an observer, with much talent and perspicacity; Mme de La Fayette, too, was connected with the court without, however, having any role to play in it. She was admirably well placed to be able to provide us with a picture of its manners and customs. Thus women, situated on the side-lines of society, are well placed to produce works of literature; and that is why there are a large number of important and successful works by women.

Nevertheless, in the case of both these women whom I have just likened to each other, there is one thing which strikes me; both remain fundamentally in agreement with the society of their time. Murasaki Shikibu, for example, goes to great lengths to tell us: I am a woman, so I do not speak Chinese. It is a lie, but she does not want to be seen as a pedantic blue-stocking; from time to time, moreover, she stops to say: I will not tell you these stories, it is not suitable for a woman to do so. In fact she plays, with great charm, by the way, the part of a traditional woman, of a woman who knows nothing, who tells a story as if by chance, but who has nothing of the pedant about her, who still conforms to the traditional image of a woman. The same is true of Mme de La Fayette, who in no way challenges the moral code and manners which she describes. She approves of them. The inequality which exists between men and women in their sexual and conjugal life is approved by her, at least in her novel. And that is why I said that women are well placed to describe the society, the world, the time to which they belong, but only to a certain extent. Truly great works are those which contest the world in its entirety. Now that is something which women just do not do. They will criticize, they will challenge certain details; but as for contesting the world in its entirety—to do that it is necessary to feel deeply responsible for the world. Now women are not responsible to the extent that it is a man's world; women do not assume responsibility for the world in the way in which great artists typically do. They do not contest the world in any radical way, which is why, throughout human history, women have never been the ones to construct major religious or philosophical or even ideological systems; to do so you must as it were make a clean sweep of all the things that are normally taken for granted—as Descartes did with all knowledge— and start from scratch. And given their situation, women are just not capable of doing that!

People will doubtless protest that all that is fine as far as women in the past are concerned, but that for women of today the situation is totally different. Women ought now to be able to take charge, to feel just as responsible for the world as men do. They should be able to contest it in just the same way, to demolish it in order to rebuild it differently. But this is not the case, because we must not underestimate the importance not only of their education but of the total context in which women's lives are inscribed, a context which remains the same today as it was in the past.

Women are conditioned, let me repeat it, not only by the education which they receive directly from their parents and teachers, but also by what they read, by the myths communicated to them through the books they read—including those written by women—they are conditioned by the traditional image of women, and to break from this mould is something which they find very difficult indeed. Women often write while remaining locked up in their private world, confined within the little universe which belongs to them: they write more or less to kill time, and in France there is an extremely unkind word used to designate these sorts of books: they are called ladies' fancy-work [*ouvrages de dame*]. And in effect, very often you get the impression that women write for the same reasons that they embroider or paint water-colours, to pass the time. Some display a certain amount of talent, that is to say, they describe reasonably effectively their own little closed and limited world; their books have a certain charm, they are read with a certain amount of pleasure, but they are of little real significance. In addition, the factors which I mentioned earlier with reference to women's careers—their timidity towards men, their fear of upsetting the tranquility of their home life if they are too successful—also play a part in this sphere. I remember a young woman who brought me a manuscript which was not at all bad; I told her that with a little more audacity, a little more confidence in herself, and a little more effort, she would be able to produce a good book. She replied:"Yes, I'd like to write a good book; but deep down I don't think I would dare: my husband is quite happy that I write in

that it keeps me at home; I do not go out; I do not flirt; all that is fine, but if I were successful, then I don't know what would happen to my marriage." I have seen other women who have written successful first books and then left it at that, because their success created difficulties between themselves and their husbands. Evidently, we are talking here about women whose vocations are not very strong. But who knows what they might have achieved had they not been hindered from the outset by a series of external considerations which had nothing whatsoever to do with literature.

Of course all women are not like this. Some reject the traditional image; they try to produce works which make considerable demands of them, works of considerable importance. They devote themselves to their writing. In France today what matters most to some women is to write, everything else is subordinated to this goal; their everyday life is organized around this basic point; in addition they are interested in the world, they are involved in social and political activities, they are the equal of many male writers, as far as their way of life and their achievements are concerned. Nevertheless, in none of them do we find what I would call a certain extremist quality, because they are all haunted by the myths of femininity. To return to the example of Giacometti; there was something crazy about him when he declared that he wanted to "wring the neck of sculpture"; it was in a sense an excessive ambition, which might seem arrogant if it were not for the fact that it was simultaneously an act of faith and a challenge to himself. When Giacometti talked about "wringing the neck of sculpture" it was beautiful because by this he meant several things: "I believe I can produce statues of a kind never before produced, resolve problems never before resolved; otherwise sculpting or painting would be pointless. The failures which are an integral part of every life's work, I will do away with them." But this act of faith was at the same time a challenge to himself, and what he really meant was: "I will not content myself with any of the busts I have carved, any of the statues I have sculpted so far, even if the whole world finds them worthy of admiration, even if I am paid thousands for them; that is not what I want. I demand more; I expect much more of myself." Such incredible faith and such exacting personal standards are characteristic of only five or six figures each century; and special conditions are necessary in order for them to blossom, to bear fruit, and the first of these conditions is to be a man. Women do not have enough faith in themselves, because others have not had faith in them; neither do they make the most extreme demands of themselves, which alone allow the individual to attain the greatest heights of achievement. For want of such exacting standards, women lack the infinite patience which Buffon described as the essence of genius. These qualities are denied them not by virtue of any flaw in their nature, but by virtue of the conditioning they have undergone.

In conclusion, therefore, I would say that many people have a totally erroneous view of the nature of creativity. They conceive of it as some sort of natural secretion; the artist, the writer, will produce works of art just as the cow produces milk. Women's nature is such that it denies them this fertility. In truth, creativity is an extremely complex process, conditioned by all aspects of society. It is clear, therefore, that as the circumstances are totally different for men and for women, and the condition of women inferior to that of men, thus giving them fewer opportunities, their achievements will be fewer as well. One really cannot claim that, given equal opportunities, women do less well than men, since opportunities really are not equal, nor have they ever been, and nowhere in the world today are they even remotely so. Perhaps the twenty-year-old women of today will astonish future generations, but we cannot tell today. What is certain, however, is that their mothers and grandmothers were conditioned by traditional models. The twenty-year-old women of today may perhaps produce works of art which in terms both of their quality and of their quantity will rank alongside those of men. It is hard to tell, since up to now equal opportunities have never existed. And if I stress this point, and if I choose it as the subject for my lecture, it is because we are caught in a vicious circle from which I want women to escape. When they are constantly told that women in the past achieved nothing of any great or lasting value, it is in order to discourage them; what is being said is basically: be sensible, you will never achieve anything of any real value, so don't waste your time trying. And given the enormous weight of public opinion, women are all too easily convinced. I want them to realize that it is not like that; that it is because they have not had a real chance that they have not done more; that if they fight for greater opportunities they are at the same time fighting for their own achievements. Women must not let themselves be intimidated by the past because in this sphere, as in all others, the past can never give the lie to the future.

The Job of Housewife

Barbara Bergmann

To be a housewife is to be a member of a very peculiar occupation, one with characteristics like no other. The nature of the duties to be performed, the method of payment, the form of supervision, the tenure system, the "market" in which the "workers" find "jobs," and the physical hazards are all very different from the way things are in other occupations. The differences are so great that one tends not to think of a housewife as belonging to an occupation in the usual sense. It is sometimes said that a housewife "doesn't work." The truth is, of course, that a housewife does work, does get a reward for her work, and not infrequently gets fired or quits. One dictionary defines an occupation as "an activity that serves as one's regular source of livelihood." Being a housewife is an activity that gets one food, clothing, and a place to live. It certainly meets the dictionary's definition of having an occupation.

By tradition and by law, the housewife is not counted as working for an "employer." The reward she gets for her work is not legally defined as a "wage." That reward may be access to goods and services rather than cash. This arrangement has implications for her status, her sense of independence, and her participation in planning the family budget. Because she has been considered to be merely an economic and social appendage of her husband, she was never

From *Economic Emergence of Women*, Chapter 9. Reprinted by permission.

taxed as other workers. Her old-age support was not arranged on the same basis as that of other workers.

In the era when all women were expected to spend their mature years as housewives, when almost all men maintained housewives, and when divorce was uncommon, none of this was thought to merit comment or was considered a problem. Now, however, we are in a transition period in which about half of the married men maintain housewives while the other half have employed spouses. The housewife's pay, taxes, postdivorce support, and provision for old age raise policy questions that paradoxically get more insistent as the housewife occupation dwindles. In some respects, housewives are gravely disadvantaged. In other respects, families with housewives are given extra advantages that families with two earners are denied. The way the tax and Social Security laws treat the housewife need examination and reform. The postdivorce situation of women who have been long-term housewives needs to be improved.

The proportion of adult women who report themselves as engaged exclusively in keeping house has been dwindling throughout this century. But even in its dwindled state, the housewife occupation is very large. In fact, it is still the largest single occupation in the United States economy. In January 1986, a total of 29.9 million women in the United States (or 32 percent of the women aged sixteen years or over) described themselves to the census taker as "keeping house."* By comparison, workers of both sexes in professional and managerial occupations—physicians, nurses, lawyers, teachers, engineers, social workers, business executives, government officials—amounted altogether to only 26.4 million. Workers of both sexes in clerical and allied jobs amounted to 17.5 million.

A housewife is a married woman who holds no paid job and who works within the home performing services for her own family. She may also contribute some unpaid volunteer work. But her principal attention is to child care, food preparation, housecleaning, laundry, grocery shopping, and a host of other chores and errands. Many if not all of these services will be performed whether the family maintains a housewife or not. However, a family that maintains a competent person devoted full time to performing these services generally benefits from having them performed well and carefully and in a timely manner. A one-earner family has a higher standard of living than a two-earner family with the same money income because of the family's greater enjoyment of high-quality services.

While the advantages of having a housewife in the family are considerable, so are the disadvantages. Most obviously, the family loses the money income that the person serving as housewife might contribute to the collective budget. There are other disadvantages, concentrated on the shoulders of the person playing the housewife role. A housewife works alone, or with only the company of small children, and many housewives are, as a result, extremely lonely. The husband of a housewife, with his monopoly of direct access to money, has the opportunity to be tyrannical. Sometimes, he acts violently toward her. He may desert, leaving her unprepared to earn a good living. For all these reasons, the housewife occupation is one of the most problem-ridden in the economy.

---

* In January 1986, 468,000 men reported that they were not in the labor force because they were keeping house.

Being a housewife is no longer a lifetime vocation for most women. Many of the women who tell the census taker they are not in the labor force because they are "keeping house" are taking a temporary spell in the housewife occupation. The shorter the time a person spends as a housewife, the less severe the problems are likely to be. When looked at objectively, the long-term housewife's occupation turns out to be one of the riskiest, both physically and financially. But even short spells as a housewife can produce severe disadvantages.

The housewife usually is thought of as outside the economy. Housewives' services are not included as part of the gross national product, and housewives lack cash payments designated as wages. But there certainly is an economic side to the housewife role. The nature and value of the productive services delivered by the housewife, the nature and value of the pay, and how these get set raise issues worthy of examination.

While there has been some agitation to include housewives' services in the gross national product and to pay them cash wages, the important issues of public policy with respect to housewives lie elsewhere. The treatment of the "displaced homemaker"—a person who has been a housewife for a long time but whose "job" has ended through separation or divorce—is a national scandal. Another set of important policy questions, debated in the Congress every few years, is the treatment of the housewife and the employed wife in matters of taxation and Social Security. Present laws favor the housewife-maintaining family in important ways and penalize the family with an employed wife. Another issue concerns the wisdom of encouraging women to assume the housewife role after the birth of a baby, by instituting generous maternity-leave policies.

THE DUTIES OF THE HOUSEWIFE

"The hand that rocks the cradle rules the world," goes one attempt to persuade women that they should rest content with being housewives. At the other extreme, John Kenneth Galbraith has called the housewife a "crypto-servant." Both of these are irritating ideas, probably intentionally so.

Many of the housewife's duties are those of the servant, and the servant job is the one closest to the housewife's in the money economy. Unlike the servant, the housewife is a family member and therefore partakes to some degree in whatever deference is due to the bank account, class position, and occupation of the husband. She also partakes, as a servant does not, of whatever luxury the husband's salary affords in living space, food, clothing, and entertainment. She does have more discretion than a servant ordinarily has, and she may have the management of the family's finances in her hands. In some respects the housewife's working conditions are more onerous than the servant's: The housewife works seven days a week and is on call twenty-four hours a day for the service of the whole family.

Personal relations are important in a regular job, but they are a much more important part of the housewife's job. The children she takes care of are her own. The housewife's relation to the husband, including their sexual relation, is a factor in her ability to keep her position as wife. Of course, the feelings of love that the housewife and her husband may share enhance the marriage and may make the performance of her work "a labor of love." Yet sexual relations are notoriously changeable in their tenor. If they go sour, the housewife may lose her position. The connection between the economic and the sexual means that the housewife's economic security is hostage to personal whims.

To continue the servant analogy, female servants in the nineteenth century, and probably throughout the course of history, had sexual duties to the father of the house and possibly to the grown sons as well. This was certainly true if they were slaves or indentured servants. These days, good servants are rare, and if unwelcome

attentions are forced on them, they can quit and go elsewhere. Only the prostitute and the housewife now have jobs in which a requirement to engage in sex relations is part of the duties. In any other job, the imposition of such a requirement is considered sexual harassment and is outlawed under the Civil Rights Act.

The sexual part of the housewife's job has become more crucial with the advent of easy and frequent divorce. When marriage was understood to go on until death, falling out of love, or meeting someone you liked better was considered no excuse to end it. In the present era, even an excuse is unnecessary. There are some other jobs besides the housewife's where a person performing competently in the technical aspects of the work will be displaced because the boss develops a sexual desire for another person. But surely, the best ones do not have that characteristic.

A great deal of what we are saying about the housewife also applies, to some degree, to many of the wives who have paid jobs. Most do housework seven days a week, in addition to their paid job. The majority of them have wages that are considerably lower than their husbands'. For a woman in that situation, the continuation of the marriage allows her to have a far higher standard of living than she could achieve independently. In this sense, she, like the housewife, gets part of her livelihood by being her husband's wife and doing whatever is necessary to maintain that status.

THE HOUSEWIFE'S MOBILITY PROBLEMS

The housewife has problems in moving from one job to another that exceed those in other jobs. For most people it is easier to move from one job to another within the same occupation than to change occupations. But the housewife, unlike nurses or carpenters or secretaries or economists, cannot search overtly for other vacancies of a similar type while occupying her present "job." For that matter, even after it has ended, she cannot search overtly for another "meal ticket"—her search must be presented to herself and to others as a search for love. If anything, her experience as a housewife is a hindrance in finding a new spot in the same profession. She now counts as secondhand merchandise, with some expensive appendages—her children by her previous husband—trailing after her. She is no longer as young as she was.

In short, gaining another housewife berth with a new husband is not easy. A survey by the Census Bureau in 1985 found that 35 percent of women who had ever been divorced had not remarried. Of those who did find new partners, the median interval between divorce and remarriage was 4.6 years.

If the housewife wants to move into another occupation—namely, a paying job—the similarity of the duties of the housewife and the duties of the servant create difficulties. Apparently most employers do not consider the experience of the housewife to be valuable in performing paid jobs. Of course, this attitude may grow out of sexism. An equivalent set of duties attached to a man's job might well be thought of as valuable experience, possibly for some managerial jobs.

The nature of the financial arrangements of housewife-maintaining families creates difficulties for the housewife if she wants to "quit her job" by quitting the marriage. It may be difficult or impossible for her to accumulate a cash reserve that would carry her through until she finds some other source of livelihood, usually a job in another occupation. If she can make such an accumulation, it may have to be done by stealth. The "live-in" feature of the housewife's job increases the difficulty of quitting by increasing the size of the cash accumulation needed to change jobs. In most other occupations a person who quits a particular job does not have to move out of his or her living quarters at the time of the quit. Such a person usually can live for a while on the goodwill built up with the landlord and on the stocks of staples in the kitchen.

To the financial difficulties of quitting a marriage must be added the formidable logistical difficulties—finding new residential quarters and arranging to move there. A housewife's lack of credit in her own name may also create problems at such a time. We are speaking here of the difficulties of a transition for the housewife from her present job to some other way of getting a living. The longer-term prospects are not good, either, principally because most of the high-paying jobs are marked off for men.

PHYSICAL HAZARDS

It is estimated that about 14 million women are injured in the home each year. Accidents are not the only source of injury. Large numbers of women are the victims of intentional violence from their husbands. A survey found that 4 percent of women living with a husband or male partner at the time of the survey had in the previous twelve months been kicked, bitten, hit with a fist, hit with an object, been beaten up, threatened with a knife or a gun, or had a knife or gun used against them. Nine percent of the women said that at some time in the past they had been victims of those kinds of abuse from the man they lived with. If we include what the survey characterized as less severe forms of violence—having something thrown at them, or being pushed, grabbed, shoved, or slapped—then 10 percent of the women reported violent abuse in the previous twelve months and 21 percent had at some time experienced it.

Police officers have not considered a husband's violent behavior against his wife to be a crime. If called to a home on a complaint of violence, apparently most police officers consider that the appropriate course of action is to conciliate the matter rather than to arrest the husband and charge him with a criminal offense. Many men, including many police officers, believe that men have the right to beat their wives. A housewife will lose her economic support if her husband has to spend time in jail, and this makes judges reluctant to jail battering husbands. Beaten-up wives themselves worry about this. A housewife often refuses to press charges, or withdraws them if they have been pressed. This kind of behavior reinforces police officers' attitude in refusing to make arrests.

There has been considerable speculation about why wives continue to live with violent spouses. Some have argued that such wives derive a masochistic enjoyment from being hurt, or feel that they have deserved punishment. Whether this is true or not, there is very likely an economic aspect to the wife's behavior. Such a woman will have no immediate way to make money, and is likely to have young children whom she feels she must keep with her and whom she would have to feed and shelter. She may not have relatives in the same city with extra space and money they would be willing to put at her disposal. To such a woman, the difficulties of leaving a violent husband may appear insurmountable. There is literally no place for her to go.

Feminists have opened up an offensive against wife-battering by bringing lawsuits against municipal authorities in cases where the police have failed to protect women from their batterers. Where permanent injury has been sustained, multimillion-dollar judgments have been obtained, and these will certainly motivate authorities to indoctrinate police officers to behave more aggressively against batterers than they have been wont to do in the past.

Feminists also have begun organizing shelters for battered women in many cities throughout the United States. These serve as a place of resort for a woman and her children with nowhere else to go. From the shelter, she can apply for welfare and look for a job and a place to live. The shelter movement has received some financial help from the federal government. Recently there has been an attack on the shelter movement from the religious right wing on the grounds that shelters are "antifamily" and "rest and recreation centers for tired housewives." Those who attack shelters want to shore up the husband's authority in the family and

apparently believe that the right to administer physical punishment to his wife is necessary or helpful to the maintenance of that authority.

MEASURING THE ECONOMIC VALUE OF THE HOUSEWIFE

The housewife's activities result in the production of a great many excellent things: meals on the table, clean rooms, clean clothes, and children cared for. We can arrive at measures of the value of the housewife's services by drawing on the obvious parallels between her activities and similar productive activities in the market economy. However, as will become apparent, there is more than one way to arrive at a measurement, and determining which method is the best is no simple matter.

There is no housework task that does not have analogies in the commercial economy. For food preparation and cooking, there are restaurant meals. For housecleaning, there are paid cleaners. For transportation of family members, there are taxis and chauffeurs. There are commercial laundries. The people who perform these tasks for pay are, of course, covered in the U.S. government's tally of production and income, the gross national product accounts. Yet the productive value of the unpaid housework by family members is not covered. Why is that?

The accounts, which were set up for the United States in the 1930s and 1940s, were envisaged primarily as a device for measuring levels of production and income generation in the money economy. Certain items not traded for money did get included, but housework services were not among them. Originally housework may have been excluded from the national income accounts because the changes in the amount performed were thought to be small and to lack relevance to policy. Sexism may also have played a part, considering some of the nontraded items that room was found for, such as the food grown by farmers that is eaten on farms.

These days, however, when catering to the self-image of housewives is considered good politics both on the right and the left, it probably is the valuation problem that has kept housework from being part of the gross national product. No less than three alternative methodologies suggest themselves for valuing housework. However, any of them if adopted might prove embarrassing to the statistical agency.

One way to estimate the value of the housework performed by a housewife would be to equate it to the salary of a full-time servant. This method of estimation probably would be considered to be in bad taste and certainly would not endear the statistical agency to housewives and their partisans. A major purpose of putting housework in the gross national product is to add dignity to the status of housewives, so such a methodology is worse than useless.

A second method of valuing the housewife's productive contribution goes to the opposite extreme. It involves listing the activities of a housewife and finding the specialized occupation in the money economy that is closest to each one. The list that proponents of this kind of measure get together usually includes cook, dishwasher, chauffeur, cleaner, interior designer, nursemaid, dietician, laundress, and so on. The housewife's time at each activity is then valued at the appropriate specialist's pay scale. Many of the occupations cited are mostly male, and many of them are high-paying, in part because women frequently are excluded from them. Housewives work long hours, so this method can easily produce an estimate higher than the average male salary and two to three times as high as the average pay of a woman working at a full-time job. The Chase Manhattan Bank published an estimate based on this method for 1972 that came to a value of $257.53 for a 100-hour work week. In that year white males employed full time averaged $172 and white females $108.

A third methodology would equate the value of housework to the wage the housewife

herself could earn on a full-time job. This method gives a different value to the housework of the college graduate and that of the high-school graduate, despite the fact that they may be doing identical housework.

Given the problem of measuring the housewife's contribution to the national economy, it certainly is no wonder that the economists and statisticians who compile the national economic accounts have been slow to include those contributions. However, those who are pressing for their inclusion might ask themselves how much real benefit would result.

Up to this point, I have emphasized the similarities between housework and services available for purchase in the money economy. However, a word ought to be said about the differences. Oscar Wilde rightly spoke against those who know the price of everything and the value of nothing. What is it worth to have one's own mother devoted to one's care twenty-four hours a day? On the other hand, what is the true cost of living for and through others, of giving up for a lifetime the possibility of achievements outside the home? Accounting for such benefits and costs by putting price tags on them would not do them justice. However, they need to be in our consciousness as we think about the housewife, contemplate the decline and eventual disappearance of the housewife occupation, and consider what might be done to replace some of the good things that are being lost in the course of that decline.

PAY FOR HOUSEWIVES

The housewife, despite the productive work she does, receives no sum of money she can call her wage. This lack of a wage has struck many people as an important injustice, which they say ought to be remedied. Perhaps what is most galling is that while the housewife's duties resemble those of a servant, the financial arrangements she has with her husband somewhat resemble those of someone even lower down on the status ladder—namely, the slave. Slaves get no sum of money designated as a wage but do get room, board, and clothing. The legal impunity with which the husband has been able to chastise the wife physically has reinforced the slave analogy. The slave who ran away might be captured and brought back by law. The housewife was constrained to stay by the poverty of the economic and social alternatives open to her. In some cultures, the bridegroom buys the bride for a considerable sum from her father.

The truth of the matter is that both the housewife and the slave do receive a recompense for their work. The slave is at the mercy of the master for the amount of the recompense and for his or her very life. By contrast, custom constrains the husband to allow the wife a standard of living similar to his own. Unless the husband has expensive vices (gambling, drink, and resort to other women are the classic ones), the wife generally cannot complain that the share he accords her is unfair. It is not the lack of recompense but the form that it takes that creates practical and psychological problems, especially if the two spouses do not have an amicable relationship.

The housewife's contributions to the family and the return she gets for making them are both obscured by legal and popular ideas that each spouse is unilaterally rendering duties to the other rather than making an exchange of economically valuable services. A husband is seen as having a duty to support the wife, with no conditions specified. The wife is seen as having a duty to keep the house, again unconditionally. The connection between the husband's monetary support and the wife's housework is further obscured by the fact that the standard of living of the wife seems to be inversely related to the amount of housework she does. Those wives who do no housework whatever often enjoy the highest standard of living. Many of those who do the most housework have the lowest standard of living.

The wives of the richest husbands get a pure grant of their living expenses from their husband. Their situation certainly is not typical but seems to have set the pattern for thinking about the economic relations of all husbands and wives. All husbands are thought of as contributing support as a pure grant. Where, as is the usual case, servants cannot be afforded, the wife "has to do the housework." The fraction of wives exempted from housework has always been small; nowadays it is minuscule. The monetary contributions of the husband are in most situations connected to the performance of the housework by the wife. After all, if she stops doing the housework, the marriage will probably end. So there is in reality an exchange of the wife's housework for the husband's continuance in the marriage, and for his continuing to supply her with room, board, and other benefits.

When the husband works, he helps his employer to produce an output and is paid by that employer in money. His income is embodied in his paycheck. Presumably, all of that paycheck becomes the family's income and goes into the family budget. It is consumed when the dollars are used for family members' expenses. The husband's recompense from his employer gets converted into consumer goods for him, consumer goods for other members of the family, and some that are enjoyed jointly, such as the family living quarters.

The housewife's productive activities also contribute to the family's ability to consume, and it is not farfetched to call that contribution an addition on her part to the family income. That contribution is as real as the monetary contribution out of the husband's paycheck. As we have seen, there is more than one way of valuing the housewife's services, but they are real and substantial nonetheless. The income contributed by the wife is consumed almost as it is being produced. By contrast, the income contributed by the husband may linger a bit in the bank before melting away in consumption.

Is the housewife paid? By analogy with the

husband, the value of her housework services constitutes an income she has earned. Granted, she immediately and automatically contributes her "income" to the family. But many husbands contribute all of their income to the family, too.

Husband and wife share both the money income and get a benefit from the housework, which we might call the "service income." In the last analysis, the recompense of each for their exertions is their share in both kinds of incomes. The recompense of the housewife includes a share in the goods and services purchased out of the family's cash budget—clothing, a roof over her head, participation in family vacations, travel, medical care, trips to the movies, and so on. She also benefits from her own services, as when she partakes of a family meal she has cooked, or gets satisfaction from the development of a child she has nurtured. She ends up with a certain total level of consumption—and whether we call that her share or her pay should not much matter.

What, then, do the "pay for housework" advocates complain of? It is attitudes they are complaining of more than material deprivation. The husband's money contribution seems more real or important than the wife's service contribution. His contribution is more visible and seems more concrete. Psychologically, a sum of money perhaps is more easily comprehended than a multitude of actions that constitute housework. The nature of the husband's contribution renders him more powerful in the family and creates the impression that he supports her with no return and that she is parasitical. If she had money to contribute to their joint budget, all of those ideas might disappear or at least be softened.

If the housewife had a wage, she might have more say over the way the family's money income gets spent. Of course, there are families in which the husband's pay is all delivered entirely to the wife's control and all spending is controlled by the wife. However, if the husband wants, he can keep control of all the money and

dole it out to the wife at his pleasure. She may have no fixed sum that is given to her for her own needs or even for household expenses. She may be in the humiliating position of continually having to ask for small sums. Informal surveys among my students whose mothers are housewives suggest that about 20 percent of them are in that situation. The opportunities for petty tyranny in such an arrangement are endless.

Suppose it became common practice for the husband of a housewife to render up to her some fraction of his cash wage and acknowledge that he was paying her a wage for housework. Each spouse could not go off and spend the money under their control independently. On the contrary, both the husband and the wife would have to put up almost all of that money for food purchases, the rent or the mortgage, car expenses, and so on. Perhaps the wife would feel freer to buy things for herself, but this is far from clear.

Another possible source of a cash wage for housework would be the government. But where would the government get the funds? One possibility would be to put a large special tax on the husbands of housewives. The money collected, with a suitable subtraction for administrative expenses, might be sent by the Internal Revenue Service to the housewives. The housewives' self-esteem might be enhanced by the receipt of the government checks, but the benefits would be entirely in terms of status.

Another scheme, which would have important substantive results, would be to send government paychecks to housewives out of the ordinary revenue of the government. Presumably there would have to be a tax increase to finance it. The additional taxes would be paid by housewife-maintaining families as well as by single people and two-earner couples. However, the latter two groups would receive no benefit from the extra taxes. The net effect would be a transfer of purchasing power from the pockets of single people and two-earner families into the pockets of families that maintained housewives.

But single-earner families are already better off in terms of living standards than two-earner couples of identical cash income. Sending the former a check for the wife's housework financed in part by taxes of the latter would be asking the less well off to contribute to the more well off. Such a scheme also would encourage women to become and remain housewives.

To sum up this discussion, those who have sought to put pay for housewives on the feminist agenda appear to have made a mistake.

MATERNITY AND CHILDREARING LEAVE

Most women who enter the housewife occupation do so when they have a baby. Not all new mothers leave their jobs. About a quarter of women currently giving birth to a baby do not leave the labor force at all, and another quarter return before the child's first birthday.

There always has been some sentiment for the allowance of long and generously paid maternity leaves for employed women. Lengths of three months, six months, a year, or even several years have been proposed. Such leaves would allow women with jobs to be housewives for considerable periods, and with pay to boot. Since they would be keeping one foot in the labor market at all times, the appearance of dependency would be avoided. Women in dead-end, boring, arduous jobs would no doubt welcome such leaves, and others might also. The leaves might be considered society's or the employer's contribution to the raising of children. They would make the life of the mother easier, allow her to devote herself to the child entirely, and would keep some very young babies out of day-care centers.

Long paid maternity and child-raising leaves are really another version of pay for housewives. The rhetoric on leaves emphasizes the welfare of the child rather than the worth of the mother's services. But in economic terms the two are very similar. However, the stipend for maternity leave is usually proportional to the wife's wage.

A policy requiring employers to give such paid leaves has important disadvantages for women. If the employer must pay a woman's salary for a long maternity leave, employers will have a further incentive to keep women out of the high-paying fields. Even more than now, women will be confined to jobs in which the duties follow an easily learned routine and in which one person can easily be replaced by another. In such jobs, the pay would be lowered to make up for the cost of the maternity leave. More women would take long maternity leaves, and every woman who has a baby would be under social pressure to take the maternity leave, at possible damage to her career. Another disadvantage of long paid maternity leaves for child-rearing is that they reinforce the idea that child care, and the other family service chores that women do when they stay home, are women's work.

An alternative to long leaves for mothers would be work-reduction arrangements for both spouses that allowed couples to share child care and housework. Both the mother and the father might reduce the intensity of their paid work for a considerable period after the birth of their baby. Perhaps both could go on half-time for two years or so, or perhaps the father and mother might take alternate weeks or months or quarters of a year off. Under such a system, neither mothers nor fathers would sacrifice career opportunities disproportionately. However, both parents would be at a disadvantage relative to one-earner couples and childless people in highly competitive fields, unless special rules were instituted to take care of that too. Such a system would restore to young children a period of nurturance passed in the quiet and (relatively germ-free) isolation of their own homes, at all times under the attention and care of a parent.

We might call such a system "two-parent nurturance leave." From many points of view, including probably that of the child, it would be superior both to the housewife-breadwinner setup, and to the two-earners-with-baby setup, with its overextended "supermom." The Swedes have taken modest steps to work toward such a system. In Sweden, the health insurance system provides for paid leave when a baby is born, which mothers and fathers may share. To encourage fathers to participate in child care, the father is entitled to ten days of leave, which does not count against the couple's allotment and which is lost if not taken. However, in Sweden only a small percentage of new fathers currently take advantage of the leave.

The Swedish example shows that instituting such a system would by no means be easy. Men have an interest in continuing to be exempt from household chores, and from career interruption. And as long as wages of women are far inferior to those of men, any scheme that involves men taking unpaid or partly paid leave is relatively expensive for the family.

*   *   *

TAX POLICY AND THE HOUSEWIFE

We turn now to the treatment of housewives and employed wives in matters of taxation.

The United States has consistently followed a system of income taxation based on two principles. One is the principle of progressive taxation—that people with higher incomes should pay higher shares of their incomes to the tax collector. The second is that a married couple should be taxed on the sum of their incomes, and the spouses not be allowed to calculate their taxes as though they were single people. In recent decades, U.S. tax laws have been revised numerous times. However all revisions, including the revisions of 1986, have kept these principles intact.

A low-income person who marries a high-income person is not allowed by the U.S. tax code to pay the low taxes that would be levied on a low-income person living alone. Rather, such a person is made to pay the higher taxes thought appropriate to a member of an affluent family. While that has a measure of justice to it, it creates a *two-earner marriage penalty*—when

TABLE 1   How Income Taxes in the United States Vary with Marital Status

THE TWO-EARNER MARRIAGE PENALTY	
Man with income of $30,000	
Woman with income of $20,000	
Their taxes as single people	
($4,638 + 2,250)	$6,888
Their tax as a married couple	7,554

THE HOUSEWIFE BONUS	
Man with income of $30,000	
His tax as a single person	$4,638
His tax if married to a housewife,	
no children	3,150

THE SINGLE PARENT PENALTY	
Tax of single mother earning	
$40,000, two-person family	$5,712
Tax of married couple earning	
$40,000, two person family	4,854

Note: Based on proposals for taxes to take affect in 1988 as detailed in *Tax Reform Act of 1986: Report of the Committee on Finance. United States Senate,* Report 99–313, May 21, 1986. The use of the standard deduction is assumed in all cases.

two people marry, and both continue to earn income, the taxes they owe as a couple may be greater than the sum of the taxes the two of them owed as single people.

In order to keep the marriage penalty from becoming more than a few thousand dollars per couple, the tax rules have been written so that a married couple with a given income pays less tax than one single person with the same income. That creates a second anomaly—the *housewife bonus.* A man married to a woman with no income pays considerably less than he would as a single person.

There is still a third anomaly in the U.S. tax code—the *single-parent penalty.* A mother who is not currently married, and is the only earner in her family, is not permitted the same generous treatment accorded to the single-earner married couple. She is treated as an intermediate case between singles and marrieds.

These tax anomalies are illustrated in Table 1. The numbers in the table are based on current plans for taxes in 1988. A two-earner couple who as single people would have paid a total of $6,888 in taxes would owe $7,554 after their marriage, thus suffering a rise in taxes of $666 or almost 10 percent. By contrast, the man who is married to a nonemployed wife would pay $1,488 less than he would as a single person, a tax reduction of almost a third. The single mother supporting a nonearning child in our example is forced to pay $858 more than a man supporting a nonearning wife, an 18 percent tax penalty.

The marriage penalty encourages people who are living together without benefit of formal marriage to stay that way. For those who do get married, the tax system encourages wives to remain housewives or to become housewives. In our example, a couple's taxes increase from $3,150 to $7,554, a sum of $4,404, if the wife takes a job that pays $20,000.

Most couples view the husband's employment as beyond question but view the wife's employment as something on which a decision might be made either way. Thus they would tend to view the $4,404 addition to their tax bill not as an extra burden on both of their salaries but as the tax on the $20,000 that the wife might earn. By that way of thinking, her salary carries a higher tax rate than the rate on husband's salary, and a rate almost double the rate she paid as a single woman.

The idea behind a progressive tax structure is that better-off people should carry a more-than-proportional share of supporting public expenditure, while the burden on lower-income people should be relatively light. The principle is straightforward when comparing individuals. When comparing individuals with married couples or comparing one- and two-earner families, however, what is fair and what is unfair becomes more problematical.

Should two-earner couples be allowed to pay taxes as though they were single? One argument against the idea is that when people marry, their expenses diminish because they share a dwelling unit, so they can afford higher

taxes. These days, however, many couples live together before their marriage. It seems unreasonable to force such couples to pay extra taxes for the act of getting married.

On balance, there is a lot to be said for requiring people to file on the basis of their own incomes without regard to the income of other family members, and for abolishing special tax rates for married people. This is the way taxes are structured in Sweden. If such a system was adopted in the United States, married single earners would have to pay considerably more tax than they currently do.

A more radical proposal, by Rolande Cuvillier, would go farther than getting rid of the tax break currently enjoyed by the one-earner couple. Cuvillier would make the one-earner couple pay extra taxes. They would be required to pay tax on the value of the services performed by the housewife. Cuvillier reasons that having a housewife increases the family's real income. She simply carries the idea of taxation to its logical conclusion and argues that the family should be taxed on that part of its real income consisting of housewife-performed services. After all, says Cuvillier, the housewife is part of the community, and public services are delivered to her at public expense. She, or her husband on her behalf, should pay her share of this public expense.

Presumably only the extra services delivered by the housewife beyond those performed by two-earner couples would be taxed. In computing taxable income, an amount equal to some fraction of a servant's wage would be added to the cash income of couples maintaining a housewife.

SOCIAL SECURITY AND THE HOUSEWIFE

The Social Security system, on which Americans depend to give them income in old age, was established in the 1930s. Each person who has ever held a job covered under Social Security has an individual account in which that person's earnings are recorded. The rhetoric used to convince a basically conservative population that the system was a reasonable one portrayed the benefits as being drawn from a fund that had been built up out of the worker's own contributions as well as contributions by the employer on the worker's behalf. In reality, benefit formulas were constructed to replace a greater portion of the wage income of the lower-earning workers than of high-earning workers, and extra benefits were paid to the retired male workers who were married.

At the time Social Security was set up and the principles of the benefit formula were established, most women spent their married years out of the labor force. If they were to receive Social Security benefits, they would have to do so in their capacity as wives or widows of male workers. The solution adopted was to award to each retired couple a "spouse benefit" equal to 50 percent of the husband's benefit. Wives who had earnings in their own right might elect to take benefits based on those earnings, or might elect the spouse benefit, but not both.

The net effect of such arrangements is that the benefits a person gets are not proportional to that person's contributions. People who have had low earnings get more Social Security benefits per dollar of contribution than high wage earners. A married man gets more than a single man who has made the same contributions. Many women who have made contributions to Social Security end up by accepting the spouse benefit, which they could have received with no contributions at all. In a sense, these women receive nothing for their contributions.

Table 2 shows examples of the results of this kind of arrangement, which have been chosen to highlight the features of the system. In the first case shown (Dennis and Deborah), the man's salary had averaged $11,000 in terms of 1985 wage levels, and the wife's salary had been the same. They have a choice of taking the benefits the two of them were entitled to on the basis of their own earnings, or taking the husband's benefit plus the 50 percent spouse benefit. Obviously they would choose the former, giving them a benefit of $10,936. By contrast, the one-earner couple (Edgar and Elsie) can retire on an annual benefit of $13,047, which includes the $8,698 the husband would have been entitled to as a retired single man, plus the 50 percent spouse benefit.

The combined earnings of the first couple are equal to those of the second couple, and the two couples would have paid identical Social

TABLE 2   Benefits to Couples Under the Social Security System for People Retiring in 1985

	AVERAGE INDEXED EARNINGS	BENEFITS FOR COUPLES BASED ON	
		OWN EARNINGS	SPOUSE BENEFITS
Dennis	$11,000	$ 5,468	$ 5,468
Deborah	11,000	5,468	2,734
Total	$22,000	$10,936	$ 8,202
Edgar	$22,000	$ 8,698	$ 8,698
Elsie	—	—	4,349
Total	$22,000	$ 8,698	$13,047

Note: Benefits are based on 1985 formulas for people retiring at 65, which give 90 percent of the first $280 per month average indexed earnings, 32 percent of earnings between $280 and $1,691, and 15 percent of earnings of between $1,691 and $3,291. Average indexed earnings are computed by taking earnings for each of the previous 25 years, adjusting them to account for changes in average salary levels between the year in question and the retirement year, and then taking the average of such adjusted earnings. The lowest 5 years are excluded from the average. Detailed information on benefit structures are contained in U.S. Department of Health and Human Services, *Social Security Handbook,* 8th ed. (1984).

Security taxes. Moreover, the first couple would have put out more work effort, and led a less comfortable life than the second couple, who would have had the services of a housewife. Nevertheless, the one-earner couple would be awarded a benefit that was 19 percent higher than that awarded the two-earner couple.

If the two wives in our example become widowed, they would get very different benefits. Elsie, who had never contributed to the Social Security system, would get a widow's benefit of $8,698. Deborah would get much less, only $5,468, despite a lifetime of contributions.

These examples suggest that the Social Security system, like the income-tax system, is more generous to families with housewives than to families of employed women. This is certainly the case if we restrict our attention to benefits going to retired married couples and to widows. The system is generous to those housewives who manage to stay married to their husbands. But it is extremely harsh to those housewives who become divorced.

Until 1978, a divorced woman who had been married to a man less than twenty years was entitled to no Social Security benefit whatsoever on the basis of her former marriage. Spouse benefits would have been payable only for the retired ex-husband's new wife, if any. If the divorced wife had been a housewife, or had a poor or spotty earnings record under her own name, her financial situation in old age would be very poor. Currently, divorced women whose marriage lasted for at least ten years qualify for benefits based on the ex-husband's earnings. However, while the ex-husband is alive, a divorced wife receives no benefits until he retires, and then is entitled only to a payment equal to the spouse benefit. Thus if Edgar divorced Elsie, he and a new wife would retire with a benefit of $13,047, but Elsie would be reduced to living on $4,349. However, if Edgar died, Elsie's benefit would rise to $8,698, the same amount the second wife would receive.

The problem of old-age support for divorced housewives has stirred suggestions that the Social Security system should give housewives direct credit for their service at home by putting "earnings" credits into their records. When wives received benefits under such a system, the benefits would be based on the woman's own credits—any earnings the woman had plus her housewife credits.

On what basis would the housewife's credits be computed? Some have suggested that credit for all the earnings of a couple be shared between spouses. Under earnings-sharing, the separate Social Security accounts of the husband and wife each would be credited with one half of their total earnings. Men married to housewives would get credit in their own accounts for only 50 percent of their earnings. This certainly would have the virtue of making explicit the economic partnership implicit in the marriage and of vesting in the wife the right to future benefits based on economic activity during the marriage. But men have been highly vocal against "giving away credits that belong to them." Other schemes that have been suggested to extend explicit coverage to housewives would allow couples to pay for extra credits to the wife's account (as is permitted in some other countries), or alternatively require them to make such payments. Still another would give the husband full credit for his earnings but would award an extra 50 percent to the wife's account. Under the latter scheme, the rest of the community would continue the current subsidies to housewife-maintaining couples.

All of these schemes involve basing pension checks on each person's "own" account. This might have the effect of giving housewives more dignity; their work would be recognized as worthy of social credit, and they would appear to be less dependent.

A still more fundamental reform of Social Security would reduce the effect of a person's earnings on the size of that person's retirement benefit check. Under a so-called two-tiered or double-decker setup, every old person would get a stipend unrelated to the person's earning history. To that stipend would be added a relatively small amount based on the earnings record. This would make the system more "like welfare" rather than the purely contributory system it appears (falsely) to most people to be. The two-tier system would help the displaced housewife more than any other. It would also reduce the unfair advantage the current system gives to the one-earner over two-earner couples with the same income. For those reasons it is the most desirable of the reforms that have been proposed.

FEMINIST THINKING ABOUT THE FULL-TIME HOMEMAKER

The role of the housewife has a major place in feminist thought. Betty Friedan's book *The Feminine Mystique*, which was influential in initiating the current wave of feminism in the United States, had as its central theme the disadvantages to women from assuming the housewife role. All feminists believe that women should not be forced into assuming that role and that alternative choices should be available.

There is a second strand of feminist thinking concerning housewives that derives from the solidarity feminists feel with all women, housewives included. This solidarity expresses itself in a concern to alleviate injuries (physical, psychological, financial) that housewives have suffered. It also leads feminists to join in efforts to shore up the dignity of the housewife.

There is still a third strand of thought about homemakers. Some people who consider themselves feminists think it would be desirable for even larger numbers of people to assume the stay-at-home housekeeper role than now do so. They see it as indispensable for the proper raising of children. They would prefer it if members of both sexes were candidates for the role, or if mothers and fathers could alternate. However, whether that were possible or not, they favor public policies making it financially easier

for families to support a full-time homemaker. They tend to favor multi-year parental leaves with pay for childrearing.

Much of the attention of feminists has gone toward trying to help the housewife. Rolande Cuvillier, quoted earlier in connection with taxation, argues that the net effect of many pro-housewife measures is not to help women at all. Rather, such measures help men to retain someone dedicated to serving them in the home, at the expense of the rest of society. Thus policy measures that encourage women to become or remain housewives, such as tax breaks for housewife-maintaining families, help perpetuate the inequality of the sexes. When the scarce resources of the feminist movement are devoted to pushing measures that have that effect, support and attention are diverted away from reforms that would help the employed woman, the single mother, or the battered housewife.

The disadvantages to playing the role of full-time homemaker are so great that it is unlikely that significant numbers of men would want to serve in it. If the occupation continues to exist, it will continue to be part of the female domain and hence inherently disadvantaged. Since this is the case, equality of the sexes and women's welfare would be better served if younger women were to avoid entering the role even temporarily and if the socially sanctioned "option" to assume the role were to disappear. Policies that reward families for having housewives, or encourage women to assume the housewife role, do harm to women and should be avoided.

After we have passed through a phase where unpaid family care services have been largely replaced by purchased substitutes, and after equality of opportunity has been established in the workplace, it will be time to consider reviving the occupation of full-time homemaker. Then we can see if it can become an honorable, safe, and secure occupation for both mothers and fathers.

The Domestic Scene

Anger and Tenderness

Adrienne Rich

. . . to understand is always an ascending movement; that is why comprehension ought always to be concrete. (one is never got out of the cave, one comes out of it.)

—Simone Weil, *First and Last Notebooks*

Entry from my journal, November 1960

My children cause me the most exquisite suffering of which I have any experience. It is the suffering of ambivalence: the murderous alternation between bitter resentment and raw-edged nerves, and blissful gratification and tenderness. Sometimes I seem to myself, in my feelings toward these tiny guiltless beings, a monster of selfishness and intolerance. Their voices wear away at my nerves, their constant needs, above all their need for simplicity and patience, fill me with despair at my own failures, despair too at my fate, which is to serve a function for which I was not fitted. And I am weak sometimes from held-in rage. There are times when I feel only death will free us from one another, when I envy the barren woman who has the luxury of her regrets but lives a life of privacy and freedom.*

And yet at other times I am melted with the sense of their helpless, charming and quite irresistible beauty—their ability to go on loving and trusting—their staunchness and decency and unselfconsciousness. *I love them*. But it's in the enormity and inevitability of this love that the sufferings lie.

April 1961

A blissful love for my children engulfs me from time to time and seems almost to suffice—the aesthetic pleasure I have in these little, changing creatures, the sense of being loved, however dependently, the sense too that I'm not an utterly unnatural and shrewish mother—much though I am!

May 1965

To suffer with and for and against a child—maternally, egotistically, neurotically, sometimes

---

From *Of Woman Born*, Chapter 1. Reprinted by permission.

* The term "barren woman" was easy for me to use, unexamined, fifteen years ago. As should be clear throughout this book, it seems to me now a

term both tendentious and meaningless, based on a view of women which sees motherhood as our only positive definition.

with a sense of helplessness, sometimes with the illusion of learning wisdom—but always, everywhere, in body and soul, *with* that child—because that child is a piece of oneself.

To be caught up in waves of love and hate, jealousy even of the child's childhood; hope and fear for its maturity; longing to be free of responsibility, tied by every fibre of one's being.

That curious primitive reaction of protectiveness, the beast defending her cub, when anyone attacks or criticizes him—And yet no one more hard on him than I!

September 1965

Degradation of anger. Anger at a child. How shall I learn to absorb the violence and make explicit only the caring? Exhaustion of anger. Victory of will, too dearly bought—far too dearly!

March 1966

Perhaps one is a monster—an anti-woman—something driven and without recourse to the normal and appealing consolations of love, motherhood, joy in others. . . .

Unexamined assumptions: First, that a "natural" mother is a person without further identity, one who can find her chief gratification in being all day with small children, living at a pace tuned to theirs; that the isolation of mothers and children together in the home must be taken for granted; that maternal love is, and should be, quite literally selfless; that children and mothers are the "causes" of each others' suffering. I was haunted by the stereotype of the mother whose love is "unconditional"; and by the visual and literary images of motherhood as a single-minded identity. If I knew parts of myself existed that would never cohere to those images, weren't those parts then abnormal, monstrous? And—as my eldest son, now aged twenty-one, remarked on reading the above passages: "You seemed to feel you ought to love us all the time. But there *is* no human relationship where you love the other person at every moment." Yes, I

tried to explain to him, but women—above all, mothers—have been supposed to love that way.

From the fifties and early sixties, I remember a cycle. It began when I had picked up a book or began trying to write a letter, or even found myself on the telephone with someone toward whom my voice betrayed eagerness, a rush of sympathetic energy. The child (or children) might be absorbed in busyness, in his own dreamworld; but as soon as he felt me gliding into a world which did not include him, he would come to pull at my hand, ask for help, punch at the typewriter keys. And I would feel his wants at such a moment as fraudulent, as an attempt moreover to defraud me of living even for fifteen minutes as myself. My anger would rise; I would feel the futility of any attempt to salvage myself, and also the inequality between us: my needs always balanced against those of a child, and always losing. I could love so much better, I told myself, after even a quarter-hour of selfishness, of peace, of detachment from my children. A few minutes! But it was as if an invisible thread would pull taut between us and break, to the child's sense of inconsolable abandonment, if I moved—not even physically, but in spirit—into a realm beyond our tightly circumscribed life together. It was as if my placenta had begun to refuse him oxygen. Like so many women, I waited with impatience for the moment when their father would return from work, when for an hour or two at least the circle drawn around mother and children would grow looser, the intensity between us slacken, because there was another adult in the house.

I did not understand that this circle, this magnetic field in which we lived, was not a natural phenomenon.

Intellectually, I must have known it. But the emotion-charged, tradition-heavy form in which I found myself cast as the Mother seemed, then, as ineluctable as the tides. And, because of this form—this microcosm in which my children and I formed a tiny, private emotional cluster, and in which (in bad weather or when someone was ill) we sometimes passed days at a time without seeing another adult except for their father—there *was* authentic need underlying my child's invented claims upon me when I seemed to be wandering away from him. He was reassuring himself that warmth, tenderness, continuity, solidity were still there for him, in my person. My singularity, my uniqueness in the world as *his mother*—perhaps more dimly also as Woman—evoked a need vaster than any single human being could satisfy, except by loving continuously, unconditionally, from dawn to dark, and often in the middle of the night.

2

In a living room in 1975, I spent an evening with a group of women poets, some of whom had children. One had brought hers along, and they slept or played in adjoining rooms. We talked of poetry, and also of infanticide, of the case of a local woman, the mother of eight, who had been in severe depression since the birth of her third child, and who had recently murdered and decapitated her two youngest, on her suburban front lawn. Several women in the group, feeling a direct connection with her desperation, had signed a letter to the local newspaper protesting the way her act was perceived by the press and handled by the community mental health system. Every woman in that room who had children, every poet, could identify with her. We spoke of the wells of anger that her story cleft open in us. We spoke of our own moments of murderous anger at our children, because there was no one and nothing else on which to discharge anger. We spoke in the sometimes tentative, sometimes rising, sometimes bitterly witty, unrhetorical tones and language of women who had met together over our common work, poetry, and who found another common ground in an unacceptable, but undeniable anger. The words are being spoken now, are being written down; the taboos are being broken, the masks of motherhood are cracking through. For centuries no one talked of these feelings. I be-

came a mother in the family-centered, consumer-oriented, Freudian-American world of the 1950s. My husband spoke eagerly of the children we would have; my parents-in-law awaited the birth of their grandchild. I had no idea of what *I* wanted, what *I* could or could not choose. I only knew that to have a child was to assume adult womanhood to the full, to prove myself, to be "like other women."

To be "like other women" had been a problem for me. From the age of thirteen or fourteen, I had felt I was only acting the part of a feminine creature. At the age of sixteen my fingers were almost constantly ink-stained. The lipstick and high heels of the era were difficult-to-manage disguises. In 1945 I was writing poetry seriously, and had a fantasy of going to postwar Europe as a journalist, sleeping among the ruins in bombed cities, recording the rebirth of civilization after the fall of the Nazis. But also, like every other girl I knew, I spent hours trying to apply lipstick more adroitly, straightening the wandering seams of stockings, talking about "boys." There were two different compartments, already, to my life. But writing poetry, and my fantasies of travel and self-sufficiency, seemed more real to me; I felt that as an incipient "real woman" I was a fake. Particularly was I paralyzed when I encountered young children. I think I felt men could be—wished to be—conned into thinking I was truly "feminine"; a child, I suspected, could see through me like a shot. This sense of acting a part created a curious sense of guilt, even though it was a part demanded for survival.

I have a very clear, keen memory of myself the day after I was married: I was sweeping a floor. Probably the floor did not really need to be swept; probably I simply did not know what else to do with myself. But as I swept that floor I thought: "Now I am a woman. This is an age-old action, this is what women have always done." I felt I was bending to some ancient form, too ancient to question. *This is what women have always done.*

As soon as I was visibly and clearly pregnant, I felt, for the first time in my adolescent and adult life, not guilty. The atmosphere of approval in which I was bathed—even by strangers on the street, it seemed—was like an aura I carried with me, in which doubts, fears, misgivings, met with absolute denial. *This is what women have always done.*

Two days before my first son was born, I broke out in a rash which was tentatively diagnosed as measles, and was admitted to a hospital for contagious diseases to await the onset of labor. I felt for the first time a great deal of conscious fear, and guilt toward my unborn child, for having "failed" him with my body in this way. In rooms near mine were patients with polio; no one was allowed to enter my room except in a hospital gown and mask. If during pregnancy I had felt in any vague command of my situation, I felt now totally dependent on my obstetrician, a huge, vigorous, paternal man, abounding with optimism and assurance, and given to pinching my cheek. I had gone through a healthy pregnancy, but as if tranquilized or sleep-walking. I had taken a sewing class in which I produced an unsightly and ill-cut maternity jacket which I never wore; I had made curtains for the baby's room, collected baby clothes, blotted out as much as possible the woman I had been a few months earlier. My second book of poems was in press, but I had stopped writing poetry, and read little except household magazines and books on child-care. I felt myself perceived by the world simply as a pregnant woman, and it seemed easier, less disturbing, to perceive myself so. After my child was born the "measles" were diagnosed as an allergic reaction to pregnancy.

Within two years, I was pregnant again, and writing in a notebook:

November 1956

Whether it's the extreme lassitude of early pregnancy or something more fundamental, I don't know; but of late I've felt, toward poetry, —both reading and writing it—nothing but boredom and indifference. Es-

pecially toward my own and that of my immediate contemporaries. When I receive a letter soliciting mss., or someone alludes to my "career," I have a strong sense of wanting to deny all responsibility for and interest in that person who writes—or who wrote.

If there is going to be a real break in my writing life, this is as good a time for it as any. I have been dissatisfied with myself, my work, for a long time.

My husband was a sensitive, affectionate man who wanted children and who—unusual in the professional, academic world of the fifties—was willing to "help." But it was clearly understood that this "help" was an act of generosity; that *his* work, *his* professional life, was the real work in the family; in fact, this was for years not even an issue between us. I understood that my struggles as a writer were a kind of luxury, a peculiarity of mine; my work brought in almost no money: it even cost money, when I hired a household helper to allow me a few hours a week to write. "Whatever I ask he tries to give me," I wrote in March 1958, "but always the initiative has to be mine." I experienced my depressions, bursts of anger, sense of entrapment, as burdens my husband was forced to bear because he loved me; I felt grateful to be loved in spite of bringing him those burdens.

But I was struggling to bring my life into focus. I had never really given up on poetry, nor on gaining some control over my existence. The life of a Cambridge tenement backyard swarming with children, the repetitious cycles of laundry, the night-wakings, the interrupted moments of peace or of engagement with ideas, the ludicrous dinner parties at which young wives, some with advanced degrees, all seriously and intelligently dedicated to their children's welfare and their husbands' careers, attempted to reproduce the amenities of Brahmin Boston, amid French recipes and the pretense of effortlessness—above all, the ultimate lack of seriousness with which women were regarded in that world—all of this defied analysis at that time, but I *knew* I had to remake my own life. I did not then understand that we—the women of that academic community—as in so many middle-class communities of the period—were expected to fill both the part of the Victorian Lady of Leisure, the Angel in the House, and also of the Victorian cook, scullery maid, laundress, governess, and nurse. I only sensed that there were false distractions sucking at me, and I wanted desperately to strip my life down to what was essential.

June 1958

These months I've been all a tangle of irritations deepening to anger: bitterness, disillusion with society and with myself; beating out at the world, rejecting out of hand. What, if anything, has been positive? Perhaps the attempt to remake my life, to save it from mere drift and the passage of time. . . .

The work that is before me is serious and difficult and not at all clear even as to plan. Discipline of mind and spirit, uniqueness of expression, ordering of daily existence, the most effective functioning of the human self—these are the chief things I wish to achieve. So far the only beginning I've been able to make is to waste less time. That is what some of the rejection has been all about.

By July of 1958 I was again pregnant. The new life of my third—and, as I determined, my last—child, was a kind of turning for me. I had learned that my body was not under my control; I had not intended to bear a third child. I knew now better than I had ever known what another pregnancy, another new infant, meant for my body and spirit. Yet, I did not think of having an abortion. In a sense, my third son was more actively chosen than either of his brothers; by the time I knew I was pregnant with him, I was not sleepwalking any more.

August 1958 (Vermont)

I write this as the early rays of the sun light up our hillside and eastern windows. Rose with [the baby] at 5:30 A.M. and have fed him and breakfasted. This is one of the few mornings on which I haven't felt terrible mental depression and physical exhaustion.
. . . I have to acknowledge to myself that I

would not have chosen to have more children, that I was beginning to look to a time, not too far off, when I should again be free, no longer so physically tired, pursuing a more or less intellectual and creative life. . . . The *only* way I can develop now is through much harder, more continuous, connected work than my present life makes possible. Another child means postponing this for some years longer—and years at my age are significant, not to be tossed lightly away.

And yet, somehow, something, call it Nature or that affirming fatalism of the human creature, makes me aware of the inevitable as already part of me, not to be contended against so much as brought to bear as an additional weapon against drift, stagnation and spiritual death. (For it is really death that I have been fearing—the crumbling to death of that scarcely-born physiognomy which my whole life has been a battle to give birth to—a recognizable, autonomous self, a creation in poetry and in life.)

If more effort has to be made then I will make it. If more despair has to be lived through, I think I can anticipate it correctly and live through it.

Meanwhile, in a curious and unanticipated way, we really do welcome the birth of our child.

There was, of course, an economic as well as a spiritual margin which allowed me to think of a third child's birth not as my own death-warrant but as an "additional weapon against death." My body, despite recurrent flares of arthritis, was a healthy one; I had good prenatal care; we were not living on the edge of malnutrition; I knew that all my children would be fed, clothed, breathe fresh air; in fact it did not occur to me that it could be otherwise. But, in another sense, beyond that physical margin, I knew I was fighting for my life through, against, and with the lives of my children, though very little else was clear to me. I had been trying to give birth to myself; and in some grim, dim way I was determined to use even pregnancy and parturition in that process.

Before my third child was born I decided to have no more children, to be sterilized. (Nothing is removed from a woman's body during this operation; ovulation and menstruation continue. Yet the language suggests a cutting- or burning-away of her essential womanhood, just as the old word "barren" suggests a woman eternally empty and lacking.) My husband, although he supported my decision, asked whether I was sure it would not leave me feeling "less feminine." In order to have the operation at all, I had to present a letter, counter-signed by my husband, assuring the committee of physicians who approved such operations that I had already produced three children, and stating my reasons for having no more. Since I had had rheumatoid arthritis for some years, I could give a reason acceptable to the male panel who sat on my case; my own judgment would not have been acceptable. When I awoke from the operation, twenty-four hours after my child's birth, a young nurse looked at my chart and remarked coldly: "Had yourself spayed, did you?"

The first great birth-control crusader, Margaret Sanger, remarks that of the hundreds of women who wrote to her pleading for contraceptive information in the early part of the twentieth century, all spoke of wanting the health and strength to be better mothers to the children they already had; or of wanting to be physically affectionate to their husbands without dread of conceiving. None was refusing motherhood altogether, or asking for an easy life. These women—mostly poor, many still in their teens, all with several children—simply felt they could no longer do "right" by their families, whom they expected to go on serving and rearing. Yet there always has been, and there remains, intense fear of the suggestion that women shall have the final say as to how our bodies are to be used. It is as if the suffering of the mother, the primary identification of woman *as* the mother—were so necessary to the emotional grounding of human society that the mitigation, or removal, of that suffering, that identification, must be fought at every level, including the level of refusing to question it at all.

3

"Vous travaillez pour l'armée, madame?" (You are working for the army?), a Frenchwoman said to me early in the Vietnam war, on hearing I had three sons.

April 1965

Anger, weariness, demoralization. Sudden bouts of weeping. A sense of insufficiency to the moment and to eternity. . . .

Paralyzed by the sense that there exists a mesh of relations, between e.g. my rejection and anger at [my eldest child], my sensual life, pacifism, sex (I mean in its broadest significance, not merely physical desire)—an interconnectedness which, if I could see it, make it valid, would give me back myself, make it possible to function lucidly and passionately—Yet I grope in and out among these dark webs—

I weep, and weep, and the sense of powerlessness spreads like a cancer through my being.

August 1965, 3:30 A.M.

Necessity for a more unyielding discipline of my life.
Recognize the uselessness of blind anger.
Limit society.
Use children's school hours better, for work & solitude.
Refuse to be distracted from own style of life.
Less waste.
Be harder & harder on poems.

Once in a while someone used to ask me, "Don't you ever write poems about your children?" The male poets of my generation did write poems about their children—especially their daughters. For me, poetry was where I lived as no-one's mother, where I existed as myself.

The bad and the good moments are inseparable for me. I recall the times when, suckling each of my children, I saw his eyes open full to mine, and realized each of us was fastened to the other, not only by mouth and breast, but through our mutual gaze: the depth, calm, passion, of that dark blue, maturely focused look. I recall the physical pleasure of having my full breast suckled at a time when I had no other physical pleasure in the world except the guilt-ridden pleasure of addictive eating. I remember early the sense of conflict, of a battleground none of us had chosen, of being an observer who, like it or not, was also an actor in an endless contest of wills. This was what it meant to me to have three children under the age of seven. But I recall too each child's individual body, his slenderness, wiriness, softness, grace, the beauty of little boys who have not been taught that the male body must be rigid. I remember moments of peace when for some reason it was possible to go to the bathroom alone. I remember being uprooted from already meager sleep to answer a childish nightmare, pull up a blanket, warm a consoling bottle, lead a half-asleep child to the toilet. I remember going back to bed starkly awake, brittle with anger, knowing that my broken sleep would make next day a hell, that there would be more nightmares, more need for consolation, because out of my weariness I would rage at those children for no reason they could understand. I remember thinking I would never dream again (the unconscious of the young mother—where does it entrust its messages, when dream-sleep is denied her for years?)

For many years I shrank from looking back on the first decade of my children's lives. In snapshots of the period I see a smiling young woman, in maternity clothes or bent over a half-naked baby; gradually she stops smiling, wears a distant, half-melancholy look, as if she were listening for something. In time my sons grew older, I began changing my own life, we began to talk to each other as equals. Together we lived through my leaving the marriage, and through their father's suicide. We became sur-

vivors, four distinct people with strong bonds connecting us. Because I always tried to tell them the truth, because their every new independence meant new freedom for me, because we trusted each other even when we wanted different things, they became, at a fairly young age, self-reliant and open to the unfamiliar. Something told me that if they had survived my angers, my self-reproaches, and still trusted my love and each other's, they were strong. Their lives have not been, will not be, easy; but their very existences seem a gift to me, their vitality, humor, intelligence, gentleness, love of life, their separate life-currents which here and there stream into my own. I don't know how we made it from their embattled childhood and my embattled motherhood into a mutual recognition of ourselves and each other. Probably that mutual recognition, overlaid by social and traditional circumstance, was always there, from the first gaze between the mother and the infant at the breast. But I do know that for years I believed I should never have been anyone's mother, that because I felt my own needs acutely and often expressed them violently, I was Kali, Medea, the sow that devours her farrow, the unwomanly woman in flight from womanhood, a Nietzschean monster. Even today, rereading old journals, remembering, I feel grief and anger; but their objects are no longer myself and my children. I feel grief at the waste of myself in those years, anger at the mutilation and manipulation of the relationship between mother and child, which is the great original source and experience of love.

On an early spring day in the 1970s, I meet a young woman friend on the street. She has a tiny infant against her breast, in a bright cotton sling; its face is pressed against her blouse, its tiny hand clutches a piece of the cloth. "How old is she?" I ask. "Just two weeks old," the mother tells me. I am amazed to feel in myself a passionate longing to have, once again, such a small, new being clasped against my body.

The baby belongs there, curled, suspended asleep between her mother's breasts, as she belonged curled in the womb. The young mother—who already has a three-year-old—speaks of how quickly one forgets the pure pleasure of having this new creature, immaculate, perfect. And I walk away from her drenched with memory, with envy. Yet I know other things: that her life is far from simple; she is a mathematician who now has two children under the age of four; she is living even now in the rhythms of other lives—not only the regular cry of the infant but her three-year-old's needs, her husband's problems. In the building where I live, women are still raising children alone, living day in and day out within their individual family units, doing the laundry, herding the tricycles to the park, waiting for the husbands to come home. There is a baby-sitting pool and a children's playroom, young fathers push prams on weekends, but child-care is still the individual responsibility of the individual woman. I envy the sensuality of having an infant of two weeks curled against one's breast; I do not envy the turmoil of the elevator full of small children, babies howling in the laundromat, the apartment in winter where pent-up seven- and eight-year-olds have one adult to look to for their frustrations, reassurances, the grounding of their lives.

4

But, it will be said, this is the human condition, this interpenetration of pain and pleasure, frustration and fulfillment. I might have told myself the same thing, fifteen or eighteen years ago. But the patriarchal institution of motherhood is not the "human condition" any more than rape, prostitution, and slavery are. (Those who speak largely of the human condition are usually those most exempt from its oppressions—whether of sex, race, or servitude.)

Motherhood—unmentioned in the histories of conquest and serfdom, wars and treaties, exploration and imperialism—has a history, it has an ideology, it is more fundamental than tribalism or nationalism. My individual, seemingly private pains as a mother, the individual, seemingly private pains of the mothers around me and before me, whatever our class or color, the regulation of women's reproductive power by men in every totalitarian system and every socialist revolution, the legal and technical control by men of contraception, fertility, abortion, obstetrics, gynecology, and extrauterine reproductive experiments—all are essential to the patriarchal system, as is the negative or suspect status of women who are not mothers.

Throughout patriarchal mythology, dream-symbolism, theology, language, two ideas flow side by side: one, that the female body is impure, corrupt, the site of discharges, bleedings, dangerous to masculinity, a source of moral and physical contamination, "the devil's gateway." On the other hand, as mother the woman is beneficent, sacred, pure, asexual, nourishing; and the physical potential for motherhood—that same body with its bleedings and mysteries—is her single destiny and justification in life. These two ideas have become deeply internalized in women, even in the most independent of us, those who seem to lead the freest lives.

In order to maintain two such notions, each in its contradictory purity, the masculine imagination has had to divide women, to see us, and force us to see ourselves, as polarized into good or evil, fertile or barren, pure or impure. The asexual Victorian angel-wife and the Victorian prostitute were institutions created by this double thinking, which had nothing to do with women's actual sensuality and everything to do with the male's subjective experience of women. The political and economic expediency of this kind of thinking is most unashamedly and dramatically to be found where sexism and racism become one. The social historian A. W. Calhoun describes the encouragement of the rape of black women by the sons of white planters, in a deliberate effort to produce more mulatto slaves, mulattos being considered more valuable. He quotes two mid-nineteenth-century southern writers on the subject of women:

"The heaviest part of the white racial burden in slavery was the African woman of strong sex instincts and devoid of a sexual conscience, at the white man's door, in the white man's dwelling." . . . "Under the institution of slavery, the attack against the integrity of white civilization was made by the insidious influence of the lascivious hybrid woman at the point of weakest resistance. In the uncompromising purity of the white mother and wife of the upper classes lay the one assurance of the future purity of the race."[1]

The motherhood created by rape is not only degraded; the raped woman is turned into the criminal, the *attacker*. But who brought the black woman to the white man's door, whose absence of a sexual conscience produced the financially profitable mulatto children? Is it asked whether the "pure" white mother and wife was not also raped by the white planter, since she was assumed to be devoid of "strong sexual instinct?" In the American South, as elsewhere, it was economically necessary that children be produced; the mothers, black and white, were a means to this end.

Neither the "pure" nor the "lascivious" woman, neither the so-called mistress nor the slave woman, neither the woman praised for reducing herself to a brood animal nor the woman scorned and penalized as an "old maid" or a "dyke," has had any real autonomy or selfhood to gain from this subversion of the female body (and hence of the female mind). Yet, because short-term advantages are often the only ones visible to the powerless, we, too, have played our parts in continuing this subversion.

5

Most of the literature of infant care and psychology has assumed that the process toward individuation is essentially the *child's* drama, played out against and with a parent or parents who are, for better or worse, givens. Nothing could have prepared me for the realization that I *was* a mother, one of those givens, when I knew I was still in a state of uncreation myself. That calm, sure, unambivalent woman who moved through the pages of the manuals I read seemed as unlike me as an astronaut. Nothing, to be sure, had prepared me for the intensity of relationship already existing between me and a creature I had carried in my body and now held in my arms and fed from my breasts. Throughout pregnancy and nursing, women are urged to relax, to mime the serenity of madonnas. No one mentions the psychic crisis of bearing a first child, the excitation of long-buried feelings about one's own mother, the sense of confused power and powerlessness, of being taken over on the one hand and of touching new physical and psychic potentialities on the other, a heightened sensibility which can be exhilarating, bewildering and exhausting. No one mentions the strangeness of attraction—which can be as single-minded and overwhelming as the early days of a love affair—to a being so tiny, so dependent, so folded-in to itself—who is, and yet is not, part of oneself.

From the beginning the mother caring for her child is involved in a continually changing dialogue, crystallized in such moments as when, hearing her child's cry, she feels milk rush into her breasts; when, as the child first suckles, the uterus begins contracting and returning to its normal size, and when later, the child's mouth, caressing the nipple, creates waves of sensuality in the womb where it once lay; or when, smelling the breast even in sleep, the child starts to root and grope for the nipple.

The child gains her first sense of her own existence from the mother's responsive gestures and expressions. It's as if, in the mother's eyes, her smile, her stroking touch, the child first reads the message: *You are there!* And the mother, too, is discovering her own existence newly. She is connected with this other being, by the most mundane and the most invisible strands, in a way she can be connected with no one else except in the deep past of her infant connection with her own mother. And she, too, needs to struggle from that one-to-one intensity into new realization, or reaffirmation, of her being-unto-herself.

The act of suckling a child, like a sexual act, may be tense, physically painful, charged with cultural feelings of inadequacy and guilt; or, like a sexual act, it can be a physically delicious, elementally soothing experience, filled with a tender sensuality. But just as lovers have to break apart after sex and become separate individuals again, so the mother has to wean herself from the infant and the infant from herself. In psychologies of child-rearing the emphasis is placed on "letting the child go" for the child's sake. But the mother needs to let it go as much or more for her own.

Motherhood, in the sense of an intense, reciprocal relationship with a particular child, or children, is one part of female process; it is not an identity for all time. The housewife in her mid-forties may jokingly say, "I feel like someone out of a job." But in the eyes of society, once having been mothers, what are we, if not always mothers? The process of "letting-go"—though we are charged with blame if we do not—is an act of revolt against the grain of patriarchal culture. But it is not enough to let our children go; we need selves of our own to return to.

To have borne and reared a child is to have done that thing which patriarchy joins with physiology to render into the definition of femaleness. But also, it can mean the experiencing of one's own body and emotions in a powerful way. We experience not only physical, fleshly changes but the feeling of a change in character. We learn, often through painful self-discipline and self-cauterization, those qualities which are supposed to be "innate" in

us: patience, self-sacrifice, the willingness to repeat endlessly the small, routine chores of socializing a human being. We are also, often to our amazement, flooded with feelings both of love and violence intenser and fiercer than any we had ever known. (A well-known pacifist, also a mother, said recently on a platform: "If anyone laid a hand on *my* child, I'd murder him.")

These and similar experiences are not easily put aside. Small wonder that women gritting their teeth at the incessant demands of child-care still find it hard to acknowledge their children's growing independence of them; still feel they must be at home, on the *qui vive*, be that car always tuned for the sound of emergency, of being needed. Children grow up, not in a smooth ascending curve, but jaggedly, their needs inconstant as weather. Cultural "norms" are marvelously powerless to decide, in a child of eight or ten, what gender s/he will assume on a given day, or how s/he will meet emergency, loneliness, pain, hunger. One is constantly made aware that a human existence is anything but linear, long before the labyrinth of puberty; because a human being of six is still a human being.

In a tribal or even a feudal culture a child of six would have serious obligations; ours have none. But also, the woman at home with children is not believed to be doing serious work; she is just supposed to be acting out of maternal instinct, doing chores a man would never take on, largely uncritical of the meaning of what she does. So child and mother alike are depreciated, because only grown men and women in the paid labor force are supposed to be "productive."

The power-relations between mother and child are often simply a reflection of power-relations in patriarchal society: "You will do this because I know what is good for you" is difficult to distinguish from "You will do this because I can *make* you." Powerless women have always used mothering as a channel—narrow but deep—for their own human will to power, their need to return upon the world what it has visited on them. The child dragged by the arm across the room to be washed, the child cajoled, bullied, and bribed into taking "one more bite" of a detested food, is more than just a child which must be reared according to cultural traditions of "a good mothering." S/he is a piece of reality, of the world, which can be acted on, even modified, by a woman restricted from acting on anything else except inert materials like dust and food.

6

When I try to return to the body of the young woman of twenty-six, pregnant for the first time, who fled from the physical knowledge of her pregnancy and at the same time from her intellect and vocation, I realize that I was effectively alienated from my real body and my real spirit by the institution—not the fact—of motherhood. This institution—the foundation of human society as we know it—allowed me only certain views, certain expectations, whether embodied in the booklet in my obstetrician's waiting room, the novels I had read, my mother-in-law's approval, my memories of my own mother, the Sistine Madonna or she of the Michelangelo *Pietà*, the floating notion that a woman pregnant is a woman calm in her fulfillment or, simply, a woman waiting. Women have always been seen as waiting: waiting to be asked, waiting for our menses, in fear lest they do or do not come, waiting for men to come home from wars, or from work, waiting for children to grow up, or for the birth of a new child, or for menopause.

In my own pregnancy I dealt with this waiting, this female fate, by denying every active, powerful aspect of myself. I became dissociated both from my immediate, present, bodily experience and from my reading, thinking, writing

life. Like a traveler in an airport where her plane is several hours delayed, who leafs through magazines she would never ordinarily read, surveys shops whose contents do not interest her, I committed myself to an outward serenity and a profound inner boredom. If boredom is simply a mask for anxiety, then I had learned, as a woman, to be supremely bored rather than to examine the anxiety underlying my Sistine tranquility. My body, finally truthful, paid me back in the end: I was allergic to pregnancy.

I have come to believe that female biology—the diffuse, intense sensuality radiating out from clitoris, breasts, uterus, vagina; the lunar cycles of menstruation; the gestation and fruition of life which can take place in the female body—has far more radical implications than we have yet to come to appreciate. Patriarchal thought has limited female biology to its own narrow specifications. The feminist vision has recoiled from female biology for these reasons; it will, I believe, come to view our physicality as a resource, rather than a destiny. In order to live a fully human life we require not only *control* of our bodies (though control is a prerequisite); we must touch the unity and resonance of our physicality, our bond with the natural order, the corporeal ground of our intelligence.

The ancient, continuing envy, awe, and dread of the male for the female capacity to create life has repeatedly taken the form of hatred for every other female aspect of creativity. Not only have women been told to stick to motherhood, but we have been told that our intellectual or aesthetic creations were inappropriate, inconsequential, or scandalous, an attempt to become "like men," or to escape from the "real" tasks of adult womanhood: marriage and childbearing. To "think like a man" has been both praise and prison for women trying to escape the body-trap. No wonder that many intellectual and creative women have insisted that they were "human beings" first and women only incidentally, have minimized their physicality and their bonds with other women. The body has been made so problematic for women that it has often seemed easier to shrug it off and travel as a disembodied spirit.

But this reaction against the body is now coming into synthesis with new inquiries into the actual—as opposed to the culturally warped—power inherent in female biology, however we choose to use it, and by no means limited to the maternal function.

My own story is only one story. What I carried away in the end was a determination to heal—insofar as an individual woman can, and as much as possible with other women—the

separation between mind and body; never again to lose myself both psychically and physically in that way. Slowly I came to understand the paradox contained in "my" experience of motherhood; that, although different from many other women's experiences it was not unique; and that only in shedding the illusion of my uniqueness could I hope, as a women, to have any authentic life at all.

NOTE

1. Arthur Calhoun, A *Social History of the American Family from Colonial Times to the Present* (Cleveland, 1917).

The Divorce Law Revolution and the Transformation of Legal Marriage

Lenore J. Weitzman

In 1970, California launched a legal revolution by instituting the first no-fault divorce law in the United States. This pioneering new law promised to free the legal process of divorce from the shackles of outmoded tradition. It embodied "modern" concepts of equity and equality, and was immediately heralded as the family law of the future.

Before 1970 all states in the United States

From *Contemporary Marriage*. Reprinted by permission.

required fault-based grounds for divorce. One party had to be judged guilty of some marital fault, such as adultery or cruelty, before a divorce could be granted. California rejected this traditional system by permitting parties to divorce when "irreconcilable differences" caused the breakdown of their marriage. This simple change transformed the legal process of divorce. By 1985, just fifteen years later, every state but South Dakota had adopted some form of no-fault divorce law.

These no-fault divorce laws are unique in several respects. First, they eliminate the need for grounds in order to obtain a divorce. (In fact, in many no-fault states it is not even necessary to obtain a spouse's consent in order to obtain a divorce.) Second, they undercut the old system of alimony and property awards for "innocent" spouses. Third, no-fault laws seek to undermine the adversary process and to reduce the acrimony and trauma of the fault system. Finally, new norms for dividing property and awarding alimony eliminate the anachronistic assumptions in the traditional law and treat wives as full and equal partners in the marital partnership.

When I first read about California's new law I was fascinated by the reformers' attempt to alter the social and psychological effects of divorce by changing the legal process. I had just completed two years as a postdoctoral fellow at Yale Law School, with a focus on family law, and I saw California's law as an exciting experiment in legal reform.

I also shared the reformers' optimism and assumed that only good could come from an end to the old fault-based system of divorce. The sham testimony and vilification that were required to prove fault insulted the dignity of the law, the courts, and all the participants. How much better, I thought, to construct a legal procedure that would eliminate vicious scenes and reduce, rather than increase, the antagonism and hostility between divorcing spouses. How much better to lessen the trauma of divorce for both parents and children. And how much better to end a marriage in a non-adversarial process that would enable the parties to fashion fair and equitable financial arrangements. If I, as a researcher, had a personal or political goal beyond my stated aim of analyzing the effects of the new law, it was to help potential reformers in other states learn from the California experience.

In the early 1970s I joined with Herma Hill Kay and Ruth B. Dixon in an interdisciplinary effort to study the social and legal consequences of California's divorce law reforms. We embarked on an analysis of court records, interviews with family law judges and lawyers, and in-depth interviews with recently divorced men and women.

As this research progressed, it became evident that the consequences of the legal reforms extended far beyond the original vision of the reformers. Without fault-based grounds for divorce, and without the need to prove adultery or mental cruelty, the reformers had not only recast the *psychological context* of divorce (and had in fact reduced some of the hostility and acrimony it generated), but they had also transformed the *economic consequences* of divorce and, in the process, had redefined the rights and responsibilities of husbands and wives in legal marriage.

Ends may influence beginnings. In a society where one-half of all first marriages are expected to end in divorce, a radical change in the rules for ending marriage inevitably affects the rules for marriage itself and the intentions and expectations of those who enter it.

THE UNINTENDED CONSEQUENCES

One unanticipated and unintended result of the no-fault reforms has been widespread economic disruption for divorced women and their children. The new rules for alimony, property, and child support shape radically different economic futures for divorced men, on the one hand, and for divorced women and their children on the other. Women, and the minor children in their households—90 percent of the children live with their mothers after divorce—experience a sharp decline in their standard of living after divorce. Men, in contrast, are usually much better off and have a higher standard of living as a result of no-fault divorce.

How could these simple changes in the rules for divorce have such far-reaching effects?

Why would a legal reform designed to create more equitable settlements end up impoverishing divorced women and their children?

In the pages that follow we will see how the new rules, rules designed to treat men and women "equally," have in practice served to deprive divorced women, especially mothers of young children and older homemakers, of the protections that the old law provided. These women have lost both the legitimacy and the financial rewards that the traditional divorce law provided for wives and mothers. Instead of recognition for their contributions as homemakers and mothers, and instead of compensation for the years of lost opportunities and impaired earning capacities, these women now face a divorce law that treats them "equally" and expects them to be equally capable of supporting themselves after divorce.

Since a woman's ability to support herself is likely to be impaired during marriage, especially if she has been homemaker and mother, she may not be equal to her former husband at the point of divorce. Rules that treat her as if she is equal simply serve to deprive her of the financial support she needs. In fact, marriage itself contributes to the economic inequalities between men and women and to the different structural opportunities that the two spouses face at divorce. While most married women give priority to their family roles, most married men give priority to their careers. She often forgoes further education and occupational gains for homemaking and child care, while he often acquires more education and on-the-job experience. As a result, her earning capacity is impaired while his earning capacity is enhanced. In both single-income and two-income families the couple, as a unit, are more likely to have given priority to the husband's career.

If the divorce rules do not allow her to share the fruits of her investment in his career (through alimony and child support awards); and if divorce rules expect her to enter the labor market as his equal—even though she may have

fewer job skills, outdated experience, no seniority, and no time for retraining; and if she continues to have the major responsibility for their children after divorce, it is easy to understand why divorced women are likely to be much worse off than their former husbands. Confronted with expectations that they will be "equally" responsible for the financial support of their children and themselves, they have typically been unequally disadvantaged by marriage and have fewer resources to meet those expectations. In addition, rules that require an equal division of marital property often force the sale of the family home and compound the financial dislocations by forcing children to change schools, neighborhoods, and friends just when they most need continuity and stability.

The result is often hardship, impoverishment, and disillusionment for divorced women and their children.

The unintended economic consequences of no-fault divorce provide the first major theme of this paper. The second major theme traces the effects of no-fault divorce on the institution of marriage.

*   *   *

THE TRANSFORMATION OF MARRIAGE

The divorce law revolution transformed more than the prior legal assumptions about divorce. It transformed the legal norms for marriage by articulating, codifying, and legitimating a new understanding of the marital partnership and marital commitment in our society. The new laws reflect, among other things, changing social realities, emerging social norms, and everyday legal practice. Ideally, that is as it should be: if law is to be effective, it must accord with social and practical reality. But the new divorce laws do not adequately or accurately reflect social reality, and they therefore exacerbate some of the grossest inequities in our society.

Traditional family law established a clear

TABLE 1   Summary of Changes in Divorce Law

Traditional Divorce	No-Fault Divorce
Restrictive law	Permissive law
To protect marriage	To facilitate divorce
Specific grounds	No grounds
Adultery, cruelty, etc.	Marital breakdown
Moral framework	Administrative framework
Guilt vs. innocence	
Fault	No-fault
One party caused divorce	Cause of divorce irrelevant
Consent of innocent spouse needed	No consent
Innocent spouse has "power"	Unilateral divorce
Can prevent/delay divorce	No consent/agreement necessary
Gender-based responsibilities	Gender-neutral responsibilities
Husband responsible for alimony	Both responsible for self-support
Wife responsible for custody	Both eligible for custody
Husband responsible for child support	Both responsible for child support
Financial awards linked to fault	Financial awards based on need and equality
Alimony for "innocent" wife	Alimony based on need
Greater share of property to "innocent" spouse	Property divided equally
Adversarial	Nonadversarial
One party guilty, one innocent	No guilty or innocent party
Financial gain improving fault	No financial gain in charges
	Amicable resolution encouraged

moral framework for both marriage and divorce: marriage was a partnership, a lifelong commitment to join together "forsaking all others," for better or for worse. Husbands and wives were assigned specific roles and responsibilities, and these obligations were reinforced by law. The moral obligations of marriage were, in theory, reinforced by alimony and property awards so that spouses who lived up to their marriage contract were rewarded, and those who had not were punished.

Of course, we now know that the reality of divorce settlements often diverged from this theoretical ideal. Alimony was the exception rather than the rule, and fathers often breached their responsibility for child support. But the old structure did give the spouse who wanted to remain married considerable bargaining power, and to that extent it reinforced marriage as against the alternative of divorce. The required grounds and the need to prove fault created barriers to divorce. In addition, because the old structure linked fault to the terms of the eco-

nomic settlement, divorce was expensive for men of means. If she was "innocent," the wife of a man with money and property could expect to be awarded a lifetime alimony, the family home, and other property to meet her needs. In addition, her husband would remain responsible for her financial support. (So, too, could the guilty wife expect to be punished and be denied alimony and property.)

The new reforms altered each of the major provisions of the traditional law, and in the process, they redefined the norms of legal marriage. No-fault laws abolished the need for grounds and the need to prove fault in order to obtain a divorce. They abandoned the gender-based assumptions of the traditional law in favor of standards for treating men and women "equally" in alimony and property awards. They negated the traditional role that fault played in financial awards and instead decreed that awards should be based on the divorcing parties' current financial needs and resources. And finally, the new rules shifted the legal criteria for divorce—and thus for viable marriage—from fidelity to the marriage contract to individual standards of personal satisfaction. The rules are thereby redefining marriage as a time-limited, contingent arrangement rather than a lifelong commitment.

From State Protection of Marriage to Facilitation of Divorce

The divorce law reforms have moved the state from a position of protecting marriage (by restricting marital dissolution) to one of facilitating divorce.

They adopt a laissez-faire attitude toward both marriage and divorce, leaving both the terms of the marriage contract—and the option to terminate it—squarely in the hands of the individual parties. The pure no-fault states also eliminate any moral dimension from the divorce: guilt and innocence, fidelity and faithlessness, no longer affect the granting of the decree or its financial consequences.

The individual's freedom to end the marriage is further bolstered in some states by no-consent rules that give either party the right to obtain a divorce without the other's agreement. Since pure no-fault—no-consent rules allow one spouse to make a unilateral decision to terminate the marriage, they transfer the economic leverage from the spouse who wants to remain married to the spouse who wants to get divorced. It is an important difference. Under the prior law the party who wanted a divorce might well have to make economic concessions or "buy" a spouse's agreement. But under the no-consent rule it is the one who hopes to preserve the marriage who must do the bargaining. Apart from the economic implications, which are considerable, these laws strengthen the hand of the party who seeks the divorce, increasing the likelihood that divorce will in fact occur.

From a Lifetime Contract to an Optional, Time-Limited Commitment

The new divorce laws no longer view marriage as a lifelong partnership, but as a union that remains only so long as it proves satisfying to both partners. In addition, the traditional obligations of marriage, like the institution itself, are increasingly being redefined by the new divorce laws as optional, time-limited, contingent, open to individual definition, and, most important, terminable upon divorce.

In contrast to the traditional marriage contract whereby a husband undertook lifelong responsibility for his wife's support, the new divorce laws suggest that this and other family responsibilities can—and may—be terminated upon divorce, or soon after divorce, as evident in the new rules for alimony, property, child support, and custody. Short-term alimony awards, discussed above, are evident throughout the United States as courts define women as "dependents" for shorter and shorter periods of time. Current awards in California average two years.

Similar in its effect is the emphasis on a speedy resolution of the spouses' property claims. My research reveals many more forced sales of family homes than in the past, to hasten the day when each spouse can "take his (or her) money and leave." Arrangements that delay the sale of the home so that minor children do not have to move are viewed with disfavor by the courts because they "tie up the father's money." The judges we interviewed asserted that each spouse is entitled to his or her share of the property and should not have to wait for it. There is also a tendency to "cash out" other shared investments such as pensions and retirement benefits to provide a "clean break" between the parties at the time of the divorce.

Even parenting is becoming increasingly optional and terminable upon divorce. Indeed, a de facto effect of the current laws is to deprive children of the care, companionship, and support of their fathers. This is evident in the courts' treatment of postdivorce visitation and child support. Furstenberg et al. found that 52 percent of the children of divorce in a nationally representative sample had not seen their fathers at all in the past year, and only 17 percent of the children had seen their fathers at least once a week. These data indicate that a majority of divorced fathers are abandoning their parental roles after divorce and are being allowed to do so without legal sanction.

In fact, one of the strongest supports for the assertion that fathers—who are 90 percent of the noncustodial parents—are legally allowed to abandon their children is the lack of a legal course of action to compel a parent to see his or her children. The implicit message is that joint parenting—and even parenting itself—is an "optional" responsibility for divorced fathers.

This message is also reflected by the law's tolerance for fathers who abandon their children financially and in the meager amounts of court-ordered child support. The courts award little child support to begin with, thereby allowing fathers to rid themselves of much of their financial responsibility for their children, and then fail to enforce child support awards once they are made.

The inadequacy of child support awards has been well documented. A 1978 U.S. Census survey found that divorced fathers paid an average of $1,951 per year per child. In 1981 they paid an average of $2,220, which represents a 16 percent decline in real dollars between 1978 and 1981. In California we found that the average child support award was typically less than the cost of day care alone—it did not approach half of the cost of actually raising children.

Past research has also more than amply documented the widespread noncompliance with child support awards. The 1981 Census survey, for example, showed that more than half (53 percent) of the millions of women who are due child support do not receive it.

While child support awards have always been inadequate and poorly enforced, what appears to be unique about the current situation is the willful disregard of court orders among middle class and upper middle class fathers. For example, our California data reveal that fathers

with incomes of $30,000 to $50,000 a year are just as likely to avoid child support payments as men with incomes of under $10,000 a year. The explanation for this lies in the legal system's lax enforcement, which has given fathers tacit approval (and financial incentives) for evading court orders.

Although 1984 federal legislation to strengthen the enforcement of child support may alter the present pattern, thus far family law judges and lawyers have been reluctant to bother with enforcement. When we collected our data the California law already contained many of the strict enforcement provisions of the 1984 federal law, but the judges we interviewed preferred not to use them.

Preston contends that the financial and social "disappearing act of fathers" after divorce is part of a larger trend: the conjugal family is gradually divesting itself of care for children in much the same way that it did earlier for the elderly. To date, indications of parental abandonment have focused on fathers. Thus far, most analysts have seen mothers as firmly committed to their children. But as the norms of the new divorce laws permeate popular awareness, this picture also may change.

The import of the new custody laws, especially those that change the maternal presumption to a joint custody preference, undermine women's incentives to invest in their children. As women increasingly recognize that they will be treated "equally" in child custody decisions, that caretaking and nurturance of children find no protection in the law and are punished by the job market, and that joint custody awards may push them into difficult, restrictive, and unrewarding postdivorce custodial arrangements, they may increasingly take to heart the new laws' implied warning that motherhood does not pay.

The optional and time-limited marital commitments embodied in the new divorce laws have a differential effect on men and women. While they free men from the responsibilities they retained under the old system, they "free" women from the security that system provided. Since women's investments in home, family, and children have typically meant lost opportunities in the paid labor force, they are more dependent on the long-term protection and security that the traditional law promised them. It is not surprising that our research finds women "suffering" more under the new laws, for these laws remove the financial safeguards of the old law—with a decline in alimony awards and a decrease in women's share of the community property—at the same time that they increase the financial burdens imposed on women after divorce.

For men, by contrast, the new legal assumption of time-limited commitments means a new freedom from family financial obligations. In fact, the new laws actually give men an incentive to divorce by offering them a release from the financial burdens of marriage. In fact, the wealthier a man is, and the longer he has been married, the more he has to gain financially from divorce.

From Protection for Housewives and Mothers to Gender-Neutral Rules

If the new legal assumptions were accompanied by provisions that enabled both spouses to choose the extent to which they would assume breadwinning and homemaking roles, and if they then gave each spouse "credit" for the roles they in fact assumed during marriage, then the law would accurately reflect the complexity and variety of marital roles in these years of "transition." But the present legal system seems to leave no room for such flexibility.

Rather, it suggests that a woman (or a man) who chooses homemaking and parenting risks a great penalty because she (or he) will pay heavily for that choice in the event of a divorce. Even if two parties agree to form an equal partnership in which they give priority to his career while she assumes the larger share of the house-

work and child care, and even if they agree that he will share his earnings and career assets with her, their agreement may have no legal standing. The woman will still be expected to be self-sufficient after divorce, and the man's promise of continued support and a share of his earnings—the promise that is implied in most marriages with a traditional division of labor—will be ignored in most courts.

The penalty can be equally severe for the woman who works during marriage, or who works part-time, but who nevertheless gives priority to her family over her work. Her claims to share her husband's income through spousal support fall on deaf ears in courts, which are concerned only with her "ability to engage in gainful employment."

Under the new legal assumptions the average divorced woman in California will be awarded no alimony, only minimal child support (which she probably will not be able to collect), exactly half of the joint tangible assets (an average of less than $10,000 worth of property), and an explicit directive to become immediately self-supporting. Even if she had married under the old law, and lived her life by the letter of the traditional marriage contract, and is forty-five or fifty-five at the time of divorce, chances are that the courts will apply the new standards of self-sufficiency to her as well. Especially disadvantaged by these new assumptions are mothers of young children and older homemakers.

Thus one implication of the present allocation of family resources at divorce is that women had better not forgo any of their own education, training, and career development to devote themselves fully or even partially to domesticity. The law assures that they will not be much rewarded for their devotion, and they will suffer greatly if their marriage dissolves.

The concept of marital roles embodied in the new divorce laws carries an equally sobering message about motherhood. Divorcing mothers of preschool children have experienced a greater decline in alimony awards than any other group of women since the no-fault laws were instituted and the vast majority of these mothers—87 percent—arc awarded no alimony at all. They are expected to find jobs immediately, to support themselves completely and, for the most part, to support their children as well.

In addition, since the age of majority children has dropped from age twenty-one to age eighteen, the divorced mother of teenage children confronts the fact that her former husband is not legally required to support their children once they reach age eighteen even if they are still in their senior year of high school, much less through college. However, both high school and college students in these post–child-support years usually remain financially dependent on their parents. It is their mothers who are much more likely to respond to their needs and to support them, even though they are typically financially less able to do so.

Finally, the woman who has raised her children to maturity and who, as a result of the priority she has given to motherhood, finds herself with no marketable skills when she is divorced at forty-five or fifty-five, typically faces the harshest deprivations after divorce. The courts rarely reward her for the job she has done. Rather, the new assumptions imply that her motherhood years were wasted and worthless, for she, too, is measured against the all-important new criterion of earning capacity.

Thus the new divorce laws are institutionalizing a set of norms that may be as inappropriate in one direction as the old norms were in another. The old law assumed that all married women were first and foremost housewives and mothers. The new law assumes that all married women are employable and equally capable of self-sufficiency after divorce. Both views are overly simplistic, impede women's options, and exert a rigidifying influence on future possibilities.

For most women in our society, marriage and career are no longer either/or choices. Most women do not expect to choose between work and marriage, or between a career and motherhood. The vast majority of American women want all three. But, as Shirley Johnson has observed, when "women who have both worked full time and carried the lioness's share of the household management and child-rearing responsibilities, find out that their dual role is not recognized or rewarded in divorce settlements, the effect of the new divorce laws is to encourage women to . . . shift their energies into the labor market." Johnson argues that the economic message in the new divorce laws is that it no longer pays for a woman to "invest in marriage-specific skills" since such investments have a relatively low payoff in a society with a high risk of marital dissolution.

From Partnership to Individualism

The new divorce laws alter the traditional legal view of marriage as a partnership by rewarding individual achievement rather than investment in the family partnership. Instead of the traditional vision of a common financial future within marriage, the no-fault and no-consent standards for divorce, and the new rules for alimony, property, custody, and child support, all convey a new vision of independence for husbands and wives in marriage. In addition, the new laws confer economic advantages on spouses who invest in themselves at the expense of the marital partnership.

This focus on the individual underlies many of the changes discussed above. It reflects not only a shift in the legal relationships between the family and its adult members but also a shift in the courts' attitudes and practices in meting out rewards at divorce.

The traditional law embodied the partnership concept of marriage by rewarding sharing and mutual investments in the marital community. Implicit in the new laws, in contrast, are incentives for investing in oneself, maintaining one's separate identity, and being self-sufficient. The new stress is on individual responsibility for one's future, rather than on joint or reciprocal responsibilities.

Once again, it is easy to see how these new assumptions reflect larger cultural themes: the rise of individualism, the emphasis on personal fulfillment, the belief in personal responsibility, and the importance we attach to individual "rights." These trends have at once been applauded for the freedom they offer and criticized as selfish, narcissistic, and amoral. Whether this change represents a decline or an advance depends on one's personal values: are we concerned with the security and stability that the old order provided or with the misery it caused for those who were forced to remain in unhappy marriages?

Our evaluation will also depend on how we see the past. The belief that the rise of individualism has fostered a decline in the family rests on the assumption that the family was stable and harmonious in the past. But historians have not yet identified an era in which families were stable and harmonious and all family members behaved unselfishly and devoted their efforts to the collective good. That "classical family of western nostalgia," to use William J. Goode's term for the stereotype, has been one of the major casualties of recent research in family history.

But historical research does suggest a change in the psychological quality of family life and a rise in what Lawrence Stone calls "affective individualism"—a growing focus on individuals as unique personalities and a political emphasis on individual rights. The rise of effective individualism has brought emotional closeness between nuclear family members and a greater appreciation for the individuality of each person in the family. Historically, this trend strengthened the husband–wife unit at the expense of the larger family and the kinship network in which it was embedded. More recently, as rising divorce rates demonstrate, the strength of the husband–wife unit has declined and values of "pure" individualism are emerging. The new divorce laws reflect this evolution in that they encourage notions of personal primacy for both husband and wife. They imply that neither spouse should invest too much in marriage or place marriage above self-interest.

Both the new rules for spousal support and the new rules for property undermine the marital partnership. Despite the partnership principles that underlie the division of property, that is, the idea that property accumulated during marriage is to be shared equally at divorce—the current bases for dividing property belie such principles.

If the major breadwinner is allowed to retain most of the new property or career assets he (or she) has acquired during marriage—assets such as a professional education or good will, or health benefits, or enhanced earning capacity—the law's implicit message is that one's own career is the only safe investment. This encourages both spouses to invest in themselves before investing in each other, or their marriage, or their children.

This is one area in which the new legal assumptions are not congruent with the attitudes and assumptions of the divorced men and women we interviewed. Our interviewees rejected the limited definition of alimony as based on "need" and minimal self-sufficiency, and instead saw alimony as a means of sharing their partnership assets—the income and earning capacity in which they had both invested, and the standard of living they expected to share. These "sharing principles" for alimony were seen as an essential element in their implicit partnership "contract."

One implication of these changes is that marriage is likely to become increasingly less central to the lives of individual men and women. The privileged status of marriage in traditional family law, as well as the protections and restrictions placed on its inception and dissolution, reinforced its importance and encouraged husbands and wives to invest in it and to make it the center of their lives. The new laws, in contrast, discourage shared investments in marriage and thereby encourage both husbands and wives to dissociate from investments in the partnership. As more men and women follow the apparent mandate of the new laws, it seems reasonable to predict that marriage will lose further ground.

Indeed, William J. Goode persuasively argues that the trend is already well in progress. He observes that for both men and women marriage is simply less important today than it was in the past, and he foresees the further "decline of individual investments in family relationships over the coming decade" because investments in one's individual life and career pay off better in modern society. As more women seek to follow men in the path of acquiring status, self-esteem, and a sense of individual accomplishment from their jobs, the importance of marriage will rest increasingly on its ability to provide individuals with psychic and emotional sustenance. This, Goode observes, is a difficult and fragile bond. In these trends he sees profound implications for the future of intimate relationships and the bearing and rearing of children in Western nations.

THE CLOUDED STATUS OF CHILDREN

A final feature of the new divorce laws is their ambiguous message about parental responsibility for children. In the past, the sustained well-being of the children of divorce was assumed to be the state's primary concern in any legal proceedings involving children. Indeed, it was this concern that dictated most of the traditional divorce law protections for women: women were recognized as the primary custodians of children, and in that capacity were to be accorded preferences and support to ensure the fulfillment of their responsibilities. Similarly, women who had devoted the productive years of their lives to child-rearing were to be rewarded for that appropriate and honorable effort.

Under the new laws, the state's concern for the welfare of children is far less in evidence. Rather, it appears that in the law's practical application, at least, the children have been all but forgotten in the courts' preoccupation with parental "equality."

The same rules that facilitate divorce facilitate the disruption of children's lives. The gender-neutral rules that encourage or force mothers to work also deprive children of the care and attention they might otherwise have. (Effectively, the fate of divorcing mothers is still the fate of the children of divorce because, sex-neutral custody standards notwithstanding, mothers still are the primary caretakers of children after divorce.) Also, the actual effects of the current laws deprive children of both the care and the support of their fathers.

In sum, under the present laws divorced fathers *may* participate more in the lives of their children if they choose to do so, but they need not so choose; and mothers *must* work outside the home whether they wish it or not, and thus *must* divide their energies between jobs and children. One might well ask what legal protections remain to insure parenting for children after divorce.

Even as the law over time evolves to reflect social reality, it also serves as a powerful force in creating social reality. Although the divorce law reformers knew that equality between the sexes was not yet a reality when they codified assumptions about equality in the law, they had seen trends in that direction and believed the new law would accelerate those trends. My research shows however, that the law actually slowed any trend toward economic equality that may have been developing. It worsened women's condition, improved men's condition, and widened the income gap between the sexes. The law has moved us toward a new reality, to be sure, but it is not, in the economic sphere at least, the hoped-for-reality.

So long as the laws remain in force in their present form and their present application, post-divorce equality between the sexes will remain an illusion.

The Feminization of Poverty

Diana Pearce

I'm going to talk about three things today. First, I'm going to give you a description of poverty trends, especially the trend towards the feminization of poverty. Second, I'm going to describe how our welfare system, not AFDC, but unemployment, etc., reinforces women's poverty. Third, I'm going to talk about what the future holds; there will be two topics under this, first, welfare reform, which we already have in the form of the Family Support Act, and secondly, housing reform, which we don't have yet, but desperately need.

The "other America," described two decades ago by Michael Harrington, is a changing neighborhood. Men are moving out, while women, many with children, are moving in. As a result, the War on Poverty, as described by Harrington and many others, was built on images and assumptions about the poor that have become increasingly invalid. I'm going to talk today about the feminization of poverty which has profoundly altered the nature of poverty and therefore the nature of the kinds of solutions that we must propose.

What is the feminization of poverty? Whether it is widows, divorcees, or unmarried mothers, women have always experienced more poverty than men. But in the last two decades, families maintained by women alone have increased from 36 percent to 51.5 percent of all

From *The Journal for Peace and Justice Studies* Vol 2. (1990). Reprinted with permission.

poor families. That is the feminization of poverty.

During the 1970s, there was a net increase each year of about 100,000 poor, woman-maintained families. Between 1979 and 1987, another almost 1 million families headed by women became poor. And of the increase in poor families between 1986 and 1987, the last year for which we have data, 2/3 were headed by women. There are now 3-1/2 million families maintained by women alone with incomes below the poverty level. If one simply extrapolated the present trends and did not take into account any other factors, all of the poor by the year 2000 would be women and children. That is the feminization of poverty.

The relative economic status of families maintained by women alone has also declined, with average income of female-headed families falling from 51 percent to 46 percent of the average male-headed family. Once poor, the female-maintained family is more likely to stay poor—ten times more likely by one estimate. That is the feminization of poverty.

These trends are even greater within the minority community. Particularly in the 1970s, the black community experienced a shift in the burden of poverty from two-parent families to families maintained by the woman alone, so that now, about three out of four poor black families are maintained by women alone. Because of racial discrimination, the statistics for minority women are even more dismal than

How does this compare to that percent of families in general?

those for majority women. This shift has increased minority poverty and exacerbated racial inequality. That is the feminization of poverty.

Basically, what has been happening are two opposite trends. First, several groups that have historically experienced disproportionate rates of poverty have been lifted out of poverty by post-war economic growth or by the development of targeted social programs. Many workers who used to be labeled the "working poor" by themselves as well as others, are now economically secure enough to be seen as the "working class" or the "middle class." Older Americans, whose poverty frequently occurred because of a health care crisis or a lack of housing and inadequate Social Security, have been given Medicare—although we've been gutting that—housing chartered specifically for the elderly, and raised and indexed Social Security benefits. As a result, the overall poverty rate for the elderly is actually less than that of the population as a whole.

The opposite trend characterizes families maintained by women alone. Although a decrease in the proportion of these families experienced poverty, about one third of all female maintained families are poor today, compared to one half in the 1960s. This gain has been overwhelmed by the large increase in the number of women-maintained families, greatly enlarging the pool of those at risk. Most people are aware that the rise in the divorce rate and the increase in the number of children born out of wedlock has increased the number of single-parent families. But this trend is also the result of the fact that, first of all, virtually every woman today is married at some point (about 94 percent of women by the age of sixty-five have tried marriage) and most ever married have children. Only 6 percent remain childless by the age of forty to forty-four in 1980. In 1950, about 20 percent remained childless by the time they got to the end of their child-bearing years. In short, more women are mothers, but fewer do so with a lifelong mate.

But this just begs the question of why women-maintained households have either not shared in either the *prosperity* of the 1950s and 1960s, or in the poverty reduction experienced by other high-risk groups. The answer lies in the following two basic phenomena. First, women's poverty is fundamentally different from that experienced by men, and second, poor women are subject to programs designed for poor men. Poor women find that these programs are not only inadequate and inappropriate, but also lock them into a life of poverty.

While many women are poor for some of the same reasons that men are poor—for example, they live in a job-poor area, and/or they lack the necessary skills or education—much of women's poverty can be traced to two causes that are basically unique to women. First, women must provide all or most of the support for their children, and secondly, they are disadvantaged in the labor market as women.

Women bear the economic as well as emotional burden of rearing their children. When a couple with children breaks up, frequently, the man becomes single, while the woman becomes a single parent. Poverty rates for households with children have always been greater than those for households that do not have children and the difference had always been greater for female-headed households. That gap is increasing: 46.1 percent of women-headed households with children under eighteen years of age are in poverty, compared with about 8 percent of households maintained by men with their children living with them. The differential is in part a product of the fact that many families never receive some or all of the support due them from the absent father. For instance, in 1985, only 43 percent of absent fathers paid child support and only about half of those who paid paid the full amount. The amounts paid are small as well, averaging only about $2,200 annually per family, not per child. At a time when the median family income is over $30,000 a year, this is less than 10 percent of average family income. According to one study, a father's child support payment averaged less than his car payment. In other words, fathers pay more to support their cars than to support their kids. What makes matters worse, payments have not kept up with inflation. In the last three years, the real value of the average payment in constant inflation adjusted dollars has fallen 16 percent. I'll talk later about some things that are starting to happen so that the child support picture won't be so dismal in the future.

Public support of dependent children is even more appalling. Using as a standard the amount of money paid a foster mother to take care of children who are not her own, we can see that we have always been more generous to children in two-parent foster homes than to children in their own, single-parent homes. Over the past eight years, however, that ratio has become worse, and now instead of the foster parent getting three times what the AFDC parent gets for food, shelter, and clothes for the child, the foster parent in the average state gets four times as much. In 1982, the average foster child payment was $197 per month while the average payment for an additional child was $49 per month. In some states, the foster parents are paid seven or eight times as much as the child's own mother is to take care of the child.

The other source of women's poverty that is unique to women is their disadvantage in the labor market, and I think most of you are pretty familiar with that. That is, the average woman only earns about 65 percent of what the average male earns for full-time work and that figure has changed very little—it's gone up and down, and it's going up a little now, but it's still within the range of where it's been since the Korean War.

In 1987, the average woman college graduate working full-time, throughout the year, earned less than the average male high school graduate. We've made some progress—we used to earn less as college graduates than the average male high school dropout.

Equally important, but less well known is another aspect of women's disadvantage in the labor market. More women than men are unable to obtain regular, full-time, year round work. About half the women in the labor force are working part-time or part year, or both, and slightly less than half the women are full-time, year round workers. Many women, especially mothers seeking to support their households on their earnings, encounter serious obstacles with full participation in the labor force, including inadequate, unavailable or unaffordable day care, and discrimination based on full-time work. And, as a result, only about 40 percent of women maintaining households alone are full-time, year-round workers, as compared to almost two thirds of male householders. About one third of women heading families alone, compared to 20 percent of the men, are not in the labor force at all. In addition, women are concentrated in a relatively small number of occupations, many of which are underpaid. As women experience occupational segregation and confinement to the pink-collar ghetto, the limitations on opportunities for income growth that accompany such segregation keep women poor. Finally, there are the economic costs of sexual harassment that are almost always borne by the woman alone. Every woman who has lost a promotion, quit to avoid further sexual harassment, or "mysteriously" walked away from an opportunity, has paid an economic as well as a psychic price for being a woman. As far as I know, no one has done a really good job of measuring the "price," the economic costs, of sexual harassment, not sex discrimination, but sexual harassment.

Even working women must work harder to avoid poverty. Eleven percent of minority women single parents who work full-time, all year, are still poor; this is the same percentage of white male householders who are poor, who do not work at all. Because of the higher poverty rates of women associated with each level of participation in the labor market, and because fewer female heads of household participate as full time workers, having a job is a much less certain route out of poverty for women than for men. Altogether, about 4 percent of families with a working male householder are in poverty, while more than 25 percent of families headed by employed women have incomes below the poverty level. And recent work that I haven't published yet shows that most of the increase in women's labor force participation over the last decade has been as low wage workers, and that's at about $5.85 an hour or less, minimum wage in the 1970s, so that most of our increase in the labor force has been at the very bottom, and it's been particularly bad for single parents. Single parents are working more now and have higher poverty rates than before so that they've now moved from being working poor to being poor.

Now let's look at the welfare system and what it does. It's supposed to provide income support for families when they have inadequate income. Our system was developed to provide income to individuals and families whose earnings are inadequate to meet their needs. But beyond that basic rule, various income support programs differ greatly in every characteristic, such as the amount of benefits, accessibility, and stigma attached to the benefit.

Using such characteristics, these programs can be divided into two broad groups. Programs found in the *primary* sector are for the deserving poor and have been characterized as a right, often but not always, a right which comes from working, from being employed. They have relatively generous benefits and are not means-tested and are not stigmatizing. By contrast, programs in the *secondary* sector are for the "undeserving poor" and frequently restrict and treat eligibility criteria depending on time and geography. These programs have a strict income limit in order to qualify, and provide benefits that are penurious in amount and stigmatizing. Programs in both sectors are based on male models, primarily a male breadwinner model for the primary sector, and a male pauper model

for the secondary sector. An example of a major program in the primary sector is the unemployment compensation program. This program is designed for a limited group of workers. You think of it as something for everybody who's unemployed, but it's not supposed to be. This group of workers is comprised of regular workers, who are presumed also to be the breadwinners in their families, in which the wife had a supporting role but was not herself in paid employment. The original aim was to help these workers, who, through no fault of their own and due to the vagaries of seasonal employment patterns, business cycles, or technological obsolescence, found themselves out of work. The group to be aided by this program was not all the unemployed, since casual workers, or those who worked part time or seasonally, could not prove their attachment to the work force and therefore were not deserving of help. Women and other minority workers were not and are not now statutorily excluded from eligibility for unemployment benefits, but many have been excluded in disproportionate numbers by virtue of their low wages, or their less than full-time status. They are considered "casual" workers, or, because they are part-time, are not eligible for unemployment compensation. This has far-reaching consequences for those who are the sole supporters of their households.

By contrast, the secondary sector is disproportionately composed of women and minorities. In spite of this demographic characteristic, the secondary sector programs are built on the male pauper model, which has its roots in the sixteenth-century poor laws of England, when paupers were ex-soldiers, beggars, and vagabond, landless peasants, and were mostly men. This model offers a simple set of principles: "Most of the poor are poor because they do not work, and most of the poor are able-bodied and could work." Therefore, the solution to poverty, according to the male pauper model, is to "put them to work." Unlike unemployment compensation, there is little concern for the quality of the job, even its monetary return, or in matching workers' skills to jobs with appropriate requirements. Rather, any job will do. When applied to women, such as AFDC mothers, the results are less than positive. First, as we've seen above, having a job is, by itself a less certain route out of poverty for women than it is for men. Second, income from earnings only partially meets the woman's needs and therefore, only partially alleviates her poverty. A woman's responsibility for children and other dependents results in economic and emotional burdens requiring additional income and fringe benefits for child care and health insurance, and flexible or part-time work arrangements, that are not available with most jobs.

The dual welfare system described above is not only inherently discriminatory against women, but also operates to reinforce their disadvantaged status in the labor market. Economists have developed a theory of institutional divisions in the labor market that conceives of the labor market as a dual system, divided into primary and secondary sectors. In the primary sector, workers hold jobs with relatively high pay and good fringe benefits, better working conditions and greater security. If they should lose their jobs, they are likely to be compensated relatively better through unemployment compensation and through other programs such as disability at rates designed to replace 50 percent of lost wages; plus, if they are members of a union, they receive supplementary union benefits. Although theoretically, workers in this sector must return to work as soon as possible, the programs are designed, not only to support the worker and his or her family during unemployment, but also to enable the worker to conduct a job search that will result in re-employment in a job that will maintain his or her skills, occupational status and income. Indeed, many people who receive unemployment do not go through a great income loss over that period of time and return to a job that pays relatively well.

...not any more...

In contrast, workers in the secondary sector find themselves at relatively low wage jobs with little job security and few fringe benefits. If they lose their jobs, which happens relatively more frequently and unpredictably than in the primary sector, these workers often find themselves ineligible for unemployment compensation. Many women in this circumstance turn to AFDC, the "poor woman's unemployment compensation." Studies show that 90 percent of welfare mothers have worked, many of them recently, and many of the women who apply for public assistance do so only after both the labor market *and* the marriage institution have failed to provide income to adequately support their families. However, they cannot even obtain this help without first impoverishing themselves, by exhausting their resources and savings. Once on welfare, they not only find it penurious in amount and stigmatizing, but they are also pushed to leave it as soon as possible, no matter how poor the new job's pay and long-term prospects, or how inadequate the child care is, or how difficult the transportation. The secondary welfare sector destroys not only one's incentive, but also one's prospects of ever working one's way out of poverty. And, of course, as soon as one's child gets sick, or a crisis happens, or, one gets fired, one's back on welfare and the cycle continues and reinforces one's position in the secondary labor market, the secondary welfare system.

"one's"? terrible writing

Disproportionate numbers of women and minorities are found in the secondary sector. While 87 percent of the recipients of primary benefits are white families headed by men or married couples, only three percent are families maintained by black women alone. Conversely, woman householders account for over two thirds of secondary sector recipients, that is, recipients of welfare and public assistance. As one might expect, there's a great difference in the poverty incidence between the two sectors. While only about 8 percent of those families whose heads have been receiving primary sector benefits, such as unemployment compensation, are poor, almost 3/4 of families with heads who receive secondary sector benefits are in poverty. Thus women, particularly minority women, are disproportionately experiencing impoverishing consequences of the dual welfare system.

I'm going to talk now about a new aspect of the problem of women and poverty, the housing crisis and women. Women are disproportionately affected by the housing crisis for all of the reasons I've been describing—their disproportionate low income and poverty incidence and the fact that they tend to be long-term poor as compared to men. One of the consequences of it is disproportionate poverty is that women are much more likely to be renters than owners. Two thirds of women-maintained families are renters, as compared to 3/4 of all other families who are owners, a tremendous dichotomy in terms of women's positions in the housing market.

The second aspect in the housing market is that women-maintained households have experienced some increase in income, but it hasn't kept up with the increases in rent. So those who are renters are getting the squeeze. Over the decade of 1975–1985, renter women-maintained households' income increased an average of 12 percent, but rents increased an average of 20 percent. As a result of this, the average percent of income that women-maintained households are spending on housing, rent and utilities, rose from 38 percent in 1974 to 58 percent in 1987. They're spending almost 60 percent of their income on housing.

This is worse for black and Hispanic women who have higher poverty rates and higher percentages which go to rent. I think one of the things to keep in mind when we're talking about this particular aspect of poverty is that when you spend money on housing, when you're very poor, you can't cut back on your housing expenditures. If you're very poor, you could skip a meal, not buy new clothes. You can't stop using your living room to cut down

on your rent costs. So as we see this increasing squeeze of higher costs and less income, women are really being squeezed by this.

The supply of low-cost housing is disappearing very fast. In 1970, there were 15 million units which were considered "affordable," that is, with an income of $5,000 or less, you could rent them for 30 percent or less of your income. Today, the number of units that are "affordable," adjusting for inflation, is now only 1.8 million. This is about one unit per every two families that are low-income.

We have also seen an increase in discrimination against families with kids, another factor which affects women in the housing market. Families with children are new clients under the Fair Housing Law, but given the effectiveness of the 1968 Fair Housing Act, in terms of race and gender discrimination, I think we shouldn't expect discrimination against families with children to disappear overnight. In fact, we're beginning to hear about new kinds of discrimination against families with children. For example, "we can't rent to families with children because there's lead paint and we don't want to poison the children." Suddenly, I guess they're concerned about children.

What are we doing in terms of public policy in this area? HUD helps about 4.3 million households, not just female headed households but all households. This is about 1/3 of the families in need, that is, families who are eligible either because of low income or inadequate housing.

Since 1981, housing for low income families has been cut more than any other low income budget item, with about 80 percent cut in that area. To give you a specific example illustrating how bad it has gotten, and what's going to happen in the near future, we have had a program called Section 8, which is where you give someone a certificate and they can go and get housing and pay only 30 percent of their income for that housing and the government pays the difference between that and the rent.

This year, about 20,000 of those certificates will expire and that means that people will suddenly have to be paying the full rent. Next year, about 200,000 of those certificates will expire and at this point, we have nothing in the budget which will deal with those issues and that's obviously a big part of the battle about housing. And after next year, there will be another several hundred thousand. It will escalate like this: almost all of the housing we built or subsidized for low income families, including Section 8 certificates, had time limits. Somehow, we thought the problem would solve itself, that somehow the local housing authority would start producing housing for low income households, or that we would no longer have poor households. Whichever assumption was made, it was all very unrealistic and it's all coming due. The more recent housing programs have even shorter time frames, so we're going over a cliff in the early nineties in terms of what's going to happen for housing.

One consequence of this squeeze in the housing market and the decline in affordable housing units and the increases in rent, is that families with children, especially women with children, are becoming homeless.

I'd like to talk now, and most of this is drawn from congressional testimony I gave earlier this week, about the problem of the invisibility of homeless families. I think one of the problems we are confronting with public housing policy today, is that women-headed families with children are the most invisible of all of our poverty population. By the way, all of the statistics I gave you on poverty, and the feminization of poverty, don't count the homeless because all those statistics are based on household surveys. If you don't have a house, you're not a household and you're not counted. So all of those official numbers underestimate poverty in the 1980s, because we don't have any count of people even in shelters, we only count people in households when doing the annual survey on income and poverty.

Families with children, most of which are women with children, are the fastest growing segment of the homeless. This is the virtually unanimous conclusion of surveys done by mayors, homeless coalitions, and others. Between 1983 and 1987, the number of women seeking shelter at battered women shelters has increased 100 percent. The proportion of homeless which are families varies widely from city to city from 25 percent to 70 percent of the homeless depending on the city and depending on the person doing the estimate. With the total estimate of up to three million homeless, the number of homeless families could well be in the neighborhood of one million.

But this is truly the proverbial tip of the iceberg. Detailed reports from a number of cities state that the ratio of those turned away to those served is highest for those families with children, with figures of three turnaways for every family served common, as those of you who work in shelters or soup kitchens probably know. For example, in Minneapolis, families with children are 28 percent of the homeless served in shelters and soup kitchens surveyed but are 72 percent of those turned away. The Coalition Against Domestic Violence reports that in 1987, 40 percent of battered women were turned away from domestic violence shelters due to a lack of space and many of the women and their children had to return to the husbands or lovers that were battering them.

Though many have no place to call home, most of these families who are turned away are considered to be "near homeless" or "precariously housed" because they're not in shelters or on the streets. Such terms marginalize these families and keep them invisible when we talk about the "real homeless." Not surprisingly, studies which only count those on the streets and in the shelters (which is, by the way, the predominant method to be used in the 1990 census to count the homeless) estimate not only much smaller numbers of homeless but a much smaller proportion who are families with children. Though they frankly express surprise when they do find women who are homeless, roughly 20–25 percent of homeless population, few if any are homeless mothers with children. And when they do find them, they are characterized as not really homeless. One of the best known studies, done in Chicago by Rossi and others, found no homeless mothers with children in the streets. Of those in the shelters, they noticed there was a "minority of young black women who were typically homeless with their children and apparently in transition from unsatisfactory housing arrangements to establishing new households with those children."

One must ask, "Are not all homeless in some sense, in transition from one housing situation to another?" In short, the more successful homeless families are at hiding their homelessness, the less likely they are to be counted as or seen as homeless, whether by academics, the census bureau, or even by economic service providers, and less likely to have access to the services and housing opportunities which they so desperately need.

It's no accident that families with children are often the invisible homeless. To be counted as homeless, one must become known to someone who is doing the counting: shelter providers, social service officials, or an academic interviewer. Many families with children who are homeless desperately do not want to be known as homeless, for to become known, is to incur the risk of losing their children. That is, if the shelters you go to, or social services you apply to, are not able to provide you with even temporary housing, or they judge your housing situation to be inadequate, officials are empowered by law to make sure the children are not without shelter, and that means putting the children in foster care. Once the children are in foster care, it is extremely difficult to get them back, for the parents are caught in a catch-22. Without their children, they are not eligible for welfare or housing assistance as families; without income and housing, it's very difficult to get the children back.

The threat of foster care is not an idle threat. The number of children in foster care has begun to increase recently, which is highly unusual during a time of economic recovery and relatively low unemployment. While the number of children in foster care each year was about 275,000 in the mid-1980s, it has suddenly increased in the last two years. The House Select Committee on Children, Youth and Families, estimated that the 1988 number will jump as much as 50 percent, from 250,000 to 395,000. In some jurisdictions, homelessness is fast becoming a major reason for children being placed in foster care. While in California, a child cannot be placed in foster care for the sole reason of homelessness, in many other places, families are losing their children to foster care. It is a policy of many jurisdictions, including the District of Columbia—I don't know what is true in Philadelphia—that a baby born to a woman who lives in a women's shelter or on the streets is automatically placed in foster care. The reasoning is that, as a homeless person, she is by definition neglecting her child by not providing food and shelter. In Michigan, families who do not pay their utility bills or rent, can be found guilty of "environmental" neglect, a new kind of neglect, and their children can be put into foster care. All too often, parents in need of counseling, medical care or food must make an awful choice between seeking help and risk losing their kids, or not seeking help and seeing them suffer.

Faced with the threat of foster care and of shelters and welfare hotels, homeless families use five strategies to cope with their situation. These strategies contribute to their not being counted and to their invisibility.

The first strategy, used by many homeless families with children, is to double up with families or friends. This is a particularly common strategy among young, single parents with one or two children. With the cutbacks in welfare payments and public housing, setting up one's own single parent household is precluded. Public housing authorities know that there are large numbers of such families. According to one study, half of the eligible applicants for public housing already live in public housing, just doubled up. According to a recent report in 1986, one third of all children in the District of Columbia, and this isn't one third of the poor children, this is one third of *all* children, now live in doubled up households. It's probably just as high in other cities.

Doubling up forestalls going to shelters or living on the streets, but only for a short time. More than one half of [Washington] DC's homeless families had been doubled up before becoming homeless. The threat of discovery, the fear of reprisals against both families by the landlord, whether public or private, plus the overcrowding, makes such housing strategies inherently short lived. At the same time, fear of discovery prevents these families from seeking access to low-income housing, for which they are eligible, when it is available. For example, applicants from doubled up households who were applying for newly furnished units in a housing development in Brooklyn, New York, if they were not in a shelter, could not give the name of a landlord or even their host as references, because they feared reprisal for themselves or their host family, and thus were effectively excluded from this opportunity. Many people simply stopped filling out their applications when they got to the landlord reference section.

A second strategy used by homeless families with children is to seek hidden housing, such as abandoned cars and empty houses. In the South, some people live in abandoned chicken coops and in the West, on and off freeways. In this and other areas, they live in parks, campgrounds and even in ravines. They are not seen in downtown areas or sleeping in crates. They seek instead the anonymity of more residential suburban and even rural areas. Perhaps

the most creative strategy was that of a Montgomery County, Maryland, woman who described her experiences during her years on a waiting list for subsidized housing. This is from a hearing:

When my husband left and I was with four children, I didn't have a job and I was not able to pay the rent. We were evicted and Community Ministries came and put our furniture in storage, but there were five of us. I went from place to place, but the shelters were full. You know, everybody's sorry. We slept anywhere we could, in basements, in vacant houses. I would find vacant houses during the week, and I'd leave a window open and go in at night. We moved about twelve times throughout the five years while we were waiting. We lived for eight months in a vacant apartment with no heat and no utilities and you don't want too many people to find out, because they'll take my kids away, so we just kept moving. I took midnight shift jobs so the kids could sleep in the building. Finally, I got my certificate, so now I have a house. But when you go to Community Ministries or when you go to the Women's Interfaith Store for your clothes, you hear the same thing: I don't know where I'm going to stay tonight. I've been there for three years and I can't ever forget.

A third strategy used by families who become homeless because of abuse or violence is to go to a shelter for battered women. But because these are not homeless shelters these women are often not thought of as homeless. Although over 300,000 women and children were sheltered last year in over 1100 shelters and safe houses, priorities for housing assistance for victims of domestic violence have not been well publicized. And even when they are, such priorities are not worth much in many communities because waiting lists are years long, or are closed altogether. This is especially a problem, since most battered women's shelters have time limits numbered in days or weeks, not years.

Fourth, homeless families with children who can't find housing together seek out private, informal alternatives to official foster care.

In a HUD study done in 1980, and surely the problem is worse now, 20 percent of the families with children ended up splitting up, that is, leaving the children with relatives while they searched for housing. Half of those families remained apart for four months or more. These families also get caught in a catch-22, as when applications for housing assistance, such as Section 8, permit the applicant to list only family members who are currently living with them. Finally, when all else fails, parents force their children to live in a shelter or welfare hotel. Some homeless parents choose to place their children voluntarily into foster care. As I said earlier, in the average state, foster parents receive four times as much per child than the parents or guardians under AFDC. If you had to choose between the kind of housing available and affordable on a welfare grant (or doubling up, or living in a vacant apartment), *versus* your child receiving four times that amount for food and shelter living in a foster home, what would be the best choice to make for your children?

When children enter foster care, homeless families become doubly invisible, for they now appear as two separate statistics, as more children in foster care *and* more homeless adults. Thus, if you go to the shelters for homeless women, you'll find that many of those women have children. In fact, many times, they are in contact with them. They phone them—but they can't get their children back. But as *homeless* families, they become invisible, they disappear. Becoming a whole family again—much less securing housing—is, needless to say, incredibly difficult once your children are in foster care.

I'd like to briefly describe the story of a woman accompanying me when I testified before the U.S. House of Representatives. This is a story from Soberton, Georgia. Her name was Cora Lee Johnson. A woman she knew was the mother of her nephew's child and had three children, including a baby. They were in church one day three weeks ago, and the baby appeared sick, feverish. When they got home and they changed the baby's diaper, they discovered there was blood in the diaper so they took the baby to the hospital. They got a ride to the hospital.

They had to go to another county. (It's in a very poor area and there was no nearby hospital). They drove thirty miles to the nearest hospital. The mother went with the baby because that is required in most places. They placed the baby in the hospital. When it came time for the baby to leave the hospital, they would not release the baby to the mother and they said that the welfare department, "the Welfare," had come and taken the baby. She called Miss Cora Lee Johnson and asked to have her help, so she came down, but by that time, "the Welfare" had taken the baby and they told the mother, "Forget about this child, you'll never see this child again."

Why did they take the child? Because the woman was living with her three children, doubled up, with another household, and they said her housing was inadequate for her to be able to take care of her children. When she returned home, her other two children had also been taken by welfare and all three children were put in different places.

They took the child out of the hospital without even getting the doctor's permission and the child got sick again and they brought it back to the hospital. The doctors said, "I never released this baby and the baby didn't finish taking the medicine. The baby's very sick and I'm afraid it's going to die. I won't take the baby back under my care because then I'd be responsible for it and I'm not the one who caused the baby to get really sick again and I'm afraid the child will die and I'll be sued."

So they had to take it to yet another hospital. The mother found out where the child was and went to try and see the baby. The posted a policeman at the hospital and refused to let her see the child. She finally was allowed to see it, informally, but was not allowed to take the child. The child did get better, miraculously, given the kind of treatment the child had had. But the Welfare placed it in yet another county. That child is still in foster care. The woman who did the testifying, who was a pretty prominent woman and very active and has worked a lot with welfare officials, helped build low-income housing, etc., *she* tried to get the baby placed with her because the baby is actually a relative of hers. They would not place the child with her, even though in Georgia, they do not pay relatives for foster care. She was going to take care of the child, take custody of the child, and they would not place it with her, even though she could do so. They're still fighting it.

As we talked about this incident, she started to tell me other stories about what is happening in terms of housing. There *is* low income housing in Soberton, Georgia, but it is segregated, into black housing projects and white housing projects. She had one woman come to her, who had one child, and she was seven months pregnant with another, and she was living in a car. When she applied for a house, they said her income wasn't high enough because she was on welfare, and these public housing project apartments were for people who were low income and employed. In Georgia, you can be pretty low income and still be employed.

So they were holding them open. There were vacant apartments and she was living in a car. It took two months and they got her in a week before the baby was born. That one ended successfully—we'll see what happens with this other story.

I could leave you there, but that's a particularly down note to leave you on. I think we will solve that particular case—but there are thousands more. Those are just a couple of stories about what's happening out there in terms of children and foster care and homelessness.

I'd like to outline for you what I think we need to do and this is a very broad concept of what we need to do, but I think we need to look at this as a broad issue that needs a broad solution. I think we as a society must begin to take

on a share of the risk of children's homelessness in a way we've never done before, except with the risks of aging.

Fifty years ago, when we instituted Social Security, we basically said that the problems of the aging should not be borne by themselves alone or by their families: "It's a risk we all must pass through and we all need to share the risk. We need to share the risk of becoming older." We need to do the same thing with children and not make women who have children and are abandoned by the fathers of those children and now are abandoned by the society as well, bear all the burden and costs of bearing children.

This kind of approach would involve the following things. We need to have universal child care, universally available the way we have public education available. Right now, we ask young parents at a point when they're just starting their careers, when their income is very low, to pay for child care out of relatively low incomes and the result, of course, is that they not only impoverish themselves in trying to work and take care of the children, they impoverish the people taking care of their children so that there's no way you can give people taking care of children decent wages, because they're being paid by people who are young parents themselves. The only way to deal with this is to begin to share the risks among those of us who are at different points in our careers and have higher incomes.

Second, we need some kind of support system for children when they are very young. This would be an annual income support that supplements child support and it should include housing as well. We should have a guarantee that no child will be placed in foster care because the family is homeless. And, in more general terms, we should guarantee that no child shall be punished in terms of poverty by lack of housing, lack of education, because they are in a single-parent as opposed to a typical two-parent family.

Third, we need to give family and medical leave universally, not just to those who are in companies that are large enough and are covered by legislation, or live in states that are covered by legislation. But when people have children, adopt children or they have an ill child or relative that they need to take time off from work, that should be covered so that they are not bearing all the burden for having to take care of that.

Fourth, we need health care for everyone. Obviously, this doesn't need a lot of explanation.

So the first thing we need to do is to create a kind of social security for our children, for our entire age span, not just for over sixty-five. The second thing we really need to do is to look at income and welfare inequality, which is growing very rapidly and has been since the early 1980s. On the income side of it, we've got to do something about minimum wage. We now have a situation where a single parent with one child has to work about fifty hours a week just to make a poverty-level wage and then she has to work about another seven hours to do the Social Security and other automatic reductions. We need to raise taxes to cover things, we need to share socially much more of our burden and not give everybody income tax breaks, because it only increases our inequality.

In the area of wealth inequality, I think we really have to do some imaginative thinking around the issue of housing. We now have a situation where people who rent are becoming poorer and poorer and have no control whatsoever. Housing is the only means of saving. Those of us who own housing are sending our kids to college, are getting wealthy, and we can retire on it; it's everything. It's our catastrophic health insurance, it's our next generation's investment; it's everything. So you cannot get away from house ownership as long as we have these things. Once we start developing policies like national health care, national child care, higher education, then we don't have to have everything, then we don't have to have every-

one be a homeowner in order to secure themselves against the future—illness, aging, college educations.

We need to develop a third kind of housing that is in between those two extremes, of private home ownership and public housing, which is shared housing programs such as mutual housing, limited equity co-op, or cooperative housing, where people share some of the benefits of owning housing and share communally some of the benefits, so we get something that's in-between. We really need to do a lot more work on that issue.

Third, we need to renew our commitment to reduce racial inequality and to increase equality of opportunity. We've had a real flagging of those efforts in terms of affirmative action, in terms of access of minority children to higher education all the way across the line. I think we particularly need to pay attention to urban education. We have dropout rates in some schools now of 50 percent, that is, of children entering eighth grade, only about 50 percent of them are finishing high school. Informal reports from people running teaching programs suggest that those who finish high school routinely have reading levels in the range of third, fourth and fifth grade. That's an awful thing to do to people. That means they have no future whatsoever.

Urban education is a euphemism—we're really talking about predominantly minority (students) and what we have not done. We started in the 1960s and early 1970s to really desegregate our school systems. The important thing about desegregation wasn't having black and white school children sitting together, but that we have black and white dollars next to each other. In other words, having an integration of the resources is essential. Until we go back to doing something like that and have real resources and real access and real equality of opportunity, we're going to have racial inequality and I think we really have to renew our efforts in that area.

And finally, we have to attack the root causes of women's poverty. We need to provide adequate support for women raising children, as I described earlier. All the way through women's lives, including earnings-sharing when people retire. At this point, if a young man takes two or three years out of his life when he's eighteen or nineteen or twenty and serves in the Armed Forces, we reward that young man (and sometimes, young woman), with all kinds of veteran's benefits, education benefits, all the way through his/her life, including health benefits all the way through, and even burial benefits.

If a young woman takes two or three years out of her life to raise children, however, she's punished. She's punished in terms of her career, she's punished in terms of Social Security, she's punished in terms of Unemployment Compensation. We do exactly the opposite from those serving in the Armed Forces. I think we have to start looking at raising children as just as much an investment in our society's future and security as having people go into the Armed Forces.

The other side to women's poverty, other than the children, is the employment side and we really need to work in those areas in terms of pay equity, in terms of getting women into non-traditional employment. We need to work on the area of part-time employment, which is a rapidly rising invisible ghetto. Two-thirds of the people in part-time employment are women— they do not get fringe benefits, they do not get any chance to grow in terms of employment, they are pretty much confined to low wages and dead-end jobs and that's a growing area.

None of this is going to happen because it *ought* to happen. It's only going to happen when we work on it so I call upon you as you talk about these issues today and after you leave today to really think about it. These things are wonderful things, but they can only happen if we really work on it. And this means we have to work on it both nationally, on such issues as the minimum wage and locally, on housing, which has to be resolved within the community and within the women's community, sister to sister.

❧ Cultural Invisibility ☙

Dancing Through the Minefield: Some Observations on the Theory, Practice, and Politics of a Feminist Literary Criticism

Annette Kolodny

During the years that I was in college, from 1958 to 1962, no one thought to ask why so few women poets and novelists appeared on required reading lists or, even less, why women's names were only rarely mentioned when we discussed the "important" or "influential" critics of the day. Where women writers were taught, as in the courses on the history of the English novel, a supposedly exceptional work might be remarked for its "large scope" or "masculine thrust"; but, more often than not, women's novels were applauded for a certain elegance of style, an attention to detail or nuance, and then they were curtly dismissed for their inevitably "feminine" lack of humor,

weighty truths, or universal significance. If possible, things were even more dismal in the American literature courses, where Anne Bradstreet was treated as a Puritan anomaly, and Emily Dickinson was presented as a case study who had offered biographer after biographer the occasion to identify the peculiar pathology which *must* explain (or explain away) her otherwise apparently incomprehensible prolific poetic output. These were the years, after all, when no one blinked at Norman Mailer's "terrible confession" that he could not read "any of the talented women who write today," and most nodded in agreement when Theodore Roethke listed among the frequent charges made against women's poetry, its "lack of range—in subject matter, in emotional tone—and a lack of a sense of humor." Elizabeth Janeway has noted that

From *Men's Studies Modified*, edited by Dale Spender (1981). Reprinted by permission.

women writers of that period quite properly attempted to reject the label "women's literature," reacting against the "automatic disparagement of their work" which it implied. For readers as for writers then, as Adrienne Rich recalled, "it seemed to be a given fact that men wrote poems and women frequently inhabited them."

But just beneath the many surface complacencies of the 1950's an anger was brewing. With the radical critiques of American society that emerged in the 1960's there emerged also, though perhaps more slowly, a gradual recognition by women that it was not just the blacks or the other minority groups who were being deprived of their basic civil rights; that women, too, regardless of their class or education, were also, in a real sense, second-class citizens. As this perception was shared, especially in the consciousness-raising groups that marked the beginning of the "new feminism" at the end of the 1960s and the beginning of the 1970s, "the sleepwalkers," as Adrienne Rich called us, began "coming awake"; and, even more important, "for the first time this awakening" took on "a collective reality." By the time I was completing my Ph.D. thesis at the University of California at Berkeley, in 1969, that new collective consciousness had permeated campus study groups and social gatherings sufficiently to make it at least uncomfortable for anyone to merely laugh at or accept as witty Norman Mailer's dismissal of women writers on the grounds "that a good novelist can do without everything but the remnant of his balls." And few of the *women* graduate students, at any rate, were willing to accept without further investigation Roethke's pronouncement that women writers had always contented themselves with 'the embroidering of trivial themes' or shown only "a concern with the mere surfaces of life—that special province of the female talent in prose—hiding from the real agonies of the spirit." That further investigation which began so tentatively at the end of the 1960s became, of course, what we now call "feminist literary criticism."

Had anyone the prescience back then to pose the question of defining a "feminist" literary criticism, she might have been told, after the appearance of Mary Ellmann's *Thinking About Women*, in 1968, that it involved exposing the sexual stereotyping of women in both our literature and our literary criticism and, as well, demonstrating the inadequacy of established critical schools and methods to deal fairly or sensitively with works written by women. And, for the most part, such a prediction would have stood well the test of time. What could not have been anticipated as the 1960s drew to a close, however, was the long-term catalyzing effect of an ideology that, for many of us, had helped to bridge the gap between the world as we found it and the world as we wanted it to be. For those of us who studied literature, a previously unspoken sense of exclusion from authorship, and a painfully personal distress at discovering whores, bitches, muses, and heroines dead in childbirth where we had once hoped to discover ourselves, could now, for the first time, begin to be understood as more than "a set of disconnected, unrealized private emotions." With a renewed courage to make public our otherwise private discontents, what had once been "felt individually as personal insecurity" came at last to be "viewed collectively as structural inconsistency" within the very disciplines we studied. Following unflinchingly the full implications of Ellmann's percipient early observations, and emboldened to do so by the liberating energy of feminist ideology—in all its various forms and guises—feminist criticism very quickly moved beyond merely "expos[ing] sexism in one work of literature after another," and promised, instead, that we might at last "begin to record new choices in a new literary history." So powerful was that impulse that we experienced it, along with Adrienne Rich, as much more than "a chapter in cultural history": it became, rather, "an act of survival." What was at stake was not so much literature or criticism *per se* but the historical, social, and ethical consequences of women's participation in, or exclusion from either enterprise.

The pace of inquiry these last ten years has been fast and furious—especially after Kate Millett's 1970 analysis of the sexual politics of literature added a note of urgency to what had earlier been Ellmann's sardonic anger—while the diversity of that inquiry easily outstripped all efforts to define feminist literary criticism as either a coherent system or a unified set of methodologies. Under its wide umbrella everything has been thrown into question: our established canons, our aesthetic criteria, our interpretive strategies, our reading habits, and, most of all, ourselves as critics and as teachers. To delineate its full scope would require nothing less than a book—a book that would be outdated even as it was being composed. For the sake of brevity, therefore, let me attempt only a summary outline.

Perhaps the most obvious success of this new scholarship has been the return to circulation of previously lost or otherwise ignored works by women writers. Following fast upon the initial success of the Feminist Press in reissuing gems like Rebecca Harding Davis' 1861 novella, *Life in the Iron Mills*, and Charlotte Perkins Gilman's 1892 *The Yellow Wallpaper*, published in 1972 and 1973 respectively, numbers of commercial trade and reprint houses vied with one another in the reprinting of anthologies of lost texts and, in some cases, in the reprinting of whole series. For those of us in American literature especially, the phenomenon promised a radical reshaping of our concepts of literary history and, at the very least, a new chapter in understanding the development of women's literary traditions. So commercially successful were these reprintings, and so attuned were the reprint houses to the political attitudes of the audiences for which they were offered, that many of us found ourselves being wooed to compose critical introductions which would find in the pages of nineteenth-century domestic and sentimental fictions some signs of either

muted rebellions or overt radicalism, in anticipation of the current wave of "new feminism." In rereading with our students these previously lost works, we inevitably raised perplexing questions as to the reasons for their disappearance from the canons of "major works," and worried over the aesthetic and critical criteria by which they had been accorded diminished status.

This increased availability of works by women writers led, of course, to an increased interest in what elements, if any, might comprise some sort of unity or connection among them. The possibility that women had developed either a unique, or at least a related tradition of their own, especially intrigued those of us who specialized in one national literature or another, or in historical periods. Nina Baym's *Women's Fiction: A Guide to Novels by and about Women in America, 1820–1870* demonstrates the Americanists' penchant for examining what were once the "best sellers" of their day, the ranks of the popular fiction writers, among which women took a dominant place throughout the nineteenth century, while the feminist studies of British literature emphasized instead the wealth of women writers who have been regarded as worthy of canonization. Not so much building upon one another's work as clarifying, successively, the parameters of the questions to be posed, Sydney Janet Kaplan, Ellen Moer, Patricia Meyer Spacks, and Elaine Showalter, among many others, concentrated their energies on delineating an internally consistent 'body of work' by women which might stand as a female counter-tradition. For Kaplan, in 1975, this entailed examining women writers' various attempts to portray feminine consciousness and self-consciousness not as a psychological category, but as a stylistic or rhetorical device; that same year, arguing essentially that literature publicizes the private, Spacks placed her consideration of a 'female imagination' within social and historical frames, to conclude that, "for readily discernible historical reasons women have characteristically concerned themselves with matters more or less peripheral to male concerns," and attributed to this fact an inevitable difference in the literary emphases and subject matters of female and male writers. The next year, Moer's *Literary Women* focused on the pathways of literary influence that linked the English novel in the hands of women. And, finally, in 1977, Showalter took up the matter of a "female literary tradition in the English novel from the generation of the Brontës to the present day" by arguing that, since women in general constitute a kind of "subculture within the framework of a larger society," the work of women writers, in particular, would thereby demonstrate a unity of "values, conventions, experiences, and behaviors impinging on each individual" as she found her sources of "self-expression relative to a dominant [and, by implication, male] society."

At the same time that women writers were being reconsidered and reread, male writers were similarly subjected to a new feminist scrutiny. The continuing result, to put ten years of difficult analysis into a single sentence, has been nothing less than an acute attentiveness to the ways in which certain power relations—usually those in which males wield various forms of influence over females—are inscribed in the texts (both literary and critical) that we have inherited, not merely as subject matter, but as the unquestioned, often unacknowledged *given* of the culture. Even more important than the new interpretations of individual texts which such attentiveness has rendered is its probings into the consequences (for women) of the conventions which inform those texts. In surveying selected nineteenth- and early twentieth-century British novels which employ what she calls "the two suitors convention," for example, Jean Kennard sought to understand why and how the structural demands of the convention, even in the hands of women writers, inevitably work to imply 'the inferiority and necessary subordination of women." Her 1978 study, *Victims of Convention*, points out that the symbolic

nature of the marriage which conventionally concludes such novels "indicates the adjustment of the protagonist to society's values, a condition which is equated with her maturity." Kennard's concern, however, is with the fact that the structural demands of the form too often sacrifice precisely those "virtues of independence and individuality," or in other words, the very "qualities we have been invited to admire in" the heroines. If Kennard appropriately cautions us against drawing from her work any simplistically reductive thesis about the mimetic relations between art and life, her approach does nonetheless suggest that what is important about a fiction is not whether it ends in a death or a marriage, but what the symbolic demands of that particular conventional ending imply about the values and beliefs of the world that engendered it.

Her work thus participates in a growing emphasis in feminist literary study on the fact of literature as a social institution, embedded not only within its own literary traditions but within the particular physical and mental artifacts of the society from which it comes. Adumbrating Millett's 1970 decision to anchor her 'literary reflections' to a preceding analysis of the historical, social, and economic contexts of sexual politics, more recent work—most notably Lillian Robinson's—begins with the premise that the process of artistic creation "consists not of ghostly happenings in the head but of a matching of the states and processes of symbolic models against the states and processes of the wider world." The power relations inscribed in the form of conventions within our literary inheritance, these critics argue, reify the encodings of those same power relations in the culture at large. And the critical examination of rhetorical codes becomes, in their hands, the pursuit of ideological codes, since both embody either value systems or the dialectic of competition between value systems. More often than not, these critics also insist upon examining not only the mirroring of life in art but, as well, the normative impact of art on life. Addressing herself to the popular arts available to working women, for example, Lillian Robinson is interested in understanding not only 'the forms it uses', but, more importantly "the myths it creates, the influence it exerts." "The way art helps people to order, interpret, mythologize, or dispose of their own experience," she declares, may be "complex and often ambiguous, but it is not impossible to define."

Whether its focus be upon the material or the imaginative contexts of literary invention; single texts or entire canons; the relations between authors, genres, or historical circumstances; lost authors or well-known names, the variety and diversity of all feminist literary criticism finally coheres in its stance of almost defensive re-reading. What Adrienne Rich had earlier called "re-vision," that is, 'the act of looking back, of seeing with fresh eyes, of entering an old text from a new critical direction," took on a more actively self-protective coloration in 1978, when Judith Fetterley called upon the woman reader to learn to 'resist' the sexist designs a text might make upon her—asking her to identify against herself, so to speak, by manipulating her sympathies on behalf of male heroes, but against female shrew or bitch characters. Underpinning a great deal of this critical re-reading has been the not-unexpected alliance between feminist literary study and those feminist studies in linguistics and language acquisition examined in the chapter by Mercilee Jenkins and Cheris Kramarae. Tillie Olsen's common sense observation of the danger of "perpetuating—by continued usage—entrenched, centuries-old oppressive power realities, early-on incorporated into language," has been given substantive analysis in the writings of feminists who study "language as a symbolic system closely tied to a patriarchal social structure." Taken together, their work demonstrates 'the importance of language in establishing, reflecting, and maintaining an asymmetrical relationship between women and men."

To consider what this implies for the fate of women who essay the craft of language is to ascertain, perhaps for the first time, the real dilemma of the poet who finds her most cherished private experience "hedged by taboos, mined with false-namings" and, as well, the dilemma of the male reader who, in opening the pages of a woman's book, finds himself entering a strange and unfamiliar world of symbolic significance. For if, as Nelly Furman insists, neither language use nor language acquisition are "gender-neutral," but, instead, are both "imbued with our sex-inflected cultural values" and if, additionally, reading is a process of "sorting out the structures of signification" in any text, then male readers who find themselves outside of and unfamiliar with the symbolic systems that constitute female experience in women's writings, will necessarily dismiss those systems as undecipherable, meaningless, or trivial. And male professors will find no reason to include such works in the canons of 'major authors'. At the same time, women writers, coming into a tradition of literary language and conventional forms already appropriated, for centuries, to the purposes of male expression, will be forced virtually to 'wrestle' with that language in an effort "to remake it as a language adequate to our conceptual processes." To all of this, feminists concerned with the politics of language and style have been acutely attentive. "Language conceals an invincible adversary," observes French critic Helene Cixous "because it's the language of men and their grammar." But equally insistent, as in the work of Sandra M. Gilbert and Susan Gubar, has been the understanding of the need for *all* readers—male and female alike—to learn to penetrate the otherwise unfamiliar universes of symbolic action that comprise women's writings, past and present.

* * *

To have attempted so many difficult questions and to have accomplished so much—even acknowledging the inevitable false starts, overlapping, and repetition—in so short a time, should certainly, one would imagine, have secured feminist literary criticism full partnership in that academic pursuit which we term, loosely enough, "critical analysis." But, in fact, as the 1979 *Harvard Guide to Contemporary American Writing* makes all too clear, our situation is, at best, ambiguous; at worst, precarious. Boasting that it 'undertakes a critical survey of the most significant writing in the United States between the end of World War II and the end of the 1970s, the *Guide's* Preface promises "first, . . . a survey of intellectual commitments and attitudes during the period" and then "an examination of the theories and practices of literary criticism which have accompanied and to some extent even influenced the writing of these decades." The opening chapter by Alan Trachtenberg on the "Intellectual Background," however, while it pays respectful and often probing attention to the social critics and the 'revolutionary criticism' which marked the 1960s and early 1970s, never mentions what remains as perhaps the most enduring legacy of that critique: the women's liberation movement. Similarly, in his overview of 'American literary criticism since 1945,' A. Walton Litz notes a 'general trend . . . from consensus to diversity,' but he fails to note feminist literary criticism as any contributor to that growing critical diversity. To be sure, the *Guide* includes two chapters by women—Elizabeth Janeway's study of 'Women's Literature' and Josephine Hendin's survey of "Experimental Fiction." And both, in different ways, point to the importance of women writers and the new feminism for current developments in American Literature. That only the women contributors marked this fact, though, suggests the continuing ghettoization of women's interests and demonstrates again how fragile has been the impact of feminist criticism on our non-feminist colleagues and on the academic mainstream in general.

Indeed, for all our efforts, instead of being welcomed into that mainstream, we've been forced to negotiate a mine-field. The very energy and diversity of our enterprise has rendered us vulnerable to attack on the grounds that we lack both definition and coherence; while our particular attentiveness to the ways in which literature encodes and disseminates cultural value systems calls down upon us imprecations which echo those heaped upon the Marxist critics of an earlier generation. If we are scholars dedicated to rediscovering a lost body of writings by women, then our finds are questioned on aesthetic grounds. And if we are critics, determined to practice revisionist readings, it is claimed that our focus is too narrow, and our results only distortions or, worse still, polemical misreadings.

The very vehemence of the outcry, coupled with the fact of our total dismissal in some quarters, suggests not our deficiencies, however, but the potential magnitude of our challenge. For what we are asking be scrutinized are nothing less than shared cultural assumptions so deeply rooted and so long ingrained that, for the most part, our critical colleagues have ceased to recognize them as such. In other words, what is really being bewailed in the claims that we distort texts or threaten the disappearance of the great western literary tradition itself is not so much the disappearance of either text or tradition but, instead, the eclipse of that particular *form* of the text, and that particular *shape* of the canon, which previously reified male readers' sense of power and significance in the world. Analogously, by asking whether, as readers, we ought to be 'really satisfied by the marriage of Dorothea Brooke to Will Ladislaw? of Shirley Keeldar to Louis Moore?' or whether, as Jean Kennard suggests, we must reckon with the ways in which "the qualities we have been invited to admire in these heroines [have] been sacrificed to structural neatness," is to raise difficult and profoundly perplexing questions about the ethical implications of our otherwise unquestioned aesthetic pleasures. It is, after all, an imposition of high order to ask the viewer to attend to Ophelia's sufferings in a scene where, before, he'd always so comfortably kept his eye fixed firmly on Hamlet. To understand all this, then, as the real nature of the challenge we have offered and, in consequence, as the motivation for the often overt hostility we've aroused, should help us learn to negotiate the mine-field, if not with grace, then with at least a clearer comprehension of its underlying patterns.

The ways in which objections to our work are usually posed, of course, serve to obscure their deeper motivations. But this may, in part, be due to our own reticence at taking full responsibility for the truly radicalizing premises that lie at the theoretical core of all we have so far accomplished. It may be time, therefore, to redirect discussion, forcing our adversaries to deal with the substantive issues and pushing ourselves into a clearer articulation of what, in fact, we are about. Up until now, I fear, we have only piecemeal dealt with the difficulties inherent in challenging the authority of established canons and then justifying the excellence of women's traditions, sometimes in accord with standards to which they have no intrinsic relation.

At the very point at which we must perforce enter the discourse—that is, claiming excellence or importance for our 'finds'—all discussion has already, we discover, long ago been closed. 'If Kate Chopin were *really* worth reading', an Oxford-trained colleague once assured me, 'she'd have lasted—like Shakespeare'; and he then proceeded to vote against the English Department's crediting a Women's Studies seminar I was offering in American women writers. The canon, for him, conferred excellence; Chopin's exclusion demonstrated only her lesser worth. As far as he was concerned, I could no more justify giving English Department credit for the study of Chopin than I could dare publicly to question Shakespeare's genius. Through hindsight, I've now come to view that discussion as not only having posed fruitless op-

positions but as having entirely evaded the much more profound problem lurking just beneath the surface of our disagreement: and that is, that the fact of canonization puts any work beyond questions of establishing its merit and, instead, invites students to offer only increasingly more ingenious readings and interpretations, the purpose of which is to validate the greatness already imputed by canonization.

Had I only understood it for what it was then, into this circular and self-serving set of assumptions I might have interjected some statement of my right to question why *any* text is revered and my need to know what it tells us about "how we live, how we have been living, how we have been led to imagine ourselves, [and] how our language has trapped as well as liberated us." The very fact of our critical training within the strictures imposed by an established canon of major works and authors, however, repeatedly deflects us from such questions; instead, we find ourselves endlessly responding to the *riposte* that the overwhelmingly male presence among canonical authors was only an accident of history—and never intentionally sexist—coupled with claims to the 'obvious' aesthetic merit of those canonized texts. It is, as I say, a fruitless exchange, serving more to obscure than to expose the territory being protected and dragging us, again and again, through the mine-field.

It is my contention that current hostilities might be transformed into a true dialogue with our critics if we at last made explicit what appear, to this observer, to constitute the three crucial propositions to which our special interests inevitably give rise. They are, moreover, propositions which, if handled with care and intelligence, could breathe new life into now moribund areas of our profession:

1. Literary history (and, with that, the historicity of literature) is a fiction;
2. insofar as we are taught how to read, what we engage are not texts but paradigms; and, finally.

3. that since the grounds upon which we assign aesthetic value to texts are never infallible, unchangeable, or universal, we must re-examine not only our aesthetics but, as well, the inherent biases and assumptions informing the critical methods which (in part) shape our aesthetic responses.

For the sake of brevity, I won't attempt to offer the full arguments for each but, rather, only sufficient elaboration to demonstrate what I see as their intrinsic relation to the potential scope of and present challenge implied by feminist literary study:

1. *Literary history (and, with that, the historicity of literature) is a fiction.* To begin with, an established canon functions as a model by which to chart the continuities and discontinuities, as well as the influences upon and the interconnections between works, genres, and authors. That model we tend to forget, however, is of our own making. It will take a very different shape, and explain its inclusions and exclusions in very different ways, if the reigning critical ideology believes that new literary forms result from some kind of ongoing internal dialectic within pre-existing styles and traditions or if, by contrast, the ideology declares that literary change is dependent upon societal development and thereby determined by upheavals in the social and economic organization of the culture at large. Indeed, whenever in the previous century of English and American literary scholarship one alternative replaced the other, we saw dramatic alterations in canonical "wisdom."

This suggests, then, that our sense of a "literary history" and, by extension, our confidence in a so-called historical canon, is rooted not so much in any definitive understanding of the past, as in our need to call up and utilize the past on behalf of a better understanding of the present. Thus, to paraphrase David Couzens Hoy, it becomes 'necessary to point out that the understanding of art and literature is such an essential aspect of the present's self-understanding that this self-understanding conditions

what even gets taken' as comprising that artistic and literary past. To quote Hoy fully, "this continual reinterpretation of the past goes hand in hand with the continual reinterpretation by the present of itself." In our own time, uncertain as to which, if any, model truly accounts for our canonical choices or accurately explains literary history, and pressured further by the feminists' call for some justification of the criteria by which women's writings were largely excluded from both that canon and history, we suffer what Harold Bloom has called "a remarkable dimming" of "our mutual sense of canonical standards."

Into this apparent impasse feminist literary theorists implicitly introduce the observation that our choices and evaluations of current literature have the effect either of solidifying or of reshaping our sense of the past. The authority of any established canon, after all, is reified by our perception that current work seems to grow, almost inevitably, out of it (even in opposition or rebellion), and is called into question when what we read appears to have little or no relation to what we recognize as coming before. So, were the larger critical community to begin to seriously attend to the recent outpouring of fine literature by women, this would surely be accompanied by a concomitant re-searching of the past, by literary historians, in order to account for the present phenomenon. In that process, literary history would itself be altered: works by seventeenth, eighteenth, or nineteenth century women writers, to which we had not previously attended, for example, might be given new importance as 'precursors' or as prior influences upon present-day authors; while selected male writers might also be granted new prominence as figures whom the women today, or even yesterday, needed to reject. I am arguing, in other words, that the choices we make in the present inevitably alter our sense of the past that led to them.

Related to this is the feminist challenge to that patently mendacious critical fallacy that we read the 'classics' in order to reconstruct the past 'the way it really was', and that we read Shakespeare and Milton in order to apprehend the meanings that they intended. Short of time machines or miraculous resurrections, there is simply no way to know, precisely or surely, what 'really was', what Homer intended when he sang, or Milton when he dictated. Critics more acute than I have already pointed up the impossibility of grounding a reading in the imputation of authorial intention, since the further removed the author is from us, so too must be his or her systems of knowledge and belief, points of view, and structures of vision (artistic and otherwise). (I omit here the difficulty of finally either proving or disproving the imputation of intentionality since, inescapably, the only appropriate authority is unavailable: deceased.) What we have really come to mean when we speak of competence in reading historical texts, therefore, is the ability to recognize literary conventions which have survived through time—so as to remain operational in the mind of the reader—and, where these are lacking, the ability to translate (or perhaps transform?) the text's ciphers into more current and recognizable shapes. But we never really reconstruct the past in its own terms. What we gain when we read the 'classics', then, is neither Homer's Greece nor George Eliot's England *as they knew it* but, rather, an approximation of an already fictively imputed past made available, through our interpretive strategies, for present concerns. Only by understanding this can we put to rest that recurrent delusion that the so-called "continuing relevance" of the classics serves as 'testimony to perennial features of human experience." The only 'perennial feature' to which our ability to read and reread texts written in previous centuries testifies is our inventiveness—in the sense that all of literary history is a fiction which we daily recreate as we reread it. What distinguishes feminists in this regard is their desire to alter and extend what we take as historically relevant from out of that vast

storehouse of our literary inheritance and, further, their recognition of the storehouse for what it really is: a resource for remodeling our literary history, past, present, and future.

2.   *Insofar as we are taught how to read, what we engage are not texts but paradigms.* To pursue the logical consequences of the first proposition leads, however uncomfortably to the conclusion that we appropriate meaning from a text according to what we need (or desire), or, in other words, according to the critical assumptions or predispositions (conscious or not) that we bring to it. And we appropriate different meanings, or report different gleanings, at different times—even from the same text—according to our changed assumptions, circumstances, and requirements. This, in essence, constitutes the heart of the second proposition. For insofar as literature is itself a social institution, so too, reading is a highly socialized—or learned—activity. What makes it so exciting, of course, is that it can be constantly relearned, so as to provide either an individual or an entire reading community, over time, infinite variations of the same text. It *can* provide that; but, I must add, too often it does not. Frequently our reading habits become fixed so that each successive reading experience functions, in effect, normatively, with one particular kind of novel stylizing our expectations of those to follow, the stylistic devices of any favorite author (or group of authors) alerting us to the presence or absence of those devices in the works of others, and so on. 'Once one has read his first poem', Murray Krieger has observed, 'he turns to his second and to the others that will follow thereafter with an increasing series of preconceptions about the sort of activity in which he is indulging. In matters of literary experience, as in other experiences', Krieger concludes, "one is a virgin but once."

For most readers, this is a fairly unconscious process, and not unnaturally, what we are taught to read well and with pleasure, when we are young, predisposes us to certain specific kinds of adult reading tastes. For the professional literary critic, the process may be no different, but it is at least more conscious. Graduate schools, at their best, are training grounds for competing interpretive paradigms or reading techniques: affective stylistics, structuralism, and semiotic analysis, to name only a few of the more recent entries. The delight we learn to take in the mastery of these interpretive strategies is then often mistakenly construed as our delight in reading specific texts, especially in the case of works that would otherwise be unavailable or even offensive to us. In my own graduate career, for example, with superb teachers to guide me, I learned to take great pleasure in *Paradise Lost*, even though as both a Jew and a feminist, I can subscribe neither to its theology nor to its hierarchy of sexual valuation. If, within its own terms (as I have been taught to understand them), the text manipulates my sensibilities and moves me to pleasure—as I will affirm it does—then, at least in part, that must be because, in spite of my real-world alienation from many of its basic tenets, I have been able to enter that text through interpretive strategies which allow me to displace less comfortable observations with others to which I have been taught pleasurably to attend. Though some of my teachers may have called this process "learning to read the *text* properly', I have now come to see it as learning to effectively manipulate the critical strategies which they taught me so well. Knowing, for example, the poem's debt to epic conventions, I am able to discover in it echoes and reworkings of both lines and situations from Virgil and Homer; placing it within the ongoing Christian debate between Good and Evil, I comprehend both the philosophic and the stylistic significance of Satan's ornate rhetoric as compared to God's majestic simplicity in Book III. But, in each case, an interpretive model, already assumed, had guided my discovery of the evidence for it.

When we consider the implications of these observations for the processes of canonformation and for the assignment of aesthetic value, we find ourselves locked in a chicken-and-egg dilemma, unable easily to distinguish as primary the importance of *what* we read as opposed to *how* we have learned to read it. For, simply put, we read well, and with pleasure, what we already know how to read; and what we know how to read is to a large extent dependent upon what we have already read (works from which we've developed our expectations and learned our interpretive strategies). What we then choose to read—and, by extension, teach and thereby "canonize"—usually follows upon our previous reading. Radical breaks are tiring, demanding, uncomfortable, and sometimes wholly beyond our comprehension.

Though the argument is not usually couched in precisely these terms, a considerable segment of the most recent feminist rereadings of women writers allows the conclusion that, where those authors have dropped out of sight, the reason may be due not to any lack of merit in the work but, instead, to an incapacity of predominantly male readers to properly interpret and appreciate women's texts—due, in large part, to a lack of prior acquaintance. The fictions which women compose about the worlds they inhabit may owe a debt to prior, influential works by other women or, simply enough, to the daily experience of the writer herself or, more usually, to some combination of the two. The reader coming upon such fiction, with knowledge of neither its informing literary traditions nor its real-world contexts, will thereby find himself hard-pressed, though he recognize the words on the page, to competently decipher its intended meanings. And this is what makes the recent studies by Spacks, Moer, Showalter, Gilbert and Gubar, and others so crucial: for, by attempting to delineate the connections and inter-relations that make for a female literary tradition, they provide us with invaluable aids for recognizing and understanding the unique literary traditions and sex-related contexts out of which women write.

The (usually male) reader who, both by experience and by reading, has never made acquaintance with those contexts—historically, the lying-in room, the parlor, the nursery, the kitchen, the laundry, and so on—will necessarily lack the capacity to fully interpret the dialogue or action embedded therein; for, as every good novelist knows, the meaning of any character's action or statement is inescapably a function of the specific situation in which it is embedded. Virginia Woolf therefore quite properly anticipated the male reader's disposition to write off what he could not understand, abandoning women's writings as offering "not merely a difference of view, but a view that is weak, or trivial, or sentimental because it differs from his own." Grappling most obviously with the ways in which male writers and male subject matter had already preempted the language of literature, in her essay on 'Women and Diction', Woolf was also tacitly commenting on the problem of (male) audience and conventional reading expectations when she speculated that the woman writer might well 'find that she is perpetually wishing to alter the established values [in literature]—to make serious what appears insignificant to a man, and trivial what is to him important." "The "competence" necessary for understanding [a] literary message . . . depends upon a great number of codices," after all; as Cesare Segre has pointed out, to be competent, a reader must either share or at least be familiar with, "in addition to the code language . . . the codes of custom, of society, and of conceptions of the world" (what Woolf meant by 'values'). Males ignorant of women's 'values' or conceptions of the world will necessarily, thereby, be poor readers of works that in any sense recapitulate their codes.

The problem is further exacerbated when the language of the literary text is largely dependent upon figuration. For it can be argued, as Ted Cohen has shown, that while "in general, and with some obvious qualifications . . . all literal use of language is accessible to all whose language it is . . . figurative use can be inaccessible to all but those who share information about one another's knowledge, beliefs, intentions, and attitudes." There was nothing fortuitous, for example, in Charlotte Perkins Gilman's decision to situate the progressive mental breakdown and increasing incapacity of the protagonist of *The Yellow Wallpaper* in an upstairs room that had once served as a nursery (with barred windows, no less). But the reader unacquainted with the ways in which women traditionally inhabited a household might not have taken the initial description of the setting as semantically relevant; and the progressive infantilization of the adult protagonist would thereby lose some of its symbolic implications. Analogously, the contemporary poet who declares, along with Adrienne Rich, the need for 'a whole new poetry beginning here' is acknowledging the fact that the materials available for symbolization and figuration from women's contexts will necessarily differ from those that men have traditionally utilized:

Vision begins to happen in such a life
as if a woman quietly walked away
from the argument and jargon in a room
and sitting down in the kitchen, began turning in her
    lap
bits of yarn, calico and velvet scraps,

        · · ·

pulling the tenets of a life together
with no mere will to mastery,
only care for the many-lived, unending
forms in which she finds herself.[1]

What, then, the fate of the woman writer whose competent reading community is composed only of members of her own sex? And what, then, the response of the male critic who, on first looking into Virginia Woolf or Doris Lessing, finds all of the interpretive strategies at his command inadequate to a full and pleasurable deciphering of their pages? Historically, the result has been the diminished status of women's products and their consequent absence from major canons. Nowadays, however, by pointing out that the act of 'interpreting language is no more sexually neutral than language use or the language system itself', feminist students of language, like Nelly Furman, help us better understand the crucial linkage between our gender and our interpretive, or reading, strategies. Insisting upon "the contribution of the . . . reader [in] the active attribution of significance to formal signifiers," Furman and others promise to shake us all—male and female alike—out of our canonized and conventional aesthetic assumptions.

3. *Since the grounds upon which we assign aesthetic value to texts are never infallible, unchangeable, or universal, we must re-examine not only our aesthetics but, as well, the inherent biases and assumptions informing the critical methods which (in part) shape our aesthetic responses.* I am, on the one hand, arguing that men will be better readers, or appreciators, of women's books when they have read more of them (as women have always been taught to become astute readers of men's texts); on the other hand, it will be noted, the impact of my remarks shifts the act of critical judgment from assigning aesthetic valuations to texts and directs it, instead, to ascertaining the adequacy of any interpretive paradigm to a full reading of both male and female writing. My third proposition—and, I admit, perhaps the most controversial—thus calls into question that recurrent tendency in criticism to establish norms for the evaluation of literary works when we might better serve the cause of literature by developing standards for evaluating the adequacy of our critical methods. This does not mean that I wish to discard aesthetic valuation. The choice, as I see it, is not between retaining or discarding aesthetic values; rather, the choice is between having some awareness of what constitutes (at least in part) the bases of our aesthetic responses and going without such an awareness. For it is my view that insofar as aesthetic responsiveness continues to be an integral aspect

of our human response system—in part spontaneous, in part learned and educated—we will inevitably develop theories to help explain, formalize, or even initiate those responses. Indeed, in a sense, this is what criticism is all about.

In challenging the adequacy of received critical opinion or the imputed excellence of established canons, therefore, feminist literary critics are essentially seeking to discover how aesthetic value is assigned in the first place, where it resides (in the text or in the reader), and, most importantly, what validity may really be claimed by our so-called aesthetic "judgments." What ends do those judgments serve, the feminist asks; and what conceptions of the world or ideological stances do they (even if unwittingly) help to perpetuate? She confronts, for example, the reader who simply cannot entertain the possibility that women's worlds are symbolically rich, the reader who, like the male characters in Susan Glaspell's 1917 short story, "A Jury of Her Peers," has already assumed the innate 'insignificance of kitchen things." Such a reader, she knows, will prove himself unable to assign significance to fictions which attend to 'kitchen things" and will, instead, judge such fictions as trivial and as aesthetically wanting. For her to take useful issue with such a reader, she must make clear that what appears to be a dispute about aesthetic merit is, in reality, a dispute about the *contexts of judgment*; and what is at issue, then, is the adequacy of the prior assumptions and reading habits brought to bear on the text. To put it bluntly: we have had enough pronouncements of aesthetic valuation for a time; it is now our task to evaluate the imputed norms and normative reading patterns that, in part, led to those pronouncements.

By and large, I think I've made my point. Only to clarify it do I add this coda: when feminists turn their attention to the works of male authors which have traditionally been accorded high aesthetic value and, where warranted, follow Tillie Olsen's advice that we assert our "right to say: this is surface, this falsifies reality, this degrades," such statements do not necessarily mean that we will end up with a diminished canon. To question the source of the aesthetic pleasures we've gained from reading Spenser, Shakespeare, Milton, *et al*, does not imply that we must deny those pleasures. It means only that aesthetic response is once more invested with epistemological, ethical, and moral concerns. It means, in other words, that readings of *Paradise Lost* which analyze its complex hierarchal structures but fail to note the implications of gender within that hierarchy; or which insist upon the inherent (or even inspired) perfection of Milton's figurative language but fail to note the consequences, for Eve, of her specifically gender-marked weakness, which, like the flowers to which she attends, requires "propping up"; or which concentrate on the poem's thematic reworking of classical notions of martial and epic prowess into Christian (moral) heroism but fail to note that Eve is stylistically edited out of that process—all such readings, however, useful, will no longer be deemed wholly adequate. The pleasures we had earlier learned to take in the poem will not be diminished thereby; but they will become part of an altered reading attentiveness.

* * *

These three propositions I believe to be at the theoretical core of all current feminist literary criticism, whether acknowledged as such or not. If I am correct in this, then that criticism represents more than a profoundly skeptical stance towards all other pre-existing and contemporaneous schools and methods, and more than an impassioned demand that the variety and variability of women's literary expression be taken into full account, rather than written off as caprice and exception, the irregularity in an otherwise regular design; it represents that locus in literary study where, in unceasing effort, female self-consciousness turns in upon itself, attempting to grasp the deepest conditions of its own unique and multiplicitous realities, in the

hope, eventually, of altering the very forms through which the culture perceives, expresses, and knows itself. For, if what the larger women's movement looks for in the future is a transformation of the structures of primarily male power which now order our society, then the feminist literary critic demands that we understand the ways in which those structures have been—and continue to be—reified by our literature and by our literary criticism. Thus, along with other so-called 'radical' critics and critical schools, though our focus remains the power of the word to both structure and mirror human experience, our overriding commitment is to a radical alteration—an improvement, we hope—in the nature of that experience.

What distinguishes our work from those similarly oriented 'social consciousness' critiques, it is said, is its lack of systematic coherence. Pitted against, for example, psychoanalytic or Marxist readings, which owe a decisive share of their persuasiveness to their apparent internal consistency as a system, the aggregate of feminist literary criticism appears woefully deficient in system, and painfully lacking in program. It is, in fact, from all quarters, the most telling defect alleged against us, the most explosive threat in the mine-field. And my own earlier observation that, as of 1976, feminist literary criticism appeared "more like a set of interchangeable strategies than any coherent school or shared goal orientation," has been taken by some as an indictment, by others as a statement of impatience. Neither was intended. I felt then, as I do now, that this would "prove both its strength *and* its weakness," in the sense that the apparent disarray would leave us vulnerable to the kind of objection I've just alluded to, while the fact of our diversity would finally place us securely where, all along, we should have been: camped out, on the far side of the mine-field, with the other pluralists and pluralisms.

In our heart of hearts, of course, most critics are really structuralists (whether or not they accept the label), since what we are seeking are patterns (or structures) that can order and explain the otherwise inchoate; thus, we invent, or believe we discover, relational patternings in the texts we read which promise transcendence from difficulty and perplexity to clarity and coherence. But, as I've tried to argue in these pages, to the imputed 'truth' or 'accuracy' of these findings, the feminist must oppose the painfully obvious truism that what is attended to in a literary work, and hence what is reported about it, is often determined not so much by the work itself as by the critical technique or aesthetic criteria through which it is filtered or, rather, read and decoded. All the feminist is asserting, then, is her own equivalent right to liberate new (and perhaps different) significances from these same texts; and, at the same time, her right to choose which features of a text she takes as relevant since she is, after all, asking new and different questions of it. In the process, she claims neither definitiveness nor structural completeness for her different readings and reading systems, but only their usefulness in recognizing the particular achievements of woman-as-author and their applicability in conscientiously decoding woman-as-sign.

That these alternate foci of critical attentiveness will render alternate readings or interpretations of the same text—even among feminists—should be no cause for alarm. Such developments illustrate only the pluralist contention that, 'in approaching a text of any complexity . . . the reader must choose to emphasize certain aspects which seem to him crucial' and 'in fact, the variety of readings which we have for many works is a function of the selection of crucial aspects made by the variety of readers'. Robert Scholes, from whom I've been quoting, goes so far as to assert that "there is no single 'right' reading for any complex literary work," and, following the Russian formalist school, he observes that "we do not speak of readings that are simply true or false, but of readings that are more or less rich, strat-

egies that are more or less appropriate." The fact that those who share the term 'feminist' nonetheless practice a diversity of critical strategies, leading, in some cases, to quite different readings, requires us to acknowledge among ourselves that sister critics, "having chosen to tell a different story, may in their interpretation identify different aspects of the meanings conveyed by the same passage." In other words, just because we will no longer tolerate the specifically sexist omissions and ignorances of earlier critical schools and methods does not mean that, in their stead, we must establish our own "party lines."

In my view, our purpose is not and should not be the formulation of any single reading method or potentially procrustean set of critical procedures nor, even less, the generation of prescriptive categories for some dreamed-of non-sexist literary canon. Instead, as I see it, our task is to initiate nothing less than a playful pluralism, responsive to the possibilities of multiple critical schools and methods, but captive of none, recognizing that the many tools needed for our work of analysis will necessarily be largely inherited and only partly of our own making. Only by employing a plurality of methods will we protect ourselves from the temptation to so oversimplify any text—and especially those particularly offensive to us—that we render ourselves unresponsive to what Robert Scholes has called "its various systems of meaning and their interaction." Any text we deem worthy of our critical attention is usually, after all, a locus of many and varied kinds of (personal, thematic, stylistic, structural, rhetorical, etc.) relationships. So, whether we tend to treat a text as a _mimesis_, in which words are taken to be recreating or representing viable worlds; or whether we prefer to treat a text as a kind of equation of communication, in which decipherable messages are passed from writers to readers; and whether we locate meaning as inherent in the text, the act of reading, or in some collaboration between reader and text—

whatever our predilection, let us generate from it not some strait jacket which limits the scope of possible analysis but, rather, an ongoing dialogue of competing potential possibilities—among feminists and, as well, between feminist and non-feminist critics.

The difficulty of what I describe does not escape me. The very idea of pluralism seems to threaten a kind of chaos for the future of literary inquiry while, at the same time, it seems to deny the hope of establishing some basic conceptual model which can organize all data—the hope which always begins any analytical exercise. My effort here, however, has been to demonstrate the essential delusions which inform such objections: If literary inquiry has historically escaped chaos by establishing canons, then it has only substituted one mode of arbitrary action for another—and, in this case, at the expense of half the population. And if feminists openly acknowledge ourselves as pluralists, then we do not give up the search for patterns of opposition and connection—probably the basis of thinking itself; what we give up is simply the arrogance of claiming that our work is either exhaustive or definitive. (It is, after all, the identical arrogance we are asking our non-feminist colleagues to abandon.) If this kind of pluralism appears to threaten both the present coherence of and the inherited aesthetic criteria for a canon of 'greats', then, as I have earlier argued, it is precisely that threat which, alone, can free us from the prejudices, the strictures, and the blind-spots of the past. In feminist hands, I would add, it is less a threat than a promise.

What unites and repeatedly reinvigorates feminist literary criticism, then, is neither dogma nor method but, as I have indicated earlier, an acute and impassioned *attentiveness* to the ways in which primarily male structures of power are inscribed (or encoded) within our literary inheritance; the consequences of that encoding for women—as characters, as readers, and as writers; and, with that, a shared analytic *concern* for the implications of that encoding

not only for a better understanding of the past, but on behalf of an improved reordering of the present and future as well. If that *concern* identifies feminist literary criticism as one of the many academic arms of the larger women's movement, then that *attentiveness*, within the halls of academe, poses no less a challenge for change, generating, as it does, the three propositions explored here. The critical pluralism which inevitably follows upon those three propositions, however, bears little resemblance to what Lillian Robinson has called "the great bourgeois theme of all, the myth of pluralism, with its consequent rejection of ideological commitment as 'too simple' to embrace the (necessarily complex) truth." Only ideological commitment could have gotten us to enter the mine-field, putting in jeopardy our careers and our livelihood. Only the power of ideology to transform our conceptual worlds, and the inspiration of that ideology to liberate long-suppressed energies and emotions, can account for our willingness to take on critical tasks that, in an earlier decade, would have been "abandoned in despair or apathy." The fact of differences among us proves only that, despite our shared commitments, we have nonetheless refused to shy away from complexity, preferring rather to openly disagree than to give up either the intellectual honesty or hard-won insights.

Finally, I would argue, pluralism informs feminist literary inquiry not simply as a description of what already exists but, more importantly, as the only critical stance consistent with the current status of the larger women's movement. Segmented and variously focussed, the different women's organizations, in the United States at least, neither espouse any single system of analysis nor, as a result, express any wholly shared, consistently articulated ideology. The ensuing loss in effective organization and political clout is a serious one, but it has not been paralyzing; in spite of our differences, we have united to *act* in areas of clear mutual concern (the push for the Equal Rights Amendment,

[ERA], is probably the most obvious example). The trade-off, as I see it, has made possible an ongoing and educative dialectic of analysis and preferred solutions, protecting us thereby from the inviting traps of reductionism and dogma. And so long as this dialogue remains active, both our politics and our criticism will be free of dogma—but never, I hope, of feminist ideology, in all its variety. For, whatever else ideologies may be—projections of unacknowledged fears, disguises for ulterior motives, phatic expressions of group solidarity' (and the women's movement, to date, has certainly been all of these, and more)—whatever ideologies express, they are, as Clifford Geertz astutely observes, 'most distinctively, maps of problematic social reality and matrices for the creation of collective conscience. And despite the fact that "ideological advocates . . . tend as much to obscure as to clarify the true nature of the problems involved," as Geertz notes, "they at least call attention to their existence and, by polarizing issues, make continued neglect more difficult. Without Marxist attack, there would have been no labor reform; without Black Nationalists, no deliberate speed"; without Senecca Falls, I would add, no enfranchisement of women, and without 'consciousness raising', no feminist literary criticism nor, even less, Women's Studies.

Ideology, however, only truly manifests its power by ordering the *sum* of our actions. If feminist criticism calls anything into question, it must be that dog-eared myth of intellectual neutrality. For, what I take to be the underlying spirit, or message, of any consciously ideologically-premised criticism—that is, that ideas are important *because* they determine the ways we live, or want to live, in the world—is vitiated by confining those ideas to the study, the classroom, or the pages of our books. To write chapters decrying the sexual stereotyping of women in our literature while closing our eyes to the sexual harassment of our women students and colleagues; to display Katherine Hepburn and Rosalind Russell in our courses on "The Image of the Independent Career Woman in Film," while managing not to notice the paucity of female administrators on our own campus; to study the women who helped make universal enfranchisement a political reality while keeping silent about our activist colleagues who are denied promotion or tenure; to include segments on 'Women in the Labor Movement' in our American Studies or Women's Studies courses while remaining wilfully ignorant of the department secretary fired for her efforts to organize a clerical workers' union; to glory in the delusions of 'merit', 'privilege', and 'status' which accompany campus life in order to insulate ourselves from the millions of women who labor in poverty—all this is not merely hypocritical; it destroys both the spirit and the meaning of what we are about. It puts us, however unwittingly, in the service of those who laid the mine-field in the first place. In my view, it is a fine thing for many of us, individually, to have traversed the mine-field; but that happy circumstance will only prove of lasting importance if, together, we expose it for what it is (the male fear of sharing power and significance with women) and deactivate its components, so that others, after us, may literally dance through the mine-field.

NOTE

1. Adrienne Rich, "Transcendental Elude" in her *The Dream of a Common Language: Poems 1974–1977* (New York: W. W. Norton & Co., 1978) pp. 76–77.

Women in History:
The Modern Period

Joan Scott

THE MODERN PERIOD

*What one wants, I thought—and why does not some brilliant student at
Newnham or Girton supply it?—is a mass of information; at what age did
she marry; how many children had she as a rule; what was her house like;
had she a room to herself; did she do the cooking; would she be likely to have
a servant? All these facts lie somewhere, presumably, in parish registers and
account books; the life of the average Elizabethan woman must be scattered
about somewhere, could one collect it and make a book of it. It would be
ambitious beyond my daring, I thought, looking about the shelves for books
that were not there, to suggest to the students of those famous colleges that
they should rewrite history, though I own that it often seems a little queer
as it is, unreal, lop-sided; but why should they not add a supplement to
history? calling it, of course, by some inconspicuous name so that women
might figure there without impropriety?*[1]

During the last decade, Virginia Woolf's call
for a history of women—written more than fifty
years ago—has been answered. Inspired directly
or indirectly by the political agenda of the women's movement, historians have documented
not only the lives of the average woman in various historical periods, but they have charted as
well changes in the economic, educational and
political positions of women of various classes
in city and country and in nation states. Book-
shelves are now being filled with biographies of
forgotten prominent women, chronicles of feminist movements, and the collected letters of
female authors; the book titles treat subjects as
disparate as suffrage and birth control. Journals
have appeared which are devoted exclusively to
women's studies and to the even more specialized area of women's history. And, at least in
the United States, there are major conferences
each year devoted entirely to the presentation of
scholarly papers on the history of women.

World Copyright: The Past and Present Society,
175 Banbury Road, Oxford, England. This article is
reprinted with permission of the Society and the author from *Past and Present: A Journal of Historical
Studies*, No. 101 (November 1983).

The production of materials is marked by extraordinary diversity in topic, method and interpretation. Indeed, it is foolish to attempt, as some historians have recently done, to reduce the field to a single interpretive or theoretical stance. Reductionism of that sort creates an illusion that the reviewer commands, indeed that he dominates, a profusion of disparate texts. At the same time, the illusion obscures the professed end of such reviews: an accurate account of the "state of the art", and of the meaning and importance of its diversity and complexity. It is precisely in the acknowledgement of its complexity and confusions that one finds both an understanding of women's history and also the basis for critical evaluation of it.

Some of the complexity comes from the sheer variety of topics studied. The confusion results from the proliferation of case studies and large interpretive attempts which neither address one another nor a similar set of questions and from the absence of a definable historiographic tradition within which interpretations are debated and revised. Instead, woman as subject has been grafted on to other traditions or studied in isolation from any of them. While some histories of women's work, for example, address contemporary feminist questions about the relationship between wage-earning and status, others frame their studies within the context of debates among Marxists and between Marxists and modernization theorists about the impact of industrial capitalism. Reproduction covers a vast terrain in which fertility and contraception are sometimes treated within the confines of historical demography as aspects of the "demographic transition." Alternately they are viewed within the context of discussions of the conflicting political analyses of Malthusian political economists and socialist labour leaders, or within the very different framework of evaluations of the impact of the nineteenth-century "ideology of domesticity" on the power of women in their families. Yet another approach stresses feminist debates about sexuality and the history of women's demands for the right to control their own bodies. Additionally, some Marxist-feminists have redefined reproduction as the functional equivalent of production in an effort to incorporate women into the corpus of Marxist theory. Investigations of politics have sought either to demonstrate simply that women were to be found "in public," or to illustrate the historical incompatibility between feminist claims and the structure and ideology of organized trade unions and political parties (the "failure" of socialism, for example, to accommodate feminism). Another quite different approach to politics examines the interior organization of women's political movements as a way of documenting the existence of a distinctively female culture.

Still, there is a common dimension to the enterprise of these scholars of different schools and that is to make women a focus of enquiry, a subject of the story, an agent of the narrative— whether that narrative is the familiar chronicle of political events (the French Revolution, the Swing riots, World War I or II) and political movements (Chartism, utopian socialism, feminism, women's suffrage), or the newer, more analytically cast account of the workings or unfoldings of large-scale processes of social change (industrialization, capitalism, modernization, urbanization, the building of nation states). The titles of some of the books that launched the "women's history movement" in the early 1970s explicitly conveyed their authors' intentions: those who had been "Hidden from History" were "Becoming Visible." Although book titles are now more circumspect (in part in order to legitimate claims to serious academic consideration), the mission of their authors remains to construct women as historical subjects. That effort goes far beyond the naive search for the heroic ancestors of the contemporary women's movement to a re-evaluation of established standards of historical significance. It culminates in a debate whose terms are contained in Woolf's phrases: can a focus on women "add a supplement to history" without also "rewriting history"? Beyond that, what does the feminist rewriting of history entail?

There are several positions in the debate, which is less a debate than a different set of approaches to the "rewriting of history." Most scholars working in women's history assume their work will transform history as it has been written and understood; they differ on the questions of how that will be accomplished. Some see the recovery of information and the focus on female subjects as sufficient to the task. Others use their research to challenge received interpretations of progress and regress. In this regard, for example, an impressive mass of evidence has been compiled to show that the Renaissance was not a renaissance for women, that technology did not lead to women's liberation either in the work place or at home, that the "Age of Democratic Revolutions" excluded women from political participation, that the "affective nuclear family" constrained women's emotional and personal development, and that the rise of medical science deprived women of autonomy and a sense of feminine community. Still others—a much smaller number at this point—attempt to join their evidence more directly to "mainstream" social and political history. Evidence about women becomes a way into examining social, economic and political relationships and the conclusions are less about women themselves than about the organization of societies, the dynamics of power, the content and meaning of historically specific politics. For this approach, a focus on women leads to the articulation of gender (or sexual difference) as a category of historical analysis, to the incorporation of gender into the historian's analytical tool box, and to a conceptual perspective that makes possible a genuine "rewriting of history."

In this essay I will examine these various approaches less in terms of their conclusions than in terms of their assumptions and methods. I will draw most heavily on North American scholarship not only because I am most

familiar with it, but because in the United States there has been produced during the past ten or twelve years the largest volume of, the most varied examples of subject and interpretation in, and the fullest elaboration of theoretical debates about women's history.

The first approach writes women's history as "her-story," a narrative of women's experience either alongside or entirely outside conventional historical frameworks. The aim in both instances is to give value as history to an experience that has been ignored and thus devalued and to insist on female agency in the "making of history." Investigations that seek to uncover women's participation in major political events and to write a women's political history attempt to fit a new subject—women—into received historical categories, interpreting their actions in terms recognizable to political and social historians. A forthcoming book on the history of the French women's suffrage movement by Steven Hause nicely exemplifies this approach. The author interprets the weakness and small size of the movement (in comparison with its English and American counterparts) as the result of the ideologies and institutions of French Catholicism, the legacy of Roman law, the conservatism of French society, and the peculiar political history of French republicanism, especially the Radical Party during the Third Republic. Hause also analyses divisions among feminists and he tells the entire story in terms of the ideas and organizations of the women leaders. Another example of this kind of approach examines a women's political movement from the perspective of its rank-and-file members rather than its leaders. In the best traditions of the social histories of labour (that were inspired by the work of E. P. Thompson) Jill Liddington and Jill Norris offer a sensitive and illuminating account of working-class women's participation in the English suffrage movement. Their material, drawn largely from Manchester records and from oral histories they collected, documents the involvement of working-class women in the campaign to win the vote (previous histories described it as almost entirely a middle-class movement) and links demands by these women for suffrage to their work and family lives and to the activities of trade union and Labour Party organizers. The predominance and wisdom of the Pankhurst wing of the movement is called into question for its élitism and its insistence on female separatism (a position rejected by the majority of suffragettes).

A different sort of investigation, still within the "her-story" position, departs from the framework of conventional history and offers a new narrative, different periodization and different causes. It seeks to illuminate the structures of ordinary women's lives as well as those of notable women, and to discover the nature of the feminist or female consciousness which motivated their behaviour. Patriarchy and class are usually assumed to be the contexts within which nineteenth- and twentieth-century women defined their experience, but these are rarely specified or examined concretely. Since these are the given contexts, however, a number of histories tend to emphasize moments of cross-class collaboration among women and those actions which directly addressed women's oppression, but such topics are not the defining characteristic of this approach. Rather the central aspect of this approach is the exclusive focus on female agency, on the causal role played by women in their history, and on the gender determinants of that role. Evidence consists of women's expressions, ideas and actions. Explanation and interpretation are framed within the terms of the female sphere: by examinations of personal experience, familial and domestic structures, collective (female) reinterpretations of social definitions of women's role, and networks of female friendship that provided emotional as well as physical sustenance. The exploration of the women's world has led to the brilliant insights of Carroll Smith-Rosenberg about the "female world of love and ritual" in nineteenth-century America, to an insistence on the

positive aspects of the domestic ideology of the same period, to a dialectical reading of the relationship between middle-class women's political action and the ideas of womanhood that confined them to domestic realms, and to an analysis of the "reproductive ideology" that constructed the world of the *bourgeoises* of northern France in the mid-nineteenth century. It has also led Carl Degler to argue that American women themselves created the ideology of their separate sphere in order to enhance their autonomy and status. In his rendering of the story, women create a world neither within nor in opposition to oppressive structures or ideas that others have imposed, but to further a set of group interests, defined and articulated from within the group itself. Although Degler has been accused of misreading the histories upon which he draws for his account, his conceptualization follows from the causality implied in "her-story's" construction of the woman as historical subject and from its frequent failure to distinguish between the valuation of women's experience (considering it worthy of study) and the positive assessment of everything women said or did.

This approach to women's history substitutes women for men, but it does not rewrite conventional history. To be sure, it raises questions that call for answers by offering documentation about women's activities—public and private—that happened, but were not included in conventional accounts. It insists as well that "personal, subjective experience" matters as much as "public and political activities," indeed that the former influences the latter. It demonstrates that sex and gender need to be conceptualized in historical terms, at least if some of the motives for women's actions are to be understood. Yet it does not then move on to challenge conventional history directly. Although women are substituted for men as the subject of historical accounts, their story remains separate—whether different questions are asked, different categories of analysis offered, or only different documents examined. For those interested there is now a growing and important history of women to supplement and enrich conventional political and social histories, but it remains embedded in the "separate sphere" that has long been associated exclusively with the female sex.

The second approach to the "rewriting of history" is most closely associated with social history. Social history offered important support for a women's history in several ways. First, it provided methodologies in quantification, in the use of details from everyday life, and in interdisciplinary borrowings from sociology, demography and ethnography. Secondly, it conceptualized as historical phenomena family relationships, fertility and sexuality. Thirdly, social history challenged the narrative line of political history ("male leaders make history") by taking as its subject large-scale social processes as they were realized in many dimensions of human experience. This led to the fourth influence, the legitimation of a focus on groups customarily excluded from political history. Social history's story is ultimately about processes or systems (such as capitalism or modernization, depending on the theoretical stance of the historian), but it is told through the lives of various groups of people who are the ostensible, though not always the actual, subjects of the narrative. Since social experience or relations of power are embodied everywhere in a society, one can choose among a variety of topics, and it is relatively easy to extend the list from workers, peasants, slaves, élites and diverse occupational or social groups to include women. Thus, for example, studies of women's work were undertaken, much as studies of workers had been, to assess capitalism's impact or to understand its operation.

These studies have led to a proliferation of that "mass of information" Virginia Woolf asked for. We know what kinds of jobs women did, what their patterns of labour force participation were, what stage of the life cycle coincided with work away from home, under what conditions they formed labour unions or went on strike, what their wages were and how all of that has changed during the past hundred and fifty years. The mass of information has, furthermore, suggested the importance of including questions about family organization and sex-segregated labour markets in analyses of working-class history, but it has stopped short of meeting the challenge to "rewrite history." That is because most of the social history of women's work has been contained within the terms of social theories based on analytic categories that are primarily economic. There are many arguments advanced about women and work. Some insist that wage-earning enhanced women's sexual identity. Others that women were exploited as a cheap labour supply and that, as a result, men perceived women as a threat to the value of their own labour. Still others point out that sex-segregation undermined women's job control and hence their ability to organize and strike. Some historians have insisted that family divisions of labour attributed economic value to a wife's domestic role, others that family conflict centered around control of wages. One recent article suggests that when women commanded sufficient resources they engaged in collective action identical to men's. In all these studies the explanation ultimately has to do with economic variables not gender. Sexual divisions, their definition and elaboration are explained as the result of economic forces when, in fact, it is equally plausible and probably more accurate to suggest that cultural definitions of gender differences permitted the implementation of economic practices such as sex-segregated labour markets or the use of women to undercut the wages of skilled craftsmen.

Some historians of women's work have used a notion of patriarchy as a way of including gender in their analyses, but the term seems insufficiently theorized. Most often political, class and family systems are described as forms of male dominance which either transcend particular historical situations and social relations *or* follow directly from economic causes.

If social history has freed historians to write about women and given them some methods by which to document the experience and agency of women in the past, it has also limited the potential of women's history to "rewrite history." Few studies of social processes or social movements have yet been fundamentally altered as a result of studies focused on women. Women are a department of social history; they are one of the groups mobilizing resources, being modernized or exploited, contending for power or being excluded from a polity; they are explained, in other words, within the terms of behaviourist or Marxist or modernizationist models. The history of women enriches and adds new perspectives, but it has not yet been central to social history's largely successful effort to reconceptualize political history. That is because the issue of gender—implicit in the materials studied—has not been sufficiently singled out as either providing qualitatively different insights or as raising different kinds of analytic questions. In a sense, if "her-story" tends to too separatist a position, much of the social history of women has been too integrationist, subsuming women within received categories of analysis. Both approaches offer supplements to history, but they have not found a way to convince or demonstrate to other historians that it is essential to take their findings into account. They have not, in other words, "rewritten history." That rewriting is the project of the third position in the "debate" I have constructed, and it builds on, indeed it is made possible by, the work of both "her-story" and the social history of women.

The third position was articulated in prescriptions for women's history by some of its most important American representatives, but it has proved difficult to put into practice. Usually beginning with a focus on women, its subject is nonetheless gender. The late Joan Kelly set as the goal for this women's history making sex "as fundamental to our analysis of the social order as other classifications such as class and race." For Natalie Zemon Davis the aim is: "to understand the significance of the sexes, of gender groups in the historical past. Our goal is to discover the range in sex roles and in sexual symbolism in different societies and periods, to find out what meaning they had and how they functioned to maintain the social order or to promote its change." The point is to examine social definitions of gender as they are developed by men and women, constructed in and affected by economic and political institutions, expressive of a range of relationships which included not only sex, but class and power. The results throw new light not only on women's experience, but on social and political practice as well. In addition, enquiries into gender permit historians to raise critical questions that lead to the "rewriting of history."

Studying gender is less a question of a single theory than of a method or procedure for investigation. It consists of examining women and men in relation to one another, of asking what the definitions or laws that apply to one imply about the other, what the comparative location and activities of men and women reveal about each, and what representations of sexual difference suggest about the structure of social, economic and political authority. Thus Temma Kaplan's *Anarchists of Andalusia* analysed the different appeals of that political movement to men and women and the different but complementary ways in which male and female peasants and workers were organized to revolutionary struggle. Her parallel treatment of men and women within anarchism illuminates gender relationships in Andalusian society in relation to the nature and meaning of this particular political movement's attack on capitalism and the state. Tim Mason developed important insight about the "reconciliatory function of the family" in Nazi Germany as a result of an enquiry into the position of women and policies towards women. The factual material he gathered about women, who were largely "non-actors" in the politics of the period, "provided an exceptionally fruitful new vantage point from which the behaviour of the actors could be—indeed, had to be—reinterpreted." Taking Foucault's suggestions in the *History of Sexuality* as her starting-point, Judith Walkowitz delved into Josephine Butler's campaign against the Contagious Diseases Acts in late Victorian England. Avoiding what might have been the temptation to write a simple heroic account of the success of a woman's movement aimed at combating the double standard of sexual morality, Walkowitz used her material for an investigation into economic, social, religious and political divisions in English society. Although she did not directly offer criticism of conventional historical accounts of the period, her book implies such criticism. The study establishes that a debate about sexual conduct took place openly, within parliament as well as outside, that it was instigated by women (and supported by men) within the terms of their moral and religious preoccupations and carried on "in public," that it resulted in institutional and legal change, in short that sex was an explicit political issue for at least several decades. These findings not only question the conventional characterization of the period as "repressed," but suggest the need for rewriting a political history that has focused largely on the contests between Disraeli and Gladstone and on issues such as Irish Home Rule. How can the debate on prostitution and sexual standards be written into that political history? What critical perspective do we gain from the fact that it has, until now, been left out? At points of contact such as these the history of gender establishes a critique of political history and the means for rewriting it.

It seems no accident that many of the best efforts at joining women's history with established history take place in studies of politics broadly defined. Political structures and political ideas—structures and ideas that create and enforce relationships of power—shape and set the boundaries of public discourse and of all aspects of life. Even those excluded from participation in the discourse and activities of politics are defined by them; "non-actors," to use Mason's term, are acting according to rules established in political realms; the private sphere is a public creation; those absent from official accounts partook nonetheless in the making of history; those who are silent speak eloquently about the meanings of power and the uses of political authority. Feminist desires to make woman a historical subject cannot be realized simply by making her the agent or principal character of a historical narrative. To discover where women have been throughout history it is necessary to examine what gender and sexual difference have had to do with the workings of power. By doing so historians will both find women and transform political history.

At this point the approach I am suggesting is best undertaken by specific studies of discrete periods, movements or events. One could, for example, recast studies of suffrage campaigns to uncover relationships between gender and power in late nineteenth-century America or England. Brian Harrison has described the opposition to suffrage and others have analysed the ideas and supporters of the movement. But there has as yet been no study which brings together in a context larger than the issues of the vote itself all the participants—militants, moderates, antis, government ministers and members of parliament. What did the debate over the vote for women signify about conceptions of authority and political rights? How are patriarchal ideas articulated and in what terms? Where do conflicts about women (really about sexual difference) fit in the distribution of social, economic and political power in a nation? What is at stake and for which groups in a society when questions of gender difference become the focus of dispute, legislative consideration and ideological conflict?

Another example stems from work on the French Revolution. Studies of women in that revolution have moved from documentation of female participation to considerations of iconography and of the question of when and why sexual difference became an issue for dispute. Darlene Levy and Harriet Applewhite have focused on the debates in 1793 which outlawed women's clubs in the name of protecting femininity and domesticity. Why did gender become a means of drawing political lines? What issues beyond those having literally to do with women's rights were being addressed in prohibitions of female political organization? What was the significance of the revolutionaries' choice of a female figure to represent liberty and the republic? Was there any connection between iconographic representations and political rights for women? How did men and women differ in their discussions of women's political role? What do the political debates about sexual difference add to our understanding of the legitimation of authority and the protection of power during the French Revolution? These questions cannot be answered without information about women, but they are not limited to woman as subject or agent. Instead they include gender as a way of gaining a new appreciation of the politics and of the social and political impact of the French Revolution.

Studies of politics in the sense in which I employ the term need not deal only with issues of power at the level of nation states for my use of the term extends to contests (expressed in language as well as institutional arrangements) about power and authority in all aspects of social life. Indeed the work of Deborah Valenze on women preachers in English popular "cottage" religion demonstrates the interconnectedness between religious ideas and gender in expressions of opposition to change in community and household economies. Leonore Davidoff explores the ways in which individuals played with culturally defined categories of gender and class in her article on Arthur J. Munby; she reminds us of the complicated ways in which personal relationships are variations on

social themes of power, status and authority. Some recent considerations of the labour and socialist movements have used questions about gender to advance discussion beyond documentation of misogyny or condemnation of male leaders and beyond reductionist economic interpretations of the ideas and actions of workers. Parallel considerations of the discourses and experiences of working men and women have led to new interpretations, in one instance emphasizing the relative openness of utopian socialism to feminism, as compared to Marxian socialism's marginalization of women. Enquiries about the significance of sexual difference have led, in addition, to readings of representations of work, which include sexual, familial and religious dimensions. Work then has meaning beyond the literal description of productive activity, and studies about the place of women in the work-force and the labour movement offer insight both about women and the sexual politics of male and female workers *and* about the nature, meaning and purpose of their organizations and collective actions. The analysis must include women's actions and experiences, ideas and policies which define their rights, and metaphoric and symbolic representations of feminine and masculine. The problem for empirical historical investigation is to select moments when all of these are somehow at issue and to ask how they illuminate not only women's experience but politics as well.

To ignore politics in the recovery of the female subject is to accept the reality of public/private distinctions and the separate or distinctive qualities of women's character and experience. It misses the chance not only to challenge the accuracy of binary distinctions between men and women in the past and present, but to expose the very political nature of a history written in those terms. Simply to assert, however, that gender is a political issue is not enough. The realization of the radical potential of women's history comes in the writing of narratives that focus on women's experience *and* analyze the ways in which politics construct gender and gender constructs politics. Female agency then becomes not the recounting of great deeds performed by women, but the exposure of the often silent and hidden operations of gender which are nonetheless present and defining forces of politics and political life.

With this approach women's history enters the terrain of political history and inevitably begins the rewriting of history.

NOTE

1. Virginia Woolf, *A Room of One's Own* (London, 1929), p. 68.

The Feminist Critique in Religious Studies

Rosemary Radford Ruether

I. SOCIOLOGICAL AND HISTORICAL CONTEXT FOR WOMEN'S STUDIES IN RELIGION

Why women's studies in religion? To answer this question one must first survey the historical and sociological reality of women's participation in religion. One must start with the fact of women's historic exclusion from religious leadership roles in Judaism and Christianity and their consequent exclusion from advanced and professional theological education preparatory for the roles of clergy and teacher in these traditions. One could document similar histories in other world religions, such as Islam, but in this discussion we will speak primarily of Judaism and Christianity.

Many examples of this exclusion of women from leadership, teaching and education can be

cited. One thinks of the dicta in Rabbinic Judaism, "cursed be the man who teaches his daughter Torah," or the comparable statement in the New Testament, "I do not permit a woman to teach or to have authority over men. She is to keep silence" (I. Tim. 2, 12). Historically women were excluded from the study of Torah and Talmud that led to the rabbinate and which, as devotion, was considered the highest calling of the Jew. In Christianity the calling of the celibate woman diverged somewhat from the traditional view of women's limitations. But the education of women in monasteries was generally inferior to that of men and usually lacked the component of secular and classical learning which was regarded as inappropriate for women. When the educational center of Christendom shifted from the monastery to the university in the twelfth century, women were generally excluded. The northern European university particularly was a male, clerical institution.

From *Soundings* (1981). Reprinted by permission.

The seminary is a later institution that developed after the Reformation, when universities began to be seen as too secular to provide proper theological formation for priests and ministers. Generally they have been slow to open up to women. Oberlin was the first. Its theological school allowed a few women to attend in the 1840s, but at first they were not permitted to speak in class. Methodist and Congregational seminaries had a few women by the late nineteenth century. But prestigious seminaries like the Harvard Divinity School did not open its doors to women until the 1950s. Jewish and Catholic women began entering their seminaries even later.

II. EFFECTS OF WOMEN'S EXCLUSION ON THEOLOGICAL CULTURE

The exclusion of women from leadership and theological education results in the elimination of women as shapers of the official theological culture. Women are confined to passive and secondary roles. Their experience is not incorporated into the official culture. Those who do manage to develop as religious thinkers are forgotten or have their stories told through male-defined standards of what women can be. In addition, the public theological culture is defined by men, not only in the absence of, but against women. Theology not only assumed male standards of normative humanity, but is filled with an ideological bias that defines women as secondary and inferior members of the human species.

Many examples of this overt bias against women in the theological tradition can be cited. There is the famous definition of woman by Thomas Aquinas as a "misbegotten male." Aquinas takes this definition of women from Aristotle's biology, which identifies the male sperm with the genetic form of the embryo. Women are regarded as contributing only the matter or "blood" that fleshes out the form of the embryo. Hence, the very existence of women must be explained as a biological accident that comes about through a deformation of the male seed by the female "matter," producing a defective human or woman who is defined as lacking normative human standing.

Women are regarded as deficient physically, lacking full moral self-control and capacity for rational activity. Because of this defective nature women cannot represent normative humanity. Only the male can exercise headship or leadership in society. Aquinas also deduces from this that the maleness of Christ is not merely a historical accident, but a necessity. In order to represent humanity Christ must be incarnated into normative humanity, the male. Only the male, in turn, can represent Christ in the priesthood.

This Thomistic view of women is still reflected in Roman Catholic canon law where it is decreed that women are "unfit matter" for ordination. If one were to ordain a woman it, quite literally, would not "take," anymore than if one were to ordain a monkey or an ox. Some recent Episcopalian conservatives who declared that ordaining a woman is like ordaining a donkey are fully within this medieval scholastic tradition. Whether defined as inferior or simply as "different," theological and anthropological justifications of women's exclusion from religious learning and leadership can be found in every period of Jewish and Christian thought. Sometimes this exclusion of women is regarded as a matter of divine law, as in Old Testament legislation. Christian theologians tend to regard it as a reflection of "natural law," or the "order of nature," which, ultimately, also is a reflection of divine intent. Secondly, women's exclusion is regarded as an expression of woman's greater proneness to sin or corruption. Thus, as in the teaching of I Timothy, women are seen as "second in creation but first in sin" (I Timothy 2, 13–14).

The male bias of Jewish and Christian theology not only affects the teaching about woman's person, nature and role, but also generates a symbolic universe based on the patriarchal hierarchy of male over female. The subordination of woman to man is replicated in the symbolic universe in the imagery of divine-human relations. God is imaged as a great patriarch over against the earth or Creation, imaged in female terms. Likewise Christ is related to the Church as bridegroom to bride. Divine-human relations in the macrocosm are also reflected in the microcosm of the human being. Mind over body, reason over the passions, are also seen as images of the hierarchy of the "masculine" over the "feminine." Thus everywhere the Christian and Jew are surrounded by religious symbols that ratify male domination and female subordination as the normative way of understanding the world and God. This ratification of male domination runs through every period of the tradition, from Old to New Testament, Talmud, Church Fathers and canon law, Reformation Enlightenment and modern theology. It is not a marginal, but an integral part of what has been received as mainstream, normative traditions.

III. THE TASK OF FEMINISM IN RELIGIOUS STUDIES

The task of women's studies in religious education is thus defined by this historical reality of female exclusion and male ideological bias in the tradition. The first task of feminist critique takes the form of documenting the fact of this male ideological bias itself and tracing its sociological roots. One thinks of works such as Mary Daly's first book, *The Church and the Second Sex*, or the book I edited, *Religion and Sexism: Images of Women in the Jewish and Christian Traditions*. These works trace male bias against women from the Scriptures, Talmud and Church Fathers through medieval, Reformation and modern theologians. They intend to show that this bias is not marginal or accidental. It is not an expression of idiosyncratic, personal views of a few writers, but runs through the

whole tradition and shapes in conscious and unconscious ways the symbolic universe of Jewish and Christian theology.

The second agenda of feminist studies in religion aims at the discovery of an alternative history and tradition that supports the inclusion and personhood of women. At the present time, there are two very distinct types of alternative traditions that are being pursued by religious feminists. Within the Jewish and Christian theological academies the alternative tradition is being sought within Judaism and Christianity. However, many feminists have come to believe that no adequate alternative can be found within these religions. They wish to search for alternatives outside and against Judaism and Christianity. Some of these feminists are academically trained religious scholars who teach in religious studies or women's studies in colleges and universities and others are more self-trained writers that relate to the popular feminist spirituality movement, such as Starhawk and Z. Budapest.

This latter group draw their sources from anthropology and historical scholarship of matriarchal societies and ancient religions centered in the worship of the Mother Goddess rather than the patriarchal God of Semitic religions. They see the worship of the Mother Goddess as a woman's religion stemming from pre-patriarchal or matriarchal societies. This religion is believed to have been suppressed by militant patriarchal religions, but survived underground in secret, women-centered, nature religions persecuted by the dominant male religion. Medieval witchcraft is believed to have been such a female religion. Modern feminist witchcraft or "Wicca" sees itself as the heir to this persecuted goddess religion.

Writers of this emergent goddess religion draw from an anthropological scholarship of matriarchal origins that developed in the nineteenth century and which many scholars today regard as outdated and historically dubious. There has not yet been an opportunity for an adequate dialogue between these counter-cultural religious feminists and academic feminist scholarship. This is doubly difficult since goddess religion is not simply a matter of correct or incorrect scholarship, but of a rival faith stance. Most goddess religionists would feel that even if an adequate historical precedent for their faith cannot be found in the past, it should be created and they are creating it now.

The question of the relation of Jewish and Christian to post-Christian feminist religion will be discussed again later in this paper. For the moment, I will discuss some aspects of the search for an alternative tradition within Judaism and Christianity and its incorporation into theological education in seminaries and religious studies departments.

There now exists a fair body of well-documented studies in alternative traditions within Scripture and Jewish and Christian history. These studies show that male exclusion of women from leadership roles and theological reflection is not the whole story. There is much ambiguity and plurality in the traditions about women and the roles women have actually managed to play. For example, evidence is growing that women in first-century Judaism were not uniformly excluded from study in the synagogues. The rabbinic dicta against teaching women Torah thus begins to appear, not as a consensus of that period, but as one side of an argument—that eventually won—against the beginnings of inclusion of women in discipleship.

Similarly, the teachings of I Timothy about women keeping silence appear, not as the uniform position of the New Testament Church, but as a second generation reaction against widespread participation of women in leadership, teaching and ministering in first-generation Christianity. Indeed, the very fact that such vehement commandments against women learning and teachings were found in the traditions should have been a clue to the existence of widespread practices to the contrary. Otherwise, the

statements would have been unnecessary. But because the documents were used as Scripture or normative tradition, rather than historical documents, this was not realized.

The participation of women in early Christianity was not simply an accident of sociology, but a conscious expression of an alternative anthropology and soteriology. The equality of men and women in the image of God was seen as restored in Christ. The gifts of the prophetic spirit, poured out again at the Messianic coming, were understood, in fulfillment of the Messianic prediction of the prophet Joel, to have been given to the "maidservants" as well as the "menservants" of the Lord (Acts 2, 17–21). Baptism overcomes the sinful divisions among people and makes us one in the Christ: Jew and Greek, male and female, slave and free (Galatians 3, 28). Thus, the inclusion of women expressed an alternative theology in direct confrontation with the theology of patriarchal subordination of women. The New Testament now must be read, not as a consensus about women's place, but rather as a conflict and struggle over two alternative understandings of the gospel that suggested different views of male and female.

This alternative theology of equality, of women as equal in the image of God, as restored to equality in Christ and as commissioned to preach and minister by the Spirit, did not just disappear with the reassertion of patriarchal norms in I Timothy. It can be traced as surfacing again and again in different periods of Christian history. The strong role played by women in ascetic and monastic life in late antiquity and the early Middle Ages reflects a definite appropriation by women of a theology of equality in Christ that was understood as being applicable particularly to the monastic life. Celibacy was seen as abolishing sex-role differences and restoring men and women to their original equivalence in the image of God. As the male Church deserted this theology, female monastics continued to cling to it and understood their own vocation out of this theology. The history of female monasticism in the late Middle Ages and the Counter-Reformation is one of a gradual success of the male Church in suppressing this latent feminism of women's communities. It is perhaps then not accidental that women in renewed female religious orders in Roman Catholicism today have become militant feminists, to the consternation of the male hierarchy.

Left-wing Puritanism in the English Civil War again becomes a period when the latent egalitarianism of Christian theology surfaces to vindicate women's right to personal inspiration, community power and public teaching. The reclericalization of the Puritan congregation can be seen as a defeat for this renewed feminism of the Reformation. The Quakers were the one Civil War sect that retained the vision of women's equality and carried it down into the beginnings of nineteenth-century feminism.

Finally, the nineteenth century becomes a veritable hotbed of new types of female participation in religion, ranging from the evangelical holiness preacher, Phoebe Palmer, to Mother Ann Lee, understood by her followers as the female Messiah. New theologies that attempt to vindicate androgyny in humanity and God express a sense of the inadequacy of the masculinist tradition of symbolization. Works such as *Women of Spirit: Female Leadership in the Jewish and Christian Traditions*, Rosemary Ruether and Eleanor McLaughlin, and *Women In American Religion*, Janet Wilson James, or the documentary history, *Women and Religion: the Nineteenth Century*, Rosemary Keller and Rosemary Ruether, trace different periods of women's recovered history in religion.

Feminists who are engaged in recovering alternative histories for women in religion recognize that they are not just supplementing the present male tradition. They are, implicitly, attempting to construct a new norm for the interpretation of the tradition. The male justification of women's subordination in Scripture and tradition is no longer regarded as nor-

mative for the gospel. Rather, it is judged as a failure to apply the authentic norms of equality in creation and redemption authentically. This is judged as a failure, in much the same way as the political corruption of the Church, the persecution of Jews, heretics or witches, or the acceptance of slavery has been judged as a failure. This does not mean that this "bad" history is suppressed or forgotten. This also would be an ideological history that tries to "save" the moral and doctrinal reputation of the Church by forgetting what we no longer like. We need to remember this history, but as examples of our fallibility, not as norms of truth.

The equality of women, as one of the touchstones for understanding our faithfulness to the vision, is now set forth as one of the norms for criticizing the tradition and discovering its best expressions. This will create a radical reappraisal of Jewish or Christian traditions, since much that has been regarded as marginal, and even heretical, must now be seen as efforts to hold on to an authentic tradition of women's equality. Much of the tradition which has been regarded as "mainstream" must be seen as deficient in this regard. We underestimate the radical intent of women's studies in religion if we do not recognize that it aims at nothing less than this kind of radical reconstruction of the normative tradition.

IV. TRANSLATION OF WOMEN'S STUDIES IN RELIGION INTO EDUCATIONAL PRAXIS

Obviously women cannot affect an educational system until they first secure their own access to it. It has taken approximately one hundred and twenty-five years for most schools of theological education to open their doors to women and then to include women in sufficient numbers for their concerns to begin to be recognized. Women began to enter theological schools of the Congregational tradition beginning with Oberlin in the 1840s and Methodist institutions in the 1870s. Only in the 1970s have some Roman Catholic and Jewish seminaries been open to women. Moreover, even liberal Protestant institutions did not experience any "critical mass" of female students until the 1970s.

Usually, access to theological education precedes winning the right to ordination. Winning the educational credentials for ordination then becomes a powerful wedge to winning the right of ordination itself. It is for that reason that there may be efforts to close Roman Catholic seminaries, at least those directly related to Rome, to women. Rumor has it (as of this writing) that a decree has been written but not yet promulgated in Rome forbidding women to attend pontificatical seminaries (which would include all Jesuit seminaries, but not most diocesan and order seminaries). Women's tenure in professional schools of theology cannot be regarded as secure until they win the right to ordination. Only then can they develop a larger number of women students and attain the moral and organizational clout to begin to make demands for changes in the context of the curriculum.

Generally, demands for feminist studies begin with the organization of a caucus of women theological students. They then begin to demand women's studies in the curriculum and women faculty who can teach such courses. In many seminaries, particularly in U.S. liberal Protestant institutions, there has been some response to these demands: some women faculty have been hired, and some women's studies incorporated into the curriculum. It is at this point that we can recognize several stages of resistance to the implied challenge to the tradition.

One standard strategy of male faculty is to seek and retain one or two women on the faculty, but to give preference to women who are "traditional scholars," not feminists. This is fairly easy to do by the established rules of the guild, while, at the same time, appearing to be "objective." Feminists studies are nontraditional. They force one to use non-traditional methods and sources and to be something of a generalist. Their content is still in flux and experimentation. Rare is the person who can fulfill the expectations of both traditional scholarship and feminist scholarship equally well. So it is easy to attack such persons as "unscholarly," and to fail to tenure them in preference to those women who prefer to be "one of the boys." As of this writing there is an alarming erosion of feminist faculty talent in theological education through precisely this method. This has forced feminist scholars in theological education to band together in a new national organization, Feminist Theology and Ministry, in order to defend the employment of feminists in existing institutions of theological education.

Efforts are also underway to create new, alternative settings for women's studies in religion. For example, groups in the Boston-Washington corridor and in Chicago (largely, but not exclusively, Roman Catholic) are seriously considering the development of autonomous feminist theology schools for women, since the existing (especially Roman Catholic) institutions have proved so unfavorable to their interests.

In some other settings a decade-long struggle for women's studies in religion is beginning to bear fruit. For example, at the Harvard Divinity School, bastion of "traditional" education, a pilot program of graduate assistants in women's studies in various fields has continued for some eight years, for much of this time under constant threat of liquidation. However, a study of the program located one of its chief flaws in the lack of prestige and respect given to the women's studies teachers by the tenured faculty. As a result, a new level of funding has been developed to allow this program to be continued and eventually to be converted into a permanent research center for women in religion, with five full-time junior and senior faculty appointments. It remains to be seen whether this expanded "prestige" will not result in some of the same pressure to prefer traditional over feminist scholars.

In the development of feminist studies in the curriculum, most institutions move through several stages. The first stage is a grudging allowance of a generalist course on women's studies in religion that is taught outside the structure of the curriculum and usually by a person marginal to the faculty. The male faculty tend to feel little respect for the content of the course (about which they generally know nothing) or its instructor, and no commitment to its continuance as a regular part of the curriculum.

The second stage is when faculty begin to acquire women in one or more regular fields who are both respected as scholars and prepared to do women's studies. Women's studies courses can then be initiated that are located in the various regular disciplines of the curriculum, such as Biblical studies, Church history, theology, ethics, pastoral psychology, preaching and liturgy or Church administration. These courses, however, are taught as occasional electives. They attract only feminist students, mostly females and a few males. The rest of the student body is not influenced by them. Most of the faculty ignore them. The new material in them does not affect the foundational curriculum. In other words, women's studies in religion goes on as a marginal and duplicate curriculum. There is now a course in "systematic theology" and a second one on "feminist" theology. The foundational courses continue as before. Therefore, implicitly, they claim the patriarchal bias in theology as the "real" or "true" theology.

The third stage would come when feminist studies begin to affect the foundational curriculum itself. Here we might detect two more stages. The third stage would be when foundational curricula continue as usual, except for an occasional "ladies' day" when women's concerns are discussed. Thus, for example, one would teach twelve weeks of traditional male Church history, and then one week in which "great women" are considered. The fourth and optimum situation would be reached when feminist critique really penetrates the whole foundational curriculum and transforms the way in which all the topics are considered. Thus, it becomes impossible to deal with any topic of theological studies without being aware of sexist and nonsexist options in the tradition and bringing that out as an integral part of one's hermeneutic. Thus, for example, one would understand St. Paul as a man whose theology is caught up in ambivalent struggle between various alternatives: between an exclusivist and a universal faith, between an historical and an eschatological faith, and between a patriarchal and an integrative faith. The way he handled the third ambiguity, moreover, conditioned fundamentally the way he handled the first two ambiguities. Thus, one cannot understand Paul as a whole without incorporating the question of sexism into the context of his theology.

Generally we can say that most seminaries who have dealt with women's studies at all are somewhere between stage one and stage two, usually at stage one. A few have done an occasional "ladies' day" in the foundational curriculum. Few have even begun to imagine what it would mean to reach the optimum incorporation of feminism into the foundational curriculum, as a normal and normative part of the interpretive context of the whole. Moreover women's studies in religion has not yet matured to the point where it is able to offer a comprehensive reconstruction of methodology and tradition in various fields. For example, a genuine feminist reconstruction of systematic theology is yet to be written.

Even further down the road is the "retraining" of male faculty who are able to take such work into account. There are exceptions. Occasionally one finds that prodigy, a male professor who early recognized the value of the feminist critique and has been able, easily and gracefully, to incorporate it into his teaching with a minimum of defensiveness or breast-beating. In general, however, one would have to say that women's studies in theological education is still marginal and vulnerable. The conservative drift of the seminaries means that increasing numbers of women students themselves are non- or anti-feminist. Cadres of explicitly hostile white male students are emerging. Constant struggle is necessary to maintain momentum or even to prevent slipback. The recent publication of the book *Your Daughters Shall Prophecy* reflects on this ten-year struggle for feminist theological education in several major educational settings.

V. ALTERNATIVE VIEWS OF FEMINISM AND RELIGIOUS STUDIES

Finally, we must say that feminists in religion are by no means united in what they understand to be the optimum feminist reconstruction of religion. We also have to reckon with the fact that religion is not simply an academic discipline. It is an integral part of popular culture. Concern with it has to do with *modus vivendi* of large numbers of people in many walks of life. It shapes mass institutions, the Church and the Synagogue, as well as alternative religious communities that emerge to fill people's need for life symbols. Thus, the interest in feminism and religion has an urgency, as well as a rancor, that is different from that in academic disciplines.

There are several different lines that are emerging both in academics and across the religious institutions and movements of popular culture today. One group, who could be identified as evangelical feminists, believe that the message of Scripture is fundamentally egalitarian. Scripture, especially the New Testament, proposes a new ideal of "mutual submission" of men and women to each other. This has been misread as the subjugation of women by the theological tradition. These feminists would hope to clean up the sexism of Scripture by better exegesis. It would be incorrect to interpret these evangelical feminists as always limited by a pre-critical method of scriptural interpretation. Their limitations are often more pastoral than personal. They are concerned to address a certain constituency, the members of the evangelical churches from which they come, with the legitimacy of an egalitarian understanding of Biblical faith. They sometimes limit themselves to this kind of exegesis because they know it is the only way to reach that constituency.

A second view, which I would call the "liberationist" position, takes a more critical view of Scripture. People with this view believe there is a conflict between the prophetic, iconoclastic message of the prophetic tradition, with its attack on oppressive and self-serving religion, and the failure to apply this message to subjugated minorities in the patriarchal family, especially the women and slaves. The vision of redemption of the Biblical tradition transcends the inadequacies of past consciousness. It goes ahead of us, pointing toward a new and yet unrealized future of liberation whose dimensions are continually expanding as we become more sensitive to injustices which were overlooked in past cultures. Liberationists would use the prophetic tradition as the norm to critique the sexism of the religious tradition. Biblical sexism is not denied, but it loses its authority. It must be denounced as a failure to measure up to the full vision of human liberation of the prophetic and gospel messages.

A third group, we mentioned earlier, feel that women waste their time salvaging positive elements of these religious traditions. They take the spokesmen of patriarchal religion at their word when they say that Christ and God are literally and essentially male, and conclude that these religions have existed for no other purpose except to sanctify male domination. Women should quit the Church and the Synagogue and move to the feminist coven to celebrate the sacrality of women through recovery of the religion of the Goddess.

Although I myself am most sympathetic to the second view, I would regard all these positions as having elements of truth. All respond to real needs of different constituencies of women (and some men). It is unlikely that any of these views will predominate, but all will work as parallel trends in the ensuing decades to reshape the face of religion.

The evangelical feminists address themselves to an important group in American religion who frequently use Scripture to reinforce traditional patriarchal family models. Evangelical feminists wish to lift up neglected traditions and to give Biblicist Christians a basis for addressing the question of equality. They will probably get the liberal wing of these churches to modify their language and exegesis. The first creation story of women's and man's equal creation in the image of God will be stressed, rather than the second creation story of Eve from Adam's rib. Galatians 3, 28 will be stressed in Paul rather than Ephesians 5, and so forth. They might get some denominations to use inclusive language for the community and maybe even for God.

The liberationist wing would want Churches to take a much more active and prophetic role in critiquing the sexism of society, not only on such issues as abortion rights, gay rights and the ERA, but also on the links between sexism and economic injustice. They would press churches with a social gospel tradition into new questions about the adequacy of a patriarchal, capitalist, and consumerist economy to promote a viable human future.

The impact of the separatist goddess religions is more difficult to predict. Traditional Jews and Christians would view these movements as "paganism," if not "satanism." The Goddess movements are likely to respond in a equally defensive way and to direct their feelings against feminists who are still working within Churches and Synagogues. A lot depends on whether some mediating ground can be developed. On the one side, there would have to be a conscious rejection of the religious exclusivism of the Jewish and Christian tradi-

tions and a recognition of the appropriateness of experiencing the divine through female symbols and body images. The Goddess worshippers, in turn, might have to grow out of some of their defensiveness toward their Jewish and Christian sisters and start thinking about how we are to create a more comprehensive faith for our sons, as well as our daughters.

This is not to be construed as a call for such feminists to become (or return) to Judaism or Christianity, but rather a growth toward that kind of maturity that can recognize the legitimacy of religious quests in several kinds of contexts. As long as "goddess" feminists can only affirm their way by a reversed exclusivism and denial of the possibility of liberating elements in the Biblical tradition, they are still tied to the same exclusivist patterns of thought in an opposite form.

A creative dialogue between these two views could be very significant. Countercultural feminist spirituality could make important contributions to the enlargement of our religious symbols and experiences. We might be able to experience God gestating the world in Her womb, rather than just "making it" through a divine phallic fiat. We would rediscover the rhythms that tie us biologically with earth, fire, air and water which have been so neglected in our anti-natural spiritualities. We would explore the sacralities of the repressed parts of our psyches and our environmental experiences. Many worlds that have been negated by patriarchal religion might be reclaimed for the enlargement of our common life.

It is not clear what all this might mean. It might well be the beginning of a new religion as momentous in its break with the past as Christianity was with the religions of the Semites and the Greeks. But if it is truly to enlarge our present options, it must also integrate the best of the insights that we have developed through Judaism and Christianity, as these religions integrated some (not all) of the best insights of the Near Eastern and Greco-Roman worlds. What is clear is this: the patriarchal repression of women and women's experience has been so massive and prevalent that to begin to take women seriously will involve a profound and radical transformation of our religions.

Re-visioning Clinical Research: Gender and the Ethics of Experimental Design

Sue V. Rosser

INTRODUCTION

Since the practice of modern medicine depends heavily on clinical research, flaws and ethical problems in this research are likely to result in poorer health care and inequity in the medical treatment of disadvantaged groups. The first purpose of this paper is to explore some ways in which clinical research has been impaired and compromised by an androcentric focus in its choice and definition of problems studied, approaches and methods used, and theories and conclusions drawn. Second, I shall describe some attempts to correct this biased focus and envision further improvement through feminist perspectives and approaches.

In scientific research, it is rarely admitted that data have been gathered and interpreted from a particular perspective. Since scientific research centers on the physical and natural world, it is presumed "objective;" therefore, the term perspective does not apply to it. However,

From *Hypatia* (1989). Reprinted by permission.

the decisions, either conscious or unconscious, regarding what questions are asked, who is allowed to do the asking, what information is collected, and who interprets that information create a particular vantage point from which the knowledge or truth is perceived.

Historians of science, particularly Thomas Kuhn and his followers, have pointed out that scientific theories are not objective and value-free but are paradigms that reflect the historical and social context in which they are conceived. In our culture, the institutionalized power, authority, and domination of men frequently result in acceptance of the male world view or androcentrism as the norm. Recognizing the influence of this androcentric perspective is particularly difficult for scientists because of their traditional belief in the objectivity of science which makes it difficult for them to admit that they actually hold any perspectives which may influence their data, approaches, and theories.

Feminist philosophers of science have described the specific ways in which the very objectivity said to be characteristic of scientific knowledge and the dichotomy between subject and object are, in fact, male ways of relating to the world, which specifically exclude women. Research has also become a masculine province in its choice and definition of problems studied, methods and experimental subjects used, and interpretation and application of experimental results.

Revealing the distortions in clinical research that emanate from the androcentric biases uncovers points at which a feminist ethics might influence this research. Feminist scientists have called for more people-oriented and patient-centered research which would be likely to provide better health care for all.

CHOICE AND DEFINITION OF PROBLEMS STUDIED

With the expense of sophisticated equipment, maintenance of laboratory animals and facilities, and salaries for qualified technicians and researchers, virtually no medical research is undertaken today without Federal or foundation support. Gone are the days when individuals had laboratories in their homes or made significant discoveries working in isolation using homemade equipment. In fiscal 1987, the National Institutes of Health (NIH) funded approximately $6.1 billion of research. Private foundations and state governments funded a smaller portion of the research.

The choice of problems for study in medical research is substantially determined by a national agenda that defines what is worthy of study, i.e., funding. As Marxist, African-American, and feminist critics of scientific research have pointed out, the scientific research that is undertaken reflects the societal bias towards the powerful who are overwhelmingly white, middle/upper class, and male in the United States. Obviously, the members of Congress who appropriate the funds for NIH and other Federal agencies are overwhelmingly white, middle/upper class, and male; they are more likely to vote funds for research which they view as beneficial to health needs, as defined from their perspective.

It may be argued that actual priorities for medical research and allocations of funds are not set by members of Congress but by leaders in medical research who are employees of NIH or other Federal agencies or who are brought in as consultants. Unfortunately the same descriptors—white, middle/upper class, and male—must be used to characterize the individuals in the theoretical and decision-making positions within the medical hierarchy and scientific establishment.

Women are lacking even at the level of the peer review committee, which is how NIH determines which of the competitive proposals submitted by researchers in a given area are funded. In the ten year interval 1975–1984, women went from 16.9 percent of NIH peer review committee members to only 17.9 percent; during this time, the total number of members nearly doubled from 733 to 1,264. Because the percentage of women post-doctoral fellows increased by 32 percent during the same time period, it seems likely that qualified women were available, but not used.

I believe that the results of having a huge preponderance of male leaders setting the priorities for medical research have definite effects on the choice and definition of problems for research:

1. Hypotheses are not formulated to focus on gender as a crucial part of the question being asked. Since it is clear that many diseases have different frequencies (heart disease, lupus), symptoms (gonorrhea), or complications (most sexually transmitted diseases) in the two sexes, scientists should routinely consider and test for differences or lack of differences based on gender in any hypothesis being tested. For example, when exploring the metabolism of a particular drug, one should routinely run tests in both males and females. Two dramatic,

widely publicized recent examples demonstrate that sex differences are *not* routinely considered as part of the question asked. In a longitudinal study of the effects of cholesterol lowering drugs, gender differences were not tested since the drug was tested on 3,806 men and no women. In a similar test of the effects of aspirin on cardio-vascular disease, which is now used widely by the pharmaceutical industry to support "taking one aspirin each day to prevent heart attacks," no females were included.

2. Some diseases which affect both sexes are defined as male diseases. Heart disease is the best example of a disease that has been so des-ignated because of the fact that heart disease occurs more frequently in men at younger ages than women. Therefore, most of the funding for heart disease has been appropriated for re-search on predisposing factors for the disease (such as cholesterol level, lack of exercise, stress, smoking, and weight) using white, middle-aged, middle-class males.

This "male disease" designation has re-sulted in very little research being directed to-wards high risk groups of women. Heart disease is a leading cause of death in older women who live an average of eight years longer than men. It is also frequent in poor black women who have had several children. Virtually no research has explored predisposing factors for these groups who fall outside the disease definition established from an androcentric perspective. Recent data indicate that the designation of AIDS as a disease of male homosexuals and drug users has led researchers and health care practitioners to fail to understand the etiology and diagnosis of AIDS in women.

3. Research on conditions specific to fe-males receives low priority, funding, and pres-tige. Some examples include dysmenorrhea, incontinency in older women, and nutrition in post-menopausal women. Effects of exercise level and duration upon alleviation of menstrual discomfort and length and amount of exposure to VDTs that have resulted in the "cluster preg-

nancies" of women giving birth to deformed babies in certain industries have also received low priority. In contrast, significant amounts of time and money are expended upon clinical research on women's bodies in connection with other aspects of reproduction. In this century up until the 1970s considerable attention was devoted to the development of devices for fe-males rather than for males. Furthermore, sub-stantial clinical research has resulted in increasing medicalization and control of preg-nancy, labor, and childbirth. Feminists have critiqued the conversion of a normal, natural process controlled by women into a clinical, often surgical, procedure controlled by men. More recently, the new reproductive technolo-gies such as amniocentesis, *in vitro* fertiliza-tion, and artificial insemination have become a major focus as means are sought to overcome infertility. Feminists have warned of the extent to which these technologies place pressure upon women to produce the "perfect" child while placing control in the hands of the male med-ical establishment.

These examples suggest that considerable resources and attention are devoted to women's health issues when those issues are directly re-lated to men's interest in controlling production of children. Contraceptive research may permit men to have sexual pleasure without the pro-duction of children; research on infertility, preg-nancy, and childbirth has allowed men to assert more control over the production of more "per-fect" children and over an aspect of women's lives over which they previously held less power.

4. Suggestions of fruitful questions for re-search based on the personal experience of women have also been ignored. In the health care area, women have often reported (and accepted among themselves) experiences that could not be documented by scientific experi-ments or were not accepted as valid by the researchers of the day. For decades, dsymen-orrhea was attributed by most health care re-searchers and practitioners to psychological or

social factors despite the reports from an over-whelming number of women that these were monthly experiences in their lives. Only after prostaglandins were "discovered" was there widespread acceptance among the male medical establishment that this experience reported by women had a biological component.

These four types of bias raise ethical issues: Health care practitioners must treat the majority of the population, which is female, based on information gathered from clinical research in which drugs may not have been tested on females, in which the etiology of the disease in women has not been studied and in which women's experience has been ignored.

APPROACHES AND METHODS

1. The scientific community has often failed to include females in animal studies in basic research as well as in clinical research unless the research centered on controlling the production of children. The reasons for the exclusion (cleaner data from males due to lack of interference from estrus or menstrual cycles, fear of inducing fetal deformities in pregnant subjects, and higher incidence of some diseases in males) are practical when viewed from a financial standpoint. However, the exclusion results in drugs that have not been adequately tested in women subjects before being marketed and lack of information about the etiology of some diseases in women.

2. Using the male as the experimental subject not only ignores the fact that females may respond differently to the variable tested, it may also lead to less accurate models even in the male. Models which *more accurately* simulate functioning complex biological systems may be derived from using female rats as subjects in experiments. Women scientists such as Joan Hoffman have questioned the tradition of using male rats or primates as subjects. With the exception of insulin and the hormones of the female reproductive cycle, traditional endo-crinological theory assumed that most of the 20-odd human hormones are kept constant in level in both males and females. Thus, the male of the species, whether rodent or primate, was chosen as the experimental subject because of his noncyclicity. However, new techniques of measuring blood hormone levels have demonstrated episodic, rather than steady, patterns of secretion of virtually all hormones in both males and females. As Hoffman points out, the rhythmic cycle of hormone secretion as also portrayed in the cycling female rat appears to be a more accurate model for the secretion of most hormones.

3. When females have been used as experimental subjects, often they are treated as not fully human. In his attempts to investigate the side effects nervousness and depression attributable to oral contraceptives, Goldzieher gave dummy pills to seventy-six women who sought treatment at a San Antonio clinic to prevent further pregnancies. None of the women was told that she was participating in research or receiving placebos. The women in Goldzieher's study were primarily poor, multiparous, Mexican Americans. Research that raises similar issues about the ethics of informed consent was carried out on poor Puerto Rican women during the initial phases of testing the effectiveness of the pill as a contraceptive.

Frequently it is difficult to determine whether these women are treated as less than human because of their gender or whether race and class are more significant variables. From the Tuskegee Syphilis Experiment in which the effects of untreated syphilis were studied in 399 men over a period of forty years, it is clear that men who are black and poor may not receive appropriate treatment or information about the experiment in which they are participating. Feminist scholars have begun to explore the extent to which gender, race and class become complex, interlocking political variables that may affect access to and quality of health care.

4. Current clinical research sets up a dis-

tance between the observer and the human object being studied. Several feminist philosophers have characterized this distancing as an androcentric approach. Distance between the observer and experimental subject may be more comfortable for men who are reared to feel more comfortable with autonomy and distance than for women who tend to value relationship and interdependency.

5.   Using only the methods traditional to a particular discipline may result in limited approaches that fail to reveal sufficient information about the problem being explored. This may be a particular difficulty for research surrounding medical problems of pregnancy, childbirth, menstruation, and menopause for which the methods of one discipline are clearly inadequate.

Methods which cross disciplinary boundaries or include combinations of methods traditionally used in separate fields may provide more appropriate approaches. For example, if the topic of research is occupational exposures that present a risk to the pregnant woman working in a plant where toxic chemicals are manufactured, a combination of methods traditionally used in social science research with methods frequently used in biology and chemistry may be the best approach. Checking the chromosomes of any miscarried fetuses, chemical analysis of placentae after birth, Apgar Scores of the babies at birth, and blood samples of the newborns to determine trace amounts of the toxic chemicals would be appropriate biological and chemical methods used to gather data about the problem. In-depth interviews with women to discuss how they are feeling and any irregularities they detect during each month of the pregnancy, or evaluation using weekly written questionnaires regarding the pregnancy progress are methods more traditionally used in the social sciences for problems of this sort. Jean Hamilton has called for interactive models that draw on both the social and natural sciences to explain complex problems:

Particularly for understanding human, gender-related health, we need more interactive and contextual models that address the actual complexity of the phenomenon that is the subject of explanation. One example is the need for more phenomenological definitions of symptoms, along with increased recognition that psychology, behavioral studies, and sociology are among the "basic sciences" for health research. Research on heart disease is one example of a field where it is recognized that both psychological stress and behaviors such as eating and cigarette smoking influence the onset and natural course of a disease process.[1]

Perhaps more women holding decision-making positions in designing and funding clinical research would result in more inter-disciplinary research to study issues of women's health care such as menstruation, pregnancy, childbirth, lactation, and menopause. Those complex phenomena fall outside the range of methods of study provided by a sole discipline. The interdisciplinary approaches developed to solve these problems might then be applied to other complex problems to benefit all health care consumers, both male and female.

THEORIES AND CONCLUSIONS DRAWN FROM THE RESEARCH

The rationale which is traditionally presented in support of the "objective" methods is that they prevent bias. Emphasis upon traditional disciplinary approaches that are quantitative and maintain the distance between observer and experimental subject supposedly removes the bias of the researcher. Ironically, to the extent that these "objective" approaches are in fact synonymous with a masculine approach to the world, they may introduce bias. Specifically, androcentric bias may permeate the theories and conclusions drawn from the research in several ways:

1.   First, theories may be presented in androcentric language. Much feminist scholarship has focussed on problems of sexism in language

and the extent to which patriarchal language has excluded and limited women. Sexist language is a symptom of underlying sexism, but language also shapes our concepts and provides the framework through which we express our ideas. The awareness of sexism and the limitations of a patriarchal language that feminist researchers have might allow them to describe their observations in less gender-biased terms.

An awareness of language should aid experimenters in avoiding the use of terms such as "tomboyism," "aggression" and "hysteria" that reflect assumptions about sex-appropriate behavior that permeate behavioral descriptions in clinical research. Once the bias in the terminology is exposed, the next step is to ask whether that terminology leads to a constraint or bias in the theory itself.

2.   An androcentric perspective may lead to formulating theories and conclusions drawn from medical research to support the status quo of inequality for women and other oppressed groups. Building upon their awareness of these biases, women scientists have critiqued the studies of brain-hormone interaction for their biological determinism used to justify women's socially inferior position. Bleier has repeatedly warned against extrapolating from one species to another in biochemical as well as behavioral traits. Perhaps male researchers are less likely to see flaws in and question biologically deterministic theories that provide scientific justification for men's superior status in society because they as men gain social power and status from such theories. Researchers from outside the mainstream (women, for example) are much more likely to be critical of such theories since they lose power from those theories. In order to eliminate bias, the community of scientists undertaking clinical research needs to include individuals from backgrounds of as much variety and diversity as possible with regard to race, class, gender, and sexual preference. Only then is it less likely that the perspective of one group

will bias research design, approaches, subjects, and interpretations.

HINTS OF RE-VISIONING

Some changes in clinical research have come about because of the recognition of flaws and ethical problems for women discussed in this paper. Some of the changes are the result of critiques made by feminists and women scientists; some of the changes have been initiated by men.

The rise of the women's health movement in the 1970's encouraged women to question established medical authority, take responsibility for their own bodies and express new demands for clinical research and for access to health care. Feminist demands have led to increased availability of health related information to women consumers. Litigation and federal affirmative action programs have resulted in an increase from about 6% to about 40% of women medical students from 1960 to the present. Consumer complaints and suggestions have fostered minor reforms in obstetrical care. The decor, ambiance, and regimens of birthing facilities have improved to provide personal and psychological support for the mother and to promote infant-parent bonding. However, concurrent with modest obstetrical modifications in hospitals, nurse midwives in most states have felt the backlash of professional efforts to control their practice and licensure status.

Efforts to increase the understanding of the biology of birth and translate that knowledge into clinical care expressed as acceptable infant mortality rates remain inadequate.

2.   Guidelines have been developed that require any research project that is Federally funded to insure humane treatment of human subjects and fully informed consent. The impetus for the formation of the National Commission for the Protection of Human Subjects

of Biomedical and Behavioral Research was the revelation of the abuses of human subjects during the Nuremberg War Crimes Trials and the Tuskegee Syphilis Experiments (Belmont Report). However, the attention drawn by men such as Veatch to unethical issues surrounding the testing of oral contraceptives in women helped to insure that women, especially pregnant women, were given particular consideration in the papers forming the basis of the Belmont Report (Levine 1978).

3. In recent years U.S. government agencies have shown increased sensitivity to clinical research surrounding women's health issues and the difficult ethical issues of including women in pharmacological research. The Public Health Service (PHS) Task Force on Women's Health Issues was commissioned to aid the PHS "as the agency works within its areas of jurisdiction and expertise to improve the health and well-being of women in the United States". In her insightful commissioned paper "Avoiding Methodological and Policy-Making Biases in Gender-Related Health Research" for the Report to the Task Force, Jean Hamilton makes strong recommendations:

PHS consensus-development conference on "Gender-related Methods for Health Research" (for the development of guidelines) should be held. . . . The feasibility of including women in certain types of research needs to be reexamined. . . . A number of working groups should be formed: A working-group to reconsider the difficult ethical issues of including women in pharmacological research (e.g., extra-protection for women as research subjects, versus other means for informed consent) . . . A working-group to identify and to consider mechanisms to enhance the kind of multi-center, *collaborative* or *clinical research center* studies that would be most efficient in advancing our understanding of women and their health . . . A working group or committee to consider ways to foster subject-selection in a way that allows for an examination of possible age, sex, and hormonal status effects.[2]

4. Some attempts at patient involvement in research design and implementation have provided a mechanism to shorten the distance between the observer and subjects observed. Elizabeth Fee describes an account of occupational health research in an Italian factory:

Prior to 1969, occupational health research was done by specialists who would be asked by management to investigate a potential problem in the factory. . . . The procedure was rigorously objective, the results were submitted to management. The workers were the individualized and passive objects of this kind of research. In 1969, however, when workers' committees were established in the factories, they refused to allow this type of investigation . . . Occupational health specialists had to discuss the ideas and procedures of research with workers' assemblies and see their "objective" expertise measured against the "subjective" experience of the workers. The mutual validation of data took place by testing in terms of the workers' experience of reality and not simply by statistical methods; the subjectivity of the workers' experience was involved at each level in the definition of the problem, the method of research, and the evaluation of solutions. Their collective experience was understood to be much more than the statistical combination of individual data; the workers had become the active subjects of research, involved in the production, evaluation, and uses of the knowledge relating to their own experience.[3]

CONCLUSION

Replacing the androcentrism in the practice of medical research and the androcentric bias in the questions asked, methods used, theories and conclusions drawn from data gathered with a feminist approach represents a major change with profound ethical implications. Lynda Birke, a feminist scientist, suggests that feminism will change science and medicine from research that is oppressive to women and potentially destructive to all towards liberation and improvement for everyone.

Perhaps this discussion of creating a feminist science seems hopelessly utopian. Perhaps. But feminism is, above all else, about wanting and working for change, change towards a better society in which women of all kinds are not devalued, or oppressed in any way. Working for change has to include changing science, which not only perpetuates our oppression at present, but threatens also to destroy humanity and all the other species with whom we share this earth.[4]

NOTES

1. Jean Hamilton, "Avoiding Methodological Biases in Gender-related Research," *Women's Health Report of the Public Health Service Task Force on Women's Health Issues*, U.S. Dept. of Health and Human Services, Public Service: Washington DC (1985) p. 62.

2. Ibid., p. 63–4.

3. Elizabeth Fee, Women's nature and scientific objectivity. In *Woman's nature, rationalizations of inequality*, Marian Lowe and Ruth Hubbard (eds.). New York: Pergamon Press. 1983 p 24.

4. Lynda Birke. *Women, Feminism and Biology*, New York: Methuen (1986) p 171.

❧ Liberal Feminism ❧

The Subjection of Women

John Stuart Mill

The object of this Essay is to explain as clearly as I am able, the grounds of an opinion which I have held from the very earliest period when I had formed any opinions at all on social or political matters, and which, instead of being weakened or modified, has been constantly growing stronger by the progress of reflection and the experience of life: That the principle which regulates the existing social relations between the two sexes—the legal subordination of one sex to the other—is wrong in itself, and now one of the chief hindrances to human improvement; and that it ought to be replaced by a principle of perfect equality, admitting no power or privilege on the one side, nor disability on the other.

The very words necessary to express the task I have undertaken show how arduous it is. But it would be a mistake to suppose that the difficulty of the case must lie in the insufficiency or obscurity of the grounds of reason on which my conviction rests. The difficulty is that which exists in all cases in which there is a mass of feeling to be contended against. So long as an opinion is strongly rooted in the feelings, it gains rather than loses in stability by having a preponderating weight of argument against it. For if it were accepted as a result of argument, the refutation of the argument might shake the solidity of the conviction; but when it rests solely on feeling, the worse it flares in argumentative contest, the more persuaded its adherents are that their feeling must have some deeper ground, which the arguments do not reach; and while the feeling remains, it is always throwing up fresh intrenchments of argument to repair any breach made in the old. And there are so many causes tending to make the feelings connected with this subject the most intense and most deeply-rooted of all those which gather round and protect old institutions and customs, that we need not wonder to find them as yet less undermined and loosened than any of the rest by the progress of the great modern spiritual and social transition; nor suppose that the barbarisms to which men cling longest must be less barbarisms than those which they earlier shake off. . . .

In the first place, the opinion in favour of the present system, which entirely subordinates the weaker sex to the stronger, rests upon theory only; for there never has been trial made of any other; so that experience, in the sense in which it is vulgarly opposed to theory, cannot be pre-

From *The Subjection of Women* first printed in 1869.

tended to have pronounced any verdict. And in the second place, the adoption of this system of inequality never was the result of deliberation, or forethought, or any social ideas, or any notion whatever of what conducted to the benefit of humanity or the good order of society. It arose simply from the fact that from the very earliest twilight of human society, every woman (owing to the value attached to her by men, combined with her inferiority in muscular strength) was found in a state of bondage to some man. Laws and systems of polity always begin by recognising the relations they find already existing between individuals. They convert what was a mere physical fact into a legal right, give it the sanction of society, and principally aim at the substitution of public and organized means of asserting and protecting these rights, instead of the irregular and lawless conflict of physical strength. Those who had already been compelled to obedience became in this manner legally bound to it. Slavery, from being a mere affair of force between the master and the slave, became regularized and a matter of compact among the masters, who, binding themselves to one another for common protection, guaranteed by their collective strength the private possessions of each, including his slaves. In early times, the great majority of the male sex were slaves, as well as the whole of the female. And many ages elapsed, some of them ages of high cultivation, before any thinker was bold enough to question the rightfulness and the absolute social necessity, either of the one slavery or of the other. . . .

If people are mostly so little aware how completely, during the greater part of the duration of our species, the law of force was the avowed rule of general conduct, any other being only a special and exceptional consequence of peculiar ties—and from how very recent a date it is that the affairs of society in general have been even pretended to be regulated according to any moral law; as little do people remember or consider, how institutions and customs which never had any ground but the law of force, last on into ages and states of general opinion which never would have permitted their first establishment. Less than forty years ago, Englishmen might still by law hold human beings in bondage as saleable property; within the present century they might kidnap them and carry them off, and work them literally to death. This absolutely extreme case of the law of force, condemned by those who can tolerate almost every other form of arbitrary power, and which, of all others, presents features the most revolting to the feelings of all who look at it from an impartial position, was the law of civilized and Christian England within the memory of persons now living: and in one half of Anglo-Saxon America three or four years ago, not only did slavery exist, but the slave trade, and the breeding of slaves expressly for it, was a general practice between slave states. Yet not only was there a greater strength of sentiment against it, but, in England at least, a less amount either of feeling or of interest in favour of it, than of any other of the customary abuses of force: for its motive was the love of gain, unmixed and undisguised; and those who profited by it were a very small numerical fraction of the country, while the natural feeling of all who were not personally interested in it was unmitigated abhorrence. So extreme an instance makes it almost superfluous to refer to any other; but consider the long duration of absolute monarchy. In England at present it is the almost universal conviction that military despotism is a case of the law of force, having no other origin or justification. Yet in all the great nations of Europe except England it either still exists, or has only just ceased to exist, and has even now a strong party favourable to it in all ranks of the people, especially among persons of station and consequence. Such is the power of an established system, even when far from universal, when not only in almost every period of history there have been great and well-known examples of the contrary system, but these have almost invariably been afforded by the most illustrious and most prosperous communities. In this case, too, the possessor of the undue power, the person directly interested in it, is only one person, while those who are subject to it and suffer from it are literally all the rest. The yoke is naturally and necessarily humiliating to all persons, except the one who is on the throne, together with, at most, the one who expects to succeed to it. How different are these cases from that of the power of men over women! I am not now prejudging the question of its justifiableness. I am showing how vastly more permanent it could not but be, even if not justifiable, than these other dominations which have nevertheless lasted down to our own time. Whatever gratification of pride there is in the possession of power, and whatever personal interest in its exercise, is in this case not confined to a limited class, but common to the whole male sex. Instead of being, to most of its supporters, a thing desirable chiefly in the abstract, or, like the political ends usually contended for by factions, of little private importance to any but the leaders; it comes home to the person and hearth of every male head of a family, and of every one who looks forward to being so. The clodhopper exercises, or is to exercise, his share of the power equally with the highest nobleman. And the case is that in which the desire of power is the strongest: for every one who desires power, desires it most over those who are nearest to him, with whom his life is passed, with whom he has most concerns in common, and in whom any independence of his authority is oftenest likely to interfere with his individual preferences. If, in the other cases specified, power manifestly grounded only on force, and having so much less to support them, are so slowly and with so much difficulty got rid of, much more must it be so with this, even if it rests on no better foundation than those. We must consider, too, that the possessors of the power have facilities in this case, greater than in any other, to prevent any uprising against it. Every one of the subjects lives under the very eye, and almost, it may be said, in the hands, of one of the masters—in closer intimacy with him than with any of her fellow-subjects; with no means of combining against him, no power of even locally overmastering him, and, on the other hand, with the strongest motives for seeking his favour and avoiding to give him offence. In struggles for political emancipation, everybody knows how often its champions are bought off by bribes, or daunted by terrors. In the case of women, each individual of the subject-class is in a chronic state of bribery and intimidation combined. In setting up the standard of resistance, a large number of the leaders, and still more of the followers, must make an almost complete sacrifice of the pleasures or the alleviations of their own individual lot. If ever any system of privilege and enforced subjection had its yoke tightly riveted on the necks of those who are kept down by it, this has. . . .

All causes, social and natural, combine to make it unlikely that women should be collectively rebellious to the power of men. They are so far in a position different from all other subject classes, that their masters require something more from them than actual service. Men do not want solely the obedience of women, they want their sentiments. All men, except the most brutish, desire to have in the woman most nearly connected with them, not a forced slave but a willing one, not a slave merely, but a favourite. They have therefore put everything in practice to enslave their minds. The masters of all other slaves rely, for maintaining obedience, on fear; either fear of themselves, or religious fears. The masters of women wanted more than simple obedience, and they turned the whole force of education to effect their purpose. All women are brought up from the very earliest years in the belief that their ideal of character is the very opposite to that of men; not self-will, and government by self-control, but submission, and yielding to the control of others. All the moralities tell them that it is the duty of women, and all the current sentimentalities that it is their nature, to live for others; to make complete abnegation of themselves, and to have no life but in their affections. And by their affections are meant the only ones they are allowed to have—those to the men with whom they are connected, or to the children who constitute an additional and indefeasible tie between them and a man. When we put together three things—first, the natural attraction between opposite sexes; secondly, the wife's entire dependence on the husband, every privilege or pleasure she has being either his gift, or depending entirely on his will; and lastly, that the principal object of human pursuit, consideration, and all objects of social ambition, can in general be sought or obtained by her only through him, it would be a miracle if the object of being attractive to men had not become the polar star of feminine education and formation of character. And, this great means of influence over the minds of women having been acquired, an instinct of selfishness made men avail themselves of it to the utmost as a means of holding women in subjection, by representing to them meekness, submissiveness, and resignation of all individual will into the hands of a man, as an essential part of sexual attractiveness. Can it be doubted that any of the other yokes which mankind have succeeded in breaking, would have subsisted till now if the same means had existed, and had been as sedulously used, to bow down their minds to it? If it had been made the object of the life of every young plebeian to find personal favour in the eyes of some patrician, of every young serf with some seigneur; if domestication with him, and a share of his personal affections, had been held out as the prize which they all should look out for, the most gifted and aspiring being able to reckon on the most desirable prizes; and if, when this prize had been obtained, they had been shut out by a wall of brass from all interests not centering in him, all feelings and desires but those which he shared or inculcated; would not serfs and seigneurs, plebeians and patricians, have been as broadly distinguished at this day as men and women are? and would not all but a thinker here and there, have believed the distinction to be a fundamental and unalterable fact in human nature?

The preceding considerations are amply sufficient to show that custom, however universal it may be, affords in this case no presumption, and ought not to create any prejudice, in favour of the arrangements which place women in social and political subjection to men. But I may go farther, and maintain that the course of history, and the tendencies of progressive human society, afford not only no presumption in favour of this system of inequality of rights, but a strong one against it; and that, so far as the whole course of human improvement up to this time, the whole stream of modern tendencies, warrants any inference on the subject, it is, that this relic of the past is discordant with the future, and must necessarily disappear.

For, what is the peculiar character of the modern world—the difference which chiefly distinguishes modern institutions, modern social ideas, modern life itself, from those of times long past? It is, that human beings are no longer born to their place in life, and chained down by an inexorable bond to the place they are born to, but are free to employ their faculties, and such favourable chances as offer, to achieve the lot which may appear to them most desirable. Human society of old was constituted on a very different principle. All were born to a fixed social position, and were mostly kept in it by law, or interdicted from any means by which they could emerge from it. As some men are born white and others black, so some were born slaves and others freemen and citizens; some were born patricians, others plebeians; some were born feudal nobles, others commoners and *roturiers*. A slave or serf could never make himself free, nor, except by the will of his master, become so. In most European countries it was not till towards the close of the middle ages, and as a consequence of the growth of regal power, that commoners could be ennobled. Even among nobles, the eldest son was born the exclusive heir to the paternal possessions, and a long time elapsed before it was fully established that the father could disinherit him. Among the industrious classes, only those who were born members of a guild, or were admitted into it by its members, could lawfully practise their calling within its local limits; and nobody could practise any calling deemed important, in any but the legal manner—by processes authoritatively prescribed. Manufacturers have stood in the pilory for presuming to carry on their business by new and improved methods. In modern Europe, and most in those parts of it which have participated most largely in all other modern improvements, diametrically opposite doctrines now prevail. Law and government do not undertake to prescribe by whom any social or industrial operation shall or shall not be conducted, or what modes of conducting them shall be lawful. These things are left to the unfettered choice of individuals. Even the laws which required that workmen should serve an apprenticeship, have in this country been repealed: there being ample assurance that in all cases in which an apprenticeship is necessary, its necessity will suffice to enforce it. The old theory was, that the least possible should be left to the choice of the individual agent; that all he had to do should, as far as practicable, be laid down for him by superior wisdom. Left to himself he was sure to go wrong. The modern conviction, the fruit of a thousand years of experience is, that things in which the individual is the person directly interested, never go right but as they are left to his own discretion; and that any regulation of them by authority, except to protect the rights of others, is sure to be mischievous. This conclusion, slowly arrived at, and not adopted until almost every possible application of the contrary theory had been made with disastrous result, now (in the industrial department) prevails universally in the most advanced countries, almost universally in all that have

pretensions to any sort of advancement. It is not that all processes are supposed to be equally good, or all persons to be equally qualified for everything; but that freedom of individual choice is now known to be the only thing which procures the adoption of the best processes, and throws each operation into the hands of those who are best qualified for it. Nobody thinks it necessary to make a law that only a strong-armed man shall be a blacksmith. Freedom and competition suffice to make blacksmiths strong-armed men, because the weak-armed can earn more by engaging in occupations for which they are more fit. In consonance with this doctrine, it is felt to be an overstepping of the proper bounds of authority to fix beforehand, on some general presumption, that certain persons are not fit to do certain things. It is now thoroughly known and admitted that if some such presumptions exist, no such presumption is infallible. Even if it be well grounded in a majority of cases, which it is very likely not to be, there will be a minority of exceptional cases in which it does not hold; and in those it is both an injustice to the individuals, and a detriment to society, to place barriers in the way of their using their faculties for their own benefit and for that of others. In the cases, on the other hand, in which the unfitness is real, the ordinary motives of human conduct will on the whole suffice to prevent the incompetent person from making, or from persisting in, the attempt.

If this general principle of social and economical science is not true; if individuals, with such help as they can derive from the opinion of those who know them, are not better judges than the law and the government, of their own capacities and vocation; the world cannot too soon abandon this principle, and return to the old system of regulations and disabilities. But if the principle is true, we ought to act as if we believed it, and not to ordain that to be born a girl instead of a boy, any more than to be born black instead of white, or a commoner instead of a nobleman, shall decide the person's position through all life—shall interdict people from all the more elevated social positions, and from all, except a few, respectable occupations. Even were we to admit the utmost that is ever pretended as to the superior fitness of men for all the functions now reserved to them, the same argument applies which forbids a legal qualification for members of Parliament. If only once in a dozen years the conditions of eligibility exclude a fit person, there is a real loss, while the exclusion of thousands of unfit persons is no gain; for if the constitution of the electoral body disposes them to choose unfit persons, there are always plenty of such persons to choose from. In all things of any difficulty and importance, those who can do them well are fewer than the need, even with the most unrestricted latitude of choice; and any limitation of the field of selection deprives society of some chances of being served by the competent, without ever saving it from the incompetent.

At present, in the more improved countries, the disabilities of women are the only case, save one, in which laws and institutions take persons at their birth, and ordain that they shall never in all their lives be allowed to compete for certain things. . . .

The social subordination of women thus stands out an isolated fact in modern social institutions; a solitary breach of what has become their fundamental law; a single relic of an old world of thought and practice exploded in everything else, but retained in the one thing of most universal interest. . . .

The least that can be demanded is that the question should not be considered as prejudged by existing fact and existing opinion, but open to discussion on its merits, as a question of justice and expediency; the decision on this, as on any of the other social arrangements of mankind, depending on what an enlightened estimate of tendencies and consequences may show to be most advantageous to humanity in general, without distinction of sex. And the discussion must be a real discussion, descending to

foundations, and not resting satisfied with vague and general assertions. It will not do, for instance, to assert in general terms, that the experience of mankind has pronounced in favour of the existing system. Experience cannot possibly have decided between two courses, so long as there has only been experience of one. If it be said that the doctrine of the equality of the sexes rests only on theory, it must be remembered that the contrary doctrine also has only theory to rest upon. All that is proved in its favour by direct experience, is that mankind have been able to exist under it, and to attain the degree of improvement and prosperity which we now see; but whether that prosperity has been attained sooner, or is now greater, than it would have been under the other system, experience does not say. On the other hand, experience does say, that every step in improvement has been so invariably accompanied by a step made in raising the social position of women, that historians and philosophers have been led to adopt their elevation or debasement as on the whole the surest test and most correct measure of the civilization of a people or an age. Through all the progressive period of human history, the condition of women has been approaching nearer to equality with men. This does not of itself prove that the assimilation must go on to complete equality; but it assuredly affords some presumption that such is the case.

Neither does it avail anything to say that the *nature* of the two sexes adapts them to their present functions and position, and renders these appropriate to them. Standing on the ground of common sense and the constitution of the human mind, I deny that any one knows, or can know, the nature of the two sexes, as long as they have only been seen in their present relation to one another. If men had ever been found in society without women, or women without men, or if there had been a society of men and women in which the women were not under the control of the men, something might have been positively known about the mental and moral differences which may be inherent in the nature of each. What is now called the nature of women is an eminently artificial thing—the result of forced repression in some directions, unnatural stimulation in others. It may be asserted without scruple, that no other class of dependents have had their character so entirely distorted from its natural proportions by their relation with their masters; for, if conquered and slave races have been, in some respects, more forcibly repressed, whatever in them has not been crushed down by an iron heel has generally been let alone, and if left with any liberty of development, it has developed itself according to its own laws; but in the case of women, a hot-house and stove cultivation has always been carried on of some of the capabilities of their nature, for the benefit and pleasure of their masters. . . .

Hence, in regard to that most difficult question, what are the natural differences between the two sexes—a subject on which it is impossible in the present state of society to obtain complete and correct knowledge—while almost everybody dogmatizes upon it, almost all neglect and make light of the only means by which any partial insight can be obtained into it. This is, an analytic study of the most important department of psychology, the laws of the influence of circumstances on character. For, however great and apparently ineradicable the moral and intellectual differences between men and women might be, the evidence of their being natural differences could only be negative. Those only could be inferred to be natural which could not possibly be artificial—the residuum, after deducting every characteristic of either sex which can admit of being explained from education or external circumstances. The profoundest knowledge of the laws of the formation of character is indispensable to entitle any one to affirm even that there is any difference, much more what the difference is, between the two sexes considered as moral and rational beings; and since no one, as yet, has

that knowledge (for there is hardly any subject which, in proportion to its importance, has been so little studied), no one is thus far entitled to any positive opinion on the subject. Conjectures are all that can at present be made; conjectures more or less probable, according as more or less authorized by such knowledge as we yet have of the laws of psychology, as applied to the formation of character.

Even the preliminary knowledge, what the differences between the sexes now are, apart from all questions as to how they are made what they are, is still in the crudest and most incomplete state. . . .

One thing we may be certain of—that what is contrary to women's nature to do, they never will be made to do by simply giving their nature free play. The anxiety of mankind to interfere in behalf of nature, for fear lest nature should not succeed in effecting its purpose, is an altogether unnecessary solicitude. What women by nature cannot do, it is quite superfluous to forbid them from doing. What they can do, but not so well as the men who are their competitors, competition suffices to exclude them from; since nobody asks for protective duties and bounties in favour of women; it is only asked that the present bounties and protective duties in favour of men should be recalled. If women have a greater natural inclination for some things than for others, there is no need of laws or social inculcation to make the majority of them do the former in preference to the latter. Whatever women's services are most wanted for, the free play of competition will hold out the strongest inducements to them to undertake. And, as the words imply, they are most wanted for the things for which they are most fit; by the apportionment of which to them, the collective faculties of the two sexes can be applied on the whole with the greatest sum of valuable result.

The general opinion of men is supposed to be, that the natural vocation of a woman is that of a wife and mother. I say, is supposed to be, because, judging from acts—from the whole of the present constitution of society—one might infer that their opinion was the direct contrary. They might be supposed to think that the alleged natural vocation of women was of all things the most repugnant to their nature; insomuch that if they are free to do anything else—if any other means of living, or occupation of their time and faculties, is open, which has any chance of appearing desirable to them—there will not be enough of them who will be willing to accept the condition said to be natural to them. If this is the real opinion of men in general, it would be well that it should be spoken out. I should like to hear somebody openly enunciating the doctrine (it is already implied in much that is written on the subject)—"It is necessary to society that women should marry and produce children. They will not do so unless they are compelled. Therefore it is necessary to compel them." The merits of the case would then be clearly defined. It would be exactly that of the slaveholders of South Carolina and Louisiana. "It is necessary that cotton and sugar should be grown. White men cannot produce them, Negroes will not, for any wages which we choose to give, *Ergo* they must be compelled." An illustration still closer to the point is that of impressment. Sailors must absolutely be had to defend the country. It often happens that they will not voluntarily enlist. Therefore there must be the power of forcing them. How often has this logic been used! and, but for one flaw in it, without doubt it would have been successful up to this day. But it is open to the retort—First pay the sailors the honest value of their labour. When you have made it as well worth their while to serve you, as to work for other employers, you will have no more difficulty than others have in obtaining their services. To this there is no logical answer except "I will not": and as people are now not only ashamed, but are not desirous, to rob the labourer of his hire, impressment is no longer advocated. Those who attempt to force women

into marriage by closing all other doors against them, lay themselves open to a similar retort. If they mean what they say, their opinion must evidently be, that men do not render the married condition so desirable to women, as to induce them to accept it for its own recommendations. It is not a sign of one's thinking the boon one offers very attractive, when one allows only Hobson's choice, "that or none." And here, I believe, is the clue to the feelings of those men, who have a real antipathy to the equal freedom of women. I believe they are afraid, not lest women should be unwilling to marry, for I do not think that any one in reality has that apprehension; but lest they should insist that marriage should be on equal conditions; lest all women of spirit and capacity should prefer doing almost anything else, not in their own eyes degrading, rather than marry, when marrying is giving themselves a master, and a master too of all their earthly possessions. And truly, if this consequence were necessarily incident to marriage, I think that the apprehension would be very well founded. I agree in thinking it probable that few women, capable of anything else, would, unless under an irresistible *entrainement*, rendering them for the time insensible to anything but itself, choose such a lot, when any other means were open to them of filling a conventionally honourable place in life: and if men are determined that the law of marriage shall be a law of despotism, they are quite right, in point of mere policy, in leaving to women only Hobson's choice. But, in that case, all that has been done in the modern world to relax the chain on the minds of women, has been a mistake. They never should have been allowed to receive a literary education. Women who read, much more women who write, are, in the existing constitution of things, a contradiction and a disturbing element: and it was wrong to bring women up with any acquirements but those of an odalisque, or of a domestic servant.

Address before the U.S. Senate Committee on Woman Suffrage

Elizabeth Cady Stanton

The point I wish plainly to bring before you on this occasion is the individuality of each human soul—our Protestant idea, the right of individual conscience and judgment—our republican idea, individual citizenship. In discussing the rights of woman, we are to consider, first, what belongs to her as an individual, in a world of her own, the arbiter of her own destiny, an imaginary Robinson Crusoe with her woman Friday on a solitary island. Her rights under such circumstances are to use all her faculties for her own safety and happiness.

Secondly, if we consider her as a citizen, as a member of a great nation, she must have the same rights as all other members, according to the fundamental principles of our Government.

Thirdly, viewed as a woman, an equal factor in civilization, her rights and duties are still the same—individual happiness and development.

Fourthly, it is only the incidental relations of life, such as mother, wife, sister, daughter, which may involve some special duties and training. In the usual discussion in regard to woman's sphere, such men as Herbert Spencer,

Frederick Harrison and Grant Allen uniformly subordinate her rights and duties as an individual, as a citizen, as a woman, to the necessities of these incidental relations, some of which a large class of women never assume. In discussing the sphere of man we do not decide his rights as an individual, as a citizen, as a man, by his duties as a father, a husband, a brother or a son, some of which he may never undertake. Moreover he would be better fitted for these very relations, and whatever special work he might choose to do to earn his bread, by the complete development of all his faculties as an individual. Just so with woman. The education which will fit her to discharge the duties in the largest sphere of human usefulness, will best fit her for whatever special work she may be compelled to do.

The isolation of every human soul and the necessity of self-dependence must give each individual the right to choose his own surroundings. The strongest reason for giving woman all the opportunities for higher education, for the full development of her faculties, her forces of mind and body; for giving her the most enlarged freedom of thought and action; a complete emancipation from all forms of bondage, of custom, dependence, superstition; from all the

From "Address before U.S. Senate Committee on Woman Suffrage" 1892.

crippling influences of fear—is the solitude and personal responsibility of her own individual life. The strongest reason why we ask for woman a voice in the government under which she lives; in the religion she is asked to believe; equality in social life, where she is the chief factor; a place in the trades and professions, where she may earn her bread, is because of her birthright to self-sovereignty; because, as an individual, she must rely on herself. . . .

To throw obstacles in the way of a complete education is like putting out the eyes; to deny the rights of property is like cutting off the hands. To refuse political equality is to rob the ostracized of all self-respect, of credit in the market place, of recompense in the world of work, of a voice in choosing those who make and administer the law, a choice in the jury before whom they are tried, and in the judge who decides their punishment. Shakespeare's play of Titus and Andronicus contains a terrible satire on woman's position in the nineteenth century—"Rude men seized the king's daughter, cut out her tongue, cut off her hands, and then bade her go call for water and wash her hands." What a picture of woman's position! Robbed of her natural rights, handicapped by law and custom at every turn, yet compelled to fight her own battles, and in the emergencies of life to fall back on herself for protection. . . .

How the little courtesies of life on the surface of society, deemed so important from man towards woman, fade into utter insignificance in view of the deeper tragedies in which she must play her part alone, where no human aid is possible!

Nothing strengthens the judgment and quickens the conscience like individual responsibility. Nothing adds such dignity to character as the recognition of one's self-sovereignty; the right to an equal place, everywhere conceded —a place earned by personal merit, not an ar-

tificial attainment by inheritance, wealth, family and position. Conceding then that the responsibilities of life rest equally on man and woman, that their destiny is the same, they need the same preparation for time and eternity. The talk of sheltering woman from the fierce storms of life is the sheerest mockery, for they beat on her from every point of the compass, just as they do on man, and with more fatal results, for he has been trained to protect himself, to resist, to conquer. . . .

In music women speak again the language of Mendelssohn, Beethoven, Chopin, Schumann, and are worthy interpreters of their great thoughts. The poetry and novels of the century are theirs, and they have touched the keynote of reform in religion, politics and social life. They fill the editor's and professor's chair, plead at the bar of justice, walk the wards of the hospital, speak from the pulpit and the platform. Such is the type of womanhood that an enlightened public sentiment welcomes to-day, and such the triumph of the facts of life over the false theories of the past.

Is it, then, consistent to hold the developed woman of this day within the same narrow political limits as the dame with the spinning wheel and knitting needle occupied in the past? No, no! Machinery has taken the labors of woman as well as man on its tireless shoulders; the loom and the spinning wheel are but dreams of the past; the pen, the brush, the easel, the chisel, have taken their places, while the hopes and ambitions of women are essentially changed.

We see reason sufficient in the outer conditions of human beings for individual liberty and development, but when we consider the self-dependence of every human soul, we see the need of courage, judgment and the exercise of every faculty of mind and body, strengthened and developed by use, in woman as well as man. . . .

Feminist Justice and the Family

James P. Sterba

Contemporary feminists almost by definition seek to put an end to male domination and to secure women's liberation. To achieve these goals, many feminists support the political ideal of androgyny. According to these feminists, all assignments of rights and duties are ultimately to be justified in terms of the ideal of androgyny. Since a conception of justice is usually thought to provide the ultimate grounds for the assignment of rights and duties in a society, I shall refer to this ideal of androgyny as "feminist justice."

THE IDEAL OF ANDROGYNY

But how is this ideal of androgyny to be interpreted? In a well-known article, Joyce Trebilcot distinguishes two forms of androgyny. The first form postulates the same ideal for everyone. According to this form of androgyny, the ideal person "combines characteristics usually attributed to men with characteristics usually attributed to women." Thus, we should expect both nurturance and mastery, openness and objectivity, compassion and competitiveness from each and every person who has the capacities for these traits.

From *Perspectives on the Family* edited by Robert Moffat and Michael Bayles, 1990. Reprinted by permission.

By contrast, the second form of androgyny does not advocate the same ideal for everyone but rather a variety of options from "pure" femininity to "pure" masculinity. As Trebilcot points out, this form of androgyny shares with the first the view that biological sex should not be the basis for determining the appropriateness of gender characterization. It differs in that it holds that "all alternatives with respect to gender should be equally available to and equally approved for everyone, regardless of sex."

It would be a mistake, however, to sharply distinguish between these two forms of androgyny. Properly understood, they are simply two different facets of a single ideal. For, as Mary Ann Warren has argued, the second form of androgyny is appropriate only "with respect to feminine and masculine traits which are largely matters of personal style and preference and which have little direct moral significance." However, when we consider so-called feminine and masculine *virtues*, it is the first form of androgyny that is required because, then, other things being equal, the same virtues are appropriate for everyone.

We can even formulate the ideal of androgyny more abstractly so that it is no longer specified in terms of so-called feminine and masculine traits. We can, for example, specify the ideal as requiring no more than that the traits that are truly desirable in society be equally available to both women and men, or in the case of virtues, equally inculcated in both women and men.

There is a problem, of course, in determining which traits of character are virtues and which traits are largely matters of personal style and preference. To make this determination, Trebilcot has suggested that we seek to bring about the second form of androgyny, where people have the option of acquiring the full range of so-called feminine and masculine traits. But surely when we already have good grounds for thinking that certain traits are virtues, such as courage and compassion, fairness and openness, there is no reason to adopt such a laissez-faire approach to moral education. Although, as Trebilcot rightly points out, proscribing certain options will involve a loss of freedom, nevertheless, we should be able to determine at least with respect to some character traits when a gain in virtue is worth the loss of freedom. It may even be the case that the loss of freedom suffered by an individual now will be compensated for by a gain of freedom to that same individual in the future once the relevant virtue or virtues have been acquired.

So understood, the class of virtues will turn out to be those desirable traits that can be justifiably inculcated in both women and men. Admittedly, this is a restrictive use of the term virtue. In normal usage, "virtue" is almost synonymous with "desirable trait." But there is good reason to focus on those desirable traits that can be justifiably inculcated in both women and men, and, for present purposes, I will refer to this class of desirable traits as virtues.

Unfortunately, many of the challenges to the ideal of androgyny fail to appreciate how the ideal can be interpreted to combine a required set of virtues with equal choice from among other desirable traits. For example, some challenges interpret the ideal as attempting to achieve "a proper balance of moderation" among opposing feminine and masculine traits and then question whether traits like feminine

gullibility or masculine brutality could ever be combined with opposing gender traits to achieve such a balance. Other challenges interpret the ideal as permitting unrestricted choice of personal traits and then regard the possibility of Total Women and Hells Angels androgynes as a *reductio ad absurdum* of the ideal. But once it is recognized that the ideal of androgyny can not only be interpreted to require of everyone a set of virtues (which need not be a mean between opposing extreme traits), but can also be interpreted to limit everyone's choice to desirable traits, then such challenges to the ideal clearly lose their force.

Actually the main challenge raised by feminists to the ideal of androgyny is that the ideal is self-defeating in that it seeks to eliminate sexual stereotyping of human beings at the same time that it is formulated in terms of the very same stereotypical concepts it seeks to eliminate. Or as Warren has put it, "Is it not at least mildly paradoxical to urge people to cultivate both 'feminine' and 'masculine' virtues, while at the same time holding that virtues ought not to be sexually stereotyped?"

But in response to this challenge, it can be argued that to build a better society we must begin where we are now, and where we are now people still speak of feminine and masculine character traits. Consequently, if we want to easily refer to such traits and to formulate an ideal with respect to how they should be distributed in society it is plausible to refer to them in the way that people presently refer to them, that is, as feminine or masculine traits.

Alternatively, to avoid misunderstanding altogether, the ideal could be formulated in the more abstract way I suggested earlier so that it no longer specifically refers to so-called feminine or masculine traits. So formulated, the ideal requires that the traits that are truly desirable in society be equally available to both women and men. So formulated the ideal would, in effect, require that men and women have in the fullest sense an equal right of self-development. The ideal would require this because an equal right to self-development can only be effectively guaranteed by equally inculcating the same virtues in both women and men and by making other desirable traits equally available to both women and men.

So characterized the ideal of androgyny represents neither a revolt against so-called feminine virtues and traits nor their exaltation over so-called masculine virtues and traits. Accordingly, the ideal of androgyny does not view women's liberation as *simply* the freeing of women from the confines of traditional roles thus making it possible for them to develop in ways heretofore reserved for men. Nor does the ideal view women's liberation as *simply* the revaluation and glorification of so-called feminine activities like housekeeping or mothering or so-called feminine modes of thinking as reflected in an ethic of caring. The first perspective ignores or devalues genuine virtues and desirable traits traditionally associated with women while the second ignores or devalues genuine virtues and desirable traits traditionally associated with men. By contrast, the ideal of androgyny seeks a broader based ideal for both women and men that combines virtues and desirable traits traditionally associated with women with virtues and desirable traits traditionally associated with men. Nevertheless, the ideal of androgyny will clearly reject any so-called virtues or desirable traits traditionally associated with women or men that have been supportive of discrimination or oppression against women or men.

DEFENSES OF ANDROGYNY

Now there are various contemporary defenses of the ideal of androgyny. Some feminists have attempted to derive the ideal from a Welfare Liberal Conception of Justice. Others have attempted to derive the ideal from a Socialist Conception of Justice. Let us briefly consider each of these defenses in turn.

In attempting to derive the ideal of andro-gyny from a Welfare Liberal Conception of Justice, feminists have tended to focus on the right to equal opportunity which is a central requirement of a Welfare Liberal Conception of Justice. Of course, equal opportunity could be interpreted minimally as providing people only with the same legal rights of access to all advantaged positions in society for which they are qualified. But this is not the interpretation given the right by welfare liberals. In a Welfare Liberal Conception of Justice, equal opportunity is interpreted to require in addition the same prospects for success for all those who are relevantly similar, where relevant similarity involves more than simply present qualifications. For example, Rawls claims that persons in his original position would favor a right to "fair equality of opportunity," which means that persons who have the same natural assets and the same willingness to use them would have the necessary resources to achieve similar life prospects. The point feminists have been making is simply that failure to achieve the ideal of androgyny translates into a failure to guarantee equal opportunity to both women and men. The present evidence for this failure to provide equal opportunity is the discrimination that exists against women in education, employment and personal relations. Discrimination in education begins early in a child's formal educational experience as teachers and school books support different and less desirable roles for girls than for boys. Discrimination in employment has been well documented. Women continue to earn only a fraction of what men earn for the same or comparable jobs and although women make up almost half of the paid labor force in the U.S., 70 percent of them are concentrated in just twenty different job categories, only five more than in 1905. Finally, discrimination in personal relations is the most entrenched of all forms of discrimination against women. It primarily manifests itself in traditional family structures in which the woman is responsible for domestic work and childcare and the man's task is "to protect against the outside world and to show how to meet this world successfully." In none of these areas, therefore, do women have the same prospects for success as compared with men with similar natural talents and similar desires to succeed.

Now the support for the ideal of androgyny provided by a Socialist Conception of Justice appears to be much more direct than that provided by a Welfare Liberal Conception of Justice. This is because the Socialist Conception of Justice and the ideal of androgyny can be interpreted as requiring the very same equal right of self-development. What a Socialist Conception of Justice purports to add to this interpretation of the ideal of androgyny is an understanding of how the ideal is best to be realized in contemporary capitalist societies. For according to advocates of this defense of androgyny, the ideal is best achieved by socializing the means of production and satisfying people's nonbasic as well as their basic needs. Thus, the general idea behind this approach to realizing the ideal of androgyny is that a cure for capitalist exploitation will also be a cure for women's oppression.

Yet despite attempts to identify the feminist ideal of androgyny with a right to equal opportunity endorsed by a Welfare Liberal Conception of Justice or an equal right of self-development endorsed by a Socialist Conception of Justice, the ideal still transcends both of these rights by requiring not only that desirable traits be equally available to both women and men but also that the same virtues be equally inculcated in both women and men. Of course, part of the rationale for inculcating the same virtues in both women and men is to support such rights. And if support for such rights is to be fairly allocated, the virtues needed to support such rights must be equally inculcated in both women and men. Nevertheless, to hold that the virtues required to support a right to equal opportunity or an equal right to self-development must be equally inculcated in both women and men is different from claim-

ing, as the ideal of androgyny does, that human virtues, sans phrase, should be equally inculcated in both women and men. Thus, the ideal of androgyny clearly requires an inculcation of virtues beyond what is necessary to support a right to equal opportunity or an equal right to self-development. What additional virtues are required by the ideal obviously depends upon what other rights should be recognized. In this regard, the ideal of androgyny is somewhat open-ended. Feminists who endorse the ideal would simply have to go along with the best arguments for additional rights and corresponding virtues. In particular, I would claim that they would have to support a right to welfare that is necessary for meeting the basic needs of all legitimate claimants given the strong case that can be made for such a right from welfare liberal, socialist and even libertarian perspectives.

Now, in order to provide all legitimate claimants with the resources necessary for meeting their basic needs, there obviously has to be a limit on the resources that will be available for each individual's self-development, and this limit will definitely have an effect upon the implementation of the ideal of androgyny. Of course, some feminists would want to pursue various possible technological transformations of human biology in order to implement their ideal. For example, they would like to make it possible for women to inseminate other women and for men to lactate and even to bring fertilized ova to term. But bringing about such possibilities would be very costly indeed. Consequently, since the means selected for meeting basic needs must be provided to all legitimate claimants including distant peoples and future generations, it is unlikely that such costly means could ever be morally justified. Rather it seems preferable radically to equalize the opportunities that are conventionally provided to women and men and wait for such changes to ultimately have their effect on human biology as well. Of course, if any "technological fixes" for achieving androgyny should prove to be cost efficient as a means for meeting people's basic needs, then obviously there would be every reason to utilize them.

Unfortunately, the commitment of a Feminist Conception of Justice to a right of equal opportunity raises still another problem for the view. For some philosophers have contended that equal opportunity is ultimately an incoherent goal. As Lloyd Thomas has put the charge, "We have a problem for those who advocate competitive equality of opportunity: the prizes won in the competitions of the first generation will tend to defeat the requirements of equality of opportunity for the next." The only way to avoid this result, Thomas claims, "is by not permitting persons to be dependent for their self-development on others at all," which obviously is a completely unacceptable solution.

But this is a problem, as Thomas points out, that exists for competitive opportunities. They are opportunities for which, even when each person does her best, there are considerably more losers than winners. With respect to such opportunities, the winners may well be able to place themselves and their children in an advantageous position with respect to subsequent competitions. But under a Welfare Liberal Conception of Justice, and presumably a Feminist Conception of Justice as well, most of the opportunities people have are not competitive opportunities at all, but rather noncompetitive opportunities to acquire the resources necessary for meeting their basic needs. These are opportunities with respect to which virtually everyone who does her best can be a winner. Of course, some people who do not do their best may fail to satisfy their basic needs, and this failure may have negative consequences for their children's prospects. But under a Welfare Liberal Conception of Justice, and presumably a Feminist Conception of Justice as well, every effort is required to insure that each generation has the same opportunities to meet their basic needs, and as long as most of the opportunities

that are available are of the noncompetitive sort, this goal should not be that difficult to achieve.

Now it might be objected that if all that will be accomplished under the proposed system of equal opportunity is, for the most part, the satisfaction of people's basic needs, then that would not bring about the revolutionary change in the relationship between women and men that feminists are demanding. For don't most women in technologically advanced societies already have their basic needs satisfied, despite the fact that they are not yet fully liberated?

In response, it should be emphasized that the concern of defenders of the ideal of androgyny is not just with women in technologically advanced societies. The ideal of androgyny is also applicable to women in Third World and developing societies, and in such societies it is clear that the basic needs of many women are not being met. Furthermore, it is just not the case that all the basic needs of most women in technologically advanced societies are being met. Most obviously, their basic needs for self-development are still not being met. This is because they are being denied an equal right to education, training, jobs and a variety of social roles for which they have the native capabilities. In effect, women in technologically advanced societies are still being treated as second-class persons, no matter how well-fed, well-clothed, well-housed they happen to be. This is why there must be a radical restructuring of social institutions even in technologically advanced societies if women's basic needs for self-development are to be met.

ANDROGYNY AND THE FAMILY

Now the primary locus for the radical restructuring required by the ideal of androgyny is the family. Here two fundamental changes are needed. First, all children irrespective of their sex must be given the same type of upbringing consistent with their native capabilities. Second, mothers and fathers must also have the same opportunities for education and employment consistent with their native capabilities.

Surprisingly, however, some welfare liberals have viewed the existence of the family as imposing an acceptable limit on the right to equal opportunity. Rawls, for example, claims the principle of fair opportunity can be only imperfectly carried out, at least as long as the institution of the family exists. The extent to which natural capacities develop and reach fruition is affected by all kinds of social conditions and class attitudes. Even the willingness to make an effort, to try, and so to be deserving in the ordinary sense is itself dependent upon happy family and social circumstances. It is impossible in practice to secure equal chances of achievement and culture for those similarly endowed, and therefore we may want to adopt a principle which recognizes this fact and also mitigates the arbitrary effects of the natural lottery itself.

Thus, according to Rawls, since different families will provide different opportunities for their children, the only way to fully achieve "fair equality of opportunity" would require us to go too far and abolish or radically modify traditional family structures.

Yet others have argued that the full attainment of equal opportunity requires that we go even further and equalize people's native as well as their social assets. For only when everyone's natural and social assets have been equalized would everyone have exactly the same chance as everyone else to attain the desirable social positions in society. Of course, feminists have no difficulty recognizing that there are moral limits to the pursuit of equal opportunity. Accordingly, feminists could grant that other than the possibility of special cases, such as sharing a surplus organ like a second kidney, it would be too much to ask people to sacrifice their native assets to achieve equal opportunity.

Rawls, however, proposes to limit the pursuit of equal opportunity still further by accepting the inequalities generated by families in any given sector of society, provided that there is still equal opportunity between the sectors or that the existing inequality of opportunity can be justified in terms of its benefit to those in the least-advantaged position. Nevertheless, what Rawls is concerned with here is simply the inequality of opportunity that exists between individuals owing to the fact that they come from different families. He fails to consider the inequality of opportunity that exists in traditional family structures, especially between adult members, in virtue of the different roles expected of women and men. When viewed from the original position, it seems clear that this latter inequality of opportunity is sufficient to require a radical modification of traditional family structures, even if the former inequality, for the reasons Rawls suggests, does not require any such modifications.

Yet at least in the United States this need radically to modify traditional family structures to guarantee equal opportunity confronts a serious problem. Given that a significant proportion of the available jobs are at least 9 to 5, families with preschool children require day care facilities if their adult members are to pursue their careers. Unfortunately, for many families such facilities are simply unavailable. In New York City, for example, more than 144,000 children under the age of six are competing for 46,000 full-time slots in day care centers. In Seattle, there is licensed day care space for 8,800 of the 23,000 children who need it. In Miami, two children, three and four years old, were left unattended at home while their mother worked. They climbed into a clothes dryer while the timer was on, closed the door and burned to death.

Moreover, even the available day care facilities are frequently inadequate either because their staffs are poorly trained or because the child/adult ratio in such facilities is too high. At best, such facilities provide little more than custodial care; at worst, they actually retard the development of those under their care. What this suggests is that at least under present conditions if pre-school children are to be adequately cared for, frequently, one of the adult members of the family will have to remain at home to provide that care. But since most jobs are at least 9 to 5, this will require that the adult members who stay at home temporarily give up pursuing a career. However, such sacrifice appears to conflict with the equal opportunity requirement of Feminist Justice.

Now families might try to meet this equal opportunity requirement by having one parent give up pursuing a career for a certain period of time and the other give up pursuing a career for a subsequent (equal) period of time. But there are problems here too. Some careers are difficult to interrupt for any significant period of time, while others never adequately reward latecomers. In addition, given the high rate of divorce and the inadequacies of most legally mandated child support, those who first sacrifice their careers may find themselves later faced with the impossible task of beginning or reviving their careers while continuing to be the primary caretaker of their children. Furthermore, there is considerable evidence that children will benefit more from equal rearing from both parents. So the option of having just one parent doing the child-rearing for any length of time is, other things being equal, not optimal.

It would seem, therefore, that to truly share child-rearing within the family what is needed is flexible (typically part-time) work schedules that also allow both parents to be together with their children for a significant period every day. Now some flexible job schedules have already been tried by various corporations. But if equal opportunity is to be a reality in our society, the option of flexible job schedules must be guaranteed to all those with preschool children. Of course, to require employers to guarantee flexible job schedules to all those with preschool children would place a significant restriction upon the rights of employers, and it may appear to move the practical requirements of Feminist Justice closer to those of Socialist Justice. But if the case for flexible job schedules is grounded on a right to equal opportunity then at least defenders of Welfare Liberal Justice will have no reason to object. This is clearly one place where Feminist Justice with its focus on equal opportunity within the family tends to drive Welfare Liberal Justice and Socialist Justice closer together in their practical requirements.

Recently, however, Christina Hoff Sommers has criticized feminist philosophers for being "against the family." Sommers' main objection is that feminist philosophers have criticized traditional family structures without adequately justifying what they would put in its place. In this paper, I have tried to avoid any criticism of this sort by first articulating a defensible version of the feminist ideal of androgyny which can draw upon support from both Welfare Liberal and Socialist Conceptions of Justice and then by showing what demands this ideal would impose upon family structures. Since Sommers and other critics of the feminist ideal of androgyny also support a strong requirement of equal opportunity, it is difficult to see how they can consistently do so while denying the radical implications of that requirement (and the ideal of androgyny that underlies it) for traditional family structures.

Outrageous Acts
and Everyday Rebellions

Gloria Steinem

Classist

The great strength of feminism—like that of the black movement here, the Gandhian movement in India, and all the organic struggles for self-rule and simple justice—has always been encouragement for each of us to act, without waiting and theorizing about some future take-over at the top. It's no accident that, when some small group does accomplish a momentous top-down revolution, the change seems to benefit only those who made it. Even with the best intentions of giving "power to the people," the revolution is betrayed.

Power can be taken, but not given. The process of the taking is empowerment in itself.

So we ask ourselves: What might a spectrum of diverse, mutually supportive tactics really look like for us as individuals, for family and community groups, for men who care about equality, for children, and for political movements as a whole? Some actions will always be unique to particular situations and thus unforeseeable. Others will be suited to times of great energy in our lives, and still others will make sense for those who are burnt out and need to know that a time of contemplation and assessment is okay. But here are some that may inspire action, if only to say, "No, that's

not right. But this is what I choose to do instead."

AS INDIVIDUALS

In the early 1970s when I was traveling and lecturing with feminist lawyer and black activist Florynce Kennedy, one of her many epigrams went like this: "Unity in a movement situation is overrated. If you were the Establishment, which would you rather see coming in the door, five hundred mice or one lion?"

Mindful of her teaching, I now often end lectures with an organizer's deal. If each person in the room promises that in the twenty-four hours beginning the very next day she or he will do at least *one outrageous thing* in the cause of simple justice, then I promise I will, too. It doesn't matter whether the act is as small as saying, "Pick it up yourself" (a major step for those of us who have been our family's servants) or as large as calling a strike. The point is that, if each of us does as promised, we can be pretty sure of two results. First, the world one day later won't be quite the same. Second, we will have such a good time that we will never again get up in the morning saying, "*Will* I do anything outrageous?" but only "*What* outrageous act will I do today?"

Here are some samples I've recorded from the outrageous acts of real life.

- Announced a permanent refusal to contribute more money to a church or synagogue until women too can become priests, ministers, and rabbis.
- Asked for a long-deserved raise, or, in the case of men and/or white folks, refused an undeserved one that is being given over the heads of others because of their race or sex.
- Written a well-reasoned critique of a sexist or racist textbook and passed it out on campus.
- Challenged some bit of woman-hating humor or imagery with the seriousness more often reserved for slurs based on religion or race.
- Shared with colleagues the knowledge of each other's salaries so that unfairnesses can be calculated. (It's interesting that employers try to keep us from telling the one fact we know.)
- Cared for a child or children so that an overworked mother could have a day that is her own. (This is especially revolutionary when done by a man.)
- Returned to a birth name or, in the case of a man, gave his children both parents' names.
- Left home for a week so that the father of your young child could learn to be a parent. (As one woman later reported calmly, "When I came home, my husband and the baby had bonded, just the way women and babies do.")
- Petitioned for a Women's Studies section in a local library or bookstore.
- Checked a corporate employer's giving programs, see if they are really inclusive by benefiting women with at least half of their dollars, and made suggestions if not.
- Personally talked to a politician who needed persuasion to support, or reward for helping, issues of equality.
- Redivided a conventional house so that each person has a space for which he or she is solely responsible, with turns taken caring for kitchen, bathroom, and other shared rooms.
- Got married to an equal, or divorced from an unequal.
- Left a violent lover or husband.
- Led a walkout from a movie that presents rape scenes or other violence as titillating and just fine.
- Made a formal complaint about working (or living) in a white ghetto. White people are also being culturally deprived.

- Told the truth to a child, or a parent.
- Said proudly, "I am a feminist." (Because this word means a believer in equality, it's especially helpful when said by a man.)
- Organized a block, apartment house, or dormitory to register and vote.
- Personally picketed and/or sued a bigoted employer/teacher/athletic coach/foreman/union boss.

[handwritten marginal note: I already do this every day]

In addition to one-time outrageous acts, these are also the regular ones that should be the bottom line for each of us: writing five letters a week to lobby, criticize, or praise anything from TV shows to a senator; giving 10 percent of our incomes to social justice; going to one demonstration a month or one consciousness-raising group a week just to keep support and energy up; and figuring out how to lead our daily lives in a way that reflects what we believe. People who actually incorporate such day-by-day changes into their lives report that it isn't difficult: five lobbying letters can be written while watching "The Late Show"; giving 10 percent of their incomes often turns out to be the best investment they ever made; meetings create a free space, friends, and an antidote to isolation; and trying to transform a job or a family or a life-style in order to reflect beliefs, instead of the other way around, gives a satisfying sense of affecting the world.

If each of us only reached out and changed *five other people in our lifetimes*, the spiral of revolution would widen enormously—and we can do much more than that.

IN GROUPS

Some of the most effective group actions are the simplest:

- Dividing membership lists according to political district, from precinct level up, so we can inform and get out the pro-equality vote.
- Asking each organization we belong to, whether community or professional, union or religious, to

support issues of equality in their formal agendas.

- Making sure that the nonfeminist groups we're supporting don't have mostly women doing the work and mostly men on their boards.
- Making feminist groups *feminist*; that is, relevant to women of the widest diversity of age, race, economics, life-styles, and political labels practical for the work at hand. (An inclusiveness that's best begun among the founders. It's much tougher to start any group and only later reach out to "others.")
- Offering support where it's needed without being asked—for instance, to the school librarian who's fighting right-wing censorship of feminist and other books; or to the new family feeling racially isolated in the neighborhood. (Would you want to have to ask people to help you?)
- Identifying groups for coalitions and allies for issues.
- Streamlining communications. If there were an emergency next week—a victim of discrimination who needed defending, a piece of sinister legislation gliding through city council—could your membership be alerted?
- Putting the group's money where its heart is, and not where it isn't. That may mean contributing to the local battered women's shelter and protesting a community fund that gives far more to Boy Scouts than to Girl Scouts; or publishing a directory of women-owned businesses; or withholding student-activity fees from a campus program that invites mostly white male speakers. (Be sure and let the other side know how much money they're missing. To be more forceful, put your contributions in an escrow account, with payment contingent on a specific improvement.)
- Organizing speak-outs and press conferences. There's nothing like personal testimonies from the people who have experienced the problem firsthand.
- Giving public awards and dinners to women (and men) who've made a positive difference.
- Bringing in speakers or Women's Studies courses to inform your members; running speakers' bureaus so your group's message gets out to the community.
- Making sure new members feel invited and welcome once they arrive, with old members assigned to brief them and transfer group knowledge.
- Connecting with other groups like yours regionally or nationally for shared experience, actions, and some insurance against reinventing the wheel.

Obviously, we must be able to choose the appropriate action from a full vocabulary of tactics, from voting to civil disobedience, from supporting women in the trades to economic boycotts and tax revolts, from congressional hearings to zap actions with humor and an eye to the evening news.

Given the feminization of poverty, however, groups are also assuming another importance. Since women are an underdeveloped, undercapitalized labor force with an unequal knowledge of technology—in other words, a Third World country wherever we are—we're beginning to realize that the Horatio Alger model of individualistic economic progress doesn't work very well for us. Probably we have more to learn about economic development from our sisters in countries recognized as the Third World. Cooperative ownership forms and communal capital formation may be as important to our future as concepts of equal pay.

So far, these experiments have started small: three single mothers who combine children and resources to buy a house not one of them could afford alone; two women who buy a truck for long-distance hauling jobs; a dozen women who pool their savings to start a bakery or a housecleaning service, or single mothers and feminist architects who transform old buildings into new homes.

But we're beginning to look at Third World examples of bigger efforts. If the poorest women in rural Kenya can pool their savings for years, buy a bus, make money from passengers, and build a cooperative store, why can't we with our greater resources help each other to do the same? If illiterate women in India can found and run their own credit cooperative, thus giving them low-interest loans for the goods they sell in the streets, how dare American women be immobilized by a poor economy? It's also a healthy reversal of the usual flow of expertise from developed to underdeveloped country that may help feminists build bridges across national chasms of condescension and mistrust. Groups and organizations have been the base of our issue-oriented, electoral, consciousness-raising, and direct-action progress. In the future, they may be our economic base as well.

AS STRATEGISTS

We've spent the first decade or so of the second wave of feminism on the riverbank, rescuing each other from drowning. In the survival areas of rape, battery, and other terrorist violence against women, for instance, we've begun to organize help through shelters, hot lines, pressure on police to provide protection, reforms in social services and legislation, and an insistence that society stop blaming the victim.

Now, some of us must go to the head of the river and keep the victims from falling in.

For instance, we can pursue new strategies that have proved effective in treating wife batterers and other violent men. Such strategies have been successful precisely because they came from experiences and feminist insight: violence is an addiction that a male-dominant society creates by teaching us that "real men" must dominate and control the world in general and women in particular. When some men inevitably become addicted to violence to prove their masculinity, conventional Freudian-style treatment has only said: "Yes, men are natural aggressors, but you must learn to control the degree." That's like telling a drug addict that he can have just a little heroin.

Treatment based on experience, on the other hand, says: "No, men are not natural aggressors; you must unhook your sense of identity and masculinity from violence, and kick the habit completely."

The few such programs that exist have been helpful to batterers, rapists and other violent men, criminals, and dangerous citizens who have been judged untreatable precisely because they saw themselves as normal men. This fundamental challenge to cultural ideas of masculinity might also hold hope for less violent ways of solving conflicts on this fragile Spaceship Earth.

That's one of hundreds of futurist examples. There are many other strategies centered around four great goals: *reproductive freedom; work redefined; democratic families; and depoliticized culture.*

Clearly, these goals can only be reached a long distance in the future. We are very far from the opposite shore.

But the image of crossing a river may be too linear to describe the reality we experience. In fact, we repeat similar struggles that seem cyclical and discouraging in the short run, yet each one is on slightly changed territory. One full revolution is not complete until it has passed through the superficiality of novelty and even law to become an accepted part of the culture. Only when we look back over a long passage of time do we see that each of these cycles has been moving in a direction. We see the spiral of history.

In my first days of activism, I thought I would do this ("this" being feminism) for a few years and then return to my real life (what my "real life" might be, I did not know). Partly, that was a naïve belief that injustice only had to be pointed out in order to be cured. Partly, it was a simple lack of courage.

But like so many others now and in movements past, I've learned that this is not just something we care about for a year or two or three. We are in it for life—and for our lives. Not even the spiral of history is needed to show the distance traveled. We have only to look back at the less complete people we ourselves used to be.

And that is the last Survival Lesson: *we look at how far we've come, and then we know—there can be no turning back.*

❧ Radical Feminism ❧

The Dialectic of Sex

Shulamith Firestone

Sex class is so deep as to be invisible. Or it may appear as a superficial inequality, one that can be solved by merely a few reforms, or perhaps by the full integration of women into the labor force. But the reaction of the common man, woman, and child—"*That?* Why you can't change *that!* You must be out of your mind!"—is the closest to the truth. We are talking about something every bit as deep as that. This gut reaction—the assumption that, even when they don't know it, feminists are talking about changing a fundamental biological condition—is an honest one. That so profound a change cannot be easily fit into traditional categories of thought, e.g., "political," is not because these categories do not apply but because they are not big enough: radical feminism bursts through them. If there were another word more all-embracing than *revolution* we would use it.

Until a certain level of evolution had been reached and technology had achieved its present sophistication, to question fundamental biological conditions was insanity. Why should a woman give up her precious seat in the cattle car for a bloody struggle she could not hope to

win? But, for the first time in some countries, the preconditions for feminist revolution exist—indeed, the situation is beginning to *demand* such a revolution.

The first women are fleeing the massacre, and, shaking and tottering, are beginning to find each other. Their first move is a careful joint observation, to resensitize a fractured consciousness. This is painful: No matter how many levels of consciousness one reaches, the problem always goes deeper. It is everywhere. The division yin and yang pervades all culture, history, economics, nature itself; modern Western versions of sex discrimination are only the most recent layer. To so heighten one's sensitivity to sexism presents problems far worse than the black militant's new awareness of racism: Feminists have to question, not just all of *Western* culture, but the organization of culture itself, and further, even the very organization of nature. Many women give up in despair: if *that's* how deep it goes they don't want to know. Others continue strengthening and enlarging the movement, their painful sensitivity to female oppression existing for a purpose: eventually to eliminate it.

Before we can act to change a situation, however, we must know how it has arisen and

From *Dialectic of Sex*. Reprinted by permission.

evolved, and through what institutions it now operates. Engels: "[We must] examine the historic succession of events from which the antagonism has sprung in order to discover in the conditions thus created the means of ending the conflict." For feminist revolution we shall need an analysis of the dynamics of sex war as comprehensive as the Marx-Engels analysis of class antagonism was for the economic revolution. More comprehensive. For we are dealing with a larger problem, with an oppression that goes back beyond recorded history to the animal kingdom itself.

In creating such an analysis we can learn a lot from Marx and Engels: Not their literal opinions about women—about the condition of women as an oppressed class they know next to nothing, recognizing it only where it overlaps with economics—but rather their analytic *method*.

Marx and Engels outdid their socialist forerunners in that they developed a method of analysis which was both *dialectical* and *materialist*. The first in centuries to view history dialectically, they saw the world as process, a natural flux of action and reaction, of opposites yet inseparable and interpenetrating. Because they were able to perceive history as movie rather than as snapshot, they attempted to avoid falling into the stagnant "metaphysical" view that had trapped so many other great minds. . . . They combined this view of the dynamic interplay of historical forces with a materialist one, that is, they attempted for the first time to put historical and cultural change on a real basis, to trace the development of economic classes to organic causes. By understanding thoroughly the mechanics of history, they hoped to show men how to master it.

Socialist thinkers prior to Marx and Engels, such as Fourier, Owen, and Bebel, had been able to do no more than moralize about existing social inequalities, positing an ideal world where class privilege and exploitation should not exist—in the same way that early feminist thinkers posited a world where male privilege and exploitation ought not exist—by mere virtue of good will. In both cases, because the early thinkers did not really understand how the social injustice had evolved, maintained itself, or could be eliminated, their ideas existed in a cultural vacuum, utopian. Marx and Engels, on the other hand, attempted a scientific approach to history. They traced the class conflict to its real economic origins, projecting an economic solution based on objective economic preconditions already present: the seizure by the proletariat of the means of production would lead to a communism in which government had withered away, no longer needed to repress the lower class for the sake of the higher. In the classless society the interests of every individual would be synonymous with those of the larger society.

But the doctrine of historical materialism, much as it was a brilliant advance over previous historical analysis, was not the complete answer, as later events bore out. For though Marx and Engels grounded their theory in reality, it was only a *partial* reality. Here is Engels' strictly economic definition of historical materialism from *Socialism: Utopian or Scientific*:

Historical materialism is that view of the course of history which seeks the *ultimate* cause and the great moving power of all historical events in the economic development of society, in the changes of the modes of production and exchange, in the consequent division of society into distinct classes, and in the struggles of these classes against one another. (Italics mine)

Further, he claims:

. . . that all past history with the exception of the primitive stages was the history of class struggles; that these warring classes of society are always the products of the modes of production and exchange—in a word, of the economic conditions of their time; that the *economic* structure of society always furnishes the real basis, starting from which we can alone work out the *ultimate* explanation of the whole superstructure of juridical and political institutions as well as of the religious, philosophical, and other ideas of a given historical period. (Italics mine)

It would be a mistake to attempt to explain the oppression of women according to this strictly economic interpretation. The class analysis is a beautiful piece of work, but limited: although correct in a linear sense, it does not go deep enough. There is a whole sexual substratum of the historical dialectic that Engels at times dimly perceives, but because he can see sexuality only through an economic filter, reducing everything to that, he is unable to evaluate in its own right.

Engels did observe that the original division of labor was between man and woman for the purposes of childbreeding; that within the family the husband was the owner, the wife the means of production, the children the labor; and that reproduction of the human species was an important economic system distinct from the means of production. . . .

But Engels has been given too much credit for these scattered recognitions of the oppression of women as·a class. In fact he acknowledged the sexual class system only where it overlapped and illuminated his economic construct. Engels didn't do so well even in this respect. But Marx was worse: There is a growing recognition of Marx's bias against women (a cultural bias shared by Freud as well as all men of culture), dangerous if one attempts to squeeze feminism into an orthodox Marxist framework—freezing what were only incidental insights of Marx and Engels about sex class into dogma. Instead, we must enlarge historical materialism to *include* the strictly Marxian, in the same way that the physics of relativity did not invalidate Newtonian physics so much as it drew a circle around it, limiting its application—but only through comparison—to a smaller sphere. For an economic diagnosis traced to ownership of the means of production,

even of the means of *re*production, does not explain everything. There is a level of reality that does not stem directly from economics.

The assumption that, beneath economics, reality is psychosexual is often rejected as ahistorical by those who accept a dialectical materialist view of history because it seems to land us back where Marx began: groping through a fog of utopian hypotheses, philosophical systems that might be right, that might be wrong (there is no way to tell), systems that explain concrete historical developments by *a priori* categories of thought; historical materialism, however, attempted to explain "knowing" by "being" and not vice versa.

But there is still an untried third alternative: We can attempt to develop a materialist view of history based on sex itself. . . .

Let us try to develop an analysis in which biology itself—procreation—is at the origin of the dualism. The immediate assumption of the layman that the unequal division of the sexes is "natural" may be well-founded. We need not immediately look beyond this. Unlike economic class, sex class sprang directly from a biological reality: men and women were created different, and not equally privileged. Although, as De Beauvoir points out, this difference of itself did not necessitate the development of a class system—the domination of one group by another—the reproductive *functions* of these differences did. The biological family is an inherently unequal power distribution. The need for power leading to the development of classes arises from the psychosexual formation of each individual according to this basic imbalance, rather than, as Freud, Norman O. Brown, and others have, once again overshooting their mark, postulated, some irreducible conflict of Life against Death, Eros vs. Thanatos.

The *biological family*—the basic reproductive unit of male/female/infant, in whatever form of social organization—is characterized by these fundamental—if not immutable—facts:

1. That women throughout history before the advent of birth control were at the continual mercy of their biology—menstruation, menopause, and "female ills," constant painful childbirth, wetnursing and care of infants, all of which made them dependent on males (whether brother, father, husband, lover, or clan, government, community-at-large) for physical survival.

2. That human infants take an even longer time to grow up than animals, and thus are helpless and, for some short period at least, dependent on adults for physical survival.

3. That a basic mother/child interdependency has existed in some form in every society, past or present, and thus has shaped the psychology of every mature female and every infant.

4. That the natural reproductive difference between the sexes led directly to the first division of labor at the origins of class, as well as furnishing the paradigm of caste (discrimination based on biological characteristics).

These biological contingencies of the human family cannot be covered over with anthropological sophistries. Anyone observing animals mating, reproducing, and caring for their young will have a hard time accepting the "cultural relativity" line. For no matter how many tribes in Oceania you can find where the connection of the father to fertility is not known, no matter how many matrilineages, no matter how many cases of sex-role reversal, male housewifery, or even empathic labor pains, these facts prove only one thing: the amazing *flexibility* of human nature. But human nature is adaptable *to* something, it is, yes, determined by its environmental conditions. And the biological family that we have described has existed everywhere throughout time. Even in matriarchies where woman's fertility is worshiped, and the father's role is unknown or unimportant, if perhaps not on the genetic father, there is still some dependence of the female and the infant on the male. And though it is true that the nuclear family is only a recent development, one which, as I shall attempt to

show, only intensifies the psychological penalties of the biological family, though it is true that throughout history there have been many variations on this biological family, the contingencies I have described existed in all of them, causing specific psychosexual distortions in the human personality.

But to grant that the sexual imbalance of power is biologically based is not to lose our case. We are no longer just animals. And the Kingdom of Nature does not reign absolute. . . .

The "natural" is not necessarily a "human" value. Humanity has begun to outgrow nature: we can no longer justify the maintenance of a discriminatory sex class system on grounds of its origins in Nature. Indeed, for pragmatic reasons alone it is beginning to look as if we *must* get rid of it.

The problem becomes political, demanding more than a comprehensive historical analysis, when one realizes that, though man is increasingly capable of freeing himself from the biological conditions that created his tyranny over women and children, he has little reason to want to give this tyranny up. As Engels said, in the context of economic revolution:

It is the law of division of labor that lies at the basis of the division into classes [Note that this division itself grew out of a fundamental biological division]. But this does not prevent the ruling class, once having the upper hand, from consolidating its power at the expense of the working class, from turning its social leadership into an intensified exploitation of the masses.

Though the sex class system may have originated in fundamental biological conditions, this does not guarantee once the biological basis of their oppression has been swept away that women and children will be freed. On the contrary, the new technology, especially fertility control, may be used against them to reinforce the entrenched system of exploitation.

So that just as to assure elimination of economic classes requires the revolt of the underclass (the proletariat) and, in a temporary dictatorship, their seizure of the means of *production*, so to assure the elimination of sexual classes requires the revolt of the underclass (women) and the seizure of control of *reproduction*: not only the full restoration to women of ownership of their own bodies, but also their (temporary) seizure of control of human fertility—the new population biology as well as all the social institutions of childbearing and childrearing. And just as the end goal of socialist revolution was not only the elimination of the economic class *privilege* but of the economic class *distinction* itself, so the end goal of feminist revolution must be, unlike that of the first feminist movement, not just the elimination of male *privilege* but of the sex *distinction* itself: genital differences between human beings would no longer matter culturally. (A reversion to an unobstructed *pansexuality*—Freud's "polymorphous perversity"—would probably supersede hetero/homo/bisexuality.) The reproduction of the species by one sex for the benefit of both would be replaced by (at least the option of) artificial reproduction: children would be born to both sexes equally, or independently of either, however one chooses to look at it; the dependence of the child on the mother (and vice versa) would give way to a greatly shortened dependence on a small group of others in general, and any remaining inferiority to adults in physical strength would be compensated for culturally. The division of labor would be ended by the elimination of labor altogether (cybernation). The tyranny of the biological family would be broken. . . .

STRUCTURAL IMPERATIVES

Before we talk about revolutionary alternatives, let's summarize—to determine the specifics that must be carefully excluded from any new structures. Then we can go on to "utopian speculation" directed by at least negative guidelines.

We have seen how women, biologically distinguished from men, are culturally distinguished from "human." Nature produced the fundamental inequality—half the human race must bear and rear the children of all of them—which was later consolidated, institutionalized, in the interests of men. Reproduction of the species cost women dearly, not only emotionally, psychologically, culturally but even in strictly material (physical) terms: before recent methods of contraception, continuous childbirth led to constant "female trouble," early aging, and death. Women were the slave class that maintained the species in order to free the other half for the business of the world—admittedly often its drudge aspects, but certainly all its creative aspects as well.

This natural division of labor was continued only at great cultural sacrifice: men and women developed only half of themselves, at the expense of the other half. The division of the psyche into male and female to better reinforce the reproductive division was tragic: the hypertrophy in men of rationalism, aggressive drive, the atrophy of their emotional sensitivity was a physical (war) as well as a cultural disaster. The emotionalism and passivity of women increased their suffering (we cannot speak of them in a symmetrical way, since they were victimized as a class by the division). Sexually men and women were channeled into a highly ordered—time, place, procedure, even dialogue—heterosexuality restricted to the genitals, rather than diffused over the entire physical being.

I submit, then, that the first demand for any alternative system must be:

1. *The freeing of women from the tyranny of their reproductive biology by every means available, and the diffusion of the childbearing and childrearing role to the society as a whole, men as well as women*. There are many degrees of this. Already we have a (hard-won) acceptance of "family planning," if not contraception for its own sake. Proposals are imminent for day-care centers, perhaps even twenty-four-hour childcare centers staffed by men as

well as women. But this, in my opinion, is timid if not entirely worthless as a transition. We're talking about *radical* change. And though indeed it cannot come all at once, radical goals must be kept in sight at all times. Day-care centers buy women off. They ease the immediate pressure without asking why that pressure is on *women*.

At the other extreme there are the more distant solutions based on the potentials of modern embryology, that is, artificial reproduction, possibilities still so frightening that they are seldom discussed seriously. We have seen that the fear is to some extent justified: in the hands of our current society and under the direction of current scientists (few of whom are female or even feminist), any attempted use of technology to "free" anybody is suspect. But we are speculating about post-revolutionary systems, and for the purposes of our discussion we shall assume flexibility and good intentions in those working out the change.

To thus free women from their biology would be to threaten the *social* unit that is organized around biological reproduction and the subjection of women to their biological destiny, the family. Our second demand will come also as a basic contradiction to the family, this time the family as an *economic* unit:

2. *The full self-determination, including economic independence, of both women and children.* To achieve this goal would require fundamental changes in our social and economic structure. This is why we must talk about a feminist socialism: in the immediate future, under capitalism, there could be at best a token integration of women into the labor force. For women have been found exceedingly useful and cheap as a transient, often highly skilled labor supply,[1] not to mention the economic value of their traditional function, the reproduction and rearing of the next generation of children, a job for which they are now patronized (literally and thus figuratively) rather than paid. But whether or not officially recognized, these are essential economic functions. Women, in this present capacity, are the very foundation of the economic superstructure, vital to its existence. The paeans to self-sacrificing motherhood have a basis in reality: Mom *is* vital to the American way of life, considerably more than apple pie. She is an institution without which the system really *would* fall apart. In official capitalist terms, the bill for her economic services might run as high as one-fifth of the gross national product. But payment is not the answer. To pay her, as is often discussed seriously in Sweden, is a reform that does not challenge the basic division of labor and thus could never eradicate the disastrous psychological and cultural consequences of that division of labor.

As for the economic independence of children, that is really a pipe dream, realized as yet nowhere in the world. And, in the case of children too, we are talking about more than a fair integration into the labor force; we are talking about the abolition of the labor force itself under a cybernetic socialism, the radical restructuring of the economy to make "work," i.e., wage labor, no longer necessary. In our post-revolutionary society adults as well as children would be provided for—irrespective of their social contributions—in the first equal distribution of wealth in history.

We have now attacked the family on a double front, challenging that around which it is organized: reproduction of the species by females and its outgrowth, the physical dependence of women and children. To eliminate these would be enough to destroy the family, which breeds the power psychology.

NOTE

1. Most bosses would fail badly had they to take over their secretaries' job, or do without them. I know several secretaries who sign without a thought their bosses' names to their own (often brilliant) solutions. The skills of college women especially would cost a fortune reckoned in material terms of male labor.

Some Reflections on Separatism and Power

Marilyn Frye

I have been trying to write something about separatism almost since my first dawning of feminist consciousness, but it has always been for me somehow a mercurial topic which, when I tried to grasp it, would softly shatter into many other topics like sexuality, man-hating, so-called reverse discrimination, apocalyptic utopianism, and so on. What I have to share with you today is my latest attempt to get to the heart of the matter.

In my life, and within feminism as I understand it, separatism is not a theory or a doctrine, nor a demand for certain specific behaviors on the part of feminists, though it is undeniably connected with lesbianism. Feminism seems to me to be kaleidoscopic—something whose shapes, structures and patterns alter with every turn of feminist creativity; and one element which is present through all the changes is an element of separation. This element has different roles and relations in different turns of the glass—it assumes different meanings, is variously conspicuous, variously determined or determining, depending on how the pieces fall and who is the beholder. The theme of separation, in its multitude variations, is there in everything from

From *The Politics of Power* (1983). Reprinted with permission.

divorce to exclusive lesbian separatist communities, from shelters for battered women to witch covens, from women's studies programs to women's bars, from expansion of daycare to abortion on demand. The presence of this theme is vigorously obscured, trivialized, mystified and outright denied by many feminist apologists, who seem to find it embarrassing, while it is embraced, explored, expanded and ramified by most of the more inspiring theorists and activists. The theme of separation is noticeably absent or heavily qualified in most of the things I take to be personal solutions and band-aid projects, like legalization of prostitution, liberal marriage contracts, improvement of the treatment of rape victims and affirmative action. It is clear to me, in my own case at least, that the contrariety of assimilation and separation is one of the main things that guides or determines assessments of various theories, actions and practices as reformist or radical, as going to the root of the thing or being relatively superficial. So my topical question comes to this: What is it about separation, in any or all of its many forms and degrees, that makes it so basic and so sinister, so exciting and so repellent?

Feminist separation is, of course, separation of various sorts or modes from men and from institutions, relationships, roles and activities which are male-defined, male-dominated and operating for the benefit of males and the maintenance of male privilege-this separation being initiated or maintained, at will, *by women*. (Masculist separatism is the partial segregation of women from men and male domains *at the will of men*. This difference is crucial.) The feminist separation can take many forms. Breaking up or avoiding close relationships or working relationships; forbidding someone to enter your house; excluding someone from your company, or from your meeting; withdrawal from participation in some activity or institution, or avoidance of participation; avoidance of communications and influence from certain quarters (not listening to music with sexist lyrics, not watching TV); withholding commitment or support; rejection of or rudeness toward obnoxious individuals.* Some separations are subtle realignments of identification, priorities and commitments, or working with agendas which only incidently coincide with the agendas of the institution one works in. Ceasing to be loyal to something or someone is a separation; and ceasing to love. The feminist's separations are rarely if ever sought or maintained directly as ultimate personal or political ends. The closest we come to that, I think, is the separation which is the instinctive and self-preserving recoil from the systematic misogyny that surrounds us.** Generally, the separations are brought about and maintained for the sake of something else like independence, liberty, growth, invention, sisterhood, safety, health, or the practice of novel or heretical customs. Often the separations in question evolve, unpremeditated, as one goes one's way and finds various persons, institutions or relationships useless, obstructive or noisome and leaves them aside or behind. Sometimes the separations are consciously planned and cultivated as necessary prerequisites or conditions for getting on with one's business. Sometimes the separations are accomplished or maintained easily, or with a sense of relief, or even joy; sometimes they are accomplished or maintained with difficulty, by dint of constant vigilance, or with anxiety, pain or grief.

Most feminists, probably all, practice some separation from males and male-dominated institutions. A separatist practices separation consciously, systematically, and probably more generally than the others, and advocates thorough and "broadspectrum" separation as part of the conscious strategy of liberation. And, contrary to the image of the separatist as a cowardly escapist, hers is the life and program which inspires the greatest hostility, disparagement, insult and confrontation and generally she is the one against whom economic sanctions operate most conclusively. The penalty for refusing to work with or for men is usually starvation (or, at the very least, doing without medical insurance); and if one's policy of noncooperation is more subtle, one's livelihood is still constantly on the line, since one is not a loyal partisan, a proper member of the team, or what have you. The penalties for being a lesbian are ostracism, harassment and job insecurity or joblessness. The penalty for rejecting men's sexual advances is often rape and, perhaps even more often, forfeit of such things as professional or job opportunities. And the separatist lives with the added burden of being assumed by many to be a morally depraved man-hating bigot. But there is a clue here: if you are doing something that is

---

* Adrienne Rich: ". . . makes me question the whole idea of 'courtesy' or 'rudeness'-surely <u>their</u> constructs, since women become 'rude' when we ignore or reject male obnoxiousness, while male 'rudeness' is usually punctuated with the 'Haven't you a sense of humor' tactic." Yes; me too. I embrace rudeness; our compulsive/compulsory politeness so often is what coerces us into their "fellowship."

** Ti-Grace Atkinson: *Should give more attention here to our vulnerability to assault and degradation, and to separation as <u>protection</u>.* Okay, but then we have to re-emphasize that it has to be separation at our behest—we've had enough of their imposed separation for our "protection." (There's no denying that in my real-life life, protection and maintenance of places for healing are major motives for separation.)

so strictly forbidden by the patriarchs, you must be doing something right.

There is an idea floating around in both feminist and antifeminist literature to the effect that females and males generally live in a relation of parasitism, a parasitism of the male on the female . . . that it is, generally speaking, the strength, energy, inspiration and nurturance of women that keeps men going, and not the strength, aggression, spirituality and hunting of men that keeps women going.

It is sometimes said that the parasitism goes the other way around, that the female is the parasite. But one can conjure the appearance of the female as parasite only if one takes a very narrow view of human living—historically parochial, narrow with respect to class and race, and limited in conception of what are the necessary goods. Generally, the female's contribution to her material support is and always has been substantial; in many times and places it has been independently sufficient. One can and should distinguish between a partial and contingent material dependence created by a certain sort of money economy and class structure, and the nearly ubiquitous spiritual, emotional and material dependence of males on females. Males presently provide, off and on, a portion of the material support of women, within circumstances apparently designed to make it difficult for women to provide them for themselves. But females provide and generally have provided for males the energy and spirit for living; the males are nurtured by the females. And this the males apparently cannot do for themselves, even partially.

The parasitism of males on females is, as I see it, demonstrated by the panic, rage and hysteria generated in so many of them by the thought of being abandoned by women. But it is demonstrated in a way that is perhaps more generally persuasive by both literary and sociological evidence. Evidence cited in Jesse Bernard's work in *The Future of Marriage* and in

George Gilder's *Sexual Suicide* and *Men Alone* convincingly shows that males tend in shockingly significant numbers and in alarming degree to fall into mental illness, petty crime, alcoholism, physical infirmity, chronic unemployment, drug addiction and neurosis when deprived of the care and companionship of a female mate, or keeper. (While on the other hand, women without male mates are significantly healthier and happier than women with male mates.). And masculist literature is abundant with indications of male cannibalism, of males deriving essential sustenance from females. Cannibalistic imagery, visual and verbal, is common in pornography: images likening women to food, and sex to eating. And, as documented in Millett's *Sexual Politics* and many other feminist analyses of masculist literature, the theme of men getting high off beating, raping or killing women (or merely bullying them) is common. These interactions with women, or rather, these actions upon women, make men feel good, walk tall, feel refreshed, invigorated. Men are drained and depleted by their living by themselves and with and among other men, and are revived and refreshed, re-created, by going home and being served dinner, changing to clean clothes, having sex with the wife; or by dropping by the apartment of a woman friend to be served coffee or a drink and stroked in one way or another; or by picking up a prostitute for a quicky or for a dip in favorite sexual escape fantasies; or by raping refugees from their wars (foreign and domestic). The ministrations of women, be they willing or unwilling, free or paid for, are what restore in men the strength, will and confidence to go on with what they call living.

If it is true that a fundamental aspect of the relations between the sexes is male parasitism, it might help to explain why certain issues are particularly exciting to patriarchal loyalists. For instance, in view of the obvious advantages of easy abortion to population control, to control of welfare rolls, and to ensuring sexual availability of women to men, it is a little surprising that the loyalists are so adamant and riled up in their objection to it. But look . . .

The fetus lives parasitically. It is a distinct animal surviving off the life (the blood) of another animal creature. It is incapable of surviving on its own resources, of independent nutrition; incapable even of symbiosis. If it is true that males live parasitically upon females, it seems reasonable to suppose that many of them and those loyal to them are in some way sensitive to the parallelism between their situation and that of the fetus. They could easily identify with the fetus. The woman who is free to see the fetus as a parasite* might be free to see the man as a parasite. The woman's willingness to cut off the life line to one parasite suggests a willingness to cut off the life line to another parasite. The woman who is capable (legally, psychologically, physically) of decisively, self-interestedly, independently rejecting the one parasite, is capable of rejecting, with the same decisiveness and independence, the like burden of the other parasite. In the eyes of the other parasite, the image of the wholly self-determined abortion, involving not even a ritual submission to male veto power, is the mirror image of death.

Another clue here is that one line of argument against free and easy abortion is the slippery slope argument that if fetuses are to be freely dispensed with, old people will be next. Old people? Why are old people next? And why the great concern for them? Most old people are women, indeed, and patriarchal loyalists are not

---

* *Caroline Whitbeck: Cross-cultural evidence suggests it's not the fetus that gets rejected in cultures where abortion is common, it is the role of motherhood, the burden, in particular, of "illegitimacy"; where the institution of illegitimacy does not exist, abortion rates are pretty low.* This suggests to me that the woman's rejection of the fetus is even more directly a rejection of the male and his world than I had thought.

generally so solicitous of the welfare of any women. Why old people? Because, I think, in the modern patriarchal divisions of labor, old people too are parasites on women. The anti-abortion folks seem not to worry about wife beating and wife murder—there is no broad or emotional popular support for stopping these violences. They do not worry about murder and involuntary sterilization in prisons, nor murder in war, nor murder by pollution and industrial accidents. Either these are not real to them or they cannot identify with the victims; but anyway, killing in general is not what they oppose. They worry about the rejection *by women, at women's discretion,* of something which lives parasitically on women. I suspect that they fret not because old people are next, but because men are next.

There are other reasons, of course, why patriarchal loyalists should be disturbed about abortion on demand; a major one being that it would be a significant form of female control of reproduction, and at least from certain angles it looks like the progress of patriarchy *is* the progress toward male control of reproduction, starting with possession of wives and continuing through the invention of obstetrics and the technology of extrauterine gestation. Giving up that control would be giving up patriarchy. But such an objection to abortion is too abstract, and requires too historical a vision, to generate the hysteria there is now in the reaction against abortion. The hysteria is, I think, to be accounted for more in terms of a much more immediate and personal presentiment of ejection by the woman-womb.

I discuss abortion here because it seems to me to be the most publicly emotional and most physically dramatic ground on which the theme of separation and male parasitism is presently being played out. But there are other locales for this play. For instance, women with newly raised consciousnesses tend to leave marriages and families, either completely through divorce, or partially, through unavailability of their cooking, housekeeping and sexual services. And women academics tend to become alienated from their colleagues and male mentors and no longer serve as sounding board, ego booster, editor, mistress or proofreader. Many awakening women become celibate or lesbian, and the others become a very great deal more choosy about when, where and in what relationships they will have sex with men. And the men affected by these separations generally react with defensive hostility, anxiety and guilt-tripping, not to mention descents into illogical argument which match and exceed their own most fanciful images of female irrationality. My claim is that they are very afraid because they depend very heavily upon the goods they receive from women, and these separations cut them off from those goods.

Male parasitism means that males *must have access* to women; it is the Patriarchal Imperative. But feminist no-saying is more than a substantial removal (redirection, reallocation) of goods and services because Access is one of the faces of Power. Female denial of male access to females substantially cuts off a flow of benefits, but it has also the form and full portent of assumption of power.

Differences of power are always manifested in asymmetrical access. The President of the United States has access to almost everybody for almost anything he might want of them, and almost nobody has access to him. The super-rich have access to almost everybody; almost nobody has access to them. The resources of the employee are available to the boss as the resources of the boss are not to the employee. The parent has unconditional access to the child's room; the child does not have similar access to the parent's room. Students adjust to professors' office hours; professors do not adjust to students' conference hours. The child is required not to lie; the parent is free to close out the child with lies at her discretion. The slave is uncondition-

ally accessible to the master. Total power is unconditional access; total powerlessness is being unconditionally accessible. The creation and manipulation of power is constituted of the manipulation and control of access.

All-woman groups, meetings, projects seem to be great things for causing controversy and confrontation. Many women are offended by them; many are afraid to be the one to announce the exclusion of men; it is seen as a device whose use needs much elaborate justification. I think this is because conscious and deliberate exclusion of men by women, from anything, is blatant insubordination, and generates in women fear of punishment and reprisal (fear which is often well-justified). Our own timidity and desire to avoid confrontations generally keep us from doing very much in the way of all-woman groups and meetings. But when we do, we invariably run into the male champion who challenges our right to do it. Only a small minority of men go crazy when an event is advertised to be for women only—just one man tried to crash our women-only Rape Speak-Out, and only a few hid under the auditorium seats to try to spy on a women-only meeting at a NOW convention in Philadelphia. But these few are onto something their less rabid com-patriots are missing. The woman-only meeting is a fundamental challenge to the structure of power. It is always the privilege of the master to enter the slave's hut. The slave who decides to exclude the master from her hut is declaring herself not a slave. The exclusion of men from the meeting not only deprives them of certain benefits (which they might survive without); it is a controlling of access, hence an assumption of power. It is not only mean, it is arrogant.

It becomes clearer now why there is always an off-putting aura of negativity about separatism—one which offends the feminine pollyanna in us and smacks of the purely defensive to the political theorist in us. It is this: First: When those who control access have made you totally accessible, your first act of taking control must be denying access, or must have denial of access as one of its aspects. This is not because you are charged up with (unfeminine or politically incorrect) negativity; it is because of the logic of the situation. When we start from a position of total accessibility there *must* be an aspect of no-saying (which is the beginning of control) in *every effective* act and strategy, the effective ones being precisely those which *shift power*, i.e., ones which involve manipulation and control of access. Second: Whether or not one says "no," or withholds or closes out or rejects, on this occasion or that, the capacity and ability to say "no" (with effect) is logically necessary to control. When we are in control of access to ourselves there will be some no-saying, and when we are more accustomed to it, when it is more common, an ordinary part of living, it will not seem so prominent, obvious, or strained . . . we will not strike ourselves or others as being particularly negative. In this aspect of ourselves and our lives, we will strike ourselves pleasingly as active beings with momentum of our own, with sufficient shape and structure—with sufficient integrity—to generate friction. Our experience of our no-saying will be an aspect of our experience of our definition.

When our feminist acts or practices have an aspect of separation, we are assuming power by controlling access and simultaneously by undertaking definition. The slave who excludes the master from her hut thereby declares herself *not a slave*. And *definition* is another face of power.

The powerful normally determine what is said and sayable. When the powerful label something or dub it or baptize it, the thing becomes what they call it. When the Secretary of Defense calls something a peace negotiation, for instance, then whatever it is that he called a peace negotiation is an instance of negotiating peace. If the activity in question is the working

out of terms of a trade-off of nuclear reactors and territorial redistributions, complete with arrangements for the resulting refugees, that is peacemaking. People laud it, and the negotiators get Nobel Peace Prizes for it. On the other hand, when I call a certain speech act a rape, my "calling" it does not make it so. At best, I have to explain and justify and make clear exactly what it is about this speech act which is assaultive in just what way, and then the others acquiesce in saying the act was *like* rape or could figuratively be called a rape. My counterassault will not be counted a simple case of self-defense. And what I called rejection of parasitism, they call the loss of the womanly virtues of compassion and "caring." And generally, when renegade women call something one thing and patriarchal loyalists call it another, the loyalists get their way.*

---

* This paragraph and the succeeding one are the passage which has provoked the most substantial questions from women who read the paper. One thing that causes trouble here is that I am talking from a stance or position that is ambiguous—it is located in two different and noncommunicating systems of thought-action. *Re* the patriarchy and the English language, there is general usage over which I/we do not have the control that elite males have (with the cooperation of all the ordinary patriarchal loyalists). *Re* the new being and meaning which are being created now by lesbian-feminists, we *do* have semantic authority, and, collectively, can and do define with effect. I think it is only by maintaining our boundaries through controlling concrete access to us that we can enforce on those who are not-us our definitions of ourselves, hence force on them *the fact of our existence* and thence open up the *possibility* of our having semantic authority with them. (I wrote some stuff that's relevant to this in the last section of my paper "Male Chauvinism—A Conceptual Analysis.") Our unintelligibility to patriarchal loyalists is a source of pride and delight, in some contexts; but if we don't have an effect on their usage while we continue, willy nilly, to be subject to theirs, being totally unintelligible to them could be fatal. (A friend of mine had a dream where the women were meeting in a cabin at the edge of town, and they had a sort of

Women generally are not the people who do the defining, and we cannot from our isolation and powerlessness simply commence saying different things than others say and make it stick. There is a humpty-dumpty problem in that. But we are able to arrogate definition to ourselves when we repattern access. Assuming control of access, we draw new boundaries and create new roles and relationships. This, though it causes some strain, puzzlement and hostility, is to a fair extent within the scope of individuals and small gangs, as outright verbal redefinition is not, at least in the first instance.

One may see access as coming in two sorts, "natural" and humanly arranged. A grizzly bear has what you might call natural access to the picnic basket of the unarmed human. The access of the boss to the personal services of the secretary is humanly arranged access; the boss exercises institutional power. It looks to me, looking from a certain angle, like institutions *are* humanly designed patterns of access— access to persons and their services. But institutions are artifacts of definition. In the case of intentionally and formally designed institutions, this is very clear, for the relevant definitions are explicitly set forth in by-laws and constitutions, regulations and rules. When one defines the term "president," one defines presidents in terms of what they can do and what is owed them by other offices, and "what they can do" is a matter of their access to the services of others. Similarly, definitions of *dean, student, judge,* and *cop* set forth patterns of access, and definitions of *writer, child, owner,* and of course, *hus-*

inspiration through the vision of one of them that they should put a sign on the door which would connect with the patriarchs' meaning-system, for otherwise the men would be too curious/frightened about them and would break the door down to get in. They put a picture of a fish on the door.) Of course, you might say that *being* intelligible to them might be fatal. Well, perhaps it's best to be in a position to make tactical decisions about when and how to be intelligible and unintelligible.

band, wife, and *man* and *girl.* When one changes the pattern of access, one forces new uses of words on those affected. The term "man" has to shift in meaning when rape is no longer possible. When we take control of sexual access to us, of access to our nurturance and to our reproductive function, access to mothering and sistering, we redefine the word "woman." The shift of usage is pressed on others by a change in social reality; it does not await their recognition of our definitional authority.

When women separate (withdraw, break out, regroup, transcend, shove aside, step outside, migrate, say *no*), we are simultaneously controlling access and defining. We are doubly insubordinate, since neither of these is permitted. And access and definition are fundamental ingredients in the alchemy of power, so we are doubly, and radically, insubordinate.

If these, then, are some of the ways in which separation is at the heart of our struggle, it helps to explain why separation is such a hot topic. If there is one thing women are queasy about it is *actually taking power.* As long as one stops just short of that, the patriarchs will for the most part take an indulgent attitude. We are afraid of what will happen to us when we really frighten them. This is not an irrational fear. It is our experience in the movement generally that the defensiveness, nastiness, violence, hostility and irrationality of the reaction to feminism tends to correlate with the blatancy of the element of separation in the strategy or project which triggers the reaction. The separations involved in women leaving homes, marriages and boyfriends, separations from fetuses, and the separation of lesbianism are all pretty dramatic. That is, they are dramatic and blatant when perceived from within the framework provided by the patriarchal world view and male parasitism. Matters pertaining to marriage and divorce, lesbianism and abortion touch individual men (and their sympathizers) because they can feel the relevance of these to themselves—they can feel the threat that they might be the next. Hence, heterosexuality, marriage, and motherhood, which are the institutions which most obviously and individually maintain female accessibility to males, form the core triad of antifeminist ideology; and all-woman spaces, all-woman organizations, all-woman meetings, all-woman classes, are outlawed, suppressed, harassed, ridiculed and punished—in the name of that other fine and enduring patriarchal institution, Sex Equality.

To some of us these issues can seem almost foreign . . . strange ones to be occupying center stage. We are busily engaged in what seem to *us* our blatant insubordinations: living our own lives, taking care of ourselves and one another, doing our work, and in particular, telling it as we see it. Still, the original sin is the separation which these presuppose, and it is that, not our art or philosophy, not our speechmaking, nor our "sexual acts" (or abstinences), for which we will be persecuted, when worse comes to worst.

Pornography, Civil Rights, and Speech

Catharine MacKinnon

. . . There is a belief that this is a society in which women and men are basically equals. Room for marginal corrections is conceded, flaws are known to exist, attempts are made to correct what are conceived as occasional lapses from the basic condition of sex equality. Sex discrimination law has concentrated most of its focus on these occasional lapses. It is difficult to overestimate the extent to which this belief in equality is an article of faith for most people, including most women, who wish to live in self-respect in an internal universe, even (perhaps especially) if not in the world. It is also

partly an expression of natural law thinking: if we are inalienably equal, we can't "really" be degraded.

This is a world in which it is worth trying. In this world of presumptive equality, people make money based on their training or abilities or diligence or qualifications. They are employed and advanced on the basis of merit. In this world of just deserts, if someone is abused, it is thought to violate the basic rules of the community. If it doesn't, victims are seen to have done something they could have chosen to do differently, by exercise of will or better judgment. Maybe such people have placed themselves in a situation of vulnerability to physical abuse. Maybe they have done something pro-

From the *Harvard Civil Rights Civil Liberties Law Review* (1985). Reprinted with permission.

vocative. Or maybe they were just unusually unlucky. In such a world, if such a person has an experience, there are words for it. When they speak and say it, they are listened to. If they write about it, they will be published. If certain experiences are never spoken about, if certain people or issues are seldom heard from, it is supposed that silence has been chosen. The law, including much of the law of sex discrimination and the First Amendment, operates largely within the realm of these beliefs.

Feminism is the discovery that women do not live in this world, that the person occupying this realm is a man, so much more a man if he is white and wealthy. This world of potential credibility, authority, security, and just rewards, recognition of one's identity and capacity, is a world that some people do inhabit as a condition of birth, with variations among them. It is not a basic condition accorded humanity in this society, but a prerogative of status, a privilege, among other things, of gender.

I call this a discovery because it has not been an assumption. Feminism is the first theory, the first practice, the first movement, to take seriously the situation of all women from the point of view of all women, both on our situation and on social life as a whole. The discovery has therefore been made that the implicit social content of humanism, as well as the standpoint from which legal method has been designed and injuries have been defined, has not been women's standpoint. Defining feminism in a way that connects epistemology with power as the politics of women's point of view, this discovery can be summed up by saying that women live in another world: specifically, a world of *not* equality, a world of inequality.

Looking at the world from this point of view, a whole shadow world of previously invisible silent abuse has been discerned. Rape, battery, sexual harassment, forced prostitution, and the sexual abuse of children emerge as common and systematic. We find that rape happens to women in all contexts, from the family, including rape of girls and babies, to students and women in the workplace, on the streets, at home, in their own bedrooms by men they do not know and by men they do know, by men they are married to, men they have had a social conversation with, and, least often, men they have never seen before. Overwhelmingly, rape is something that men do or attempt to do to women (44 percent of American women according to a recent study) at some point in our lives. Sexual harassment of women by men is common in workplaces and educational institutions. Based on reports in one study of the federal workforce, up to 85 percent of women will experience it, many in physical forms. Between a quarter and a third of women are battered in their homes by men. Thirty-eight percent of little girls are sexually molested inside or outside the family. Until women listened to women, this world of sexual abuse was *not spoken* of. It was the unspeakable. What I am saying is, if you *are* the tree falling in the epistemological forest, your demise doesn't make a sound if no one is listening. Women did not "report" these events, and overwhelmingly do not today, because no one is listening, because no one believes us. This silence does not mean nothing happened, and it does not mean consent. It is the silence of women of which Adrienne Rich has written, "Do not confuse it with any kind of absence."

Believing women who say we are sexually violated has been a radical departure, both methodologically and legally. The extent and nature of rape, marital rape, and sexual harassment itself, were discovered in this way. Domestic battery as a syndrome, almost a habit, was discovered through refusing to believe that when a woman is assaulted by a man to whom she is connected, that it is not an assault. The sexual abuse of children was uncovered, Freud notwithstanding, by believing that children were not making up all this sexual abuse. Now what is striking is that when each discovery is made, and somehow made real in the world, the response has been: it happens to men too. If women are hurt, men are hurt. If women are raped, men are raped. If women are sexually harassed, men are sexually harassed. If women are battered, men are battered. Symmetry must be reasserted. Neutrality must be reclaimed. Equality must be reestablished.

The only areas where the available evidence supports this, where anything like what happens to women also happens to men, involve children—little boys are sexually abused—and prison. The liberty of prisoners is restricted, their freedom restrained, their humanity systematically diminished, their bodies and emotions confined, defined, and regulated. If paid at all, they are paid starvation wages. They can be tortured at will, and it is passed off as discipline or as means to a just end. They become compliant. They can be raped at will, at any moment, and nothing will be done about it. When they scream, nobody hears. To be a prisoner means to be defined as a member of a group for whom the rules of what can be done to you, of what is seen as abuse of you, are reduced as part of the definition of your status. To be a woman is that kind of definition and has that kind of meaning.

Men *are* damaged by sexism. (By men I mean the status of masculinity that is accorded to males on the basis of their biology but is not itself biological.) But whatever the damage of sexism to men, the condition of being a man is not defined as subordinate to women by force. Looking at the facts of the abuses of women all at once, you see that a woman is socially defined as a person who, whether or not she is or has been, can be treated in these ways by men at any time, and little, if anything, will be done about it. This is what it means when feminists say that maleness is a form of power and femaleness is a form of powerlessness.

In this context, all of this "men too" stuff means that people don't really believe that the things I have just said are true, though there really is little question about their empirical ac-

curacy. The data are extremely simple, like women's pay figure of fifty-nine cents on the dollar. People don't really seem to believe that either. Yet there is no question of its empirical validity. This is the workplace story: what women do is seen as not worth much, or what is not worth much is seen as something for women to do. *Women* are seen as not worth much, is the thing. Now why are these basic realities of the subordination of women to men, for example, that only 7.8 percent of women have never been sexually assaulted, not effectively believed, not perceived as real in the face of all this evidence? Why don't *women* believe our own experiences? In the face of all this evidence, especially of systematic sexual abuse—subjection to violence with impunity is one extreme expression, although not the only expression, of a degraded status—the view that basically the sexes are equal in this society remains unchallenged and unchanged. The day I got this was the day I understood its real message, its real coherence: *This is equality for us.*

I could describe this, but I couldn't explain it until I started studying a lot of pornography. In pornography, there it is, in one place, all of the abuses that women had to struggle so long even to begin to articulate, all the *unspeakable* abuse: the rape, the battery, the sexual harassment, the prostitution, and the sexual abuse of children. Only in the pornography it is called something else: sex, sex, sex, sex, and sex, respectively. Pornography sexualizes rape, battery, sexual harassment, prostitution, and child sexual abuse; it thereby celebrates, promotes, authorizes, and legitimizes them. More generally, it eroticizes the dominance and submission that is the dynamic common to them all. It makes hierarchy sexy and calls that "the truth about sex" or just a mirror of reality. Through this process pornography constructs what a woman is as what men want from sex. This is what the pornography means.

Pornography constructs what a woman is in terms of its view of what men want sexually, such that acts of rape, battery, sexual harassment, prostitution, and sexual abuse of children become acts of sexual equality. Pornography's world of equality is a harmonious and balanced place. Men and women are perfectly complementary and perfectly bipolar. Women's desire to be fucked by men is equal to men's desire to fuck women. All the ways men love to take and violate women, women love to be taken and violated. The women who most love this are most men's equals, the most liberated; the most participatory child is the most grown-up, the most equal to an adult. Their consent merely expresses or ratifies these preexisting facts.

The content of pornography is one thing. There, women substantively desire dispossession and cruelty. We desperately want to be bound, battered, tortured, humiliated, and killed. Or, to be fair to the soft core, merely taken and used. This is erotic to the male point of view. Subjection itself, with self-determination ecstatically relinquished, is the content of women's sexual desire and desirability. Women are there to be violated and possessed, men to violate and possess us, either on screen or by camera or pen on behalf of the consumer. On a simple descriptive level, the inequality of hierarchy, of which gender is the primary one, seems necessary for sexual arousal to work. Other added inequalities identify various pornographic genres or subthemes, although they are always added through gender: age, disability, homosexuality, animals, objects, race (including anti-Semitism), and so on. Gender is never irrelevant.

What pornography *does* goes beyond its content: it eroticizes hierarchy, it sexualizes inequality. It makes dominance and submission into sex. Inequality is its central dynamic; the illusion of freedom coming together with the reality of force is central to its working. Perhaps because this is a bourgeois culture, the victim must look free, appear to be freely acting. Choice is how she got there. Willing is what she is when she is being equal. It seems equally important that then and there she actually be forced and that forcing be communicated on some level, even if only through still photos of her in postures of receptivity and access, available for penetration. Pornography in this view is a form of forced sex, a practice of sexual politics, an institution of gender inequality.

From this perspective, pornography is neither harmless fantasy nor a corrupt and confused misrepresentation of an otherwise natural and healthy sexual situation. It institutionalizes the sexuality of male supremacy, fusing the erotization of dominance and submission with the social construction of male and female. To the extent that gender is sexual, pornography is part of constituting the meaning of that sexuality. Men treat women as who they see women as being. Pornography constructs who that is. Men's power over women means that the way men see women defines who women can be. Pornography is that way. Pornography is not imagery in some relation to a reality elsewhere constructed. It is not a distortion, reflection, projection, expression, fantasy, representation, or symbol either. It is a sexual reality.

In Andrea Dworkin's definitive work, *Pornography: Men Possessing Women*, sexuality itself is a social construct gendered to the ground. Male dominance here is not an artificial overlay upon an underlying inalterable substratum of uncorrupted essential sexual being. Dworkin presents a sexual theory of gender inequality of which pornography is a constitutive practice. The way pornography produces its meaning constructs and defines men and women as such. Gender has no basis in anything other than the social reality its hegemony constructs. Gender is what gender means. The process that gives sexuality its male supremacist meaning is the same process through which gender inequality becomes socially real.

In this approach, the experience of the (overwhelmingly) male audiences who consume pornography is therefore not fantasy or simulation or catharsis but sexual reality, the level of reality on which sex itself largely operates. Understanding this dimension of the problem does not require noticing that pornography models are real women to whom, in most cases, something real is being done; nor does it even require inquiring into the systematic infliction of pornography and its sexuality upon women, although it helps. What matters is the way in which the pornography itself provides what those who consume it want. Pornography *participates* in its audience's eroticism through creating an accessible sexual object, the possession and consumption of which *is* male sexuality, as socially constructed; to be consumed and possessed as which, *is* female sexuality, as socially constructed; pornography is a process that constructs it that way.

The object world is constructed according to how it looks with respect to its possible uses. Pornography defines women by how we look according to how we can be sexually used. Pornography codes how to look at women, so you know what you can do with one when you see one. Gender is an assignment made visually, both originally and in everyday life. A sex object is defined on the basis of its looks, in terms of its usability for sexual pleasure, such that both the looking—the quality of the gaze, including its point of view—and the definition according to use become eroticized as part of the sex itself. This is what the feminist concept "sex object" means. In this sense, sex in life is no less mediated than it is in art. Men have sex with their image of a woman. It is not that life and art imitate each other; in this sexuality, they *are* each other.

To give a set of rough epistemological translations, to defend pornography as consistent with the equality of the sexes is to defend the subordination of women to men as sexual equality. What in the pornographic view is love and romance looks a great deal like hatred and torture to the feminist. Pleasure and eroticism become violation. Desire appears as lust for dominance and submission. The vulnerability

of women's projected sexual availability, that acting we are allowed (that is, asking to be acted upon), is victimization. Play conforms to scripted roles. Fantasy expresses ideology, is not exempt from it. Admiration of natural physical beauty becomes objectification. Harmlessness becomes harm. Pornography is a harm of male supremacy made difficult to see because of its pervasiveness, potency, and principally, because of its success in making the world a pornographic place. Specifically, its harm cannot be discerned, and will not be addressed, if viewed and approached neutrally, because it *is* so much of "what is." In other words, to the extent pornography succeeds in constructing social reality, it becomes invisible as harm. If we live in a world that pornography creates through the power of men in a male-dominated situation, the issue is not what the harm of pornography is, but how that harm is to become visible.

Obscenity law provides a very different analysis and conception of the problem of pornography. In 1973 the legal definition of obscenity became that which the average person, applying contemporary community standards, would find that, taken as a whole, appeals to the prurient interest; that which depicts or describes in a patently offensive way—you feel like you're a cop reading someone's *Miranda* rights—sexual conduct specifically defined by the applicable state law; and that which, taken as a whole, lacks serious literary, artistic, political or scientific value. Feminism doubts whether the average person gender-neutral exists; has more questions about the content and process of defining what community standards are than it does about deviations from them; wonders why prurience counts but powerlessness does not and why sensibilities are better protected from offense than women are from exploitation; defines sexuality, and thus its violation and expropriation, more broadly than does state law; and questions why a body of law that has not in practice been able to tell rape from intercourse should, without further guidance, be entrusted with telling pornography from anything less. Taking the work "as a whole" ignores that which the victims of pornography have long known: legitimate settings diminish the perception of injury done to those whose trivialization and objectification they contextualize. Besides, and this is a heavy one, if a woman is subjected, why should it matter that the work has other value? Maybe what redeems the work's value is what enhances its injury to women, not to mention that existing standards of literature, art, science, and politics, examined in a feminist light, are remarkably consonant with pornography's mode, meaning, and message. And finally—first and foremost, actually—although the subject of these materials is overwhelmingly women, their contents almost entirely made up of women's bodies, our invisibility has been such, our equation as a sex *with* sex has been such, that the law of obscenity has never even considered pornography a women's issue.

Obscenity, in this light, is a moral idea, an idea about judgments of good and bad. Pornography, by contrast, is a political practice, a practice of power and powerlessness. Obscenity is ideational and abstract; pornography is concrete and substantive. The two concepts represent two entirely different things. Nudity, excess of candor, arousal or excitement, prurient appeal, illegality of the acts depicted, and unnaturalness or perversion are all qualities that bother obscenity law when sex is depicted or portrayed. Sex forced on real women so that it can be sold at a profit and forced on other real women; women's bodies trussed and maimed and raped and made into things to be hurt and obtained and accessed, and this presented as the nature of women in a way that is acted on and acted out, over and over; the coercion that is visible and the coercion that has become invisible—this and more bothers feminists about pornography. Obscenity as such probably does little harm. Pornography is integral to attitudes and behav-

iors of violence and discrimination that define the treatment and status of half the population.

At the request of the city of Minneapolis, Andrea Dworkin and I conceived and designed a local human rights ordinance in accordance with our approach to the pornography issue. We define pornography as a practice of sex discrimination, a violation of women's civil rights, the opposite of sexual equality. Its point is to hold those who profit from and benefit from that injury accountable to those who are injured. It means that women's injury—our damage, our pain, our enforced inferiority—should outweigh their pleasure and their profits, or sex equality is meaningless.

We define pornography as the graphic sexually explicit subordination of women through pictures or words that also includes women dehumanized as sexual objects, things, or commodities; enjoying pain or humiliation or rape; being tied up, cut up, mutilated, bruised, or physically hurt; in postures of sexual submission or servility or display; reduced to body parts, penetrated by objects or animals, or presented in scenarios of degradation, injury, torture; shown as filthy or inferior; bleeding, bruised, or hurt in a context that makes these conditions sexual. Erotica, defined by distinction as not this, might be sexually explicit materials premised on equality. We also provide that the use of men, children, or transsexuals in the place of women is pornography. The definition is substantive in that it is sex-specific, but it covers everyone in a sex-specific way, so is gender neutral in overall design. . . .

This law aspires to guarantee women's rights consistent with the First Amendment by making visible a conflict of rights between the equality guaranteed to all women and what, in some legal sense, is now the freedom of the pornographers to make and sell, and their consumers to have access to, the materials this ordinance defines. Judicial resolution of this conflict, if the judges do for women what they have done for others, is likely to entail a balancing of the rights of women arguing that our lives and opportunities, including our freedom of speech and action, are constrained by—and in many cases flatly precluded by, in and through—pornography, against those who argue that the pornography is harmless, or harmful only in part but not in the whole of the definition; or that it is more important to preserve the pornography than it is to prevent or remedy whatever harm it does.

In predicting how a court would balance these interests, it is important to understand that this ordinance cannot now be said to be either conclusively legal or illegal under existing law or precedent, although I think the weight of authority is on our side. This ordinance enunciates a new form of the previously recognized governmental interest in sex equality. Many laws make sex equality a governmental interest. Our law is designed to further the equality of the sexes, to help make sex equality real. Pornography is a practice of discrimination on the basis of sex, on one level because of its role in creating and maintaining sex as a basis for discrimination. It harms many women one at a time and helps keep all women in an inferior status by defining our subordination as our sexuality and equating that with our gender. It is also sex discrimination because its victims, including men, are selected for victimization on the basis of their gender. But for their sex, they would not be so treated.

The harm of pornography, broadly speaking, is the harm of the civil inequality of the sexes made invisible as harm because it has become accepted as the sex difference. Consider this analogy with race: if you see Black people as different, there is no harm to segregation; it is merely a recognition of that difference. To neutral principles, separate but equal was equal. The injury of racial separation to Blacks arises "solely because [they] choose to put that construction upon it." Epistemologically translated: how you see it is not the way it is. Similarly, if

you see women as just different, even or especially if you don't know that you do, subordination will not look like subordination at all, much less like harm. It will merely look like an appropriate recognition of the sex difference.

Pornography does treat the sexes differently, so the case for sex differentiation can be made here. But men as a group do not tend to be (although some individuals may be) treated the way women are treated in pornography. As a social group, men are not hurt by pornography the way women as a social group are. Their social status is not defined as *less* by it. So the major argument does not turn on mistaken differentiation, particularly since the treatment of women according to pornography's dictates makes it all too often accurate. The salient quality of a distinction between the top and the bottom in a hierarchy is not difference, although top is certainly different from bottom; it is power. So the major argument is: subordinate but equal is not equal.

Particularly since this is a new legal theory, a new law, and "new" facts, perhaps the situation of women it newly exposes deserves to be considered on its own terms. Why do the problems of 53 percent of the population have to look like somebody else's problems before they can be recognized as existing? Then, too, they can't be addressed if they do look like other people's problems, about which something might have to be done if something is done about these. This construction of the situation truly deserves inquiry. Limiting the justification for this law to the situation of the sexes would serve to limit the precedential value of a favorable ruling.

Its particularity to one side, the *approach* to the injury is supported by a whole array of prior decisions that have justified exceptions to First Amendment guarantees when something that matters is seen to be directly at stake. What unites many cases in which speech interests are raised and implicated but not, on balance, protected, is harm, harm that counts. In some existing exceptions, the definitions are much more open-ended than ours. In some the sanctions are more severe, or potentially more so. For instance, ours is a civil law; most others, although not all, are criminal. Almost no other exceptions show as many people directly affected. Evidence of harm in other cases tends to be vastly less concrete and more conjectural, which is not to say that there is necessarily less of it. None of the previous cases addresses a problem of this scope or magnitude—for instance, an eight-billion-dollar-a-year industry. Nor do other cases address an abuse that has such widespread legitimacy. Courts have seen harm in other cases. The question is, will they see it here, especially given that the pornographers got there first. I will confine myself here to arguing from cases on harm to people, on the supposition that, the pornographers notwithstanding, women are not flags. . . .

To reach the magnitude of this problem on the scale it exists, our law makes trafficking in pornography—production, sale, exhibition, or distribution—actionable. Under the obscenity rubric, much legal and psychological scholarship has centered on a search for the elusive link between harm and pornography defined as obscenity. Although they were not very clear on what obscenity was, it was its harm they truly could not find. They looked high and low—in the mind of the male consumer, in society or in its "moral fabric," in correlations between variations in levels of antisocial acts and liberalization of obscenity laws. The only harm they have found has been harm to "the social interest in order and morality." Until recently, no one looked very persistently for harm to women, particularly harm to women through men. The rather obvious fact that the sexes *relate* has been overlooked in the inquiry into the male consumer and his mind. The pornography doesn't just drop out of the sky, go into his head, and stop there. Specifically, men rape, batter, prostitute, molest, and sexually harass women. Un-

der conditions of inequality, they also hire, fire, promote, and grade women, decide how much or whether we are worth paying and for what, define and approve and disapprove of women in ways that count, that determine our lives.

If women are not just born to be sexually used, the fact that we are seen and treated as though that is what we are born for becomes something in need of explanation. If we see that men relate to women in a pattern of who they see women as being, and that forms a pattern of inequality, it becomes important to ask where that view came from or, minimally, how it is perpetuated or escalated. Asking this requires asking different questions about pornography than the ones obscenity law made salient.

Now I'm going to talk about causality in its narrowest sense. Recent experimental research on pornography shows that the materials covered by our definition cause measurable harm to women through increasing men's attitudes and behaviors of discrimination in both violent and nonviolent forms. Exposure to some of the pornography in our definition increases the immediately subsequent willingness of normal men to aggress against women under laboratory conditions. It makes normal men more closely resemble convicted rapists attitudinally, although as a group they don't look all that different from them to start with. Exposure to pornography also significantly increases attitudinal measures known to correlate with rape and self-reports of aggressive acts, measures such as hostility toward women, propensity to rape, condoning rape, and predicting that one would rape or force sex on a woman if one knew one would not get caught. On this latter measure, by the way, about a third of all men predict that they would rape, and half would force sex on a woman.

As to that pornography covered by our definition in which normal research subjects seldom perceive violence, long-term exposure still makes them see women as more worthless, trivial, nonhuman, and objectlike, that is, the way those who are discriminated against are seen by those who discriminate against them. Crucially, all pornography by our definition acts dynamically over time to diminish the consumer's ability to distinguish sex from violence. The materials work behaviorally to diminish the capacity of men (but not women) to perceive that an account of a rape is an account of a rape. The so-called sex-only materials, those in which subjects perceive no force, also increase perceptions that a rape victim is worthless and decrease the perception that she was harmed. The overall direction of current research suggests that the more expressly violent materials accomplish with less exposure what the less overtly violent—that is, the so-called sex-only materials—accomplish over the longer term. Women are rendered fit for use and targeted for abuse. The only thing that the research cannot document is which individual women will be next on the list. (This cannot be documented experimentally because of ethics constraints on the researchers—constraints that do not operate in life.) Although the targeting is systematic on the basis of sex, for individuals it is random. They are selected on a roulette basis. Pornography can no longer be said to be just a mirror. It does not just reflect the world or some people's perceptions. It *moves* them. It increases attitudes that are lived out, circumscribing the status of half the population.

What the experimental data predict will happen actually does happen in women's real lives. You know, it's fairly frustrating that women have known for some time that these things do happen. As Ed Donnerstein, an experimental researcher in this area, often puts it, "We just quantify the obvious." It is women, primarily, to whom the research results have been the obvious, because we live them. But not until a laboratory study predicts that these things *will* happen do people begin to believe you when you say they *did* happen to you. There is no—*not any*—inconsistency between the patterns the laboratory studies predict and the data on what actually happens to real

women. Show me an abuse of women in society, I'll show it to you made sex in the pornography. If you want to know who is being hurt in this society, go see what is being done and to whom in pornography and then go look for them other places in the world. You will find them being hurt in just that way. We did in our hearings.

In our hearings women spoke, to my knowledge for the first time in history in public, about the damage pornography does to them. We learned that pornography is used to break women, to train women to sexual submission, to season women, to terrorize women, and to silence their dissent. It is this that has previously been termed "having no effect." The way men inflict on women the sex they experience through the pornography gives women no choice about seeing the pornography or doing the sex. Asked if anyone ever tried to inflict unwanted sex acts on them that they knew came from pornography, 10 percent of women in a recent random study said yes. Among married women, 24 percent said yes. That is a lot of women. A lot more don't know. Some of those who do testified in Minneapolis. One wife said of her ex-husband, "He would read from the pornography like a textbook, like a journal. In fact when he asked me to be bound, when he finally convinced me to do it, he read in the magazine how to tie the knots." Another woman said of her boyfriend, "[H]e went to this party, saw pornography, got an erection, got me . . . to inflict his erection on. . . . There is a direct causal relationship there." One woman, who said her husband had rape and bondage magazines all over the house, discovered two suitcases full of Barbie dolls with rope tied on their arms and legs and with tape across their mouths. Now think about the silence of women. She said, "He used to tie me up and he tried those things on me." A therapist in private practice reported:

Presently or recently I have worked with clients who have been sodomized by broom handles, forced to have sex with over 20 dogs in the back seat of their car, tied up and then electrocuted on their genitals. These are children, [all] in the ages of 14 to 18, all of whom [have been directly affected by pornography,] [e]ither where the perpetrator has read the manuals and manuscripts at night and used these as recipe books by day or had the pornography present at the time of the sexual violence.[1]

One woman, testifying that all the women in a group of exprostitutes were brought into prostitution as children through pornography, characterized their collective experience: "[I]n my experience there was not one situation where a client was not using pornography while he was using me or that he had not just watched pornography or that it was verbally referred to and directed me to pornography." "Men," she continued, "witness the abuse of women in pornography constantly and if they can't engage in that behavior with their wives, girl friends or children, they force a whore to do it."

Men also testified about how pornography hurts them. One young gay man who had seen *Playboy* and *Penthouse* as a child said of such heterosexual pornography: "It was one of the places I learned about sex and it showed me that sex was violence. What I saw there was a specific relationship between men and women. . . . [T]he woman was to be used, objectified, humiliated and hurt; the man was in a superior position, a position to be violent. In pornography I learned that what it meant to be sexual with a man or to be loved by a man was to accept his violence." For this reason, when he was battered by his first lover, which he described as "one of the most profoundly destructive experiences of my life," he accepted it.

Pornography also hurts men's capacity to relate to women. One young man spoke about this in a way that connects pornography—not the prohibition on pornography—with fascism. He spoke of his struggle to repudiate the thrill of dominance, of his difficulty finding connection with a woman to whom he is close. He said: "My point is that if women in a society filled by pornography must be wary for their physical selves, a man, even a man of good intentions, must be wary for his mind. . . . I do not want to be a mechanical, goose-stepping follower of the Playboy bunny, because that is what I think it is. . . . [T]hese are the experiments a master race perpetuates on those slated for extinction." The woman he lives with is Jewish. There was a very brutal rape near their house. She was afraid; she tried to joke. It didn't work. "She was still afraid. And just as a well-meaning German was afraid in 1933, I am also very much afraid."

Pornography stimulates and reinforces, it does not cathect or mirror, the connection between one-sided freely available sexual access to women and masculine sexual excitement and sexual satisfaction. The catharsis hypothesis is fantasy. The fantasy theory is fantasy. Reality is: pornography conditions male orgasm to female subordination. It tells men what sex means, what a real woman is, and codes them together in a way that is behaviorally reinforcing. This is a real five-dollar sentence, but I'm going to say it anyway: pornography is a set of hermeneutical equivalences that work on the epistemological level. Substantively, pornography defines the meaning of what a woman is seen to be by connecting access to her sexuality with masculinity through orgasm. What pornography means *is* what it does.

So far, opposition to our ordinance centers on the trafficking provision. This means not only that it is difficult to comprehend a group injury in a liberal culture—that what it *means* to be a woman is defined by this and that it is an injury for all women, even if not for all women equally. It is not only that the pornography has got to be accessible, which is the bottom line of virtually every objection to this law. It is also that power, as I said, is when you say something, it is taken for reality. If you talk about rape, it will be agreed that rape is awful. But rape is a conclusion. If a victim describes the facts of a rape, maybe she was asking for it or enjoyed it or at least consented to it, or the man might have thought she did, or maybe she had had sex before. It is now agreed that there is something wrong with sexual harassment. But describe what happened to you, and it may be trivial or personal or paranoid, or maybe you should have worn a bra that day. People are against discrimination. But describe the situation of a real woman, and they are not so sure she wasn't just unqualified. In law, all these disjunctions between women's perspective on our injuries and the standards we have to meet go under dignified legal rubrics like burden of proof, credibility, defenses, elements of the crime, and so on. These standards all contain a definition of what a woman is in terms of what sex is and the low value placed on us through it. They reduce injuries done to us to authentic expressions of who we are. Our silence is written all over them. So is the pornography.

We have as yet encountered comparatively little objection to the coercion, force, or assault provisions of our ordinance. I think that's partly because the people who make and approve laws may not yet see what they do as that. They *know* they use the pornography as we have described it in this law, and our law defines that, the reality of pornography, as a harm to women. If they suspect that they might on occasion engage in or benefit from coercion or force or assault, they may think that the victims won't be able to prove it—and they're right. Women who charge men with sexual abuse are not believed. The pornographic view of them is: they want it; they all want it. When women bring charges of sexual assault, motives such as venality or sexual repression must be invented, because we cannot really have been hurt. Under the trafficking provision, women's lack of credibility cannot be relied upon to negate the harm. There's no woman's story to destroy, no credibility-based decision on what happened. The hearings establish the harm. The definition sets the standard. The grounds of reality definition are authoritatively shifted. Pornography is bigotry, *period*. We are now—the world pornography

has decisively defined—having to meet the burden of proving, once and for all, for all of the rape and torture and battery, all of the sexual harassment, all of the child sexual abuse, all of the forced prostitution, *all* of it that the pornography is part of and that is part of the pornography, that the harm *does happen* and that when it happens it looks like this. Which may be why all this evidence never seems to be enough.

It is worth considering what evidence has been enough when other harms involving other purported speech interests have been allowed to be legislated against. By comparison to our trafficking provision, analytically similar restrictions have been allowed under the First Amendment, with a legislative basis far less massive, detailed, concrete, and conclusive. Our statutory language is more ordinary, objective, and precise and covers a harm far narrower than the legislative record substantiates. Under *Miller*, obscenity was allowed to be made criminal in the name of the "danger of offending the sensibilities of unwilling recipients or exposure to juveniles." Under our law, we have direct evidence of harm, not just a conjectural danger, that unwilling women in considerable numbers are not simply offended in their sensibilities, but are violated in their persons and restricted in their options. Obscenity law also suggests that the applicable standard for legal adequacy in measuring such connections may not be statistical certainty. The Supreme Court has said that it is not their job to resolve empirical uncertainties that underlie state obscenity legislation. Rather, it is for them to determine whether a legislature could reasonably have determined that a connection might exist between the prohibited material and harm of a kind in which the state has legitimate interest. Equality should be such an area. The Supreme Court recently recognized that prevention of sexual exploitation and abuse of children is, in their words, "a governmental objective of surpassing importance." This might also be the case for sexual exploitation and abuse of women, although I think a civil remedy is initially more appropriate to the goal of empowering adult women than a criminal prohibition would be.

Other rubrics provide further support for the argument that this law is narrowly tailored to further a legitimate governmental interest consistent with the goals underlying the First Amendment. Exceptions to the First Amendment—you may have gathered from this—exist. The reason they exist is that the harm done by some speech outweighs its expressive value, if any. In our law a legislature recognizes that pornography, as defined and made actionable, undermines sex equality. One can say—and I have—that pornography is a causal factor in violations of women; one can also say that women will be violated so long as pornography exists; but one can also say simply that pornography violates women. Perhaps this is what the woman had in mind who testified at our hearings that for her the question is not just whether pornography causes violent acts to be perpetrated against some women. "Porn is already a violent act against women. It is our mothers, our daughters, our sisters, and our wives that are for sale for pocket change at the newsstands in this country." *Chaplinsky v. New Hampshire* recognized the ability to restrict as "fighting words" speech which, "by [its] very utterance inflicts injury." Perhaps the only reason that pornography has not been "fighting words"—in the sense of words that by their utterance tend to incite immediate breach of the peace—is that women have seldom fought back, yet.

Some concerns that are close to those of this ordinance underlie group libel laws, although the differences are equally important. In group libel law, as Justice Frankfurter's opinion in *Beauharnais* illustrates, it has been understood that an individual's treatment and alternatives in life may depend as much on the reputation of the group to which that person belongs as on their own merit. Not even a partial analogy can be made to group libel doctrine

without examining the point made by Justice Brandeis and recently underlined by Larry Tribe: would more speech, rather than less, remedy the harm? In the end, the answer may be yes, but not under the abstract system of free speech, which only enhances the power of the pornographers while doing nothing substantively to guarantee the free speech of women, for which we need civil equality. The situation in which women presently find ourselves with respect to the pornography is one in which more *pornography* is inconsistent with rectifying or even counterbalancing its damage through speech, because so long as the pornography exists in the way it does there *will not be more speech by women*. Pornography strips and devastates women of credibility, from our accounts of sexual assault to our everyday reality of sexual subordination. We are stripped of authority and reduced and devalidated and silenced. Silenced here means that the purposes of the First Amendment, premised upon conditions presumed and promoted by protecting free speech, do not pertain to women because they are not our conditions. Consider them: individual self-fulfillment—how does pornography promote our individual self-fulfillment? How does sexual inequality even permit it? Even if she can form words, who listens to a woman with a penis in her mouth? Facilitating consensus—to the extent pornography does so, it does so one-sided by silencing protest over the injustice of sexual subordination. Participation in civic life—central to Professor Meiklejohn's theory—how does pornography enhance women's participation in civic life? Anyone who cannot walk down the street or even lie down in her own bed without keeping her eyes cast down and her body clenched against assault is unlikely to have much to say about the issues of the day, still less will she become Tolstoy. Facilitating change—*this law* facilitates the change that existing First Amendment theory had been used to throttle. Any system of freedom of expression that does not address a problem where the free speech of men silences the free speech of women, a real conflict between speech interests as well as between people, is not serious about securing freedom of expression in this country.

For those of you who still think pornography is only an idea, consider the possibility that obscenity law got one thing right. Pornography is more actlike than thoughtlike. The fact that pornography, in a feminist view, furthers the idea of the sexual inferiority of women, which is a political idea, doesn't make the pornography itself into a political idea. One can express the idea a practice embodies. That does not make the practice into an idea. Segregation expresses the idea of the inferiority of one group to another on the basis of race. That does not make segregation an idea. A sign that says "Whites Only" is only words. Is it therefore protected by the First Amendment? Is it not an act, a practice, of segregation because what it means is inseparable from what it does? *Law* is only words.

The issue here is whether the fact that words and pictures are the central link in the cycle of abuse will immunize that entire cycle, about which we cannot do anything without doing something about the pornography. As Justice Stewart said in *Ginsburg*, "When expression occurs in a setting where the capacity to make a choice is absent, government regulation of that expression may coexist with and *even implement* First Amendment guarantees." I would even go so far as to say that the pattern of evidence we have closely approaches Justice Douglas' requirement that "freedom of expression can be suppressed if, and to the extent that, it is so closely brigaded with illegal action as to be an inseparable part of it." Those of you who have been trying to separate the acts from the speech—that's an act, that's an act, there's a law against that act, regulate that act, don't touch the speech—notice here that the illegality of the acts involved doesn't mean that the speech that is "brigaded with" it *cannot* be regulated. This is when it *can* be.

I take one of two penultimate points from Andrea Dworkin, who has often said that pornography is not speech for women, it is the silence of women. Remember the mouth taped, the woman gagged, "Smile, I can get a lot of money for that." The smile is not her expression, it is her silence. It is not her expression not because it didn't happen, but because it *did* happen. The screams of the women in pornography are silence, like the screams of Kitty Genovese, whose plight was misinterpreted by some onlookers as a lovers' quarrel. The flat expressionless voice of the woman in the New Bedford gang rape, testifying, is silence. She was raped as men cheered and watched, as they do in and with the pornography. When women resist and men say, "Like this, you stupid bitch, here is how to do it" and shove their faces into the pornography, this "truth of sex" is the silence of women. When they say, "If you love me, you'll try," the enjoyment we fake, the enjoyment we learn is silence. Women who submit because there is more dignity in it than in losing the fight over and over live in silence. Having to sleep with your publisher or director to get access to what men call speech is silence. Being humiliated on the basis of your appearance, whether by approval or disapproval, because you have to look a certain way for a certain job, whether you get the job or not, is silence. The absence of a woman's voice, everywhere that it cannot be heard, is silence. And anyone who thinks that what women say in pornography is women's speech—the "Fuck me, do it to me, harder," all of that—has never heard the sound of a woman's voice.

The most basic assumption underlying First Amendment adjudication is that, socially, speech is free. The First Amendment says Congress shall not abridge the freedom of speech. Free speech, get it, *exists*. Those who wrote the First Amendment *had* speech—they wrote the Constitution. *Their* problem was to keep it free from the only power that realistically threatened it: the federal government. They designed the

First Amendment to prevent government from constraining that which, if unconstrained by government, was free, meaning *accessible to them*. At the same time, we can't tell much about the intent of the framers with regard to the question of women's speech, because I don't think we crossed their minds. It is consistent with this analysis that their posture toward freedom of speech tends to presuppose that whole segments of the population are not systematically silenced socially, prior to government action. If everyone's power were equal to theirs, if this were a nonhierarchical society, that might make sense. But the place of pornography in the inequality of the sexes makes the assumption of equal power untrue.

This is a hard question. It involves risks. Classically, opposition to censorship has involved keeping government off the backs of people. Our law is about getting some people off the backs of other people. The risks that it will be misused have to be measured against the risks of the status quo. Women will never have that dignity, security, compensation that is the promise of equality so long as the pornography exists as it does now. The situation of women suggests that the urgent issue of our freedom of speech is not primarily the avoidance of state intervention as such, but getting affirmative access to speech for those to whom it has been denied.

NOTES

1. *Public Hearings on Ordinances to Add Pornography as Discrimination Against Women*, Committee on Governmental Operations, City Council, Minneapolis MN, December 12–13, 1983.

❧ Psychoanalytic Feminism ❧

Family Structure and Feminine Personality

Nancy Chodorow

I propose here a model to account for the reproduction within each generation of certain general and nearly universal differences that
characterize masculine and feminine personality and roles. My perspective is largely
psychoanalytic. Cross-cultural and social-
psychological evidence suggests that an argument drawn solely from the universality of
biological sex differences is unconvincing. At
the same time, explanations based on patterns of
deliberate socialization (the most prevalent kind
of anthropological, sociological, and social-
psychological explanation) are in themselves insufficient to account for the extent to which
psychological and value commitments to sex differences are so emotionally laden and tena-
ciously maintained, for the way gender identity
and expectations about sex roles and gender consistency are so deeply central to a person's consistent sense of self.

Reprinted from *Woman, Culture, and Society*,
edited by Michelle Zimbalist Rosaldo and Louise
Lamphere with the permission of the publishers,
Stanford University Press. © 1974 by the Board of
Trustees of the Leland Stanford Junior University.

This paper suggests that a crucial differentiating experience in male and female development arises out of the fact that women,
universally, are largely responsible for early
child care and for (at least) later female socialization. This points to the central importance of
the mother-daughter relationship for women,
and to a focus on the conscious and unconscious effects of early involvement with a female
for children of both sexes. The fact that males
and females experience this social environment
differently as they grow up accounts for the
development of basic sex differences in personality. In particular, certain features of the
mother-daughter relationship are internalized
universally as basic elements of feminine ego
structure (although not necessarily what we normally mean by "femininity").

Specifically, I shall propose that, in any
given society, feminine personality comes to define itself in relation and connection to other
people more than masculine personality does.
(In psychoanalytic terms, women are less individuated than men; they have more flexible ego
boundaries.) Moreover, issues of dependency

are handled and experienced differently by men and women. For boys and men, both individuation and dependency issues become tied up with the sense of masculinity, or masculine identity. For girls and women, by contrast, issues of femininity, or feminine identity, are not problematic in the same way. The structural situation of child rearing, reinforced by female and male role training, produces these differences, which are replicated and reproduced in the sexual sociology of adult life.

The paper is also a beginning attempt to rectify certain gaps in the social-scientific literature, and a contribution to the reformulation of psychological anthropology. Most traditional accounts of family and socialization tend to emphasize only role training, and not unconscious features of personality. Those few that rely on Freudian theory have abstracted a behaviorist methodology from this theory, concentrating on isolated "significant" behaviors like weaning and toilet training. The paper advocates instead a focus on the ongoing interpersonal relationships in which these various behaviors are given meaning.

More empirically, most social-scientific accounts of socialization, child development, and the mother-child relationship refer implicitly or explicitly only to the development and socialization of boys, and to the mother-son relationship. There is a striking lack of systematic description about the mother-daughter relationship, and a basic theoretical discontinuity between, on the one hand, theories about female development, which tend to stress the development of "feminine" qualities in relation to and comparison with men, and on the other hand, theories about women's ultimate mothering role. This final lack is particularly crucial, because women's motherhood and mothering role seem to be the most important features in accounting for the universal secondary status of women. The present paper describes the development of psychological qualities in women that are central to the perpetuation of this role.

In a formulation of this preliminary nature, there is not a great body of consistent evidence to draw upon. Available evidence is presented that illuminates aspects of the theory—for the most part psychoanalytic and social-psychological accounts based almost entirely on highly industrialized Western society. Because aspects of family structure are discussed that are universal, however, I think it is worth considering the theory as a general model. In any case, this is in some sense a programmatic appeal to people doing research. It points to certain issues that might be especially important in investigations of child development and family relationships, and suggests that researchers look explicitly at female vs. male development, and that they consider seriously mother-daughter relationships even if these are not of obvious "structural importance" in a traditional anthropological view of that society.

THE DEVELOPMENT OF GENDER PERSONALITY

According to psychoanalytic theory, personality is a result of a boy's or girl's social-relational experiences from earliest infancy. Personality development is not the result of conscious parental intention. The nature and quality of the social relationships that the child experiences are appropriated, internalized, and organized by her/him and come to constitute her/his personality. What is internalized from an ongoing relationship continues independent of that original relationship and is generalized and set up as a permanent feature of the personality. The conscious self is usually not aware of many of the features of personality, or of its total structural organization. At the same time, these are important determinants of any person's behavior, both that which is culturally expected and that which is idiosyncratic or unique to the individual. The conscious aspects of personality, like a person's general self-concept and, importantly, her/his gender identity, require and depend upon the consistency and stability of its unconscious organization. In what follows I shall describe how contrasting male and female experiences lead to differences in the way that the developing masculine or feminine psyche resolves certain relational issues.

Separation and Individuation (Preoedipal Development). All children begin life in a state of "infantile dependence" upon an adult or adults, in most cases their mother. This state consists first in the persistence of primary identification with the mother: the child does not differentiate herself/himself from her/his mother but experiences a sense of oneness with her. (It is important to distinguish this from later forms of identification, from "secondary identification," which presuppose at least some degree of experienced separateness by the person who identifies.) Second, it includes an oral-incorporative mode of relationship to the world, leading, because of the infant's total helplessness, to a strong attachment to and dependence upon whoever nurses and carries her/him.

Both aspects of this state are continuous with the child's prenatal experience of being emotionally and physically part of the mother's body and of the exchange of body material through the placenta. That this relationship continues with the natural mother in most societies stems from the fact that women lactate. For convenience, and not because of biological necessity, this has usually meant that mothers, and females in general, tend to take all care of babies. It is probable that the mother's continuing to have major responsibility for the feeding and care of the child (so that the child interacts almost entirely with her) extends and intensifies her/his period of primary identification with her more than if, for instance, someone else were to take major or total care of the child. A child's earliest experience, then, is usually of identity with and attachment to a single mother, and always with women.

For both boys and girls, the first few years

are preoccupied with issues of separation and individuation. This includes breaking or attenuating the primary identification with the mother and beginning to develop an individuated sense of self, and mitigating the totally dependent oral attitude and attachment to the mother. I would suggest that, contrary to the traditional psychoanalytic model, the preoedipal experience is likely to differ for boys and girls. Specifically, the experience of mothering for a woman involves a double identification. A woman identifies with her own mother and, through identification with her child, she (re/)experiences herself as a cared-for child. The particular nature of this double identification for the individual mother is closely bound up with her relationship to her own mother. As Deutsch expresses it, "In relation to her own child, woman repeats her own mother-child history." Given that she was a female child, and that identification with her mother and mothering are so bound up with her being a woman, we might expect that a woman's identification with a girl child might be stronger; that a mother, who is, after all, a person who is a woman and not simply the performer of a formally defined role, would tend to treat infants of different sexes in different ways.

There is some suggestive sociological evidence that this is the case. Mothers in a women's group in Cambridge, Massachusetts, say that they identified more with their girl children than with boy children. The perception and treatment of girl vs. boy children in high-caste, extremely patriarchal, patrilocal communities in India are in the same vein. Families express preference for boy children and celebrate when sons are born. At the same time, Rajput mothers in North India are "as likely as not" to like girl babies better than boy babies once they are born, and they and Havik Brahmins in South India treat their daughters with greater affection and leniency than their sons. People in both groups say that this is out of sympathy for the future plight of their daughters, who will have to leave their natal family for a strange and usually oppressive postmarital household. From the time of their daughters' birth, then, mothers in these communities identify anticipatorily, by re-experiencing their own past, with the experiences of separation that their daughters will go through. They develop a particular attachment to their daughters because of this and by imposing their own reaction to the issue of separation on this new external situation.

It seems, then, that a mother is more likely to identify with a daughter than with a son, to experience her daughter (or parts of her daughter's life) as herself. Fliess's description of his neurotic patients who were the children of ambulatory psychotic mothers presents the problem in its psychopathological extreme. The example is interesting, because, although Fliess claims to be writing about people defined only by the fact that their problems were tied to a particular kind of relationship to their mothers, an overwhelmingly large proportion of the cases he presents are women. It seems, then, that this sort of disturbed mother inflicts her pathology predominantly on daughters. The mothers Fliess describes did not allow their daughters to perceive themselves as separate people, but simply acted as if their daughters were narcissistic extensions or doubles of themselves, extensions to whom were attributed the mothers' bodily feelings and who became physical vehicles for their mothers' achievement of autoerotic gratification. The daughters were bound into a mutually dependent "hypersymbiotic" relationship. These mothers, then, perpetuate a mutual relationship with their daughters of both primary identification and infantile dependence.

A son's case is different. Cultural evidence suggests that insofar as a mother treats her son differently, it is usually by emphasizing his masculinity in opposition to herself and by pushing him to assume, or acquiescing in his assumption of, a sexually toned male-role relation to her. Whiting and Whiting [and others] suggest that mothers in societies with mother-child

sleeping arrangements and postpartum sex taboos may be seductive toward infant sons. Slater describes the socialization of precarious masculinity in Greek males of the classical period through their mothers' alternation of sexual praise and seductive behavior with hostile deflation and ridicule. This kind of behavior contributes to the son's differentiation from his mother and to the formation of ego boundaries (I will later discuss certain problems that result from this).

Neither form of attitude or treatment is what we would call "good mothering." However, evidence of differentiation of a pathological nature in the mother's behavior toward girls and boys does highlight tendencies in "normal" behavior. It seems likely that from their children's earliest childhood, mothers and women tend to identify more with daughters and to help them to differentiate less, and that processes of separation and individuation are made more difficult for girls. On the other hand, a mother tends to identify less with her son, and to push him toward differentiation and the taking on of a male role unsuitable to his age, and undesirable at any age in his relationship to her.

For boys and girls, the quality of the preoedipal relationship to the mother differs. This, as well as differences in development during the oedipal period, accounts for the persisting importance of preoedipal issues in female development and personality that many psychoanalytic writers describe. Even before the establishment of gender identity, gender personality differentiation begins.

Gender Identity (Oedipal Crisis and Resolution). There is only a slight suggestion in the psychological and sociological literature that preoedipal development differs for boys and girls. The pattern becomes explicit at the next developmental level. All theoretical and empirical accounts agree that after about age three (the beginning of the "oedipal" period, which focuses on the attainment of a stable gender identity) male and female development becomes radically different. It is at this stage that the father, and men in general, begin to become important in the child's primary object world. It is, of course, particularly difficult to generalize about the attainment of gender identity and sex-role assumption, since there is such a wide variety in the sexual sociology of different societies. However, to the extent that in all societies women's life tends to be more private and domestic, and men's more public and social, we can make general statements about this kind of development.

In what follows, I shall be talking about the development of gender personality and gender identity in the tradition of psychoanalytic theory. Cognitive psychologists have established that by the age of three, boys and girls have an irreversible conception of what their gender is. I do not dispute these findings. It remains true that children (and adults) may know definitely that they are boys (men) or girls (women), and at the same time experience conflicts or uncertainty about "masculinity" or "femininity," about what these identities require in behavioral or emotional terms, etc. I am discussing the development of "gender identity" in this latter sense.

A boy's masculine gender identification must come to replace his early primary identification with his mother. This masculine identification is usually based on identification with a boy's father or other salient adult males. However, a boy's father is relatively more remote than his mother. He rarely plays a major caretaking role even at this period in his son's life. In most societies, his work and social life take place farther from the home than do those of his wife. He is, then, often relatively inaccessible to his son, and performs his male role activities away from where the son spends most of his life. As a result, a boy's male gender identification often becomes a "positional" identification, with aspects of his father's clearly or not-so-clearly defined male role, rather than a more generalized "personal" identification—a diffuse identification with his father's personality, values, and behavioral traits—that could grow out of a real relationship to his father.

Mitscherlich, in his discussion of Western advanced capitalist society, provides a useful insight into the problem of male development. The father, because his work takes him outside of the home most of the time, and because his active presence in the family has progressively decreased, has become an "invisible father." For the boy, the tie between affective relations and masculine gender identification and role learning (between libidinal and ego development) is relatively attenuated. He identifies with a fantasied masculine role, because the reality constraint that contact with his father would provide is missing. In all societies characterized by some sex segregation (even those in which a son will eventually lead the same sort of life as his father), much of a boy's masculine identification must be of this sort, that is, with aspects of his father's role, or what he fantasies to be a male role, rather than with his father as a person involved in a relationship to him.

There is another important aspect to this situation, which explains the psychological dynamics of the universal social and cultural devaluation and subordination of women. A boy, in his attempt to gain an elusive masculine identification, often comes to define this masculinity largely in negative terms, as that which is not feminine or involved with women. There is an internal and external aspect to this. Internally, the boy tries to reject his mother and deny his attachment to her and the strong dependence upon her that he still feels. He also tries to deny the deep personal identification with her that has developed during his early years. He does this by repressing whatever he takes to be feminine inside himself, and, importantly, by denigrating and devaluing whatever he considers to be feminine in the outside world. As a societal member, he also appropriates to himself and defines as superior particular social activities and cultural (moral, religious, and creative) spheres—possibly, in fact, "society" and "culture" themselves.

Freud's description of the boy's oedipal crisis speaks to the issues of rejection of the feminine and identification with the father. As his early attachment to his mother takes on phallic-sexual overtones, and his father enters the picture as an obvious rival (who, in the son's fantasy, has apparent power to kill or castrate his son), the boy must radically deny and repress his attachment to his mother and replace it with an identification with his loved and admired, but also potentially punitive, therefore feared, father. He internalizes a superego.

To summarize, four components of the attainment of masculine gender identity are important. First, masculinity becomes and remains a problematic issue for a boy. Second, it involves denial of attachment or relationship, particularly of what the boy takes to be dependence or need for another, and differentiation of himself from another. Third, it involves the repression and devaluation of femininity on both psychological and cultural levels. Finally, identification with his father does not usually develop in the context of a satisfactory affective relationship, but consists in the attempt to internalize and learn components of a not immediately apprehensible role.

The development of a girls' gender identity contrasts with that of a boy. Most important, femininity and female role activities are immediately apprehensible in the world of her daily life. Her final role identification is with her mother and women, that is, with the person or people with whom she also has her earliest relationship of infantile dependence. The development of her gender identity does not involve a rejection of this early identification, however. Rather, her later identification with her mother is embedded in and influenced by their ongoing relationship of both primary identification and preoedipal attachment. Because her mother is around, and she has had a genuine relationship

to her as a person, a girl's gender and gender role identification are mediated by and depend upon real affective relations. Identification with her mother is not positional—the narrow learning of particular role behaviors—but rather a personal identification with her mother's general traits of character and values. Feminine identification is based not on fantasied or externally defined characteristics and negative identification, but on the gradual learning of a way of being familiar in everyday life, and exemplified by the person (or kind of people—women) with whom she has been most involved. It is continuous with her early childhood identifications and attachments.

The major discontinuity in the development of a girl's sense of gender identity, and one that has led Freud and other early psychoanalysts to see female development as exceedingly difficult and tortuous, is that at some point she must transfer her primary sexual object choice from her mother and females to her father and males, if she is to attain her expected heterosexual adulthood. Briefly, Freud considers that all children feel that mothers give some cause for complaint and unhappiness: they give too little milk; they have a second child; they arouse and then forbid their child's sexual gratification in the process of caring for her/him. A girl receives a final blow, however: her discovery that she lacks a penis. She blames this lack on her mother, rejects her mother, and turns to her father in reaction.

Problems in this account have been discussed extensively in the general literature that has grown out of the women's movement, and within the psychoanalytic tradition itself. These concern Freud's misogyny and his obvious assumption that males possess physiological superiority, and that a woman's personality is inevitably determined by her lack of a penis. The psychoanalytic account is not completely unsatisfactory, however. A more detailed consideration of several theorists reveals important features of female development, especially about the mother-daughter relationship, and at the same time contradicts or mitigates the absoluteness of the more general Freudian outline.

These psychoanalysts emphasize how, in contrast to males, the female oedipal crisis is not resolved in the same absolute way. A girl cannot and does not completely reject her mother in favor of men, but continues her relationship of dependence upon and attachment to her. In addition, the strength and quality of her relationship to her father is completely dependent upon the strength and quality of her relationship to her mother. Deutsch suggests that a girl wavers in a "bisexual triangle" throughout her childhood and into puberty, normally making a very tentative resolution in favor of her father, but in such a way that issues of separation from and attachment to her mother remain important throughout a woman's life:

It is erroneous to say that the little girl gives up her first mother relation in favor of the father. She only gradually draws him into the alliance, develops from the mother-child exclusiveness toward the triangular parent-child relationship and continues the latter, just as she does the former, although in a weaker and less elemental form, all her life. Only the principal part changes: now the mother, now the father plays it. The ineradicability of affective constellations manifests itself in later repetitions. [1]

We might suggest from this that a girl's internalized and external object-relations become and remain more complex, and at the same time more defining of her, than those of a boy. Psychoanalytic preoccupation with constitutionally based libidinal development, and with a normative male model of development, has obscured this fact. Most women are genitally heterosexual. At the same time, their lives always involve other sorts of equally deep and primary relationships, especially with their children, and, importantly, with other women. In

these spheres also, even more than in the area of heterosexual relations, a girl imposes the sort of object-relations she has internalized in her preoedipal and later relationship to her mother.

Men are also for the most part genitally heterosexual. This grows directly out of their early primary attachment to their mother. We know, however, that in many societies their heterosexual relationships are not embedded in close personal relationship but simply in relations of dominance and power. Furthermore, they do not have the extended personal relations women have. They are not so connected to children, and their relationships with other men tend to be based not on particularistic connection or affective ties, but rather on abstract, universalistic role expectations.

Building on the psychoanalytic assumption that unique individual experiences contribute to the formation of individual personality, culture and personality theory has held that early experiences common to members of a particular society contribute to the formation of "typical" personalities organized around and preoccupied with certain issues: "Prevailing patterns of child-rearing must result in similar internalized situations in the unconscious of the majority of individuals in a culture, and these will be externalized back into the culture again to perpetuate it from generation to generation." In a similar vein, I have tried to show that to the extent males and females, respectively, experience similar interpersonal environments as they grow up, masculine and feminine personality will develop differently.

I have relied on a theory which suggests that features of adult personality and behavior are determined, but which is not biologically determinist. Culturally expected personality and behavior are not simply "taught," however. Rather, certain features of social structure, supported by cultural beliefs, values, and perceptions, are internalized through the family and the child's early social object-relationships. This largely unconscious organization is the context in which role training and purposive socialization take place.

SEX-ROLE LEARNING AND ITS SOCIAL CONTEXT

Sex-role training and social interaction in childhood build upon and reinforce the largely unconscious development I have described. In most societies (ours is a complicated exception) a girl is usually with her mother and other female relatives in an interpersonal situation that facilitates continuous and early role learning and emphasizes the mother-daughter identification and particularistic, diffuse, affective relationships between women. A boy, to a greater or lesser extent, is also with women for a large part of his childhood, which prevents continuous or easy masculine role identification. His development is characterized by discontinuity.

* * *

The content of boys' and girls' role training tends in the same direction as the context of this training and its results. Barry, Bacon, and Child, in their well-known study, demonstrate that the socialization of boys tends to be oriented toward achievement and self-reliance and that of girls toward nurturance and responsibility. Girls are thus pressured to be involved with and connected to others, boys to deny this involvement and connection.

* * *

EGO BOUNDARIES AND THE MOTHER-DAUGHTER RELATIONSHIP

The care and socialization of girls by women ensures the production of feminine personalities founded on relations and connection, with flexible rather than rigid ego boundaries, and with a comparatively secure sense of gender identity. This is one explanation for how women's relative embeddedness is reproduced from generation to generation, and why it exists within almost every society. More specific investigation of different social contexts suggests, however, that there are variations in the kind of relationship that can exist between women's role performance and feminine personality.

Various kinds of evidence suggest that separation from the mother, the breaking of dependence, and the establishment and maintenance of a consistently individuated sense of self remain difficult psychological issues for Western middle-class women (i.e., the women who become subjects of psychoanalytic and clinical reports and social-psychological studies). Deutsch in particular provides extensive clinical documentation of these difficulties and of the way they affect women's relationships to men and children and, because of their nature, are reproduced in the next generation of women. Mothers and daughters in the women's group mentioned above describe their experiences of boundary confusion or equation of self and other, for example, guilt and self-blame for the other's unhappiness; shame and embarrassment at the other's actions; daughters' "discovery" that they are "really" living out their mothers' lives in their choice of career; mothers' not completely conscious reactions to their daughters' bodies as their own (over-identification and therefore often unnecessary concern with supposed weight or skin problems, which the mother is really worried about in herself); etc.

A kind of guilt that Western women express seems to grow out of and to reflect lack of adequate self/other distinctions and a sense of inescapable embeddedness in relationships to others. Tax describes this well (italics mine):

Since our awareness of others is considered our duty, the price we pay when things go wrong is guilt and self-hatred. And things always go wrong. We respond with apologies; we continue to apologize long after the event is forgotten—and *even if it had no causal relation to anything we did to begin with*. If the rain spoils someone's picnic, we apologize. We apologize for taking up space in a room, for living.[2]

As if the woman does not differentiate herself clearly from the rest of the world, she feels a sense of guilt and responsibility for situations that did not come about through her actions and without relation to her actual ability to determine the course of events. This happens, in the most familiar instance, in a sense of diffuse responsibility for everything connected to the welfare of her family and the happiness and success of her children. This loss of self in overwhelming responsibility for and connection to others is described particularly acutely by women writers (in the work, for instance, of Simone de Beauvoir, Kate Chopin, Doris Lessing, Tillie Olsen, Christina Stead, Virginia Woolf).

Slater points to several studies supporting the contention that Western daughters have particular problems about differentiation from their mother. These studies show that though most forms of personal parental identification correlate with psychological adjustment (i.e., freedom from neurosis or psychosis, *not* social acceptability), personal identification of a daughter with her mother does not. The reason is that the mother-daughter relation is the one form of personal identification that, because it results so easily from the normal situation of child development, is liable to be excessive in the direction of allowing no room for separation or difference between mother and daughter.

The situation reinforces itself in circular fashion. A mother, on the one hand, grows up without establishing adequate ego boundaries or a firm sense of self. She tends to experience boundary confusion with her daughter, and does not provide experiences of differentiating ego development for her daughter or encourage the breaking of her daughter's dependence. The daughter, for her part, makes a rather unsatisfactory and artificial attempt to establish boundaries: she projects what she defines as bad within her onto her mother and tries to take what is good into herself. (This, I think, is the best way to understand the girl's oedipal "rejection" of her mother.) Such an arbitrary mechanism cannot break the underlying psychological unity, however. Projection is never more than a temporary solution to ambivalence or boundary confusion.

The implication is that, contrary to Gutmann's suggestion, "so-called ego pathology" may not be "adaptive" for women. Women's biosexual experiences (menstruation, coitus, pregnancy, childbirth, lactation) all involve some challenge to the boundaries of her body ego ("me"/"not-me" in relation to her blood or milk, to a man who penetrates her, to a child once part of her body). These are important and fundamental human experiences that are probably intrinsically meaningful and at the same time complicated for women everywhere. However, a Western woman's tenuous sense of individuation and of the firmness of her ego boundaries increases the likelihood that experiences challenging these boundaries will be difficult for her and conflictive.

Nor is it clear that this personality structure is "functional" for society as a whole. The evidence presented in this paper suggests that satisfactory mothering, which does not reproduce particular psychological problems in boys and girls, comes from a person with a firm sense of self and of her own value, whose care is a freely chosen activity rather than a reflection of a conscious and unconscious sense of inescapable connection to and responsibility for her children.

SOCIAL STRUCTURE AND THE MOTHER-DAUGHTER RELATIONSHIP

Clinical and self-analytic descriptions of women and of the psychological component of mother-daughter relationships are not available from societies and subcultures outside of the Western middle class. However, accounts that are primarily sociological about women in other societies enable us to infer certain aspects of their psychological situation. In what follows, I am not claiming to make any kind of general statement about what constitutes a "healthy society," but only to examine and isolate specific features of social life that seem to contribute to the psychological strength of some members of a society. Consideration of three groups with matrifocal tendencies in their family structure . . . highlights several dimensions of importance in the developmental situation of the girl.

Young and Willmott describe the daily visiting and mutual aid of working-class mothers and daughters in East London. In a situation where household structure is usually nuclear, like the Western middle class, grown daughters look to their mothers for advice, for aid in childbirth and child care, for friendship and companionship, and for financial help. Their mother's house is the ultimate center of the family world. Husbands are in many ways peripheral to family relationships, possibly because of their failure to provide sufficiently for their families as men are expected to do. This becomes apparent if they demand their wife's disloyalty toward or separation from her mother: "The great triangle of childhood is mother-father-child; in Bethnal Green the great triangle of adult life is Mum-wife-husband."

Geertz and Jay describe Javanese nuclear families in which women are often the more powerful spouse and have primary influence upon how kin relations are expressed and to whom (although these families are formally centered upon a highly valued conjugal relationship based on equality of spouses). Financial and decision-making control in the family often rests largely in the hands of its women. Women are potentially independent of men in a way that men are not independent of women. Geertz points to a woman's ability to participate

in most occupations, and to own farmland and supervise its cultivation, which contrasts with a man's inability, even if he is financially independent, to do his own household work and cooking.

Women's kin role in Java is important. Their parental role and rights are greater than those of men; children always belong to the woman in case of divorce. When extra members join a nuclear family to constitute an extended family household, they are much more likely to be the wife's relatives than those of the husband. Formal and distant relations between men in a family, and between a man and his children (especially his son), contrast with the informal and close relations between women, and between a woman and her children. Jay and Geertz both emphasize the continuing closeness of the mother-daughter relationship as a daughter is growing up and throughout her married life. Jay suggests that there is a certain amount of ambivalence in the mother-daughter relationship, particularly as a girl grows toward adulthood and before she is married, but points out that at the same time the mother remains a girl's "primary figure of confidence and support."

Siegel describes Atjehnese families in Indonesia in which women stay on the homestead of their parents after marriage and are in total control of the household. Women tolerate men in the household only as long as they provide money, and even then treat them as someone between a child and a guest. Women's stated preference would be to eliminate even this necessary dependence on men: "Women, for instance, envision paradise as the place where they are reunited with their children and their mothers; husbands and fathers are absent, and yet there is an abundance all the same. Quarrels over money reflect the women's idea that men are basically adjuncts who exist only to give their families whatever they can earn." A woman in this society does not get into conflicts in which she has to choose between her mother and her husband, as happens in the Western working class, where the reigning ideology supports the nuclear family.

In these three settings, the mother-daughter tie and other female kin relations remain important from a woman's childhood through her old age. Daughters stay closer to home in both childhood and adulthood, and remain involved in particularistic role relations. Sons and men are more likely to feel uncomfortable at home, and to spend work and play time away from the house. Male activities and spheres emphasize universalistic, distancing qualities: men in Java are the bearers and transmitters of high culture and formal relationships; men in East London spend much of their time in alienated work settings; Atjehnese boys spend their time in school, and their fathers trade in distant places.

Mother-daughter ties in these three societies, described as extremely close, seem to be composed of companionship and mutual cooperation, and to be positively valued by both mother and daughter. The ethnographies do not imply that women are weighed down by the burden of their relationships or by overwhelming guilt and responsibility. On the contrary, they seem to have developed a strong sense of self and selfworth, which continues to grow as they get older and take on their maternal role. The implication is that "ego strength" is not completely dependent on the firmness of the ego's boundaries.

Guntrip's distinction between "immature" and "mature" dependence clarifies the difference between mother-daughter relationships and women's psyche in the Western middle class and in the matrifocal societies described. Women in the Western middle class are caught up to some extent in issues of infantile dependence, while the women in matrifocal societies remain in definite connection with others, but in relationships characterized by mature dependence. As Guntrip describes it *"Mature dependence* is characterized by full differentiation of ego and object (emergence from primary identification) and therewith a capacity for valuing the object for its own sake and for giving as well as receiving; a condition which should be described not as independence but as mature dependence."* This kind of mature dependence is also to be distinguished from the kind of forced independence and denial of need for relationship that I have suggested characterizes masculine personality, and that reflects continuing conflict about infantile dependence (my italics): "Maturity is not equated with independence though it includes a certain capacity for independence. . . . The independence of the mature person is simply that he does not collapse when he has to stand alone. It is not an independence of needs for other persons with whom to have relationship: *that would not be desired by the mature."*

Depending on its social setting, women's sense of relation and connection and their embeddedness in social life provide them with a kind of security that men lack. The quality of a mother's relationship to her children and maternal self-esteem, on the one hand, and the nature of a daughter's developing identification with her mother, on the other, make crucial differences in female development.

Women's kin role, and in particular the mother role, is central and positively valued in Atjeh, Java, and East London. Women gain status and prestige as they get older; their major role is not fulfilled in early motherhood. At the same time, women may be important contributors to the family's economic support, as in Java and East London, and in all three societies they have control over real economic resources. All these factors give women a sense of self-esteem independent of their relationship to their children. Finally, strong relationships exist between women in these societies, expressed in mutual cooperation and frequent contact. A mother, then, when her children are young, is likely to spend much of her time in the company of other women, not simply isolated with her children.

These social facts have important positive effects on female psychological development. (It must be emphasized that all the ethnographies indicate that these same social facts make male development difficult and contribute to psychological insecurity and lack of ease in interpersonal relationships in men.) A mother is not invested in keeping her daughter from individuating and becoming less dependent. She has other ongoing contacts and relationships that help fulfill her psychological and social needs. In addition, the people surrounding a mother while a child is growing up become mediators between mother and daughter, by providing a daughter with alternative models for personal identification and objects of attachment, which contribute to her differentiation from her mother. Finally, a daughter's identification with her mother in this kind of setting is with a strong woman with clear control over important spheres of life, whose sense of self-esteem can reflect this. Acceptance of her gender identity involves positive valuation of herself, and not an admission of inferiority. In psychoanalytic terms, we might say it involves identification with a preoedipal, active, caring mother. Bibring points to clinical findings supporting this interpretation: "We find in the analysis of the women who grew up in this 'matriarchal' setting the rejection of the feminine role less frequently than among female patients coming from the patriarchal family culture."

There is another important aspect of the situation in these societies. The continuing structural and practical importance of the mother-daughter tie not only ensures that a daughter develops a positive personal and role identification with her mother, but also requires that the close psychological tie between mother and daughter become firmly grounded in real role expectations. These provide a certain constraint and limitation upon the relationship, as well as an avenue for its expression through common spheres of interest based in the external social world.

All these societal features contrast with the situation of the Western middle-class woman. Kinship relations in the middle class are less important. Kin are not likely to live near each other, and, insofar as husbands are able to provide adequate financial support for their families, there is no need for a network of mutual aid among related wives. As the middle-class woman gets older and becomes a grandmother, she cannot look forward to increased status and prestige in her new role.

The Western middle-class housewife does not have an important economic role in her family. The work she does and the responsibilities that go with it (household management, cooking, entertaining, etc.) do not seem to be really necessary to the economic support of her family (they are crucial contributions to the maintenance and reproduction of her family's class position, but this is not generally recognized as important either by the woman herself or by the society's ideology). If she works outside the home, neither she nor the rest of society is apt to consider this work to be important to her self-definition in the way that her housewife role is.

Child care, on the other hand, is considered to be her crucially important responsibility. Our post-Freudian society in fact assigns to parents (and especially to the mother) nearly total responsibility for how children turn out. A middle-class mother's daily life is not centrally involved in relations with other women. She is isolated with her children for most of her workday. It is not surprising, then, that she is likely to invest a lot of anxious energy and guilt in her concern for her children and to look to them for her own self-affirmation, or that her self-esteem, dependent on the lives of others than herself, is shaky. Her life situation leads her to an overinvolvement in her children's lives.

A mother in this situation keeps her daughter from differentiation and from lessening her infantile dependence. (She also perpetuates her son's dependence, but in this case society and his father are more likely to interfere in order to assure that, behaviorally, at least, he doesn't *act* dependent.) And there are not other people around to mediate in the mother-daughter relationship. Insofar as the father is actively involved in a relationship with his daughter and his daughter develops some identification with him, this helps her individuation, but the formation of ego autonomy through identification with and idealization of her father may be at the expense of her positive sense of feminine self. Unlike the situation in matrifocal families, the continuing closeness of the mother-daughter relationship is expressed only on a psychological, interpersonal level. External role expectations do not ground or limit it.

It is difficult, then, for daughters in a Western middle-class family to develop self-esteem. Most psychoanalytic and social theorists claim that the mother inevitably represents to her daughter (and son) regression, passivity, dependence, and lack of orientation to reality, whereas the father represents progression, activity, independence, and reality orientation. Given the value implications of this dichotomy, there are advantages for the son in giving up his mother and identifying with his father. For the daughter, feminine gender identification means identification with a devalued, passive mother, and personal maternal identification is with a mother whose own self-esteem is low. Conscious rejection of her oedipal maternal identification, however, remains an unconscious rejection and devaluation of herself, because of her continuing preoedipal identification and boundary confusion with her mother.

Cultural devaluation is not the central issue, however. Even in patrilineal, patrilocal societies in which women's status is very low, women do not necessarily translate this cultural devaluation into low self-esteem, nor do girls have to develop difficult boundary problems with their mother. In the Moslem Moroccan family, for example, a large amount of sex segregation and sex antagonism gives women a separate (domestic) sphere in which they have a real productive role and control, and also a life situation in which any young mother is in the company of other women. Women do not need to invest all their psychic energy in their children, and their self-esteem is not dependent on their relationship to their children. In this and other patrilineal, patrilocal societies, what resentment women do have at their oppressive situation is more often expressed toward their sons, whereas daughters are seen as allies against oppression. Conversely, a daughter develops relationships of attachment to and identification with other adult women. Loosening her tie to her mother therefore does not entail the rejection of all women. The close tie that remains between mother and daughter is based not simply on mutual overinvolvement but often on mutual understanding of their oppression.

CONCLUSION

Women's universal mothering role has effects both on the development of masculine and feminine personality and on the relative status of the sexes. This paper has described the development of relational personality in women and of personalities preoccupied with the denial of relation in men. In its comparison of different societies, it has suggested that men, while guaranteeing to themselves sociocultural superiority over women, always remain psychologically defensive and insecure. Women, by contrast, although always of secondary social and cultural status, may in favorable circumstances gain psychological security and a firm sense of worth and importance in spite of this.

Social and psychological oppression, then, is perpetuated in the structure of personality. The paper enables us to suggest what social arrangements contribute (and could contribute) to social equality between men and women and their relative freedom from certain sorts of psychological conflict. Daughters and sons must be able to develop a personal identification with more than one adult, and preferably one embedded in a role relationship that gives it a social context of expression and provides some limitation upon it. Most important, boys need to grow up around men who take a major role in child care, and girls around women who, in addition to their child-care responsibilities, have a valued role and recognized spheres of legitimate control. These arrangements could help to ensure that children of both sexes develop a sufficiently individuated and strong sense of self, as well as a positively valued and secure gender identity, that does not bog down either in ego-boundary confusion, low self-esteem, and overwhelming relatedness to others, or in compulsive denial of any connection to others or dependence upon them.

NOTES

1. Helen Deutsch, *Psychology of Women*, Vol I, II New York (1944) p. 205.
2. Meredith Tax, *Woman and Her Mind*, Boston (1970) p. 2.

Gender in the Context of Race and Class: Notes on Chodrow's "Reproduction of Mothering"

Elizabeth V. Spelman

Much of feminist theory has proceeded on the assumption that gender is indeed a variable of human identity independent of other variables such as race and class, that whether one is a woman is unaffected by what class or race one is. Feminists have also assumed that sexism is distinctly different from racism and classism,

From *Inessential Woman*, edited for inclusion in this volume. Reprinted by permission of the author.

that whether and how one is subject to sexism is unaffected by whether and how one is subject to racism or classism.

The work of Nancy Chodorow has seemed to provide feminist theory with a strong foundation for these arguments. It has explicitly and implicitly been used to justify the assumption that there is nothing problematic about trying to examine gender independently of other variables such as race, class, and ethnicity. Though Chodorow's writings have received sometimes scathing criticism from feminists, more often they have been seen by feminist scholars in many different disciplines as providing a particularly rich understanding of gender. Indeed, Chodorow offers what appears to be a very promising account of the relations between gender identity and other important aspects of identity such as race and class. For while she treats gender as separable from race and class, she goes on to suggest ways in which the sexist oppression intimately connected to gender differences is related to racism and classism.

I hope to show that while Chodorow's work is very compelling, it ought to be highly problematic for any version of feminism that demands more than lip service to the significance of race and class, racism and classism, in the lives of the women on whom Chodorow focuses. The problem, as I see it, is not that feminists have taken Chodorow seriously, but that we have not taken her seriously enough. Her account points to a more complicated understanding of gender and the process of becoming gendered than she herself develops. She tells us to look at the social context of mothering in order to understand the effect of mothering on the acquisition of gender identity in children; but if we follow her advice, rather than her own practice, we are led to see that gender identity is not neatly separable from other aspects of identity such as race and class. They couldn't be if, as Chodorow insists, the acquisition of gender occurs in and helps perpetuate the "hierarchical and differentiated social worlds" we inhabit.

I

According to *The Reproduction of Mothering*, there are systematic differences between girls and boys, between women and men, that are biological; but there also are systematic differences in behavior and in what some psychologists refer to as "intrapsychic structures." The latter differences cannot be accounted for by the biological differences. But neither can they be explained by reference to learning to behave in certain ways, whether by exposure to role models, ideological messages, or coercion. Neither account enables us to understand the psychological investment girls and boys come to have in becoming women and men and the psychological investment women and men have in reproducing girls and boys. In particular, we have to understand the different "relational capacities" and "senses of self" in girls and boys, women and men. These differences are produced by the sexual division of labor in which women, and not men, mother; and that division of labor is in turn reproduced by these differences. The sexual division of labor can reproduce itself because through it are produced women and men who "develop personalities which tend to guarantee that they will get gratification or satisfaction from those activities which are necessary to the reproduction" of the sexual division of labor.

In short, we can't adequately describe gender differences without focusing on the different senses of self women and men have that are linked to their thinking or not thinking of themselves in ways that prepare them for mothering; at the same time, neither can we explain how these gender differences come about without focusing on the fact that it is women and not men who mother. For it is the mothering of girls and boys that women do that explains why girls and boys develop different relational capacities and different senses of self—why girls in turn go on to mother and boys not only do not mother but demean mothers and mothering.

Our becoming girl-gendered or boy-gendered, then, is a process mediated by our mothers:

An account of the early mother-infant relationship in contemporary Western society reveals the overwhelming importance of the mother in everyone's psychological development, in their sense of self, and in their basic relational stance. It reveals that becoming a person [girl or boy] is the same thing as becoming a person in relationship and in social context.[1]

But mothering itself is a mediated activity. "Women's mothering does not exist in isolation." It is an intricate part of the sexual division of labor; it is part of a "social organization" that "includes male dominance, a particular family system, and women's dependence on men's income." It is "informed by [the woman's] relationship to her husband, her experience of financial dependence, her expectations of marital inequality, and her expectations about gender roles."

Chodorow believes that "all societies are constituted around a structural split . . . between the private, domestic world of women and the public, social world of men." There is a division of labor between the public, "nonrelational" sphere, where men have their primary location, and a private, "relational" sphere, where women have their "primary social and economic location." Mothering in such a context is a process geared to producing girls who will be fit denizens of the private sphere and boys who will participate in the public world—the "capitalist world of work" in Western society. How does this happen?

In answering this, Chodorow is trying to carry out the promise contained in the subtitle of the book: "psychoanalysis and the sociology of gender." Her focus on the social context of gender and mothering makes use of Freud and object-relation theorists. Briefly, mothers see their daughters as "more like and continuous with" themselves than their sons are. Girls are not called upon to individuate themselves, to see themselves as distinct from their mothers, as early, as firmly, or as finally as boys are. A girl's sense of self is not as threatened by her ties to her mother as a boy's is; the resolution of his oedipal stage means he must give up his mother in a way his sister does not have to. At the same time, because a girl learns what it is to be a woman by identifying with her mother, and be-

cause the asymmetrical organization of parenting means the mother is present, this process of identification takes place in the context of a personal relationship. However, part of the asymmetrical organization of parenting is that the boy's father is not present in the way the mother is; learning what it is to be masculine hence happens, not in the context of a personal relationship, but "through identification with cultural images of masculinity and men chosen as masculine models." Because of the context in which mothering takes place, mothers have different kinds of relationships with their daughters than they do with their sons. And these different kinds of relationships produce different psychic configurations in girls and boys—configurations that prepare the growing girls and boys to come to find satisfaction in the very same division of labor in the context of which mothering occurs.

According to Chodorow, then, the most significant difference between girls and boys, women and men, is in terms of the degree to which they see themselves as related to and connected with others. "The basic feminine sense of self is connected to the world, the basic masculine sense of self is separate." This is the psychological counterpart of the roles women and men are expected to play: "Women in our society are primarily defined as wives and mothers, thus in particularistic relation to someone else, whereas men are defined primarily in universalistic occupational terms." As long as it is only women who mother, in the social context in which they do, these differences in women and men will continue to exist. If we want to change or to put an end to such differences, the institution of mothering has to change.

Chodorow says in a later article in the feminist journal *Signs* that any feminist ought to want to eliminate those kinds of differences between men and women, because "a treating of women as others, or objects, rather than subjects, or selves" not only adversely affects women but "extends to our culture as a whole."

The boy comes to define his self more in opposition than through a sense of his wholeness or continuity. He becomes the self and experiences his mother as the other. The process also extends to his trying to dominate the other in order to ensure his sense of self. Such domination begins with mother as the object, extends to women, and is then generalized to include the experience of all others as objects rather than subjects. This stance, in which people are treated and experienced as things, becomes basic to male Western culture.[2]

Here Chodorow elaborates on a quotation from Lévi-Strauss she placed at the beginning of her 1979 article, "Gender, Relation, and Difference in Psychoanalytic Perspective":

I would go so far as to say that even before slavery or class domination existed, men built an approach to women that would serve one day to introduce differences among us all.[3]

Though Chodorow does not take it upon herself to explain or defend these points in any more detail, it seems fairly clear that she takes sexism to be independent of racism and classism but at the same time to be both the model for them (the domination of male over female is adapted for the purposes of other forms of domination) and the cause of them (if men weren't so insecure about their sense of self vis-à-vis their mothers, they wouldn't need to define anyone else as Other).

II

As mentioned earlier, Chodorow's feminist critics have not been shy about pointing to what they take to be particularly vulnerable aspects of her account of gender acquisition: her reliance on some of the more troubling aspects of Freud, her uncritical use of the distinction between "public" and "private" spheres, her assumption of women's heterosexuality. Though I share her critics' concerns, I want to focus on aspects of her work that have not received sufficient atten-

tion. But first I shall describe what I take to be some of the initially more helpful directions of Chodorow's work and some of the questions she leaves unanswered.

Perhaps the most politically significant part of Chodorow's account is her reminder that mothering occurs in a particular social context. It is informed, she notes, by the mother's relation to her husband, her economic dependence on him, her experience of male dominance. But why does Chodorow focus on only these elements of the larger social context? After all, most societies—including that of contemporary North America, about which she is most concerned—are also characterized by other forms of dominance, other sorts of hierarchies. Women mother in societies that may be racist and classist as well as sexist and heterosexist. Are we to believe that a woman's mothering is informed only by her relation to a husband or male lover and her experience of living in a male-dominated society, but not by her relation to people of other classes and races and her experience of living in a society in which there are race and class hierarchies? Chodorow wants us to think about the "specific implications of the actual social context in which the child learns." But if I do that, then it does not seem accurate to describe what my mother nurtured in me, and what I learned, as being simply a "girl." I was learning to be a white, middle-class Christian and "American" girl. Chodorow rails against the view that "feminine biology shapes psychic life without mediation of culture." But does only one part of the culture mediate mothering?

"Families," Chodorow says, "create children gendered, heterosexual, and ready to marry"—or anyway they are supposed to. But do families have no racial or class or ethnic identity? Do they create children prepared to marry anyone, no matter the person's race, class, ethnicity, religion? Is the creation of children in the ways Chodorow lists the only thing families are supposed to do? As Chodorow herself so usefully points out, the socialization that must take place in order for the society to continue to reproduce itself "must lead to the assimilation and internal organization of generalized capacities for participation in a hierarchical and differentiated social world." Families are organized so as to produce new beings who will "get gratification or satisfaction from those activities which are necessary to the reproduction of the larger social structure." But is this true for only certain elements of that larger social structure? If children are said to be prepared to participate in a sexually unequal society, why aren't they also said to be prepared to participate in a society where there are racial, class, and other forms of inequality?

As we've seen, Chodorow certainly is not unaware of forms of domination other than sexism, and undoubtedly she would acknowledge that the raising of children contributes in some ways (and presumably in different ways in different families) to the perpetuation of racism, classism, and other forms of oppression. She probably would respond to the questions above by saying that the production of gender identity in families is separate from, even if at some point in tandem with, the production of other aspects of identity such as race or ethnicity or class. But let us look in more detail at what she means by "gender" and see whether what she tells us about gender indeed means that it can or must be specified independently of elements of identity such as race and class.

Chodorow refers to a "core gender identity" that, along with a sense of self, is established in the first two years. This core gender identity is a "cognitive sense" of oneself as male or female. As we saw above, according to Chodorow the distinction between a "basic feminine sense of self" and a "basic masculine sense of self" involves seeing oneself as connected to or seeing oneself as separate from the world. But she also describes gender in more specific terms:

I am using *gender* here to stand for the mother's particular psychic structure and relational sense, for her (probable) heterosexuality, and for her conscious and unconscious acceptance of the ideology, meanings, and expectations that go into being a gendered member of our society and understanding what gender means.[4]

Part of gender ideology is that men are superior to women, for male superiority is built "into the definition of masculinity itself." Gendered senses of self have to be politically loaded, since they prepare girls and boys to enter a world in which there is a sexual division of labor that is itself politically loaded: male domination couldn't continue, Chodorow reasons, unless gender differentiation included gender hierarchy. Whether or not Chodorow thinks that the engendering of baby humans *causes* sexual domination, she clearly thinks that coming to be and think of oneself as masculine or feminine involves assuming one's place (and having a sense of one's place) in a world in which masculine beings dominate feminine ones. Mothering in a sexist context reproduces sexism insofar as it creates young humans well adapted psychologically to take their place in a sexist world.

Chodorow begins her book with the claim that "women's mothering is one of the few universal and enduring elements of the sexual division of labor." She means by this that no matter how else cultures and subcultures differ with respect to the division of labor along sexual lines, the work of mothering is always done by women. At the same time Chodorow says that mothering "is not an unchanging transcultural universal." By this she seems to mean that as the world into which children enter changes over time, so the responsibilities of women preparing children for entry into the world change. For example, "the development of industrial capitalism in the West entailed that women's role in the family become increasingly concerned with personal relations and psychological stability." Together these two claims suggest that while it is women who everywhere mother—that is, who not only feed and clean infants but provide them with "affective bonds and a diffuse, multifaceted, ongoing personal relationship" —the kind of development they unconsciously and consciously encourage in their children will depend on the particular requirements of the world in which they live and for which they must prepare the children. To learn one's gender identity is among other things to learn what work one is supposed to do and also to want to do that work (or at least not *not* want to because it isn't the kind of work one is supposed to do).

There are, then, according to Chodorow two universals: a sexual division of labor and, within that division, the assignment of mothering to women. Two things are not universal: the particular tasks (other than mothering) that are assigned along sexual lines and the content of mothering. Indeed, Chodorow says that class differences within a society—below she is speaking of modern capitalist societies—are reflected in "parental child-rearing values":

Working-class parents are more likely to value obedience, conformity to external authority, neatness, and other "behavioral" characteristics in their children; middle-class parents emphasize more "internal" and interpersonal characteristics like responsibility, curiosity, self-motivation, self-control, and consideration. [5]

Whether or not Chodorow's descriptions of class differences are accurate, it is important to note that she does think class may make an important difference to mothering. "We know almost nothing" about effects of class differences on mothering, she cautions, and admits that "all claims about gender differences gloss over important differences within genders and similarities between genders." Moreover, in a later response to critics, she says that among the things she would stress more than she did in her book is

how women's mothering and early infantile development is tied to the treatment of people as things and rigid self-other distinctions that characterize our culture and thought. That is, I would examine the link between what seems exclusively gender related and the construction of other aspects of society, politics and culture [and also would encourage study of] class and ethnic differences, differences in family and household structure, differences in sexual orientation of parents, and historical and cross-cultural variations in these relationships. [6]

From this further foray into Chodorow's account of gender, several things emerge: that according to her analysis, sexual hierarchy is built into definitions of masculine and feminine, and that we know little about the effect of class differences on the mothering practices that reproduce gender identities. But if she says these things about gender, it makes it harder rather than easier to show that gender is isolatable from other elements of identity.

First of all, what kind of difference could the study of class and ethnic differences make to the study of gender identity and the role of mothering in its production and reproduction? Unless Chodorow thinks they might make a significant difference, she presumably will not think it important to investigate any further. Her own theory reveals something of her answer to this question. One of the major functions of families, she told us, is to produce beings who will "get gratification or satisfaction from those activities which are necessary to the reproduction of the larger social structure." But investigation of ethnicity and class and race within that social structure might make us consider the possibility that what one learns when one learns one's gender identity is the gender identity appropriate to one's ethnic, class, national, and racial identity. Understanding gender, Chodorow told us, includes understanding "the ideology, meanings, and expectations that go into being a gendered member of our society." But if, for example, masculine identity is rich enough to include the notion of male superiority, as Chodorow says it is, then we are not barred from asking whether it doesn't also include notions of class or race superiority. In a racist society such as the United States, is the ideological content of masculinity the idea that any man is superior to any woman?

The ideology of masculinity in the United States hardly includes the idea that Black men are superior to white women. So if gender is supposed to include ideology, and if learning one's gender identity prepares one for what is expected of a person gendered in the way one is, then we can't describe masculinity as including simply the notion that men are superior to women. If a poor Black boy in the United States thinks that being "masculine" entitles him to dominate white women, since he's male and they are female, he's not been prepared well for the society into which he's been born (and as we shall discuss below, it is highly unlikely that his mother would be unaware of this). This is not to say that he may not wish to dominate white women (along with Black women), but rather to remind us that if Emmet Till had been white, he wouldn't have been murdered by white men for talking to a white woman, nor would his murderers have been acquitted.

*   *   *

IV

Chodorow invites us to consider the difference class makes to parenting and suggests that the sexism built into the context of early psychological development has some role to play in the maintenance, perhaps even in the creation, of racial and class hierarchies. Her account thus raises some very crucial methodological questions for anyone who thinks that a complete feminist analysis of sexism ought to include at least some examination of the relation between sexism and other forms of oppression. The methodological questions have to do with where and how issues about race and racism, class and classism, enter into the analysis. As we have

seen, Chodorow herself suggests at least two places they might intersect. Starting with her suggestions and thinking of other points of entry, we can generate a fairly long list of the ways we might begin to examine connections between issues of race and class and those of gender:

1. Does race or class identity affect gender identity? For example, are there elements of race and class in notions of masculinity and femininity?

Isn't the idea of superiority built, as Chodorow affirms, into the notion of "masculinity" understood to apply only under certain conditions? Does the ideology packed into the notion of masculinity include the notion that any man is superior to any woman? Does the ideology packed into the notion of femininity include the notion that any woman is inferior to any man, that all women are inferior in just the same way to all men?

2. Does a child's sense of self include a conscious or unconscious sense of race or class? (This is closely connected to question 1.)

If we are looking for an account of psychosocial development that explains how children come to be psychologically and socially prepared for the positions set for them in a hierarchically ordered political and social and economic world, we might do well to ask whether children learn what it means to be men or women by learning what it is to be men or women of their race, class, ethnicity.

3. What are the hierarchies in the world into which children are born and socialized? Is sexual privilege or domination affected by the race and class of the men and women in question?

The world into which the children enter is one in which race and class identity cuts across gender identity (men can be Anglo- or Afro-

American, women can be upper class or working class, and so on), and racism and classism cut across sexism (there are significant differences in the situations of highly educated well-to-do women with tenured jobs and poor women on welfare). It would be much easier to account for how children are prepared for entry into such a complex world if what they learned when they learned their gender identity was not simply that they were boys or girls but something more complicated—for example, that they were white male or female, Black male or female, and so forth.

4. What are the ways in which sexism might be related to other forms of oppression? For example, is sexism a support for or cause of racism or classism? Or is it in some sense more closely intertwined with them?

Perhaps we can begin to account for the reproduction of racism by taking our task to be not simply to explain how men have come to think of themselves as superior to women, but rather to explain how children learn that the superiority built into "masculine" is meant to be the prerogative of a certain group of men; and to explain how it is possible for a group of women thinking of themselves as inferior to "men" to also think of themselves as superior to some men and some women.

*   *   *

X

It is a general principle of feminist inquiry to be sceptical about any account of human relations that fails to mention gender or consider the possible effects of gender differences: for in a world in which there is sexism, obscuring the workings of gender is likely to involve—whether intentionally or not—obscuring the workings of sexism. We thus ought to be sceptical about any account of gender relations that fails to mention race and class or to consider the possible effects of race and class differences on gender: for in a world in which there is racism and classism, obscuring the workings of race and class is likely to involve—whether intentionally or not—obscuring the workings of racism and classism.

For this reason alone we may have a lot to learn from the following questions about any account of gender relations that presupposes or otherwise insists on the separability of gender, race, and class: Why does it seem possible or necessary to separate them? Whatever the motivations for doing so, does it serve the interests of some people and not others? Does methodology ever express race or class privilege—for example, do any of the methodological reasons that might be given for trying to investigate gender in isolation from race and class in fact serve certain race or class interests?

These questions are not rhetorical. For very good and very important reasons, feminists have insisted on asking how gender affects or is affected by every branch of human inquiry (even those such as the physical sciences, which seem to have no openings for such questions). And with very good reason we have been annoyed by the absence of reference to gender in inquires about race or class, racism and classism. Perhaps it seems the best response, to such a state of affairs, first to focus on gender and sexism and then to go on to think about how gender and sexism are related to race and racism, class and classism. Hence the appeal of the work of Nancy Chodorow and the variations on it by others. But however logically, methodological, and politically sound such inquiry seems, it obscures the ways in which race and class identity may be intertwined with gender identity. Moreover, since in a racist and classist society the racial and class identity of those who are subject to racism and classism are not obscured, all it can really mask is the racial and class identity of white middle-class women. It is because white middle-class women have something at stake in not having their racial and class identity made and kept visible that we must question accepted feminist positions on gender identity.

If feminism is essentially about gender, and gender is taken to be neatly separable from race and class, then race and class don't need to be talked about except in some peripheral way. And if race and class are peripheral to women's identities as women, then racism and classism can't be of central concern to feminism. Hence the racism and classism some women face and other women help perpetuate can't find a place in feminist theory unless we keep in mind the race and class of all women (not just the race and class of those who are the victims of racism and classism). I have suggested here that one way to keep them in mind is to ask about the extent to which gender identity exists in concert with these other aspects of identity. This is quite different from saying either (1) we need to talk about race and class instead of gender or (2) we need to talk about race and class in addition to gender. Some feminists may be concerned that focus on race and class will deflect attention away from gender and from what women have in common and thus from what gives feminist inquiry its distinctive cast. This presupposes not only that we ought not spend too much time on what we don't have in common but that we have gender in common. But do we have gender identity in common? In one sense, of course, yes: all women are women. But in another sense, no: not if gender is a social construction and females become not simply women but particular kinds of women. If I am justified in thinking that what it means for me to be a woman must be exactly the same as what it means for you to be a woman (since we both are women), I needn't bother to find out anything from you or about you in order to find out what it means for you to be a woman: I can simply deduce what it means from my own case. On the other hand, if the meaning of what we apparently have in common (being women) depends in some ways on the meaning of what we don't have in common (for example, our different racial or class identities), then far from distracting us from issues of gender, attention to race and class in fact helps us to understand gender. In this sense it is only if we pay attention to how we differ that we come to an understanding of what we have in common.

NOTES

1. Chodorow, Nancy, *The Reproduction of Mothering*, Berkeley: University of California Press (1978) p. 76.

2. Chodorow, Reply to "On The Reproduction of Mothering: A Methodological Debate" *Signs* 6, No. 3 (1981).

3. Chodorow, "Gender, Relation and Difference, in *The Future of Difference*, edited by Hester Eisenstein, New Brunswick: Rutgers University Press (1985).

4. *Op. cit.*, p. 98.

5. *Ibid.*, 176.

6. Chodorow, "Reply", 514.

❧ Marxist/Socialist Feminism ❧

The Origin of the Family, Private Property, and the State

Friedrich Engels

The study of primitive history reveals conditions where the men live in polygamy and their wives in polyandry at the same time, and their common children are therefore considered common to them all—and these conditions in their turn undergo a long series of changes before they finally end in monogamy. The trend of these changes is to narrow more and more the circle of people comprised within the common bond of marriage, which was originally very wide, until at last it includes only the single pair, the dominant form of marriage today.

Reconstructing thus the past history of the family, Morgan, in agreement with most of his colleagues, arrives at a primitive stage when unrestricted sexual freedom prevailed within the tribe, every woman belonging equally to every man and every man to every woman

* * *

From *The Origin of the Family, Private Property and the State*. First printed 1884.

According to Morgan, from this primitive state of promiscuous intercourse there developed, probably very early:

1. The Consanguine Family, the First Stage of the Family

Here the marriage groups are separated according to generations: all the grandfathers and grandmothers within the limits of the family are all husbands and wives of one another; so are also their children, the fathers and mothers; the latter's children will form a third circle of common husbands and wives; and their children, the great-grandchildren of the first group, will form a fourth. In this form of marriage, therefore, only ancestors and progeny, and parents and children, are excluded from the rights and duties (as we should say) of marriage with one another. Brothers and sisters, male and female cousins of the first, second, and more remote degrees, are all brothers and sisters of one another, and *precisely for that reason* they are all husbands and wives of one another. At this stage the relationship of brother and sister also includes as a matter of course the practice of sexual intercourse with one another. In its typical form, such a family would consist of the descendants of a single pair, the descendants of these descendants in each generation being again brothers and sisters, and therefore husbands and wives, of one another.

The consanguine family is extinct. Even the most primitive peoples known to history provide no demonstrable instance of it. But that it *must* have existed, we are compelled to admit; for the Hawaiian system of consanguinity still prevalent today throughout the whole of Polynesia expresses degrees of consanguinity which could only arise in this form of family; and the whole subsequent development of the family presupposes the existence of the consanguine family as a necessary preparatory stage.

2. The Punaluan Family

If the first advance in organization consisted in the exclusion of parents and children from sexual intercourse with one another, the second was the exclusion of sister and brother. On account of the greater nearness in age, this second advance was infinitely more important, but also more difficult, than the first. It was effected gradually, beginning probably with the exclusion from sexual intercourse of one's own brothers and sisters (children of the same mother) first in isolated cases and then by degrees as a general rule (even in this century exceptions were found in Hawaii), and ending with the prohibition of marriage even between collateral brothers and sisters, or, as we should say, between first, second, and third cousins. It affords, says Morgan, "a good illustration of the operation of the principle of natural selection." There can be no question that the tribes among whom inbreeding was restricted by this advance were bound to develop more quickly and more fully than those among whom marriage between

brothers and sisters remained the rule and the law. How powerfully the influence of this advance made itself felt is seen in the institution which arose directly out of it and went far beyond it—the gens, which forms the basis of the social order of most, if not all, barbarian peoples of the earth and from which in Greece and Rome we step directly into civilization.

After a few generations at most, every original family was bound to split up. The practice of living together in a primitive communistic household which prevailed without exception till late in the middle stage of barbarism set a limit, varying with the conditions but fairly definite in each locality, to the maximum size of the family community. As soon as the conception arose that sexual intercourse between children of the same mother was wrong, it was bound to exert its influence when the old households split up and new ones were founded (though these did not necessarily coincide with the family group). One or more lines of sisters would form the nucleus of the one household and their own brothers the nucleus of the other. It must have been in some such manner as this that the form which Morgan calls the punaluan family originated out of the consanguine family. According to the Hawaiian custom, a number of sisters, natural or collateral (first, second or more remote cousins) were the common wives of their common husbands, from among whom, however, their own brothers were excluded. These husbands now no longer called themselves brothers, for they were no longer necessarily brothers, but *punalua*—that is, intimate companion, or partner. Similarly, a line of natural or collateral brothers had a number of women, *not* their sisters, as common wives, and these wives called one another *punalua*. This was the classic form of family structure [*Familienformation*], in which later a number of variations was possible, but whose essential feature was the mutually common possession of husbands and wives within a definite family circle, from which, however, the brothers of the wives—first one's own and later also collateral—and conversely also the sisters of the husbands, were excluded.

* * *

In all forms of group family, it is uncertain who is the father of a child; but it is certain who its mother is. Though she calls *all* the children of the whole family her children and has a mother's duties toward them, she nevertheless knows her own children from the others. It is therefore clear that in so far as group marriage prevails, descent can only be proved on the *mother's* side and that therefore only the *female* line is recognized. And this is in fact the case among all peoples in the period of savagery or in the lower stage of barbarism. . . .

If we now take one of the two standard groups of the punaluan family, namely a line of natural and collateral sisters (that is, one's own sisters' children in the first, second or more remote degree), together with their children and their own collateral brothers on the mother's side (who, according to our assumption, are *not* their husbands), we have the exact circle of persons whom we later find as members of a gens, in the original form of that institution. They all have a common ancestral mother, by virtue of their descent from whom the female offspring in each generation are sisters. The husbands of these sisters, however, can no longer be their brothers and therefore cannot be descended from the same ancestral mother; consequently, they do not belong to the same consanguine group, the later gens. The children of these sisters, however, do belong to this group, because descent on the mother's side alone counts, since it alone is certain. As soon as the ban had been established on sexual intercourse between all brothers and sisters, including the most remote collateral relatives on the mother's side, this group transformed itself into a gens—that is, it constituted itself as a firm circle of blood relations in the female line between whom marriage was prohibited; and henceforward by other common institutions of a social

and religious character, it increasingly consolidated and differentiated itself from the other gentes of the same tribe (more of this later). When we see, then, that the development of the gens follows, not only necessarily, but also perfectly naturally from the punaluan family, we may reasonably infer that at one time this form of family almost certainly existed among all peoples among whom the presence of gentile institutions can be proved—that is, practically all barbarians and civilized peoples.

* * *

3. The Pairing Family

A certain amount of pairing, for a longer or shorter period, already occurred in group marriage or even earlier; the man had a chief wife among his many wives (one can hardly yet speak of a favorite wife), and for her he was the most important among her husbands. This fact has contributed considerably to the confusion of the missionaries, who have regarded group marriage sometimes as promiscuous community of wives, sometimes as unbridled adultery. But these customary pairings were bound to grow more stable as the gens developed and the classes of "brothers" and "sisters" between whom marriage was impossible became more numerous. The impulse given by the gens to the prevention of marriage between blood relatives extended still further. Thus among the Iroquois and most of the other Indians at the lower stage of barbarism, we find that marriage is prohibited between *all* relatives enumerated in their system—which includes several hundred degrees of kinship. The increasing complication of these prohibitions made group marriages more and more impossible; they were displaced by the *pairing family*. In this stage, one man lives with one woman, but the relationship is such that polygamy and occasional infidelity remain the right of the men, even though for economic reasons polygamy is rare, while from the woman the strictest fidelity is generally demanded throughout the time she lives with the man and adultery on her part is cruelly punished. The marriage tie can, however, be easily dissolved by either partner; after separation, the children still belong as before to the mother alone.

*   *   *

Thus the history of the family in primitive times consists in the progressive narrowing of the circle, originally embracing the whole tribe, within which the two sexes have a common conjugal relation. The continuous exclusion, first of nearer, then of more and more remote relatives, and at last even of relatives by marriage, ends by making any kind of group marriage practically impossible. Finally, there remains only the single, still loosely linked pair, the molecule with whose dissolution marriage itself ceases. This in itself shows what a small part individual sex love, in the modern sense of the word, played in the rise of monogamy. Yet stronger proof is afforded by the practice of all peoples at this stage of development. Whereas in the earlier forms of the family, men never lacked women but, on the contrary, had too many rather than too few, women had now become scarce and highly sought after. Hence it is with the pairing marriage that there begins the capture and purchase of women—widespread *symptoms*, but no more than symptoms, of the much deeper change that had occurred.

*   *   *

The pairing family, itself too weak and unstable to make an independent household necessary or even desirable, in no wise destroys the communistic household inherited from earlier times. Communistic housekeeping, however, means the supremacy of women in the house; just as the exclusive recognition of the female parent, owing to the impossibility of recognizing the male parent with certainty, means that the women—the mothers—are held in high respect. One of the most absurd notions taken over from 18th century enlightenment is that in the beginning of society woman was the slave of man. Among all savages and all barbarians of the lower and middle stages, and to a certain extent of the upper stage also, the position of women is not only free, but honorable. As to what it still is in the pairing marriage, let us hear the evidence of Ashur Wright, for many years missionary among the Iroquois Senecas:

As to their family system, when occupying the old long houses [communistic households comprising several families], it is probable that some one clan [gens] predominated, the women taking in husbands, however, from the other clans [gentes]. . . . Usually, the female portion ruled the house. . . . The stores were in common; but woe to the luckless husband or lover who was too shiftless to do his share of the providing. No matter how many children, or whatever goods he might have in the house, he might at any time be ordered to pick up his blanket and budge; and after such orders it would not be healthful for him to attempt to disobey. The house would be too hot for him; and . . . he must retreat to his own clan [gens]; or, as was often done, go and start anew matrimonial alliance in some other. The women were the great power among the clans [gentes]; as everywhere else. They did not hesitate, when occasion required, "to knock off the horns," as it was technically called, from the head of a chief, and send him back to the ranks of the warriors.

The communistic household, in which most or all of the women belong to one and the same gens, while the men come from various gentes, is the material foundation of that supremacy of the women which was general in primitive times, and which it is Bachofen's third great merit to have discovered. The reports of travelers and missionaries, I may add, to the effect that women among savages and barbarians are overburdened with work in no way contradict what has been said. The division of labor between the two sexes is determined by quite other causes than by the position of woman in society. Among peoples where the women have to work far harder than we think suitable, there is often much more real respect for women than among our Europeans. The lady of civilization, surrounded by false homage and estranged from all real work, has an infinitely lower social position than the hard-working woman of barbarism, who was regarded among her people as a real lady (lady, *frowa*, *Frau*—mistress) and who was also a lady in character.

* * *

The first beginnings of the pairing family appear on the dividing line between savagery and barbarism; they are generally to be found already at the upper stage of savagery, but occasionally not until the lower stage of barbarism. The pairing family is the form characteristic of barbarism, as group marriage is characteristic of savagery and monogamy of civilization. To develop it further, to strict monogamy, other causes were required than those we have found active hitherto. In the single pair the group was already reduced to its final unit, its two-atom molecule: one man and one woman. Natural selection, with its progressive exclusions from the marriage community, had accomplished its task; there was nothing more for it to do in this direction. Unless new, *social* forces came into play, there was no reason why a new form of family should arise from the single pair. But these new forces did come into play.

We now leave America, the classic soil of the pairing family. No sign allows us to conclude that a higher form of family developed here or that there was ever permanent monogamy anywhere in America prior to its discovery and conquest. But not so in the Old World.

Here the domestication of animals and the breeding of herds had developed a hitherto unsuspected source of wealth and created entirely new social relations. Up to the lower stage of barbarism, permanent wealth had consisted almost solely of house, clothing, crude ornaments and the tools for obtaining and preparing food— boat, weapons, and domestic utensils of the simplest kind. Food had to be won afresh day by day. Now, with their herds of horses, camels, asses, cattle, sheep, goats, and pigs, the advancing pastoral peoples—the Semites on the Euphrates and the Tigris, and the Aryans in the Indian country of the Five Streams (Punjab), in the Ganges region, and in the steppes then much more abundantly watered by the Oxus and the Jaxartes—had acquired property which only needed supervision and the rudest care to reproduce itself in steadily increasing quantities and to supply the most abundant food in the form of milk and meat. All former means of procuring food now receded into the background; hunting, formerly a necessity, now became a luxury.

But to whom did this new wealth belong? Originally to the gens, without a doubt. Private property in herds must have already started at an early period, however. Is it difficult to say whether the author of the so-called first book of Moses regarded the patriarch Abraham as the owner of his herds in his own right as head of a family community or by right of his position as actual hereditary head of a gens. What is certain is that we must not think of him as a property owner in the modern sense of the word. And it is also certain that at the threshold of authentic history we already find the herds everywhere separately owned by heads of families, as are the artistic products of barbarism (metal implements, luxury articles and, finally, the human cattle—the slaves).

For now slavery had also been invented. To the barbarian of the lower stage, a slave was valueless. Hence the treatment of defeated enemies by the American Indians was quite different from that at a higher stage. The men were killed or adopted as brothers into the tribe of the victors; the women were taken as wives or otherwise adopted with their surviving children. At this stage human labor power still does not produce any considerable surplus over and above its maintenance costs. That was no longer the case after the introduction of cattle breeding, metalworking, weaving and, lastly, agriculture. Just as the wives whom it had formerly been so easy to obtain had now acquired an exchange value and were bought, so also with labor power, particularly since the herds had definitely become family possessions. The family did not multiply so rapidly as the cattle. More people were needed to look after them; for this purpose use could be made of the enemies captured in war, who could also be bred just as easily as the cattle themselves.

Once it had passed into the private possession of families and there rapidly begun to augment, this wealth dealt a severe blow to the society founded on pairing marriage and the matriarchal gens. Pairing marriage had brought a new element into the family. By the side of the natural mother of the child it placed its natural and attested father with a better warrant of paternity, probably, than that of many a "father" today. According to the division of labor within the family at that time, it was the man's part to obtain food and the instruments of labor necessary for the purpose. He therefore also owned the instruments of labor, and in the event of husband and wife separating, he took them with him, just as she retained her household goods. Therefore, according to the social custom of the time, the man was also the owner of the new source of subsistence, the cattle, and later of the new instruments of labor, the slaves. But according to the custom of the same society, his children could not inherit from him. For as regards inheritance, the position was as follows:

At first, according to mother right—so long, therefore, as descent was reckoned only in the female line—and according to the original custom of inheritance within the gens, the gentile relatives inherited from a deceased fellow member of their gens. His property had to remain within the gens. His effects being insignificant, they probably always passed in practice to his nearest gentile relations—that is, to his blood relations on the mother's side. The children of the dead man, however, did not belong

to his gens, but to that of their mother; it was from her that they inherited, at first conjointly with her other blood-relations, later perhaps with rights of priority; they could not inherit from their father because they did not belong to his gens within which his property had to remain. When the owner of the herds died, therefore, his herds would go first to his brothers and sisters and to his sister's children, or to the issue of his mother's sisters. But his own children were disinherited.

Thus on the one hand, in proportion as wealth increased it made the man's position in the family more important than the woman's, and on the other hand created an impulse to exploit this strengthened position in order to overthrow, in favor of his children, the traditional order of inheritance. This, however, was impossible so long as descent was reckoned according to mother right. Mother right, therefore, had to be overthrown, and overthrown it was. This was by no means so difficult as it looks to us today. For this revolution—one of the most decisive ever experienced by humanity—could take place without disturbing a single one of the living members of a gens. All could remain as they were. A simple decree sufficed that in the future the offspring of the male members should remain within the gens, but that of the female should be excluded by being transferred to the gens of their father. The reckoning of descent in the female line and the matriarchal law of inheritance were thereby overthrown, and the male line of descent and the paternal law of inheritance were substituted for them. As to how and when this revolution took place among civilized peoples, we have no knowledge. It falls entirely within prehistoric times. But that it *did* take place is more than sufficiently proved by the abundant traces of mother right which have been collected.

* * *

The overthrow of mother right was the world historical defeat of the female sex. The man took command in the home also; the woman was degraded and reduced to servitude; she became the slave of his lust and a mere instrument for the production of children. This degraded position of the woman, especially conspicuous among the Greeks of the heroic and still more of the classical age, has gradually been palliated and glossed over, and sometimes clothed in a milder form; in no sense has it been abolished.

The establishment of the exclusive supremacy of the man shows its effects first in the patriarchal family, which now emerges as an intermediate form. . . .

Its essential features are the incorporation of unfree persons and paternal power; hence the perfect type of this form of family is the Roman. The original meaning of the word "family" (*familia*) is not that compound of sentimentality and domestic strife which forms the ideal of the present-day philistine; among the Romans it did not at first even refer to the married pair and their children but only to the slaves. *Famulus* means domestic slave, and *familia* is the total number of slaves belonging to one man. . . . The term was invented by the Romans to denote a new social organism whose head ruled over wife and children and a number of slaves, and was invested under Roman paternal power with rights of life and death over them all.

* * *

Such a form of family shows the transition of the pairing family to monogamy. In order to make certain of the wife's fidelity and therefore of the paternity of the children, she is delivered over unconditionally into the power of the husband; if he kills her, he is only exercising his rights.

* * *

4. The Monogamous Family

It develops out of the pairing family, as previously shown, in the transitional period between the upper and middle stages of barbarism; its decisive victory is one of the signs that civiliza-

tion is beginning. It is based on the supremacy of the man, the express purpose being to produce children of undisputed paternity; such paternity is demanded because these children are later to come into their father's property as his natural heirs. It is distinguished from pairing marriage by the much greater strength of the marriage tie, which can no longer be dissolved at either partner's wish. As a rule, it is now only the man who can dissolve it and put away his wife. The right of conjugal infidelity also remains secured to him, at any rate by custom. . . .

We meet this new form of the family in all its severity among the Greeks. While the position of the goddesses in their mythology, as Marx points out, refers to an earlier period when the position of women was freer and more respected, in the heroic age we find the woman already being humiliated by the domination of the man and by competition from girl slaves. Note how Telemachus in the *Odyssey* silences his mother. In Homer young women are booty and are handed over to the pleasure of the conquerors, the handsomest being picked by the commanders in order of rank; the entire *Iliad*, it will be remembered, turns on the quarrel of Achilles and Agamemnon over one of these slaves. If a hero is of any importance, Homer also mentions the captive girl with whom he shares his tent and his bed. These girls were also taken back to Greece and brought under the same roof as the wife, as Cassandra was brought by Agamemnon in Aeschylus; the sons begotten of them received a small share of the paternal inheritance and had the full status of freemen. Teucer, for instance, is a natural son of Telamon by one of these slaves and has the right to use his father's name. The legitimate wife was expected to put up with all this, but herself to remain strictly chaste and faithful. In the heroic age a Greek woman is, indeed, more respected than in the period of civilization, but to her husband she is after all nothing but the mother of his legitimate children and heirs, his chief housekeeper and the supervisor of his female slaves, whom he can and does take as concubines if he so fancies. It is the existence of slavery side by side with monogamy, the presence of young, beautiful slaves belonging unreservedly to the *man*, that stamps monogamy from the very beginning with its specific character of monogamy *for the woman only*, but not for the man. And that is the character it still has today.

* * *

In *Euripides* [Orestes] a woman is called an *oikurema*, a thing (the word is neuter) for looking after the house, and, apart from her business of bearing children, that was all she was for the Athenian—his chief female domestic servant. The man had his athletics and his public business from which women were barred; in addition, he often had female slaves at his disposal and during the most flourishing days of Athens an extensive system of prostitution which the state at least favored. It was precisely through this system of prostitution that the only Greek women of personality were able to develop, and to acquire that intellectual and artistic culture by which they stand out as high above the general level of classic womanhood as the Spartan women by their qualities of character. But that a woman had to be a *hetaera* before she could be a woman is the worst condemnation of the Athenian family.

* * *

This is the origin of monogamy as far as we can trace it back among the most civilized and highly developed people of antiquity. It was not in any way the fruit of individual sex love, with which it had nothing whatever to do; marriages remained as before marriages of convenience. It was the first form of the family to be based not on natural but on economic conditions—on the victory of private property over primitive, natural communal property. The Greeks themselves put the matter quite frankly: the sole exclusive aims of monogamous marriage were to make the man supreme in the family and to propagate, as the future heirs to his wealth, children indisputably his own. Otherwise, marriage was

a burden, a duty which had to be performed whether one liked it or not to gods, state, and one's ancestors. In Athens the law exacted from the man not only marriage but also the performance of a minimum of so-called conjugal duties.

Thus when monogamous marriage first makes its appearance in history, it is not as the reconciliation of man and woman, still less as the highest form of such a reconciliation. Quite the contrary monogamous marriage comes on the scene as the subjugation of the one sex by the other; it announces a struggle between the sexes unknown throughout the whole previous prehistoric period. In an old unpublished manuscript written by Marx and myself in 1846, I find the words: "The first division of labor is that between man and woman for the propagation of children." And today I can add: The first class opposition that appears in history coincides with the development of the antagonism between man and woman in monogamous marriage, and the first class oppression coincides with that of the female sex by the male. Monogamous marriage was a great historical step forward; nevertheless, together with slavery and private wealth, it opens the period that has lasted until today in which every step forward is also relatively a step backward, in which prosperity and development for some is won through the misery and frustration of others. It is the cellular form of civilized society in which the nature of the oppositions and contradictions fully active in that society can be already studied.

* * *

If monogamy was the only one of all the known forms of the family through which modern sex love could develop, that does not mean that within monogamy modern sexual love developed exclusively or even chiefly as the love of husband and wife for each other. That was precluded by the very nature of strictly monogamous marriage under the rule of the man. Among all historically active classes—that is, among all ruling classes—matrimony remained what it had been since the pairing marriage, a matter of convenience which was arranged by the parents. The first historical form of sexual love as passion, a passion recognized as natural to all human beings (at least if they belonged to the ruling classes), and as the highest form of the sexual impulse—and that is what constitutes its specific character—this first form of individual sexual love, the chivalrous love of the middle ages, was by no means conjugal. Quite the contrary, in its classic form among the Provençals, it heads straight for adultery, and the poets of love celebrated adultery. The flowers of Provençal love poetry are the Albas [songs of dawn], in German, *Tagelieder*. They describe in glowing colors how the knight lies in bed beside his love—the wife of another—while outside stands the watchman who calls to him as soon as the first gray of dawn (*alba*) appears so that he can get away unobserved; the parting scene then forms the climax of the poem. The northern French and also the worthy Germans adopted this kind of poetry together with the corresponding fashion of chivalrous love. . . . Sex love in the relationship with a woman becomes and can only become the real rule among the oppressed classes, which means today among the proletariat—whether this relation is officially sanctioned or not. But here all the foundations of typical monogamy are cleared away. Here there is no property, for the preservation and inheritance of which monogamy and male supremacy were established; hence there is no incentive to make this male supremacy effective. What is more, there are no means of making it so. Bourgeois law, which protects this supremacy, exists only for the possessing class and their dealings with the proletarians. The law costs money and, on account of the worker's poverty, it has no validity for his relation to his wife. Here quite other personal and social conditions decide. And now that large-scale industry has taken the wife out of the home onto the labor market and into the factory, and made her often the breadwinner of the family, no basis for any kind of male supremacy is left in the proletarian household, except, perhaps, for something of the brutality toward women that has spread since the introduction of monogamy. The proletarian family is therefore no longer monogamous in the strict sense, even where there is passionate love and firmest loyalty on both sides and maybe all the blessings of religious and civil authority. Here, therefore, the eternal attendants of monogamy, hetaerism and adultery, play only an almost vanishing part. The wife has in fact regained the right to dissolve the marriage, and if two people cannot get on with one another, they prefer to separate. In short, proletarian marriage is monogamous in the etymological sense of the word, but not at all in its historical sense.

Our jurists, of course, find that progress in legislation is leaving women with no further ground of complaint. Modern civilized systems of law increasingly acknowledge first, that for a marriage to be legal it must be a contract freely entered into by both partners and secondly, that also in the married state both partners must stand on a common footing of equal rights and duties. If both these demands are consistently carried out, say the jurists, women have all they can ask.

This typically legalist method of argument is exactly the same as that which the radical republican bourgeois uses to put the proletarian in his place. The labor contract is to be freely entered into by both partners. But it is considered to have been freely entered into as soon as the law makes both parties equal on *paper*. The power conferred on the one party by the difference of class position, the pressure thereby brought to bear on the other party—the real economic position of both—that is not the law's business. Again, for the duration of the labor contract, both parties are to have equal rights in so far as one or the other does not expressly surrender them. That economic relations compel the worker to surrender even the last semblance of equal rights—here again, that is no concern of the law.

In regard to marriage, the law, even the most advanced, is fully satisfied as soon as the partners have formally recorded that they are entering into the marriage of their own free consent. What goes on in real life behind the juridical scenes, how this free consent comes about—that is not the business of the law and the jurist. And yet the most elementary comparative jurisprudence should show the jurist what this free consent really amounts to. In the countries where an obligatory share of the paternal inheritance is secured to the children by law and they cannot therefore be disinherited —in Germany, in the countries with French law and elsewhere—the children are obliged to obtain their parents' consent to their marriage. In the countries with English law, where parental consent to a marriage is not legally required, the parents on their side have full freedom in the testamentary disposal of their property and can disinherit their children at their pleasure. It is obvious that in spite and precisely because of this fact freedom of marriage among the classes with something to inherit is in reality not a whit greater in England and America than it is in France and Germany.

As regards the legal equality of husband and wife in marriage, the position is no better. The legal inequality of the two partners bequeathed to us from earlier social conditions is not the cause but the effect of the economic oppression of the woman. In the old communistic household, which comprised many couples and their children, the task entrusted to the women of managing the household was as much a public, a socially necessary industry as the procuring of food by the men. With the patriarchal family and still more with the single monogamous family, a change came. Household management lost its public character. It no longer concerned society. It became a *private service*; the wife became the head servant, excluded from all participation in social production. Not until the coming of modern large-scale industry was the road to social production opened to her again—and then only to the proletarian wife. But it was opened in such a manner that, if she carries out her duties in the private service of her family, she remains excluded from public production and unable to earn; and if she wants to take part in public production and earn independently, she cannot carry out family duties. And the wife's position in the factory is the position of women in all branches of business, right up to medicine and the law. The modern individual family is founded on the open or concealed domestic slavery of the wife, and modern society is a mass composed of these individual families as its molecules.

In the great majority of cases today, at least in the possessing classes, the husband is obliged to earn a living and support his family, and that in itself gives him a position of supremacy without any need for special legal titles and privileges. Within the family he is the bourgeois, and the wife represents the proletariat. In the industrial world, the specific character of the economic oppression burdening the proletariat is visible in all its sharpness only when all special legal privileges of the capitalist class have been abolished and complete legal equality of both classes established. The democratic republic does not do away with the opposition of the two classes; on the contrary, it provides the clear field on which the fight can be fought out. And in the same way, the peculiar character of the supremacy of the husband over the wife in the modern family, the necessity of creating real social equality between them and the way to do it, will only be seen in the clear light of day when both possess legally complete equality of rights. Then it will be plain that the first condition for the liberation of the wife is to bring the whole female sex back into public industry, and that this in turn demands that the characteristic of the monogamous family as the economic unit of society be abolished.

* * *

We are now approaching a social revolution in which the economic foundations of monogamy as they have existed hitherto will disappear just as surely as those of its complement—prostitution. Monogamy arose from the concentration of considerable wealth in the hands of a single individual—a man—and from the need to bequeath this wealth to the children of that man and of no other. For this purpose, the monogamy of the woman was required, not that of the man, so this monogamy of the woman did not in any way interfere with open or concealed polygamy on the part of the man. But by transforming by far the greater portion, at any rate, of permanent, heritable wealth—the means of production—into social property, the coming social revolution will reduce to a minimum all this anxiety about bequeathing and inheriting. Having arisen from economic causes, will monogamy then disappear when these causes disappear?

One might answer, not without reason: far from disappearing, it will on the contrary begin to be realized completely. For with the transformation of the means of production into social property there will disappear also wage labor, the proletariat, and therefore the necessity for a certain—statistically calculable—number of women to surrender themselves for money. Prostitution disappears; monogamy, instead of collapsing, at last becomes a reality—also for men.

In any case, therefore, the position of men will be very much altered. But the position of women, of *all* women, also undergoes significant change. With the transfer of the means of production into common ownership, the single family ceases to be the economic unit of society. Private housekeeping is transformed into a social industry. The care and education of the children becomes a public affair; society looks after all children alike, whether they are legitimate or not. This removes all the anxiety about the "consequences," which today is the most essential social—moral as well as economic—factor that prevents a girl from giving herself completely to the man she loves. Will not that suffice to bring about the gradual growth of unconstrained sexual intercourse and with it a more tolerant public opinion in regard to a maiden's honor and a woman's shame? And finally, have we not seen that in the modern world monogamy and prostitution are indeed contradictions, but inseparable contradictions, poles of the same state of society? Can prostitution disappear without dragging monogamy with it into the abyss?

Here a new element comes into play, an element which at the time when monogamy was developing existed at most in embryo—individual sex love.

* * *

As sexual love is by its nature exclusive—although at present this exclusiveness is fully realized only in the woman—the marriage based on sexual love is by its nature individual marriage. . . . If now the economic considerations disappear which made women put up with the habitual infidelity of their husbands—concern for their own means of existence and still more for their children's future—then, according to all previous experience, the equality of woman thereby achieved will tend infinitely more to make men really monogamous than to make women polyandrous.

But what will quite certainly disappear from monogamy are all the features stamped upon it through its origin in property relations; these are, in the first place, supremacy of the man and secondly, the indissolubility of marriage. The supremacy of the man in marriage is the simple consequence of his economic supremacy, and with the abolition of the latter will disappear of itself. The indissolubility of marriage is partly a consequence of the economic situation in which monogamy arose, partly tradition from the period when the connection between this economic situation and monogamy was not yet fully understood and was carried to extremes under a religious form. Today it is already broken through at a thousand points. If only the marriage based on love is moral, then also only the marriage is moral in which love continues. But the intense emotion of individual sex love varies very much in duration from one individual to another, especially among men, and if affection definitely comes to an end or is supplanted by a new passionate love, separation is a benefit for both partners as well as for society—only people will then be spared having to wade through the useless mire of a divorce case.

What we can now conjecture about the way in which sexual relations will be ordered after the impending overthrow of capitalist production is mainly of a negative character, limited for the most part to what will disappear. But what will there be new? That will be answered when a new generation has grown up: a generation of men who never in their lives have known what it is to buy a woman's surrender with money or any other social instrument of power; a generation of women who have never known what it is to give themselves to a man from any other considerations than real love or to refuse to give themselves to their lover from fear of the economic consequences. When these people are in the world, they will care precious little what anybody today thinks they ought to do; they will make their own practice and their corresponding public opinion about the practice of each individual—and that will be the end of it.

The Unhappy Marriage of Marxism and Feminism: Towards a More Progressive Union

Heidi Hartmann

The "marriage" of marxism and feminism has been like the marriage of husband and wife depicted in English common law: marxism and feminism are one, and that one is marxism. Recent attempts to integrate marxism and feminism are unsatisfactory to us as feminists because they subsume the feminist struggle into the "larger" struggle against capital. To continue our simile further, either we need a healthier marriage or we need a divorce.

The inequalities in this marriage, like most social phenomena, are no accident. Many marxists typically argue that feminism is at best less important than class conflict and at worst divisive of the working class. This political stance produces an analysis that absorbs feminism into the class struggle. Moreover, the analytic power of marxism with respect to capital has obscured its limitations with respect to sexism. We will argue here that while marxist anal-

Reprinted from *Women and Revolution* edited by Lydia Sargent and *Feminist Theory: From Margin to Center* by Bell Hooks with permission from the publisher, South End Press, 116 Saint Botolph St., Boston, MA 02115 U.S.A.

ysis provides essential insight into the laws of historical development, and those of capital in particular, the categories of marxism are sex-blind. Only a specifically feminist analysis reveals the systemic character of relations between men and women. Yet feminist analysis by itself is inadequate because it has been blind to history and insufficiently materialist. Both marxist analysis, particularly its historical and materialist method, and feminist analysis, especially the identification of patriarchy as a social and historical structure, must be drawn upon if we are to understand the development of western capitalist societies and the predicament of women within them. In this essay we suggest a new direction for marxist feminist analysis.

* * *

1. MARXISM AND THE WOMAN QUESTION

The woman question has never been the "feminist question." The feminist question is directed at the causes of sexual inequality between women and men, of male dominance over women. Most marxist analyses of women's position take as their question the relationship of women to the economic system, rather than that of women to men, apparently assuming the latter will be explained in their discussion of the former. Marxist analysis of the woman question has taken several forms. All see women's oppression in our connection (or lack of it) to production. Defining women as part of the working class, these analyses consistently subsume women's relation to men under workers' relation to capital.

*   *   *

All attempt to include women in the category working class and to understand women's oppression as another aspect of class oppression. In doing so all give short shrift to the object of feminist analysis, the relations between women and men. While our "problems" have been elegantly analyzed, they have been misunderstood. The focus of marxist analysis has been class relations; the object of marxist analysis has been understanding the laws of motion of capitalist society. While we believe marxist methodology *can* be used to formulate feminist strategy, these marxist feminist approaches discussed above clearly do not do so; their marxism clearly dominates their feminism.

As we have already suggested, this is due in part to the analytical power of marxism itself. Marxism is a theory of the development of class society, of the accumulation process in capitalist societies, of the reproduction of class dominance, and of the development of contradictions and class struggle. Capitalist societies are driven by the demands of the accumulation process, most succinctly summarized by the fact that production is oriented to exchange, not use. In a capitalist system production is important only insofar as it contributes to the making of profits, and the use value of products is only an incidental consideration. Profits derive from the capitalists' ability to exploit labor power, to pay laborers less than the value of what they produce. The accumulation of profits systematically transforms social structure as it transforms the rela-

tions of production. The reserve army of labor, the poverty of great numbers of people and the near-poverty of still more, these human reproaches to capital are by-products of the accumulation process itself. From the capitalist's point of view, the reproduction of the working class may "safely be left to itself." At the same time, capital creates an ideology, which grows up along side it, of individualism, competitiveness, domination, and in our time, consumption of a particular kind. Whatever one's theory of the genesis of ideology one must recognize these as the dominant values of capitalist societies.

Marxism enables us to understand many aspects of capitalist societies: the structure of production, the generation of a particular occupational structure, and the nature of the dominant ideology. Marx's theory of the development of capitalism is a theory of the development of "empty places." Marx predicted, for example, the growth of the proletariat and the demise of the petit bourgeoisie. More precisely and in more detail, Braverman among others has explained the creation of the "places" clerical worker and service worker in advanced capitalist societies. Just as capital creates these places indifferent to the individuals who fill them, the categories of marxist analysis, class, reserve army of labor, wage-laborer, do not explain why particular people fill particular places. They give no clues about why *women* are subordinate to *men* inside and outside the family and why it is not the other way around. *Marxist categories, like capital itself, are sex-blind.* The categories of marxism cannot tell us who will fill the empty places. Marxist analysis of the woman question has suffered from this basic problem.

*   *   *

II. RADICAL FEMINISM AND PATRIARCHY

The great thrust of radical feminist writing has been directed to the documentation of the slogan "the personal is political." Women's discontent, radical feminists argued, is not the neurotic lament of the maladjusted, but a response to a social structure in which women are systematically dominated, exploited, and oppressed. Women's inferior position in the labor market, the male-centered emotional structure of middle class marriage, the use of women in advertising, the so-called understanding of women's psyche as neurotic—popularized by academic and clinical psychology—aspect after aspect of women's lives in advanced capitalist society was researched and analyzed. The radical feminist literature is enormous and defies easy summary. At the same time, its focus on psychology is consistent. The New York Radical Feminists' organizing document was "The Politics of the Ego." "The personal is political" means for radical feminists, that the original and basic class division is between the sexes, and that the motive force of history is the striving of men for power and domination over women, the dialectic of sex.

Accordingly, Firestone rewrote Freud to understand the development of boys and girls into men and women in terms of power. Her characterizations of what are "male" and "female" character traits are typical of radical feminist writing. The male seeks power and domination; he is egocentric and individualistic, competitive and pragmatic; the "technological mode," according to Firestone, is male. The female is nurturant, artistic, and philosophical; the "aesthetic mode" is female.

No doubt, the idea that the aesthetic mode is female would have come as quite a shock to the ancient Greeks. Here lies the error of radical feminist analysis: the dialectic of sex as radical feminists present it projects male and female characteristics as they appear in the present back into all of history. Radical feminist analysis has greatest strength in its insights into the present. Its greatest weakness is a focus on the psychological which blinds it to history.

The reason for this lies not only in radical feminist method, but also in the nature of pa-triarchy itself, for patriarchy is a strikingly resilient form of social organization. Radical feminists use patriarchy to refer to a social system characterized by male domination over women. Kate Millett's definition is classic:

our society . . . is a patriarchy. The fact is evident at once if one recalls that the military, industry, technology, universities, science, political offices, finances—in short, every avenue of power within the society, including the coercive force of the police, is entirely in male hands.[1]

This radical feminist definition of patriarchy applies to most societies we know of and cannot distinguish among them. The use of history by radical feminists is typically limited to providing examples of the existence of patriarchy in all times and places. For both marxist and mainstream social scientists before the women's movement, patriarchy referred to a system of relations between men, which formed the political and economic outlines of feudal and some pre-feudal societies, in which hierarchy followed ascribed characteristics. Capitalist societies are understood as meritocratic, bureaucratic, and impersonal by bourgeois social scientists; marxists see capitalist societies as systems of class domination. For both kinds of social scientists neither the historical patriarchal societies nor today's western capitalist societies are understood as systems of relations between men that enable them to dominate women.

Towards a Definition of Patriarchy

We can usefully define patriarchy as a set of social relations between men, which have a material base, and which, though hierarchical, establish or create interdependence and solidarity among men that enable them to dominate women. Though patriarchy is hierarchical and men of different classes, races, or ethnic groups have different places in the patriarchy, they also are united in their shared relationship of dominance over their women; they are dependent on each other to maintain that domination. Hierarchies "work" at least in part because they create vested interests in the status quo. Those at the higher levels can "buy off" those at the lower levels by offering them power over those still lower. In the hierarchy of patriarchy, all men, whatever their rank in the patriarchy, are bought off by being able to control at least some women. There is some evidence to suggest that when patriarchy was first institutionalized in state societies, the ascending rulers literally made men the heads of their families (enforcing their control over their wives and children) in exchange for the men's ceding some of their tribal resources to the new rulers. Men are dependent on one another (despite their hierarchical ordering) to maintain their control over women.

The material base upon which patriarchy rests lies most fundamentally in men's control over women's labor power. Men maintain this control by excluding women from access to some essential productive resources (in capitalist societies, for example, jobs that pay living wages) and by restricting women's sexuality. Monogamous heterosexual marriage is one relatively recent and efficient form that seems to allow men to control both these areas. Controlling women's access to resources and their sexuality, in turn, allows men to control women's labor power, both for the purpose of serving men in many personal and sexual ways and for the purpose of rearing children. The services women render men, and which exonerate men from having to perform many unpleasant tasks (like cleaning toilets) occur outside as well as inside the family setting. Examples outside the family include the harrassment of women workers and students by male bosses and professors as well as the common use of secretaries to run personal errands, make coffee, and provide "sexy" surroundings. Rearing children, whether or not the children's labor power is of immedi-

ate benefit to their fathers, is nevertheless a crucial task in perpetuating patriarchy as a system. Just as class society must be reproduced by schools, work places, consumption norms, etc., so must patriarchal social relations. In our society children are generally reared by women at home, women socially defined and recognized as inferior to men, while men appear in the domestic picture only rarely. Children raised in this way generally learn their places in the gender hierarchy well. Central to this process, however, are the areas outside the home where patriarchal behaviors are taught and the inferior position of women enforced and reinforced: churches, schools, sports, clubs, unions, armies, factories, offices, health centers, the media, etc.

The material base of patriarchy, then, does not rest solely on childrearing in the family, but on all the social structures that enable men to control women's labor. The aspects of social structures that perpetuate patriarchy are theoretically identifiable, hence separable from their other aspects. Gayle Rubin has increased our ability to identify the patriarchal element of these social structures enormously by identifying "sex/gender systems":

a "sex/gender system" is the set of arrangements by which a society transforms biological sexuality into products of human activity, and in which these transformed sexual needs are satisfied.[2]

We are born female and male, biological sexes, but we are created woman and man, socially recognized genders. *How* we are so created is that second aspect of the *mode* of production of which Engels spoke, "the production of human beings themselves, the propagation of the species."

How people propagate the species is socially determined. If, biologically, people are sexually polymorphous, and society were organized in such a way that all forms of sexual expression were equally permissible, reproduction would result only from some sexual encounters, the heterosexual ones. The strict division of labor by sex, a social invention common to all known societies, creates two very separate genders and a need for men and women to get together for economic reasons. It thus helps to direct their sexual needs toward heterosexual fulfillment, and helps to ensure biological reproduction. In more imaginative societies, biological reproduction might be ensured by other techniques, but the division of labor by sex appears to be the universal solution to date. Although it is theoretically possible that a sexual division of labor not imply inequality between the sexes, in most known societies, the socially acceptable division of labor by sex is one which accords lower status to women's work. The sexual division of labor is also the underpinning of sexual subcultures in which men and women experience life differently; it is the material base of male power which is exercised (in our society) not just in not doing housework and in securing superior employment, but psychologically as well.

How people meet their sexual needs, how they reproduce, how they inculcate social norms in new generations, how they learn gender, how it feels to be a man or a woman—all occur in the realm Rubin labels the sex/gender system. Rubin emphasizes the influence of kinship (which tells you with whom you can satisfy sexual needs) and the development of gender specific personalities via childrearing and the "oedipal machine." In addition, however, we can use the concept of the sex/gender system to examine all other social institutions for the roles they play in defining and reinforcing gender hierarchies. Rubin notes that theoretically a sex/gender system could be female dominant, male dominant, or egalitarian, but declines to label various known sex/gender systems or to periodize history accordingly. We choose to label our present sex/gender system patriarchy, because it appropriately captures the notion of hierarchy and male dominance which we see as central to the present system.

Economic production (what marxists are used to referring to as *the* mode of production) and the production of people in the sex/gender sphere both determine "the social organization under which the people of a particular historical epoch and a particular country live," according to Engels. The whole of society, then, can be understood by looking at both these types of production and reproduction, people and things. There is no such thing as "pure capitalism," nor does "pure patriarchy" exist, for they must of necessity coexist. What exists is patriarchal capitalism, or patriarchal feudalism, or egalitarian hunting/gathering societies, or matriarchal horticultural societies, or patriarchal horticultural societies, and so on. There appears to be no necessary connection between *changes* in the one aspect of production and changes in the other. A society could undergo transition from capitalism to socialism, for example, and remain patriarchal. Common sense, history, and our experience tell us, however, that these two aspects of production are so closely intertwined, that change in one ordinarily creates movement, tension, or contradiction in the other.

Racial hierarchies can also be understood in this context. Further elaboration may be possible along the lines of defining color/race systems, arenas of social life that take biological color and turn it into a social category, race. Racial hierarchies, like gender hierarchies, are aspects of our social organization, of how people are produced and reproduced. They are not fundamentally ideological; they constitute that second aspect of our mode of production, the production and reproduction of people. It might be most accurate then to refer to our societies not as, for example, simply capitalist, but as patriarchal capitalist white supremacist. In Part III below, we illustrate one case of capitalism adapting to and making use of racial orders and several examples of the interrelations between capitalism and patriarchy.

Capitalist development creates the places

for a hierarchy of workers, but traditional marxist categories cannot tell us who will fill which places. Gender and racial hierarchies determine who fills the empty places. *Patriarchy is not simply hierarchical organization*, but hierarchy in which *particular* people fill *particular* places. It is in studying patriarchy that we learn why it is women who are dominated and how. While we believe that most known societies have been patriarchal, we do not view patriarchy as a universal, unchanging phenomenon. Rather patriarchy, the set of interrelations among men that allow men to dominate women, has changed in form and intensity over time. It is crucial that the hierarchy among men, and their differential access to patriarchal benefits, be examined. Surely, class, race, nationality, and even marital status and sexual orientation, as well as the obvious age, come into play here. And women of different class, race, national, marital status, or sexual orientation groups are subjected to different degrees of patriarchal power. Women may themselves exercise class, race, or national power, or even patriarchal power (through their family connections) over men lower in the patriarchal hierarchy than their own male kin.

To recapitulate, we define patriarchy as a set of social relations which has a material base and in which there are hierarchical relations between men and solidarity among them which enable them in turn to dominate women. The material base of patriarchy is men's control over women's labor power. That control is maintained by excluding women from access to necessary economically productive resources and by restricting women's sexuality. Men exercise their control in receiving personal service work from women, in not having to do housework or rear children, in having access to women's bodies for sex, and in feeling powerful and being powerful. The crucial elements of patriarchy as we *currently* experience them are: heterosexual marriage (and consequent homophobia), female childrearing and housework, women's

economic dependence on men (enforced by arrangements in the labor market), the state, and numerous institutions based on social relations among men—clubs, sports, unions, professions, universities, churches, corporations, and armies. All of these elements need to be examined if we are to understand patriarchal capitalism.

Both hierarchy and interdependence among men and the subordination of women are *integral* to the functioning of our society; that is, these relationships are *systemic*. We leave aside the question of the creation of these relations and ask, can we recognize patriarchal relations in capitalist societies? Within capitalist societies we must discover those same bonds between men which both bourgeois and marxist social scientists claim no longer exist or are, at the most, unimportant leftovers. Can we understand how these relations among men are perpetuated in capitalist societies? Can we identify ways in which patriarchy has shaped the course of capitalist development?

III. THE PARTNERSHIP OF PATRIARCHY AND CAPITAL

How are we to recognize patriarchal social relations in capitalist societies? It appears as if each woman is oppressed by her own man alone; her oppression seems a private affair. Relationships among men and among families seem equally fragmented. It is hard to recognize relationships among men, and between men and women, as *systematically* patriarchal. We argue, however, that patriarchy as a system of relations between men and women exists in capitalism, and that in capitalist societies a healthy and strong partnership exists between patriarchy and capital. Yet if one begins with the concept of patriarchy and an understanding of the capitalist mode of production, one recognizes immediately that the partnership of patriarchy and capital was not inevitable; men and capitalists often have conflicting interests, particularly over the use of women's labor power. Here is one way in which this conflict might manifest itself: the vast majority of men might want their women at home to personally service them. A smaller number of men, who are capitalists, might want most women (not their own) to work in the wage labor market. In examining the tensions of this conflict over women's labor power historically, we will be able to identify the material base of patriarchal relations in capitalist societies, as well as the basis for the partnership between capital and patriarchy.

Industrialization and the Development of Family Wages

Marxists made quite logical inferences from a selection of the social phenomena they witnessed in the nineteenth century. But marxists ultimately underestimated the strength of the preexisting patriarchal social forces with which fledgling capital had to contend and the need for capital to adjust to these forces. The industrial revolution was drawing all people into the labor force, including women and children; in fact the first factories used child and female labor almost exclusively. That women and children could earn wages separately from men both undermined authority relations (as discussed in Part I above) and kept wages low for everyone. Kautsky, writing in 1892, describes the process this way:

[Then with] the wife and young children of the working-man . . . able to take care of themselves, the wages of the male worker can safely be reduced to the level of his own personal needs without the risk of stopping the fresh supply of labor power.
The labor of women and children, moreover, affords the additional advantage that these are less capable of resistance than men [sic]; and their introduction into the ranks of the workers increases tremendously the quantity of labor that is offered for sale in the market.
Accordingly, the labor of women and children . . . also diminishes [the] capacity [of the male

worker] for resistance in that it overstocks the market; owing to both these circumstances it lowers the wages of the working-man.[3]

The terrible effects on working class family life of low wages and of forced participation of all family members in the labor force were recognized by marxists. Kautsky wrote:

The capitalist system of production does not in most cases destroy the single household of the working-man, but robs it of all but its unpleasant features. The activity of woman today in industrial pursuits . . . means an increase of her former burden by a new one. *But one cannot serve two masters.* The household of the working-man suffers whenever his wife must help to earn the daily bread.[4]

Working men as well as Kautsky recognized the disadvantages of female wage labor. Not only were women "cheap competition" but working women were their very wives, who could not "serve two masters" well.

Male workers resisted the wholesale entrance of women and children into the labor force, and sought to exclude them from union membership and the labor force as well. In 1846 the *Ten Hours' Advocate* stated:

It is needless for us to say, that all attempts to improve the morals and physical condition of female factory workers will be abortive, unless their hours are materially reduced. Indeed we may go so far as to say, that married females would be much better occupied in performing the domestic duties of the household, than following the never-tiring motion of machinery. We therefore hope the day is not distant, when the husband will be able to provide for his wife and family, without sending the former to endure the drudgery of a cotton mill.[5]

In the United States in 1854 the National Typographical Union resolved not to "encourage by its act the employment of female compositors." Male unionists did not want to afford union protection to women workers; they tried to exclude them instead. In 1879 Adolph Strasser, president of the Cigarmakers International Union, said: "We cannot drive the females out of the trade, but we can restrict their daily quota of labor through factory laws."

While the problem of cheap competition could have been solved by organizing the wage earning women and youths, the problem of disrupted family life could not be. Men reserved union protection for men and argued for protective labor laws for women and children. Protective labor laws, while they may have ameliorated some of the worst abuses of female and child labor, also limited the participation of adult women in many "male" jobs. Men sought to keep high wage jobs for themselves and to raise male wages generally. They argued for wages sufficient for their wage labor alone to support their families. This "family wage" system gradually came to be the norm for stable working class families at the end of the nineteenth century and the beginning of the twentieth. Several observers have declared the non-wage-working wife to be part of the standard of living of male workers. Instead of fighting for equal wages for men and women, male workers sought the family wage, wanting to retain their wives' services at home. In the absence of patriarchy a unified working class might have confronted capitalism, but patriarchal social relations divided the working class, allowing one part (men) to be bought off at the expense of the other (women). Both the hierarchy between men and the solidarity among them were crucial in this process of resolution. Family wages may be understood as a resolution of the conflict over women's labor power which was occurring between patriarchal and capitalist interests at that time.

Family wages for most adult men imply men's acceptance, and collusion in, lower wages for others, young people, women and socially defined inferior men as well (Irish, blacks, etc., the lowest groups in the patriarchal hierarchy who are denied many of the patriarchal benefits). Lower wages for women and children and inferior men are enforced by job segregation in the labor market, in turn maintained by unions and management as well as by auxiliary institutions like schools, training programs, and even families. Job segregation by sex, by insuring that women have the lower paid jobs, both assures women's economic dependence on men and reinforces notions of appropriate spheres for women and men. For most men, then, the development of family wages, secured the material base of male domination in two ways. First, men have the better jobs in the labor market and earn higher wages than women. The lower pay women receive in the labor market both perpetuates men's material advantage over women and encourages women to choose wifery as a career. Second, then, women do housework, childcare, and perform other services at home which benefit men directly. Women's home responsibilities in turn reinforce their inferior labor market position.

The resolution that developed in the early twentieth century can be seen to benefit capitalist interests as well as patriarchal interests. Capitalists, it is often argued, recognized that in the extreme conditions which prevailed in the early nineteenth century industrialization, working class families could not adequately reproduce themselves. They realized that housewives produced and maintained healthier workers than wage-working wives and that educated children became better workers than noneducated ones. The bargain, paying family wages to men and keeping women home, suited the capitalists at the time as well as the male workers. Although the terms of the bargain have altered over time, it is still true that the family and women's work in the family serve capital by providing a labor force and serve men as the space in which they exercise their privilege. Women, working to serve men and their families, also serve capital as consumers. The family is also the place where dominance and submission are learned, as Firestone, the Frankfurt School, and many others have explained. Obedient children become obedient workers; girls and boys each learn their proper roles.

While the family wage shows that capitalism adjusts to patriarchy, the changing status of children shows that patriarchy adjusts to capital. Children, like women, came to be excluded from wage labor. As children's ability to earn money declined, their legal relationship to their parents changed. At the beginning of the industrial era in the United States, fulfilling children's need for their fathers was thought to be crucial, even primary, to their happy development; fathers had legal priority in cases of contested custody. As children's ability to contribute to the economic well-being of the family declined, mothers came increasingly to be viewed as crucial to the happy development of their children, and gained legal priority in cases of contested custody. Here patriarchy adapted to the changing economic role of children: when children were productive, men claimed them; as children became unproductive, they were given to women.

The Family and the Family Wage Today

We argued above, that, with respect to capitalism and patriarchy, the adaptation, or mutual accommodation, took the form of the development of the family wage in the early twentieth century. The family wage cemented the partnership between patriarchy and capital. Despite women's increased labor force participation, particularly rapid since World War II, the family wage is still, we argue, the cornerstone of the present sexual division of labor—in which women are primarily responsible for housework and men primarily for wage work. Women's lower wages in the labor market (combined with the need for children to be reared by someone) assure the continued existence of the family as a necessary income pooling unit. The family, supported by the family wage, thus allows the control of women's labor by men both within and without the family.

Though women's increased wage work may cause stress for the family (similar to the stress Kautsky and Engels noted in the nineteenth century), it would be wrong to think that as a consequence, the concepts and the realities of the family and of the sexual division of labor will soon disappear. The sexual division of labor reappears in the labor market, where women work at women's jobs, often the very jobs they used to do only at home—food preparation and service, cleaning of all kinds, caring for people, and so on. As these jobs are low-status and low-paying patriarchal relations remain intact, though their material base shifts somewhat from the family to the wage differential, from family-based to industrially-based patriarchy.

Industrially based patriarchal relations are enforced in a variety of ways. Union contracts which specify lower wages, lesser benefits, and fewer advancement opportunities for women are not just atavistic hangovers—a case of sexist attitudes or male supremacist ideology—they maintain the material base of the patriarchal system. While some would go so far as to argue that patriarchy is already absent from the family (see, for example, Stewart Ewen, *Captains of Consciousness*), we would not. Although the terms of the compromise between capital and patriarchy are changing as additional tasks formerly located in the family are capitalized, and the location of the deployment of women's labor power shifts, it is nevertheless true, as we have argued above, that the wage differential caused by extreme job segregation in the labor market reinforces the family, and, with it, the domestic division of labor, by encouraging women to marry. The "ideal" of the family wage—that a man can earn enough to support an entire family—may be giving way to a new ideal that both men and women contribute through wage earning to the cash income of the family. The wage differential, then, will become increasingly necessary in perpetuating patriarchy, the male control of women's labor power. The wage differential will aid in *defining* women's work as secondary to men's at the same time it necessitates women's actual continued economic dependence on men. The sexual division of labor in the labor market and elsewhere should be understood as a manifestation of patriarchy which serves to perpetuate it.

Many people have argued that though the partnership between capital and patriarchy exists now, it may *in the long run* prove intolerable to capitalism; capital may eventually destroy both familial relations and patriarchy. The argument proceeds logically that capitalist social relations (of which the family is not an example) tend to become universalized, that women will become increasingly able to earn money and will increasingly refuse to submit to subordination in the family, and that since the family is oppressive particularly to women and children, it will collapse as soon as people can support themselves outside it.

We do not think that the patriarchal relations embodied in the family can be destroyed so easily by capital, and we see little evidence that the family system is presently disintegrating. Although the increasing labor force participation of women has made divorce more feasible, the incentives to divorce are not overwhelming for women. Women's wages allow very few women to support themselves and their children independently and adequately. The evidence for the decay of the traditional family is weak at best. The divorce rate has not so much increased, as it has evened out among classes; moreover, the remarriage rate is also very high. Up until the 1970 census, the first-marriage age was continuing its historic decline. Since 1970 people seem to have been delaying marriage and childbearing, but most recently, the birth rate has begun to increase again. It is true that larger proportions of the population are now living outside traditional families.

Young people, especially, are leaving their parents' homes and establishing their own households before they marry and start traditional families. Older people, especially women, are finding themselves alone in their own households, after their children are grown and they experience separation or death of a spouse. Nevertheless, trends indicate that the new generations of young people will form nuclear families at some time in their adult lives in higher proportions than ever before. The cohorts, or groups of people, born since 1930 have much higher rates of eventual marriage and childrearing than previous cohorts. The duration of marriage and childrearing may be shortening, but its incidence is still spreading.

The argument that capital destroys the family also overlooks the social forces which make family life appealing. Despite critiques of nuclear families as psychologically destructive, in a competitive society the family still meets real needs for many people. This is true not only of long-term monogamy, but even more so for raising children. Single parents bear both financial and psychic burdens. For working class women, in particular, these burdens make the "independence" of labor force participation illusory. Single parent families have recently been seen by policy analysts as transitional family formations which become two-parent families upon remarriage.

It could be that the effects of women's increasing labor force participation are found in a declining sexual division of labor within the family, rather than in more frequent divorce, but evidence for this is also lacking. Statistics on who does housework, even in families with wage-earning wives, show little change in recent years; women still do most of it. The double day is a reality for wage-working women. This is hardly surprising since the sexual division of labor outside the family, in the labor market, keeps women financially dependent on men—even when they earn a wage themselves. The future of patriarchy does not, however, rest solely on the future of familial relations. For patriarchy, like capital, can be surprisingly flexible and adaptable.

Whether or not the patriarchal division of labor, inside the family and elsewhere, is "ultimately" intolerable to capital, it is shaping capitalism now. As we illustrate below, patriarchy both legitimates capitalist control and delegitimates certain forms of struggle against capital.

Ideology in the Twentieth Century

Patriarchy, by establishing and legitimating hierarchy among men (by allowing men of all groups to control at least some women), reinforces capitalist control, and capitalist values shape the definition of patriarchal good.

*   *   *

If we examine the characteristics of men as radical feminists describe them—competitive, rationalistic, dominating—they are much like our description of the dominant values of capitalist society.

This "coincidence" may be explained in two ways. In the first instance, men, as wage laborers, are absorbed in capitalist social relations at work, driven into the competition these relations prescribe, and absorb the corresponding values. The radical feminist description of men was not altogether out of line for capitalist societies. Secondly, even when men and women do not actually behave in the way sexual norms prescribe, men *claim for themselves* those characteristics which are valued in the dominant ideology. So, for example, the authors of *Crestwood Heights* found that while the men, who were professionals, spent their days manipulating subordinates (often using techniques that appeal to fundamentally irrational motives to elicit the preferred behavior), men and women characterized men as "rational and pragmatic." And while the women devoted great energies to studying

scientific methods of child-rearing and child development, men and women in Crestwood Heights characterized women as "irrational and emotional."

This helps to account not only for "male" and "female" characteristics in capitalist societies, but for the particular form sexist ideology takes in capitalist societies. Just as women's work serves the dual purpose of perpetuating male domination and capitalist production, so sexist ideology serves the dual purpose of glorifying male characteristics/capitalist values, and denigrating female characteristics/social need. If women were degraded or powerless in other societies, the reasons (rationalizations) men had for this were different. Only in a capitalist society does it make sense to look down on women as emotional or irrational. As epithets, they would not have made sense in the renaissance. Only in a capitalist society does it make sense to look down on women as "dependent." "Dependent" as an epithet would not make sense in feudal societies. Since the division of labor ensures that women as wives and mothers in the family are largely concerned with the production of use values, the denigration of these activities obscures capital's inability to meet socially determined need at the same time that it degrades women in the eyes of men, providing a rationale for male dominance. An example of this may be seen in the peculiar ambivalence of television commercials. On one hand, they address themselves to the real obstacles to providing for socially determined needs: detergents that destroy clothes and irritate skin, shoddily made goods of all sorts. On the other hand, concern with these problems must be denigrated; this is accomplished by mocking women, the workers who must deal with these problems.

A parallel argument demonstrating the partnership of patriarchy and capitalism may be made about the sexual division of labor in the work force. The sexual division of labor places women in low-paying jobs, and in tasks thought to be appropriate to women's role. Women are teachers, welfare workers, and the great majority of workers in the health fields. The nurturant roles that women play in these jobs are of low status because capitalism emphasizes personal independence and the ability of private enterprise to meet social needs, emphases contradicted by the need for collectively provided social services. As long as the social importance of nurturant tasks can be denigrated because women perform them, the confrontation of capital's priority on exchange value by a demand for use values can be avoided. In this way, it is not feminism, but sexism that divides and debilitates the working class.

IV. TOWARDS A MORE PROGRESSIVE UNION

Many problems remain for us to explore. Patriarchy as we have used it here remains more a descriptive term than an analytic one. If we think marxism alone inadequate, and radical feminism itself insufficient, then we need to develop new categories. What makes our task a difficult one is that the same features, such as the division of labor, often reinforce both patriarchy and capitalism, and in a thoroughly patriarchal capitalist society, it is hard to isolate the mechanisms of patriarchy. Nevertheless, this is what we must do. We have pointed to some starting places: looking at who benefits from women's labor power, uncovering the material base of patriarchy, investigating the mechanisms of hierarchy and solidarity among men. The questions we must ask are endless.

*   *   *

Feminism and the Class Struggle

*   *   *

The struggle against capital and patriarchy cannot be successful if the study and practice of the issues of feminism is abandoned. A struggle aimed only at capitalist relations of oppression will fail, since their underlying supports in pa-

triarchal relations of oppression will be overlooked. And the analysis of patriarchy is essential to a definition of the kind of socialism useful to women. While men and women share a need to overthrow capitalism they retain interests particular to their gender group. It is not clear—from our sketch, from history, or from male socialists—that the socialism being struggled for is the same for both men and women. For a humane socialism would require not only consensus on what the new society should look like and what a healthy person should look like, but more concretely, it would require that men relinquish their privilege.

As women we must not allow ourselves to be talked out of the urgency and importance of our tasks, as we have so many times in the past. We must fight the attempted coercion, both subtle and not so subtle, to abandon feminist objectives.

This suggests two strategic considerations. First, a struggle to establish socialism must be a struggle in which groups with different interests form an alliance. Women should not trust men to liberate them after the revolution, in part, because there is no reason to think they would know how; in part, because there is no necessity for them to do so. In fact their immediate self-interest lies in our continued oppression. Instead we must have our own organizations and our own power base. Second, we think the sexual division of labor within capitalism has given women a practice in which we have learned to understand what human interdependence and needs are. While men have long struggled *against* capital, women know what to struggle *for*. As a general rule, men's position in patriarchy and capitalism prevents them from recognizing both human needs for nurturance, sharing, and growth, and the potential for meeting those needs in a nonhierarchical, nonpatriarchal society. But even if we raise their consciousness, men might assess the potential gains against the potential losses and choose the status quo. Men have more to lose than their chains.

As feminist socialists, we must organize a practice which addresses both the struggle against patriarchy and the struggle against capitalism. We must insist that the society we want to create is a society in which recognition of interdependence is liberation rather than shame, nurturance is a universal, not an oppressive practice, and in which women do not continue to support the false as well as the concrete freedoms of men.

NOTES

1. Kate Millett, *Sexual Politics* (New York: Avon Books, 1971), p. 25.

2. Gayle Rubin, "The Traffic in Women," in *Anthropology of Women*, ed. Reiter, p. 159.

3. Karl Kautsky, *The Class Struggle* (New York: Norton, 1971), pp. 25-26.

4. We might add, "outside the household," Kautsky, *Class Struggle*, p. 26, our emphasis.

5. Cited in Neil Smelser, *Social Change and the Industrial Revolution* (Chicago: University of Chicago Press. 1959), p. 301.

Comparable Worth, Incomparable Pay

Teresa Amott and Julie Matthaei

A central issue in the Yale strike was "comparable worth." Local 34, 82 percent women, demanded pay increases on the basis of the argument that their clerical and technical work receives lower pay than other jobs at Yale which require a comparable level of skill, training, and responsibility—because it is done by women. For example, clerical workers average $13,424, compared to $18,500 for Yale truck drivers. After one year of work, a lab assistant is paid $10,208, compared to $14,394 for a dishwasher. This the workers claim, is unjust, a not-so-subtle form of sex discrimination. As the largest group of predominantly female workers to strike over the issue of comparable worth, Local 34 is at the forefront of the feminist-inspired battle for "pay equity." What follows is an introduction to the concept of comparable worth, and a discussion of its strengths and limitations. We feel that comparable worth can contribute to a socialist-feminist agenda by raising fundamental questions about the worth of work and by increasing the income of many women workers. Nonetheless, it suffers from the limitations of any piecemeal reform and needs to be pursued as part of a broader program of demands.

From *Radical America* (1984). Reprinted by permission.

The Emergence of the Comparable Worth Strategy

When the Equal Pay Act of 1963 prohibited unequal pay for equal work and the broader Civil Rights Act of 1964 set affirmative action into motion, many assumed that the gap between men and women's wages would close. Instead, the average salary for a woman working full-time year-round remained roughly 60 percent of the salary earned by a man. The constancy of the wage gap in the face of anti-discrimination legislation drew attention to the fact that women and men rarely hold the same jobs. Traditional sex roles and outright sex discrimination by employers and workers have had the result of excluding women from most occupations other than homemaking and its labor market extensions. Those paid occupations open to women shared low pay, few opportunities for advancement, and often centered around nurturing and serving others. Throughout the decade of the 1970s, over 40 percent of all women workers were concentrated in ten occupations, most of which were over 70 percent female—for example, nursing, secretarial and clerical work, teaching, and food service. In contrast, men, especially white men, had more job options and more opportunity for high pay and promotion. For instance, stock clerks, predominantly male, earn more than bank tellers, who are predominantly female, and registered nurses earn less than mail carriers. As a result of this occupational segregation, legislation prohibiting unequal pay for equal jobs failed to address the heart of pay inequity between the sexes: men and women earning unequal pay for different jobs.

The idea of comparable worth was devised to raise women's wages in female-dominated occupations up to the level paid in male occupations of "comparable worth." Also known as pay equity, comparable worth means that jobs deemed to be of "equal value to the employer" should pay the same, regardless of their sex or race-typing. The first wage comparability case before the courts was based on race. However, subsequent attempts to apply the Civil Rights Act to non-identical jobs have focused on wage differences origins from gender-based job segregation.

Some of the first attempts to broaden the concept of equal pay emerged during World War II, when unions such as the UAW and the IUE fought differential pay for men and women workers in order to prevent an overall reduction in pay scales and to generate greater unity between men and women workers. Since then, the ranks of pay equity advocates have grown and a more feminist construction has been placed on the concept. Women's rights groups, working women's organizations and unions representing women workers are currently pursuing three strategies for achieving comparable worth corrections to pay inequities based on sex or color: litigation, collective bargaining, and legislation. Often a combination of these strategies is utilized by pay equity advocates.

Litigation. Prior to a 1981 Supreme Court decision, the courts were uniformly unfriendly to charges of sex discrimination in pay across different jobs. In Denver, where nurses charged discrimination because the city paid them less than tree trimmers and sign painters, the judge ruled against the nurses, arguing that the doctrine of comparable worth was "pregnant with the possibility of disrupting the entire economic system." In 1981, however, the Supreme Court ruled that Title VII of the 1964 Civil Rights Act could be applied to prohibit wage differences in similar, but not identical, jobs. Since then, there have been lower court decisions, such as one in the state of Washington, which have awarded back pay to women whose jobs have been systematically undervalued.

Collective Bargaining. A variety of unions, including AFSCME, CWA, IUE, SEIU, UAW, UE and others, have adopted pay equity as a goal in bargaining, as well as in membership education and lobbying. Most efforts have focused on public employees, largely because information on pay scales is more accessible, and state agencies may be more vulnerable to public pressure brought through community-labor alliances. Local 101 of AFSCME in San Jose, California, is one of the public sector success stories. These city employees struck to win a substantial pay increase and "special adjustments" to upgrade jobs held predominantly by women. Unions often combine litigation with bargaining, as in the case of an IUE local which won pay equity raises for women workers employed at a Massachusetts General Electric plant.

Legislation. Many states have adopted legislation calling for a pay equity study of state employment, and others, including California, Minnesota and Washington, have passed statutes which require public sector wages to be set on the basis of comparable worth. In Idaho, a law which assigns pay in state positions on the basis of skill and responsibility has produced a 16 percent increase in pay for female clerical workers. Other states have begun to raise wages in predominantly women's jobs without explicit recourse to comparable worth. In New Mexico, for instance, over $3 million was appropriated in 1983 to raise the wages of the lowest paid state employees, over 80 percent of them women, even though a job evaluation study has not yet been completed.

Implementing Comparable Worth

The primary mechanism for implementing comparable worth in wage structures is the job analysis/job evaluation study, and efforts for pay equity usually involve ridding an existing study of inherent sex bias and/or demanding a formal job evaluation study where one does not exist.

Job evaluation studies were in use long before pay equity advocates recognized their potential in comparable worth struggles. Generally speaking, most large, bureaucratic firms and state agencies do not negotiate a wage directly with each employee, but rather assign an employee to a particular rung of a job ladder. The worker's position on the job ladder determines his or her wages. Workers in the same job would thus receive the same salary, while workers in different jobs would be paid differently. To determine pay scales, large firms use fairly systematic job analysis/evaluation schemes, often prepared by outside consultants. The first step of the study analyzes jobs through examination of job descriptions and, sometimes, discussions with workers. In the most common type of evaluation, known as a point-factor system, points are assigned to each job on the basis of criteria (factors) such as skills, effort, responsibility, and working conditions. In the final stage of the process, dollar values are assigned to the points in each category. The same procedures, and often the same consultants, are used for job evaluations in pay equity cases. In smaller firms, the process is much more informal, but rankings of jobs are still undertaken.

Despite the aura of objectivity surrounding these studies, there is no objective way to determine the relative productivity of jobs. Due to the division of labor, a myriad of different workers contribute to the output of any product, and it is impossible to distinguish their different contributions. How can one technically measure the relative importance of dietitians, nurses, or pharmacological staff to a hospital? Normally, hospital administrators pay market wages—the amount needed to attract workers—and infer the relative worth of these different workers from their wage rates. Job evaluation studies, on the other hand, attempt to determine relative productivity of jobs apart from the market. To do this, they must subjectively choose a set of factors and weights. There are many ways in which sex, race, and class bias can enter into the calculations.

One critical area is the selection and definition of factors to be evaluated. For example, it is common to define responsibility as supervisory responsibility over other workers, machines, or money. In this case, child care workers would receive low points for "responsibility" even though their jobs entail enormous responsibility for children under their care. Similarly, skilled activities such as nurturing and guidance are rarely counted, causing traditional women's jobs to receive lower points than men's jobs. Boredom from routinized work is not commonly considered worthy of point as an adverse working condition, although outdoor work and heavy lifting are.

Another critical area is the weighting of different factors, accomplished either through the number of points allocated to each factor or by the method which assigns dollars to points. This has the effect of determining the relative worth of different factors, and generally involves sophisticated statistical techniques such as multiple regression analysis. In effect, consulting firms specializing in job evaluations rely on previous correlations between existing pay scales and measured factor points to predict for new clients what a job's salary should be. From the perspective of the employer, the best point rankings are those which duplicate the existing pay hierarchy as closely as possible, since this seemingly "objective" technique can then be used to legitimize pay differentials. This means that job evaluation schemes usually embody existing pay practices, complete with sex, race, or gender bias. For example, the maximum number of points assigned for responsibility may be 2000, while adverse working conditions are awarded only a maximum of 200 points; this would ensure that managerial jobs pay more than service or operative jobs.

Despite these biased methods, current methods of evaluating jobs can still be used to win pay raises for those in "undervalued" work. For example, most studies have found that male and female jobs with equal point evaluations are paid differently because of the weighing of different factors mentioned above or because firms use different ranking schemes for different types of jobs. In these cases, legislation or bargaining agreements mandating equal pay for jobs of equal point value (under the same ranking scheme) can achieve somewhere between five and 25 percent pay increases.

Much more can be won by eliminating bias from the technique. This requires wide access to information about existing or contemplated job evaluation studies. We need to disseminate information on how consulting firms such as Hay Associates, which serves approximately 40 percent of the Fortune 500 companies, conduct their studies, and we need to bargain for input at all stages of the evaluation process. The more we involve ourselves in the technique, taking power from the technocrats, the more success we will have. Progress has already been achieved in this area. Most unions have staff members who are experts on the technique and feminist proponents of comparable worth are currently at work expanding the definitions of factors so as to recognize the value of women's traditional work skills. (One of the most important redefinitions has been the inclusion of responsibility for children as a compensable factor.) More work needs to be done to rid the method of race and class bias.

How Radical Is Comparable Worth?

While comparable worth directly challenges sexual inequality in the labor market, it may also have the potential for other radical change.

Comparable worth promises to undermine male supremacy outside the labor market as well. Feminists have long noted the way in which the lower wages of women have reinforced the traditional nuclear family and women's responsibility for unpaid work in the home.

As long as women are denied access to men's jobs, and few women's jobs pay a living wage, women are under strong economic pressure to marry. Married women's financial dependence upon their husbands contributes to sexual inequality within marriage. The economic costs of leaving or being left by one's husband are illustrated by the high percentage of women heading families on their own who live in poverty. The risk of poverty is highest for women of color; in 1982, 56.2 percent of black and 55.4 percent of Latino families headed by women were poor.

In addition, comparable worth subjects the pay structure to scrutiny it rarely receives. Conventional economic wisdom argues that in the "perfectly competitive market economy," workers are paid according to their "marginal product," that is, according to their contributions to the production process. (In graduate school, one of our teachers built models which assumed that women were 60 percent as productive as men, justifying this with the fact that full-time women workers earned on average, 60 percent as much as men!) Comparable worth debunks such convenient rationalizations of the pay structure, and the sexist assumptions they both reflect and create, by showing that the force behind pay differences has not been productivity differences but rather power and discrimination. Thus, it presents a radical critique of our system of income distribution through the "free market," and presents an alternative way of achieving what the market had promised: the distribution of income to workers according to their contributions in a manner which is fair and incentive-creating at the same time.

Finally, while comparable worth does not directly attack occupational segregation by sex, it may do so indirectly. On the one hand, by making traditionally feminine jobs palatable to women, comparable worth may reduce the incentives for women to seek entrance into male-dominated, more privileged jobs. On the other hand, as traditionally feminine jobs begin to offer wages comparable to those of masculine jobs, more men will find them attractive. Also, as women begin to fight for and expect working conditions comparable to those of men, they may find men's jobs more desirable, and be more willing to fight to get them.

Broadening the Comparable Worth Agenda

Comparable worth gains effectiveness and constituency when combined with other progressive demands.

Conservative economists have warned that raising wages for women's work would create uncontrollable inflation. While firms will try to increase their prices (and state agencies, their tax revenues), the inflationary impact would depend upon the magnitude and speed of the pay equity adjustment, as well as the ability of firms and governments to pass on the costs. (This, in turn, depends upon the degree of monopoly power and citizen resistance to tax increases.) Finally, inflation is not the worst of all evils, and can be limited by the use of wage price controls, long a demand of progressives.

What is more worrisome are the other possible reactions of firms and state agencies to an increase in the price of women's labor: automation, elimination of state programs, and runaway shops to countries in which women still provide a super-exploitable labor force. Already, computerization is threatening clerical workers

and job flight has created massive structural unemployment in the U.S. In order for comparable worth struggles not to exacerbate these problems, they must be pursued in conjunction with demands for job security, retraining, and plant-closing legislation.

So as to aid all undervalued workers, pay equity must also be extended to include comparisons between comparable but racially segregated jobs. Even this extension will not solve all workers' problems. Workers without jobs will not benefit, nor will workers in those jobs calculated to have the least worth. Since these are the main job problems faced by men of color, comparable worth offers little to them. Raising pay for women in certain jobs reduces inequality between women and men on the same level of the job hierarchy, but increases the relative poverty of those at the bottom of the hierarchy. Their problems can only be solved by a more comprehensive restructuring of work and by a deeper and more radical discussion of the worth of work.

As currently practiced, the doctrine of comparable worth accepts the idea of a hierarchy of workers, more or less "worthy" on the basis of some objective criteria. However, as radicals become involved in decisions about what factors should merit higher pay, we may well begin to question the rationale for the hierarchy itself. If the discussion of what makes work worthy is extended to the grass roots, we may well determine that all jobs are equally worthy. We may decide that workers in unskilled, routinized jobs may be doing the hardest work of all, for such work saps and denies their very humanity. Why should those whose jobs give them the most opportunity to develop and use their abilities also be paid the most? The traditional argument—that higher pay must be offered as an incentive for workers to gain skills and training—is contradicted by the fact that our highly paid jobs attract many more workers than employers demand. And given unequal access to education and training, a hierarchical pay scheme becomes a mechanism for the intergen-erational transmission of wealth privilege, with its historically-linked racism, sexism, and clas-sism.

We see comparable worth as one of the most innovative and promising approaches to redressing sexual inequality. In fact, given the present reactionary climate, it is one of the few struggles in which tangible progress against in-justice is being achieved. Furthermore, as we have pointed out, it raises larger questions about the fairness of the "free market" system, ques-tions which may even undermine the rationale for income inequality.

❧ Postmodern Feminism ❧

Woman's Word

Annie Leclerc

Nothing exists that has not been made by man—not thought, not language, not words. Even now, there is nothing that has not been made by man, not even me: especially not me.

We have to invent everything anew. Things made by man are not just stupid, deceitful and oppressive. More than anything else, they are sad, sad enough to kill us with boredom and despair.

We have to invent a woman's word. But not "of" woman, "about" woman, in the way that man's language speaks "of" woman. Any woman who wants to use a language that is specifically her own, cannot avoid this extraordinary, urgent task: we must invent woman.

It is crazy, I know. But it is the only thing that keeps me sane.

Whose voice is speaking these words? Whose voice has always spoken? Deafening tumult of important voices; and not one a woman's voice. I haven't forgotten the names of the great talk-ers. Plato, Aristotle and Montaigne, Marx and Freud and Nietzche. I know them because I've lived among them and among them alone. These strong voices are also those who have reduced me the most effectively to silence. It is these superb speakers who, more than any others, have forced me into silence.

Whose voice do we hear in those great, wise books we find in libraries? Who speaks in the Capitol? Who speaks in the temple? Who speaks in the lawcourts and whose voice is it that we hear in laws? Men's.

The world is man's word. Man is the word of the world.

No, no, I'm not making any demands. I am not tempted by the dignity of Man's status; it amuses me. When I consider Man, I am only playing.

And I say to myself: Man? What is Man? Man is what man brings into the world. We made children, they made Man.

They turned the specific into the universal. And the universal looks just like the specific.

Universality became their favourite ploy. One voice for all. With one voice, only one can speak. Man.

All I want is my voice.

You let me speak, yes, but I don't want

Reprinted from *French Connections: Voices from the Women's Movement in France*, ed., trnsl. by Claire Duchen (Amherst: University of Massachusetts Press, 1987) copyright © 1987 by Claire Duchen your voice. I want my own voice, I don't trust yours any more.

It is no longer enough to speak *about* myself for me to find a voice that is my own. Woman's literature: feminine literature, very feminine, with its exquisite feminine sensitivity. Man's literature is not masculine, with its exquisite masculine sensitivity. A man speaks in the name of Man. A woman in the name of women. But as it is man who has set out the 'truth' about us all, the truth about women, it is still man who speaks through woman's mouth.

The whole of feminine literature has been whispered to women in man's language. The whole range, all the melodies, of femininity, have already been played out.

Is it possible to invent anything new?

We have to invent: otherwise we'll perish.

This stupid, military, evil-smelling world marches on alone towards its destruction. Man's voice is a fabric full of holes, torn, frayed; a burned out voice.

However wide we open our eyes, however far we stretch our ears, from now on, the summits from where laws are made, male summits with all their sacred values, are lost in the thick fog of indifference and boredom. Which is when women open their mouths and begin to speak. From now on, no man's voice will come to cover up the multiple, vigorous voices of women.

But we still aren't there. In fact we won't get there unless woman manages to weave a fabric, whole and new, made of a voice springing from within herself. Because the voice can be new, but the words worn out. Watch out woman, pay attention to your words.

Let me say first of all where all this comes from. It comes from me, woman, from my woman's belly. It began in my belly, with small, slight, signs, hardly audible, when I was pregnant. I began to listen to this timid voice which had no words.

Who could tell me, could I ever express (and what words would I use), to speak of the extraordinary joy of pregnancy, the immense, terrible joy of childbirth.

That is how I first learned that my woman's body was the site of Dionysian celebrations of life.

So then I looked at men. For man, there is only one celebration of sexuality: intercourse. He doesn't want to hear about the others, the multiple celebrations of my body.

And this one celebration of his, he wants it all for himself. He demands that my necessary presence remain discreet and totally devoted to his pleasure.

Well it's too bad for him, but I must talk about the pleasures of my body, no, not those of my soul, my virtue or my feminine sensitivity, but the pleasures of my woman's belly, my woman's vagina, my woman's breasts, luxuriant pleasures that you can't even imagine.

I must talk about it, because only by talking about it will a new language be born, a woman's word.

I have to reveal everything that you have so determinedly hidden, because it was with that repression that all the others began. Everything that was ours, you converted to dirt, pain, duty, bitchiness, small-mindedness, servitude.

Once you had silenced us, you could do whatever you wanted with us, turn us into maid, goddess, plaything, mother hen, *femme fatale*. The only thing you demand really insistently is our silence: in fact, you could hardly demand anything more; beyond silence, you would have to demand our death.

It is our silence and the triumphant sound of your voice that authorized the theft of our labour, the rape of our bodies and all our silent slavery, our silent martyrdom. How can it be that we are now coming out of our coma, and that our tongues, though still sticky with respect for your values, are loosening up, slowly?

You had proclaimed the universality of

your language. Very good for asserting your power, but not so good for keeping it.

We listen, convinced, to those who say 'All men are born free and remain equal in their rights.'

And slowly we discover that the person who has nothing, has the right to nothing. Not to equality, nor to freedom. And we end up by demanding the letter of the law. Equality. Freedom.

My body flows with the vast rhythmic pulsation of life. My body experiences a cycle of changes. Its perception of time is cyclical, but never closed or repetitive.

Men, as far as I can judge, have a linear perception of time. From their birth to their death, the segment of time they occupy is straight. Nothing in their flesh is aware of time's curves. Their eyes, their pulse, neglect the seasons. They can only see History, they fight only for History. Their sexuality is linear: their penis becomes erect, stretches, ejaculates and becomes limp. That which makes them live kills them. They escape death only by a new life that in turn, kills them again.

My body speaks to me of another sense of time, another adventure. Thirteen times a year, I experience the cyclical changes of my body. Sometimes my body is completely forgotten. Not thinking about its pains or its pleasures, I come, I go, I work, I speak and my body is an abstraction. Sometimes, my body is there, present.

Ten, twelve days before my period, my breasts swell, become hardened. This seems, in my case, to follow ovulation, fertility. I can't say that this is always so, because other women say they experience this during their period or just before.

The nipple is tender, bright red, very sensitive. The slightest contact makes it harder. You say, friends say to each other, "My breasts are sore." Especially if you are worried that your period is late, and you are looking for any hopeful signs, you weigh your breasts in your hands, feel them, press them with anxious care, trying to force them to admit that they hurt, you say, you repeat, oh yes, they are sore. But it's not that. They don't hurt, it's just that we can feel them. They are alive, aroused, open to pain but not sore. They are also open to caresses, much more so than usual; continually caressable, strangely open to pleasure. When my period is due, my breasts are loving, avid, sensitive.

I haven't finished talking about my body yet. For it experiences still more wonders. Just because you aren't involved with them, does it mean that I must hide them under a hideous mask of pain and suffering? Do I have to feel bad because I take pleasure in experiences you can't know, to the point of denying myself this pleasure too?

You have poisoned my life. For centuries. Deprived of my body, I only knew how to live through you. Badly, hardly living. Slaving away, enduring, being silent and being pretty. My body there for work and for pleasing you; never for my own pleasure. My body, never my own, for me. Mouth sewn up, face made up. Vagina open when you want it, closed up with Tampax. Scoured, scraped, made hygienic, deodorized and re-odorized with rose-smelling perfume, it's too much, it's stifling me, I need my own body. That is what I mean by living.

You could say, well what are women complaining about since you say there are so many possibilities for them to be happy? It is because these possibilities that we have here and now are merely an anticipation of what could be possible in a radically different society, in which woman's status would also be changed. As would the way in which she is perceived by others.

I'm not saying to women, be happy; but only, do you know that you are capable of happiness?

But we have to understand everything that denies women's happiness—and which is not only her economic, sexual and familial oppression.

We know full well, because it is glaringly obvious, that women are denied happiness because they are overburdened with domestic tasks and with anxieties that postpone their pleasure in life indefinitely, almost until her death. When does a woman really have the chance to take pleasure in herself, in man, in the sun, the rain, the wind, in children, in the seasons, even in the home, when she is constantly harassed by the need to take care of—the housework, the dishes, the washing, the shopping, the ironing, the cooking?

When can she even glimpse the possibility of happiness when, already rushed off her feet, she adds the hardship and humiliation of a badly-paid job? We can't pretend that we don't know about all this, because it can't be hidden, we can *see it*.

But do we know enough about what else denies a woman happiness, maybe even more radically? Do we know the extent of a tyranny we can't see—we can't see it because we can see neither the person exercising it nor how it operates, nor exactly on what it operates?

Do we understand that, excluded from her body, kept in ignorance about the pleasures it contains, it is the ability to experience happiness that is missing?

If women are so politically apathetic, so persistently conservative, is it not also because they are incapable of imagining what their pleasure in living could be?

The only bodily pleasure they are aware of missing is the one which they see men indulge in, more often and better than they do: a properly sexual pleasure. But is their imagination so limited that they can't think of other pleasures? Are they so shortsighted that they can't see the source of their problems? Are they too humble, too lazy? If only they learned to find in themselves those joys from which the world is cut off, would their struggle not acquire a new vigour and a new, indispensable rigour? If only they knew that, if man made this world which is an oppressive world, it is up to women to prepare the coming of a different world, which would at last be a world of life.

Women will not be liberated as long as they do not also want to be liberating, by denouncing and by fighting *all* oppression, those that come from man, from power, from work, but also those that come from themselves and operate on themselves, on others and particularly on their children: disincarnated women, de-sexualized women, disinfected, disaffected, glossy magazine women, puppet women, but also women who are men's accomplices, accomplices of the strong man, the husband, boss, cop, and also jealous women, capricious and vengeful, bourgeois women, mean women, finally and above all, women the dragon of the family, women martyrs of devotion, voracious mother-hens, possessive and murderous mothers, odious step-mothers.

As long as we are somehow in complicity with man's oppressions, as long as we perpetuate them on to our children, turning them into vigorous oppressors or into docile victims, we will never, never be free.

Sorties

Hélène Cixous

Where is she?

> Activity/passivity,
> Sun/Moon,
> Culture/Nature,
> Day/Night,

> Father/Mother,
> Head/heart,
> Intelligible/sensitive,
> Logos/Pathos.

Form, convex, step, advance, seed, progress.
Matter, concave, ground—which supports the step, receptacle.

Man
_____

Woman

Always the same metaphor: we follow it, it transports us, in all of its forms, wherever a discourse is organized. The same thread, or double tress leads us, whether we are reading or speaking, through literature, philosophy, criticism, centuries of representation, of reflection.

_____
Reprinted from *New French Feminisms*, Elaine Marks and Isabelle de Courtivoron, eds. (Amherst: University of Massachusetts Press, 1980), copyright © 1980 by The University of Massachusetts Press.

Thought has always worked by opposition,
Speech/Writing
High/Low

By dual, *hierarchized*[1] oppositions. Superior/Inferior. Myths, legends, books. Philosophical systems. Wherever an ordering intervenes, a law organizes the thinkable by (dual, irreconcilable; or mitigable, dialectical) oppositions. And all the couples of oppositions are *couples*. Does this mean something? Is the fact that logocentrism subjects thought—all of the concepts, the codes, the values—to a two-term system, related to "the" couple man/woman?

> Nature/History,
> Nature/Art,
> Nature/Mind,
> Passion/Action.

Theory of culture, theory of society, the ensemble of symbolic systems—art, religion, family, language, —everything elaborates the same systems. And the movement by which each opposition is set up to produce meaning is the movement by which the couple is destroyed. A universal battlefield. Each time a war breaks out. Death is always at work.

Father/son   Relationships of authority, of privilege, of force.

Logos/writing   Relationships: opposition, conflict, relief, reversion.

Master/slave   Violence. Repression.

And we perceive that the "victory" always amounts to the same thing: it is hierarchized. The hierarchization subjects the entire conceptual organization to man. A male privilege, which can be seen in the opposition by which it sustains itself, between *activity* and *passivity*. Traditionally, the question of sexual difference is coupled with the same opposition: activity/passivity.

That goes a long way. If we examine the history of philosophy—in so far as philosophical discourse orders and reproduces all thought—we perceive[2] that: it is marked by an absolute constant, the orchestrator of values, which is precisely the opposition activity/passivity.

In philosophy, woman is always on the side of passivity. Every time the question comes up; when we examine kinship structures; whenever a family model is brought into play; in fact as soon as the ontological question is raised; as soon as you ask yourself what is meant by the question "What is it?"; as soon as there is a will to say something. A will: desire, authority, you examine that, and you are led right back—to the father. You can even fail to notice that there's no place at all for women in the operation! In the extreme the world of "being" can function to the exclusion of the mother. No need for mother—provided that there is something of the maternal: and it is the father then who acts as—is—the mother. Either the woman is passive; or she doesn't exist. What is left is unthinkable, unthought of. She does not enter into the oppositions, she is not coupled with the father (who is coupled with the son).

There is Mallarmé's[3] tragic dream, a father lamenting the mystery of paternity, which mourning tears out of the poet, the mourning of mournings, the death of the beloved son: this dream of a union between the father and the son—and no mother then. Man's dream is the face of death. Which always threatens him differently than it threatens woman.

"an alliance
a union, superb   And dream of masculine
—and the life   filiation, dream of God the father
remaining in me   emerging from himself
I shall use it   in his son, —and
to—   no mother then
so no mother then?"

She does not exist, she may be nonexistent; but there must be something of her. Of woman, upon whom he no longer depends, he retains only this space, always virginal, matter subjected to the desire that he wishes to imprint.

And if you examine literary history, it's the same story. It all refers back to man to *his* torment, his desire to be (at) the origin. Back to the father. There is an intrinsic bond between the philosophical and the literary (to the extent that it signifies, literature is commanded by the philosophical) and phallocentrism. The philosophical constructs itself starting with the abasement of woman. Subordination of the feminine to the masculine order which appears to be the condition for the functioning of the machine.

The challenging of this solidarity of logocentrism and phallocentrism has today become insistent enough—the bringing to light of the fate which has been imposed upon woman, of her burial—to threaten the stability of the masculine edifice which passed itself off as eternal-natural; by bringing forth from the world of femininity reflections, hypotheses which are necessarily ruinous for the bastion which still holds the authority. What would become of logocentrism, of the great philosophical systems, of world order in general if the rock upon which they founded their church were to crumble?

If it were to come out in a new day that the

logocentric project had always been, undeniably, to *found* (fund)[4] phallocentrism, to insure for masculine order a rationale equal to history itself?

Then all the stories would have to be told differently, the future would be incalculable, the historical forces would, will, change hands, bodies; another thinking as yet not thinkable will transform the functioning of all society. Well, we are living through this very period when the conceptual foundation of a millenial culture is in process of being undermined by millions of a species of mole as yet not recognized.

When they awaken from among the dead, from among the words, from among the laws. . . .

What does one give?

The specific difference that has determined the movement of history as a movement of property is articulated between two economies that define themselves in relation to the problematics of giving.

The (political) economy of the masculine and of the feminine is organized by different requirements and constraints, which, when socialized and metaphorized, produce signs, relationships of power, relationships of production and of reproduction, an entire immense system of cultural inscription readable as masculine or feminine.

I am careful here to use the *qualifiers* of sexual difference, in order to avoid the confusion man/masculine, woman/feminine: for there are men who do not repress their femininity, women who more or less forcefully inscribe their masculinity. The difference is not, of course, distributed according to socially determined "sexes." Furthermore, when I speak of political economy and of libidinal economy, in putting the two together, I am not bringing into play the false question of origin, that tall tale sustained by male privilege. We must guard against falling complacently or blindly into the essentialist ideological interpretation, as, for example, Freud and Jones, in different ways, ventured to do; in their quarrel over the subject of feminine sexuality, both of them, starting from opposite points of view, came to support the awesome thesis of a "natural," anatomical determination of sexual difference-opposition. And from there on, both implicitly support phallocentrism's position of power.

Let us review the main points of the opposing positions: [Ernest] Jones (in *Early Feminine Sexuality*), using an ambiguous approach, attacks the Freudian theses that make of woman an imperfect man.

For Freud:

1. the "fatality" of the feminine situation is a result of an anatomical "defectiveness."
2. there is only one libido, and its essence is male; the inscription of sexual difference begins only with a phallic phase which both boys and girls go through. Until then, the girl has been a sort of little boy: the genital organization of the infantile libido is articulated by the equivalence activity/masculinity; the vagina has not as yet been "discovered."
3. the first love object being, for both sexes, the mother, it is only for the boy that love of the opposite sex is "natural."

For Jones: Femininity is an autonomous "essence."

From the outset (starting from the age of six months) the girl has a *feminine* desire for her father; an analysis of the little girl's earliest fantasms would in fact show that, in place of the breast which is perceived as disappointing, it is the penis that is desired, or an object of the same form (by an analogical displacement). It follows, since we are already into the chain of substitutions, that in the series of partial objects, in place of the penis, would come the child—for in order to counter Freud, Jones docilely returns to the Freudian terrain. And then some. From the equation breast-penis-child, he concludes that the little girl experiences with regard to the father a primary desire. (And this would include the desire to have a child by the father as well.) And, of course, the girl also has a primary love for the opposite sex. She too, then, has a right to her Oedipal complex as a primary formation, and to the threat of mutilation by the mother. At last she is a woman, anatomically, without defect: her clitoris is not a minipenis. Clitoral masturbation is not, as Freud claims, a masculine practice. And it would seem in light of precocious fantasms that the vagina is discovered very early.

In fact, in affirming that there is a specific femininity (while in other respects preserving the theses of an orthodoxy) it is still phallocentrism that Jones reinforces, on the pretext of taking the part of femininity (and of God, who he recalls created them male and female—!). And bisexuality vanishes into the unbridged abyss that separates the opponents here.

As for Freud, if we subscribe to what he sets forth when he identifies with Napoleon in his article of 1933 on *The Disappearance of the Oedipus Complex*: "anatomy is destiny," then we participate in the sentencing to death of woman. And in the completion of all History.

That the difference between the sexes may have psychic consequences is undeniable. But they are surely not reducible to those designated by a Freudian analysis. Starting with the relationship of the two sexes to the Oedipal complex, the boy and the girl are oriented toward a division of social roles so that women "inescapably" have a lesser productivity, because they "sublimate" less than men and because symbolic activity, hence the production of culture, is men's doing.[5]

Freud moreover starts from what he calls the *anatomical* difference between the sexes. And we know how that is pictured in his eyes: as the difference between having/not having the phallus. With reference to these precious parts. Starting from what will be specified, by Lacan, as the transcendental signifier.

But *sexual difference* is not determined merely by the fantasized relationship to anatomy, which is based, to a great extent, upon the point of *view*, therefore upon a strange importance accorded [by Freud and Lacan] to exteriority and to the specular in the elaboration of sexuality. A voyeur's theory, of course.

No, it is at the level of sexual pleasure [*jouissance*] in my opinion that the difference makes itself most clearly apparent in as far as woman's libidinal economy is neither identifiable by a man nor referable to the masculine economy.

For me, the question "What does she want?" that they ask of woman, a question that in fact woman asks herself because they ask it of her, because precisely there is so little place in society for her desire that she ends up by dint of not knowing what to do with it, no longer knowing where to put it, or if she has any, conceals the most immediate and the most urgent question: "How do I experience sexual pleasure?" What is feminine *sexual pleasure*, where does it take place, how is it inscribed at the level of her body, of her unconscious? And then how is it put into writing?

We can go on at length about a hypothetical prehistory and about a matriarchal era. Or we can, as did Bachofen,[6] attempt to reconstitute a gynecocratic society, and to deduce from it poetic and mythical effects that have a powerfully subversive import with regard to the family and to male power.

All the other ways of depicting the history of power, property, masculine domination, the constitution of the State, the ideological apparatus have their effectiveness. But the change taking place has nothing to do with question of "origin." Phallocentrism *is*. History has never produced, recorded anything but that. Which does not mean that this form is inevitable or natural. Phallocentrism is the enemy. Of *everyone*. Men stand to lose by it, differently but as seriously as women. And it is time to transform. To invent the other history.

There is no such thing as "destiny," "nature," or essence, but living structures, caught up, sometimes frozen within historicocultural limits which intermingle with the historical scene to such a degree that it has long been impossible and is still difficult to think or even to imagine something else. At present, we are living through a transitional period—where the classical structure appears as if it might crack.

To predict what will happen to sexual difference—in another time (in two or three hundred years?) is impossible. But there should be no misunderstanding: men and women are caught up in a network of millenial cultural determinations of a complexity that is practically unanalyzable: we can no more talk about "woman" than about "man" without getting caught up in an ideological theater where the multiplication of representations, images, reflections, myths, identifications constantly transforms, deforms, alters each person's imaginary order and in advance, renders all conceptualization null and void.

There is no reason to exclude the possibility of radical transformations of behavior, mentalities, roles, and political economy. The effects of these transformations on the libidinal economy are unthinkable today. Let us imagine simultaneously a *general* change in all of the structures of formation, education, framework, hence of reproduction, of ideological effects, and let us imagine a real liberation of sexuality, that is, a transformation of our relationship to our body (—and to another body), an approximation of the immense material organic sensual universe that we are, this not being possible, of course, without equally radical political transformations (imagine!). Then "femininity," "masculinity," would inscribe their effects of difference, their economy, their relationships to expenditure, to deficit, to giving, quite differently. That which appears as "feminine" or "masculine" today would no longer

amount to the same thing. The general logic of difference would no longer fit into the opposition that still dominates. The difference would be a crowning display of new differences.

But we are still floundering about—with certain exceptions—in the Old order.

The masculine future:

There are exceptions. There always have been those uncertain, poetic beings, who have not let themselves be reduced to the state of coded mannequins by the relentless repression of the homosexual component. Men or women, complex, mobile, open beings. Admitting the component of the other sex makes them at once much richer, plural, strong, and to the extent of this mobility, very fragile. We invent only on this condition: thinkers, artists, creators of new values, "philosophers" of the mad Nietzschen sort, inventors and destroyers of concepts, of forms, the changers of life cannot but be agitated by singularities—complementary or contradictory. This does not mean that in order to create you must be homosexual. But there is no *invention* possible, whether it be philosophical or poetic, without the presence in the inventing subject of an abundance of the other, of the diverse: persons-detached, persons-thought, peoples born of the unconscious, and in each desert, suddenly animated, a springing forth of self that we did not know about—our women, our monsters, our jackals, our Arabs, our fellow-creatures, our fears.[7] But there is no invention of other I's, no poetry, no fiction without a certain homosexuality (interplay therefore of bisexuality) making in me a crystallized work of my ultrasubjectivities. I is this matter, personal, exuberant, lively masculine, feminine, or other in which I delights me and distresses me. And in the concert of personalizations called I, at the same time that you repress a certain homosexuality, symbolically, substitutively, it comes out through various signs—

traits, comportments, manners, gestures—and it is seen still more clearly in writing.

Thus, under the name of Jean Genet,[8] what is inscribed in the movement of a text which divides itself, breaks itself into bits, regroups itself, is an abundant, maternal, pederastic femininity. A phantasmatical mingling of men, of males, of messieurs, of monarchs, princes, orphans, flowers, mothers, breasts, gravitates around a marvelous "sun of energy" love, which bombards and disintegrates these ephemeral amorous singularities so that they may recompose themselves in other bodies for new passions. . . .

NOTES

1. The translation is faithful to Hélène Cixous's many neologisms.—Translator.

2. This is what all of Derrida's work traversing—investigating the history of philosophy—seeks to make apparent. In Plato, Hegel, Nietzsche, the same process goes on, repression, exclusion, distancing of woman. Murder which intermingles with history as a manifestation and representation of masculine power.

3. *Pour un tombeau d' Anatole* (Editions du Seuil, 1961, p. 138) tomb in which Mallarmé preserves his son, guards him, he himself the mother, from death.

4. *Fonder* in French means both "to found" and "to fund."—Translator.

5. Freud's thesis is the following: when the Oedipal complex disappears the superego becomes its heir. At the moment when the boy begins to feel the threat of castration, he begins to overcome the Oedipus complex, with the help of a very severe superego. The Oedipus complex for the boy is a primary process: his first love object, as for the girl, is the mother. But the girl's development is inevitably controlled by the pressure of a less severe superego: the discovery of her castration results in a less vigorous superego. She never completely overcomes the Oedipus complex. The feminine Oedipus complex is not a primary process: the pre-Oedipal attachment to the mother entails for the girl a difficulty from which, says Freud, she never recovers: the necessity of changing objects (to love the father), in mid-stream is a painful conversion, which is accompanied by an additional renunciation: the passage from pre-Oedipal sexuality to "normal" sexuality implies the abandonment of the clitoris in order to move on to the vagina. When this "destiny" is fulfilled, women have a reduced symbolic activity: they have nothing to lose, to gain, to defend.

6. J.-J. Bachofen (1815–1887) Swiss historian of "gynecocracy," "historian" of a nonhistory. His project is to demonstrate that the nations (Greek, Roman, Hebrew) went through an age of "gynecocracy," the reign of the Mother, before arriving at a patriarchy. This epoch can only be deduced, as it has no history. Bachofen advances that this state of affairs, humiliating for men, must have been repressed, covered over by historical forgetfulness. And he attempts to create (in *Das Mutterrecht* in particular, 1861) an archaeology of the matriarchal system, of great beauty, starting with a reading of the first historical texts, at the level of the symptom, of their unsaid. Gynecocracy, he says, is well-ordered materialism.

7. The French here, *nos semblables, nos frayeurs*, plays on and with the last line of Baudelaire's famous poem "Au lecteur" [To the reader]: "Hypocrite lecteur,—mon semblable,—mon frère."—Translator.

8. Jean Genet, French novelist and playwright, to whose writing Hélène Cixous refers when she gives examples of the inscription of pederastic femininity.—Translator.

Questions

Luce Irigaray

What is a woman?

I believe I've already answered that there is no way I would "answer" that question. The question "what is . . . ?" is the question—the metaphysical question—to which the feminine does not allow itself to submit. . . .

Over and beyond the deconstruction of the Freudian theory of femininity, can one (can you) elaborate another concept of femininity: with a different symbolics, a different unconscious, that would be "of woman" (that is, entirely other and not the inverse, the negative, the complement of that of man)? Can you sketch its content?

Can anyone, can I, elaborate another, a different, concept of femininity? There is no question of another *concept* of femininity.

To claim that the feminine can be expressed in the form of a concept is to allow oneself to be caught up again in a system of "masculine" representations, in which women are trapped in a system of meaning which serves the auto-affection of the (masculine) subject. If it is really a matter of calling "femininity" into question, there is still no need to elaborate another "concept"—unless a woman is renouncing her sex and wants to speak like men. For the

elaboration of a theory of woman, men, I think, suffice. In a woman('s) language, the concept as such would have no place. . . .

* * *

Strictly speaking, political practice, at least currently, is masculine through and through. In order for women to be able to make themselves heard, a "radical" evolution in our way of conceptualizing and managing the political realm is required. This, of course, cannot be achieved in a single "stroke."

What mode of action is possible today, then, for women? Must their interventions remain marginal with respect to social structure as a whole?

What do you mean by "marginal"?

I am thinking especially about *women's liberation movements*. Something is being elaborated there that has to do with the "feminine," with what women-among-themselves might be, what a "women's society" might mean. If I speak of marginality, it is because, first of all, these movements to some extent keep themselves deliberately apart from institutions and from the play of forces in power, and so forth. "Outside" the already-existing power relations. Sometimes they even reject intervention—including intervention "from without"—against any institution whatsoever.

This "position" is explained by the difficulties women encounter when they try to make

From *This Sex Which Is Not One* (1985). Reprinted by permission.

their voices heard in places already fixed within and by a society that has simultaneously used and excluded them, and that continues in particular to ignore the specificity of their "demands" even as it recuperates some of their themes, their very slogans. This position can be understood, too, through women's need to constitute a place to be among themselves, in order to learn to formulate their desires, in the absence of overly immediate pressures and oppressions.

Of course, certain things have been achieved for women, in large part owing to the liberation movements: liberalized contraception, abortion, and so on. These gains make it possible to raise again, differently, the question of what the social status of women might be—in particular through its differentiation from a simple reproductive-maternal function. But these contributions may always just as easily be turned against women. In other words, we cannot yet speak, in this connection, of a feminine politics, but only of certain conditions under which it may be possible. The first being an end to silence concerning the exploitation experienced by women: the systematic refusal to "keep quiet" practiced by the liberation movements. . . .

* * *

In the interview with Liberation, *you object to the notion of equality. We agree. What do you think of the notion of "woman power"? If woman were to come to pass (in history and in the unconscious . . . what would result: would a feminine power be purely and simply substituted for masculine power? Or would there be peaceful coexistence? Or what?*

* * *

It clearly cannot be a matter of substituting feminine power for masculine power. Because this reversal would still be caught up in the economy of the same, in the same economy—in which, of course, what I am trying to designate as "feminine" would not

emerge. There would be a phallic "seizure of power." Which, moreover, seems impossible: women may "dream" of it, it may sometimes be accomplished marginally, in limited groups, but for society as a whole, such a substitution of power, such a reversal of power, is impossible.

Peaceful Coexistence? I don't know just what that means. I don't think peaceful coexistence exists. It is the decoy of an economy of power and war. The question we might raise instead is this one: even though everything is in place and operating as if there could be nothing but the desire for "sameness," *why would there be no desire for "otherness"?* No desire for a difference that would not be repeatedly and eternally co-opted and trapped within an economy of "sameness." You may very well say that that is my dream, that it is just another dream. But why? Once again, the reversal or transfer of power would not signify the "advent" of the other, of a "feminine" other. But why would it be impossible for there to be any desire for difference, any desire for the other? Moreover, does not all reabsorption of otherness in the discourse of sameness signify a desire for difference, but a desire that would always—to speak a shamefully psychological language—"be frightening"? And which by that token would always keep "veiled"—in its phobia—the question of the difference between the sexes and of the sexual relation.

* * *

Why speak (dialogue) here with a man, and a man whose craft is after all philosophy?

Why try to speak with a man? Because what I want, in fact, is not to create a theory of woman, but to secure a place for the feminine within sexual difference. That difference—masculine/feminine—has always operated "within" systems that are representative, self-representative, of the (masculine) subject. Moreover, these systems have produced many other differences that appear articulated to compensate for an operative sexual indifference. For one sex and its lack, its atrophy, its negative, still does not add up to two. In other words, the feminine has never been defined except as the inverse, indeed the underside, of the masculine. So for woman it is not a matter of installing herself within this lack, this negative, even by denouncing it, nor of reversing the economy of sameness by turning the feminine into *the standard for "sexual difference"*; it is rather a matter of trying to practice that difference. Hence these questions: what other mode of reading or writing, of interpretation and affirmation, may be mine inasmuch as I am a woman, with respect to you, a man? Is it possible that the difference might not be reduced once again to a process of *hierarchization? Of subordinating the other to the same?*

As for philosophy, so far as the question of woman is concerned—and it comes down to the question of sexual difference—this is indeed what has to be brought into question. Unless we are to agree naively—or perhaps strategically—to limit ourselves to some narrow sphere, some marginal area that would leave intact the discourse that lays down the law to all the others: philosophical discourse. The philosophical order is indeed the one that has to be questioned, and *disturbed*, inasmuch as it covers over sexual difference. . . .

*   *   *

What is the signification of this gesture with respect to everything that may be called today, on whatever basis, a "women's liberation movement"? Why is this separatist breaking away of "women-among-themselves"?

The signification of this gesture with respect to women's liberation movements? Let's say that at first glance it may look like a breaking away, as you put it. This would mean that the empirical fact of remaining always and only

among women would be necessary and even sufficient to put one on the side of "women's liberation," politically. . . . But wouldn't it still be maintaining an idealist logic to pose the alternative in those terms: women either function alongside men, where they will be no more than objects, images, ideas, aspects of a feeling-matter appropriated by and for men, or else—but isn't this "or else" in danger of amounting finally to the same thing?—women remain among themselves. Which is not to say that they have no compelling need to do this. As a political tactic in particular. Women—as the stakes of private property, of appropriation by and for discourse—have always been put in a position of mutual rivalry. So to make their own efforts more effective, they have had to constitute a place where they could be "among themselves." A place for individual and collective "consciousness-raising" concerning the specific oppression of women, a place where the desire of women by and for each other could be recognized, a place for them to regroup. But, for me, that place is in danger of becoming a utopia of historical reversal, a dream of reappropriation of power—particularly phallic power—by women if it closes itself in on the circle of its demands and even desires. And besides, it would just be copying the society of men among themselves, with women remaining once again in the role assigned to them. Except that women could do without men while they are elaborating their own society?

So the "breaking away" of which you speak—and which, for me, is not one—seems strategically necessary, too, for two reasons at least (1) Women cannot work on the question of their own oppression without an analysis and even an experience of institutions—institutions governed by men. (2) What poses a problem—a fundamental one?—for the feminine, hence the necessity and usefulness of this angle of approach, is the operation of discursive logic. For example, in its oppositions, its schisms, between empirical and transcendental, perceptible and intelligible, matter and idea, and so on. That hierarchical structure has always put the feminine in a position of inferiority, of exploitation, of exclusion with respect to language. But, in the same stroke, as it were, it has confirmed the impracticable character of the sexual relation. For this relation boils down to man's self-affection mediated by the feminine, which he has appropriated into his language. The reciprocal not being "true." Thus it is necessary to turn again to this "proper" character of language, analyzing it not only in its dual movement of appropriation and disappropriation with respect to the masculine subject alone, but also in what remains mute, and deprived of any possibility of "self-affection," of "self-representation," for the feminine. If the only response to men-among-themselves is women-among-themselves, whatever subtends the functioning of the logic of presence, of being, of property—and thus maintains the effacement of the difference between the sexes—is very likely to perpetuate and even reinforce itself. Rather than maintaining the masculine-feminine opposition, it would be appropriate to seek a possibility of *nonhierarchical* articulation of that difference in language. This explains what you call the breaking away of "women-among-themselves"; such a break is equally necessary where "men-among-themselves" are concerned, even though it is more difficult to bring about, since that state of affairs underlies the contemporary forms of their power.

One cannot fail to have at least a sense that your first concern is to avoid a naive positioning of "the question of women." One that would be, for example, a pure and simple reversal of the masculine positioning of the question (a pure and simple reversal of "phallogocentrism," and so forth).

To this question I think I have in fact already replied, both in answering the preceding questions and in writing *Speculum*. Which is obviously not a book *about* woman; and it is still less-whatever one may think about it, or even project from it as a hope for the reversal of values—a "studied gynecocentrism," a "place of the monopolization of the symbolic" to the benefit of a woman, or of some women. Such naive judgments overlook the fact that from a feminine locus nothing can be articulated without a questioning of the symbolic itself. But we do not escape so easily from reversal. We do not escape, in particular, by thinking we can dispense with a rigorous interpretation of phallogocentrism. There is no simple manageable way to leap to the outside of phallogocentrism, *nor any possible way to situate oneself there, that would result from the simple fact of being a woman.* And in *Speculum*, if I was attempting to move back through the "masculine" imaginary, that is, our cultural imaginary, it is because that move imposed itself, both in order to demarcate the possible "outside" of this imaginary and to allow me to situate myself with respect to it as a woman, implicated in it and at the same time exceeding its limits. But I see this excess, of course, as what makes the sexual relation possible, and not as a reversal of phallic power. And my "first" reaction to this excess is to laugh. Isn't laughter the first form of liberation from a secular oppression? *Isn't the phallic tantamount to the seriousness of meaning?* Perhaps woman, and the sexual relation, transcend it "first" in laughter?

Besides, women among themselves begin by laughing. To escape from a pure and simple reversal of the masculine position means in any case not to forget to laugh. Not to forget that the dimension of desire, of pleasure, is untranslatable, unrepresentable, irrecuperable, in the "seriousness"—the adequacy, the univocity, the truth . . .—of a discourse that claims to state its meaning. Whether it is produced by men or women. Which is not to assert that one has to give in to saying just anything at all, but that *speaking the truth constitutes the prohibition on woman's pleasure, and thus on the sexual rela-tion.* The covering-up of its forcefulness, of force itself, under the lawmaking power of dis-course. Moreover, it is right here that the most virulent issue at stake in the oppression of women is located today: men want to hold onto the initiative of discourse about sexual pleasure, and thus also about *her* pleasure.

Can you say something about your work in re-lation to the women's liberation movement?

Before attempting to answer your question, I should like to clarify two things:

—First, that I can't tell you what is happening in the liberation movement. Even granting that I might wish to answer your question, what is happening in the women's liberation movement cannot simply be surveyed, described, related "from the outside."

—Second, that I prefer to speak, in the plural, of women's liberation movements. In fact, there are multiple groups and tendencies in women's struggles today, and to reduce them to a single movement involves a risk of introducing phe-nomena of hierarchization, claims of ortho-doxy, and so on.

To come back to my work: I am trying, as I have already indicated, to go back through the mas-culine imaginary, to interpret the way it has reduced us to silence, to muteness or mimicry, and I am attempting, from that starting-point and at the same time, to (re)discover a possible space for the feminine imaginary.

But it is obviously not simply an "individ-ual" task. A long history has put all women in the same sexual, social, and cultural condition. Whatever inequalities may exist among women, they all undergo, even without clearly realizing it, the same oppression, the same ex-ploitation of their body, the same denial of their desire.

That is why it is very important for women to be able to join together, and to join together "among themselves." In order to begin to es-cape from the spaces, roles, and gestures that they have been assigned and taught by the so-ciety of men. In order to love each other, even though men have organized a *de facto* rivalry among women. In order to discover a form of "social existence" other than the one that has always been imposed upon them. The first issue facing liberation movements is that of making each woman "conscious" of the fact that what she has felt in her personal experience is a con-dition shared by all women, thus *allowing that experience to be politicized.*

But what does "political" mean, here? No "women's politics" exists, not yet, at least not in the broad sense. And, if such a politics comes into existence one of these days, it will be very different from the politics instituted by men. For the questions raised by the exploitation of wom-en's bodies exceed the stakes, the schemas, and of course the "parties" of the politics known and practiced up to now. Obviously, that does not prevent political parties from wanting to "co-opt" the woman question by granting women a place in their ranks, with the aim of aligning them—one more time . . .—with their "pro-grams," which, most of the time, have nothing to do with them, in the sense that these programs fail to take into consideration the *specific exploi-tation* of women. For the exploitation of women does not constitute a *limited* question, within politics, one which would concern only a "sec-tor" of the population, or a "part" of the "body politic." When women want to escape from ex-ploitation, they do not merely destroy a few "prejudices," they disrupt the entire order of dominant values, economic, social, moral, and sexual. They call into question all existing the-ory, all thought, all language, inasmuch as these are monopolized by men and men alone. They challenge *the very foundation of our social and cultural order,* whose organization has been pre-scribed by the patriarchal system.

The patriarchal foundation of our social existence is in fact overlooked in contemporary politics, even leftist politics. Up to now *even Marxism has paid very little attention to the problems of the specific exploitation of women, and women's struggles most often seem to disturb the Marxists.* Even though these struggles could be interpreted with the help of the schemas for the analysis of social exploitation to which Marxist political programs lay specific claim. Provided, of course, that these schemas be used differently. But no politics has, up to now, questioned its own relation to phallocratic power . . .

In concrete terms, that means that women must of course continue to struggle for equal wages and social rights, against discrimination in employment and education, and so forth. But that is not enough: women merely "equal" to men would be "like them," therefore not women. Once more, the difference between the sexes would be in that way canceled out, ignored, papered over. So it is essential for women among themselves to invent new modes of organization, new forms of struggle, new challenges. The various liberation movements have already begun to do this, and a "women's international" is beginning to take shape. But here too, innovation is necessary: institutions, hierarchy, and authority—that is, the existing forms of politics—are men's affairs. Not ours.

That explains certain difficulties encountered by the liberation movements. If women allow themselves to be caught in the trap of power, in the game of authority, if they allow themselves to be contaminated by the "paranoid" operations of masculine politics, they have nothing more to say or do *as women.* That is why one of the tasks in France today is to try to regroup the movement's various tendencies around a certain number of specific themes and actions: rape, abortion, the challenge to the prerogative of the father's name in the case of juridical decisions that determine "to whom children belong," the full-fledged participation of women in legislative decisions and actions, and so on. And yet all that must never disguise the fact that it is in order to bring their difference to light that women are demanding their rights.

For my part, I refuse to let myself be locked into a single "group" within the women's liberation movement. Especially if such a group becomes ensnared in the exercise of power, if it purports to determine the "truth" of the feminine, to legislate as to what it means to "be a woman," and to condemn women who might have immediate objectives that differ from theirs. I think the most important thing to do is to expose the exploitation common to all women and to find the struggles that are appropriate for each woman, right where she is, depending upon her nationality, her job, her social class, her sexual experience, that is, upon the form of oppression that is for her the most immediately unbearable.

*   *   *

❧ Methodological Postscripts ❧

Have We Got a Theory for You!
Feminist Theory,
Cultural Imperialism
and the Demand for
"The Woman's Voice"

Maria Lugones
Elizabeth Spelman

Prologue

(In an Hispana voice)

A veces quisiera mezclar en una voz el sonido canyenge, tristón y urbano del porteñismo que llevo adentro con la candecia apacible, serrana y llena de corage de la hispana nuevo mejicana. Contrastar y unir

el piolín y la cuerda
el traé y el pepéname

el camión y la troca
la lluvia y el llanto

Pero este querer se me va cuando veo que he confundido la solidaridad con la falta de diferencia. La solidaridad requiere el reconocer, comprender, respetar y amar lo que nos lleva a llorar en distintas cadencias. El imperialismo cultural desea lo contrario, por eso necesitamos muchas voces. Porque una sola voz nos mata a las dos.

No quiero hablar por ti sino contigo. Pero si no aprendo tus modos y tu los mios la conversación es sólo aparente. Y la apariencia se levanta como una barrera sín sentido entre las

From *Women's Studies* (1983). Reprinted by permission.

dos. Sin sentido y sin sentimiento. Por eso no me debes dejar que te dicte tu ser y no me dictes el mio. Porque entonces ya no dialogamos. El diálogo entre nosotras requiere dos voces y no una.

Tal vez un día jugaremos juntas y nos hablaremos no en una lengua universal sino que vos me habalarás mi voz y yo la tuya.

Preface

This paper is the result of our dialogue, of our thinking together about differences among women and how these differences are silenced. (Think, for example, of all the silences there are connected with the fact that this paper is in English—for that is a borrowed tongue for one of us.) In the process of our talking and writing together, we saw that the differences between us did not permit our speaking in one voice. For example, when we agreed we expressed the thought differently; there were some things that both of us thought were true but could not express as true of each of us; sometimes we could not say "we"; and sometimes one of us could not express the thought in the first person singular, and to express it in the third person would be to present an outsider's and not an insider's perspective. Thus the use of two voices is central both to the process of constructing this paper and to the substance of it. We are both the authors of this paper and not just sections of it but we write together without presupposing unity of expression or of experience. So when we speak in unison it means just that—there are two voices and not just one.

I. INTRODUCTION

In the voice of a white/Anglo woman who has been teaching and writing about feminist theory)

Feminism is, among other things, a response to the fact that women either have been left out of, or included in demeaning and disfiguring ways in what has been an almost exclusively male account of the world. And so while part of what feminists want and demand for women is the right to move and to act in accordance with our own wills and not against them, another part is the desire and insistence that we give our *own* accounts of these movements and actions. For it matters to us what is said about us, who says it, and to whom it is said: having the opportunity to talk about one's life, to give an account of it, to interpret it, is integral to leading that life rather than being led through it; hence our distrust of the male monopoly over accounts of women's lives. To put the same point slightly differently, part of human life, human living, is talking about it, and we can be sure that being silenced in one's own account of one's life is a kind of amputation that signals oppression. Another reason for not divorcing life from the telling of it or talking about it is that as humans our experiences are deeply influenced by what is said about them, by ourselves or powerful (as opposed to significant) others. Indeed, the phenomenon of internalized oppression is only possible because this is so: one experiences her life in terms of the impoverished and degrading concepts others have found it convenient to use to describe her. We can't separate lives from the accounts given of them; the articulation of our experience is part of our experience.

Sometimes feminists have made even stronger claims about the importance of speaking about our own lives and the destructiveness of others presuming to speak about us or for us. First of all, the claim has been made that on the whole men's accounts of women's lives have been at best false, a function of ignorance; and at worst malicious lies, a function of a knowledgeable desire to exploit and oppress. Since it matters to us that falsehood and lies not be told about us, we demand, of those who have been responsible for those falsehoods and lies, or those who continue to transmit them, not just that we speak but that they learn to be able to hear us. It has also been claimed that talking about one's life, telling one's story, in the company of those doing the same (as in consciousness-raising sessions), is constitutive of feminist method.

And so the demand that the woman's voice be heard and attended to has been made for a variety of reasons: not just so as to greatly increase the chances that true accounts of women's lives will be given, but also because the articulation of experience (in myriad ways) is among the hallmarks of a self-determining individual or community. There are not just epistemological, but moral and political reasons for demanding that the woman's voice be heard, after centuries of androcentric din.

But what more exactly is the feminist demand that the woman's voice be heard? There are several crucial notes to make about it. First of all, the demand grows out of a complaint, and in order to understand the scope and focus of the demand we have to look at the scope and focus of the complaint. The complaint does not specify *which* women have been silenced, and in one way this is appropriate to the conditions it is a complaint about: virtually no women have had a voice, whatever their race, class, ethnicity, religion, sexual alliance, whatever place and period in history they lived. And if it is as women that women have been silenced, then of course the demand must be that women as women have a voice. But in another way the complaint is very misleading, insofar as it suggests that it is women as women who have been silenced, and that whether a woman is rich or poor, Black, brown or white, etc. is irrelevant to what it means for her to be a woman. For the demand thus simply made ignores at least two related points: (1) it is only possible for a woman who does not feel highly vulnerable with respect to other parts of her identity, e.g. race, class, ethnicity, religion, sexual alliance, etc., to conceive of her voice simply or essentially as a 'woman's voice'; (2) just because not all women are equally vulnerable with respect to race, class, etc., some women's voices are more

likely to be heard than others by those who have heretofore been giving—or silencing—the accounts of women's lives. For all these reasons, the women's voices most likely to come forth and the women's voices most likely to be heard are, in the US anyway, those of white, middle-class, heterosexual Christian (or anyway not self-identified non-Christian) women. Indeed, many Hispanas, Black women, Jewish women —to name a few groups—have felt it an invitation to silence rather than speech to be requested —if they are requested at all—to speak about being "women" (with the plain wrapper—as if there were one) in distinction from speaking about being Hispana, Black, Jewish, working-class, etc., women.

The demand that the "woman's voice" be heard, and the search for the "woman's voice" as central to feminist methodology, reflects nascent feminist theory. It reflects nascent empirical theory insofar as it presupposes that the silencing of women is systematic, shows up in regular, patterned ways, and that there are discoverable causes of this widespread observable phenomenon; the demand reflects nascent political theory insofar as it presupposes that the silencing of women reveals a systematic pattern of power and authority; and it reflects nascent moral theory insofar as it presupposes that the silencing is unjust and that there are particular ways of remedying this injustice. Indeed, whatever else we know feminism to include—e.g. concrete direct political action—theorizing is integral to it: theories about the nature of oppression, the causes of it, the relation of the oppression of women to other forms of oppression. And certainly the concept of the woman's voice is itself a theoretical concept, in the sense that it presupposes a theory according to which our identities as human beings are actually compound identities, a kind of fusion or confusion of our otherwise separate identities as women or men, as Black or brown or white, etc. That is no less a theoretical stance than Plato's division of the person into soul and body or Aristotle's parcelling of the soul into various functions.

The demand that the "woman's voice" be heard also invites some further directions in the exploration of women's lives and discourages or excludes others. For reasons mentioned above, systematic, sustained reflection on being a woman—the kind of contemplation that "doing theory" requires—is most likely to be done by women who vis-à-vis other women enjoy a certain amount of political, social and economic privilege because of their skin color, class membership, ethnic identity. There is a relationship between the content of our contemplation and the fact that we have the time to engage in it at some length—otherwise we shall have to say that it is a mere accident of history that white middle-class women in the United States have in the main developed "feminist theory" (as opposed to "Black feminist theory," "Chicana feminist theory," etc.) and that so much of the theory has failed to be relevant to the lives of women who are not white or middle class. Feminist theory—of all kinds—is to be based on, or anyway touch base with, the variety of real life stories women provide about themselves. But in fact, because, among other things, of the structural political and social and economic inequalities among women, the tail has been wagging the dog: feminist theory has not for the most part arisen out of a medley of women's voices; instead, the theory has arisen out of the voices, the experiences, of a fairly small handful of women, and if other women's voices do not sing in harmony with the theory, they aren't counted as women's voices—rather, they are the voices of the woman as Hispana, Black, Jew, etc. There is another sense in which the tail is wagging the dog, too: it is presumed to be the case that those who do the theory know more about those who are theorized than vice versa: hence it ought to be the case that if it is white/Anglo women who write for and about all other women, then white/Anglo women must know more about all other women than other women

know about them. But in fact just in order to survive, brown and Black women have to know a lot more about white/Anglo women—not through the sustained contemplation theory requires, but through the sharp observation stark exigency demands.

(In an Hispana voice)

I think it necessary to explain why in so many cases when women of color appear in front of white/Anglo women to talk about feminism and women of color, we mainly raise a complaint: the complaint of exclusion, of silencing, of being included in a universe we have not chosen. We usually raise the complaint with a certain amount of disguised or undisguised anger. I can only attempt to explain this phenomenon from a Hispanic viewpoint and a fairly narrow one at that: the viewpoint of an Argentinian woman who has lived in the US for sixteen years, who has attempted to come to terms with the devaluation of things Hispanic and Hispanic people in "America" and who is most familiar with Hispano life in the Southwest of the US. I am quite unfamiliar with daily Hispano life in the urban centers, though not with some of the themes and some of the salient experiences of urban Hispano life.

When I say "we," I am referring to Hispanas. I am accustomed to use the 'we' in this way. I am also pained by the tenuousness of this "we" given that I am not a native of the US. Through the years I have come to be recognized and I have come to recognize myself more and more firmly as part of this "we." I also have a profound yearning for this firmness since I am a displaced person and I am conscious of not being of and I am unwilling to make myself of— even if this were possible—the white/Anglo community.

When I say "you" I mean not the non-Hispanic but the white/Anglo women that I address. "We" and "you" do not capture my relation to other non-white women. The complexity of that relation is not addressed here, but it is vivid to me as I write down my thoughts on the subject at hand.

I see two related reasons for our complaint-full discourse with white/Anglo women. Both of these reasons plague our world, they contaminate it through and through. It takes some hardening of oneself, some self-acceptance of our own anger to face them, for to face them is to decide that maybe we can change our situation in self-constructive ways and we know fully well that the possibilities are minimal. We know that we cannot rest from facing these reasons, that the tenderness towards others in us undermines our possibilities, that we have to fight our own niceness because it clouds our minds and hearts. Yet we know that a thoroughgoing hardening would dehumanize us. So, we have to walk through our days in a peculiarly fragile psychic state, one that we have to struggle to maintain, one that we do not often succeed in maintaining.

We and you do not talk the same language. When we talk to you we use your language: the language of your experience and of your theories. We try to use it to communicate our world of experience. But since your language and your theories are inadequate in expressing our experiences, we only succeed in communicating our experience of exclusion. We cannot talk to you in our language because you do not understand it. So the brute facts that we understand your language and that the place where most theorizing about women is taking place is your place, both combine to require that we either use your language and distort our experience not just in the speaking about it, but in the living of it, or that we remain silent. Complaining about exclusion is a way of remaining silent.

You are ill at ease in our world. You are ill at ease in our world in a very different way than we are ill at ease in yours. You are not of our world and again, you are not of our world in a very different way than we are not of yours. In the intimacy of a personal relationship we appear to you many times to be wholly there, to have broken through or to have dissipated the barriers that separate us because you are Anglo and we are raza. When we let go of the psychic state that I referred to above in the direction of sympathy, we appear to ourselves equally whole in your presence but our intimacy is thoroughly incomplete. When we are in your world many times you remake us in your own image, although sometimes you clearly and explicitly acknowledge that we are not wholly there in our being with you. When we are in your world we ourselves feel the discomfort of having our own being Hispanas disfigured or not understood. And yet, we have had to be in your world and learn its ways. We have to participate in it, make a living in it, live in it, be mistreated in it, be ignored in it, and rarely, be appreciated in it. In learning to do these things or in learning to suffer them or in learning to enjoy what is to be enjoyed or in learning to understand your conception of us, we have had to learn your culture and thus your language and self-conceptions. But there is nothing that necessitates that you understand our world: understand, that is, not as an observer understands things, but as a participant, as someone who has a stake in them understands them. So your being ill at ease in our world lacks the features of our being ill at ease in yours precisely because you can leave and you can always tell yourselves that you will be soon out of there and because the wholeness of your selves is never touched by us, we have no tendency to remake you in our image.

But you theorize about women and we are women, so you understand yourselves to be theorizing about us and we understand you to be theorizing about us. Yet none of the feminist theories developed so far seem to me to help Hispanas in the articulation of our experience. We have a sense that in using them we are distorting our experiences. Most Hispanas cannot even understand the language used in these theories—and only in some cases the reason is that the Hispana cannot understand English. We do not recognize ourselves in these theories. They create in us a schizophrenic split between our concern for ourselves as women and ourselves as Hispanas, one that we do not feel otherwise. Thus they seem to us to force us to assimilate to some version of Anglo culture, however revised that version may be. They seem to ask that we leave our communities or that we become alienated so completely in them that we feel hollow. When we see that you feel alienated in your own communities, this confuses us because we think that maybe every feminist has to suffer this alienation. But we see that recognition of your alienation leads many of you to be empowered into the remaking of your culture, while we are paralyzed into a state of displacement with no place to go.

So I think that we need to think carefully about the relation between the articulation of our own experience, the interpretation of our own experience, and theory making by us and other non-Hispanic women about themselves and other "women."

The only motive that makes sense to me for your joining us in this investigation is the motive of friendship, out of friendship. A non-imperialist feminism requires that you make a real space for our articulating, interpreting, theorizing and reflecting about the connections among them—a real space must be a noncoerced space—and/or that you follow us into our world out of friendship. I see the "out of friendship" as the only sensical motivation for this following because the task at hand for you is one of extraordinary difficulty. It requires that you be willing to devote a great part of your life to it and that you be willing to suffer alienation and self-disruption. Self-interest has been proposed as a possible motive for entering this task. But self-interest does not seem to me to be a realistic motive, since whatever the benefits you may accrue from such a journey, they cannot be concrete enough for you at this time and they may not be worth your while. I do not think that you have any obligation to understand us. You do have an obligation to abandon your imperialism, your universal claims, your reduc-

tion of us to your selves simply because they seriously harm us.

I think that the fact that we are so ill at ease with your theorizing in the ways indicated above does indicate that there is something wrong with these theories. But what is it that is wrong? Is it simply that the theories are flawed if meant to be universal but accurate so long as they are confined to your particular group(s)? Is it that the theories are not really flawed but need to be translated? Can they be translated? Is it something about the process of theorizing that is flawed? How do the two reasons for our complaint–full discourse affect the validity of your theories? Where do *we* begin? To what extent are our experience and its articulation affected by our being a colonized people, and thus by your culture, theories and conceptions? Should we theorize in community and thus as part of community life and outside the academy and other intellectual circles? What is the point of making theory? Is theory making a good thing for us to do at this time? When are we making theory and when are we just articulating and/or interpreting our experiences?

II. SOME QUESTIONABLE ASSUMPTIONS ABOUT FEMINIST THEORIZING

(*Unproblematically in María's and Vicky's voice*)

Feminist theories aren't just about what happens to the female population in any given society or across all societies; they are about the meaning of those experiences in the lives of women. They are about beings who give their own accounts of what is happening to them or of what they are doing, who have culturally constructed ways of reflecting on their lives. But how can the theorizer get at the meaning of those experiences? What should the relation be between a woman's own account of her experiences and the theorizer's account of it?

Let us describe two different ways of arriving at an account of another woman's experience. It is one thing for both me and you to observe you and come up with our different accounts of what you are doing; it is quite another for me to observe myself and others much like me culturally and in other ways and to develop an account of myself and then use that account to give an account of you. In the first case you are the "insider" and I am the "outsider." When the outsider makes clear that she is an outsider and that this is an outsider's account of your behavior, there is a touch of honesty about what she is doing. Most of the time the "interpretation by an outsider" is left understood and most of the time the distance of outsidedness is understood to mark objectivity in the interpretation. But why is the outsider as an outsider interpreting your behavior? Is she doing it so that you can understand how she sees you? Is she doing it so that other outsiders will understand how you *are*? Is she doing it so that *you* will understand how you are? It would seem that if the outsider wants you to understand how she sees you and you have given your account of how you see yourself to her, there is a possibility of genuine dialogue between the two. It also seems that the lack of reciprocity could bar genuine dialogue. For why should you engage in such a one-sided dialogue? As soon as we ask this question, a host of other conditions for the possibility of a genuine dialogue between us arise: conditions having to do with your position relative to me in the various social, political and economic structures in which we might come across each other or in which you may run face to face with my account of you and my use of your account of yourself. Is this kind of dialogue necessary for me to get at the meaning of your experiences? That is, is this kind of dialogue necessary for feminist theorizing that is not seriously flawed?

Obviously the most dangerous of the understanding of what I—an outsider—am doing in giving an account of your experience is the one that describes what I'm doing as giving an account of who and how you are whether it be given to you or to other outsiders. Why should you or anyone else believe me; that is why should you or anyone else believe that you are as I say you are? Could I be right? What conditions would have to obtain for my being right? That many women are put in the position of not knowing whether or not to believe outsiders' accounts of their experiences is clear. The pressures to believe these accounts are enormous even when the woman in question does not see herself in the account. She is thus led to doubt her own judgment and to doubt all interpretation of her experience. This leads her to experience her life differently. Since the consequences of outsiders' accounts can be so significant, it is crucial that we reflect on whether or not this type of account can ever be right and if so, under what conditions.

The last point leads us to the second way of arriving at an account of another woman's experience, viz. the case in which I observe myself and others like me culturally and in other ways and use that account to give an account of you. In doing this, I remake you in my own image. Feminist theorizing approaches this remaking insofar as it depends on the concept of women as women. For it has not arrived at this concept as a consequence of dialogue with many women who are culturally different, or by any other kind of investigation of cultural differences which may include different conceptions of what it is to be a woman; it has simply presupposed this concept.

Our suggestion in this paper, and at this time it is no more than a suggestion, is that only when genuine and reciprocal dialogue takes place between "outsiders" and "insiders" can we trust the outsider's account. At first sight it may appear that the insider/outsider distinction disappears in the dialogue, but it is important to notice that all that happens is that we are now both outsider and insider with respect to each other. The dialogue puts us both in position to give a better account of each other's and our own experience. Here we should again note that white/Anglo women are much less prepared for this dialogue with women of color than women of color are for dialogue with them in that women of color have had to learn white/Anglo ways, self-conceptions, and conceptions of them.

But both the possibility and the desirability of this dialogue are very much in question. We need to think about the possible motivations for engaging in this dialogue, whether doing theory jointly would be a good thing, in what ways and for whom, and whether doing theory is in itself a good thing at this time for women of color or white/Anglo women. In motivating the last question let us remember the hierarchical distinctions between theorizers and those theorized about and between theorizers and doers. These distinctions are endorsed by the same views and institutions which endorse and support hierarchical distinctions between men/women, master race/inferior race, intellectuals/manual workers. Of what use is the activity of theorizing to those of us who are women of color engaged day in and day out in the task of empowering women and men of color face to face with them? Should we be articulating and interpreting their experience for them with the aid of theories? Whose theories?

III. WAYS OF TALKING OR BEING TALKED ABOUT THAT ARE HELPFUL, ILLUMINATING, EMPOWERING, RESPECTFUL

(*Unproblematically in María's and Vicky's voice*)

Feminists have been quite diligent about pointing out the ways in which empirical, philosophical and moral theories have been androcentric. They have thought it crucial to ask, with respect to such theories: who makes them? for whom do they make them? about what or whom are the theories? why? how are theories tested? what are the criteria for such tests and where did the criteria come from? Without posing such questions and trying to answer them, we'd never have been able to begin to mount evidence for our claims that particular theories are androcentric, sexist, biased, paternalistic, etc. Certain philosophers have become fond of—indeed, have made their careers on—pointing out that characterizing a statement as true or false is only one of many ways possible of characterizing it; it might also be, oh, rude, funny, disarming, etc.; it may be intended to soothe or to hurt; or it may have the effect, intended or not, of soothing or hurting. Similarly, theories appear to be the kinds of things that are true or false; but they also are the kinds of things that can be, e.g., useless, arrogant, disrespectful, ignorant, ethnocentric, imperialistic. The immediate point is that feminist theory is no less immune to such characterizations than, say, Plato's political theory, or Freud's theory of female psychosexual development. Of course this is not to say that if feminist theory manages to be respectful or helpful it will follow that it must be true. But if, say, an empirical theory is purported to be about "women" and in fact is only about certain women, it is certainly false, probably ethnocentric, and of dubious usefulness except to those whose position in the world it strengthens (and theories, as we know, don't have to be true in order to be used to strengthen people's positions in the world).

Many reasons can be and have been given for the production of accounts of people's lives that plainly have nothing to do with illuminating those lives for the benefit of those living them. It is likely that both the method of investigation and the content of many accounts would be different if illuminating the lives of the people the accounts are about were the aim of the studies. Though we cannot say ahead of time how feminist theory-making would be different if all (or many more) of those people it is meant to be about were more intimately part of the theory-making process, we do suggest some specific ways being talked about can be helpful:

1. The theory or account can be helpful if it enables one to see how parts of one's life fit together, for example, to see connection among parts of one's life one hasn't seen before. No account can do this if it doesn't get the parts right to begin with, and this cannot happen if the concepts used to describe a life are utterly foreign.

2. A useful theory will help one locate oneself concretely in the world, rather than add to the mystification of the world and one's location in it. New concepts may be of significance here, but they will not be useful if there is no way they can be translated into already existing concepts. Suppose a theory locates you in the home, because you are a woman, but you know full well that is not where you spend most of your time? Or suppose you can't locate yourself easily in any particular class as defined by some version of marxist theory?

3. A theory or account not only ought to accurately locate one in the world but also enable one to think about the extent to which one is responsible or not for being in that location. Otherwise, for those whose location is as oppressed peoples, it usually occurs that the oppressed have no way to see themselves as in any way self-determining, as having any sense of being worthwhile or having grounds for pride, and paradoxically at the same time feeling at fault for the position they are in. A useful theory will help people sort out just what is and is not due to themselves and their own activities as opposed to those who have power over them.

It may seem odd to make these criteria of a useful theory, if the usefulness is not to be at odds with the issue of the truth of the theory: for the focus on feeling worthwhile or having pride seems to rule out the possibility that the truth might just be that such-and-such a group of people has been under the control of others for centuries and that the only explanation of that is that they are worthless and weak people, and

will never be able to change that. Feminist theorizing seems implicitly if not explicitly committed to the moral view that women *are* worthwhile beings, and the metaphysical theory that we are beings capable of bringing about a change in our situations. Does this mean feminist theory is "biased"? Not any more than any other theory, e.g., psychoanalytic theory. What is odd here is not the feminist presupposition that women are worthwhile but rather that feminist theory (and other theory) often has the effect of empowering one group and demoralizing another.

Aspects of feminist theory are as unabashedly value-laden as other political and moral theories. It is not just an examination of women's positions, for it includes, indeed begins with, moral and political judgements about the injustice (or, where relevant, justice) of them. This means that there are implicit or explicit judgements also about what kind of changes constitute a better or worse situation for women.

4. In this connection a theory that is useful will provide criteria for change and make suggestions for modes of resistance that don't merely reflect the situation and values of the theorizer. A theory that is respectful of those about whom it is a theory will not assume that changes that are perceived as making life better for some women are changes that will make, and will be perceived as making, life better for other women. This is NOT to say that if some women do not find a situation oppressive, other women ought never to suggest to the contrary that there might be very good reasons to think that the situation nevertheless *is* oppressive. But it is to say that, e.g., the prescription that life for women will be better when we're in the workforce rather than at home, when we are completely free of religious beliefs with patriarchal origins, when we live in complete separation from men, etc., are seen as slaps in the face to women whose life would be better if they could spend more time at home, whose identity is inseparable from their religious beliefs and cul-

tural practices (which is not to say those beliefs and practices are to remain completely uncriticized and unchanged), who have ties to men— whether erotic or not—such that to have them severed in the name of some vision of what is "better" is, at that time and for those women, absurd. Our visions of what is better are always informed by our perception of what is bad about our present situation. Surely we've learned enough from the history of clumsy missionaries, and the white suffragists of the nineteenth century (who couldn't imagine why Black women "couldn't see" how crucial getting the vote for "women" was) to know that we can clobber people to destruction with our visions, our versions, of what is better. BUT: this does not mean women are not to offer supportive and tentative criticism of one another. But there is a very important difference between (a) developing ideas together, in a "pre-theoretical" stage, engaged as equals in joint enquiry, and (b) one group developing, on the basis of their own experience, a set of criteria for good change for women—and then reluctantly making revisions in the criteria at the insistence of women to whom such criteria seem ethnocentric and arrogant. The deck is stacked when one group takes it upon itself to develop the theory and then have others criticize it. Categories are quick to congeal, and the experiences of women whose lives do not fit the categories will appear as anomalous when in fact the theory should have grown out of them as much as others from the beginning. This, of course, is why any organization or conference having to do with "women"—with no qualification—that seriously does not want to be "solipsistic" will from the beginning be multi-cultural or state the appropriate qualifications. How we think and what we think about does depend in large part on who is there—not to mention who is expected or encouraged to speak. (Recall the boys in the *Symposium* sending the flute girls out.) Conversations and criticism take place in particular circumstances. Turf matters. So does the fact of

who if anyone already has set up the terms of the conversations.

5.   Theory cannot be useful to anyone interested in resistance and change unless there is reason to believe that knowing what a theory means and believing it to be true have some connection to resistance and change. As we make theory and offer it up to others, what do we assume is the connection between theory and consciousness? Do we expect others to read theory, understand it, believe it, and have their consciousness and lives thereby transformed? If we really want theory to make a difference to people's lives, how ought we to present it? Do we think people come to consciousness by reading? only by reading? Speaking to people through theory (orally or in writing) is a *very* specific context-dependent activity. That is, theory-makers and their methods and concepts constitute a community of people and of shared meanings. Their language can be just as opaque and foreign to those not in the community as a foreign tongue or dialect. Why do we engage in *this* activity and what effect do we think it ought to have? As Helen Longino has asked: "Is 'doing theory' just a bonding ritual for academic or educationally privileged feminists/women?" Again, whom does our theory-making serve?

IV. SOME SUGGESTIONS ABOUT HOW TO DO THEORY THAT IS NOT IMPERIALISTIC, ETHNOCENTRIC, DISRESPECTFUL

(Problematically in the voice of a woman of color)

What are the things we need to know about others, and about ourselves, in order to speak intelligently, intelligibly, sensitively, and helpfully about their lives? We can show respect, or lack of it, in writing theoretically about others no less than in talking directly with them. This is not to say that here we have a well-worked out concept of respect, but only to suggest that together all of us consider what it would mean to theorize in a respectful way.

When we speak, write, and publish our theories, to whom do we think we are accountable? Are the concerns we have in being accountable to "the profession" at odds with the concerns we have in being accountable to those about whom we theorize? Do commitments to "the profession," method, getting something published, getting tenure, lead us to talk and act in ways at odds with what we ourselves (let alone others) would regard as ordinary, decent behavior? To what extent do we presuppose that really understanding another person or culture requires our behaving in ways that are disrespectful, even violent? That is, to what extent do we presuppose that getting and/or publishing the requisite information requires or may require disregarding the wishes of others, lying to them, wresting information from them against their wills? Why and how do we think theorizing about others provides *understanding* of them? Is there any sense in which theorizing about others is a short-cut to understanding them?

Finally, if we think doing theory is an important activity, and we think that some conditions lead to better theorizing than others, what are we going to do about creating those conditions? If we think it not just desirable but necessary for women of different racial and ethnic identities to create feminist theory jointly, how shall that be arranged for? It may be the case that at this particular point we ought not even try to do that—that feminist theory by and for Hispanas needs to be done separately from feminist theory by and for Black women, white women, etc. But it must be recognized that white/Anglo women have more power and privilege than Hispanas, Black women, etc., and at the very least they can use such advantage to provide space and time for other women to speak (with the above caveats about implicit restrictions on what counts as "the woman's voice"). And once again it is important to re-member that the power of white/Anglo women vis-à-vis Hispanas and Black women is in inverse proportion to their working knowledge of each other.

This asymmetry is a crucial fact about the background of possible relationships between white women and women of color, whether as political co-workers, professional colleagues, or friends.

If white/Anglo women and women of color are to do theory jointly, in helpful, respectful, illuminating and empowering ways, the task ahead of white/Anglo women because of this asymmetry, is a very hard task. The task is a very complex one. In part, to make an analogy, the task can be compared to learning a text without the aid of teachers. We all know the lack of contact felt when we want to discuss a particular issue that requires knowledge of a text with someone who does not know the text at all. Or the discomfort and impatience that arise in us when we are discussing an issue that presupposes a text and someone walks into the conversation who does not know the text. That person is either left out or will impose herself on us and either try to engage in the discussion or try to change the subject. Women of color are put in these situations by white/Anglo women and men constantly. Now imagine yourself simply left out but wanting to do theory with us. The first thing to recognize and accept is that you disturb our own dialogues by putting yourself in the left-out position and not leaving us in some meaningful sense to ourselves.

You must also recognize and accept that you must learn the text. But the text is an extraordinarily complex one: viz. our many different cultures. You are asking us to make ourselves more vulnerable to you than we already are before we have any reason to trust that you will not take advantage of this vulnerability. So you need to learn to become unintrusive, unimportant, patient to the point of tears, while at the same time open to learning any possible lessons. You will also have to come to terms with the sense of alienation, of not belonging, of having your world thoroughly disrupted, having it criticized and scrutinized from the point of view of those who have been harmed by it, having important concepts central to it dismissed, being viewed with mistrust, being seen as of no consequence except as an object of mistrust.

Why would any white/Anglo woman engage in this task? Out of self-interest? What in engaging in this task would be, not just in her interest, but perceived as such by her before the task is completed or well underway? Why should we want you to come into our world out of self-interest? Two points need to be made here. The task as described could be entered into with the intention of finding out as much as possible about us so as to better dominate us. The person engaged in this task would act as a spy. The motivation is not unfamiliar to us. We have heard it said that now that Third World countries are more powerful as a bloc, westerners need to learn more about them, that it is in their self-interest to do so. Obviously there is no reason why people of color should welcome white/Anglo women into their world for the carrying out of this intention. It is also obvious that white/Anglo feminists should not engage in this task under this description since the task under this description would not lead to joint theorizing of the desired sort: respectful, illuminating, helpful and empowering. It would be helpful and empowering only in a one-sided way.

Self-interest is also mentioned as a possible motive in another way. White/Anglo women sometimes say that the task of understanding women of color would entail self-growth or self-expansion. If the task is conceived as described here, then one should doubt that growth or expansion will be the result. The severe self-disruption that the task entails should place a doubt in anyone who takes the task seriously about her possibilities of coming out of the task whole, with a self that is not as fragile as the selves of those who have been the victims of racism. But also, why should women of color embrace white/Anglo women's self-betterment without reciprocity? At this time women of color cannot afford this generous affirmation of white/Anglo women.

Another possible motive for engaging in this task is the motive of duty, "out of obligation", because white/Anglos have done people of color wrong. Here again two considerations: coming into Hispano, Black, Native American worlds out of obligation puts white/Anglos in a morally self-righteous position that is inappropriate. You are active, we are passive. We become the vehicles of your own redemption. Secondly, we couldn't want you to come into our worlds "out of obligation". That is like wanting someone to make love to you out of obligation. So, whether or not you have an obligation to do this (and we would deny that you do), or whether this task could even be done out of obligation, this is an inappropriate motive.

Out of obligation you should stay out of our way, respect us and our distance, and forego the use of whatever power you have over us—for example, the power to use your language in our meetings, the power to overwhelm us with your education, the power to intrude in our communities in order to research us and to record the supposed dying of our cultures, the power to engrain in us a sense that we are members of dying cultures and are doomed to assimilate, the power to keep us in a defensive posture with respect to our own cultures.

So the motive of friendship remains as both the only appropriate and understandable motive for white/Anglo feminists engaging in the task as described above. If you enter the task out of friendship with us, then you will be moved to attain the appropriate reciprocity of care for your and our well-being as whole beings, you will have a stake in us and in our world, you will be moved to satisfy the need for reciprocity of understanding that will enable you to follow us in our experiences as we are able to follow you in yours.

We are not suggesting that if the learning of the text is to be done out of friendship, you must enter into a friendship with a whole community and for the purpose of making theory. In order to understand what it is that we are suggesting, it is important to remember that during the description of her experience of exclusion, the Hispana voice said that Hispanas experience the intimacy of friendship with white/Anglo women friends as thoroughly incomplete. It is not until this fact is acknowledged by our white/Anglo women friends and felt as a profound lack in our experience of each other that white/Anglo women can begin to see us. Seeing us in our communities will make clear and concrete to you how incomplete we really are in our relationships with you. It is this beginning that forms the proper background for the yearning to understand the text of our cultures that can lead to joint theory-making.

Thus, the suggestion made here is that if white/Anglo women are to understand our voices, they must understand our communities and us in them. Again, this is not to suggest that you set out to make friends with our commu-nities, though you may become friends with some of the members, nor is it to suggest that you should try to befriend us for the purpose of making theory with us. The latter would be a perversion of friendship. Rather, from within friendship you may be moved by friendship to undergo the very difficult task of understanding the text of our cultures by understanding our lives in our communities. This learning calls for circumspection, for questioning of your-selves and your roles in your own culture. It necessitates a striving to understand while in the comfortable position of not having an official calling card (as "scientific" observers of our communities have); it demands recognition that you do not have the authority of knowledge; it requires coming to the task without ready-made theories to frame our lives. This learning is then extremely hard because it requires openness (in-cluding openness to severe criticism of the white/Anglo world), sensitivity, concentration, self-questioning, circumspection. It should be clear that it does not consist in a passive immer-sion in our cultures, but in a striving to under-stand what it is that our voices are saying. Only then can we engage in a mutual dialogue that does not reduce each one of us to instances of the abstraction called "women."

Sisterhood: Political Solidarity Between Women

Bell Hooks

Women are the group most victimized by sexist oppression. As with other forms of group oppression, sexism is perpetuated by institutional and social structures; by the individuals who dominate, exploit, or oppress; and by the victims themselves who are socialized to behave in ways that make them act in complicity with the status quo. Male supremacist ideology encourages women to believe we are valueless and obtain value only by relating to or bonding with men. We are taught that our relationships with one another diminish rather than enrich our experience. We are taught that women are "natural" enemies, that solidarity will never exist between us because we cannot, should not, and do not bond with one another. We have learned these lessons well. We must unlearn them if we are to build a sustained feminist movement. We must learn to live and work in solidarity. We must learn the true meaning and value of Sisterhood.

Although contemporary feminist movement should have provided a training ground for women to learn about political solidarity, Sisterhood was not viewed as a revolutionary

Reprinted form *Women and Revolution* edited by Lydia Sargent and *Feminist Theory: from Margin to Center* by Bell Hooks with permission from the publisher. South End Press, 116 Saint Botolph St., Boston, MA 02115 U.S.A.

accomplishment women would work and struggle to obtain. The vision of Sisterhood evoked by women's liberationists was based on the idea of common oppression. Needless to say, it was primarily bourgeois white women, both liberal and radical in perspective, who professed belief in the notion of common oppression. The idea of "common oppression" was a false and corrupt platform disguising and mystifying the true nature of women's varied and complex social reality. Women are divided by sexist attitudes, racism, class privilege, and a host of other prejudices. Sustained woman bonding can occur only when these divisions are confronted and the necessary steps are taken to eliminate them. Divisions will not be eliminated by wishful thinking or romantic reverie about common oppression despite the value of highlighting experiences all women share.

In recent years Sisterhood as slogan, motto, rallying cry no longer evokes the spirit of power in unity. Some feminists now seem to feel that unity between women is impossible given our differences. Abandoning the idea of Sisterhood as an expression of political solidarity weakens and diminishes feminist movement. Solidarity strengthens resistance struggle. There can be no mass-based feminist movement to end sexist oppression without a united front—women must take the initiative and demonstrate the power of solidarity. Unless we can show that barriers separating women can be eliminated, that solidarity can exist, we cannot hope to change and transform society as a whole. The shift away from an emphasis on Sisterhood has occurred because many women, angered by the insistence on "common oppression," shared identity, sameness, criticized or dismissed feminist movement altogether. The emphasis on Sisterhood was often seen as the emotional appeal masking the opportunism of manipulative bourgeois white women. It was seen as a cover-up hiding the fact that many women exploit and oppress other women. Black woman activist lawyer Florynce Kennedy wrote an essay, published in the anthology *Sisterhood is Powerful,* voicing her suspicions about the existence of solidarity between women as early as 1970:

It is for this reason that I have considerable difficulty with the sisterhood mystique: "We are sisters," "Don't criticize a 'sister' publicly," etc. When a female judge asks my client where the bruises are when she complains about being assaulted by her husband (as did Family Court Judge Sylvia Jaffin Liese), and makes smart remarks about her being overweight, and when another female judge is so hostile that she disqualifies herself but refuses to order a combative husband out of the house (even though he owns property elsewhere with suitable living quarters)— these judges are not my sisters.

Women were wise to reject a false Sisterhood based on shallow notions of bonding. We are mistaken if we allow these distortions or the women who created them (many of whom now tell us bonding between women is unimportant) to lead us to devalue Sisterhood.

Women are enriched when we bond with one another but we cannot develop sustaining ties or political solidarity using the model of Sisterhood created by bourgeois women's liberationists. According to their analysis, the basis for bonding was shared victimization, hence the emphasis on common oppression. This concept of bonding directly reflects male supremacist thinking. Sexist ideology teaches women that to

be female is to be a victim. Rather than repudiate this equation (which mystifies female experience—in their daily lives most women are not continually passive, helpless, or powerless "victims"), women's liberationists embraced it, making shared victimization the basis for woman bonding. This meant that women had to conceive of themselves as "victims" in order to feel that feminist movement was relevant to their lives. Bonding as victims created a situation in which assertive, self-affirming women were often seen as having no place in feminist movement. It was this logic that led white women activists (along with black men) to suggest that black women were so "strong" they did not need to be active in feminist movement. It was this logic that led many white women activities to abandon feminist movement when they no longer embraced the victim identity. Ironically, the women who were most eager to be seen as "victims," who overwhelmingly stressed the role of victim, were more privileged and powerful than the vast majority of women in our society. An example of this tendency is some writing about violence against women. Women who are exploited and oppressed daily cannot afford to relinquish the belief that they exercise some measure of control, however relative, over their lives. They cannot afford to see themselves solely as "victims" because their survival depends on continued exercise of whatever personal powers they possess. It would be psychologically demoralizing for these women to bond with other women on the basis of shared victimization. They bond with other women on the basis of shared strengths and resources. This is the woman bonding feminist movement should encourage. It is this type of bonding that is the essence of Sisterhood.

Bonding as "victims," white women liberationists were not required to assume responsibility for confronting the complexity of their own experience. They were not challenging one another to examine their sexist attitudes towards women unlike themselves or exploring the impact of race and class privilege on their relationships to women outside their race/class groups. Identifying as "victims," they could abdicate responsibility for their role in the maintenance and perpetuation of sexism, racism, and classism, which they did by insisting that only men were the enemy. They did not acknowledge and confront the enemy within. They were not prepared to forego privilege and do the "dirty work" (the struggle and confrontation necessary to build political awareness as well as the many tedious tasks to be accomplished in day to day organizing) that is necessary in the development of radical political consciousness. Sisterhood became yet another shield against reality, another support system. Their version of Sisterhood was informed by racist and classist assumption about white womanhood, that the white "lady" (that is to say bourgeois woman) should be protected from all that might upset or discomfort her and shielded from negative realities that might lead to confrontation. Their version of Sisterhood dictated that sisters were to "unconditionally" love one another; that they were to avoid conflict and minimize disagreement; that they were not to criticize one other, especially in public. For a time these mandates created an illusion of unity suppressing the competition, hostility, perpetual disagreement, and abusive criticism (trashing) that was often the norm in feminist groups. Today many splinter groups who share common identities (e.g. Wasp working class; white academic faculty women; anarchist feminists, etc.) use this same model of Sisterhood, but participants in these groups endeavor to support, affirm, and protect one another while demonstrating hostility (usually through excessive trashing) towards women outside the chosen sphere. Bonding between a chosen circle of women who strengthen their ties by excluding and devaluing women outside their group closely resembles the type of personal bonding between women that has always occurred under patriarchy: the one difference being the interest in feminism.

To develop political solidarity between women, feminist activists cannot bond on the terms set by the dominant ideology of the culture. We must define our own terms. Rather than bond on the basis of shared victimization or in response to a false sense of a common enemy, we can bond on the basis of our political commitment to a feminist movement that aims to end sexist oppression. Given such a commitment, our energies would not be concentrated on the issue of equality with men or solely on the struggle to resist male domination. We would no longer accept a simplistic good girls/bad boys account of the structure of sexist oppression. Before we can resist male domination we must break our attachment to sexism; we must work to transform female consciousness. Working together to expose, examine, and eliminate sexist socialization within ourselves, women would strengthen and affirm one another and build a solid foundation for developing political solidarity.

Between women and men, sexism is most often expressed in the form of male domination which leads to discrimination, exploitation, or oppression. Between women, male supremacist values are expressed through suspicious, defensive, competitive behavior. It is sexism that leads women to feel threatened by one another without cause. While sexism teaches women to be sex objects for men, it is also manifest when women who have repudiated this role feel contemptuous and superior in relation to those women who have not. Sexism leads women to devalue parenting work while inflating the value of jobs and careers. Acceptance of sexist ideology is indicated when women teach children that there are only two possible behavior patterns: the role of dominant or submissive being. Sexism teaches women woman-hating, and both consciously and unconsciously we act out this hatred in our daily contact with one another.

Although contemporary feminist activists, especially radical feminists, called attention to women's absorption in sexist ideology, ways that women who are advocates of patriarchy, as well as women who uncritically accept sexist assumptions, could unlearn that socialization were not stressed. It was often assumed that to support feminism was synonymous with repudiation of sexism in all its forms. Taking on the label "feminist" was accepted as a sign of personal transformation; as a consequence, the process by which values were altered was either ignored or could not be spelled out because no fundamental change had occurred. Sometimes consciousness-raising groups provided space for women to explore their sexism. This examination of attitudes towards themselves and other women was often a catalyst for transformation. Describing the function of rap groups in *The Politics of Women's Liberation*, Jo Freeman explains:

Women came together in small groups to share personal experiences, problems, and feelings. From this public sharing comes the realization that what was thought to be individual is in fact common: that what was thought to be a personal problem has a social cause and a political solution. The rap group attacks the effects of psychological oppression and helps women to put it into a feminist context. Women learn to see how social structures and attitudes have molded them from birth and limited their opportunities. They ascertain the extent to which women have been denigrated in this society and how they have developed prejudices against themselves and other women. They learn to develop self-esteem and to appreciate the value of group solidarity.

As consciousness-raising groups lost their popularity new groups were not formed to fulfill similar functions. Women produced a large quantity of feminist writing but placed little emphasis on ways to unlearn sexism.

Since we live in a society that promotes fadism and temporary superficial adaptation of different values, we are easily convinced that changes have occurred in arenas where there has been little or no change. Women's sexist attitudes towards one another are one such arena. All over the United States, women spend hours of their time daily verbally abusing other women, usually through malicious gossip (not to be confused with gossip as positive communication). Television soap operas and night time dramas continually portray woman-to-woman relationships as characterized by aggression, contempt, and competitiveness. In feminist circles sexism towards women is expressed by abusive trashing, total disregard and lack of concern or interest in women who have not joined feminist movement. This is especially evident at university campuses where feminist studies is often seen as a discipline or program having no relationship to feminist movement. In her commencement address at Barnard College in May, 1979, black woman writer Toni Morrison told her audience:

I want not to ask you but to tell you not to participate in the oppression of your sisters. Mothers who abuse their children are women, and another woman, not an agency, has to be willing to stay their hands. Mothers who set fire to school buses are women, and another woman, not an agency, has to tell them to stay their hands. Women who stop the promotion of other women in careers are women, and another woman must come to the victim's aid. Social and welfare workers who humiliate their clients may be women, and other women colleagues have to deflect their anger.

I am alarmed by the violence that women do to each other: professional violence, competitive violence, emotional violence. I am alarmed by the willingness of women to enslave other women. I am alarmed by a growing absence of decency on the killing floor of professional women's worlds.

To build a politicized, mass-based feminist movement, women must work harder to overcome the alienation from one another that exists when sexist socialization has not been unlearned, e.g. homophobia, judging by appearance, conflicts between women with diverse sexual practices. So far, feminist movement has not transformed woman-to-woman relationships, especially between women who are strangers to one another or from different backgrounds, even though it has been the occasion for bonding between individuals and groups of women. We must renew our efforts to help women unlearn sexism if we are to develop affirming personal relationships as well as political unity.

Racism is another barrier to solidarity between women. The ideology of Sisterhood as expressed by contemporary feminist activists indicated no acknowledgement that racist discrimination, exploitation, and oppression of multi-ethnic women by white women had made it impossible for the two groups to feel they shared common interests or political concerns. Also, the existence of totally different cultural backgrounds can make communication difficult. This has been especially true of black and white female relationships. Historically, many black women experienced white women as the white supremacist group who most directly exercised power over them, often in a manner far more brutal and dehumanizing than that of racist white men. Today, despite predominant rule by white supremacist patriarchs, black women often work in situations where the immediate supervisor, boss, or authority figure is a white woman. Conscious of the privileges white men as well as white women gain as a consequence of racial domination, black women were quick to react to the feminist call for Sisterhood by pointing to the contradiction—that we should join with women who exploit us to help liberate them. The call for Sisterhood was heard by many black women as a plea for help and support for a movement that did not address us. As Toni Morrison explains in her article "What the Black Woman Thinks About Women's Lib," many black women do not respect bourgeois white women and could not imagine supporting a cause that would be for their benefit.

Black women have been able to envy white women (their looks, their easy life, the attention they seem to get from their men); they could fear them (for the economic control they have had over black women's lives); and even love them (as mammies and domestic workers can); but black women have found it impossible to respect white women . . . Black women have no abiding admiration of white women as competent, complete people, whether vying with them for the few professional slots available to women in general, or moving their dirt from one place to another, they regarded them as willful children, pretty children, mean children, but never as real adults capable of handling the real problems of the world.

White women were ignorant of the facts of life— perhaps by choice, perhaps with the assistance of men, but ignorant anyway. They were totally dependent on marriage or male support (emotionally and economically). They confronted their sexuality with furtiveness, complete abandon, or repression. Those who could afford it gave over the management of the house and the rearing of children to others. (It is a source of amusement even now to black women to listen to feminist talk of liberation while somebody's nice black grandmother shoulders the daily responsibility of child rearing and floor mopping, and the liberated one comes home to examine the housekeeping, correct it, and be entertained by the children.) If Women's Lib needs those grandmothers to thrive, it has a serious flaw.

Many perceived that women's liberation movement as outlined by bourgeois white women would serve their interests at the expense of poor and working class women, many of whom are black. Certainly this was not a basis for Sisterhood and black women would have been politically naive had we joined such a movement. However, given the struggles of black women's participation historically and currently in political organizing, the emphasis could have been on the development and clarification of the nature of political solidarity.

White females discriminate against and exploit black women while simultaneously being envious and competitive in their interactions with them. Neither process of interaction creates conditions wherein trust and mutually reciprocal relationships can develop. After constructing feminist theory and praxis in such a way as to omit focus on racism, white women shifted the responsibility for calling attention to race onto others. They did not have to take the initiative in discussions of racism or race privilege but could listen and respond to non-white women discussing racism without changing in any way the structure of feminist movement, without losing their hegemonic hold. They could then show their concern with having more women of color in feminist organizations by encouraging greater participation. They were not confronting racism. In more recent years, racism has become an accepted topic in feminist discussions not as a result of black women calling attention to it (this was done at the very onset of the movement), but as a result of white female input validating such discussions, a process which is indicative of how racism works. Commenting on this tendency in her essay "The Incompatible Menage À Trois: Marxism, Feminism, and Racism," Gloria Joseph states:

To date feminists have not concretely demonstrated the potential or capacity to become involved in fighting racism on an equal footing with sexism. Adrienne Rich's recent article on feminism and racism is an exemplary one on this topic. She reiterates much that has been voiced by black female writers, but the acclaim given her article shows again that it takes whiteness to give even Blackness validity.

Focus on racism in feminist circles is usually directed at legitimating the "as is" structure of feminist theory and praxis. Like other affirmative action agendas in white supremacist capitalist patriarchy, lengthy discussions of racism or lip-service to its importance tend to call attention to the "political correctness" of current feminist movement; they are not directed at an overall struggle to resist racist oppression in our society (not just racism in feminist movement). Discussions of racism have been implicitly sexist because of the focus on guilt and personal behavior. Racism is not an issue simply because white women activists are individually racist. They represent a small percentage of women in this society. They could have all been anti-racist from the outset but eliminating racism would still need to be a central feminist issue. Racism is fundamentally a feminist issue because it is so inter-connected with sexist oppression. In the West, the philosophical foundations of racist and sexist ideology are similar. Although ethnocentric white values have led feminist theorists to argue the priority of sexism over racism, they do so in the context of attempting to create an evolutionary notion of culture, which in no way corresponds to our lived experience. In the United States, maintaining white supremacy has always been as great if not a greater priority than maintaining strict sex role divisions. It is no mere coincidence that interest in white women's rights is kindled whenever there is mass-based anti-racist protest. Even the most politically naive person can comprehend that a white supremacist state, asked to respond to the needs of oppressed black people and/or the needs of white women (particularly those from the bourgeois classes), will find it in its interest to respond to whites. Radical movement to end racism (a struggle that many have died to advance) is far more threatening than a women's movement shaped to meet the class needs of upwardly mobile white women.

It does not in any way diminish the value of or the need for feminist movement to recognize the significance of anti-racist struggle. Feminist theory would have much to offer if it showed women ways in which racism and sexism are immutably connected rather than pitting one struggle against the other or blatantly dismissing racism. A central issue for feminist activists has been the struggle to obtain for women the right to control their bodies. The very concept of white supremacy relies on the perpetuation of a white race. It is in the interest of continued white racist domination of the planet for white patriarchy to maintain control over all women's bodies. Any white female activist who works daily to help women gain control over their bodies and is racist negates and undermines her own effort. When white women attack white supremacy they are simultaneously participating in the struggle to end sexist oppression. This is just one example of the intersecting, complementary nature of racist and sexist oppression. There are many others that need to be examined by feminist theorists.

Racism allows white women to construct feminist theory and praxis in such a way that it is far removed from anything resembling radical struggle. Racist socialization teaches bourgeois white women to think they are necessarily more capable of leading masses of women than other groups of women. Time and time again, they have shown that they do not want to be part of feminist movement—they want to lead it. Even though bourgeois white women liberationists probably know less about grassroots organizing than many poor and working class women, they were certain of their leadership ability, as well as confident that theirs should be the dominant role in shaping theory and praxis. Racism teaches an inflated sense of importance and value, especially when coupled with class privilege. Most poor and working class women or even individual bourgeois non-white women would not have assumed that they could launch a feminist movement without first having the support and participation of diverse groups of women. Elizabeth Spelman stresses this impact of racism in her essay, "Theories of Race and Gender: The Erasure of Black Women":

. . . this is a racist society, and part of what this means is that, generally, the self-esteem of white people is deeply influenced by their difference from and supposed superiority to black people. White people may not think of themselves as racists, because they do not own slaves or hate blacks, but that does not mean that much of what props up white people's sense of self-esteem is not based on the racism which unfairly distributes benefits and burdens to whites and blacks.

One reason white women active in feminist movement were unwilling to confront racism was their arrogant assumption that their call for Sisterhood was a non-racist gesture. Many white women have said to me, "we wanted black women and other non-white women to join the movement," totally unaware of their perception that they somehow "own" the movement, that they are the "hosts" inviting us as "guests."

Despite current focus on eliminating racism in feminist movement, there has been little change in the direction of theory and praxis. While white feminist activists now include writings by women of color on course outlines, or hire one woman of color to teach a class about her ethnic group, or make sure one or more women of color are represented in feminist organizations, (even though this contribution of women of color is needed and valuable) more often than not they are attempting to cover up the fact that they are totally unwilling to surrender their hegemonic dominance of theory and praxis, a dominance which they would not have established were this not a white supremacist, capitalist state. Their attempts to manipulate women of color, a component of the process of dehumanization, do not always go unnoticed. In the July 1983 issue of *In These Times*, a letter written by Theresa Funiciello was published on the subject of poor women and the women's movement which shows the nature of racism within feminist movement:

Prior to a conference some time ago on the Urban Woman sponsored by the New York City chapter of NOW, I received a phone call from a NOW representative (whose name I have forgotten) asking for a welfare speaker with special qualifications. I was asked that she not be white—she might be "too articulate"—(i.e. not me), that she not be black, she might be "too angry." Perhaps she could be Puerto Rican? She should not say anything political or analytical but confine herself to the subject of "what the women's movement has done for me."

Funiciello responded to this situation by organizing a multiracial women's takeover of the conference. This type of action shows the spirit of Sisterhood.

Another response to racism has been the establishment of unlearning racism workshops, which are often led by white women. These workshops are important, yet they tend to focus primarily on cathartic individual psychological acknowledgement of personal prejudice without stressing the need for corresponding change in political commitment and action. A woman who attends an unlearning racism workshop and learns to acknowledge that she is racist is no less a threat than one who does not. Acknowledgement of racism is significant when it leads to transformation. More research, writing, and practical implementation of findings must be done on ways to unlearn racist socialization. Many white women who daily exercise race privilege lack awareness that they are doing so (which explains the emphasis on confession in unlearning racism workshops). They may not have conscious understanding of the ideology of white supremacy and the extent to which it shapes their behavior and attitudes towards women unlike themselves. Often, white women bond on the basis of shared racial identity without conscious awareness of the significance of their actions. This unconscious maintenance and perpetuation of white supremacy is dangerous because none of us can struggle to change racist attitudes if we do not recognize that they exist. For example, a group of white feminist activists who do not know one another may be present at a meeting to discuss feminist theory. They may feel they are bonded on the basis of shared womanhood, but the atmosphere will noticeably change when a woman of color enters the room. The white women will become

tense, no longer relaxed, no longer celebratory. Unconsciously, they felt close to one another because they shared racial identity. The "whiteness" that bonds them together is a racial identity that is directly related to the experience of non-white people as "other" and as a "threat." Often when I speak to white women about racial bonding, they deny that it exists; it is not unlike sexist men denying their sexism. Until white supremacy is understood and attacked by white women there can be no bonding between them and multi-ethnic groups of women.

Women will know that white feminist activists have begun to confront racism in a serious and revolutionary manner when they are not simply acknowledging racism in feminist movement or calling attention to personal prejudice, but are actively struggling to resist racist oppression in our society. Women will know they have made a political commitment to eliminating racism when they help change the direction of feminist movement, when they work to unlearn racist socialization prior to assuming positions of leadership or shaping theory or making contact with women of color so that they will not perpetuate and maintain racial oppression or, unconsciously or consciously, abuse and hurt non-white women. These are the truly radical gestures that create a foundation for the experience of political solidarity between white women and women of color.

White women are not the only group who must confront racism if Sisterhood is to emerge. Women of color must confront our absorption of white supremacist beliefs, "internalized racism," which may lead us to feel self-hate, to vent anger and rage at injustice at one another rather than at oppressive forces, to hurt and abuse one another, or to lead one ethnic group to make no effort to communicate with another. Often women of color from varied ethnic groups have learned to resent and hate one another, or to be competitive with one another. Often Asian, Latina, or Native American Indian groups find they can bond with whites by hating blacks. Black people respond to this by perpetuating racist stereotypes and images of these ethnic groups. It becomes a vicious cycle. Divisions between women of color will not be eliminated until we assume responsibility for uniting (not solely on the basis of resisting racism) to learn about our cultures, to share our knowledge and skills, and to gain strength from our diversity. We need to do more research and writing about the barriers that separate us and the ways we can overcome such separation. Often the men in our ethnic groups have greater contact with one another than we do. Women often assume so many job-related and domestic responsibilities that we lack the time or do not make the time to get to know women outside our group or community. Language differences often prevent us from communicating; we can change this by encouraging one another to learn to speak Spanish, English, Japanese, Chinese, etc.

One factor that makes interaction between multi-ethnic groups of women difficult and sometimes impossible is our failure to recognize that a behavior pattern in one culture may be unacceptable in another, that it may have different signification cross-culturally. Through repeated teaching of a course titled "Third World Women in the United States," I have learned the importance of learning what we called one another's cultural codes. An Asian-American student, of Japanese heritage, explained her reluctance to participate in feminist organizations by calling attention to the tendency among feminist activists to speak rapidly without pause, to be quick on the uptake, always ready with a response. She had been raised to pause and think before speaking, to consider the impact of one's words, a characteristic which she felt was particularly true of Asian-Americans. She expressed feelings of inadequacy on the various occasions she was present in feminist groups. In our class, we learned to allow pauses and appreciate them. By sharing this cultural code, we created an atmosphere in

the classroom that allowed for different communication patterns. This particular class was peopled primarily by black women. Several white women students complained that the atmosphere in the class was "too hostile." They cited the noise level and direct confrontations that took place in the room prior to class starting as an example of this hostility. Our response was to explain that what they perceived as hostility and aggression, we considered playful teasing and affectionate expressions of our pleasure at being together. Our tendency to talk loudly we saw as a consequence of being in a room with many people speaking as well as cultural background: many of us were raised in families where individuals speak loudly. In their upbringing as white, middle class females, the complaining students had been taught to identify loud and direct speech with anger. We explained that we did not identify loud or blunt speech in this way, and encouraged them to switch codes, to think of it as an affirming gesture. Once they switched codes, they not only began to have a more creative, joyful experience in the class, but they also learned that silence and quiet speech can in some cultures indicate hostility and aggression. By learning one another's cultural codes and respecting our differences, we felt a sense of community, of Sisterhood. Respecting diversity does not mean uniformity or sameness.

A crucial concern in these multi-racial classroom settings was recognition and acknowledgement of our differences and the extent to which they determine how we will be perceived by others. We had to continually remind one another to appreciate difference since many of us were raised to fear it. We talked about the need to acknowledge that we all suffer in some way but that we are not all oppressed nor equally oppressed. Many of us feared that our experiences were irrelevant because they were not as oppressive or as exploited as the experience of others. We discovered that we had a greater feeling of unity when people focused truthfully on their own experiences without comparing them with those of others in a competitive way. One student, Isabel Yrigoyei, wrote:

We are not equally oppressed. There is no joy in this. We must speak from within us, our own experiences, our own oppressions—taking someone else's oppression is nothing to feel proud of. We should never speak for that which we have not felt.

When we began our communication by focusing on individual experiences, we found them to be varied even among those of us who shared common ethnic backgrounds. We learned that these differences mean we have no monolithic experiences that we can identity as "Chicana experience," "Black experience," etc. A Chicana growing up in a rural environment in a Spanish-speaking home has a life experience that differs from that of a Chicana raised in an English-speaking family in a bourgeois, predominantly white New Jersey suburb. These two women will not automatically feel solidarity. Even though they are from the same ethnic group, they must work to develop Sisterhood. Seeing these types of differences, we also confronted our tendency to value some experiences over others. We might see the Spanish-speaking Chicana as being more "politically correct" than her English-speaking peer. By no longer passively accepting the learned tendency to compare and judge, we could see value in each experience. We could also see that our different experiences often meant that we had different needs, that there was no one strategy or formula for the development of political consciousness. By mapping out various strategies, we affirmed our diversity while working towards solidarity. Women must explore various ways to communicate with one another cross-culturally if we are to develop political solidarity. When women of color strive to learn with and about one another we take responsibility for building Sisterhood. We need not rely on white women to lead the way to solidarity; all too often oppor-

tunistic concerns point them in other directions. We can establish unity among ourselves with anti-racist women. We can stand together united in political solidarity, in feminist movement. We can restore to the idea of Sisterhood its true meaning and value.

Cutting across racial lines, class is a serious political division between women. It was often suggested in early feminist literature that class would not be so important if more poor and working class women would join the movement. Such thinking was both a denial of the existence of class privilege gained through exploitation as well as a denial of class struggle. To build Sisterhood, women must criticize and repudiate class exploitation. The bourgeois woman who takes a less privileged "sister" to lunch or dinner at a fancy restaurant may be acknowledging class but she is not repudiating class privilege—she is exercising it. Wearing second hand clothing and living in low-cost housing in a poor neighborhood while buying stock is not a gesture of solidarity with those who are deprived or under-privileged. As in the case of racism in feminist movement, the emphasis on class has been focused on individual status and change. Until women accept the need for redistribution of wealth and resources in the United States and work towards the achievement of that end, there will be no bonding between women that transcends class.

It is terribly apparent that feminist movement so far has primarily served the class interests of bourgeois white women and men. The great majority of women from middle class situations who recently entered the labor force (an entry encouraged and promoted by feminist movement) helped strengthen the economy of the 1970s. In *The Two-Paycheck Marriage*, Caroline Bird emphasizes the extent to which these women (most of whom are white) helped bolster a waning economy:

Working wives helped families maintain that standard of living through inflation. The Bureau of Labor Statistics has concluded that between 1973 and 1974 the real purchasing power of single-earner families dropped 3 percent compared with only 1 percent for families in which the wife was working . . . Women especially will put themselves out to defend a standard of living they see threatened.

Women did more than maintain standards. Working women lifted millions of families into middle class life. Her pay meant the difference between an apartment and a house, or college for the children . . .

. . . Working wives were beginning to create a new kind of rich—and . . . a new kind of poor.

More than ten years later, it is evident that large numbers of individual white women (especially those from middle class backgrounds) have made economic strides in the wake of feminist movement support of careerism, and affirmative action programs in many professions. However, the masses of women are as poor as ever, or poorer. To the bourgeois "feminist," the million dollar salary granted newscaster Barbara Walters represents a victory for women. To working class women who make less than the minimum wage and receive few if any benefits, it means continued class exploitation.

Leah Fritz's *Dreamers and Dealers* is a fine example of the liberal woman's attempt to gloss over the fact that class privilege is based on exploitation, that rich women support and condone that exploitation, that the people who suffer most are poor, under-privileged women and children. Fritz attempts to evoke sympathy for all upper class women by stressing their psychological suffering, their victimization at the hands of men. She concludes her chapter "Rich Women" with the statement:

Feminism belongs as much to the rich woman as to the poor woman. It can help her to understand that her own interests are linked with the advancement of all womankind; that comfort in dependency is a trap; that the golden cage has bars, too; and that, rich and poor, we are all wounded in the service of the patriarchy, although our scars are different. The inner turmoil that sends her to a psychoanalyst can generate energy for the movement which alone may heal her, by setting her free.

Fritz conveniently ignores that domination and exploitation are necessary if there are to be rich women who may experience sexist discrimination or exploitation. She conveniently ignores class struggle.

Women from lower class groups had no difficulty recognizing that the social equality women's liberationists talked about equated careerism and class mobility with liberation. They also knew who would be exploited in the service of this liberation. Daily confronting class exploitation, they cannot conveniently ignore class struggle. In the anthology *Women of Crisis*, Helen, a working class white woman, who works as a maid in the home of a bourgeois white "feminist" expresses her understanding of the contradiction between feminist rhetoric and practice:

I think the missus is right: everyone should be equal. She keeps on saying that. But then she has me working away in her house, and I'm not equal with her— and she doesn't want to be equal with me; and I don't blame her, because if I was her I'd hold on to my money just like she does. Maybe that's what the men are doing—they're holding on to their money. And it's a big fight, like it always is about money. She should know. She doesn't go throwing big fat pay checks at her "help." She's fair; she keeps on reminding us—but she's not going to "liberate" us, any more than the men are going to "liberate" their wives or their secretaries or the other women working in their companies

Women's liberationists not only equated psychological pain with material deprivation to de-emphasize class privilege; they often suggested it was the more severe problem. They managed to overlook the fact that many women suffer both psychologically and materially and for that reason alone changing their social status merited greater attention than careerism. Certainly the bourgeois woman who is suffering psychically is more likely to find help than the woman who is suffering material deprivation as well as emotional pain. One of the basic differences in perspective between the bourgeois woman and the working class or poor woman is that the latter know that being discriminated against or exploited because one is female may be painful and dehumanizing, but it may not necessarily be as painful, dehumanizing, or threatening as being without food or shelter, as starvation, as being deathly ill but unable to obtain medical care. Had poor women set the agenda for feminist movement, they might have decided that class struggle would be a central feminist issue; that poor and privileged women would work to understand class structure and the way it pits women against one another.

Outspoken socialist feminists, most of whom are white women, have emphasized class but they have not been effective in changing attitudes towards class in feminist movement. Despite their support of socialism, their values, behaviors, and lifestyles continue to be shaped by privilege. They have not developed collective strategies to convince bourgeois women who have no radical political perspective that eliminating class oppression is crucial to efforts to end sexist oppression. They have not worked hard to organize with poor and working class women who may not identify as socialists but do identify with the need for redistribution of wealth in the United States. They have not worked to raise the consciousness of women collectively. Much of their energy has been spent addressing the white male left, discussing the connections between marxism and feminism, or explaining to other feminist activists that socialist feminism is the best strategy for revolution. Emphasis on class struggle is often incorrectly deemed the sole domain of socialist feminists. Although I call attention to directions and strategies they have not employed, I wish to emphasize that these issues should be addressed by all activists in feminist movement. When

women face the reality of classism and make political commitments to eliminating it, we will no longer experience the class conflicts that have been so apparent in feminist movement. Until we focus on class divisions between women, we will be unable to build political solidarity.

Sexism, racism, and classism divide women from one another. Within feminist movement, divisions and disagreements about strategy and emphasis led to the formation of a number of groups with varied political positions. Splintering into different political factions and special interest groups has erected unnecessary barriers to Sisterhood that could easily be eliminated. Special interest groups lead women to believe that only socialist feminists should be concerned about class; that only lesbian feminists should be concerned about the oppression of lesbians and gay men; that only black women or other women of color should be concerned about racism. Every woman can stand in political opposition to sexist, racist, heterosexist, and classist oppression. While she may choose to focus her work on a given political issue or a particular cause, if she is firmly opposed to all forms of group oppression, this broad perspective will be manifest in all her work irrespective of its particularity. When feminist activists are anti-racist and against class exploitation, it will not matter if women of color are present or poor women, etc. These issues will be deemed important and will be addressed, although the women most personally affected by particular exploitations will necessarily continue in the forefront of those struggles. Women must learn to accept responsibility for fighting oppressions that may not directly affect us as individuals. Feminist movement, like other radical movements in our society, suffers when individual concerns and priorities are the only reason for participation. When we show our concern for the collective, we strengthen our solidarity.

Solidarity was a word seldom used in contemporary feminist movement. Much greater emphasis was placed on the idea of "support."

Support can mean upholding or defending a position one believes is right. It can also mean serving as a prop or a foundation for a weak structure. This latter meaning had greater significance in feminist circles. Its value emerged from the emphasis on shared victimization. Identifying as "victims," women were acknowledging a helplessness and powerlessness as well as a need for support, in this case the support of fellow feminist activists, "sisters." It was closely related to the shallow notion of Sisterhood. Commenting on its usage among feminist activists in her essay "With All Due Respect," Jane Rule explains:

Support is a much used word in the women's movement. For too many people it means giving and receiving unqualified approval. Some women are awfully good at withdrawing it at crucial moments. Too many are convinced they can't function without it. It's a false concept which has produced barriers to understanding and done real emotional damage. Suspension of critical judgement is not necessary for offering real support, which has to do instead with self-respect and respect for other people even at moments of serious disagreement.

Women's legacy of woman-hating which includes fierce, brutal, verbal tearing apart of one another has to be eliminated if women are to make critiques and engage in disagreements and arguments that are constructive and caring, with the intention of enriching rather than diminishing. Woman-to-woman negative, aggressive behavior is not unlearned when all critical judgement is suspended. It is unlearned when women accept that we are different, that we will necessarily disagree, but that we can disagree and argue with one another without acting as if we are fighting for our lives, without feeling that we stand to lose all self-esteem by verbally trashing someone else. Verbal disagreements are often the setting where women can demonstrate their engagement with the win-or-lose competitiveness that is most often associated with male interactions, especially in the

arena of sports. Women, like men, must learn how to dialogue with one another without competition. Jane Rule suggests that women can disagree without trashing if they realize they do not stand to lose value or self-worth if they are criticized: "No one can discredit my life if it is in my own hands, and therefore I do not have to make anyone carry the false burden of my frightened hostility."

Women need to come together in situations where there will be ideological disagreement and work to change that interaction so communication occurs. This means that when women come together, rather than pretend union, we would acknowledge that we are divided and must develop strategies to overcome fears, prejudices, resentments, competitiveness, etc. The fierce negative disagreements that have taken place in feminist circles have led many feminist activists to shun group or individual interaction where there is likely to be disagreement which leads to confrontation. Safety and support have been redefined to mean hanging out in groups where the participants are alike and share similar values. While no woman wants to enter a situation in which she will be psychically annihilated, women can face one another in hostile confrontation and struggle and move beyond the hostility to understanding. Expression of hostility as an end in itself is a useless activity, but when it is the catalyst pushing us on to greater clarity and understanding, it serves a meaningful function.

Women need to have the experience of working through hostility to arrive at understanding and solidarity if only to free ourselves from the sexist socialization that tells us to avoid confrontation because we will be victimized or destroyed. Time and time again, I have had the experience of making statements at talks that anger a listener and lead to assertive and sometimes hostile verbal confrontation. The situation feels uncomfortable, negative, and unproductive because there are angry voices, tears, etc. and yet I may find later that the experience has led to greater clarity and growth on my part and on the part of the listener. On one occasion, I was invited by a black woman sociologist, a very soft-spoken individual, to speak in a class she was teaching. A young Chicana woman who could pass for white was a student in the class. We had a heated exchange when I made the point that the ability to pass for white gave her a perspective on race totally different from that of someone who is dark-skinned and can never pass. I pointed out that any person meeting her with no knowledge of her ethnic background probably assumes that she is white and relates to her accordingly. At the time the suggestion angered her. She became quite angry and finally stormed out of the class in tears. The teacher and fellow students definitely saw me as the "bad guy" who had failed to support a fellow sister and instead reduced her to tears. They were annoyed that our get together had not been totally pleasurable, unemotional, dispassionate. I certainly felt miserable in the situation. The student, however, contacted me weeks later to share her feelings that she had gained new insights and awareness as a result of our encounter which aided her personal growth. Incidents like this one, which initially appear to be solely negative because of tension or hostility, can lead to positive growth. If women always seek to avoid confrontation, to always be "safe," we may never experience any revolutionary change, any transformation, individually or collectively.

When women actively struggle in a truly supportive way to understand our differences, to change misguided, distorted perspectives, we lay the foundation for the experience of political solidarity. Solidarity is not the same as support. To experience solidarity, we must have a community of interests, shared beliefs and goals around which to unite, to build Sisterhood. Support can be occasional. It can be given and just as easily withdrawn. Solidarity requires sustained, ongoing commitment. In feminist movement, there is need for diversity, disagreement, and difference if we are to grow. As Grace Lee Boggs and James Boggs emphasize in *Revolution and Evolution in the Twentieth Century*:

The same appreciation of the reality of contradiction underlies the concept of criticism and self-criticism. Criticism and self-criticism is the way in which individuals united by common goals can consciously utilize their differences and limitations, i.e., the negative, in order to accelerate their positive advance. The popular formulation for this process is "changing a bad thing into a good thing . . ."

Women do not need to eradicate difference to feel solidarity. We do not need to share common oppression to fight equally to end oppression. We do not need anti-male sentiments to bond us together, so great is the wealth of experience, culture, and ideas we have to share with one another. We can be sisters united by shared interests and beliefs, united in our appreciation for diversity, united in our struggle to end sexist oppression, united in political solidarity.

❧ Suggested Reading ❧

Problems of Gender Inequality

ALLEN, JEFFNER. *Lesbian Philosophy: Explorations*. Palo Alto: Institute of Lesbian Studies, 1986.

AUERBACH, STEVANNE. *Confronting the Childcare Crisis*. Boston: Beacon Press, 1979.

BARRY, KATHLEEN. *Female Sexual Slavery*. Englewood Cliffs, NJ: Prentice-Hall, 1979.

BERK, SARAH F., ED. *Women and Household Labor*. Beverly Hills: Sage Publications, 1980.

BERNARD, JESSIE SHIRLEY, ED. *Future of Marriage*. New Haven: Yale University Press, 1982.

CURLEY, JAYME. *The Balancing Act II: A Career and a Family*. Chicago: Chicago Review Press, 1981.

DALY, MARY. *The Church and the Second Sex*. Boston: Beacon Press, 1985.

DAVIS, ANGELA Y. *Women, Race and Class*. New York: Random House, 1981.

DE LAURETIS, TERESA. *Technologies of Gender: Essays on Theory, Film and Fiction*. Bloomington: Indiana University Press, 1987.

DEGLER, CARL N. *At Odds: Women and the Family in America from the Revolution to the Present*. New York: Oxford University Press, 1980.

DWORKIN, ANDREA. *Our Blood: Prophecies and Discourses on Sexual Politics*. New York: Harper and Row, 1976.

DWORKIN, ANDREA. *Pornography: Men Possessing Women*. New York: E. P. Dutton, 1989.

EPSTEIN, CYNTHIA. *Women in Law*. Garden City, NY: Anchor Press/Doubleday, 1983.

FOX, VIVIAN C., AND MARTIN H. QUITT. *Loving, Parenting, and Dying: The Family Cycle in England and America, Past and Present*. New York: Psychohistory Press, 1980.

FRYE, MARILYN. *The Politics of Reality: Essays in Feminist Theory*. Trumansburg, NY: Crossing Press, 1983.

GILLIGAN, CAROL. *In a Different Voice: Psychological Theory and Woman's Development*. Cambridge: Harvard University Press, 1982.

HARDING, SANDRA, AND JEAN F. O'BARR, EDS. *Sex and Scientific Inquiry*. Chicago: University of Chicago Press, 1987.

HARDING, SANDRA. *The Science Question in Feminism*. Ithaca: Cornell University Press, 1986.

HARLEY, SHARON, AND ROSALYN TERBORG-PENN, EDS. *The Afro-American Woman: Struggles and Images*. Port Washington, NY: Kennikat Press, 1978.

HARRIS, ANN SUTHERLAND, AND LINDA NOCHLIN. *Women Artists 1550–1950*. Los Angeles: Los Angeles County Museum of Art, 1976.

HOOKS, BELL. *Ain't I a Woman: Black Women and Feminism*. Boston: South End Press, 1981.

HUBBARD, RUTH, ET AL. *Biological Woman—the Convenient Myth: A Collection of Feminist Essays*. Cambridge: Schenkman Publishing Company, 1982.

KELLER, EVELYN FOX. *Reflections on Gender and Science*. New Haven: Yale University Press, 1985.

KESSLER-HARRIS, ALICE. *Out to Work: A History of Wage-Earning Women in America*. New York: Oxford University Press, 1982.

LEDERER, LAURA, ED. *Take Back the Night: Women on Pornography*. New York: William Morrow, 1980.

MATTHAEI, JULIE A. *An Economic History of Women in America: Women's Work, the Sexual Division of Labor, and the Development of Capitalism*. New York: Schocken Books, 1982.

MELOSH, BARBARA. *"The Physician's Hand": Work Culture and Conflict in American Nursing*. Philadelphia: Temple University Press, 1982.

MELVILLE, MARGARITA B., ED. *Twice a Minority: Mexican-American Women*. St. Louis: Mosby, 1980.

MILLER, JEAN BAKER, ED. *Toward a New Psychology of Women*. Boston: Beacon Press, 1986.

MOORE, HENRIETTA L. *Feminism and Anthropology*. Minneapolis: University of Minnesota Press, 1988.

NEWTON, JUDITH AND DEBORAH ROSENFELT, EDS. *Feminist Criticism and Social Change: Sex, Class and Race in Literature and Crisis*. New York: Methuen, 1985.

O'NEIL, ONORA, AND WILLIAM RUDDICK. *Having Children: Philosophical and Legal Reflections on Parenthood*. New York: Oxford University Press, 1979.

PARKER, ROZSIKA, AND GRISELDA POLLOCK. *Old Mistresses: Women, Art, and Ideology*. New York: Pantheon Books, 1981.

RAPOPORT, RHONA AND ROBERT, WITH JANICE BUMSTEAD. *Working Couples*. London: Routledge Chapman and Hall, 1978.

REUTHER, ROSEMARY. *Women of Spirit: Female Leadership in the Jewish and Christian Traditions*. New York: Simon and Schuster, 1979.

RICH, ADRIENNE. *Of Women Born: Motherhood as Experience and Institution*. New York: Norton, 1986.

RUDDICK, SARA, AND PAMELA DANIELS. *Working It Out: Twenty-Three Women Writers, Artists, Scientists and Scholars Talk About Their Lives and Work*. New York: Pantheon Books, 1977.

SACKS, KAREN. *Sisters and Wives: The Past and the Future of Sexual Equality*. Westport, CT: Greenwood Press, 1979.

SCHAEF, ANNE WILSON. *Women's Reality: Emerging Female System in the White Male Society*. Minneapolis: Winston Press, 1985.

SILVERMAN, KAJA. *The Acoustic Mirror: The Female Voice in Psychoanalysis and Cinema*. Bloomington: Indiana University Press, 1988.

SMITH, DOROTHY E. *The Everyday World as Problematic: A Feminist Sociology*. Boston: Northeastern University Press, 1987.

STAPLES, ROBERT. *The Black Woman in America: Sex, Marriage and the Family*. Chicago: Nelson-Hall Publishers, 1973.

STRASSER, SUSAN. *Never Done: A History of American Housework*. New York: Pantheon Books, 1982.

TILLY, LOUISE, AND JOAN SCOTT. *Women, Work, and Family*. New York: Routledge Chapman and Hall, 1989.

TREBILCOT, JOYCE, ED. *Mothering: Essays in Feminist Theory*. Totowa, NJ: Rowman and Littlefield, 1990.

VANCE, CAROLE S., ED. *Pleasure and Danger: Exploring Female Sexuality*. Boston: Routledge Chapman and Hall, 1984.

WALLACE, RUTH A. *Feminism and Sociological Theory*. Newbury Park, CA: Sage Publications, 1989.

WEIDEGER, PAULA. *Menstruation and Menopause: The Physiology and Psychology, the Myth and the Reality*. New York: Dell, 1977.

WEITZ, SHIRLEY. *Sex Roles: Biological, Psychological and Social Foundations*. New York: Oxford University Press, 1977.

WOOLF, VIRGINIA. *A Room of One's Own*. New York: Harcourt Brace Jovanovich, 1989.

Feminist Theories and Applications

ALLEN, JEFFNER, AND MARION YOUNG, EDS. *The Thinking Muse: Feminism and Modern French Philosophy.* Bloomington: Indiana University Press, 1989.

BUNCH, CHARLOTTE. *Passionate Politics: Feminist Theory in Action, Essays 1968–1986.* New York: St. Martin's Press, 1987.

CHODOROW, NANCY. *The Reproduction of Mothering: Psychoanalysis and the Sociology of Gender.* Berkeley: University of California Press, 1978.

CLARK, LORENNE M. G. "Women and Locke: Who Owns the Apples in the Garden of Eden?" *The Sexism of Social and Political Theory: Women and Reproduction from Plato to Nietzsche.* Eds. Lorenne M. G. Clark and Lynda Lange. Toronto: University of Toronto Press, 1979.

DALY, MARY. *Gyn/ecology: The Metaethics of Radical Feminism.* Boston: Beacon Press, 1990.

DE BEAUVOIR, SIMONE. *The Second Sex.* New York: Alfred A. Knopf, 1975.

DIAMOND, IRENE, AND GLORIA ORENSTEIN, EDS. *Reweaving the World: The Emergence of Ecofeminism.* San Francisco: Sierra Club Books, 1990.

DINNERSTEIN, DOROTHY. *The Mermaid and the Minotaur: Sexual Arrangements and Human Malaise.* New York: Harper and Row, 1976.

EISENSTEIN, ZILLAH R. *The Radical Future of Liberal Feminism.* Boston: Northeastern University Press, 1981.

ELSHTAIN, JEAN BETHKE. *Public Man, Private Woman: Woman in Social and Political Thought.* Princeton: Princeton University Press, 1981.

FELDBERG, ROSLYN L. "Comparable Worth: Toward Theory and Practice in the United States." *Signs: Journal of Women in Culture and Society* 10 (2), Winter 1984, pp. 311–328.

FIRESTONE, SHULAMITH. *The Dialectic of Sex: The Case for Feminist Revolution.* New York: William Morrow, 1974.

FLAX, JANE. "Do Feminists Need Marxism?" *Building Feminist Theory: Essays from "Quest," A Feminist Quarterly.* New York: Longman, 1981, pp. 174–185.

FLAX, JANE. *Thinking Fragments: Psychoanalysis, Feminism, and Postmodernism in the Contemporary West.* Berkeley: University of California Press, 1989.

FRASER, NANCY. *Unruly Practices: Power, Discourse, and Gender in Contemporary Social Theory.* Minneapolis: University of Minnesota Press, 1989.

FRIEDAN, BETTY. *The Feminine Mystique.* New York: Dell, 1984.

GALLOP, JANE. *The Daughter's Seduction: Feminism and Psychoanalysis.* Ithaca: Cornell University Press, 1982.

HARAWAY, DONNA. "A Manifesto for Cyborgs: Science, Technology, and Socialist Feminism in the 1980's." *Feminism/Postmodernism.* Ed. Linda J. Nicholson. New York: Routledge Chapman and Hall, 1989.

HARTMANN, HEIDI. "Capitalism, Patriarchy, and Job Segregation by Sex." *Signs: Journal of Women in Culture and Society* 1 (3), part 2, 1976, pp. 773–776.

HARTMANN, HEIDI. "The Family as the Locus of Gender, Class, and Political Struggle: The Example of Housework." *Signs: Journal of Women in Culture and Society* 6 (3), 1981, pp. 336–394.

HARTSOCK, NANCY. "Staying Alive." *Quest* 3 (3), Winter 1976–1977, pp. 111–122.

HIRSCH, MARIANNE, AND EVELYN FOX KELLER, EDS. *Conflicts in Feminism.* New York: Routledge Chapman and Hall, 1990.

HOOKS, BELL. *Talking Back: Thinking Feminist, Thinking Black.* Boston: South End Press, 1989.

JAGGAR, ALISON M. *Feminist Politics and Human Nature.* Totowa, NJ: Rowman and Littlefield, 1983.

JAGGAR, ALISON M., AND SUSAN R. BORDO, EDS. *Gender/Body/Knowledge: Feminist Reconstruction of Being and Knowing.* New Brunswick, NJ: Rutgers University Press, 1989.

JONES, KATHLEEN B., AND ANNA G. JONASDOTTIR. *The Political Interests of Gender: Developing Theory and Research with a Feminist Face.* London: Sage Publications, 1988.

KITTAY, EVA FEDER, AND DIANA T. MEYERS, EDS. *Women and Moral Theory.* Totowa, NJ: Rowman and Littlefield, 1987.

LORDE, AUDRE. *A Burst of Light.* Ithaca: Firebrand Books, 1988.

LORDE, AUDRE. *Sister Outsider: Essays and Speeches.* Trumansburg, NY: Crossing Press, 1984.

MACKINNON, CATHARINE A. *Toward a Feminist Theory of the State.* Cambridge: Harvard University Press, 1989.

MILLETT, KATE. *Sexual Politics.* New York: Ballantine, 1978.

MITCHELL, JULIET. *Psychoanalysis and Feminism.* New York: Pantheon Books, 1974.

MITCHELL, JULIET. *Woman's Estate.* New York: Pantheon Books, 1972.

MOI, TORIL, ED. *French Feminist Thought: A Reader.* New York: Basil Blackwell, 1987.

NICHOLSON, LINDA J. *Gender and History: The Limits of Social Theory in the Age of the Family.* New York: Columbia University Press, 1986.

NICHOLSON, LINDA J., ED. *Feminism/Postmodernism.* New York: Routledge Chapman and Hall, 1989.

NYE, ANDREA. *Feminist Theory and the Philosophies of Man.* New York: Routledge Chapman and Hall, 1988.

OKIN, SUSAN MOLLER. *Justice, Gender and the Family.* New York: Basic Books, 1989.

OKIN, SUSAN MOLLER. *Women in Western Political Thought.* Princeton: Princeton University Press, 1979.

PATEMAN, CAROLE. *The Sexual Contract.* Stanford: Stanford University Press, 1988.

PLANT, JUDITH, ED. *Healing the Wounds: The Promise of Ecofeminism.* Philadelphia: New Society Publications, 1989.

ROSENBERG, ROSALIND. *Beyond Separate Spheres: Intellectual Roots of Modern Feminism.* New Haven: Yale University Press, 1982.

ROSSI, ALICE, ED. *The Feminist Papers: From Adams to de Beauvoir.* New York: Columbia University Press, 1973.

ROWBOTHAM, SHEILA. *Woman's Consciousness, Man's World.* Harmondsworth: Penguin, 1973.

RUDDICK, SARA. *Maternal Thinking: Toward a Politics of Peace.* Boston: Beacon Press, 1989.

SPELMAN, ELIZABETH V. *Inessential Woman: Problems of Exclusion in Feminist Thought.* Boston: Beacon Press, 1988.

TONG, ROSEMARIE. *Feminist Thought: A Comprehensive Introduction.* Boulder: Westview Press, 1989.

WARREN, KAREN J. "Feminism and Ecology: Making Connections." *Environmental Ethics* 12 (2), Summer 1990, pp. 125–146.

WEEDON, CHRIS. *Feminist Practice and Poststructuralist Theory.* New York: Basil Blackwell, 1987.

ZIMMERMAN, MICHAEL E. "Feminism, Deep Ecology, and Environmental Ethics." *Environmental Ethics* 9 (1), Spring 1987, pp. 21–44.